Translating Truth

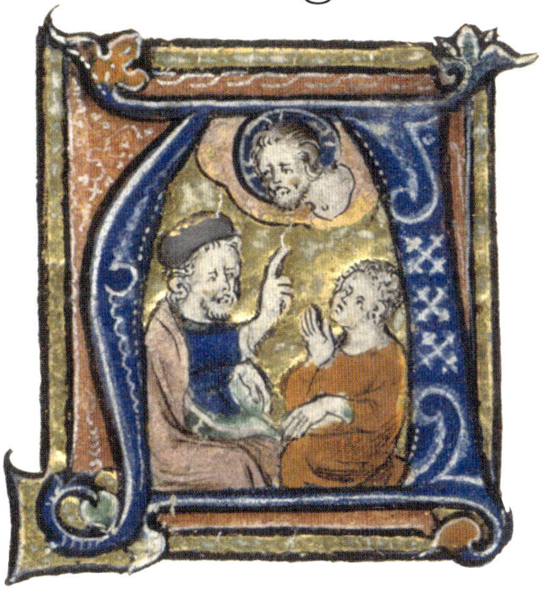

Translating Truth

Ambitious Images and Religious Knowledge in Late Medieval France and England

ADEN KUMLER

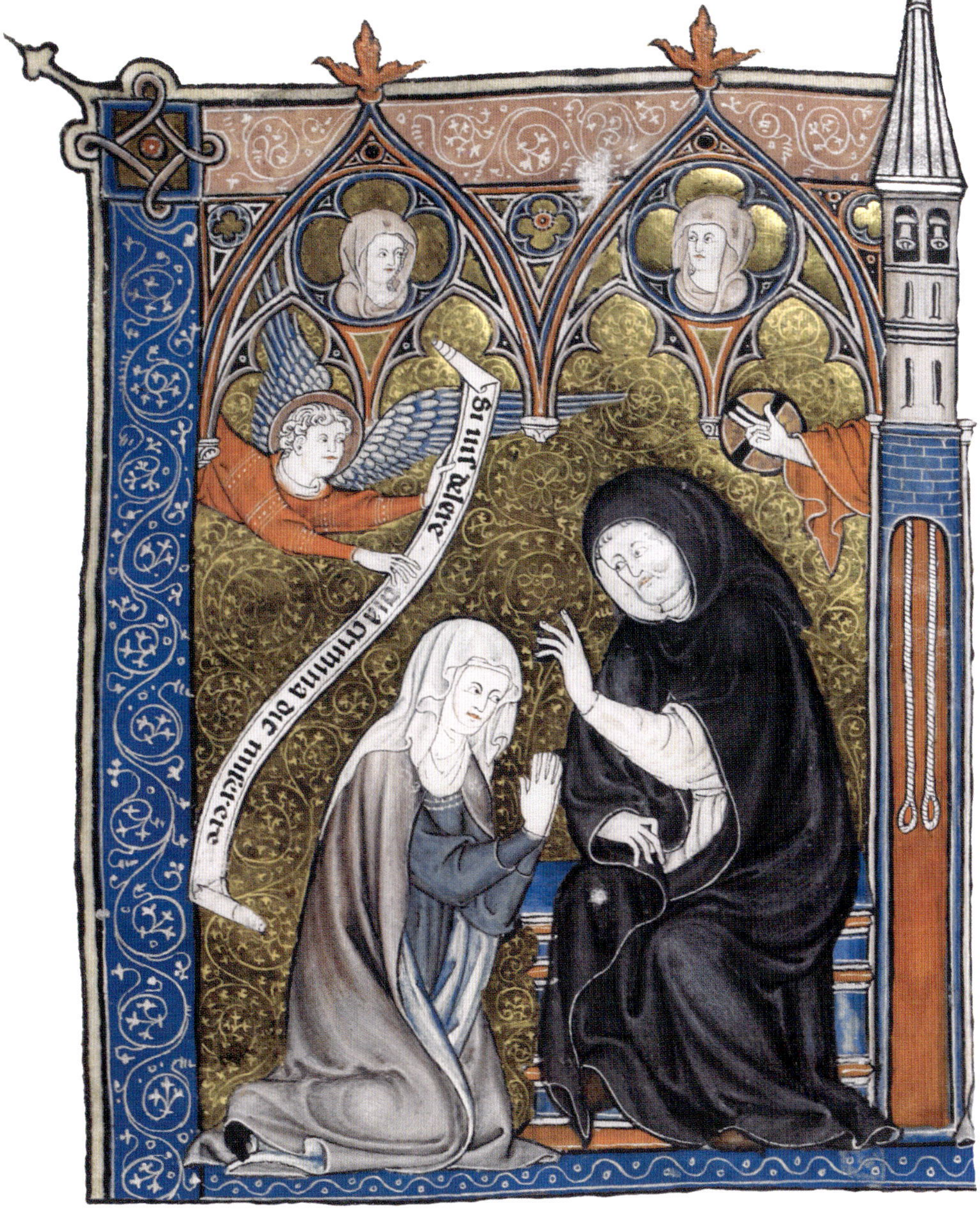

Yale University Press
New Haven and London

For JDP, for everything

Publication of this book has been aided by a grant from
the Medieval Academy of America.

Designed and set in Whitney by Laura Lindgren
Printed in China through Asia Pacific Offset

Library of Congress Cataloging-in-Publication Data
Kumler, Aden.
Translating truth : ambitious images and religious knowledge in late medieval France and England / Aden Kumler.
p. cm.
Includes bibliographical references and index.
ISBN 978-0-300-16493-0 (cloth : alk. paper)
1. Christian art and symbolism. 2. Christianity and art. 3. Image (Theology) 4. Communication—Religious aspects—Christianity. 5. Communication in art. 6. Illuminated manuscripts of the Middle Ages. 7. Church history—Middle Ages, 600–1500. I. Title. II. Title: Ambitious images and religious knowledge in late medieval France and England.
BV150.K77 2011
246.0941—dc22 2010049538

A catalogue record for this book is available from the British Library.

This paper meets the requirements of ANSI/NISO Z39.48–1992 (Permanence of Paper).

10 9 8 7 6 5 4 3 2 1

P. i: detail from fig. 53; *p. iii:* detail from fig. 80; *p. vi:* detail from fig. 14
Jacket illustrations: (front) detail from fig. 80; (back) detail from fig. 50

. . . ars est artium regimen animarum.
—Pope Gregory the Great

Vus savez, nus sumus tuz crié pur une fin,
ço est a saver, pur Deu conustre, amer e aver.
—St. Edmund of Abingdon

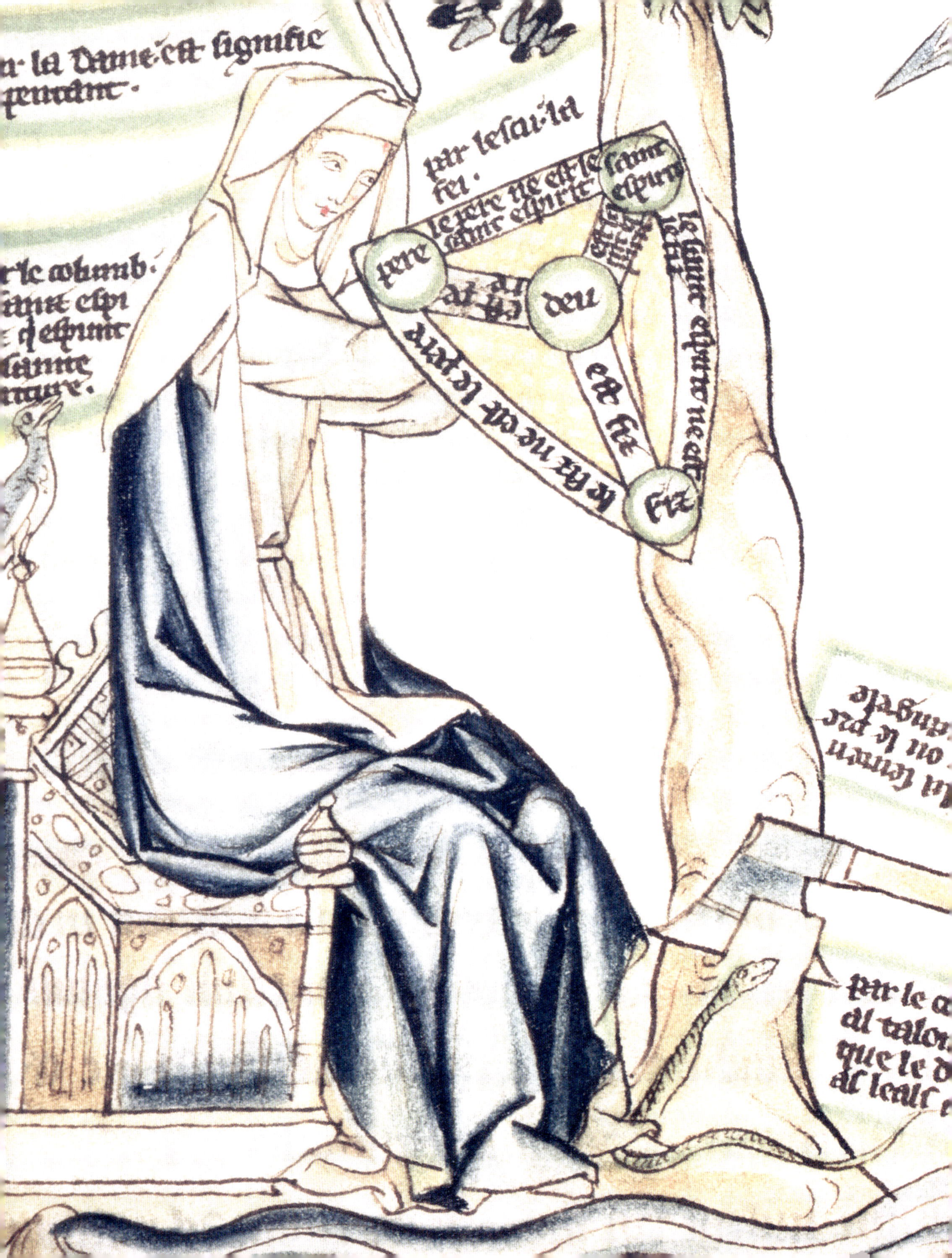

pere
deu
fiz
seint espirit

CONTENTS

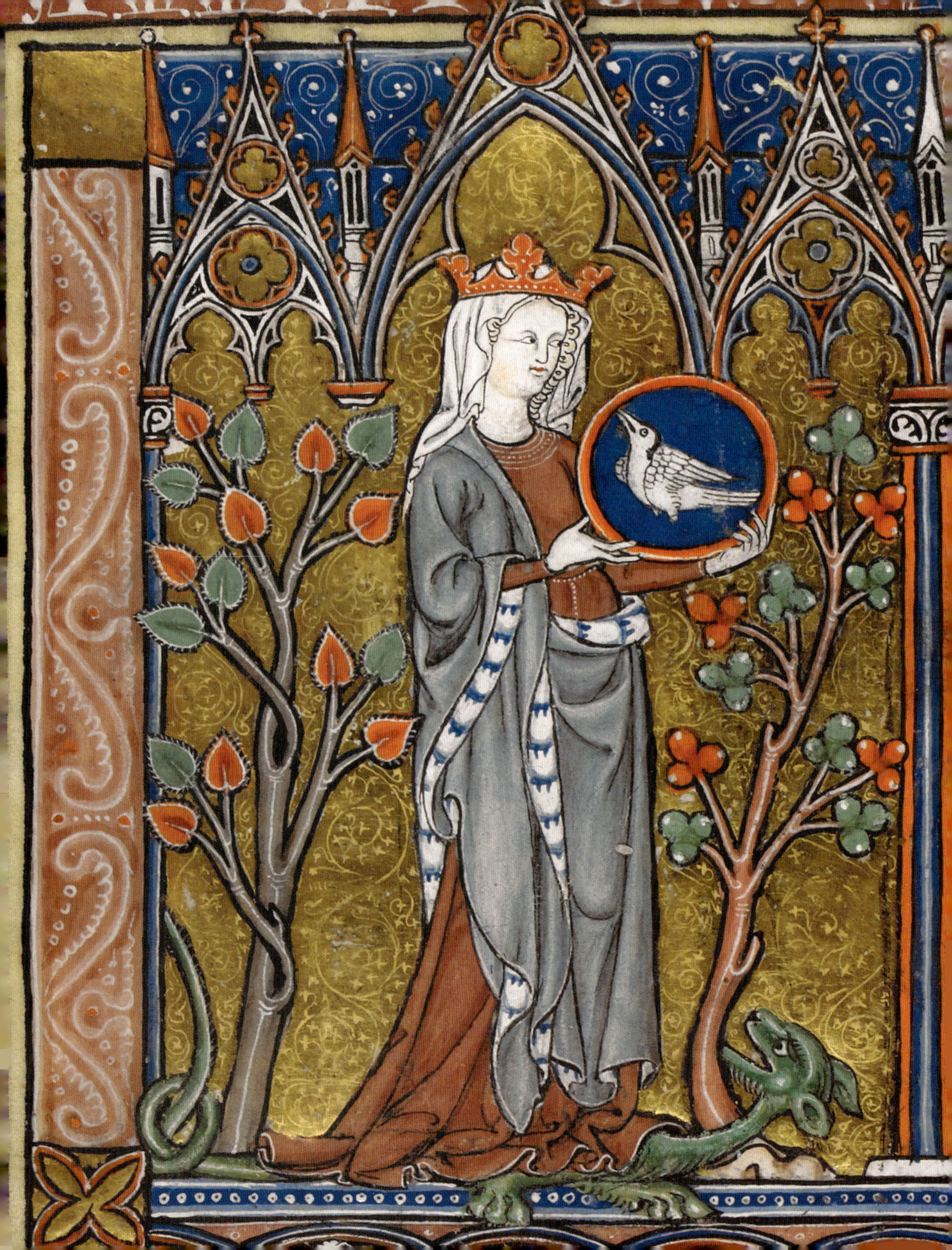

ACKNOWLEDGMENTS

Although a great historical distance divides the making of this book from the making of the medieval books it examines, like those manuscripts my own work would not have been possible were it not for the contributions, collaboration, and generosity of many friends and colleagues. Manuscript research incurs many debts of gratitude to the keepers of medieval books, and it gives me great pleasure to thank Martin Kauffmann, Michelle Brown, Peter Kidd, Kathleen Doyle, Gill Cannell, Jonathan Harrison, Stella Panayotova, Anne Korteweg, as well as the staff of the reading rooms of the Bibliothèque royale de Belgique, the Bibliothèque de l'Arsenal, the Bibliothèque Mazarine, and the Bibliothèque nationale de France's département des Manuscrits (division occidentale) for allowing me to consult manuscripts entrusted to their care. I would also like to thank Patricia Stirnemann and the erudite and helpful *chercheurs* at the Institut de recherche et d'histoire des textes (IRHT), Section romane (Paris), for making the IRHT's invaluable resources available to me.

The initial research and writing of this study was generously supported by a Frederick Sheldon Traveling Fellowship from Harvard University and a David E. Finley Predoctoral Fellowship from the Center for Advanced Study in the Visual Arts at the National Gallery in Washington, D.C., where a year in residence, filled with art historical conversation and camaraderie, contributed significantly to the development of this study. I completed the book during a year of leave spent at the Pontifical Institute of Mediaeval Studies (PIMS) as a visiting Mellon fellow, and I am very grateful to the fellows and staff of the PIMS, the PIMS Library, and the wonderful librarians of the Kelly Library of St. Michael's College, particularly Manda Vrkljan, for their considerable support as I was ending one project and beginning another. Jérôme Gazzano volunteered for the thankless task of obtaining images and permissions for the book: I am very grateful to him for all of his hard work.

Detail from Fig. 56

The publication of this book was made possible by generous subventions from the Medieval Academy of America and the Humanities Division of the University of Chicago and through the tireless efforts of Joel Snyder, for whom, I have come to believe, nothing is impossible. Also at the University of Chicago, special thanks are due to Tara Morin and Rebecca Kosick in the Art History Department; Megan Macken, Amanda Rybin, and the staff of the Visual Resources Center; and Nancy Spiegel and Catherine Mardikes of the Regenstein Library for their considerable help as I worked on this book. At Yale University Press I am grateful to Patricia Fidler, my editor, for her expert and always tactful guidance; to Jessie Hunnicutt, my manuscript editor, for improving this text in countless ways; to Laura Lindgren for her sensitive design of the book; and to Sarah Henry and Heidi Downey for deftly seeing my manuscript through the publication process. I cannot adequately express my gratitude to the three anonymous readers who reviewed my manuscript for Yale University Press. The care with which they read, the generosity of their critiques, and the intelligence of their suggestions were nothing short of revelatory.

This study has been shaped by time spent in several intellectual communities, and it is a pleasure to thank the friends and colleagues who have shared their knowledge, improved my thinking, and helped me in countless other ways as the project evolved, particularly Anthony Adams, Ladan Akbarnia, Mary Clare Altenhofen, Jonathan Bailey, Odilia Bonebakker, Leo Carruthers, Elizabeth Cropper, Chanchal Dadlani, Tom Dale, Deanna Dalrymple, Jamison Duffield, Rick Emmerson, Brendan Fay, Damian Fleming, Amy Freund, John Gagné, Paul Galvez, Spruill Harder, Magda Hayton, Anne D. Hedeman, Seth Hindin, Amy Houston, Deborah Howard, Beth Johnson, Danielle Joyner, Beverly Kienzle, Gaku Kondo, Christine Kralik, Michelle Kuo, Megan Luke, Peter Lukehart, Meredith Martin, Christopher Moisan, Ted Moore, Christina Neilson, Rob Nelson, Jonathan Newman, Jess Paehlke, Nigel Palmer, Sylvia Parsons, Benjamin Paul, Verity Platt, Jennifer Pruitt, Sarah Rentz, Elizabeth Ross, Scott Rothkopf, David Roxburgh, Elizabeth Rudy, Claire Sherman, Daniel Sherman, William Stoneman, Fred Unwalla, Alicia Walker, and Molly Warnock. Nicholas Watson and Tom Cummins helped to shape my thinking about this project when it was still an unruly dissertation, and I hope they will be able to discern the salutary effects of their comments and suggestions on its final form. My family was the very first community of ideas and argument to which I belonged, and they continue to be a source of important questions, trenchant critique, and moral support. As I worked on this book my mother, Kally Kumler, continuously reminded me of the pleasures of curiosity and the rewards of philology: I am grateful for these lessons and for all that she has taught me.

The intellectual engagement and excellent company of my colleagues in Art History at the University of Chicago—Niall Atkinson, Persis Berlekamp, Charles Cohen,

Darby English, Ping Foong, Chelsea Foxwell, Cécile Fromont, Matthew Jesse Jackson, Richard Neer, Joel Snyder, Katherine Taylor, Marty Ward, and Wu Hung—make Hyde Park one of the most exciting places for thinking, reading, talking, and looking that I know. Rebecca Zorach and Jaś Elsner were generous interlocutors as I was working on this study, and I benefited from their characteristically incisive and insightful comments on earlier states of this text. The contributions made in the past three years by Sean Keller, Christine Mehring, Maja Nef, and Ralph Ubl to my thinking about the interpretation of historical and contemporary works of all kinds cannot be adequately acknowledged: I happily remain in their debt.

My medievalist colleagues at the University of Chicago have generously shared their own work and varied commitments to the study of the medieval past. It is a pleasure to thank Michael Allen, Rachel Fulton Brown, Ryan Giles, Jonathan Lyon, Bernard McGinn, Christina von Nolcken, Willemien Otten, Anne Robertson, and Justin Steinberg for lively conversations about all things medieval. Special thanks are owed to Daisy Delogu, David Nirenberg, and Lucy Pick, who have challenged and sustained my thinking and writing at Chicago in ways that often surprise and delight me.

I owe a special and continuing debt of gratitude to Jeffrey Hamburger. It was thanks to Jeffrey that I first set eyes on the illumination that provoked this study, and his encouragement, criticism, and guidance made possible the *translatio* of that initial moment of seeing into this book. Jeffrey has been my exemplar of intellectual rigor, erudition, and discerning bibliomania for more than a decade; I am no less grateful for his kindness, humor, and friendship.

Finally, how to acknowledge Jacob Proctor? As words fail me, I can only dedicate this book to him as a material trace of our collaboration in all things.

It was my hope when I first started this project that it might one day be something I could send to Michael Camille, whose classes at the University of Chicago convinced me as an undergraduate that there was nothing more exhilarating, more challenging, and more surprisingly relevant than medieval art. As I worked on this book I often returned to his words, both on the printed page and in my memory. I am grateful for what they continue to teach me.

NOTE ON TRANSCRIPTIONS AND TRANSLATIONS

In transcriptions from manuscripts I have silently expanded abbreviations, regularized u/v and i/j, and supplied diacriticals, while otherwise preserving orthography. In translations, I have regularized capitalization and punctuation for clarity of sense. In transcriptions and translations, scriptural quotations are set in italics, as are any nonscriptural Latin phrases or quotations found in otherwise vernacular texts. Editorial clarifications and scriptural references are enclosed in square brackets. Latin scriptural texts are cited from the Vulgate (Robert Weber and Bonifatius Fischer, eds., *Biblia Sacra iuxta vulgatam versionem,* 4th ed. [Stuttgart: Deutsche Bibelgesellschaft, 1994]); English translations of scripture are cited from the Douay-Rheims Bible (rev. ed., translated by Bishop Richard Challoner [Rockford, Ill.: Tan Books, 2000]). All other translations are my own, unless otherwise noted. In shelfmarks, the abbreviations "BL" and "BnF" refer to the British Library and the Bibliothèque nationale de France, respectively.

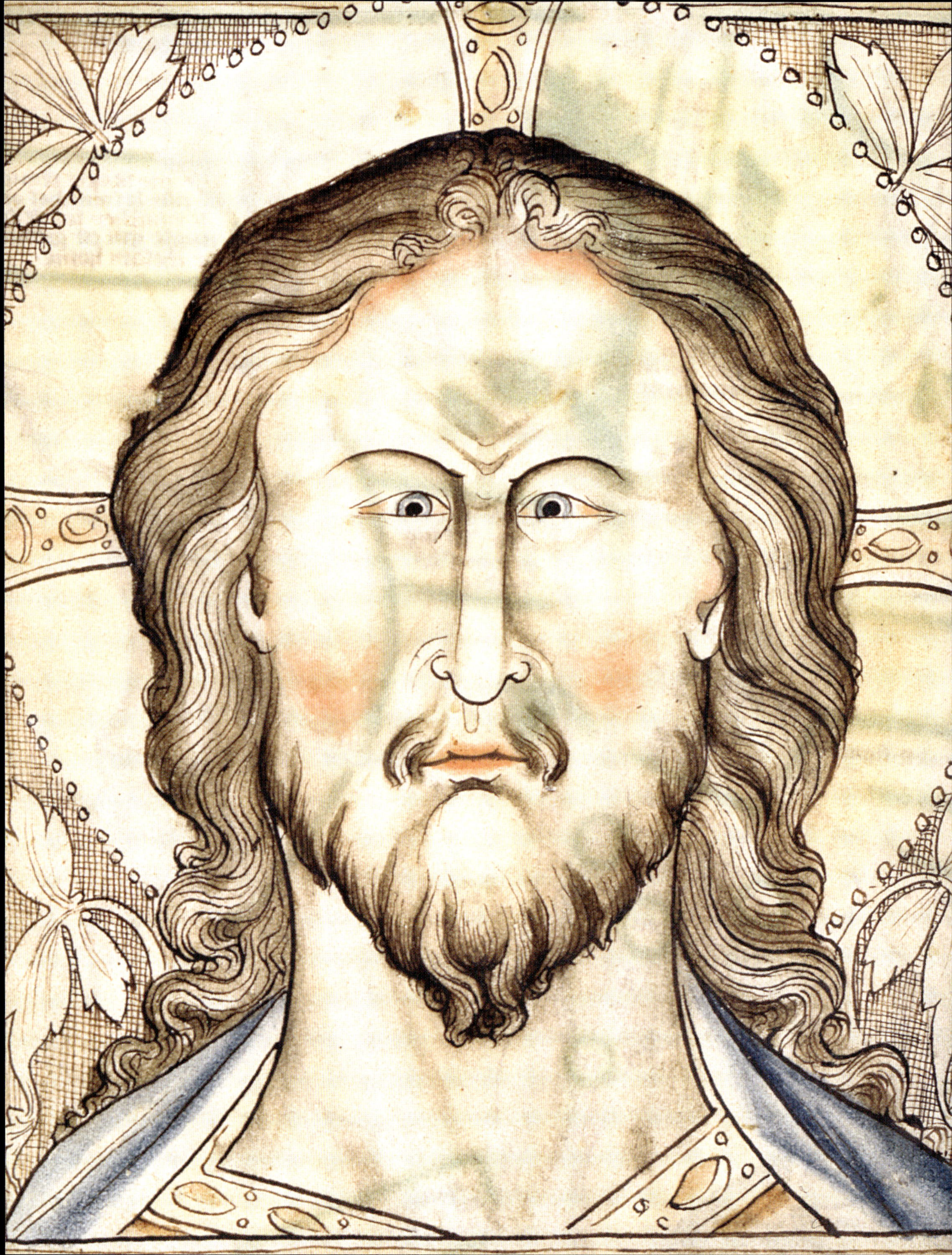

Introduction

Accounting for Medieval Religious Images

In the Middle Ages—in keeping with traditions that may be traced back beyond the inception of the Christian era—images were generally held to be lesser order artifacts.[1] Vision might reign as the queen of the senses, but her visible objects were theorized as belonging to a terrestrial world of imperfect mimetic approximation and mute pantomime. In medieval Europe, religious images were often considered crutches for—or worse, the bad habits of—the theologically uninitiated: non-Christians, novices, illiterates, and women. At their most dangerous, religious images were thought to divert *latria,* the worship reserved for God, from the Logos, promoting themselves, through an aggressive aesthetic appropriation of proper veneration, into idols, the usurpers of Judeo-Christian traditions of textual authority.[2] More innocuously, images could define a salutary starting point, an initiatory terminus for the journey to verbal theology or else the anagogical destination of pure, even apophatic, encounter with the Divine.

Varied, even contradictory, these Western medieval accounts of the power and limitations of visual representation, and of the image as a material artifact, define a Christian historical tradition that appropriated the Old Testament and was variously textually articulated and revised by countless figures, among them Augustine of Hippo, Pseudo-Dionysius, Gregory the Great, the authors of the *Opus Caroli regis contra synodum* (*Libri Carolini*), Bernard of Clairvaux, Suger of Saint-Denis, Hugh of Saint-Victor, and William Durandus. Principally as footnotes to other arguments, the place of the religious image and its powers was textually pinned down, circumscribed, rehearsed, and defined as either danger or supplement. Within the broad contours of this tradition of textual account, human-made visual representation participated in the register of the truthful only by virtue of its formal attempts at mimesis, its *imitatio* of the appearance of reality.[3] Suprasensible realities, hidden truths, sacred dicta, and the invisible secrets of divinity existed elsewhere: images produced by human artifice were innocent of these central arcana, or else they were false claimants to their authority and power.

Detail from Fig. 19

In the medieval West, the correctitude of religious images was often evaluated against the measure of the Gregorian dictum, Pope Gregory the Great's famous sixth-century injunction that images should serve as books for the illiterate, affective stimuli to pious compunction and ardent devotion.[4] The very analogy employed by the Gregorian dictum, however, opened up a new horizon of possibility for the power of images in the medieval context, claiming in a deeply ambiguous fashion that images could take the place of books for the illiterate. Some scholars have seen this as a definitive denigration, a defense of the image that damns it with faint praise, relegating it to the provincial and provisional sidelines of logocentric Christian culture. To compare an image with a book, however, is to grant to the image the considerable authority associated with text and with codices, in particular, within this religion of the book.

In the sixth century, as in the fourteenth, books were not simply repositories for sacred stories and technologies for instruction; they were also, at times, sacred objects, carried by cloth-covered hands and metaphorically aligned with the very body of God. In this respect, Gregory's assertion that images can take the place of books, albeit for the plebs rather than the presbyter, is astonishing. Implicitly, it lays the groundwork for a radical rethinking of what images can do, and should do, within Christian culture. In subsequent centuries Gregory's invitation to a reimagined, reinvigorated Christian visuality would be accepted, extended, and continually renewed. Significantly, much of this work would be done not in the medium of textual discourse, but rather by the making and viewing of images themselves.

Indeed, although the conception of the religious image, its authority, and its capacities that I have sketched dominated discussion of the manufactured visible throughout the Middle Ages, it cannot adequately account for medieval practices of visual representation and the receptions they solicited. The testimonies of objects, artifacts, and images that survive from the period suggest instead that medieval representations frequently did what they were not—according to the writers of texts—supposed to do. It seems appropriate, then, to describe the medieval image as situated within, or, more accurately, as generating, at least two parallel discursive regimes. We have the prescriptive and prohibitive discourse of texts that tell us what images should and should not do, how images should and should not be viewed, where images, confronted with the ineffable, inevitably fail. At the same time, we have the images themselves, silently but visibly articulating arguments about precisely those verities that texts tell us they could not and should not presume to treat.[5]

In the past twenty years, powerful accounts of medieval images have challenged the logocentric emphases of much of the medieval textual record. In the wake of David Freedberg's and Hans Belting's landmark studies, the cult image and the practices that surrounded it in the period became an influential paradigm for our understanding of what medieval religious images could do and how devotees responded to visual and material instantiations of the Divine in the period.[6] Indeed, the last two decades have witnessed a veritable *renovatio* of scholarly interest in medieval religious images, in forms of visual piety, and in the spiritual efficacy (and limitations) of vision in the period.[7] Many recent interpretations of religious images in the European Middle Ages have focused on the visual and material articulation of forms of presence, be it the auratic presence of the cult image, the narrative presence of pictorial hagiography, or the affective, embodied presence of the devotee gazing at the devotional image.[8] As a result, our accounts of religious images in the Middle Ages have primarily been organized around and articulated through questions and conceptions of ontology.[9]

In the thirteenth and fourteenth centuries, the terms of Christian participation in religious life altered significantly. Among the many changes that can be traced across European society in this period, the pastoral reform movement, given a papal imprimatur by the canons of the Fourth Lateran Council (1215), significantly raised the epistemological bar for Christians, both clerical and lay. Indeed, as Jean Wirth has explored in relation to changes in Gothic art, the late twelfth and thirteenth centuries were permeated by a profound "epistemological optimism," a tendency that can be discerned not only in the scholastic studium but also in the explosion of texts and images designed for the spiritual instruction of Christian readers and beholders.[10] Emphasizing, as never before, the importance of religious knowledge to the proper practice of religion and Christian living, thirteenth-century efforts to reform the *cura animarum* (the ecclesiastical care of souls) epistemologically transformed late medieval ideals of Christian identity and participation.

Michel Foucault identified the Fourth Lateran Council as a watershed in the history of truth's production.[11] For Foucault, Pope Innocent III's great pastoral council transformed the Western episteme through its legislation on confession: the verbal formulation of religious and moral truth couched in the discourse of sin and transgression.[12] Pursuing Foucault's claim, I think a closer reading of the Council's canons reveals an even broader investment in the project of "truth production," a project pursued through the Council's creedal statement, its mandating of annual communion preceded by confession, as well as its delineation of a body of religious knowledge to be mastered by priests and conveyed to their parishioners. With the promulgation of the Council's canons a new horizon of expectation was established, a syllabus of pastoral knowledge was drawn up, and a repertoire of pastoral techniques was defined. This broad project of ecclesiastical reform and outreach effectively redefined the knowledge necessary to salvation, raising the bar when it came to clerical and lay participation in the sacramental life of the church.

For lay elites in the period, however, the pastoral syllabus defined by ecclesiastical reformers was only a point of departure, a baseline of institutionalized expectation that was, rapidly and aggressively, surpassed by royal and aristocratic pursuit of religious knowledge and distinction, a phenomenon that Nicole Rice has aptly glossed as "spiritual ambition."[13] As this book will explore, images played a decisive part in this epistemological transformation of what it meant to be a good—even an excellent—Christian, not, primarily, as instantiations of the sacred or mediators of divine presence, but as things to think with, important elements in a broader late medieval project to translate religious truths.

Pastoral Reform as Translation

The pastoral reform movement codified in the canons of the Fourth Lateran Council was an ambitious attempt to translate religious ideals into quotidian realities. When, in 1213, Innocent III summoned prelates and princes from all over Europe to his general council, he announced its pastoral goals as the "uprooting of vices and the planting of virtues, the correction of deviations and the reformation of morals, the elimination of heresy and the strengthening of faith."[14] The Fourth Lateran Council was, however, only the latest and "greatest" (in quantitative and institutional terms) in a series of ecclesiastical councils to focus on promoting a serious reform of clerical and lay religious formation and participation. As I explore in chapter 1, Innocent's Council went further than its regional and local predecessors in explicitly articulating its vision of a reformed church in terms of a "trickle-down" model of institutional, spiritual, and moral correction. This paradigm for institutional and spiritual change presumed and prescribed a conceptual and bureaucratic translation of the new standards of Christian knowledge and performance, a set of revised expectations that reformist archbishops and bishops would transmit to the parochial clergy, from whom the new standards and ideals would migrate, in mediated forms, to the faithful.

In pragmatic terms, Lateran IV envisioned a very literal translation of reformed religious expectations and obligations. In its ninth canon, the Council explicitly acknowledged that the Christian faithful were *populi diversarum linguarum* (peoples of diverse languages) requiring multilingual forms of religious instruction.[15] Thirteenth- and fourteenth-century provincial and synodal legislation reveals that reformist legislators throughout France and England were sensitive to questions of linguistic intelligibility, specifying over and over again that the peoples' religious instruction and sacramental participation could and should be conducted *in lingua vulgari* (in the language of the people).[16]

The translation of the pastoral project, of its goals, and of the substance of its syllabus of belief (*credenda*) and performance (*perficienda*) was, however, never envisioned as a strictly linguistic undertaking. As Paul Binski has masterfully explored in the English context, the reformers imagined a pastorally regulated *ecclesia,* a legislative vision that was as ideological, behavioral, and (not least) aesthetic as it was spiritual in its tenor and ambitions.[17] It was also, perhaps inevitably, a dream of religious and ethical order that manifested itself in a series of aesthetic forms: liturgy, music, literature, and—not least—architecture and the visual arts.

The proliferation of *pastoralia*—the literature of pastoral care—in the wake of Innocent's Council was one such manifestation of the reform impulse and its energetic embrace of new forms and revision of old ones. First identified as a coherent if heterogeneous body of literary production by Leonard Boyle, pastoralia responded to the intellectual, moral, spiritual, and pragmatic needs of the cura animarum.[18] In Boyle's formulation, pastoralia encompasses "any literary aid or manual which can be of help to the priest in the *Cura animarum,* whether with respect to his own education as pastor or to the education of the people in his charge."[19] Although pastoralia were produced in the interconciliar period (1179–1215), it was in the forty-five years following Lateran IV that the literature of the cura animarum proliferated, diversified, and began to circulate widely.[20]

The second half of the thirteenth century witnessed the efflorescence of pastoralia addressed to lay audiences directly and in the vernacular. Concurrently, an antecedent focus on sin, penance, and the extirpation of vice yielded to a more complex vision of spiritual care, often described in constructive terms: the fostering of the virtues, the rewards of moral rectitude, the mastery of religious knowledge, and the pursuit of salvation.[21] Thus, with a work of vernacular pastoralia in his or her hands, a literate layperson of sufficient means could, quite literally, handle religious truth. The church's sacramental system still necessitated the presence of the priest, but for the first time laypeople were granted access to the means of production within the economy of salvation. They could learn the pastoral syllabus at home, they could practice the examination of their consciences within the privacy of their bedchambers, they could master the Decalogue and teach their children about the conduct of a moral life. Vernacular pastoralia made all of this possible. The illumination of that literature of spiritual instruction made religious formation—and reformation—a process of seeing religious truth painted on the page.

Visual Translation

The illumination of pastoralia did not involve a simple shift from text to image, a laying down of the pen and picking up of the brush. Rather than merely marking where text begins or ends, or even providing a visual recapitulation or amplification of the vernacular contents of a given treatise or poem, images in the luxury manuscripts examined in this study make their own arguments about the sacraments, the Trinity, religious perfection, and the practice of the faith. Collaborating with the texts they accompany, at times contradicting or revising them, these illuminations appropriated the contents of the pastoral syllabus, rendering saving truths into visible forms and contributing to the pastoral project in ways that often surpassed ecclesiastical expectations of lay religious formation.

The substantive contribution of these programs of images and their complex relationships to textual forms of spiritual instruction defy the subordinate status of the "illustration." I have, instead, interpreted them as practicing an ambitious form of translation: a *visual* translation that involved formal and semantic transformations, aggressive forms of appropriation, and the authorizing claims of fidelity, transparency, and veridicality.[22] When the illuminators of these images began painting they were, effectively, intervening in the very basis of religious knowledge: appealing to the seeing as well as the reading eye, marshalling color, pattern, brushstroke, composition, and iconography in the translation of religious truths.[23]

The truths visually translated by the manuscript paintings examined in the chapters that follow were understood to exist before and beyond textual and visual instantiation. Despite a long and continuing tradition of textual translations of sacred and saving verities, illuminations in these luxury manuscripts do not primarily—or most importantly—translate the texts they accompany. Their point of departure remains, instead, that which countless medieval texts before and after them also communicated and commented upon: the sacred and saving truths that defined the theory and practice of medieval Christian religion.

From Divine Truth to Christian Faith: Obligation, Virtue, Act

In the Middle Ages, the *summa et prima veritas* (supreme and first truth) was God.[24] *Fons et origo* of all sacred verities, the deity was truth itself, an existential mode of veridicality that admitted no falsehood, qualification, or change over time. And yet religious truth also had a history and a historicity in the period. At certain decisive historical moments sacred truth had been transformed: when God created man he created him with the truth of his image impressed like a seal in wax; when Moses received the Ten Commandments he received a canon of truths, inscribed by the finger of God. Above all, the Incarnation marked a watershed in the history of sacred and saving truth. In the incarnate Christ religious truth was again transformed, now bodied forth in an immaculate corporeality, soon subjected to torment and death, later resurrected, glorified, and ascended. In the Incarnation truth became visible, and in the era of grace inaugurated by Christ's conception Christians came to possess a more complete revelation, a more

complete truth, surpassing the shadowy figuration of the Mosaic Law and Levitical observations. In turn, the texts of the New Testament expanded the canon of written truth, preserving Christ's words and deeds as a veridical legacy for future Christians.

To this scriptural canon, a host of accessory truths were added in the Middle Ages: supplements to the divine word, but deemed no less necessary to salvation. As the pastoral reform movement placed increasing emphasis on religious education, it simultaneously disseminated and promoted an authorized canon of religious truths, a syllabus to be taught and believed. Terse formulations of this corpus of religious truth were recited by the faithful in every Sunday and festal Mass through the words of the Nicene-Constantinopolitan Creed and at the baptismal font and in extraliturgical devotion in the form of the Apostles' Creed.[25]

Couched in a series of first-person statements ("I believe"), each *Credo* was more than a catalog of religious axioms; literally and semantically, the Creeds articulated the faith, dividing the canon of essential religious truth into individual articles and putting those articles in the mouths (and minds) of the faithful. Recitation of the Credo, in church or in prayer elsewhere, verbally committed the devotee to propositions that exceeded rational probation or sensory confirmation. The *Lumere as lais* (Light for Laypeople), a thirteenth-century verse summa designed for the edification of the laity, explains,

> Les articles de la fei saver covint. Ke seint escripture plusurs contint.
> E mut de ceus veirement. Sunt outre humeine entendement.
> Nepurquant ki veut dieu plere. Les conveint fermement [c]rere.
> Trestuz les articles generaument. Mes nepurkaunt especiaument.
> Convint les articles saver. Ki a dreit se veut sauver. Que les aposteles
> entre eus feseient. E en la crede deposeient.[26]
>
> (It is necessary to know the articles of the faith, which Holy Scripture contains severally. And many of these [articles] are truly beyond human understanding. Nevertheless, whoever wishes to please God must believe them firmly—[that is,] all the articles in a general way; but nevertheless, to anyone who wishes to save his or her soul, it is especially necessary to know the articles that the apostles devised among themselves and set down in the Credo.)

Necessary truths, the articles of the faith were obligations that could never be fully known. Surpassing human understanding, they required a special act of adhesion, a willing assent (in Augustine's formulation) to the rationally unknown.[27]

Faith was also, in the period, theorized as a virtue, a power in the soul that made such unknowing but willed assent possible. As Jean de Joinville explained in the vernacular and visual creed he composed circa 1250–1251 (a work we will revisit in chapter 2), faith was "une vertuz qui fait croire fermement ce que hons ne voit ne ne set mais que par oïr dire" (a virtue that makes man firmly believe what he does not see and knows only by hearsay).[28] Here Joinville succinctly points to the seeming tautology that defined the relationship between faith and belief in the later Middle Ages: faith as virtue *fait croire* (makes belief). The object of that belief—the unseen, the unknown—distinguishes belief as an unusual, virtuosic act, an act that proceeds from articulated, yet invisible and literally unintelligible, propositions and arrives at a state of willed assent to religious truth.

Late medieval theologians, pastors, and eager devotees thus found themselves caught in a difficult bind. The cura animarum promoted a notion of faith as an object of memorization, recitation, and internalization. Its didactic enthusiasm encouraged an epistemological mastery of faith, understood as a syllabus of belief. At the same time, however, a long line of authorities asserted unequivocally that faith—both the act and its object—only began where reason (and ordinary human cogitation) stopped. As the *Lumere as lais* told its reader,

> E si reisun [t]rez de ta creaunce. Ceo nous est solaz saunz dutaunce. Mes ceo ke seint eglise nous enseigne. Creez plus ke ta resun demeine. Creez la chose premerement. Kar ceo est le profit pleinemet [*sic*]. E pus si resun truvez. De ceo en serrez reconfortez. Mes si rien creere ne volez. Saunz ceo que par resun nel provez. Ne durrai mie pour votre creaunce. De une fige la vaillaunce. Kar dunck ne creez vereaiment. For dunt avez espeirement. Pur teu creere. merite ne glorie. N'averez cum di seint gregorie.[29]
>
> (And if you [draw] reason from your belief this is a comfort to us, no doubt. But that which Holy Church teaches us, believe more than what your reason shows. Believe the things first of all, for that is fully the benefit. And then if you find a reason, from this you shall be comforted. But if you do not wish to believe anything, without proving it by reason, I will not give for your belief the worth of a fig. For thus you don't truly believe, except that which you have experienced. For such belief you shall have neither reward nor glory, as Saint Gregory says.)[30]

And it was not reason alone that was excluded from the act of faith. Medieval theologians insisted, again and again, that the evidence of the senses was inadmissible in the court of belief. No less an authority than Augustine supplied an oft-repeated proof text for this position: "Quid est enim fides, nisi credere quod non vides?" (What is faith, if not to believe what you do not see?)[31]

"Sine fide autem inpossibile placere Deo" (without faith it is impossible to please God; Hebrews 11:6)—and yet the practice of faith in the later Middle Ages was arduous.[32] The faithful were caught between the epistemological expectations of the pastoral reform movement and the established teaching that acts of cogitation foreclosed the possibility and merit of belief. In this way, *scientia* and *savoir*—forms of knowledge proceeding from the visible and the reasoned—existed in an uneasy, even agonistic relation with the Credo and with the saving acts of *fides* (faith) and *creance* (belief). Given the authority of traditional valorizations of faith above reason, of a belief in invisible verities over a confidence in visible evidence, it is all the more startling to recognize that in the wake of the Fourth Lateran Council a host of images rushed into this gap between savoir and creance.

From the expansive field of vernacular pastoralia, this study attends to one rarefied and brilliant thread: a series of luxury manuscripts containing vernacular texts and painted images, books that I believe can bear the pressure of exemplifying how illuminated pastoralia translated, and so transformed, religious truth for elite laymen and women in France and England in the thirteenth and fourteenth centuries.

For many late medieval elites—both lay and ecclesiastic—the English Channel, in Malcolm Vale's words, "served as highway rather than barrier."[33] Despite a scholarly tendency to treat the Channel as something of an impermeable barrier in the later Middle Ages, I have taken my cues from ecclesiastical reformers and lay aristocrats in the period, many of whom cultivated local forms of familial and institutional identity while participating in common Anglo-French networks of patronage, education, gift exchange, marriage, and political alliance, as well as the mutually implicating agon of cultural rivalry, territorial contestation, and, in the fourteenth century, sustained warfare.

The linguistic proximity of Anglo-Norman, Old French, and, subsequently, Middle French further facilitated communication, exchange, and the movement of people and ideas across the shifting territorial bounds that divided England and northern France. It must be acknowledged, however, that linguistic conditions differed significantly in the kingdoms of France and England in the period. In the French royal domains, two languages prevailed: Latin and langue d'oïl. Over the course of the thirteenth and fourteenth centuries the relationship between the two languages shifted considerably, and the vernacular became increasingly recognized as a *langue savante,* a language to which weighty truths—be they legal, scientific, historical, or theological—could be entrusted.[34] In thirteenth- and fourteenth-century England, by contrast, the linguistic landscape was complexly trilingual.[35] Latin persisted as a language of sacred and ecclesiastical authority as well as juridical record. By 1215, however, Anglo-Norman also began to be used in legal instruments and civil administration, becoming, in Michael Clanchy's formulation, "a language worthy of record."[36] Anglo-Norman also served as a language of elite social and spiritual formation, a language of social prestige and didactic authority.[37] Although, in the period treated by this study, Middle English was making significant gains in authority and prestige, the illumination of Middle English literature was a rather later development, a cultural and art-historical phenomenon with its own specificity that cannot be treated here.[38]

Despite these differences in the socio-linguistic landscapes of northern France and England in the later Middle Ages, a culture of aristocratic spiritual self-fashioning flourished on both sides of the Channel. This was an elite culture that made extensive (but certainly not exclusive) use of continental and insular forms of French in its pursuit of ideals of lay excellence and distinction, both spiritual and worldly.[39] The manuscripts I examine in the following chapters participated variously in this elite culture of vernacular readership, image consumption, and spiritual ambition: it was the reception context for which they were made, but it was also a cultural context that they helped to shape and to authorize.

Royal and aristocratic reader-viewers desiring spiritually improving illuminated vernacular literature had many choices in the thirteenth and fourteenth centuries. Lay elites invested in manuscripts designed to make devotion rigorous, beautiful, even (at least in the margins) amusing. Psalters, psalter-hours, breviaries, and missals—manuscripts that had been associated with monastic and clerical practices of prayer and devotion—became fixtures of elite lay libraries in the period. Of course, the lay prayer-book par excellence was the book of hours.[40] Like the psalter-hours before it, the book of hours often functioned as a devotional vade mecum, containing not only the paraliturgical offices that have come to define the genre but also a host of accessory occasional prayers. Implicitly, a wealth of religious knowledge and precept was encoded in these devotional manuscripts. Explicitly, they were organized around the goal of the devout performance of praise and petition.

Other texts, and their visual programs, offered elite reader-viewers more overtly epistemological points of access to religious truth in vernacular text and painted image.[41] The period witnessed a remarkable flowering of the literature of moral-religious instruction.[42] Although many texts were repurposed from traditions of monastic circulation and reception and reconstituted in the vernacular for new lay audiences, a host of newly composed vernacular texts also appeared on the scene and were provided with visual programs in manuscripts destined for elite reader-viewers.[43] Bestiaries, vernacular saints' lives, Gauthier de Coincy's *Miracles de Nostre-Dame,* the *Vie des Peres, Ci nous dit, Mirour du monde, Lucidaire, Lumere as lais, Somme le roi,* the monumental *Bibles moralisées, Bibles historiales completées,* Apocalypses, as well as a host of other, still little-known texts in prose and verse circulated in the vernacular with visual programs that ranged from simple decorated initials to extensive programs of half- and full-page illuminations.

Many of these texts circulated in compendia, manuscripts in which curated collections of texts (and sometimes images) were assembled by careful planning. Already in the twelfth century, the compendium had emerged as a favored and formative manuscript type for the preservation of vernacular texts. It was in compendia that the earliest corpus of vernacular texts, primarily treating aspects of religious performance and knowledge, had been preserved in writing, a manuscript phenomenon first attested in England and subsequently in France.[44] Circulating among royal and aristocratic men and women, vernacular compendia continued to find favor with lay patrons and audiences in the thirteenth and fourteenth centuries and beyond.

Although these types of manuscripts continue to be cataloged and discussed as "miscellanies," I have deliberately avoided this term and its connotations of the ad hoc and miscellaneous.[45] The manuscripts I examine are anything but miscellaneous. The products of careful curation and planning by patrons, *libraires,* scribes, and artists, these books were bespoke creations, tailored to meet the expectations, wishes, and needs of particular recipients.[46] Moreover, close examination of their texts and images reveals that considerable thought and labor were invested in the forging of conceptual connections between individual textual and visual components. In this respect, the manuscripts explored in the following chapters might best be described as overdetermined in the disposition and interrelationship of their vernacular and visual contents.

All but one of the illuminated manuscripts examined in this study were designed, from the beginning, as compendia. From an art-historical perspective, these vernacular luxury compendia presented their makers and reader-viewers with particular challenges and opportunities. With the exception of the *Somme le roi* (examined in chapter 4), none of the texts found in the manuscripts I examine already possessed an iconographic program when these books were illuminated. Accordingly, the production of these particular manuscripts challenged patrons, bookmen (and women), and illuminators to devise pleasing and powerful programs of images for new textual and historical situations.[47] These conditions of production called for ingenuity, careful planning, and considerable artistic initiative.

Designed to intervene in the spiritual formation of their reader-viewers, these manuscripts exerted extra hermeneutic pressure on the codicological and conceptual situation of the compendium. The overt preoccupations and promises of these compendia, in particular, claimed a certain efficacy and coherence for their contents. These were books designed to improve their reader-viewers in the ways that mattered most. Their very considerable cost and their edifying ambitions invited close reading, close viewing, and strong interpretation. In this way, in the manuscripts I have chosen to examine, both patronal choice and formal necessity drove the creation of *new* visual forms for older (and more recent) ideas of religious truth and salvific knowledge. Accordingly, I understand each of these manuscripts to belong to a rarefied corpus defined primarily by its shared visual and vernacular ways and means and—above all else—its hermeneutic and spiritual ambitions.

The question that drives this study—how did images produce religious truth in the later Middle Ages?—admits of several answers. Indeed, the ways in which images generated religious truth varied tremendously in the period. Collaborating and, at times, competing with texts, medieval images reinflected the truths that they claimed for themselves time and again. A multiplicity of images thus gives rise to a multiplicity of truths, and the truths produced by manuscript painting were irreducibly local verities, intimately bound up with their particular manuscript contexts and indissolubly linked to the visual ways and means employed in their production. In this respect my study insists on the contextual basis of truth's production in the period. Rather than cataloging a transcendent body of knowledge that might characterize the fruits of didactic representation in the later Middle Ages, I have, instead, attempted to attend to the specific strategies, rhetorics, and claims of the manuscripts I examine, granting each book a certain hermeneutic autonomy while nonetheless paying attention to the broader project of pastoral formation in which each of these books participated.

Chapter 1 surveys the pastoral horizon of possibility that made ambitious works of vernacular illuminated pastoralia relevant, powerful, and persuasive in the later Middle Ages. Rereading pastoral legislation as a fantasy of trickle-down epistemological reform, I juxtapose this clerical vision of the cura animarum with the vision of the pastoral project articulated in the images and vernacular text of the first *Bible moralisée,* an important, precocious witness to late medieval lay spiritual ambition. The following chapters build on this foundation. Rather than pursuing a chronological trajectory, I have instead organized chapters 2, 3, and 4 according to late medieval conceptions of spiritual progress, passing from catechesis to confession, from confession to communion, from communion to a foretaste of spiritual perfection. In chapter 2 I examine how six manuscripts variously translate the dialogic and representational mode of confession as a paradigm for the viewer's relationship to the manuscript page and to religious truth. Chapter 3 examines a range of late medieval visual translations of the Eucharist before focusing on how a visual translation of the Mass in one fourteenth-century English compendium promotes the epistemological and spiritual efficacy of vision itself. Finally, in chapter 4, I explore how one exceptional thirteenth-century French compendium translates forms of spiritual excellence and authority associated with the cloister to an audience in the world, offering the reader-viewer a model of spiritual perfection to be realized within the invisible architecture of his or her soul.

This study examines how certain late medieval images solicited belief and participated in the production of religious truth. It explores how paintings in luxury manuscripts were understood to give access to saving truths, how the eye could be engaged in the work of salvation. This is not a study of success or failure. Certainly, these didactic manuscripts and their illuminations were designed to do work; like all literature of spiritual instruction they were charged with transforming their reader-viewer, taking him or her from an imperfect "before" to an "after" state of spiritual excellence. Yet I cannot make claims for the success of the books I study. No traces remain of a direct reader response to their pages. Instead, I have focused my analyses on the strategies of solicitation that define the verbal and visual rhetoric of these manuscripts, examining the receptions they solicited, exploring how they invited their reader-viewers to the discovery of religious truth. These are serious books with serious ambitions: the provision of saving knowledge, the reform of moral-spiritual interiority, the sacramentalization of vision itself. In my analyses I have taken seriously their pretensions, granting them the authority of their ambitions.

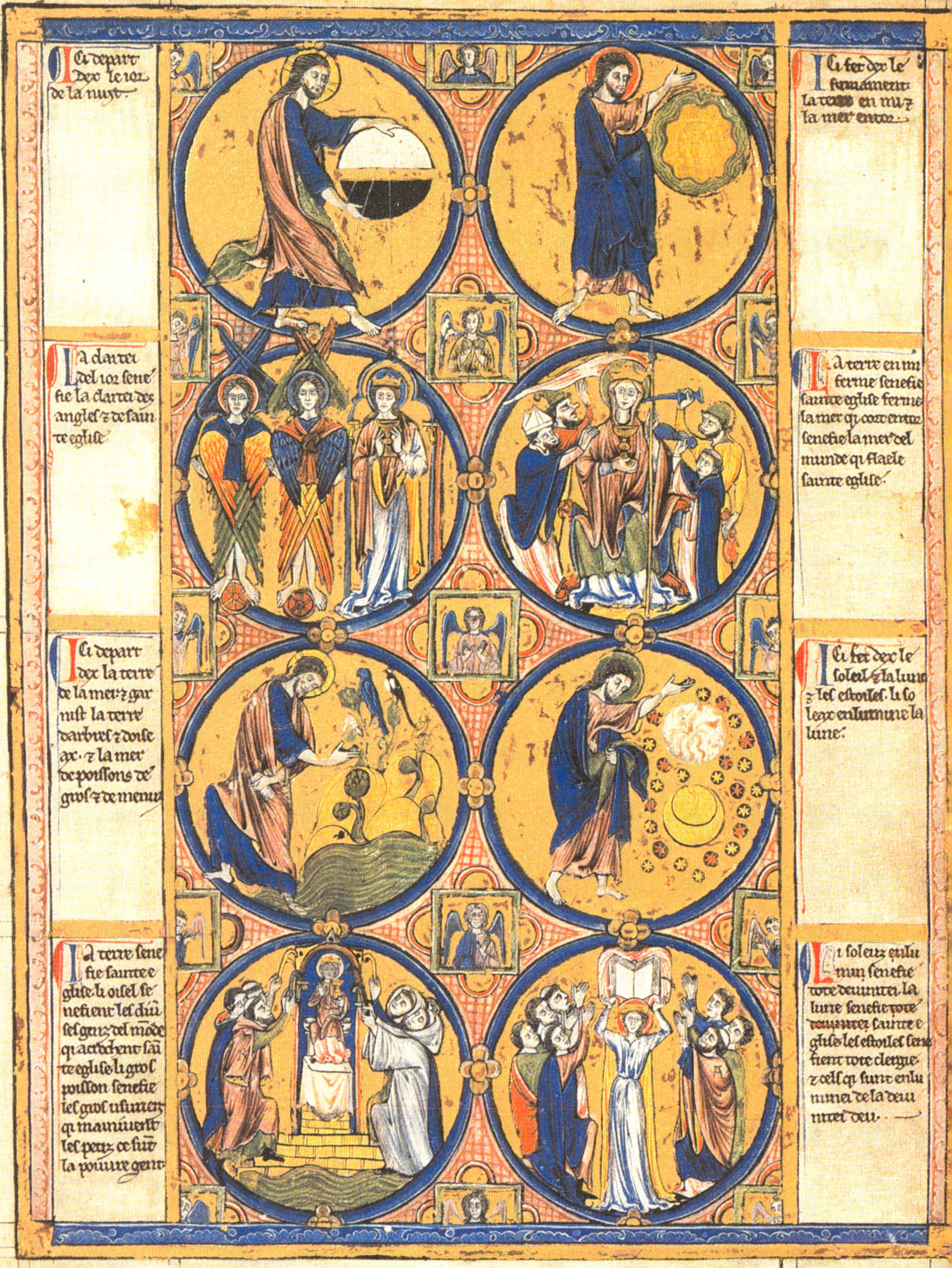
Ici depart dex le ior de la nuyt.
La clartei del ior senefie la clartei des angles ⁊ de sainte eglise.
Ici depart dex la terre de la mer ⁊ garnist la terre darbres ⁊ doisiax. ⁊ la mer de poissons de gros ⁊ de menus
La terre senefie sainte eglise. li oisel senefient les diuises genz del monde qi acrochent sainte eglise. li gros poisson senefie les gros usuriers qi mainiuent les petiz ce sunt la pouure gent.
Ici fet dex le firmament. la terre en mi ⁊ la mer entor.
La terre en mi ferme senefie sainte eglise ferme. la mer qi cort entor senefie la mer del munde qi flaele sainte eglise.
Ici fet dex le soleil ⁊ la lune ⁊ les estoiles. li soleax enlumine la lune.
Li soleuz enluminant senefie tote deuinitei. la lune senefie tote deuinitei sainte eglise. les estoiles senefient tote clergie ⁊ cels qi sunt enluminei de la deuinitei deu.

CHAPTER ONE

From Necessary Truths to Spiritual Ambitions

On the first recto of a famous thirteenth-century vernacular manuscript, religious truth appears in the authorized and authorizing form of a book (fig. 1). Shrouded in a rosy veil, this sacred book within the book requires special handling, even from the personification of *Sainte Eglise* (Holy Church) painted within the roundel.[1] Indeed, the authority of this codex is openly acclaimed by the gesticulating clerics who flank Holy Church. This *adventus* of divine truth on the manuscript page is presented within the circular limits of a medallion belonging to the instantly recognizable mise en page of a *Bible moralisée,* described by John Lowden as a "particular type of picture book of the Bible" in which scriptural text and exegetical commentary share the page with illuminations that translate—in the broadest and most argumentative sense—both Holy Writ and its exposition.[2] As Lowden has persuasively argued, the manuscript in which this medallion is found was made in the early 1220s for Blanche of Castile, queen of France, wife of Louis VIII, and mother of Louis IX.[3] It is the first of a series of such moralized Bibles, a royal manuscript tradition that extended well into the fourteenth century, reaching beyond the kingdom of France to the royal courts of England and Castile.[4]

In Blanche of Castile's manuscript (Vienna, Österreichische Nationalbibliothek, Cod. Vind. 2554; henceforth Vienna 2554), Sainte Eglise and her book visually and hermeneutically illuminate Genesis 1:14–16—God's creation of the sun, the moon, and the stars. The scriptural episode is given visual form in the roundel directly above and paraphrased in Old French in an adjacent textual compartment. The exegetical image of the divine book below receives its own vernacular gloss in a compartment to the right of the roundel: "Li soleuz senefie tote devinitei la lune senefie sainte eglise les estoiles senefient tote clergie et cels qi sunt enluminei de la devinitei deu" (The sun signifies all theology. The moon signifies Holy Church. The stars signify all of the clergy and those who are illuminated by the divinity of God).[5] As Sainte Eglise raises the book of *tote devinitei* (all theology) high above her head so that it is visible to all, including the reader-viewer inspecting the thirteenth-century manuscript page, a complex, even contradictory

Fig. 1. The book of devinitei *displayed in Blanche of Castile's Bible moralisée, early 1220s. Vienna, Österreichische Nationalbibliothek, Cod. Vind. 2554, f. 1r: 344 x 260 mm.*

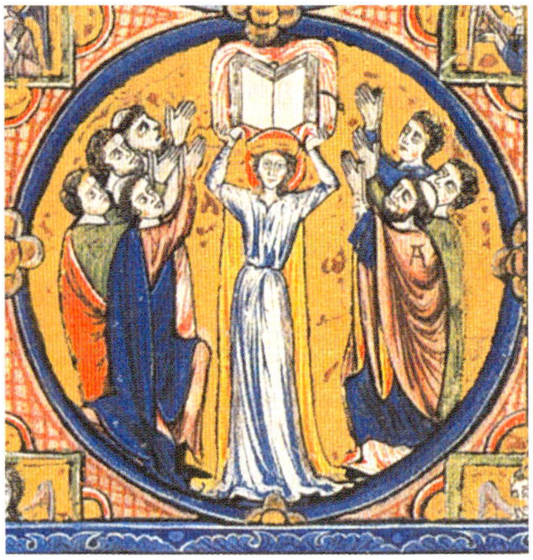

Detail from Fig. 1.

account of religious knowledge and authority is articulated in this corner of the page.[6] The elevation of the immaculate white book evokes another elevation, also first attested in Paris, namely the *elevatio* of the consecrated host in the hands of the celebrant in the Mass.[7] Like the sacrament of the altar, the book of devinitei is celebrated as an incarnation of the Divine in the world, a source of salvation hedged about by clerical figures. And like an article of faith—a mysterium—it is offered to the lay reader-viewer in a veiled and resolutely blank form: something to be gazed upon, rather than read and epistemologically apprehended.

Indeed, the vernacular texts arrayed around the edges of this painted page are the only legible texts offered to the royal reader. In this way Blanche's Bible moralisée reverses the layout of other contemporary books of scripture and commentary, scholastic volumes belonging to those masters of the sacred page who made thirteenth-century Paris a center of theological gravity, attracting students from all over Europe. Moreover, as several commentators have observed, the vernacular paraphrase of scripture inscribed beside Vienna 2554's illuminations is, at times, hopelessly errant. This was not a scriptural text that could have passed muster in the Parisian schools.[8]

In the Capetian queen's vernacular bible, visual spectacle comes first. Not only were the manuscript's images painted before its short texts were written, but, even more decisively, visual representation dominates each recto and verso, reducing scriptural text and commentary to an auxiliary role.[9] Accordingly, we might interpret the vignette painted in the last commentary roundel of Vienna 2554's first recto as a metonymic distillation of the hermeneutic situation of the volume as a whole. Blanche of Castile's Bible moralisée offered its royal audience a highly mediated access to Holy Writ, an aestheticized vision of religious truth as a kind of gleaming object in ecclesiastical hands, a source of salvation to be known only secondhand, after it was translated, sometimes beyond recognition, into visual representation and vernacular caption. And yet, as the queen inspected the glittering gold grounds of the page's medallions and read the vernacular paraphrase and exposition of scripture that flanked them, wasn't she also illuminated by devinitei?

A testament to the seemingly inexhaustible resources of Gothic manuscript painting, an index of the authority of moral theology in the period, and perhaps even the catalyst for the production of the first complete Old French translation of the Bible, Vienna 2554 is an unimpeachable witness to what ambition—patronal, artistic, linguistic, and religious—could accomplish in the first third of the thirteenth century.[10]

Historians and art historians have discussed Blanche of Castile's vernacular Bible moralisée in its own generic terms, as the first exemplar in a series of Bibles moralisées, or else the volume has been interpreted as witnessing to a broader Capetian ideological and spiritual interest in sacred history and kingship.[11] Several scholars have suggested that the Bibles moralisées may also have functioned as "mirrors of princes," a form of advice literature designed to guide the moral, spiritual, and worldly conduct of rulers.[12] It has not yet been recognized that Blanche of Castile's manuscript is also an important early example of vernacular illuminated pastoralia.[13]

With fully half of its texts and images devoted to moral exhortation, condemnation, and analysis, the manuscript's textual-visual presentation of scripture functions primarily as an authorizing foundation for sustained moral-theological examination of contemporary Christian society. Pursuing the moral-spiritual instruction of the reader-viewer by visual as well as vernacular means, Blanche's Bible moralisée represents a precocious example of illuminated "second-wave" pastoralia, literature of spiritual improvement that brought the pastoral reform movement into great households and the hands of royal and aristocratic laymen and women in the later Middle Ages.[14]

The volume's staggering quantity of illumination, its extensive use of gold, its ambitious program of innovative iconography, and its bespoke vernacular texts all suggest a project that could only have been initiated and sustained by royal patronage. Although Vienna 2554 certainly speaks volumes about the unbridled aesthetic, literary, and spiritual ambition of its royal patron, the manuscript promotes a rather retiring vision of lay spiritual excellence, of what good Christians should do and know, and of how they should pursue their salvation. In this respect, Blanche's Bible moralisée is a transitional monument. At times its textual-visual contents perpetuate older notions of the role of the laity in the scheme of salvation, and yet the manuscript as a whole exemplifies the gathering force of new desires for religious knowledge, new expressions of spiritual ambition, and new ideals of lay spiritual excellence that were just beginning to make themselves felt in royal and aristocratic circles.

Before Blanche's illuminated vernacular bible could be made, and before it could be meaningful to its anticipated audience, a horizon of expectation had to be established for the truths that were necessary to salvation and the faithful's mastery of their lessons—for all those aspects of spiritual guidance, exhortation, participation, and excellence that made the prospect of salvation imaginable, even attainable. In the twelfth and thirteenth centuries, the laity's pursuit of salvation became the object of considerable ecclesiastic attention, and the cura animarum, a system of pastoral care, was developed to systematize, regularize, and reform the sacramental and spiritual life of the faithful.

In this chapter I survey the pastoral conditions of possibility that made ambitious works of vernacular illuminated pastoralia, like Vienna 2554, relevant, powerful, and persuasive in the thirteenth and fourteenth centuries. The terrain I map in this chapter is largely charted through the orthopractical discourse of ecclesiastical legislation: the conciliar, provincial, and diocesan prescriptions and mandates drafted and promulgated by pastoral reformers. The disjunct between pastoral theory and parochial practice in the later Middle Ages was considerable; my analyses do not attempt to evaluate the success of pastoral reform on the ground. Rather, I am interested in how ecclesiastic reformers pursued a fantasy of "top-down" reform that simultaneously promoted a profound revision of the role epistemology could and should play in the religious formation of the faithful. My extended consideration of statutory measures parses late medieval pastoral legislation as a discursive regime attempting to produce a reformed church in the image of its religious knowledge.

This twinned institutional fantasy—of trickle-down reform and epistemological transformation—was formative for the cultivation and expression of elite lay spiritual ambition. In this chapter I selectively examine Vienna 2554 as an early and important witness to the translation of ecclesiastical pastoral ideals beyond the synod or pulpit. Ultimately, however, royal and aristocratic desires for religious knowledge would exceed ecclesiastical expectations, a tendency that already surfaces, if subtly, in Vienna 2554. As subsequent chapters explore, the "necessary truths" that pastoral reformers defined as essential to the laity's salvation soon became points of departure, rather than destinations, for elite lay devotees' pursuit of religious knowledge and distinction.

The Pastoral Prospect before 1215

In 1207 Robert de Courson—student of Peter the Chanter, papal legate, and pastoral reformer—described the uninstructed clergy as "toothless" and "hammering at the gates of theology" for *cibum solidiorem* (more solid food).[15] De Courson's vivid evocation of a contemporary clerical hunger for religious knowledge is a sympathetic indictment of a pastoral system that he, and many of his ecclesiastical contemporaries, felt was in need of an overhaul.

The problem of administering the cura animarum was an old one. In the late eighth and ninth centuries, Carolingian reformers laid much of the groundwork for a regulated and regulating system of ecclesiastical jurisdictions and officers, and as early as the sixth century, synodal statutes had legislated on issues of pastoral practice.[16]

In the centuries that intervened between the *capitula* issued by Carolingian bishops and archbishops and the statutes promulgated by thirteenth-century reformers like de Courson, however, a series of intertwined eleventh- and twelfth-century developments had significantly altered the spiritual landscape.

The "Gregorian" reform's assertion of ecclesiastical independence and authority in the eleventh century regularized the jurisdictions of constituent divisions of the church and, in the process, made ambitious claims for the ecclesiastical bureaucracy's integrity, authority, and utility.[17] An ever-growing corpus of canon law and swelling ranks of canonists developed a systematized and prescriptive vision of how ecclesiastical matters should be handled, and the reforming and legislating popes of the twelfth and thirteenth century actively pursued the transmission and application of this vision throughout western Europe.[18]

In the twelfth century, the development of a "universal" set of precepts and practices for the administration of the church was matched by a desire for interior reform—a reform of the self and the soul fostered within monastic centers, but with resonance beyond the monastery's walls. Conjoining the imperative *scito te ipsum* (know yourself) with a Christocentric piety that stressed emulation of Christ in fervent charity and apostolic *conversio,* the "spirituality of reform" in the twelfth century, as Giles Constable has aptly described it, promoted a vision of Christian excellence in which the active life of good works in community was intertwined with a profound awareness of *homo interior* as a work in progress.[19]

At the same time, in the schools of Laon and in the Parisian schools of the cathedral of Notre-Dame and la Monte-Sainte-Geneviève, theologians increasingly turned their attention to the interior space of the conscience and began to refine and elaborate theological considerations of intention, will, disposition, sin, virtue, and grace.[20] The emergence of a properly moral theology was accompanied by a parallel development of sacramental theology, developments in medieval theology and Christian philosophy that exerted a determinative influence over the pastoral reform efforts pursued in the thirteenth century (and in subsequent centuries), not least because so many of the reformer bishops and archbishops who undertook the rehabilitation of the clergy and laity in their care had been students at these centers of moral and sacramental theology themselves.[21]

Finally, the first quarter of the thirteenth century witnessed the formation of the Friars Preachers and the Friars Minor. These religious orders became important—if at times controversial—contributors to the reform of the cura animarum. The Dominicans, dedicated first to preaching but soon also recognized as an "Order of Confessors,"[22] developed a rigorous system of education and pastoral training designed to produce effective preachers.[23] In time they, like the Franciscans after them, became teachers not only of the laity (through their preaching, hearing of confessions, and production of pastoralia) but also of the secular clergy, who attended lectures in mendicant schools scattered across England and France.[24]

As often as not, however, when ecclesiastic reformers surveyed the spiritual landscape about them, they found much room for improvement. Absenteeism, pluralism, ignorance (often willful) of the dictates of ecclesiastical law, and a lack of proper education—even illiteracy—are repeatedly decried in statutes. The priest who abandoned his parish for a more lucrative benefice was but one specter that haunted reformist bishops and archbishops; they were equally alarmed about priestly fornicators, clerical concubines, curates who pawned or sold outright ecclesiastical vessels and other church properties, priests who scarcely celebrated Mass at all, clergy who exacted payment before administering the sacraments, and wicked priests who obstinately refused to leave their homes to hear deathbed confessions. These were not new problems in the thirteenth and fourteenth centuries, but they were flaws in the pastoral prospect that the ambitious program of reform mandated by the Fourth Lateran Council in 1215 brought into sharp focus.

The Fourth Lateran Council and the Dream of Trickle-Down Reform

The Fourth Lateran Council, summoned by Innocent III in April 1213 and convened in November 1215, focused ecclesiastical attention on a sweeping pastoral reform of the Western church.[25] Convened to galvanize support for a crusade to the Holy Land and a reconversion of European Christendom—"ad recuperationem videlicet terrae sanctae ac reformationem universalis Ecclesiae" (namely, for the recovery of the Holy Land and the reformation of the universal church)—Innocent's general council proposed a serious reshaping of what it meant to be a good Christian, both clerical and lay.[26] As recent analyses have emphasized, Lateran IV's pastoral program built on antecedent developments, conferring a papal imprimatur on reform efforts that were already under way in France and England.[27] Nonetheless, the rhetorical and conceptual impact of the Council was considerable. Lateran IV's concerted legislative articulation of what an effective and well-regulated system of pastoral care might look like effectively created an idea and ideal of the cura animarum that would animate ecclesiastical reform for centuries to come.[28]

Two elements were essential to this idealizing and prescriptive vision: the formation of an educated and effective parochial clergy and the more active participation of the faithful. In the pastoral program outlined by Lateran IV's canons these two desiderata were profoundly intertwined, causally connected in a legislative fantasy of trickle-down reform. In the sermon he addressed to gathered ecclesiastics, monastics, and lay authorities in the Lateran basilica on November 11, Innocent III confronted the problem facing reformers:[29]

> *Tempus enim est,* sicut beatus apostolus ait, *ut judicium incipiat a domo Domini* [1 Pet. 4:17]. Nam omnis in populo corruptela principaliter procedit a clero: quia *si sacerdos, qui est unctus, peccaverit, facit delinquere populum* [Lev. 4:3] quippe dum laici vident turpiter et enormiter excedentes, et ipsi eorum exemplo ad iniquitatem et scelera prolabuntur. Cumque reprehenduntur ab aliquo, protinus se excusant, dicentes: *Non potest filius facere, nisi quod viderit patrem facientem* [John 5:19]; et: *Sufficit discipulo, si sit sicut magister ejus* [Matt. 10:25]. Impletum est illud propheticum: *Erit sicut populus, sic sacerdos* [Hosea 4:9]: quinimo, *erubesce, Sidon, ait mare* [Isa. 23:4]. Hinc etiam mala provenerunt in populo Christiano. Perit fides, religio deformatur, libertas confunditur, justitia conculcatur, haeretici pullulant, insolescunt schismatici, perfidi saeviunt, praevalent Agareni.[30]
>
> (Indeed, *It is time,* as the blessed apostle said, *for judgment to begin at the house of the Lord* [1 Pet. 4:17]. For all corruption in the people comes first from the clergy, because *if the priest, who is anointed, sins, he makes the people guilty* [Lev. 4:3]. It is certain that when the laity see [the clergy] sinning shamelessly and outrageously they also will fall into sins and ungodliness because of the [clergy's] example. And when they are reproved by anyone, they immediately make excuses for themselves saying, *The Son can do only what he has seen the Father doing* [John 5:19] and *It is enough for the disciple if he is like his master* [Matt. 10:25]. So this prophecy is fulfilled, *The people will be just like the priest* [Hosea 4:9]. Indeed now the sea says, *blush with shame, O Sidon* [Isa. 23:4] for this is where evils have come into the Christian people: faith decays, religion grows deformed, liberty is thwarted, justice is trampled underfoot, heretics emerge, schismatics grow haughty, the faithless rage, the Agarenes conquer.)[31]

In the pontiff's diagnosis, corruption spread downward, from its clerical point of origin, to infect the faithful. By its bad example, a delinquent clergy inspired lay infraction, irreverence, even heresy. And a lengthy series of canons confirmed this perception of the ubiquity of clerical bad behavior. The Council prohibited clerical incontinence, drunken carousing, tavern going, and gambling.[32] Simony, absenteeism, the neglect of liturgical performance, and the extortion of payment for the sacraments were similarly confronted with canonical penalties.[33]

This dark vision of a church corrupted from within was, however, also implicitly a vision of how the pastoral prospect could be brightened, reformed, perfected. If the clergy currently disseminated corruption and the germs of religious decline, with some reformist intervention, could they not become disseminators of Christian rectitude and spiritual excellence? *Erit sicut populus, sic sacerdos* (the people will be just like the priest). According to the Council's fantasy of top-down reform, a concerted intervention at the level of the parochial clergy would, inevitably, result in a profound renovation of the people.

Like so many of the pastoral reformers, Innocent III was a product of the schools and believed that education would be a powerful catalyst for the renovation of the clergy.[34] Accordingly, Innocent, as well as his successors Honorius III and Boniface VIII, took measures to allow promising young priests the chance to study in Paris and Oxford, while also encouraging forums for remedial clerical study closer to parochial homes.[35] Innocent III and his fellow churchmen were, however, aware that the torch of clerical education had been taken up before, and to little effect. Indeed, the eleventh canon of Lateran IV notes that the Third Lateran Council (1179) had decreed that each cathedral church should provide a beneficed master to instruct the cathedral clergy and *aliosque scholares pauperes* (other poor scholars) without charge:

> Verum quoniam in multis ecclesiis id minime observatur, nos praedictum roborantes statutum, adicimus ut non solum in qualibet cathedrali ecclesia sed etiam in aliis, quarum sufficere poterunt facultates, constituatur magister idoneus a praelato . . . qui clericos ecclesiarum ipsarum et aliarum gratis in grammaticae facultate ac aliis instruat iuxta posse. Sane metropolitana ecclesia theologum nihilominus habeat, qui sacerdotes et alios in sacra pagina doceat et in his praesertim informet, quae ad curam animarum spectare noscuntur.[36]
>
> (This decree, however, is very little observed in many churches. We therefore confirm it and add that not only in every cathedral church but also in other churches with sufficient resources, a suitable master . . . shall be appointed by the prelate to teach grammar and other branches of study, as far as is possible, to the clerics of those and other churches. The metropolitan church shall have a theologian to teach scripture to priests and others and especially to instruct them in matters which are recognized as pertaining to the cure of souls.)[37]

In this canon we glimpse Lateran IV's legislative dream of a didactic reformation: a reshaping of the clergy accomplished by the study of grammar and even theology.

Couched as a help to parish priests, the canon also effectively raised the epistemological bar. If education would henceforth be the bedrock of an effective cura animarum, it would also, in the prescriptive vision of the Council, become the calling card, even the essential credential, of the good priest. According to Lateran IV's mandates, priests entrusted with the care of souls must have a modicum of learning. Even more ambitiously, the Council's eleventh canon mandated that pastors should have regular access to the resources of theology.[38]

The creedal statement promulgated as the Fourth Lateran Council's first canon was itself a serious theological document, intended for distribution to a clerical audience throughout Europe. Opening with the words "Firmiter credimus" (We firmly believe), the canon amplified antecedent formulations of the articles of belief and symbolically inaugurated Innocent's canonical vision of a reformed church with a creedal self-representation, an image of a perfected church constructed in the language of religious truth and adherence. This manifesto-like overture to Innocent III's campaign for pastoral correction and outreach also made good (albeit in a highly condensed form) the promise of theological formation and nourishment that would be reiterated and valorized in the canons that followed.

Invoking no less a pastoral authority than Pope Gregory the Great, the Council's twenty-seventh canon proclaimed that "sit ars artium regimen animarum" (the governance of souls is the art of arts). This lionizing vision of the cura animarum required significant translation, both pragmatic and conceptual, in the high and later Middle Ages—both for pastors and for the souls in their care.

Councils and Synods: Fantasies of Dissemination

Lateran IV's confidence in the trickle-down dissemination of virtue, belief, and sacramental participation was matched by its faith in the organizational efficacy of the ecclesiastical hierarchy and bureaucracy. In its sixth canon, the Council stipulated that metropolitans were henceforth to convene annual provincial councils at which clerical behavior and morals would be reviewed and corrected.[39] At these provincial councils, the canon specifies, "maxime quae statuta sunt in hoc generali concilio relegentes, ut eas faciant observari" (let them recite the canonical rules, especially those which have been laid down by this general council, so as to secure their observance).[40] Subsequent canons identify various venues (for example, cathedral chapters, monastic chapters, inquests) in which clerical offenses should be scrutinized, corrected, and punished.[41]

Episcopal and diaconal visitations also offered a means of auditing pastoral regularity and compliance on the parochial level. The Fourth Lateran Council did not neglect this instrument of pastoral control: in canon thirty-three, the supervisory mechanism of the visitation is given special consideration. Denouncing the reception of procurations without proper visitations, the Council affirmed the purposes of visitation as preaching, exhortation, correction, and reformation.[42] Described alternatively in terms of encouragement and outright punishment, the sum of these measures was a top-down supervision of curates by the upper echelons of the regional ecclesiastic hierarchy. These mechanisms of bureaucratic dissemination and enforcement do not dim the pastoral dream elaborated by Lateran IV's canons, but rather serve to substantiate, authorize, and concretize fantasy and ambition in the language of administration, organization, and order.

Not all reformers subscribed to the letter of Innocent's law. It has often been observed that the keystone of Innocent's structure for pastoral supervision—the annual provincial council prescribed in canon six—failed to find favor among archiepiscopal and episcopal legislators in France and England. Statutes issued in England after Lateran IV reveal that the canon was only erratically disseminated, and even less frequently implemented.[43] Similarly, as Raymonde Foreville has observed, the stipulation remained a "dead letter" in the Province of Rouen until the second half of the thirteenth century, despite the province's otherwise eager adoption and enforcement of other of the Council's canons.[44]

Nonetheless, both before and after Lateran IV, councils and synods played an important role in the reform of the pastoral system. It was particularly in synods that parochial clergy were introduced to new canons, both through the recital of canons in synods and through the provision of synodal exemplars that were copied and carried home by attending clergy.[45] In England, bishops Richard Poore, Alexander of Stavensby, William de Blois, Walter de Cantilupe, Richard de Wich, and Peter Quinel, and in France, bishops Eudes de Sully, Nicolas Gellent, and Guillaume le Maire decreed that the clergy must possess a correct copy of their synodal statutes.[46] Several bishops, among them Walter de Cantilupe and Guilluame le Maire, further insisted that the copy—and its possessor—be examined at a subsequent synod or visitation.[47]

The synod did not, however, simply provide an opportunity for quizzing the clergy; it was also, at times, exploited as an explicitly pedagogical forum in which parish priests could bring questions to their supervisors and receive instruction from them. In 1272, Nicolas Gellent, bishop of Angers (1260–1281), mandated that an annual gathering of the diocesan clergy be dedicated to their continuing education, particularly in relation to synodal precepts.[48] Gellent's statutes prescriptively describe a constructive seminar of sorts, in which priests would be able to consult their ecclesiastic superiors "super hiis de quibus dubitarent ad synodalem quaternum vel statute synodalia pertinentibus" (regarding these things, pertaining to the statutes or to the quarterly synod, about which they entertain doubts).[49]

Councils and synods provided a series of bureaucratic structures within which the reform of the clergy could be enacted and audited by pastoral reformers. Emphasizing both the correction of clerical infraction and the edification of the clergy, reform-minded archbishops and bishops imagined these ecclesiastic meetings as occasions for top-down formation, conformation, and reformation of the parochial clergy. Not least, councils and synods were conceived of as opportunities for clerical edification, gatherings in which pastors would display, or else improve, their mastery of the basic syllabus of religious knowledge, those necessary truths that animated the cura animarum and accomplished the salvation of souls.

The Clergy's *Clergie*

What were the parochial clergy required to know? Through the very order and structure of the topics they treat, many thirteenth- and early fourteenth-century statutes construct an ersatz syllabus of clerical knowledge consisting of *perficienda* (things that must be done) and *credenda* (things that must be believed). Synodal statutes generally reiterated the clerical obligations that had been defined by Lateran IV. Outlining the proper administration of the sacraments and the performance of ritual, these conciliar precepts defined the sine qua non of clerical performance.[50]

The epistemological foundation and demands of proper presbyteral performance were also very much on the minds of pastoral reformers. To take an influential early example, Eudes de Sully's statutes for the diocese of Paris, issued before his death in 1208, provided the clergy in his jurisdiction with a broad orientation to their parochial duties. Discussing each of the sacraments in detail, the Parisian statutes also articulate a code of clerical conduct.[51] Anticipating the emphases of Lateran IV and establishing a basis from which subsequent French and English statutes would build, Eudes de Sully's legislation reframed sacerdotal privilege and responsibility in terms of pastoral performance.

Subsequent statutes in France and England expanded on this emergent vision of what a priest should do and, with increasing emphasis, what he should know. The statutes promulgated in the "Synodal de l'Ouest" (1216–1219) incorporated a lengthy discussion of penance that offered clerical readers an up-to-date crash course in the forensic and ritual conduct of the sacrament of confession.[52] In England, Richard Poore's statutes for Salisbury (1217–1219) examined each sacrament individually and in depth, providing parish priests with both a general orientation to sacramental performance and detailed information about the particular requirements of each sacrament.[53] As in so many other statutes issued in the wake of *Omnis utriusque sexus*, Poore's statutes attest to a particular concern with penance.[54] How should a confession be heard? How should sins be evaluated? How should an appropriate penance be determined? These are some of the questions that drove statutory dilation in the period.

At times, the elaboration of the required canon of credenda and perficienda could take on a life of its own. Fully the final third of the legislation compiled in the "Synodal de l'Ouest" treats the catechetical syllabus, expounding the Trinity, the Incarnation, each of the sacraments, the articles of faith, and each of the principal sins, in turn.[55] Of this class of expansive didactic statutes, the constitutions issued by Archbishop John Pecham at the Council of the province of Canterbury convened at Lambeth in 1281 were arguably the most influential and substantial. The ninth decree of Pecham's constitutions, singled out in several manuscripts by the titulus "de informatione simplicium sacerdotum" (concerning the edification of simple priests), took the form of a pastoral tract in miniature, outlining the essential elements of the parish priest's duties.[56] The considerable appeal and utility of this pastoral vade mecum embedded in Pecham's statutes—both at the time it was issued and well into the next century—are borne out by its extensive independent circulation under the title of its incipit, *Ignorantia sacerdotum* (The Ignorance of Priests).[57]

Pecham's condensed pastoral manual identifies and expounds the syllabus of knowledge required of clergy in the province of Canterbury: the twelve articles of faith, the Ten Commandments, the two evangelical precepts, the seven works of mercy, the seven capital sins (with their "progeny"), the seven cardinal virtues, and the seven sacraments. Although *Ignorantia sacerdotum* was addressed to the clergy of the province of Canterbury, Pecham explicitly required curates to transmit its contents to their parishioners "quater in anno" (four times during the year): "hoc est, semel in qualibet quarta anni, die una sollempni vel pluribus, per se vel per alium exponat populo vulgariter, absque cuiuslibet subtilitatis textura fantastica" (that is, once in every quarter on one or several solemn days, either personally or through another, they [parish priests] must explain [the contents of the syllabus] to the people in the vernacular, without any fancifully woven subtleties).[58] Insisting that the syllabus of religious knowledge required of the clergy should be translated and transmitted to parishioners, *Ignorantia sacerdotum* exemplifies a contemporary tendency toward higher epistemological expectations and increased concern for intelligibility in late medieval English and French pastoral statutes.

Indeed, the canon of knowledge required of pastors in the period is regularly defined as the very syllabus that curates should follow when they instruct the laity. It is, I think, worth emphasizing that pastoral statutes issued in the wake of the Fourth Lateran Council routinely identify the canon of religious truths to be taught to the laity with the syllabus of religious knowledge to which they hold curates. In French and

English statutes issued in the thirteenth and fourteenth centuries, the pastoral syllabus is imagined as a curriculum for the clergy and the laity alike.

Revelations for the Laity: Truth Veiled and Unveiled

When pastoral reformers exhorted the curates in their jurisdiction to teach the laity, explicitly and repeatedly, the religious truths that defined the faith, they were, effectively, parting ways with an established, rather dimmer view of the epistemological capacity of the faithful. In his highly influential *Sententiae* (c. 1155–1158), Peter Lombard had formulated a decidedly less optimistic and less demanding assessment of what the faithful needed to know to be saved.[59] Responding to a question concerning how Old Testament patriarchs, prophets, and heroes could be justified or saved, since they had not had access to the full revelation of Christ's incarnation, passion, and resurrection, Peter Lombard made an influential distinction:

> Dici potest nullum fuisse iustum vel salvum, cui non esset facta revelatio, vel distincta, vel velata: in aperto, vel in mysterio. Distincta, ut Abrahae et Moysi aliisque maioribus, qui distinctionem articulorum fidei habebant. Velata, ut simplicibus quibus revelatum erat ea esse credenda, quae credebant illi maiores et docebant, sed eorum distinctionem apertam non habebant. Sicut et in Ecclesia aliqui minus capaces sunt, qui articulos Symboli distinguere et assignare non valent, omnia tamen credunt quae in Symbolo continentur: credunt enim quae ignorant, habentes fidem velatam in mysterio; ita et tunc minus capaces, ex revelatione sibi facta, maioribus credendo inhaerebant, quibus fidem suam quasi committebant.[60]
>
> (It may be said that no one would have been just or saved to whom a revelation was not made, whether manifest or veiled, openly or under a mystery: manifest, as to Abraham and Moses and the other ancestors, who had knowledge of the articles of faith in a distinct form; veiled, as to the simple, to whom it was revealed that they should believe the same things as those elders believed and taught, but who did not have knowledge in the same manifest form. In the church also there are some who are less able, and so cannot distinguish and explain the articles of faith, but who nevertheless believe all that is contained in the Creed; these believe what they do not know, having a faith veiled under a mystery. In the same way, in that earlier time, too, those who were less able, on the strength of a revelation made to them, adhered in faith to the elders, to whom they, as it were, entrusted their faith.)[61]

The Lombard's argument that two kinds of faith could be salvific was, theologically speaking, an attempt to maintain the possibility of salvation for those members of the Christian community who lacked the literacy, pastoral care, or epistemological resources to participate intellectually or even mnemonically in the sapiential life of the church. It was also, inevitably, an account of the relationship between forms of knowledge and belief that authorized and even valorized an utterly mediated and subordinated lay relationship to salvation and religious knowledge.[62] Describing a mode of adhesion in which epistemology played no part, this conception of a *fides implicita* (implicit faith) bracketed the Augustinian emphasis on voluntary assent and in its place substituted a trickle-down form of creedal participation that effectively excluded the "simple" from an intellectual or fully willed participation in the creedal life of the church and the pursuit of salvation.

Later medieval pastoral reformers did not explicitly theorize the epistemological obligations they placed on "simple" clerics and the lay faithful alike. Nonetheless, a set of premises and conclusions can be discerned in their promotion of the pastoral syllabus and, through it, a common canon of religious knowledge. It has long been recognized that late twelfth- and thirteenth-century pastorally minded ecclesiastics promoted a revised vision of the church, one in which the laity was involved in sacramental participation, dominical obligation, and the inward reform of the soul and conscience as never before. What has, I think, been inadequately emphasized is the profound rewriting of the established epistemological horizon of possibility that this pastoral turn involved. In effect, the pastoral reform movement articulated an alternative account of the role that religious knowledge could play in the life of the faithful and—more generally—in the corporate church's pursuit of salvation.[63]

Thus in the thirteenth century we find at least two significantly different accounts of how religious truth was necessary to salvation, of how religious truth must necessarily be attained by the faithful, and, in the broadest view, of the role epistemology should play in Christian formation and salvation. On the one hand, an older tradition, exemplified by Peter Lombard, emphasized the necessity of lay adhesion and *imitatio:* the laity could achieve salvation through an unknowing emulation of clerical exemplars. In this account, Latin-literate spiritual experts would do the epistemological heavy lifting on behalf of their simpler, less intellectually capable fellow Christians, and the relationship between religious knowledge, religious truth, and salvation was obviated, in so far as the laity were concerned.

On the other hand, many pastoral reformers promoted a very different conception of the role of religious knowledge in the life of the church and the pursuit of salvation. Consistently raising the epistemological bar, much thirteenth-century reformist legislation and pastoralia in France and England expected the parochial clergy to master a canon of religious knowledge and, in turn, to teach from that syllabus in the pulpit and the sacrament of confession. The emphasis in this account is on the transformative power of edification. In statute after statute, reformist legislators cumulatively express the conviction that each Christian can be reformed in the image of his or her religious knowledge.

The reformers' prescriptive imagining of a universal church epistemologically, morally, and behaviorally reformed by the cura animarum advanced a powerfully optimistic conception of what religious edification could accomplish. According to this vision, the acquisition of religious truth would transform the faithful, and the top-down translation of such truth was indeed possible. In Blanche's Bible moralisée we find painted proof that the reformers' confidence in the transformative effects of religious knowledge echoed beyond the synod and the schoolroom, making itself heard in the corridors of lay power and the pages of luxury manuscripts.

From ABC to the Altar: Picturing a More Explicit Faith

The reformers' prescriptive vision of a laity transformed by pastoral pedagogy is rehearsed and endorsed on folio 26v of Blanche of Castile's Bible moralisée (fig. 2). In the lower half of the manuscript page, text and image take up the trope of veiled revelation mobilized by the implicit faith thesis and visually reinterpret it in keeping with the new pastoral expectations of the thirteenth century. The page's fifth medallion depicts Exodus 34:32–35, in which Moses, returned from Mount Sinai with the tablets of the Law, appears to the Israelites transformed by his conversation with the deity.

According to the scriptural account, the brilliance of Moses's face so terrified the Israelites that he covered it when speaking with the people. In the medallion depicting the episode we see Moses gesturing in admonition toward a group of Israelites. His face, which is presented to the reader-viewer in profile, is shielded from the Israelites' view by an expanse of white cloth draped over his head. The paraphrase of the scriptural source that accompanies the medallion tersely explains that the veiling of Moses's face allows the Israelites to listen and understand him as he communicates God's commandments.[64] Immediately below, the commentary roundel and its accompanying text offer an exegetical interpretation of this biblical vignette: "Ce que moyses prist le voil et le mist devant lui et retint sa clartei en soi senefie le boen devin qi retient sa subtilitei a soi et parole au pueple grossement selonc ce qe il sunt."[65] (That Moses took the veil and put it before him and kept his light to himself signifies the good theologian who keeps his subtlety to himself and speaks to the people plainly according to who they are.)[66] Thus far, the manuscript's exegesis and pastoral precepts

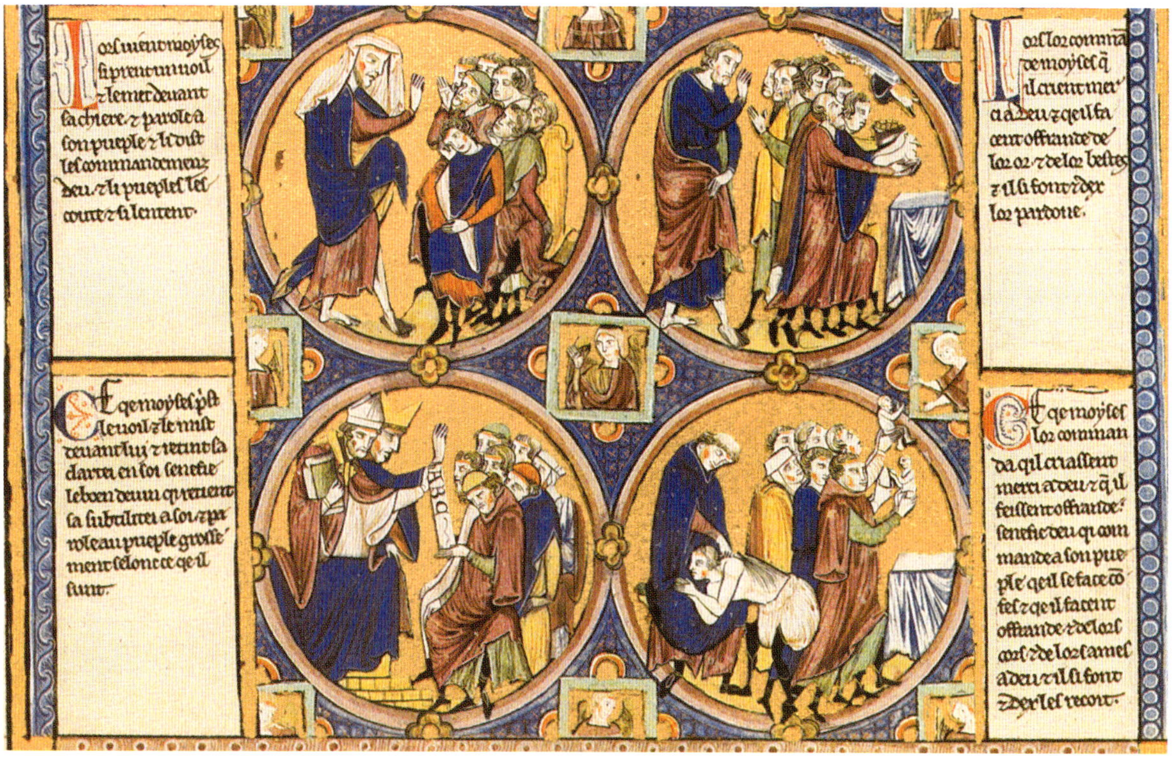

Fig. 2. Religious knowledge and righteous practice in Blanche of Castile's Bible moralisée. Vienna, Österreichische Nationalbibliothek, Cod. Vind. 2554, f. 26v (detail).

seem consonant with the Lombard's discussion of the *revelatio velata* (veiled revelation) that saved the Old Testament patriarchs and was appropriate to the implicit faith expected of simple lay believers.[67] The medallion that accompanies this vernacular exegesis, however, significantly reinflects the text beside it and the inherited wisdom it communicates.

Rather than depicting the single *devin* referenced in the text, the roundel instead features two bishops or archbishops, distinguished by their mitres from the scholastic clerics that populate so many of the manuscript's images. These figures of pastoral authority address a small crowd of laymen and one aristocratic laywoman. Holding a closed book to his breast with one hand, the ecclesiastic in the foreground retains the top of a scroll with the other. The bottom edge of the scroll is grasped by a layman and in between we read the letters "ABC": the beginner's text par excellence. Although the roundel encodes a two-tier model of religious knowledge within which the episcopal book is clearly distinguished from the laity's primer roll, this is hardly a visualization of the unknowing, unwilled assent envisaged by Peter Lombard under the rubric of fides implicita.[68] The medallion instead presents a vision of spiritual edification in which pastoral pedagogy invites a literate response from its lay audience, in which even the communication of divine truths *grossement* creates a textual community.[69]

Juxtaposed immediately to the right of the scene of pastoral pedagogy, the folio's final medallion depicts laypeople putting religious knowledge into righteous practice, a progress from knowing to doing that complicates older ideals of unthinking lay imitatio of clerical exemplars. Elaborating a visual exegesis of the commentary roundel in which Moses commands the Israelites that they should beg God's mercy and make offerings of their gold and beasts (a significantly modified interpretation of Exodus 35:4–9 and 20–22), the commentary roundel translates the sacrifices of the Israelites into the pious practices of thirteenth-century Christians.[70] On the left a layman, stripped to the waist, bends forward with his hands raised in prayer as his tonsured confessor disciplines him with a switch. At the center of the medallion, a group of six laymen and women stand before a clothed altar. The two foremost laypeople hold out tiny naked figures—representations of the soul—toward the deity, who gestures in recognition from the halved square set over a quatrefoil in the interstice above and to the right of the roundel.

The Bible moralisée's vernacular exegesis interprets this episode from the Exodus narrative as signifying how God commands "son pueple qe il se face confes et qe il facent offrande et de lors cors et de lors ames a deu et il si font et dex les reçoit" (his people to confess and to make offerings of their bodies and their souls to God and they do so and God receives them).[71] As they offer their souls to God, the laypeople at the altar do enact an overt imitatio of their clerical "betters," but the specific form of this imitation would, I think, have made Peter Lombard distinctly uncomfortable.

The laity's gestures of oblation evoke contemporary representations of the celebrant offering his soul at the altar, a scene that came to be associated with the initial A of *Ad te levavi,* the introit chant for the first Sunday in Advent.[72] In a missal painted in Paris around 1300 for the use of a Dominican convent, almost certainly the royal foundation of Poissy, we see the celebrant making just such an offering as he presents his soul to the face of the deity above the altar (fig. 3).[73] The lay figures painted in Vienna 2554 are contemporary with the earliest examples of the iconography of sacerdotal soul offering and suggest an artistic awareness of the new pastoral valorization of lay religious formation and participation.

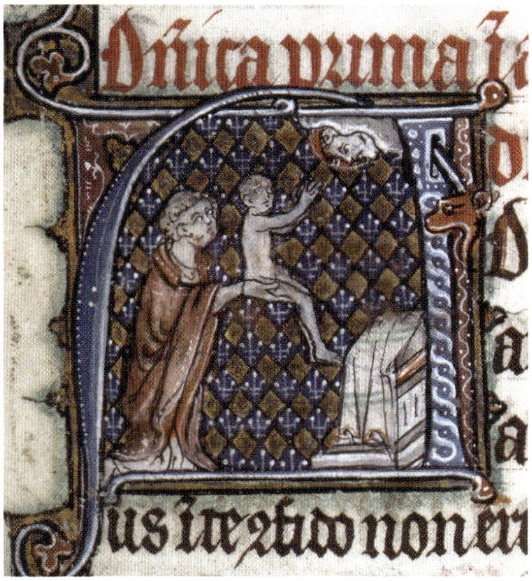

Fig. 3. A priest offers his soul at the altar in a Dominican missal, c. 1300. Princeton University Library, Department of Rare Books and Special Collections, Manuscripts Division, Garrett Medieval MS 41, f. 5r (detail): 214 x 145 mm.

Within the space of the medallion the laity is depicted as possessed of real spiritual competence. Authorized by their inclusion in a textual community of religious truth and pastoral instruction, laymen and women are prepared to make pleasing sacrifices to the deity, offerings that require epistemological engagement and preparation, as well as the practice of corporeal and devotional regimes of piety and worship. Reversing the older tradition and its insistence on implicit faith, within the Bible moralisée it is the mastery of religious knowledge that leads the laity to acts of spiritual adhesion. What, then, were good Christian laypeople expected to know?

Pastoral Production of a Faithful Laity

The reformers' revised syllabus for lay religious knowledge and performance focused on three interrelated topics: sacramental participation, the content of religious knowledge, and forms and forums for the religious education of the faithful. Over the course of the thirteenth and fourteenth centuries, pastoral legislation demonstrated an ongoing concern with both the content of the laity's religious knowledge and the shaping of that religious knowledge by the cura animarum.

Omnis utriusque sexus, the Fourth Lateran Council's twenty-first canon, is certainly the best known of these pastoral interventions in the life of the lay mind and the laity's practice of religion.[74] In it, the Council determined that all Christian men and women of the age of discernment would henceforth be required to receive the Eucharist at least once a year and further specified that confession would be a prerequisite for communication. Failure to comply with the canon's requirement of annual confession and communion would have terrible consequences: violators would be barred from entering any church during their lifetime and deprived of their right to a Christian burial.[75] Both the obligations confirmed by the canon and the punishments provided for dereliction were to be announced "frequenter" (frequently) in churches, so that no one "ignorantiae caecitate velamen excusationis assumat" (may find the pretence of an excuse in the blindness of ignorance).[76]

Omnis utriusque sexus did not legislate an innovation: by custom and (in many dioceses) by episcopal decree, Christians in France and England had been confessing their sins and receiving the Eucharist on an annual basis before 1215.[77] Indeed, in parts of western Europe—most notably England—the faithful had previously been expected to confess and communicate three times a year, a practice maintained in English statutes and attested in French legislation issued after Lateran IV.[78] In addition to the practice of more frequent festal communication (usually associated with Easter, Pentecost, and Christmas), elite Christians also received the Eucharist on an occasional basis: baptisms, knightings, coronations, and other social-religious events often involved lay communion.[79] Although Lateran IV's prescription of annual communion was hardly a break with established practice in France and England, it did decisively and unequivocally associate communion with confession, an association that would have epistemological implications for the laity's reception of the Eucharist.[80]

The Fourth Lateran Council's twenty-first canon did not simply oblige Christians to confess before their annual communion; it also specified what they should confess, in what manner they should confess, to whom they should confess, and how the confession should be conducted. All the faithful were to confess all their sins (*omnia sua peccata*) in a faithful fashion (*fideliter*) to their own priest (*proprio sacerdoti*).[81] According to the Council, confession of sins was to be made at least once a year, and penitents were enjoined to perform the penance imposed upon them by the confessor to the best of their ability (*iniunctam sibi poenitentiam studeat pro viribus adimplere*).[82] In short, Lateran IV attempted to legislate not simply the frequency of penance, or its outward procedure, but even its truthfulness, completeness, and affective character. Shifting the emphasis from an older ideal of quantified acts and public behaviors to the auditing of the invisible soul and the recital of ugly truths, the Council upped the epistemological ante, demanding that pastors and penitents bring intellectual discipline as well as compunction to the practice of the sacrament.

This emphasis on the intellectual demands of religious participation is also evident in statutory discussions of the content of the laity's religious knowledge. Typically, the obligatory minimum of religious knowledge expected of the laity was coterminous with three texts employed in liturgical and paraliturgical worship: the Pater Noster, the Ave Maria, and the Credo (or Symbol).[83] These texts had a double function. Recited during the Mass or at appointed hours of the day, they functioned as professions of belief, verbal prayers, and acts of worship. At the same time, they served as the basic set texts of lay religious education, a terse catechetical curriculum in which the cura animarum was to enroll the faithful.

The importance of these three texts to lay religious formation and practice even led some reformers to require that they be posted in plain view within churches. Thus, statutes issued for the diocese of Cambrai in 1260 require that the full texts of the Pater Noster, Ave Maria, and Credo be displayed on the doors of the choir or chancel, "videlicet in publico loco, aperte et dilucide in grossa et bene distincta littera, ita quod a longe bene possit legi" (namely in a public place, plainly and distinctly, in large and clearly articulated letters, thus so that it [the text] can definitely be read from afar).[84] In statutes issued for the diocese of Chichester (1245–1252), Bishop Richard de Wich likewise emphasized the Lord's Prayer, the angelic salutation, and the Apostles' Creed:

> Volumus etiam ut a propriis sacerdotibus laici moneantur ut dominicam orationem et symbolum apostolorum addiscant, et salutationem beate virginis; et hec sacerdotes parochianos in lingua saltim materna diligenter et frequenter doceant et in ecclesiis orationibus vacent et otiosis fabulis non intendant.[85]
>
> (We also wish that the laity should be admonished by their own [that is, their parish's] priest that they should learn the Lord's Prayer, the Apostles' Creed, and the Hail Mary; and parish priests should diligently and frequently teach their parishioners these things, at least in their native language, and [that] in churches they should pass their time in prayer and they should not attend to idle chatter.)

The provision for instruction "in lingua materna" in de Wich's statutes suggests that reformers were concerned not simply that all the faithful should mouth the same set texts in unison, but that they should also have some understanding of the words they recited. Although, as Jean-Claude Schmitt has emphasized, late medieval statutes do not specify that the Pater Noster, Ave Maria, and Credo should be recited in the vernacular by the people, only that they should be expounded by curates in the vernacular, it is clear that reformers were concerned that the semantic content of these three texts should be mastered by lay devotees.[86] Later medieval reformers did not conceive of the laity's profession and practice of the faith as a purely formal exercise—that is, as a rote memorization and recital of authorized but linguistically impenetrable texts. Rather, in the thirteenth and fourteenth centuries the laity's creedal participation was increasingly envisaged as an exercise in knowledge *and* adhesion, the mastery of a canon of religious truths *and* a willed conformity to pastoral precepts.

Many pastoral reformers imagined a daily routine for the laity in which the set texts of religious truth would have a regulated and recurring place. Statutes issued for the diocese of Cambrai (1273–1289) specify that priests should instruct the laity to recite the Pater Noster, Ave Maria, and Credo twice daily: once in the morning and once at night.[87] Bishop Alexander of Stavensby's statutes for the diocese of Coventry and Lichfield (1224–1237) outline even more ambitious expectations for the laity's creedal engagement:

> Item, precipimus ut quilibet christianus et quelibet christiana dicat omni die septies Pater noster, quia septies debet laudare deum, unde psalmista: *Septies in die laudem dixi tibi* [Ps. 118:164] Similiter in die septies Ave Maria et bis Credo, et ad hoc faciendum moneantur frequenter, et ad sciendum cogantur.[88]

(Item, we order that each and every Christian man and woman should say the Our Father seven times a day, every day; for one ought to praise god sevenfold, whence the Psalmist: *seven times a day I have given praise to thee* [Ps. 118:164]. Likewise, [they should say] the Hail Mary seven times a day and the Credo twice a day, and they should be frequently admonished to do this and they should be compelled to know how to do so.)

In Alexander of Stavensby's legislative vision, lay epistemological involvement in the pastoral syllabus was intensified by a process of multiplication. As new items were added to the list of obligatory credenda and perficienda, the laity's catechetical and devotional onus was subjected to a kind of spiritual inflation.

The Decalogue also figures implicitly and explicitly in the corpus of religious knowledge in which laypeople were to be instructed. Stressing the sanctity of the Sabbath, Bishops Nicolas Gellent and Guillaume le Maire enjoined curates to exhort the faithful to refrain from any forms of labor on Sundays and feast days.[89] Le Maire observed that salvation depends on the observance of the commandments, so the clergy must take care to instruct the laity in the keeping of the commandments, both by word and by example.[90]

Pastoral reformers also set their sights on regularizing and multiplying occasions for the religious formation of the laity and the forums in which that religious education could be pursued. Seizing on existing opportunities and imagining new pedagogical situations, ecclesiastic legislators encouraged curates to turn pastoral interactions into edifying encounters. Eudes de Sully envisioned Sundays and feast days as particular occasions for the spiritual education of the laity by the delivery of sermons.[91] In the diocese of Paris, preaching was to be taken as an opportunity not only to disseminate the syllabus but also to justify its integrity and importance through exegetical elaboration. The sermons imagined by Eudes's legislation are not simply an oral "publication" of itemized lists of credenda; rather, they are discursive initiations into both a canon of belief and a canonical way of understanding its significance.

In several sets of thirteenth-century statutes, lay attendance at Sunday services is given particular emphasis. The didactic value of the Sunday sermon and the broader social and spiritual import of participation in the Mass (if only through attendance) likely form a subtext for ecclesiastical attempts to swell the ranks of Sunday Mass-goers. In his 1245–1252 statutes for the diocese of Chichester, Richard de Wich takes a leaf from Eudes de Sully's synodal *libellus:*

> Preterea volumus quod fideles laici diebus dominicis et aliis sollempnibus saltem intersint celebrationi divinorum, nisi valitudine aut aliqua causa necessaria fuerint occupati, ne forte per hoc quod ab auditione divinorum cessaverint corda eorum indurescant.[92]
>
> (Moreover, we wish that the lay faithful should at least attend the divine services on Sundays and other solemnities, unless they shall have been taken ill or [for] some other pressing reason, lest perchance their hearts should harden because they have left off listening to divine things.)

The laity's Sunday attendance is directly associated with their ongoing spiritual reformation in this statute. Weekly sermons and churchgoing will keep lay hearts malleable and ready to receive a pastoral imprimatur; by allusion and intent, de Wich's legislation casts dominical catechesis and pastoral exhortation as formative exertions. The early fourteenth-century *Antiqua statuta* of Tournai also present Sundays and feast days as opportunities for religious formation and edification.[93] Echoing contemporary legislation in England and France, the Tournai statutes mandate that curates should expound the articles of the faith to lay churchgoers on the days of obligation, confirming and clarifying the creedal syllabus with the authority of scripture (*authoritatibus Sacre Scripture*).[94]

The ceremonial framework of the Mass and of festal observations was not the only forum designated by ecclesiastical legislators for the spiritual education and formation of the laity. Several thirteenth-century statutes also explicitly provide for the religious education of children. Robert Grosseteste enjoins rectors and parish priests to look to the spiritual education of the *pueri* of their churches:

> Provideant etiam attentius ecclesiarum rectores et sacerdotes parochiales ut pueri parochiarum suarum diligenter doceantur et sciant orationem dominicam, et symbolum, et salutationem beate virginis, et cruces signaculo se recte consignare.[95]
>
> (Let rectors of churches and parish priests make preparations so that the boys [or children] of their parishes may be diligently taught; and let them [the pueri] know the Lord's Prayer, the Creed, the Hail Mary, and how to properly cross themselves.)

As Grosseteste's synodal admonition continues, he notes with dismay that many adults do not know this canonical repertoire of prayer and gesture. The bishop's response is to require that "cum laici ad confessionem accedunt, diligenter examinentur utrum scierint predicta, et secundum quod expedit in eis a sacerdotibus instruantur" (when laypeople come to confession, they should be diligently examined as to whether they know the aforementioned things and, according to what is useful, let them be instructed in these things by priests).[96] In Grosseteste's ambitious scheme, catechetical schooling will properly form a younger generation of parishioners; their elders, however, require the remedial instruction made possible by a relatively new vision of what could and should be accomplished in the sacrament of confession. Grosseteste's faith in the didactic potential of the confessional encounter is not anomalous; many of his contemporaries and successors clearly conceived of confession as both a powerful sacrament and a kind of spiritual tutorial.[97]

As statute after statute reveals, for French and English pastoral reformers it was not enough that the laity should believe implicitly, unknowingly adhering to the superior, explicit faith of their spiritual shepherds. Thirteenth-century reformers instead stressed the mastery of uniform minimums of religious knowledge, minimums that were, over the course of the century, subjected to gradual but constant revision, expansion, and inflation. As archbishops and bishops added elements to the required syllabus of religious knowledge, they also extended the parameters of pastoral education to embrace more frequent and diversified occasions for teaching and—perhaps most significantly—higher standards for epistemological engagement in the work of Christian formation.

Over the course of the thirteenth century much of the substance of the syllabus of religious truth and obligation prescribed to parish priests became a canon of credenda and perficienda for which the laity was also held responsible. Nonetheless, despite this shared body of religious knowledge, pastoral reformers clung to a vision, promoted forcefully and perhaps fantastically by the canons of the Fourth Lateran Council, that religious truth—inevitably and ideally—would be translated from top to bottom, a migration of religious knowledge managed by the clergy to the benefit, even the salvation, of the souls in their care. Even as pastoral reformers promoted an epistemologically optimistic view of the laity—and of Christian perfectibility, more generally—they still insisted that sacred truths required careful handling, clerical framing, and periodic sacerdotal auditing.

Of course, as pastoral legislators themselves recognized, the downward dissemination of religious knowledge was only as good as the clerical conduits through which sacred truths were to pass. Within the orthopractical discourse of canons and statutes, clerical lassitude or incompetence is always the "before" state of reform, an error in the pastoral schema that reformist measures emend. The paradigm of top-to-bottom transformation—the very structural premise that conceptually guaranteed the efficacy of reformist legislation—remains unchallenged and largely unexamined in these texts. Elsewhere, however, such flaws in the pastoral prospect were made visible, examined, and addressed.

Like Water from a Rock: Religious Knowledge and Spiritual Thirst

The lower half of folio 22v in Blanche's Bible moralisée elaborates an account of spiritual need and pastoral response that scrutinizes the trickle-down paradigm and, simultaneously, reframes it in terms of lay demands for religious knowledge (fig. 4). In an exegesis of the Israelites' great thirst in the desert (Exod. 17:2–3) and Moses's divinely inspired striking of water from the rock (Exod. 17:5–6), the page's final medallions represent a before-and-after sequence of frustrated spiritual demand and beneficent pastoral supply. On the bottom left, a crowd of lay figures, with a tonsured cleric at their head, petition two bishops. The tonsured cleric echoes the Israelites painted in the medallion above, pointing to their example with one hand, while gesturing toward his mouth with the other. All the laymen standing behind him crane their necks and lean forward, save a solitary figure on the far left of the group. Leaning to the left, away from his fellow petitioners, this youth cups his face in his hand, a gesture that signals his despair.

The medallion clearly encapsulates a pathetic scene of pastoral need. As the tonsured curate seeks the *clergie* (clerical learning) required by the souls in his care, his ecclesiastic supervisors hoard their religious knowledge, guarding their monopoly on book learning, despite the entreaties of the faithful. This visual critique of the dysfunction that could, quite easily, derail the top-down reform ideal is given voice by the vernacular text that accompanies the roundel. Here we are told that the thirsting Israelites "senefie les boens crestiens qi vienent devant lors ninces prelaz et dient qi muerent de soif d'oïr la parole deu et cil tienent loes livres clos et dient qe il ne lor sevent qe doneir"[98] (signify the good Christians who come before their worthless prelates and say that they are dying of thirst to hear the word of God and those ones hold closed their books and say that they don't know what to give them).[99]

Together, the Old French commentary and the painted medallion play quite pointedly with the expected categories of ignorance and knowledge, the dissemination of religious truth, and the grateful reception of the verities that save. As the bookish bishops hypocritically feign ignorance in order to shirk their pastoral obligations, their exemplarity is exposed as a sham. It is instead those lesser figures in the hierarchy of

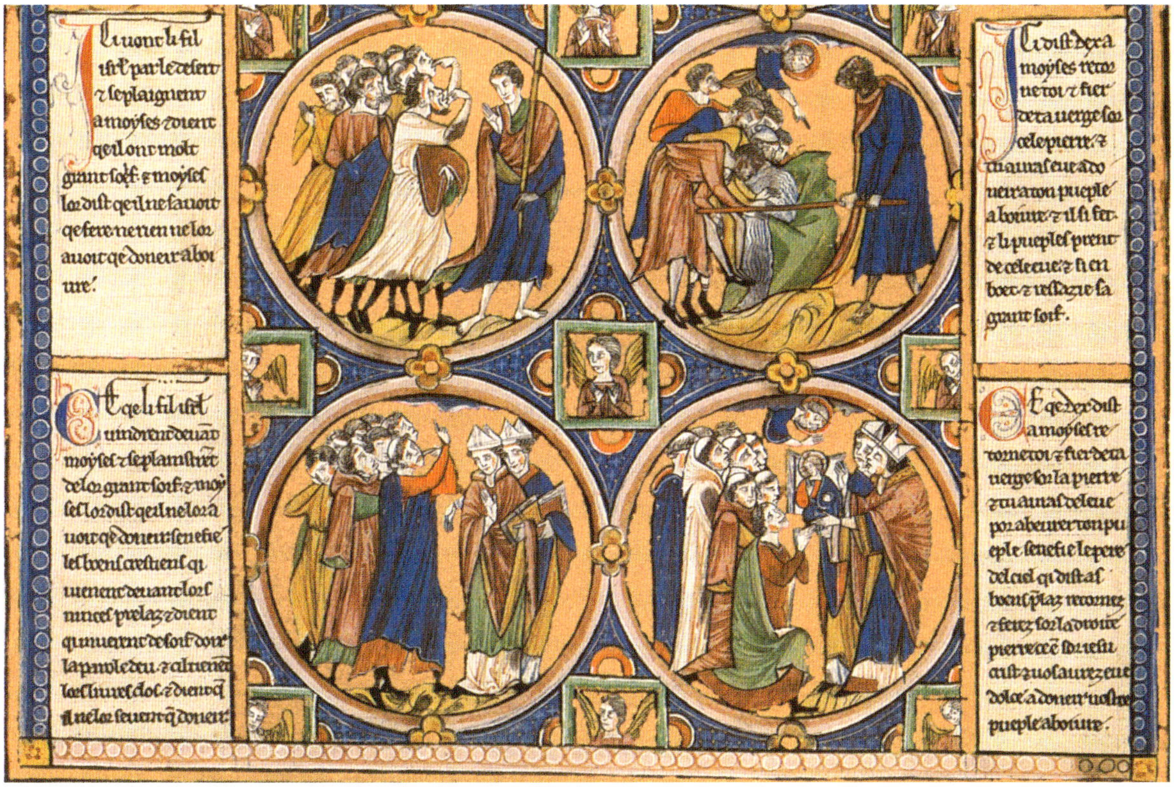

Fig. 4. Spiritual thirst and satiating religious knowledge in Blanche of Castile's Bible moralisée. Vienna, Österreichische Nationalbibliothek, Cod. Vind. 2554, f. 22v (detail).

the cura animarum—the pastor and his flock—who manifest the desire for saving truth, pastoral ambition, and the thirst for religious knowledge.

This medallion is, however, only the first term in a didactic distinction of pastoral performance. In the last roundel on the page, we see quite a different scenario. Commenting on Exodus 17:5–6, in which Moses, instructed by God, strikes the rock and provides the thirsting Israelites with water to drink, the medallion presents the dissemination of saving truth in altogether different terms. As the vernacular commentary explains, "Ce qe Dex dist a moyses retorne toi et fier de ta verge sor la pierre et tu avras de l'eue por abevrer ton pueple senefie le pere del ciel qi dist as boens prelaz retornez et ferez sor la droite pierre ce est sor iesu crist et vos aurez eue dolce a doneir vostre peuple a boivre."[100] (That God said to Moses: Return and strike your rod on the stone and you will have water for your people signifies the Father of heaven who says to the good prelates: Return and strike on the right stone which is on Jesus Christ and you will have sweet water to give your people to drink.)[101]

In the adjacent roundel we see the *boens prelaz* in action. Here the transmission of religious knowledge is deliberately presented as a clerical affair: two bishops energetically offer a crowd of tonsured figures yet another book of devinitei. In this case, the book of religious knowledge is glorified as an incarnation of Christic presence: a half-length figure of Christ appears against the foil of the codex's white pages and together with the clergy about him receives the benediction of God the Father who condescends from a cloud bank above. The medallion celebrates a fraternal order of exemplars: divine, codicological, episcopal, and clerical. Within this textual community, the thirst for religious knowledge and the desire for the word of God are satisfied by the most authorized and authorizing instantiation of a trickle-down transmission of sacred and saving truth.

There is, however, a noticeable absence in the image: no laymen or women figure among those whose thirst for the sweet water of religious knowledge has been slaked. Like the book of devinitei in the manuscript's first folio, the Christological codex of folio 22v is destined for a clerical audience; its further transmission to the laity remains out of sight, a promise or implication rather than a pastoral performance witnessed by the beholder of the page.

The pastoral fantasy of the top-down dissemination of religious precept, knowledge, and practice is thus subjected to real scrutiny in Blanche's Bible moralisée. Certainly these medallions do not indict the cura animarum; they are far from expressing anti-clerical sentiment or agitated discontent. They do, however, speak directly to the frailty of the pastoral project, to the distance between orthopractical vision and contemporary spiritual realities. And their simultaneous celebration of pastoral excellence and condemnation of pastoral failure suggest that the ambitions and limitations of the movement to reform the church and the faithful was a matter of considerable interest to the manuscript's anticipated audience.

Conclusion: Looking beyond *Minima*

The critical view of the pastoral prospect afforded to Blanche of Castile by her Bible moralisée visually and textually echoes the exhortations and condemnations voiced by late medieval bishops and archbishops when they stood back and surveyed the pastoral landscape. John Pecham, archbishop of Canterbury (1279–1292), expressed just such an assessment in the constitutions that he issued at the Council of Lambeth in 1281. Forcefully articulating both the persistent ideals and lingering disappointments of the pastoral reform movement almost seventy years after Innocent's great Council and some sixty years after Blanche's Bible moralisée was completed, Pecham wrote:

> Ignorantia sacerdotum populum precipitat in foveam erroris; et clericorum stultitia vel ruditas, qui diffinitione canonica filios fidelium instruere iubentur, magis aliquando ad errorem proficit quam doctrinam. Quidam etiam ceci predicantes non semper loca visitant que magis constat veritatis lumine indigere; testante propheta, quia *parvuli petierunt panem*, nec *erat qui frangeret* [Lam. 4:4], et alio clamante quia *egeni et pauperes querunt aquas, lingua eorum siti arruit* [Isa. 41:17].[102]
>
> (The ignorance of priests casts the people down into the ditch of error, and the foolishness and lack of learning of clerics, whom the decrees of canon law order to teach the sons of the faithful, is all the worse when it leads to error instead of knowledge. For some blind preachers do not always see the places which stand in greatest need of the light of truth; the prophet testifies that *the little ones have asked for bread, and there was none to break unto them* [Lam. 4:4], and another cries that *the needy and the poor seek for waters, and there are none: their tongue hath been dry with thirst* [Isa. 41:17].)[103]

Despite its patent frustration with the clerical status quo, Pecham's polemic clearly upholds a vision of pastoral reform as an epistemological project. In terms that cannot fail to evoke the thirsting curate and his despairing lay flock in Vienna 2554, Pecham laments how the intellectual failures and pedagogic lassitude of the clergy threaten the faithful "little ones." After several decades of reformist legislation, the illumination of religious knowledge had not burned brightly enough.

Although Pecham laments the continuing imperfections of the cura animarum, he still adheres to Lateran IV's fantasy of a trickle-down dissemination of reform ideals and realities and to its belief in the efficacy of clerical exemplarism. In 1215 this confidence in reformist imitatio, the conformation of the folk to their spiritual fathers, drove both bureaucratic measures and the prescription of new standards for religious participation and identity. At Lambeth in 1281, the archbishop decried the same trickle-down paradigm as the means by which the contagion of clerical error was spread to the faithful. The efficacy of the model was not in doubt, but for Pecham it had become terribly perverted.

Pecham's condemnation of the clergy's failings, and the statutes he issued in response, cast a long shadow in subsequent decades. From a slightly different perspective, however, it is clear that his critique was already outmoded, at least within certain royal households and princely courts, by the last quarter of the thirteenth century. In both France and England, the spiritual ambitions of elite reader-viewers were no longer coterminous with the "common" forms of religious knowledge promoted in statutory measures and prescribed by other forms of ecclesiastic authority. Necessary truths were no longer enough; new spiritual ambitions desired new forms of spiritual excellence.

Archbishop Pecham must have been well aware that royal and aristocratic spiritual ambition had outstripped ecclesiastically defined *minima* of lay religious knowledge, for it was to Pecham that Queen Eleanor of Castile (d. 1290), wife of Edward I, turned for a vernacular précis of Pseudo-Dionysius's *De celesti hierarchia* in the 1280s.[104] The *Jerarchie,* the treatise that Pecham produced for the queen, has been described by Mary Dominica Legge as a rather "puerile" exposition of the apophatic theologian's account of the angelic orders, analogized to the hierarchy of the royal court.[105] Nonetheless, Eleanor's request reveals that she was well aware of contemporary theological conversations and of the texts that were generating intellectual heat in scholastic circles.[106] The queen's desire for an archiepiscopally authored vernacular translation of the Latin text suggests that she wanted, in some fashion, to be part of the clerical conversation.

Queens like Eleanor of Castile and Blanche of Castile, as well as their less-exalted male and female aristocratic counterparts, were encouraged by the pastoral reform movement to seek out and master the truths that saved. As Vienna 2554 demonstrates, however, they do not seem to have been content with the syllabus of necessary truths that the cura animarum translated to all of the faithful. Instead, mobilizing the resources of vernacular language and the visual arts, they set about redefining the canon of religious knowledge deemed appropriate to their station. With wealth, prestige, and ready access to scribes, artists, and exemplars, elite laypeople pursued a more ambitious vision of spiritual excellence, a vision given form and voice in the pages of luxury manuscripts of spiritual instruction.

Within this aggrandized (and self-aggrandizing) pursuit of spiritual ambition, the pastoral syllabus still served as a foundation for spiritual edification. Similarly, royal and aristocratic conceptions of spiritual formation and pious practice did not dispense with corporate forms of religious expression, with sacramental participation, or with the patronage of religious institutions. As I explore in the chapters that follow, the translation of religious truth and the acquisition of religious knowledge pursued by lay elites in the thirteenth and fourteenth centuries is better understood as an artful appropriation of religious authority than as a rejection of the cura animarum, its pastoral personnel, or the collective forms of worship and devotion they promoted.

The manuscripts examined in the following chapters reveal that royal and aristocratic laypeople were intent on gaining access to authorized religious truths, mastering practices associated with spiritual experts like confessors and monastics, and learning to better discern divinity's presence in the church. Significantly, these acts of spiritual appropriation survive today in the very material and visible forms of luxury manuscripts, codices filled with vernacular texts and vivid images. Artifacts of lay spiritual ambition, these manuscripts allow us to glimpse late medieval religious truth in the process of its translation, a transformative movement from the Latinate canons, Creeds, and catechetical minima of the trickle-down reformist fantasy to the varied, sometimes vexed, often captivating forms of vernacular text and painted image.

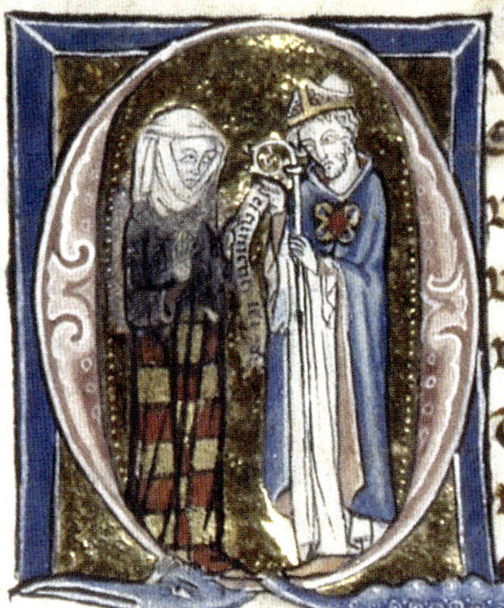

ui bien pense bien puet dire.
Sanz penser ne puet suffire
De nul bon ouere comencer.
Deu n' doint de lui penser
De qui par q en qui sunt
Tuz les biens que s' el mūd.
Deu le pere e deu le fiz
E deu li seint esperiz
Persones treis en trinite
E un soul deu en unite
Sanz fin e sanz comencement
A qui honour e glorie apent
Il nus doint ses ovres fere
E nus defende de contraire
Tout avom mester de aye
Mes tres touz ne porront mie
Saver le langage en fin
De ebreu, de gru, ne de latin
Pur loer lor creatur
Ne bouche de chanteur
Ne seit clos de deu loer
E son seint noun mercier
Ke chescun en son langage
Le conoise sanz folage
Son deu e sa redemption
En romanz comence ma reison
Pur ceus qui ne sevent mie
Ne lectrure ne clergie
De principio creationis mundi
Del mond dirai p' quoi fu feit
E puis coment donez esteit
A adam nostre primer pere

CHAPTER TWO

Translating the Modus Confitendi

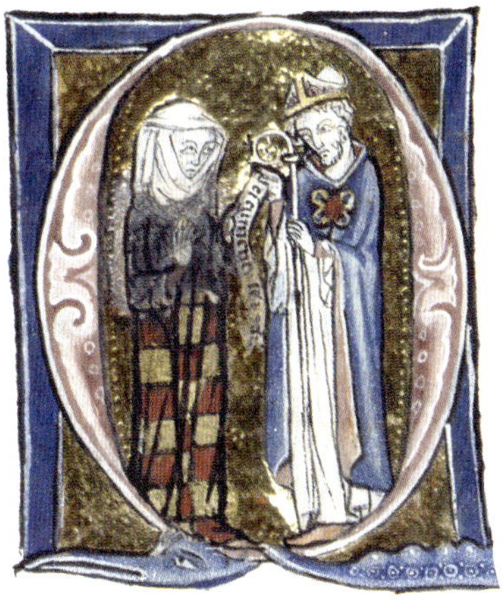

Pastor and parishioner engage in an intimate dialogue within the space of an initial introducing Robert Grosseteste's *Château d'amour* in a compendium made circa 1280–1298 for the spiritual instruction of Baroness Joan Tateshal (d. 1310; fig. 5). At left we see Joan, a Lincolnshire noblewoman, and Robert Grosseteste, bishop of Lincoln, holding a scroll inscribed "Ci cumence ici," a phrase that locates the beginning of pastoral instruction inside the painted space of the initial.[1] Facing each other across this miniature incipit, Joan and Robert engage in a vernacular colloquy, one initiated by Robert, whose hand grasps the scroll at its upper edge, but continued by Joan as she supports the scroll's unfurling descent.

When Joan had herself pictured in this initial her exemplary pastor was already dead.[2] The illuminated letter thus presents a fiction of the cura animarum, an impossible ministerial moment that commemorates Grosseteste's memory by feigning his presence. In the company of the famed bishop, Joan appears as the recipient of his pastoral care, ministered to by the figure of Grosseteste and by his "succinct survey of Christian doctrine" in verse, which she read from this page for her own spiritual improvement.[3] The image represents a moment of pastoral dialogue, a dialogue that would have been enacted by Joan and her book as she mouthed Grosseteste's words and gazed at his image. In this way the initial's representational fiction makes possible an imagined pastoral encounter and Grosseteste's ministry is granted new life and efficacy.

In illuminated manuscripts of spiritual instruction like Joan's compendium, representation was enlisted in the project of spiritual reform and images were made into the bearers of creedal instruction, moral correction, and religious formation. The performance of these images assumes a dialogic relationship between painting and viewer.[4]

Fig. 5. Joan Tateshal and her pastor Robert Grosseteste inhabit his Château d'amour, *c. 1280–1298. Princeton University Library, Department of Rare Books and Special Collections, Manuscripts Division, Taylor Medieval MS 1, f. 173r: 245 x 125 mm.*

Beholders were expected to come to visual pastoralia with intent eyes, ready to ask questions of belief and to receive salvific answers. This dialogic solicitation of the viewer links the moment of viewing with contemporary paradigms for the *modus confitendi*—the proper conduct of confession—a sacramental exercise couched in questions and answers, designed to produce representations of sin and religious truth.

This chapter argues that changes in pastoral conceptions of the sacrament of penance promoted dialogue as a practice fundamental to the exercise of the late medieval cura animarum and, by extension, as a paradigm for modes of address and solicited reception mobilized in works of visual pastoralia.[5] My analysis begins by examining how penance was revisited and revised in the twelfth and thirteenth centuries, resulting in a new theory and practice of confession as a sacramental encounter involving the representation of sin, of religious truth, of the penitent and his or her confessor. From the spoken dialogue of confession I turn to the dialogic performance of a series of illuminated manuscripts of spiritual instruction, exploring how dialogic modes of address shape their visual translations of religious truth. These books, I argue, solicit and reward the introspective and representational practices cultivated by the conduct of late medieval confession, inviting reader-viewers to the care of the spiritual self, practiced in the company of images.[6]

A New Penitential Regime

Developments in moral and sacramental theology over the course of the twelfth and thirteenth centuries altered and refined theological and pastoral understandings of the sacrament of penance—and of confession's place within that spiritual exercise.[7] As theologians, pastors, and monastics increasingly turned their attention to the problem of sin (and virtue), penance and penitence became conceptually distinguished as never before.

No single historical development suffices to explain why penance's inner and outer workings should have been revisited so thoroughly at this particular point in the history of Christian theology and pastoral practice; undoubtedly, a complex constellation of historical factors was at work. Among them, we may identify a reformist concern for conversio, initially elaborated within monastic circles—most notably among the Cistercians—and soon felt throughout European society. Certainly, the exegetical and theological ferment of the schools of Laon and of Paris (not to mention other less populous centers of learning in France, England, and Italy) testify not only to the collaborative energies brought to theological problems but also to the cumulative effect produced by continuous interchange among an international assembly of scholars and students. Finally, though by no means exhaustively, we may note that the project of collecting, reconciling, and commenting upon both civil and canon law, undertaken with real zeal by twelfth-century canonists and jurists, contributed both the example of a systematized framework and much raw *ad casus* material to the moral-theological enterprise.

Twelfth-century theologians did not, however, fabricate their vision of sacramental penance from whole cloth. Peter the Chanter and his "circle," as well as other contributors to the conversation (and at times, heated debate) about penance and its sacramental character—like Peter Lombard, Bernard of Clairvaux, Peter Abelard, and Alan of Lille—were the conscious inheritors of several centuries of Christian teaching on and practice of penance.[8] A principal element in this inheritance was the system of tariffed penance, codified and disseminated in the *libri paenitentiales*.[9] These manuals, which are thought to have first flowered in sixth-century Ireland, listed sins and their corollary penances (the penitential tariff). Although the penitentials have often been disparaged as mechanistic in their approach and excessively—even impossibly—severe in their demands, they made an important contribution to later revisions of the sacrament of penance. The penitentials authorized an approach to sin and its remedies that recognized the heterogeneity of infraction and the importance of circumstance (the who, when, where, what, and with whom of sin); moreover, they were designed for a practice of sacramental penance that involved an individual penitent, an inquiring minister, and reiterable sacramental participation.[10]

From this foundation, twelfth-century theologians and pastors elaborated a new vision of the sacrament of penance. In general terms, penance had been distinguished into three parts: repentance, confession, and satisfaction. Over the course of the twelfth and thirteenth centuries each of these terms would come under greater scrutiny and would be significantly reinflected, both in terms of its character or substance and with respect to its role in the outward and inward practice of sacramental penance.

Twelfth-century debates about contrition exerted tremendous pressure on the sacrament of penance. Arguably the most influential voice in this discussion, Abelard affirmed the ethically neutral character of acts, emphasizing the invisible, interior, and ordinarily inscrutable character of sin as an act of will. Within the Abelardian conception of sin and its sacramental remedy, sin is construed as an interior act of consent to the improper—a mental act of contempt for God, which only God can discern and absolve. True repentance, for Abelard (and for those who followed his line of thought on this point), is likewise a mental-spiritual event: contrition, like sin, is fundamentally irreducible to acts, and it too happens interiorly. In this fashion, Abelard posited that sacramental penance's goal—the reconciliation of the wrongdoer to God—is accomplished in an entirely inward or interior fashion: "Cum hoc autem gemitu et contritione cordis, quam ueram penitentiam dicimus . . . statim . . . Deo reconciliamur et precedentis peccati ueniam assequimur" (With this sigh and contrition of the heart which we call true repentance . . . we are instantly reconciled to God and we gain pardon for the

duties within the confessional courtroom. Accused, the penitent also served as (self-) accuser; pledged to faithful sacramental participation, he or she was also cast as a star witness for the prosecution.[23]

Both the medicus animae trope and the elaboration of the judicial analogy, while ostensibly affirming the expertise and authority of the confessor-priest, simultaneously inscribe the penitent at the sacramental center of penance. Certainly, without a penitent there could be no penance. Aquinas, a fervent advocate of the causal power of sacerdotal absolution, understood this basic axiom and, accordingly, afforded the penitent a contributory role in the production of the sacrament. Nonetheless, there is a significant difference between Aquinas's conception of the penitent and the role afforded him or her in both of the tropes discussed above. As metaphoric patient or participant in a quasi-juridical investigation, the penitent emerges as the contributor of more than the "matter of sin"; he or she is, at least implicitly, the confessor's partner in the modus confitendi, a performance employing representational means to an epistemological and sacramental end.

Practicing Confessional Dialogue: Quinel's *Summula*

In the wake of the Fourth Lateran Council, many French and English archbishops and bishops repeated *Omnis utriusque sexus*'s medical and judicial metaphors in their statutes.[24] Some statutes went beyond these analogic framings of confession and confessors, offering their clerical readers a more fully developed orientation to confession's aims and its conduct. The statutes and pastoral *summula* issued in 1287 by Bishop Peter Quinel for the diocese of Exeter are a case in point.[25]

Quinel's summula elaborates a confessional syllabus that will be employed in the production of a complete confession, by priest and penitent alike:

> Cum autem satisfacere debeat delinquens non secundum arbitrium proprium sed potius ad arbitrium eius contra quem deliquit, misericordius enim volens agere nobiscum dominus, sacerdotem quasi iudicem posuit inter ipsum et nos, cuius in hoc arbitrium debemus sequi. . . . Sed ut iste sciat quid nobis iniungere debeat, nos omnia debemus confiteri, quia nostras per se non potest conscientias intueri. Et quoniam ad transgressionem decem dictorum mandatorum tota reduci potest criminum multitudo, dicta mandata scire tenentur et penitentes et penitentias iniungens.[26]
>
> (Since the sinner ought to make satisfaction not according to his own judgment but rather in keeping with the judgment of him

> against whom he sinned, the merciful Lord, desiring to act on our behalf, placed the priest between himself and us, like a judge, whose judgment in this matter we ought to follow. . . . But, in order that that one [the priest] may know what he ought to enjoin upon us [as penance], we ought to confess everything, because he is not able, of himself, to see into our consciences. And because all the multitude of sins can be reduced to the transgression of the said commandments, both penitents and the one imposing penances are required to know the said commandments.)

The summula's framework for the production of a confession is inherently dialogic. The penitent comes before the priest just as a defendant comes to account before a judge, and the priest, standing between the penitent and divine judgment, listens to and approves a confession in which the penitent represents sin in the image of transgressed commandments. Providing an initial, fundamental armature for the production of a good confession, knowledge of the Ten Commandments is required of both the penitent and the priest. Working from their shared knowledge of the pastoral syllabus, confessor and sinner collaboratively produce the full and true confession necessary for the sacramental remission of sins.

As the summula continues, it takes up each of the commandments in turn. It then discusses each of the seven deadly sins, before expounding how, and to what effect, the circumstances of sin must be considered. Significantly, the systematic progress through the syllabus prescribed by the summula is explicitly identified as the penitent's onus. The section examining transgressions against the first commandment reads, "Recurrat igitur penitens ad primum mandatum, et sollicite videat in se ipso si transgressus fuerit illud" (Therefore the penitent should return to the first commandment, and he should carefully examine [literally, "look in"] himself, as to whether he shall have transgressed that [commandment]).[27] In the next two sections of the treatise, addressing the second and third commandments, this injunction is repeated: the penitent must look inward, inspecting the contents of his conscience and spying out any infractions he may have committed.[28]

When it moves on to the fourth commandment, however, the treatise's prescriptive language changes voice: "Quarto considerandum est si transgressus fuerit quartum mandatum" (Fourth, it must be considered if the fourth commandment shall have been transgressed).[29] Shifting the emphasis from penitential self-scrutiny to a more distanced, impersonal investigation of transgression, this change of grammatical construction is motivated by a traditional distinction, explicitly evoked in the text, between the first three commandments and the seven commandments that follow them. As the summula explains, "Tria vero precedentia mandata, scilicet iam dicta, deo debita sunt; septem sequentia ad proximum referuntur" (The three preceding commandments, namely those already stated, are owed to God; the seven following [commandments] relate to [one's] neighbor).[30] An implicit psychology of penitential agency and responsibility is articulated in the summula's differentiated phrasing. The discovery of sins against God depends, first and foremost, on the penitent's diligent introspection. Sins against the Christian community, however, are exterior sins, sins with a kind of social visibility that more readily exposes itself to the confessor's expert scrutiny.[3]

Although Quinel promotes the tract as an aid to confessors in his diocese, in its form and content the summula offers the parish priest precious few interrogatives. The intensive introspection demanded by the summula's systematic progress through the pastoral syllabus is a burden that must be shouldered by the penitent. As the summula itself recognizes, although the confessor possesses the power to absolve, "nostras per se non potest conscientias intueri" (he is not able, of himself, to see into our consciences)[32] The summula is composed as a response to this fundamental difficulty.

The penitent and confessor, confronted with the intrinsic hiddenness of sin, must find a way to make sin visible and utterable. The summula suggests that this project must proceed from a shared set of terms, a framework common to confessor and penitent, and it identifies that conceptual common ground in the pastoral syllabus. Detailing the commandments, delineating the sins, and defining the articles of the faith, the summula constructs an organized and coherent conceptual architecture within which a confession can be produced by a penitent and interpreted, evaluated, and ultimately accepted by a priest.

The summula allows that not all penitents will have sufficiently mastered the syllabus to adequately participate in the confessional procedure it elaborates. In the sections of the treatise devoted to the conferral of absolution and penance, the summula supplies a remedy for this problem:

> Consideret autem sacerdos, absolvere volens penitentem, si penitens sit christianus, id est si fidem habeat. Quo invento doceat eum sacerdos articulos fidei quos ignorat. Deinde doceat eum quod habeat contritionem amaram cordis, et discretam cum moderamine, ne sit dolor irrationabilis, et perseverantem cum proposito semper abstinendi, et generalem, scilicet pro omnibus commissis et omissis, et hoc precipue propter deum. . . . Doceat etiam sacerdos penitentem

> quorumlibet spiritualium remedia peccatorum secundum quod dominus ei inspiraverit ex auctoritate scriptuarum.[33]
>
> (But the priest, wishing to absolve the penitent, should consider if the penitent is Christian, that is, if he has faith. Once this is ascertained, the priest should teach him the articles of the faith that he does not know. Then let him teach [the penitent] that he should have bitter contrition of heart and prudent [contrition] with moderation, lest it should be an irrational grief, and persistent [contrition] with the intent of always abstaining [from sin], and general [contrition], that is, for all sins of commission and of omission, and this chiefly for God's sake. . . . Also the priest should teach the penitent any relevant remedies for spiritual sins, according to what God inspires in him, with recourse to scripture's authority.)

The double function of the confessional encounter emerges clearly in this passage. Penance is a disciplinary, subtractive process in which sins are named, and ultimately absolved. It is also a didactic exchange, a dialogue in which the penitent draws on his catechetical knowledge in the production of a confession, and the priest—overseeing the procedure—supplies those elements from the syllabus that the penitent does not yet know. The composition and recital of the confession thus has an accessory effect, beyond the spiritual purification and reconciliation effected by sacerdotal absolution: the sacramental encounter provides the occasion for both a dialogic auditing of the penitent's mastery of the syllabus and—as needed—a dialogic reformation and extension of that knowledge. The practice of confession is thus a redoubled moral-spiritual visitation: the penitent must examine and disclose his or her conscience, and the priest is expected to examine and correct the penitent's knowledge.

Embedded within the systematizing framework of the pastoral syllabus, the summula promotes a second, subsidiary schema through which the penitent, coached by the confessor, may discover sin and coordinate its recital: the *circumstantes.* The summula expounds the circumstantes immediately following its discourse on each of the deadly sins:

> Sed quia confessio est curatio vulnerum anime, sicut oportet vulnera carnis ostendere medico vel cirurgico omnia nudata, sic oportet omnia vulnera mentis spirituali medico revelare, id est in omnibus circumstantiis et cum omnibus que peccatum possunt aliquatenus aggravare. Notantur autem circumstantie per hunc versum: Quis, quid, ubi, quibus auxiliis, cur, quomodo, quando.[34]

(However, since confession is a healing of the wounds of the soul, just as it is proper to show the doctor or surgeon all the wounds of the flesh stripped naked, so too it is proper to reveal all the wounds of the mind to the spiritual doctor, that is, in every circumstance and with all things that are able to aggravate sin to any degree. And the circumstances are distinguished through this verse: who, what, where, by what means, why, how, and when.)

Invoking the medicus animae trope, the summula rehearses a well-established characterization of sin as symptom and confession as a clinical disclosure in which the penitent is stripped naked before the confessor's discerning gaze. The trope here reveals the profoundly revelatory character of the sacramental encounter: analogically, confession produces a visible truth, a veridical index of transgression that may be displayed and inspected. The transgressive and wounded sinful self is thus produced as a kind of representation, an object fashioned by the penitent and the confessor by means of the interrogative circumstantes. In this way penitential questions solicit properly penitential answers, and confessional dialogue yields a representation not only of sin but also of its circumstances.

The modus confitendi described in this scene is a profoundly constructive process; properly employed, the circumstantes provide the penitent with the mnemonic and rhetorical means by which he or she may produce a complete confession. Indeed, as several scholars have observed, the list of interrogatives that define the circumstantes aligns the intellectual and oral production of confession with the expert performance of the *rhetor*. Inherited from Cicero (by way of Victorinus and Boethius), the circumstantes served both heuristic and compositional ends in the practice of confession.[35] As a mnemonic schema, they afforded the penitent and the confessor an organized and organizing procedure for inward scrutiny.

Working through the list of interrogatives, the penitent or confessor encountered questions capable of guiding and structuring a penitential introspection that was also, necessarily, a retrospection. Indeed, in its discussion of the final circumstance, *quando* (when), the summula explicitly promotes the circumstantes as a powerful technique for interior mnemonic *inventio*, a process involving both categorization and discovery:

Debet enim reverti in se ad exordium vite sue quomodo se gesserit, cogitans de omnibus annis vite sue qui possunt sue occurrere memorie, et sollicite quid quibus annis fecerit et diebus et in quibus locis, quia locus est principium memorie. Per loca enim reducimus sepe ad memoriam que tradidimus oblivioni.[36]

> (For he [the penitent] ought to recall within himself how he conducted himself at the beginning of his life, thinking about all the years of his life that are able to present themselves to his memory, and carefully [considering] what he did in those years and days and in what places, because place is the starting point of memory. Indeed, by means of places, we may often retrieve those things that we had surrendered to oblivion.)

At the same time, the circumstantes offered the penitent an inventional schema capable of producing a more vivid and verisimilar (if not absolutely truthful) *narratio* of recollected sin. The summula prefaces its discussion of each of the circumstances with a general assertion of the importance of specificity in the recollection and recital of sins. Sins must be identified not *in genere* but in all their precise, aggravating circumstances. One consequence of this axiom is that the sinner confronts his transgressions in all their loathsome particularity, and this inward discovery has its own rhetorical consequences: "Et vere penitens multum odio habet peccatum. Et qui aliquid odio habet turpissimo nomine quo potest illud nominat, et sic debet penitens vocare peccatum suum, dum tamen verum dicat" (And truly, the penitent hates his sin intensely. And he who hates something denounces it with the worst name he can, and thus should the penitent name his sin, provided that he speaks the truth).[37] Guided by the circumstantes to a closer inspection and more complete discovery of sin, the penitent is prompted by this process of self-disclosure into a more vivid, more verisimilar—and, therefore, more rhetorically compelling—narration of the hidden contents of his conscience.

The incorporation of the circumstantes in the summula—and in countless other contemporary guides to the sacrament of penance—renders the practice of confession an explicitly rhetorical performance constructed (at least in part) by means of a penitential *ars memorativa* (art of memory), and addressed to both the penitent (self-discovery) and the confessor (disclosure of the discovered self). Diligent penitential introspection should result in an inventio of sin, but sacramental penance requires a further translation: as Dallas Denery explains, the penitent's inward vision must be translated into a confession that can stand "between the penitent and confessor as the intermediary through which that hidden life of sin appears."[38] In this way the conscience—be it good or bad—is produced in language as a third term, a representation to be scrutinized dialogically by the penitent and the confessor.

Significantly, the rhetorical performance that unites priest and parishioner in a sacramental practice of representation and interpretation is a performance accomplished in the vernacular. Exchanging questions and answers in the vernacular, the confessor and penitent translate the summula's monological Latin narration of the sins and their circumstances into the dialogic practice of the sacrament. The pastoral syllabus provides a framework within which the diligent penitent may look inward and discover sin, and the circumstantes delineate a rhetorically charged mode of inventio and narratio, but without an adequate vernacular representation of the hidden contents of the conscience, uttered in the presence of the confessor, no absolution is possible and no appropriate penance may be enjoined. In short, the sacrament cannot be completed.

The challenge of the confessional project comes into sharper focus if we consider that the transformation-translation of an inchoate interior presence of sin into a defined verbal representation was not the only representation at stake in the practice of penance. Bishop Quinel's statutes recognize that a different order of representation, a representation effected in bodily decorum—and potentially in the violation of that decorum—was equally operative in the modus confitendi. In the section of his statutes dealing with penance, Quinel instructs each clergyman of the diocese of Exeter to attend closely to the penitent and to himself:

> Qualitatem igitur et contritionem confitentium diligenter attendant; audiant quicquid dixerint, ac eos supportent in spiritu lenitatis; nec verbis exasperent nec aspectu, sed solicite inducant ut integre confiteantur. Vagos non habeant oculos sed pronos in terram, non respicientes faciem confitentis, nisi quatenus ipsius cordis contritionem et erubescentiam que est maxima pars penitentie valeant estimare, que non tam verbis sicut vultus aspectu poterunt deprehendi.[39]
>
> (Therefore they [priests] should diligently attend to the quality and contrition of those confessing; let them listen to whatever they have said, and they should tolerate them in a spirit of gentleness, they should not irritate with word or appearance, but carefully they should lead them to confess completely. They should not have wandering eyes, but rather [let them have their] eyes trained on the ground; nor should they look at the face of the one confessing, unless it is only so that they may be able to judge the contrition of his heart and [his] shame, which is the greatest part of penitence, which can be detected not so much from words as from the appearance of the face.)

Two visible performances are considered here: that of the confessor and that of the penitent. The encounter prescribed by Quinel is a visible discourse or dialogue of shame and responsive gentleness, of contrition and sacerdotal toleration. Quinel's instructions objectify both of these performances, turning question and response into a spectacle that is, in turn, inspected, scrutinized, and regulated.

Quinel's vision of the confessional encounter rehearses well-established advice to confessors.[40] The confessor's regulation of his bodily responses to the penitent and his or her confession must be coupled with a careful regulation of his verbal response. Confessors were urged to be circumspect in their questioning lest they introduce penitents to unusual sins through particular lines of questioning.[41] Quinel repeats this advice in his statutes, adding that the confessor must conceal such *peccata inusitata* (unusual sins) under a cloak of euphemism and vague allusion, so that penitents innocent of this class of exceptional sins will not be provided with an *occasio delinquendi* (opportunity for sinning).[42]

The confessor, caught between his responsibility to solicit and shape a complete confession and the need to preserve whatever moral-spiritual innocence the penitent retains, must—no less than the penitent—scrutinize his own conduct within the sacramental encounter, regulating his bodily and verbal rhetoric and constantly considering the penitent's response to his pastoral performance. Penitent and confessor are thus implicated in a reciprocal exchange. The confessor solicits a confession through the mobilization of the interrogative circumstantes; at the same time, the confessional serves as a pedagogic forum in which the penitent's questions about moral and spiritual conduct receive didactic responses. In both cases, a truthful representation of sin and its remedy must be produced by verbal and visible (gestural, physiognomic) means. Penitent and confessor come together to collaborate dialogically in the production of this spiritual truth, be it the truth of the penitent's transgression or the truth of a didactic answer to penitential questioning.

Confessional Dialogue as a Representational Practice

As we have seen, the immediate dyadic relationship of confessor to penitent involved a complex array of representational practices, practices that were constituent of the sacramental transaction. The dialogic exchange between priest and penitent, however, was itself open to scrutiny; indeed, the prescriptions of bishops like Eudes of Sully and Peter Quinel required that the sacrament take place in full view of *omnium* (everyone present). At the same time, the Fourth Lateran Council and subsequent ecclesiastical legislation demanded that this highly visible performance maintain a certain opacity. Confessors were strictly enjoined "ne verbo vel signo vel alio quovis modo prodat aliquatenus peccatorem" (not to betray the sinner at all by word or sign or in any other way).[43]

The practice of confession thus demanded that both penitent and priest should collaborate to produce a verbal representation of sin adequate to the demands of the sacrament, while simultaneously and constantly scrutinizing, adjusting, and regulating their individual and collective self-presentation, aware that it was always potentially the object of an external, social scrutiny.[44] As Denery insightfully observes,

> the individual constructed in confession was not the private self which has so inspired or aggravated modern philosophers. Rather, it was the individual self understood through its endless self-presentations, the individual as taken up into and formed through the very system of interrogation which could then claim to have discovered that individual as an object for consideration in the first place. Confessors and penitents alike sought the individual; they had to settle with its infinitely changing appearance, its infinitely deferred presence.[45]

The sacramental truths produced by the penitent and confessor were, necessarily, produced in the style of the sacrament. That is, they were shaped by the syllabus of credenda and perficienda and similarly formed in the image of sin or religious confusion. In this way confessional questions anticipated penitential answers, and, by the same token, the penitent's response was fashioned, in advance, to conform to the systematic armature of the circumstantes. From this perspective, confession emerges as a discursive genre, one that is capable of producing a representation in a certain, generically defined form. Thus the truth of this representation—the truth of the good confession—is both a content and a style, a discursive substance and the form (verbal, gestural, visible) in which it is uttered.

The internal and external pressures that defined the confessional performance go far in explaining why bishops like Peter Quinel found it necessary to legislate on the conduct of the sacrament and to provide their clergy with further guidance in the form of *summulae, summae confessionis, summae confessorum,* and other pastoral treatises.[46] For most lay penitents, however, the principal (if not the only) instruction they received about how to confess was that offered to them in the course of sacramental confession itself. Through confession they were initiated into a process of epistemological reformation, of rhetorical self-fashioning, and, no less, of translating the self in terms of the pastoral syllabus.

Scholars of medieval penance have observed that the penitential self articulated—quite literally—through the utterance and reception of a sacramental confession was de facto the sum of its sins. Historians—focused for the most part on the summae confessorum, libri paenitentiales, and other texts written to instruct clerical audiences in the conduct of the sacrament—have emphasized how the practice of confession

interpellated penitents as sinners.[47] Although the conduct of the sacrament certainly "produced" sinners and inscribed the epistemological work of self-discovery within a framework dominated by the taxonomy of sin, I would suggest that this historical analysis cannot adequately account for the dialogic translations undertaken in the sacramental encounter—translations that produced penitents as "masters" of the authorizing canon of credenda.[48] Successful vernacular representation of sin required both a rigorous ars memorativa and an assimilation of rhetorical technique. Moreover, as contemporary statutes repeatedly insist, confession was an important occasion for pastoral education and dialogue between priest and parishioner.[49] Whereas participation in the sacrament of penance produced a representation of the self as the sum of its transgressions, late medieval pastoral reformers clearly expected that confession would also reform the penitent's self-representation in the image of his or her religious knowledge.

In the thirteenth century, confession was increasingly conceived of as a dialogic process resulting in a moral-spiritual dialectic capable of encompassing both fault and faith. This was an ambitious vision, and one that made tremendous demands of the confessor and, perhaps, even greater demands of the penitent. Like the priest, the penitent was expected to come to the confessional encounter prepared with contrition and with knowledge of the pastoral syllabus—that is, with a mastery of the didactic schemas and dialogic techniques required to produce a contrite, complete, and coherent confession.

The proliferation of pastoralia addressed to clerical audiences in the first half of the thirteenth century provided confessors with the means to shape the discursive production of confessions; in time, these conceptual schemas and techniques were translated—textually and visually—for the instruction of lay reader-viewers beyond the sacramental encounter. What remains to be seen is how images contributed to these newly ambitious conceptions of the formative power of pastoral dialogue.

Dialogic Images and the Care of the Self

AN EXEMPLARY MIRROR FOR MONASTICS: THE *SPECULUM VIRGINUM*

The dialogic solicitation of reader-viewers in practices of moral-spiritual introspection, correction, and self-representation that is the focus of this chapter has its textual and visual roots in monastic practices of self-examination and regulation. Long before the pastoral reform movement made works of visual pastoralia a dialogic means of penitential reform, monastic readers and viewers had employed text and image in the distinction of inward virtue from vice and the cultivation of a more perfect spiritual self. The *Speculum virginum,* a twelfth-century compilation of text and image designed for the spiritual instruction of nuns (or canonesses), is a case in point.[50] The text of this "mirror of virgins" and, even more, its images would seem to have exerted a significant influence over future efforts to represent outwardly and didactically the inward contents and structure of the moral-spiritual self.

Couched as a dialogue between a male monastic, Peregrinus, and his female religious student, Theodora, the *Speculum virginum* takes the form of a didactic exchange on the qualities, duties, and prerogatives of the religious life. In keeping with its governing structural metaphor—the mirror—the *Speculum* emphasizes and extends important elements of its didactic program in a series of reflective visual representations; among these, the work makes special use of the figure of the tree. In the earliest identified manuscript of the text (London, BL, Arundel MS 44), produced circa 1140–1150, a Tree of Jesse provides a fitting visual corollary to the first book's exhortative instruction in virginity's spiritual fecundity (fig. 6).[51] Two further trees, prefacing the *Speculum*'s fourth book, forcefully visualize the opposition between vice and virtue, and their antithetical fruits (see figs. 7 and 8).

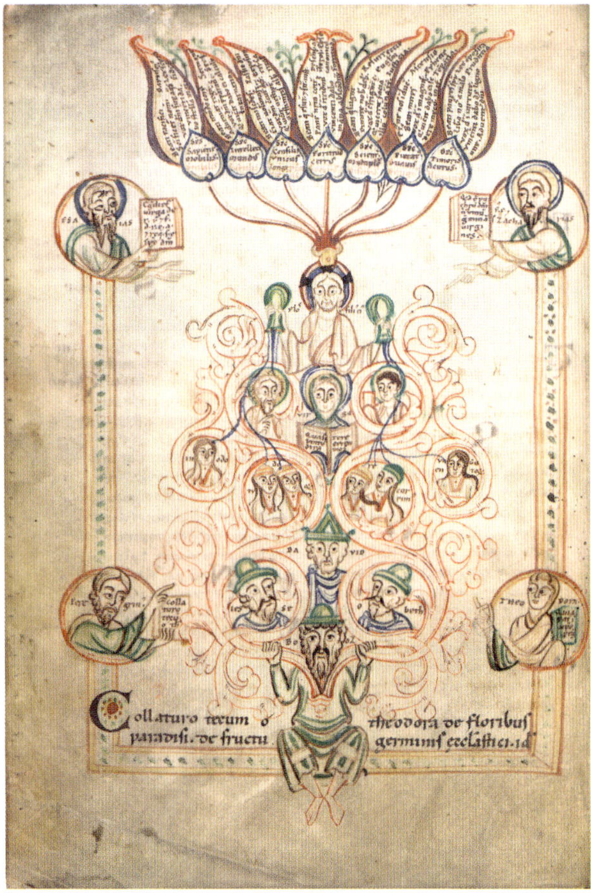

Fig. 6. The Tree of Jesse in the Speculum virginum*, c. 1140–1150. London, BL, Arundel MS 44, f. 2v: 280 x 185 mm.*

The *Speculum virginum*'s images are integral to the text's dialogic procedure. At various points in the text, Peregrinus refers to the images, adducing them as visual helps for Theodora as she seeks to understand his moral-spiritual instruction. Morgan Powell has observed that the text's "repeated allusion to difficulty with *scriptura* as a justification for *pictura*" aligns the pedagogic function of the *Speculum*'s images—and their anticipated female audience—with the Gregorian dictum and its distinction of the textually literate and those less-learned people (typically, the laity, women, novices, children) who require oral instruction and visual aids.[52] As Powell emphasizes, Peregrinus's apologiae for the *Speculum*'s images "more often than not, conceal more ambitious ideas on the real value and role of the images."[53]

The relationship between the *Speculum virginum*'s metaphoric structure—epitomized in its title—and its marshalling of visual means to facilitate spiritual (re)formation is a case in point and, we will see, was still conceptually potent when late medieval producers of visual pastoralia turned to the *Speculum* and similar works as authoritative exemplars. In the letter that prefaces the text Peregrinus activates a signifying series of

specular allusions: "Sunt enim specula mulierum eloquia diuina uisibus obiecta sanctarum animarum, in quibus semper considerant, quomodo sponso eterno aut placeant decore sancte conscientie aut displiceant peccati feditate."[54] (Now the mirrors of the women are divine words set before the eyes of holy souls, in which they may see at all times how they either please the eternal bridegroom with the beauty of a holy conscience or displease him with the ugliness of sin.)[55] Alluding to the mirrors that Moses appropriated and refashioned into the tabernacle basin (Exod. 38:8 and 40:89), Peregrinus constructs a relay of exegetical reflections. As the Israelite women's mirrors are remade as a basin containing an equally reflective surface of water, the women's reflections are displaced by the sacerdotal images of Aaron and his sons performing their ritual ablutions.

This exegetical *jeu de miroir* leads to a series of moral reflections. The *divina eloquia* (divine discourse) parsed and allegorized by the exegete cedes priority of referential place to the moral mirror of the *Speculum virginum* itself. In the *Speculum*'s dialogic reflection, the reader-viewer-listener should find her moral-spiritual mirror image, in all its deity-pleasing beauty or sinful disfiguration. Of course, as the text's anticipated virginal reader contemplates the *Speculum virginum,* she is confronted with more than a series of mirroring metaphors or allusions; on the smooth surface of its pages she also encounters a series of images, designed to provoke further reflection. The interplay between the *Speculum*'s title, its textual concatenation of mirror-references and moral-spiritual reflections, and—most decisively—its incorporation of moralizing images invites the reader-viewer to contemplate diagrammatic representations as visible forms of moral-spiritual insight.

Within the *Speculum*'s allusive architecture of text and image, book four presents the reader-viewer with two visions of the self as vicious or virtuous arboreal growth (see figs. 7 and 8). As Peregrinus tells Theodora,

> Speculum, filia, queris. Ecce quantum profeceris uel defeceris, in alterutro fructu speculari poteris. Hic enim, si te queris, reperis. Speculum dici non potest nisi quod intuentis imaginem representat. Igitur ex consideratione sacre scripture te ipsam consule, et aliqua uel uirtutum uel uiciorum uestigia reperis impressa conscientie tue.[56]
>
> (You ask for a mirror, daughter. Here you can behold in the one fruit and the other how much you have progressed and where you are still wanting. Here, indeed, if you seek, you will find yourself. Nothing can be called a mirror unless it reveals the image of its beholder. Therefore, advise yourself through the consideration of Holy Scripture, and you will discover the signs of the vices and virtues impressed on your conscience.)[57]

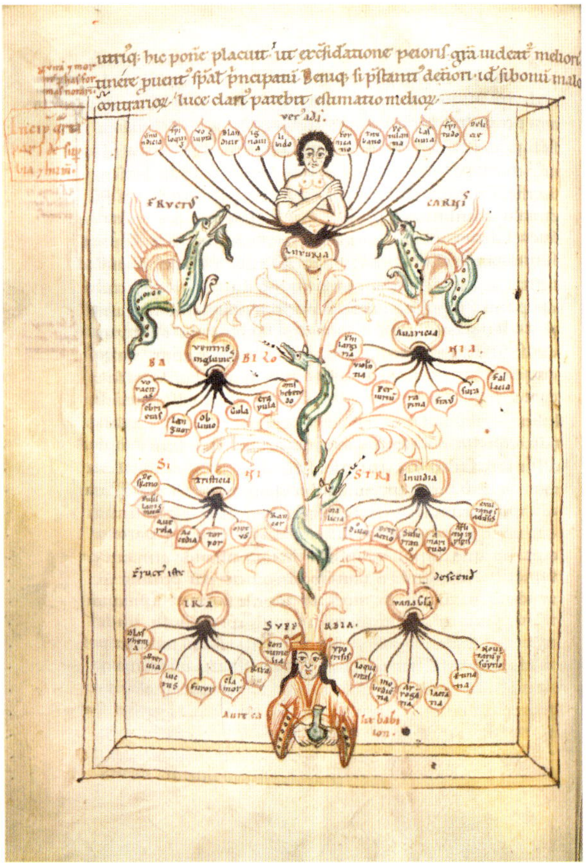

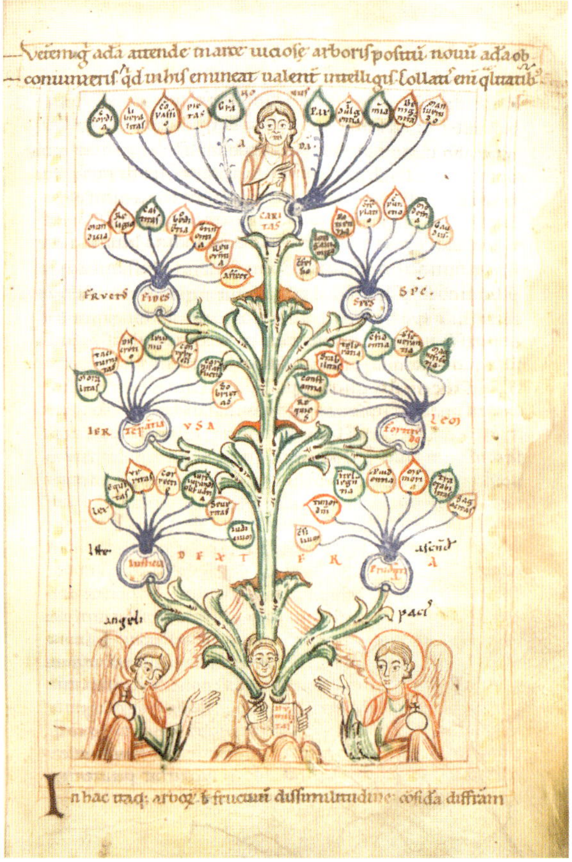

Fig. 7. The tree of vices, heavy with the fruits of the flesh in the Speculum virginum. *London, BL, Arundel MS 44, f. 28v.*

Fig. 8. The tree of virtues, yielding the fruits of the spirit in the Speculum virginum. *London, BL, Arundel MS 44, f. 29r.*

Peregrinus explicitly identifies the mode of reading and viewing solicited by the manuscript and its specular structure: Theodora—and the reader-viewer—is asked to contemplate the work's painted representations and to see in them a veridical reflection of the spiritual self.

The truthfulness of the *Speculum virginum*'s images does not depend on an illusionistic naturalism, but rather on each representation's capacity to render the invisible contents of the moral-spiritual interior in visible terms. As the tree of vices extends upward, from its root in *Superbia* to its flowering crown of *Luxuria,* it yields the drooping fruits of the flesh (*fructus carnis*)—overripe, vicious, and aligned with *Babilonia* and the sinister side (fig. 7). Across the opening, the tree of virtues springs from the personification of *Humilitas* (fig. 8). Here the *fructus spiritus* (fruits of the spirit) stretch upward toward Christ, the new Adam. Identified with Jerusalem, and the dexter side, this tree models a virtuous, vegetative mode of ascent. Considered together as a single opening, the two trees define a garden of spiritual antitheses and a mutually defined double vision of moral state.

The didactic efficacy of the *Speculum*'s images is activated by the intent, inquisitive gaze of the viewer. Like all mirrors, these representations claim to reflect what is set before them; in the *Speculum virginum* that intervening object is defined as the moral subject, the viewer who turns to the page in order to better see him- or herself. In this fashion, the construction of the viewer-image relationship is itself an extension of the dialogue form employed in the *Speculum*'s text, much as Theodora's questions solicit responses from her *magister*.

By design and by generic designation, the *Speculum*'s representations of virtue and vice anticipate the viewer and yield their reflections on moral-spiritual rectitude when activated by her questioning gaze. Authorized by its monastic pedigree, the practice of moral reflection by means of painted representation encouraged by the *Speculum virginum* and the refashioning of the inward self in dialogue with outward exemplars—both textual and visual—that it promotes would exert a significant influence over subsequent attempts to engage the reader-viewer in a pastoral exchange with the manuscript page.

ENCOUNTERING THE *VRIGIET DE SOLAS*'S MORALIZED MIRROR

At the turn of the thirteenth century, the *Vrigiet de solas* (Paris, BnF, MS fr. 9220), an illuminated compendium produced in northern France, emulated the *Speculum*'s authoritative example, while inverting its metaphoric structure.[58] The resulting work, which takes the form of a series of sixteen unusually large full-page illuminations, describes a metaphoric orchard in which the viewer encounters a didactic mirror of life and death (see fig. 9).[59]

The *Vrigiet*'s debt to its twelfth-century monastic forebears is most evident in the paired trees of virtue and vice painted for the manuscript, and this appropriation of the monastic arborescent tradition also echoes in its opening four-line address to the reader-viewer: "Cest livre puet on apieler vrigiet de solas. Car ki vioult y entrer par penser et par estude il i trueve arbres plaisans et fruis suffisans pour arme nourrir et pour cors duire et apprendre."[60] (This book can be called [the] "Orchard of Solace." For he who desires to enter it through thought and study finds in it pleasing trees and fruit enough to nourish the soul and to guide and teach the body.) Despite these self-authorizing gestures toward the monastic tradition exemplified by the *Speculum virginum,* the *Vrigiet* quite deliberately extroverts the *Speculum*'s metaphoric structure, transforming the Latin work's reflected trees of virtue and vice into an arboreal organizational structure. Entering this vernacular orchard (*vrigiet*) full of moral-spiritual fruit, the thirteenth-century manuscript's reader-viewer discovers an arresting moralized mirror.

The *Vrigiet*'s mirror of life and death (*miroirs de vie et de mort*) dominates folio 10r (fig. 9).[61] Set against a chiastic arrangement of patterned blue and orange fields, this oversized roundel, filled with a brilliant plane of burnished gold, puns—formally and materially—on its iconographic designation. The painted figures and Latin inscriptions arrayed against its reflective surface offer a visual and textual reflection of the human condition at its most fallen. Indeed, in a visual mise en abîme of the compendium's arboreal structure and specular contents, a further tree appears in this mirror, bridging the divide between the roundel's upper and lower hemispheres.[62] A Latin inscription written so as to hover behind the tree's trunk identifies it as "arbor peccati sub qua sumus arbore nati" (the tree of sin under which we are born).[63]

The crown of the tree defines a leafy bower for an enthroned female figure, identified as *Vita mundi* (Life of the World). Seated frontally within this arboreal embrasure, the figure cannot fail to evoke another crowned woman who inhabits a very different tree in the *Vrigiet*'s visual program: the Virgin Mary painted within the manuscript's Tree of Jesse image (fig. 10). A comparison of these two regal women exposes Vita mundi's attractions as deceptions; in Emile Mâle's terms, Vita mundi is revealed to be "une anti-Vierge, une Vierge du mal" (an anti-Virgin, a Virgin of evil).[64] Moreover, unlike the Virgin, Vita mundi's supremacy is soon to end: on her right, *Mors humana* (Human Death) ascends a ladder carrying a coffin. Urged upward by the devil, Human Death reaches out to topple Life from her throne.[65]

Following the tree trunk as it descends beyond the horizontal division of the roundel's upper and lower halves, the viewer discovers the tree's seven roots, from which seven hideous serpents seem to suckle. Each creature extends downward and outward, like the spokes of a wheel, to terminate in female figures who actively embody the seven deadly sins. The personification of Superbia is aligned directly below the enthroned figure of Vita mundi. Crowned and holding a scepter, Superbia touches the strap of her mantle in a diminutive gestural echo of Vita mundi above her. The filiation of Pride, Queen of the Vices, and the regal Vita mundi could not be clearer.

Contemplating the mirror of human life and death, the viewer is confronted with the corrupt vegetative growth of sin, its flowering in the rule of earthly concerns, and its racination in the vices and their debased actions. In spatial terms, the image subverts a medieval tendency to range good above evil; within *li miroirs de vie et de mort* there is no moral high ground. The composition does not reject signifying spatial values, but rather it exploits them in order to construct a vision in which the appearance of a signifying compositional hierarchy is revealed, upon closer inspection, to be morally inoperative.

If Vita mundi's complacent smile and hieratic frontality hardly betray the inherent instability of the personification's privileged place and her imminent displacement at the

Fig. 9. The Vrigiet de solas*'s mirror of life and death, c. 1290–1300. Paris, BnF, MS fr. 9220, f. 10r: 440 x 310 mm.*

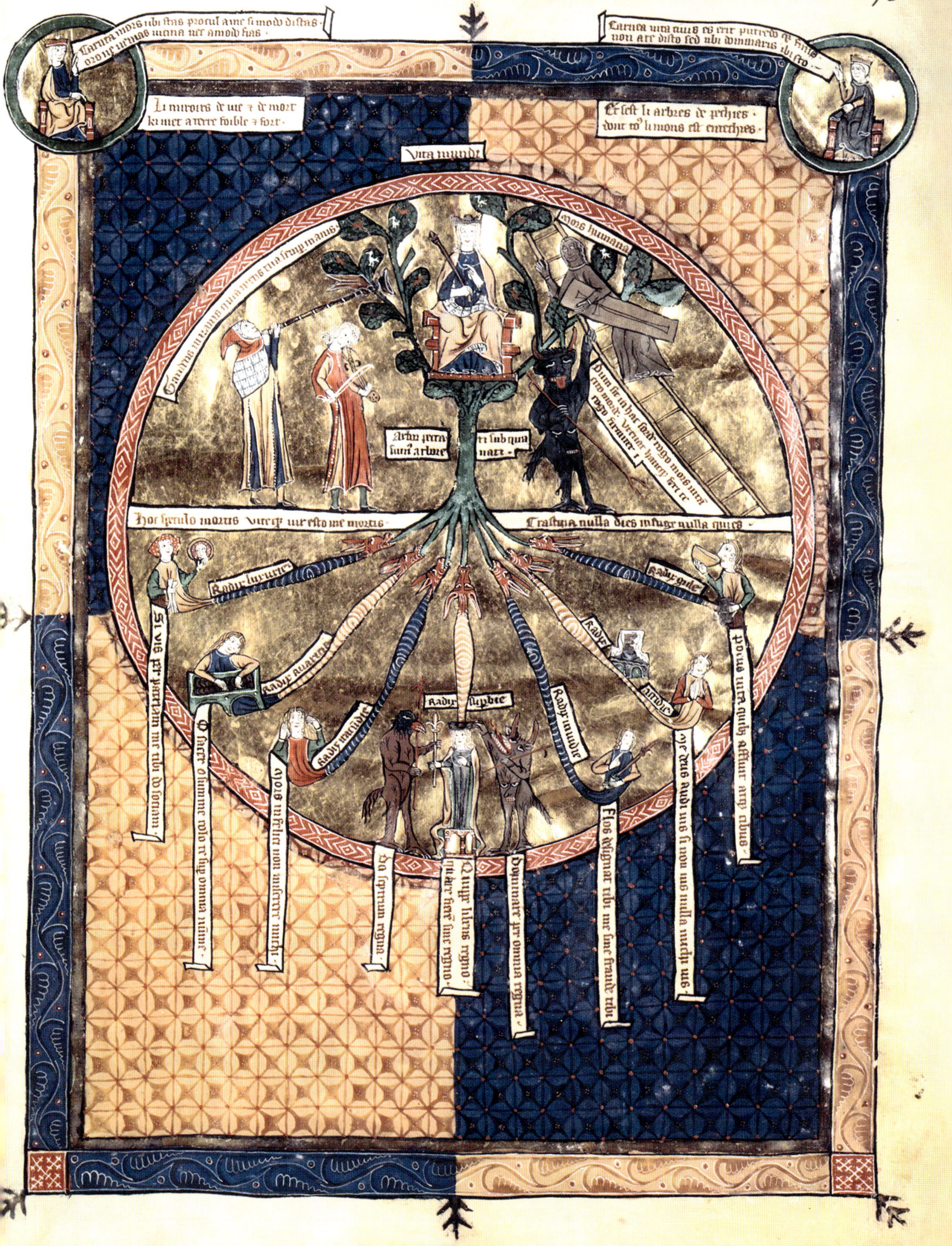
Li miroirs de vie et de mort
ki met a terre foible et fort
Vita mundi
Mors humana
Radix luxurie
Radix avaricie
Radix iracundie
Radix superbie
Radix invidie
Radix gule

hands of ascendant Death, other elements within the image invite the viewer to hasten that process of eviction. Although several of the Latin inscriptions within the pictorial field of the miniature read horizontally from left to right, many of the image's inscriptions skew from the horizontal, and the *textura* forms of their letters demand that the viewer follows the line of text as it curves, bends, and slants. Attending to the implicit movement of the inscriptions, the reader-viewer effectively sets the mirror in motion.

The inscription above the two musicians who play for Vita mundi in the upper hemisphere—"Gaudens in vanis quia mens tua semper inanis" (Rejoicing in vain things because your mind is always empty)—follows the arc of the roundel's upper edge from left to right, thus leading to the central figure of Vita mundi and implying that the vacuity of her smile reveals an inner emptiness. The titulus identifying Mors humana draws the eye past Vita mundi to the devil's three lines of speech, arrayed in parallel to Death's ladder, which descend a strong diagonal to the profile of the personification of *Gula* (Gluttony) below. Reading from inscription to inscription, the viewer must crane her neck, or perhaps even rotate the manuscript page before her. Certainly, the strips of inscriptions that descend from each of the personified vices in the lower hemisphere of the roundel require that the reader-viewer reorient either her posture or the position of the page before her by 180 degrees. In short, the *mise en miroir* of the inscriptions invites an engaged—even physically active—response from the viewer.

Within the fixed structure of its rectilinear frame, the mirror of life and death is set in motion by the reader-viewer as she attempts to parse its contents. As the page is rotated, the mirror becomes a kind of wheel of fortune in the reader-viewer's hands, and Vita mundi is displaced from her privileged position at its apex. Manipulation of the page, however, cannot replace vice with virtue: the mirror's contents provide no morally or spiritually viable point of identification or rest for the viewer. This, of course, is the mirror of life and death's circular message; as the long horizontal inscription that divides the roundel's upper and lower hemispheres proclaims, "Hoc speculo mortis viteque vir esto me mortis. Crastina nulla dies in fuge nulla quies" (In me, this looking glass of death and life, thou shall be a man of death! There is no tomorrow; in flight there is no rest).[66] With this menacing direct address the manuscript interpolates the reader-viewer into the reflective gold-leaf surface of its specular full-page image.

The *Vrigiet de solas*'s illuminated mirror is a virtuosic exteriorization of precisely the kind of introspective surveillance of the self that was expected of penitents in the later Middle Ages. The viewer inspecting the image was provided with a didactic—and perhaps threatening—vision of the contents of the uncorrected soul. Combining a mnemonically useful delineation of the vices with an implicit drama of worldly ambition menaced by the onslaught of death, the Vrigiet's gleaming mirror engages its viewer

Fig. 10. The Virgin framed within the Vrigiet de solas*'s* Tree of Jesse*. Paris, BnF, MS fr. 9220, f. 1v.*

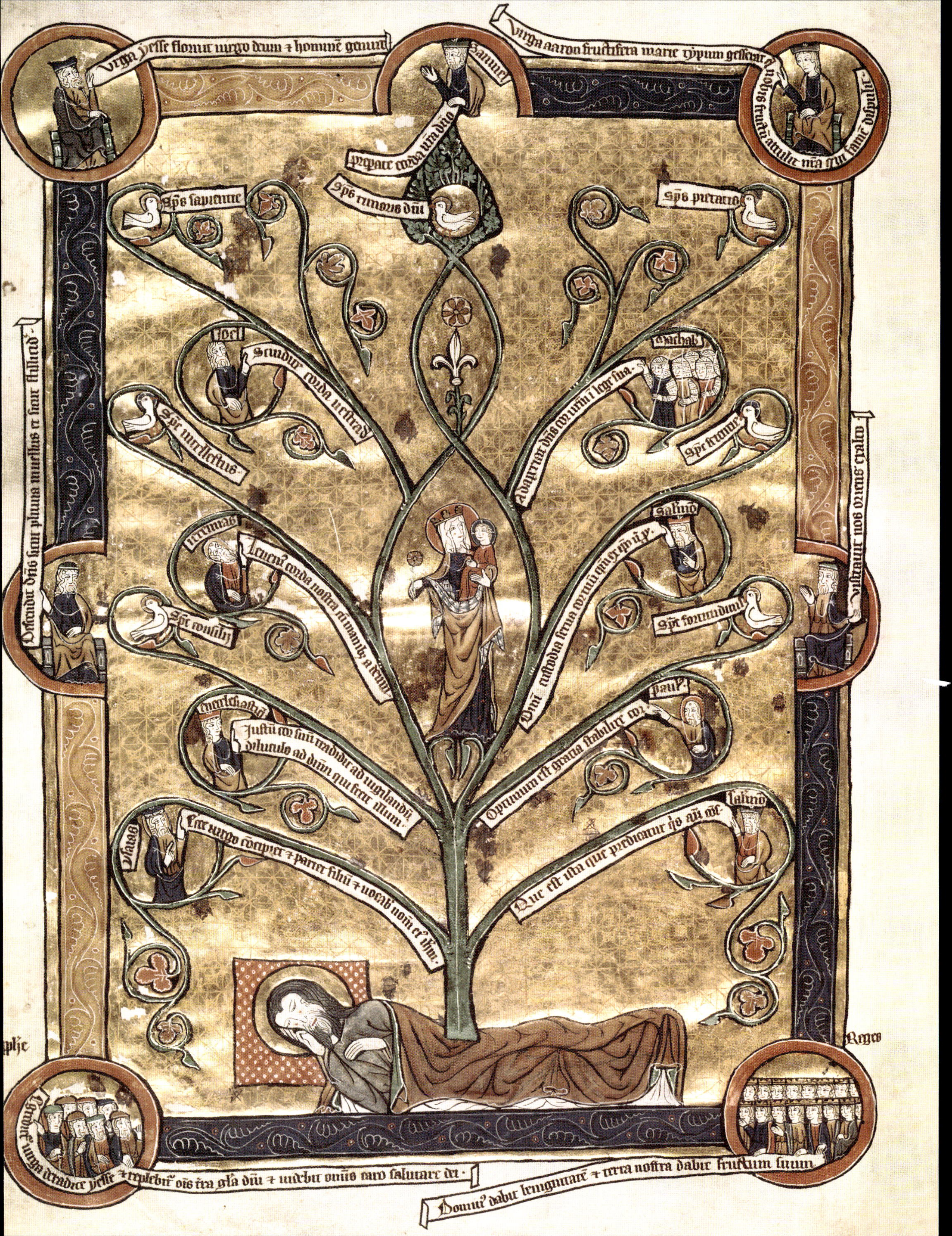

in a didactic dialogue about sin, its forms and consequences, and the inevitability of death, followed, of course, by judgment. As the mirror invites the viewer to look, the authoritative (if at times garbled) language of its Latin inscriptions chastises them for what they see.

Although the inscriptions that appear within the *miroirs de vie et de mort* image are in Latin, other images in the manuscript employ a macaronic approach, mingling Latin and Picard French. The bilingual character of the work, considered in tandem with the impressive size and imposing facture of its images, has led several interpreters to propose a lay audience for the manuscript. In an extended analysis of the manuscript's intended use and reception, Lynn Ransom has emphasized the presence of markers of Franciscan influence throughout the *Vrigiet:* in addition to the core group of so-called *Speculum theologiae* diagrams, the *Vrigiet de solas* incorporates several compositions that may also be associated with the Franciscan order and with Franciscan spirituality, more generally.[67]

As Ransom suggests, these indices of Franciscan involvement in the manuscript's design and an intended lay audience for its instruction suggest that the *Vrigiet*'s images anticipated two beholders: a friar-confessor and a lay penitent, a pastoral community of two gathered together for confessional dialogue, with the silent but eloquent presence of the book as a third participant in their colloquy. Perhaps, then, it is inadequate to describe the *Vrigiet* as designed for dialogue; rather, the *Vrigiet* challenges us to think more flexibly about the dialogic representation of sin and infraction when images visibly and materially translate the ugliness of transgression into the brilliant, if menacing, form of an illumination.

FAITH, *POINT, ET ESCRIT*: JOINVILLE'S *ROMANS AS YMAGES*

The *Vrigiet de solas*'s painted mirror reflects the dismaying inward contents of the soul in order that they may be dialogically cataloged, scrutinized, and ultimately dismissed through the workings of the sacrament of penance. This visual intervention in the pursuit of spiritual correction presumes the ultimate presence of a priest-confessor, a spiritual father who is empowered to bring the hermeneutic labor of the penitent and the didactic exhortation of the image to a sacramental conclusion.

Some forty years before the *Vrigiet* was completed, Jean de Joinville (1224?–1317), Seneschal of Champagne and biographer of Louis IX, made his own, quasi-paternal contribution to the pastoral struggle for Christian rectitude: a *Romans as ymages des poinz de nostre foi*—a vernacular exposition, with images, of the Apostles' Creed.[68] Composed between August 1250 and April 1251, while Joinville was on crusade with King Louis IX, his *Romans* was designed to be read and shown to dying Christians in order to strengthen their faith against the devil's final assaults.[69] Although the original manuscript executed in Acre no longer survives, a manuscript dated to circa 1287 (Paris, BnF, MS n. a. fr. 4509; henceforth BnF naf 4509), has preserved most of the textual and visual program that Joinville devised to instruct and defend his fellow Christians.[70]

Joinville's work buttresses its text-image exposition of the Apostles' Creed with references to *prophecies par euvres* (prophecies in deed) and *par paroles* (in words).[71] As Lionel Friedman has noted, "The situation in the *Credo* is that the articles of the Creed may serve as the fundamental basis representing the minimum required of the faithful for salvation, but the actual unit of composition is the 'point of faith' seen to be contained in or derived from the article."[72] This distinction between the articles of the Creed and the *poinz de nostre foi* (points of our faith) has two implications for the work. First, at times Joinville divides the material he expounds into units larger or smaller than those typically recognized by established *distinctiones* of the Apostles' Creed. Second, the *Romans* does not present its reader-viewer with a close parsing of the Credo per se, but rather offers an elaboration of Joinville's conception of the canon of credenda and perficienda required for salvation. Accordingly, in Joinville's treatise, *foi* (faith) is a capacious category, discursively and visually elaborated from the armature of the Apostles' Creed. Joinville performs a triplex translation of the Credo in his *Romans as ymages:* he translates each line of the Latin profession into the vernacular, he translates salient scriptural referents (including, at times, prophetic "confirmation") into visual form, and, finally and most holistically, he translates the Creed from letter to spirit, producing a work that occasionally exceeds the terms of its source text in its pursuit of an ideal of Christian excellence adequate to salvation.

Joinville's *Romans as ymages* is a profoundly dialogic work. Each principal tenet of the Christian faith is provided with a textual and visual representation designed to speak from the page to the weakened eyes and ears of the dying Christian. Joinville explicitly envisions his work as a conduit for *creance* (belief), a means of filling the dying man with the fortifying substance of faith, of responding to his deathbed doubts and confusions with a reassuring syllabus of belief. The dialogic character of the book's proposed intervention is echoed by the antiphonal relationship of its texts and images. Juxtaposed on the page, text and miniatures are arranged into quasi-typological constellations, sites of textual instruction and visual *amplificatio*. In the *Romans as ymages* word and image collaborate to exhort the reader-viewer, to solicit the gaze, and to rescue him or her from the failure of belief.

BnF naf 4509 preserves many internal references to the images planned as illustrations of each Creedal *point* and to each *point*'s prophetic announcement in text and deed; several of these internal references even allude to the *ordinatio* (organizing layout) of text and image in specific pages of the work. The opening of the creedal exposition is a case in point. The first article of the Creed appears as a rubric on folio 1v: "Je croi en dieu le pere tout poissant le creator dou ciel et de la terre" (I believe in God the Father omnipotent, the creator of heaven and earth). The text immediately following addresses the reader-viewer directly, explaining,

> Sa grant poissance poez veoir en la creation dou monde que vous veez ci aprés pointe. . . . Sa grant poissance poons veoir par les anges qui ci aprés sont point qu'il trabucha dou ciel en enfer et de si biaus et de si gloriex come il estoient les fist il si lait et si hideus.[73]
>
> (You can see his great power in the creation of the world, which you see hereafter expounded/painted. . . . We can see his great power in the angels that hereafter are expounded/painted, that he cast down from heaven into hell and as beautiful and glorious as they were, he made them just as ugly and hideous.)

The text refers to the image on the facing recto (fig. 11). In the upper left compartment of the miniature, God sits enthroned with the orb of dominion in his right hand. On his left, a line of angels stand upright with their hands raised in prayer. In the lower half of the image, an angelic explosion erupts as the rebel angels fall from grace, their wings extending in every direction across the lower edges of the frame. Despite the claim of the text on the preceding recto, this painting is the only visual representation provided for the first *article;* BnF naf 4509 does not make good on Joinville's promise of a representation of God's *poissance* in the creation of the world. In a further omission, Joinville does not adduce any prophecies for this *point*.

The absence of prophetic authorities at this point in the text-image scheme is explained in a few lines set above the image: "Des prophecies n'a il nules sor ceste premiere page pour ce que le touche de l'encomencement dou monde que cil fist qui est comencement et qui durra sanz fin" (There are no prophecies on this page because it touches on the beginning of the world which was accomplished by him who is the beginning and who continues without end).[74] When the text resumes below the miniature it turns to the next article of the Creed: "Et en ihesu crit son fil nostre seignor" (And in Jesus Christ his son, our Lord).[75] The reader-viewer is told that on "la seconde page dou credo ci aprés" (the second page of the Credo, following) there will be prophecies of Christ's advent, including the three angels welcomed by Abraham.[76] Turning the folio, the reader-viewer encounters an image of Moses kneeling before a medallion in which Christ gestures in benediction. In the miniature below, we see the annunciation, accompanied by a roundel inhabited by a prophetic figure holding a blank banderole. The visual complement of the page is completed by a small roundel housing another prophetic figure, who gestures in speech toward a second roundel in which Mary rests after giving birth; Christ appears swaddled in the manger above her. Abraham and the three angels simply do not appear on "la seconde page dou credo."

As this brief review of the manuscript's opening folios reveals, BnF naf 4509 suppresses certain visual elements that are explicitly referenced in the text; on two occasions blank space is left for miniatures that were never executed.[77] In many cases, the manuscript dispenses with representations of the prophecies or prophets that are anticipated by the text. Moreover, as the treatise progresses, the pacing of text and image becomes asynchronous: as it is preserved in BnF naf 4509, Joinville's carefully conceived coordination of text and image has become not a little discombobulated.[78] Despite these difficulties, the *Romans as ymages* retains its coherency. That the manuscript's scribe and illuminator were not entirely up to the challenges of the mise en page required by Joinville's project does not, in the end, undermine the efficacy of the manuscript's didactic mission. The ambitions of the work—and the import of its coordinated campaign of text and image—come into focus if we consider the final suite of *poinz* in conjunction with the work's prefatory and concluding statements of purpose and procedure.

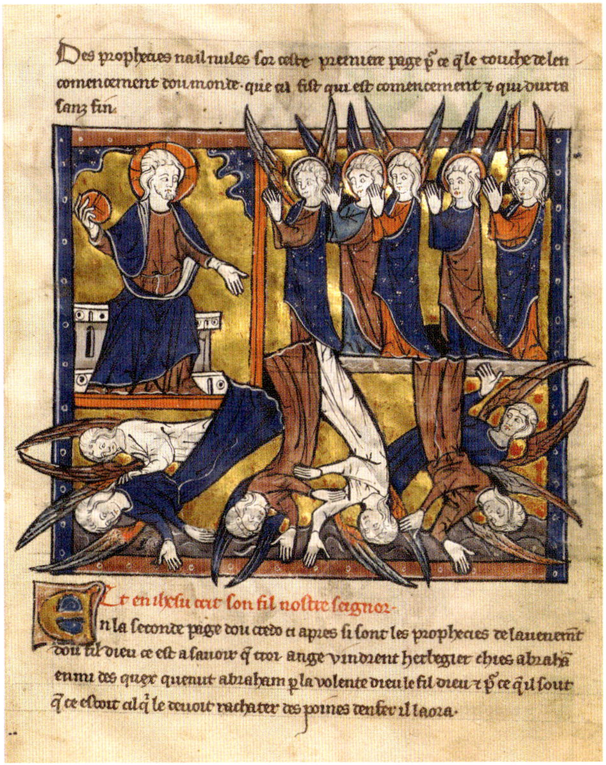

Fig. 11. Dieu le pere tout poissant *and the fall of the rebel angels in Jean de Joinville's* Romans as ymages, *c. 1287. Paris, BnF, MS n. a. fr. 4509, f. 2r: 192 x 130 mm.*

The first ten "points," extending from belief in God the Father, through the principal elements of the *vita Christi,* to belief in the Holy Spirit, are (with one exception) provided with images derived from scripture.[79] Collectively, these miniatures delineate a narrative that proceeds from the fall of the rebel angels through the principal events of Christ's life (including his apocalyptic return), supplemented with representations of select Old Testament scenes included for their prophetic-typological significance. When the work turns to the eleventh *point,* "Et ou pardon des pechiez qui nous est fait par les sacremens de sainte eglise" (And in the forgiveness of sins which is accomplished for us through the sacraments of Holy Church), the program of illumination mobilizes a different iconographic repertoire.[80]

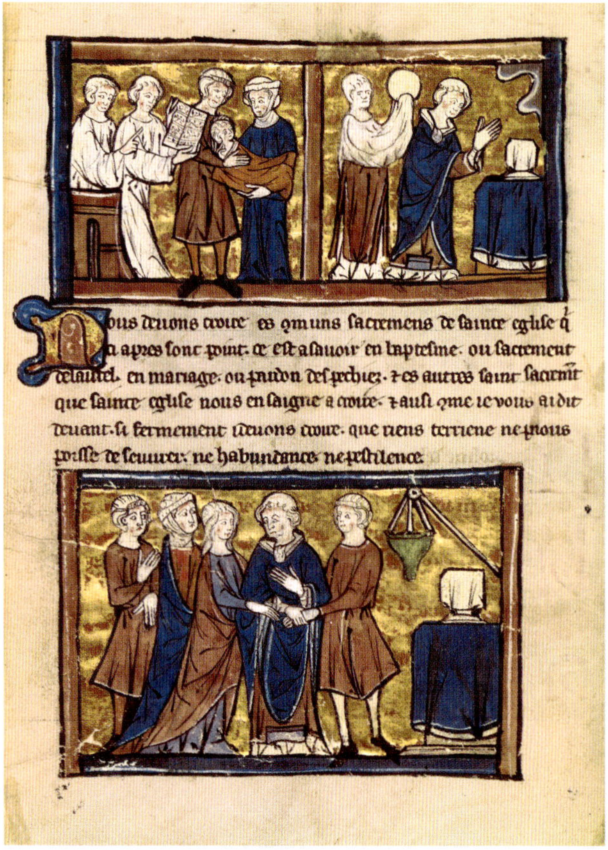

Fig. 12. *The shared sacraments of Holy Church in Jean de Joinville's* Romans as ymages. *Paris, BnF, MS n. a. fr. 4509, f. 10v.*

On folio 10v, the viewer is presented with a tripartite epitome of the sacraments: above, baptism and the Eucharist are represented in a two-compartment miniature; below, a priest solemnizes a marriage, as a single lamp hangs above a veiled chalice set on an altar (fig. 12). In the space between these sacramental scenes Joinville addresses his own instruction in the sacraments to the reader-viewer:

Nous devons croire es communs sacremens de sainte eglise qui ci aprés sont point. ce est a savoir en baptesme. ou sacrement de l'autel. en mariage. ou pardon des pechiez. et es autres saint sacrement que sainte eglise nous ensaigne a croire. et ausi comme je vous ai dit devant si fermement i devons croire. que riens terriene ne [n]ous poisse deseuvrer. ne habundance ne pestilence.[81]

(We must believe in the shared sacraments of Holy Church, which are expounded [also implying "painted"] hereafter: that is, in baptism, in the sacrament of the altar, in marriage, in the remission of sins, and in other holy sacraments that Holy Church teaches us to believe. And also, as I told you before, so firmly must we believe in them that nothing terrestrial may be able to separate us [from our belief], neither abundance, nor pestilence.)

A slight but signifying divergence between text and image may be discerned in this folio. Although Joinville's textual commentary identifies the sacraments *point* (painted or expounded) on the page as "communs sacremens," the third sacrament depicted—marriage—is, strictly speaking, not held in common by all Christians. The representation of the marriage rite in this folio certainly speaks to the concerns of the lay audience anticipated by Joinville's exposition; it may also have been selected as a formal response to the image that follows it within the opening (fig. 13).

Here the viewer encounters an episode from the Old Testament: Jacob's benediction of Joseph's sons, Ephraim and Manasses (Gen. 48:13–20). Despite Joseph's wishes, it was Ephraim who received the benediction of Jacob's right hand, a slight to

Manasses, the older of the two boys. In Joinville's commentary, the episode is invoked as a *profecie de l'uevre* (prophecy in deed): Jacob's crossed hands and inverted blessing signify that "diex osteroit sa beneiçon de la loi des juis . . . et meteroit sa beneiçon sor la nostre loi crestienne et ce apert tout cler. car il n'oint ne rois ne evesque en oint et nous les avons" (God removed his benediction from the law of the Jews . . . and conferred his benediction upon our Christian law, and this is readily apparent, for they do not have anointed kings or bishops, but we have them).[82] In the miniature, Jacob's attenuated crossed arms drive this typological argument home, but they also form a gestural foil to the exchange of hands, facilitated by the priest, in the preceding marriage scene. Christian nuptial pledges and the sacerdotal blessing they receive are thus juxtaposed with the biblical gesture that Joinville's polemical typology constructs as a prophetic announcement of the preeminence of the Christian sacraments.

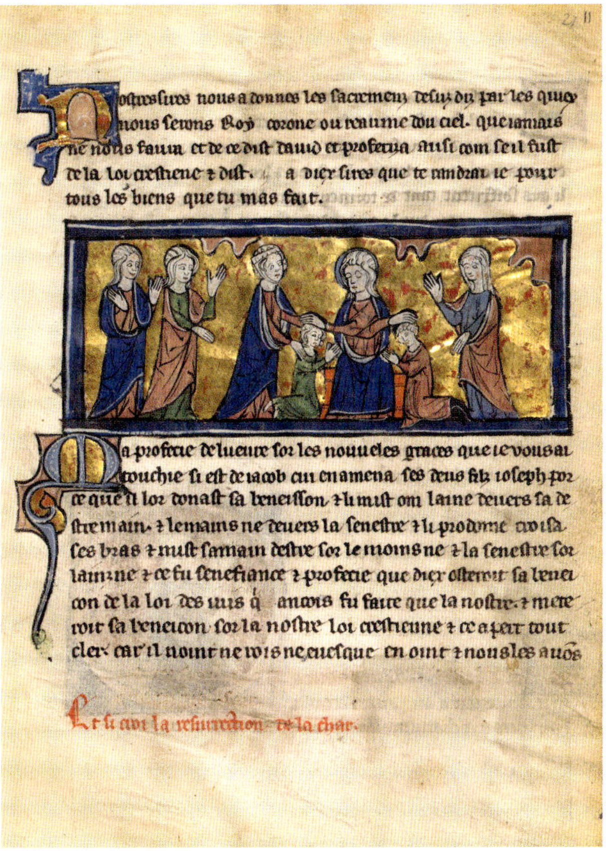

Fig. 13. A prophecy in deed: Jacob's benediction of Ephraim and Manasses in Jean de Joinville's Romans as ymages*. Paris, BnF, MS n. a. fr. 4509, f. 11r.*

Significantly, the text's chief proof of Christian exceptionality is decidedly not one of the "communs sacremens de sainte eglise"; rather, it concerns the ceremonial anointing of French kings.[83] In this opening, Joinville takes the exposition of a creedal *point* as an opportunity to go beyond the letter of the Christological narrative, even beyond the flexible frame of typological exegesis, making an argument in text and image that speaks to the manuscript's anticipated audience of French laypeople in the terms of their own religious formation and sense of spiritual exceptionality. As this example suggests, the needs and expectations of his audience are not peripheral concerns for Joinville. Indeed, in the introductory and concluding sections of his Credo, Joinville addresses his reader-viewers directly, justifying his work and its textual and visual procedure.

In the prologue to his creedal exposition, Joinville explains that because man is encumbered with sin he is deprived of a direct contemplation of "la clarté soveraine" (the supreme divine light or glory) during his lifetime.[84] Given that God, the Trinity, and the Holy Spirit remain beyond man's powers of exposition, Joinville instead tells the reader, "poez veoir ci aprés point et escrit les articles de nostre foi par letres et par ymages selonc ce que on puet poindre selonc l'umanité ihesu crit et selonc la nostre" (you can see hereafter the articles of our faith painted and written, in letters and images, in keeping with what one can expound concerning the humanity of Christ and our own humanity).[85] He begins his exposition by defining faith as "une vertuz qui fait croire fermement ce que hons ne voit ne ne set mais que par oïr dire" (a virtue that makes man firmly believe what he does not see and knows only by hearsay).[86] In the continuation of the prologue, Joinville recounts two *exempla,* each associated with St. Louis.

The first, he notes, was a story about his contemporary, Amaury VI de Montfort, told to him by Louis IX. Count Amaury VI was approached by two *aubrigois* (Albigensians) who asked him to come see a miraculous host that had been transformed into bleeding flesh.[87] Amaury refused, telling them, "alez le veoir qui ne le creez car en droit de moi le croi je bien desouz le pain et desouz le vin ausinc come sainte eglise m'enseigne" (go see it, you who don't believe it; for as concerns myself, I truly believe in it beneath the bread and beneath the wine, just as Holy Church teaches me).[88] When the Albigensians pressed him, Amaury further rebuked them: "et dist que se il creoit ce que diex et li sainz li enseignoient qu'il en atendoit plus grant guerredon et plus grant corone ou ciel que de toutes autres bone oevres qu'il porroit faire en ceste mortel vie" (and he said that if he believed what God and the saints taught him, he would receive a greater reward and a greater crown in heaven than from all the good works that he could do in this mortal life).[89]

In the second *exemplum,* Joinville recounts how Louis IX taught him that salvation depends on "bones euvres faire et fermement croire" (doing good works and believing steadfastly).[90] We are told that the king warned Joinville that the devil constantly attempts to undermine faith; the specific example mentioned by the king concerned doubts about the Eucharist. Louis IX instructed Joinville that when he was tempted by doubts about the host he should rebuke the devil, saying, "enemis ne te vaut que ja a l'aide de dieu de la foi crestiene tu ne me osteras nes se tu me feisses touz les membres tranchier" (enemy, this will get you nowhere! For never, with God's help, will you take me from the Christian faith, not even if you should cut off all my limbs).[91]

There is inherent tension between these very contemporary exhortations and the textual-visual exposition of the Creed that follows. In the prologue, Joinville asserts that faith transcends reason and the sensory, a traditional position that echoes the teachings of St. Augustine, Hugh of Saint-Victor, and Peter Lombard, among others.[92] Joinville's vernacular, lay authorities—Amaury VI and Louis IX—confirm this view, refusing to compromise the integrity of their faith through any concession to the evidence of the senses. Insisting on the superiority of Eucharistic *credenda* (things to be believed) to *videnda* (things to be seen), both of Joinville's exemplars refuse the testimony of vision.

The definition of faith promoted by Joinville and his role models is entirely canonical; it would seem, however, to implicitly reject the textual-visual procedure of the *Romans as ymages* itself.

Indeed, in this same prefatory section of the text, Joinville's use of the verb *poindre* points to a deliberate concatenation of visual representation and doctrinal exposition. In Joinville's lexicon, *point* would equally seem to mean "painted," "expounded," and "article of belief." How then may we understand his *Romans as ymages des poinz de nostre foi*? What moral-spiritual efficacy can its images have if *ferme creance* (firm belief) is an unseeing belief in insensible things? Joinville himself supplies an answer to this question in the concluding section of the treatise. In a vivid account of how the devil assails dying men, hoping to tempt them into unbelief, Joinville explains that

> devant lou malade façons lire le romant qui devise et enseigne les poinz de nostre foi si que par les eux et les oreilles mete lon lou cuer dou malade si plain de la verraie cognoissance que li anemis ne la ne aillour ne puisse riens metre ou malade dou sien dou quel diex nous gart a celle jornee de la mort et aillors.[93]
>
> (before [that is, in the presence of] the sick man we have the *romant* that distinguishes and teaches the points of our faith read so that, through the eyes and the ears, the heart of the sick man is made so full of true knowledge that the enemy may not put anything of his own in the sick man, there or elsewhere, from whom [the devil] may God protect us on that day of death and otherwise.)

Here, addressing the most dire and spiritually charged of circumstances, Joinville insists upon the efficacy of hearing and vision. The underlying premise is stated baldly: it is precisely the vernacular text and visual representations of Joinville's Credo that will effectively block the devil's sensory ingress and its terrible result, unbelief. An audio-visual dose of similia similibus, Joinville's work solicits the eye and the ear in order to counter demonic assault on the weakest point of the dying man's defenses—his senses of sight and of hearing.

Although the tension between Joinville's prefatory comments about faith and his concluding promotion of the *Romans as ymages*'s power of sensory solicitation is never neatly resolved, the significance of his textual-visual catechesis nonetheless remains clear. The clamorous dialogue in which the illuminated *Romans* engages the senses of the dying man will drown out demonic insinuation; its visual and verbal affirmation and exposition of the creed will involve the vulnerable Christian in the call and response of faithful profession. Compelling the dying man's eyes and ears to assent to the articles of the faith, Joinville's *Romans* transforms sensory weakness into a powerful weapon in the battle for salvation.

Joinville's *Romans as ymages* epitomizes a new development in the promotion and intended reception of works of visual pastoralia. Although in the body of his creedal exposition Joinville marshals scriptural authorities and the canonical weight of the Apostles' Creed itself, the prologue and conclusion to his work rely on a different canon of *auctoritates*. Here, important spiritual lessons are taught by three laymen: Amaury VI de Montfort; Louis IX, king of France and—within Joinville's lifetime—saint; and Jean de Joinville himself—aristocrat, intimate of Louis IX, and the leader of men on crusade. Moreover, at least within the terms of the *Romans as ymages,* Joinville's exegetical and doctrinal authority is assumed. In the deathbed battle for the Christian soul, who better to take up the fight for the faith than a former crusader, albeit one who refused to take up the cross a second time. Armed with his *Romans as ymages,* Joinville comes to the rescue of his fellow Christians, revealing that, by the end of the thirteenth century, the cura animarum was a dialogic responsibility that lay elites had enthusiastically taken upon themselves.

THE HEROICS OF RELIGIOUS KNOWLEDGE

As Joinville implicitly extends his conception of crusade to encompass the battlefield of Christian interiority and its vulnerable sensory frontier, he valorizes vernacular text and visual representation as essential weapons in the waging of spiritual warfare. This militaristic conceit is not Joinville's invention; like the *Vrigiet de solas*'s moralizing mirror, the trope appears in antecedent monastic practices of prayer, visual piety, and the production of images.[94] Joinville's work, with its bellicose evocation of devilish onslaught and the dangers of unbelief, is, however, a monument for a new moment. In Joinville's lifetime a repertoire of heroic ideals, associated with literate lay elites, significantly reinflected established Christian conceptions of spiritual-moral conflict. In Joinville's work the fight for ferme creance is waged by exemplary male members of the highest echelons of French society. In an image produced for Eleanor de Quincy, countess of Winchester, circa 1260 or shortly afterward—that is, approximately a decade after Joinville's *Romans as ymages*—the penitential Christian *miles* (soldier) undergoes a further translation (fig. 14).

Fig. 14. Penance as spiritual combat in Eleanor de Quincy's Lambeth Apocalypse, c. 1260. London, Lambeth Palace Library MS 209, f. 53r: 272 x 196 mm.

This full-page image is one of a series of fifteen folios of additional images appended to the Lambeth Apocalypse (London, Lambeth Palace Library, MS 209) shortly after the manuscript's apocalypse cycle was painted.[95] The painting, executed in line and wash on a reserved parchment ground, is a complex allegory of the spiritual

par le coc en lesbre · est signifie le precheur
qui desfule e le peche el despire ·

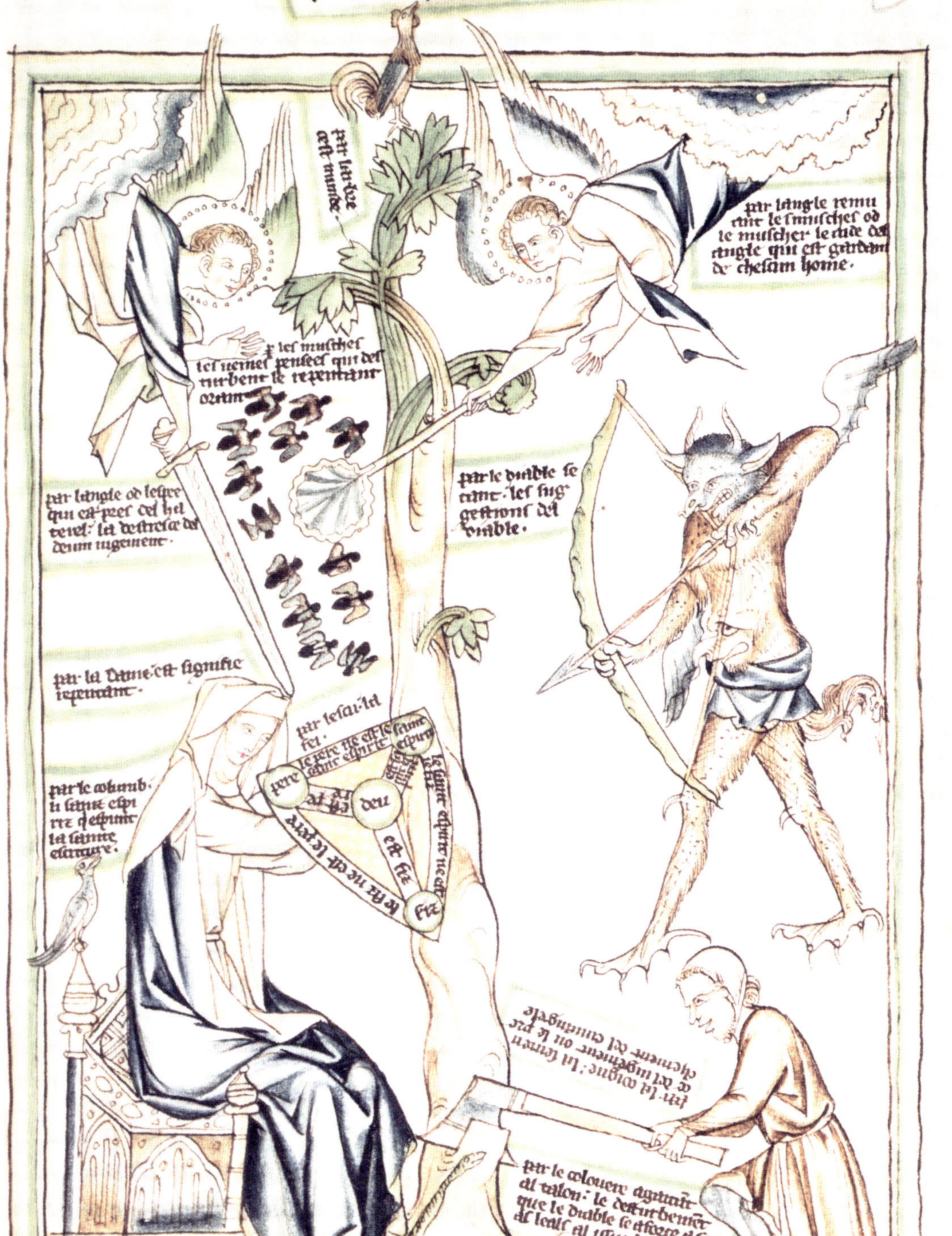

par louwe: deuine escriture la quele le precheur deministre ·

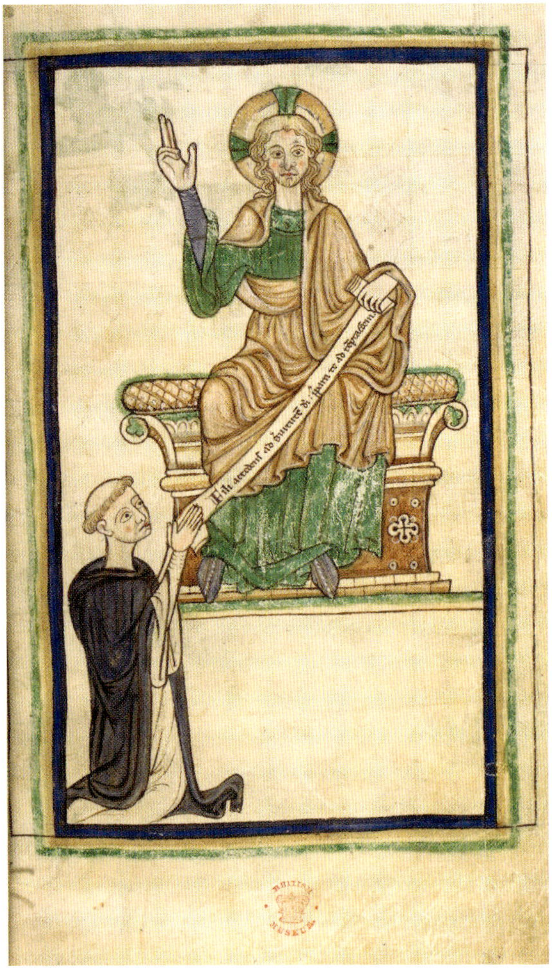

Fig. 16. *"Come to the service of God; prepare yourself for temptation": Christ exhorts a friar in a pastoral compendium. London, BL, Harley MS 3244, f. 27r.*

painted on the preceding recto (fig. 16). As the friar kneels before Christ in this full-page image, enthroned deity and Dominican each hold one end of a banderole. The inscribed text functions as a speech scroll, in which Christ addresses the book owner directly: "Fili accedens ad servitutem dei. prepara te ad temptacionem" (Oh son, come to the service of God; prepare yourself for temptation). Christ's exhortation to the kneeling friar is couched in a condensed citation of Ecclesiasticus 2:1. Significantly, this text reappears prominently in another Dominican context, the *Libellus de instructione et consolatione novitiorum* (Booklet Concerning the Instruction and Comforting of Novices) adopted by the Dominican general chapter in 1283 as a manual for the training of novices.[106] As Michèle Mulchahey has discussed, the tract's anonymous Dominican author appropriates Ecclesiasticus 2:1 to structure his training manual, organizing his exposition of the four-part formation of a friar around a fourfold distinction of this scriptural passage.[107]

Thus, in Harley 3244, Christ addresses the kneeling friar with a text identifying the foundation of Dominican conversio with service to God and the struggle against temptation. This fictive encounter between the mendicant book owner and Christ is, however, only the first moment in a dialogue between devotee and deity. In this image the book owner is invited to enter the agon of Christian life well prepared by religious discipline. In the painting that follows (see fig. 15), we see an allegorical representation of the good friar's response: the kneeling Dominican assumes the role of the spiritual warrior, a combatant not simply for his own soul but also for the souls entrusted to his care.

Although Evans stresses the idiosyncrasy of the opening's specific constituent elements and its importance as one of a very limited number of representations of the miles christianus in the period before the Reformation, the Harley manuscript's visual allegory witnesses to a broader efflorescence of "knightly allegories" charged with a moral-spiritual surplus and designed for didactic aims.[108] Clothing penitential practice in the guise of chivalric ideals, both the Harley opening and the Lambeth image are

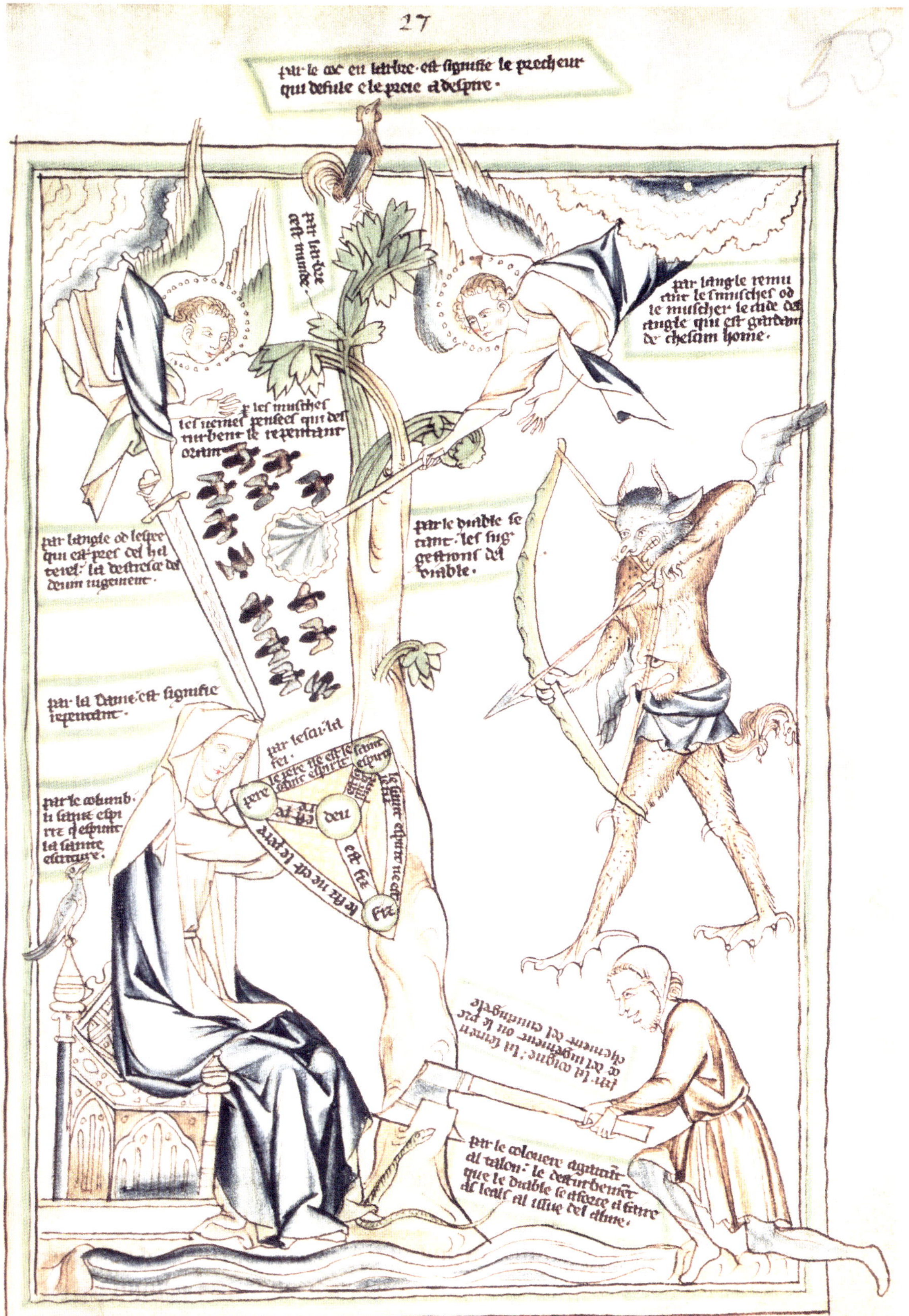
27
par le coc en letrbre est signifie le precheur
qui desule e le preie el despire.
par langle remu
ent les musches od
le muscher le eide del
angle qui est gardein
de chescun home.
par le diable se
neinte. les sug
gestions del
diable.
par le colouere agaitant
al talon: le destorbemet
que le diable se afforce a fere
al leals al issue del alme.
par le vaine: devine escriture la quele le prechein demustre.

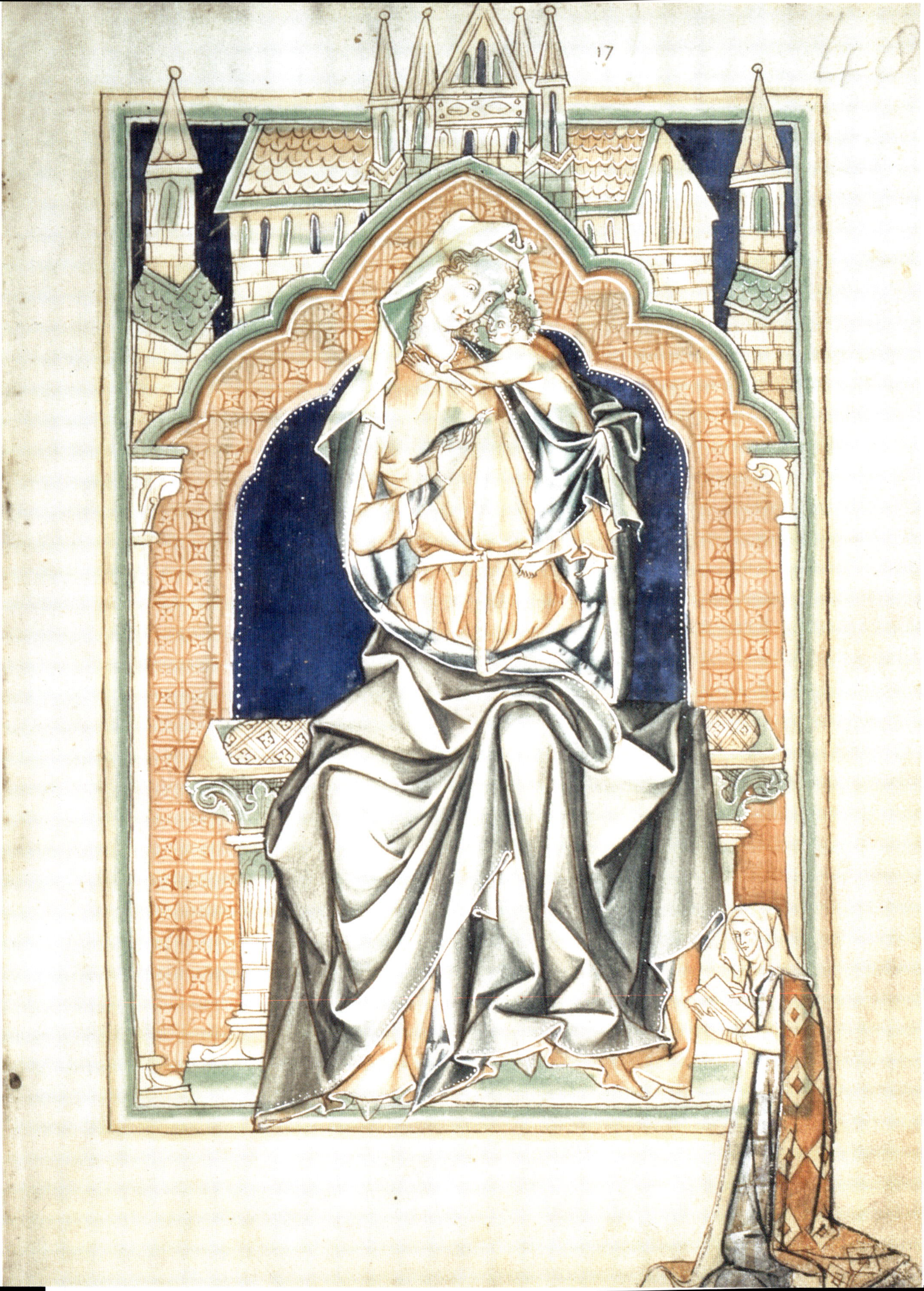

the series of images added to the manuscript's Apocalypse sequence deftly solicit the intellectual and contemplative engagement of Eleanor de Quincy, the book's female owner. In her interpretation of the manuscript's allegory of penitence, Lewis discerns an "interactive synthesis of words and images closely analogous to the 'reading' and absorption of the illustrated glossed Apocalypse."[111] This observation leads Lewis to conclude that the female heroine of the image's drama of spiritual-moral struggle,

> like John on Patmos . . . finds herself in a transitory, liminal world inhabited by angels and demons, but, unlike the visionary on Patmos, she is guided by the voices of birds (cock and dove), preaching against the world and expounding Holy Scripture, rather than what she sees. Indeed, the penitent woman looks inward behind her emblematized spiritual armor, absorbing the disparate images surrounding her into an internal vision of spiritual and moral understanding.[112]

But does the image's female penitent look inward, refusing the *visibilia* that surround her? No less than the figure of Eleanor de Quincy contemplating an open book in the presence of the Virgin and Child (see fig. 17), or the figure of Mary Magdalene gazing upon the risen Christ in an image on folio 49r (fig. 18), the penitent woman has her eyes wide open (see fig. 14). Looking up and to the right—directly at her demonic assailant—this guerriere crestiene does not flinch from the hideous aggression of her spiritual enemies.

As the manuscript's allegory of penance interpellated Eleanor de Quincy as its penitent heroine, it also offered her an initial translation of the invisible experience of moral struggle. Exteriorizing inner conflict, the image flattered her in heroic terms, urging her to take up the arms of an intellectual mastery of the faith and to recognize her most important allies in the officers of the cura animarum. In this way the image demands of its viewer a hermeneutic oscillation between the internal and external referents of its allegory—that is, between the conflict waged within the soul and the sensible world of preaching, reading, listening, and, not least, looking.

In the allegory of penitence's rhetoric—and in its procedure—the cultivation and maintenance of the devotee's moral-spiritual vigilance depends on hearing and understanding, on seeing and discerning. Within the broader context of the manuscript's visual and textual program, the image reminds its reader-viewer that the visionary is not the only mode by which moral and spiritual insight may be attained. Like Joinville's *Romans as ymages,* the Lambeth Apocalypse's allegory of penance and faith valorizes hearing and sight as "weapons in the daily battle."[113]

Fig. 17. Eleanor de Quincy in the presence of the Virgin and Child in the Lambeth Apocalypse. London, Lambeth Palace Library MS 209, f. 48r.

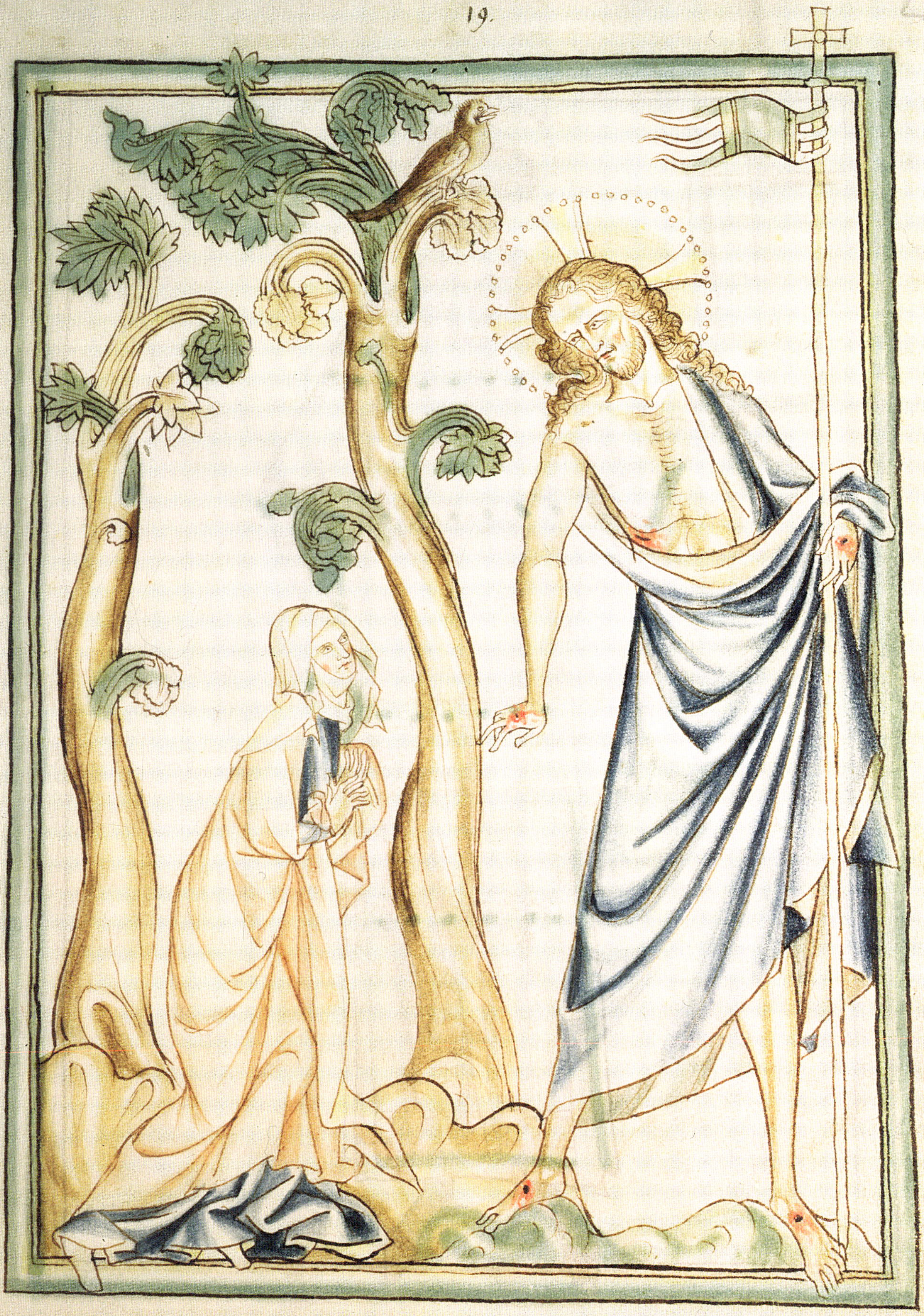

ELEANOR'S VERONICA: ILLUMINATION, INTERROGATION, AND THE *IMAGO DEI*

Like the dialogic practice of confession developed and refined over the course of the thirteenth century, the Lambeth Apocalypse's allegory of penance attempts to engage its reader-viewer in a recursive process whereby the interior space of the soul is translated into visible and verbal form, and, in turn, image and text give access to a spiritually penetrating vision of the self. This back-and-forth between image and reader-viewer is not a disembodied, asensory mode of vision; it is, instead, predicated on a vision of the manuscript page.

As Eleanor de Quincy turned the folio on which the allegory of penance is painted, she was forcefully reminded of the corporeal character of her own seeing, of its spiritual efficacy, and of its finitude. Christ's holy face confronts the viewer from the verso of folio 53 (fig. 19). The incarnate deity is presented frontally in a close-up view, with only the tops of his shoulders, draped in a blue mantle, visible above the bottom edge of the frame. Staring sternly at the beholder, Christ's face is set against, or within, a background whose crosshatched articulation identifies it as a fictive textile.[114] This is not just any iconic representation of the incarnate deity: the Holy Face appears on folio 53v in the very specific form of the Veronica.[115]

The material referent for the Lambeth Apocalypse's painting was a piece of cloth preserved in St. Peter's in Rome that bore the miraculous impress of Christ's face.[116] The Veronica was understood to be a *vera icon* (true image), a sacred artifact endowed with the authority and sacred ontology of a relic and possessed of the image's power of mimetic representation.[117] In the Lambeth Apocalypse, a short Latin office and prayer, thought to have been composed by Innocent III in honor of the Roman relic, accompany the representation of the Veronica.[118] First attested in English manuscripts of the mid-thirteenth century, the prayer circulated with a ten-day indulgence for its recital.[119] As Flora Lewis has noted, the indulgence was granted for recitation of the prayer alone; no visual surrogate for the Veronica relic was required.[120] Nonetheless, the indulgence came to be associated not simply with the verbal performance of the prayer text but also with the veneration of the accompanying image.

Reciting the words of the office and prayer inscribed below the image, Eleanor de Quincy was once again implicated in a dialogic relationship to what she saw on the page of the manuscript before her. Opening with Psalm 4:7—"Signatum est super nos lumen vultus tui domine deus dedisti leticiam in corde meo" (the light of thy countenance is signed [or sealed] upon us; thou hast given gladness in my heart)[121]—the text of the short office takes up the trope of the impression, implicit in the representation of the Veronica above, and extends it to the relationship between devotee and deity. Just as the Veronica received the impression of Christ's countenance, so too the Christian

Fig. 18. Mary Magdalene and the risen Christ in the Lambeth Apocalypse. London, Lambeth Palace Library MS 209, f. 49r.

contemplating the image and reciting the prayer is transformed, spiritually marked by his or her vision of the Holy Face. This celebration of the impression-translation of the divine image to the devotee cannot fail to recall Genesis 1:27, which describes God creating man "ad imaginem suam" (after his own image). The devotee's contemplation of the Veronica, and his or her illumination by that act of visual piety, is thus cast as a process of reformation, quite literally: a reforming of the soul that recapitulates the original moment of humanity's sinless creation.

In the prayer that follows, the devotee addresses the deity directly and confronts the conditions of the spiritual encounter that the Veronica—both relic and representation—makes possible:

> Deus qui nobis signatis lumine vultus tui memoriale tuum ad instanciam beate veronice ymaginem tuam sudario inpressam relinquere voluisti per passioniem eius et crucem tribue nobis quaesumus ut ita nunc in terris *per speculum et in enigmate* [1 Cor. 13:12] ipsam venerari adorare et honorari valeamus ut te tunc facie ad faciem securi videamus iudicem venientem super nos dominum nostrum ihesum christum.[122]
>
> (O God, at the urging of the blessed Veronica, you desired to leave behind your image impressed on the sudarium as your memorial for us, [who are] sealed with the light of your countenance. Through his passion and cross, grant us, we ask, that now, on earth—*through a mirror, darkly* [1 Cor. 13:12]—we should be able to venerate, adore, and honor that very [image] so that then, face to face, with confidence we might see the judge coming upon us, our Lord Jesus Christ.)

The prayer's appeal to the deity articulates a complex spiritual and visual economy. It describes the image-relic of the Veronica as manifesting the divine countenance, offering the faithful a source of spiritual illumination on earth. At the same time, in keeping with its material form, the Veronica is described as veiling that divine presence, offering only the muffled, mediated vision of 1 Corinthian's "speculum in enigmate." The prayer thus dialogically confronts the exceptional status of the Veronica painted above it: it is both a representation, a mediating translation of the appearance of an absent relic, and an efficacious presence in its own right, an artifact possessed of its own mode of presence, authority, and spiritual power.

Fig. 19. The Veronica—image and interrogator—in the Lambeth Apocalypse. London, Lambeth Palace Library MS 209, f. 53v.

In this Veronica, Eleanor de Quincy's penitential labor found its reward—not simply through the indulgence attached to the image and its prayer, but also through its tantalizing evocation of the beatific vision awaiting the saved at the last judgment.

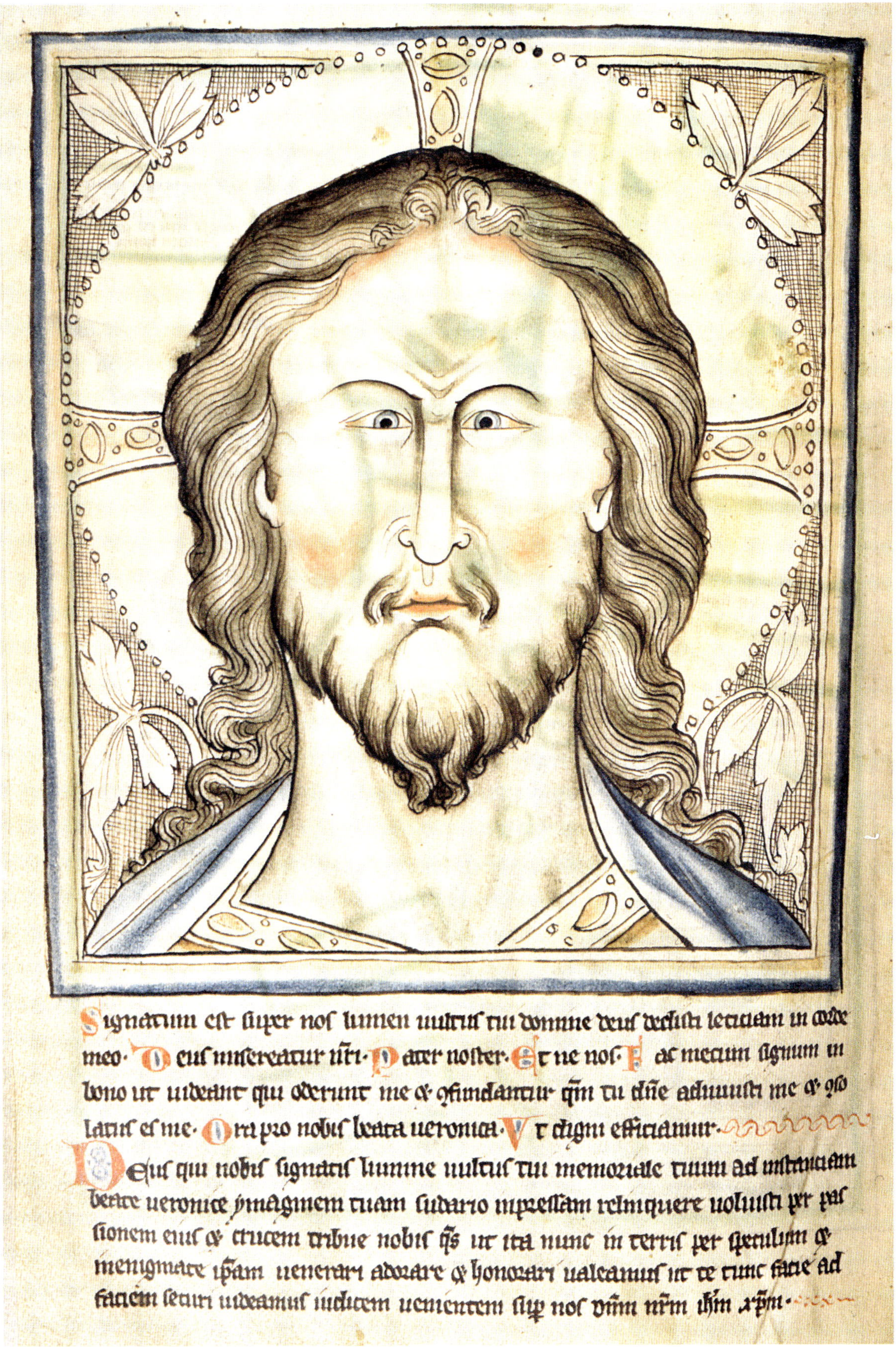
Signatum est super nos lumen uultus tui domine deus dedisti leticiam in corde
meo. Deus misereatur nostri. Pater noster. Et ne nos. Fac mecum signum in
bono ut uideant qui oderunt me et confundantur quoniam tu domine adiuuisti me et conso
latus es me. Ora pro nobis beata ueronica. Ut digni efficiamur.
Deus qui nobis signatis lumine uultus tui memoriale tuum ad instanciam
beate ueronice ymaginem tuam sudario impressam relinquere uoluisti per pas
sionem eius et crucem tribue nobis quesumus ut ita nunc in terris per speculum et
menigmate ipsam uenerari adorare et honorari ualeamus ut te tunc facie ad
faciem securi uideamus iudicem uenientem super nos dominum nostrum ihesum christum.

At the same time, however, this imposing, insistently artifactual representation of Christ subjected the penitential viewer to divine scrutiny. As the image translated its viewer from seeing subject into an object of divine vision, it forcibly reinscribed her in a further exchange.

Translating textile into painting, relic into representation, veil into revelation, Eleanor de Quincy's manuscript offered her a dialogic surface, a darkened mirror in which her penitential gaze was encouraged to see two visions simultaneously. As the prayer told her, she was sealed by the memorial of Christ's countenance painted on the page, and, illuminated by its impressed image, she might still make out the dimmed, even damaged imprint of the *imago dei* (image of God) that she bore, if imperfectly, in her soul.[123] Contemplation of the image of the Veronica was thus a form of self-discovery, a mirroring reflection designed (in the language of Psalm 4:7) to give gladness to the devotee's heart. Indeed, as Gerhard Wolf has argued, contemplation of the Veronica might even be understood as a means of polishing the inward, specular imago dei "so that it becomes true, a remedy to make the mirror brilliant by means of the holy cloth."[124]

At the same time, however, the forbidding image stared back. From the surface of the folio, rendered in more vivifying colored washes against the monochrome simulated textile, Christ—divine scrutator, illuminating exemplar, and *deus in imagine*—met Eleanor de Quincy's gaze. Rather than defining a quiescent terminus for her penitential practice, or a respite from the hermeneutic demands of the allegory of penance that precedes it on the recto, Christ's confrontational incarnation in the Veronica involved Eleanor de Quincy, like the Dominican friar who owned Harley 3244, in a dialogue with the Divine that was itself a kind of moral-spiritual agon. Dialogically framed by the practice of penance and its promised rewards, by prayerful invocation and artifactual simulation, the Holy Face in the Lambeth manuscript redoubled the terms of speaker and spoken to, mirror and beholder, rendering Eleanor de Quincy both the privileged beholder of the page and a penitential petitioner, exposed to divine inspection.

COMMUNITIES OF CATECHESIS

The last image in the Lambeth Apocalypse stages the divine surveillance of the soul in terms that are both confrontational and authorizing. In this respect the indulgenced image makes visible a premise that informs all the manuscripts examined in this chapter, and many other works of visual pastoralia besides: namely, that the viewer is invited to a moral-spiritual scrutiny of the self that will, they are promised, earn a salvific reward. Like the practice of confession, many works of visual pastoralia rely on a dialogical strategy that engages the viewer in a back and forth hermeneusis of question and answer, soliciting a knowledge of sin and of the self produced in the terms of religious truth. As Eleanor de Quincy's Veronica makes quite clear, such scrutiny of the self was also understood as taking place under the deity's watchful gaze. In addition to such explicit visualizations of divine surveillance, the visual programs of works of pastoralia also describe the labor of religious formation and reformation as a social undertaking, a moral-spiritual labor that inscribes the viewer in a community of Christian observance and knowledge.

In a little known compendium produced in England in the second half of the fourteenth century (Paris, BnF, MS fr. 400; henceforth BnF fr. 400), the reader-viewer's mastery of the pastoral syllabus is ingeniously reframed as integrating her or him into an exceptionally authorized, and authorizing, textual community.[125] In the first of a sequence of eight pages dedicated to communicating elements of the canon of catechetical knowledge, the manuscript's reader-viewer encounters the full-length figure of Moses centered in the upper half of the page (fig. 20). A titulus distinguished by a pen-flourished initial at the top of the page identifies the representation below as a presentation scene: "Le prophete moyses nous moustre lez diz comandementz et lez diz conseils de bien" (The prophet Moses shows us the Ten Commandments and the ten counsels of the good).

The two scrolls that Moses holds open do indeed display the commandments and counsels referenced in the titulus. Inscribed in Latin, the Ten Commandments appear on the left, while on the right, the three evangelical counsels of chastity, poverty, and obedience are joined by seven other virtuous Christian observances to form a pendant ten-point list.[126] The typological relationship between the two ten-part programs is emphasized by the banderole hovering behind Moses's head. Reading "decem precepta veteris legis" (the ten precepts of the old law) on the left and "decem consilia nove legis" (the ten counsels of the new law) on the right, this terse gloss mobilizes an established distinction between Old Testament *praecepta* (precepts) and New Testament *consilia* (counsels). In this typological paradigm, the Mosaic Law was understood to define observances that were necessary for salvation, minimal practices required by God of all people; by contrast, the consilia of the era of grace were deemed elective practices, divine counsels that Thomas Aquinas described as concerning "illis per quae melius et expeditius potest homo consequi" (those things through which man may better and more readily arrive) at eternal blessedness.[127]

In a further translation of revelation across historical and linguistic epochs, the bottom third of the page is occupied by an Anglo-Norman translation of these Latin mandates, a further aid to the reader-viewer's more efficient pursuit of salvation. The vernacular text is given over to recapitulating the Latin texts written above it, with two

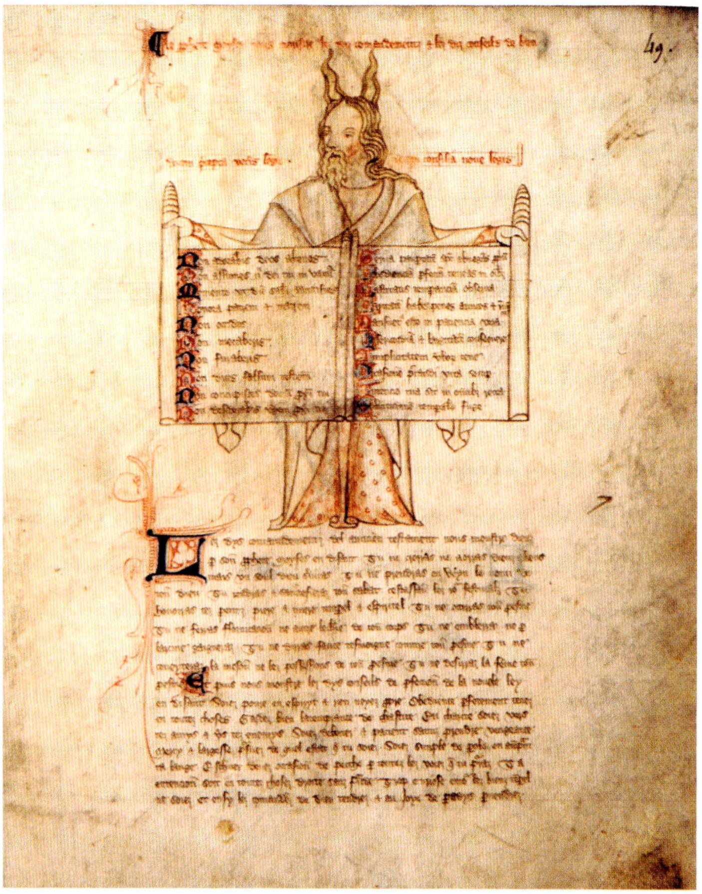

small but significant additions. In two short phrases, prefacing the translation of each list, the reader-viewer is told: "Lez dys comaundementz del auncien testament nous moustre dieuz par soun prophete moyses en disant . . ." (God shows us the Ten Commandments of the Old Testament through his prophet Moses, saying . . .); "Et puis nous moustre lez dys conseils de perfec-cioun de la novele ley en disant . . ." (And then [God] shows us the ten counsels of perfection of the New Law, saying . . .).[128]

Taken as a whole, the page proposes a typological revision of Moses's descent from Mount Sinai with the tablets of the law. As in the Bible moralisée roundel examined in chapter 1, Moses is presented as transfigured by his encounter with the deity; in BnF fr. 400, the coruscating "horns" atop Moses's head indicate the fearsome brilliance of his countenance.[129] Unlike the Bible moralisée's representation of this episode, in BnF fr. 400 Moses appears unveiled. No longer the bearer of Old Testament precepts alone but also the purveyor of the counsels that lead the devotee above and beyond the *minima* of religious necessity to spiritual perfection, the leader of the Israelites is conscripted as a kind of herald—both typological and textual—summoning the reader-viewer to the pursuit of Christian excellence.

Fig. 20. Moses with the Ten Commandments and the ten counsels of the good, c. 1350–1400. Paris, BnF, MS fr. 400, f. 49r: 337 x 248 mm.

Turning the manuscript page, the reader-viewer turns from *prophete* to pontiff, from Mosaic Law and evangelical counsels to the practices that defined late medieval Christian participation in the life of the church (fig. 21). Like Moses, St. Peter is presented as a full-length figure wearing a single tiara-mitre, the cross-pinnacle of which punctuates the titulus spanning the top of the page: "Seint piere nous moustre les sept sacramentz de seinte eglise" (St. Peter shows us the seven sacraments of Holy Church). With both hands, Peter holds open an expanse of scroll in which single Latin phrases describe each of the seven sacraments in terms of its effect; thus we learn that

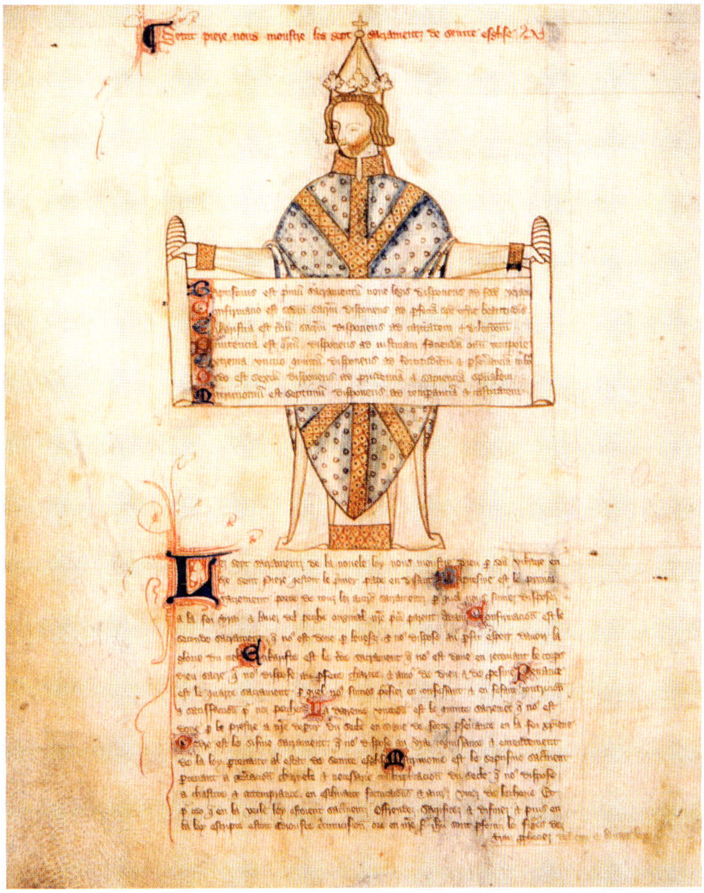

Fig. 21. St. Peter with the seven sacraments. Paris, BnF, MS fr. 400, f. 49v.

baptism disposes to the true faith, confirmation to the perfect spirit of eternal beatitude, the Eucharist to charity and love, and so forth. The Anglo-Norman text block below the papal figure offers a slightly different annotated catalog of the sacraments. In the vernacular paragraph, each of the sacraments is listed in the order employed in the Latinate scroll and glossed in terms of its dispositive effect, but the details of the inventory differ in small ways from the text above.

BnF fr. 400 represents Peter vested in mitre and chasuble, appropriate liturgical vestments for his sacerdotal administration of sacramental knowledge on the page. As in the glossing of the figure of Moses on the recto, the first sentence of the Anglo-Norman text inscribed below the pontiff describes him speaking the religious knowledge he transmits: "Lez sept sacramentz de la novele loy nous moustre dieu par soun vikaire en terre seint Piere q'estoit le primer pape en disant . . ." (God shows us the seven sacraments of the New Law through his vicar on earth Saint Peter who was the first pope, saying . . .).[130] The consistent use of the first person plural pronoun *nous* and the text's emphasis on an originary oral moment of revelatory transmission designate these catechetical exhibitions as dialogical overtures to the beholder, asking him or her to look, to read, and so to imaginatively join the community of religious knowledge visually and hermeneutically constituted in the sequence of folios within which Moses and Peter appear.

Images play a decisive role in the formation of this community. As in all of the manuscript's folios, figuration preceded inscription on recto and verso.[131] The drawing of the pope and of the unfurled roll in his hands, like the delineation of Moses on the recto, was set down before any text was written within the bounds of the fictive scroll or on the ruled expanse of the manuscript page below. As a consequence of this mode of production and in formal terms, the Latin catechetical texts held by Moses and Peter are framed as both drawing and text, representation and inscription. Circumscribed within the drawn form of a speech-scroll, these texts are marked out, like the Veronica in Eleanor de Quincy's Apocalypse manuscript, as visual artifacts, meta-representations that nonetheless remain legible, authorized, and authorizing. Framing divine verities and figuring Moses's and Peter's charismatic presence, visual representation powerfully mediates religious authority and truth for the beholder. Consequently, the fellowship to which the figures of Moses and Peter invite the viewer is not an exclusively textual community; it is also a form of religious belonging that is perfected in the beholder's visual witnessing of sacred truth.

Employing the same mise en page, subsequent folios introduce the manuscript's beholder to other members of this authorizing collectivity: on folio 50r St. Paul displays a scroll inscribed with the seven theological and cardinal virtues; on folio 50v the Virgin and Christ child unfurl a roll bearing the seven gifts of the Holy Spirit; on folio 51r the Archangel Gabriel holds in both hands a scroll listing the seven *beneuretez* (blessednesses) of the perfect life (a modification of the eight beatitudes); and on folio 53v John the Baptist, like Moses before him, displays two scrolls, one inscribed with the spiritual works of mercy and the other with the corporeal.

This sequence of individual exemplars is momentarily interrupted in the opening composed of folios 51v–52r (figs. 22 and 23). Dominated by a redoubled representation of the second person of the Trinity, these facing pages present the text of the Apostles' Creed in two Christological installments: articles that touch on Christ's deity are presented on the verso, and articles treating his humanity appear on the recto opposite. Departing from the traditional twelve-part division, the opening distinguishes Christian belief into fourteen articles, a division of the Credo also employed by Thomas Aquinas in his Commentary on the Sentences and the *Summa theologiae*.[132] Despite this fourteen-point presentation of the Creed, the opening maintains the tradition of ascribing individual articles to each of the apostles.[133] In the paragraphs of Anglo-Norman text inscribed in the lower section of verso and recto, the reader-viewer is first offered a vernacular translation of each line of the Creed and then a rapid designation of each article's apostolic author.

The opening's hypostatic disposition of the articles of the faith is made instantly apparent by the differentiated representations of Christ that appear on verso and recto. On the left side of the opening we see Christ impassible in his divinity, holding in his left hand an orb of dominion surmounted by a triumphant vexillum and in his right hand a scroll bearing a Latinate inventory of the seven articles that treat his divinity. The representation that dominates the facing recto, by contrast, describes an emphatically passible and pathetic Christ. With blood flecking his body and pouring

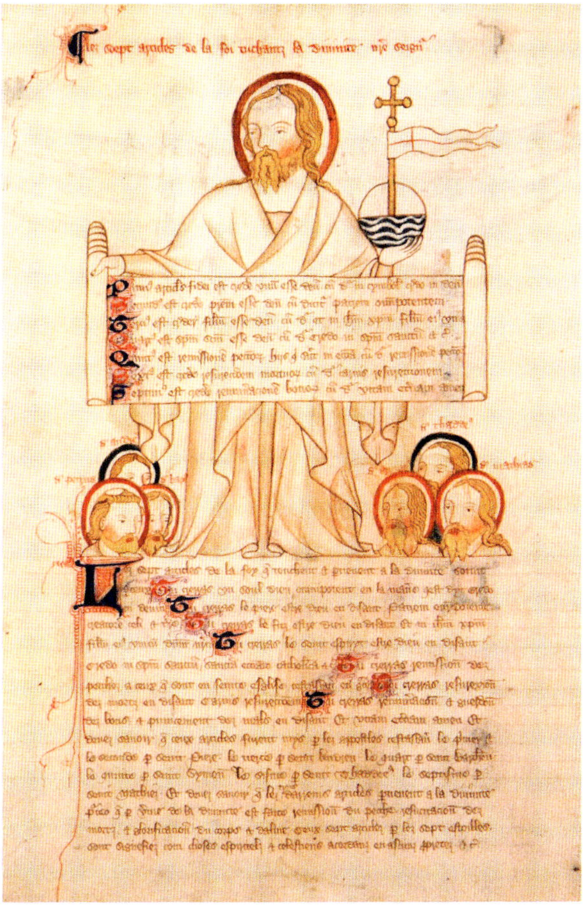

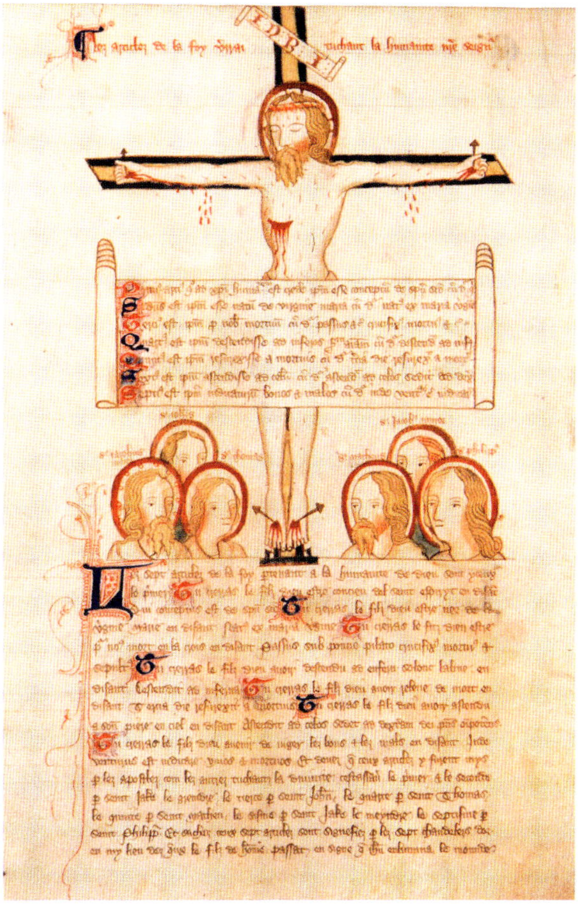

copiously from the lance wound and the four nail wounds (a rather archaizing touch), Christ in his humanity appears stretched out upon the cross, while the text of the articles treating his humanity hovers unfurled, like an ersatz winding sheet, before his hips and groin.

Fig. 22. The Apostles' Creed: Christ in his deity. Paris, BnF, MS fr. 400, f. 51v.

Fig. 23. The Apostles' Creed: Christ in his humanity. Paris, BnF, MS fr. 400, f. 52r.

The binocular tableau of verso and recto stages a textual and visual apperception of the truth of the second person of the Trinity, a truth to which the opening visually reorients the entire substance of the Creed.[134] Significantly, the Anglo-Norman texts inscribed in the lower half of each page do not reiterate the claim to derive from some mediated divine utterance that punctuates the vernacular text blocks of previous folios. Instead, the beholder of the opening encounters the divine *verbum* translated again and again—drawn in his deity; represented in his visible, incarnate form; transliterated into the Latin affirmations of the Apostles' Creed; and translated once more into Anglo-Norman text.

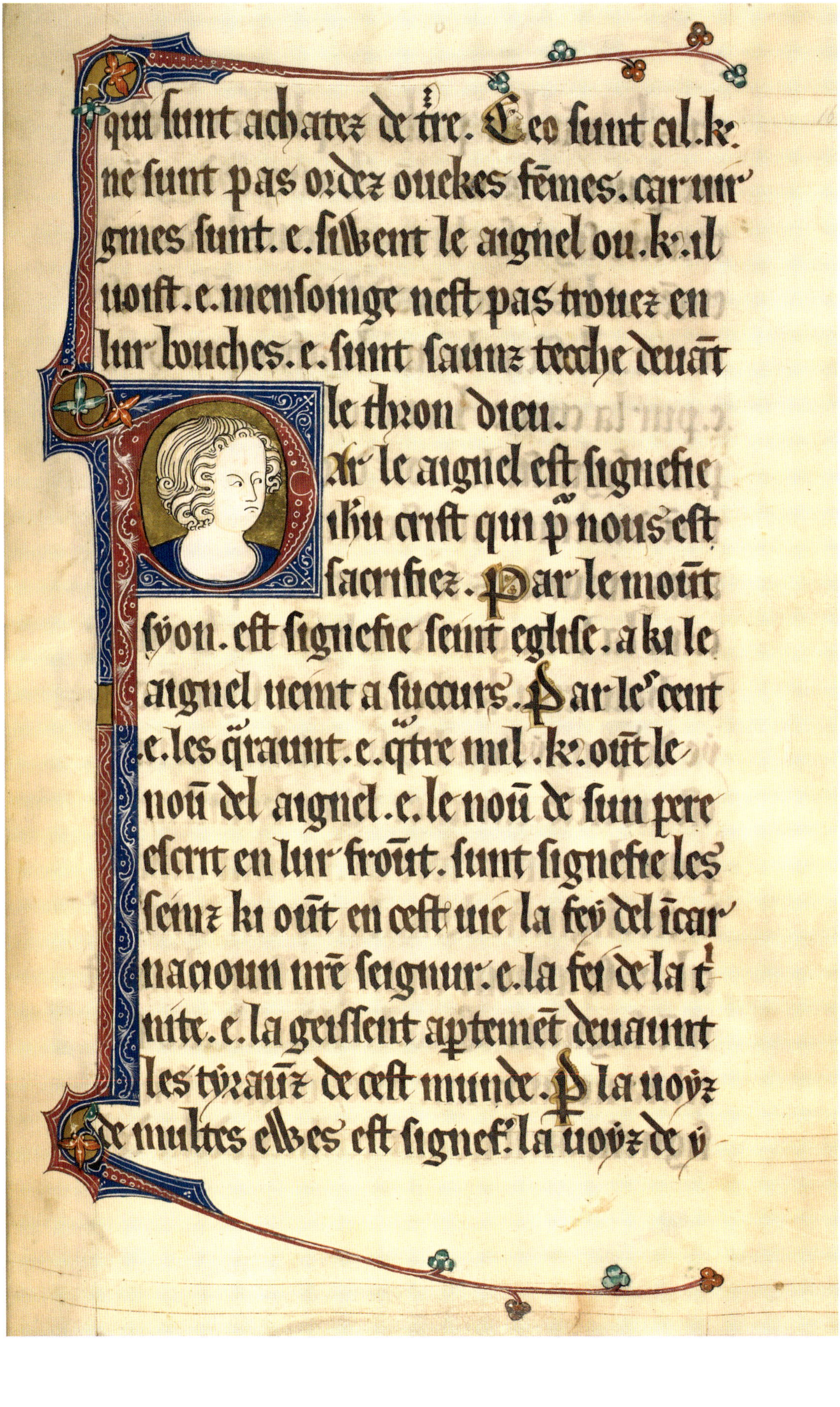

qui sunt achatez de tre. Ceo sunt cil .k.
ne sunt pas ordez ouekes fēmes. car uir
gines sunt. e. siwent le aignel ou .k. il
uoist. e. mensoinge nest pas trouez en
lur bouches. e. sunt saunz teche deuāt
le thron dieu.
Par le aignel est signefie
ihu crist qui p̄ nous est
sacrifiez. Par le mount
syon. est signefie seint eglise. a ki le
aignel uient a succurs. Par les cent
e. les quaraunt. e. quatre mil .k. ount le
noū del aignel. e. le noū de sun pere
escrit en lur frount. sunt signefie les
seinz ki ount en cest uie la fey del incar
nacioun nre seignur. e. la fei de la tri
nite. e. la geissent aptemēt deuaunt
les tyraunz de cest munde. P la uoyz
de multes ewes est signef. la uoyz de v

scene (fig. 26). Within the space of the illuminated letter O, the student makes his point forcefully, pointing with his index finger to the palm of his other hand. On the right, the seated master listens, gesturing with his open hand that he has a reply for the querulous student. The winged hybrids whose bodies constitute the framing letterform figure the tension of pedagogical give-and-take: their twining tails act as a visual metaphor for the imbrication of question and answer, just as their confronted heads gloss the animated tête-à-tête of pupil and teacher. Celebrating clerical pedagogy and emulating the *clergie* of the Latinate schoolroom, as well as its traditions of disputation, Royal 15.D.II visually translates the *Lumere* as a spectacular space appropriated to the laity's needs, purposes, and ambitions—both spiritual and social. Composed of pseudoscholastic disputation and visionary revelation, the textual-visual architecture inhabited by the manuscript's painted population of men and women, youths and maidens, was an authorizing armature.

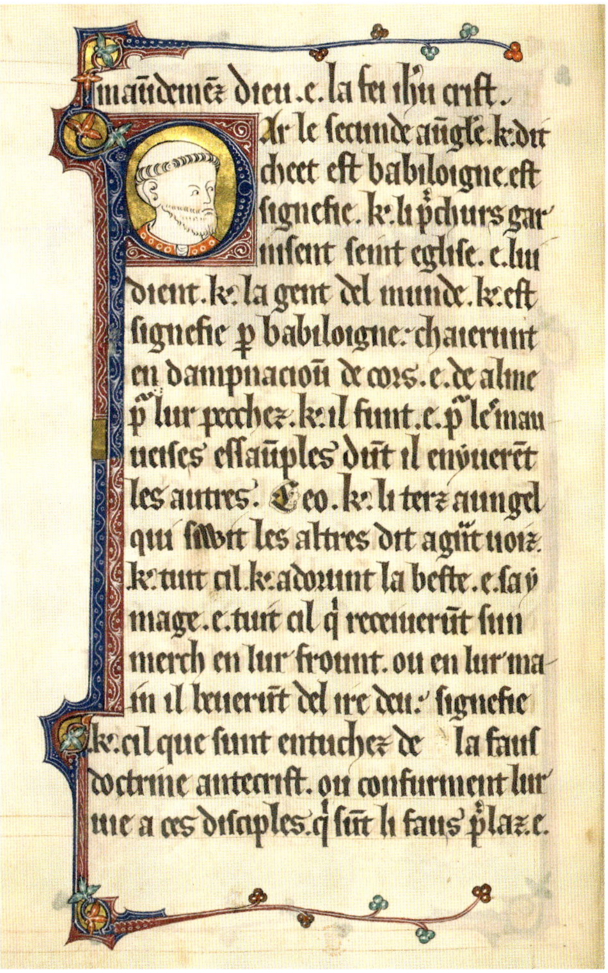

Fig. 25. A tonsured master of the vernacular page in a compendium, c. 1310. London, BL, Royal MS 15.D.II, f. 163r.

Acting as a fictive and idealizing mirror of Christian society, the compendium's initials visually describe a community unified in its relationship to religious knowledge, yet still possessed of the marks of social distinction. Was the manuscript's original owner enlightened by the didactic *lumere* of its texts and dazzled by the illuminated letters that grace almost every recto and verso? Certainly, the compendium mounted an ambitious campaign of solicitation, inviting the reader-viewer to join a company of men and women distinguished by their stature on the page and by the authorizing texts they inhabited. As the book owner voiced the words inscribed on a recto or paused to inspect a painted face, the dialogic question and answer of the *Lumere*'s text amplified, proliferated, and swelled into a polyphony of imagined voices and gazes. In this volume, the dialogic practice of spiritual reformation was figured as a sociable affair, a collective undertaking that welcomed the manuscript's owner into a garrulous community of religious knowledge and worldly distinction.

OPPOSITE: Fig. 24. A lay youth inhabits the didactic letter of a compendium, c. 1310. London, British Library, Royal MS 15.D.II, f. 165v: 445 x 308 mm.

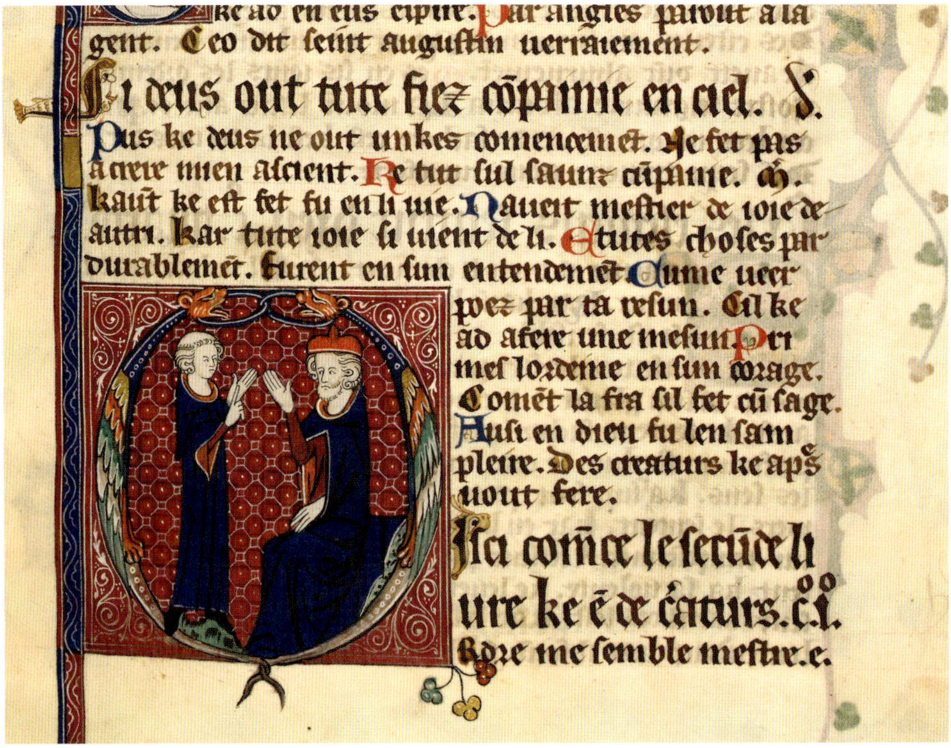

Fig. 26. Pedagogic dialog in the Lumere as lais, *c. 1310. London, BL, Royal MS 15.D.II, f. 8r (detail).*

Conclusion

Inviting reader-viewers to a dialogue of question and response, soliciting religious knowledge and ignorance from their audiences, and, in return, offering them ways of knowing, forms of profession, and the promise of penitential transformation, many works of visual pastoralia appropriated the modus confitendi to new, extrasacramental ends. Diligent inspection of the images painted in these illuminated manuscripts of spiritual instruction involved the book owner in a hermeneusis that was also an ambitious project of moral-spiritual self-fashioning.

Soliciting the senses in order to reform the soul, these manuscripts recast religious knowledge and its effects in a series of visual tropes, be it the specular structure of the mirror, the chivalric combat of penance, or the figuration of Christian community. Visual translation in these books is both process and paradigm: a formal strategy that transforms the invisible semantic substance of credenda into the visible surface of the manuscript page and, simultaneously, an implicit metaphor for the transformation of the moral-spiritual self, from sin to a state of grace, from the singularity of transgression to the distinguished fellowship of the faithful.

If, within this penitential and creedal economy, visual translation performed a quasi-sacerdotal function—mediating invisible sacred truths and so effecting a unifying communion of the faithful—then each image drawn or painted in these books might be understood as enjoying a quasi-sacramental efficacy, a capacity to make saving truths present on the page. And yet, the dialogic address of these visual representations would seem to implicate the beholder in an irresolvable paradox: how could faith—a belief in the unseen—be shaped, reformed, and perfected by visible means? In the pages that follow we will pursue how the late medieval Mass confronted medieval Christians—clerical and lay—with precisely this problem, and how one fourteenth-century artist responded, translating sacramental paradox into a powerful account of what it might mean to see images made by human hands.

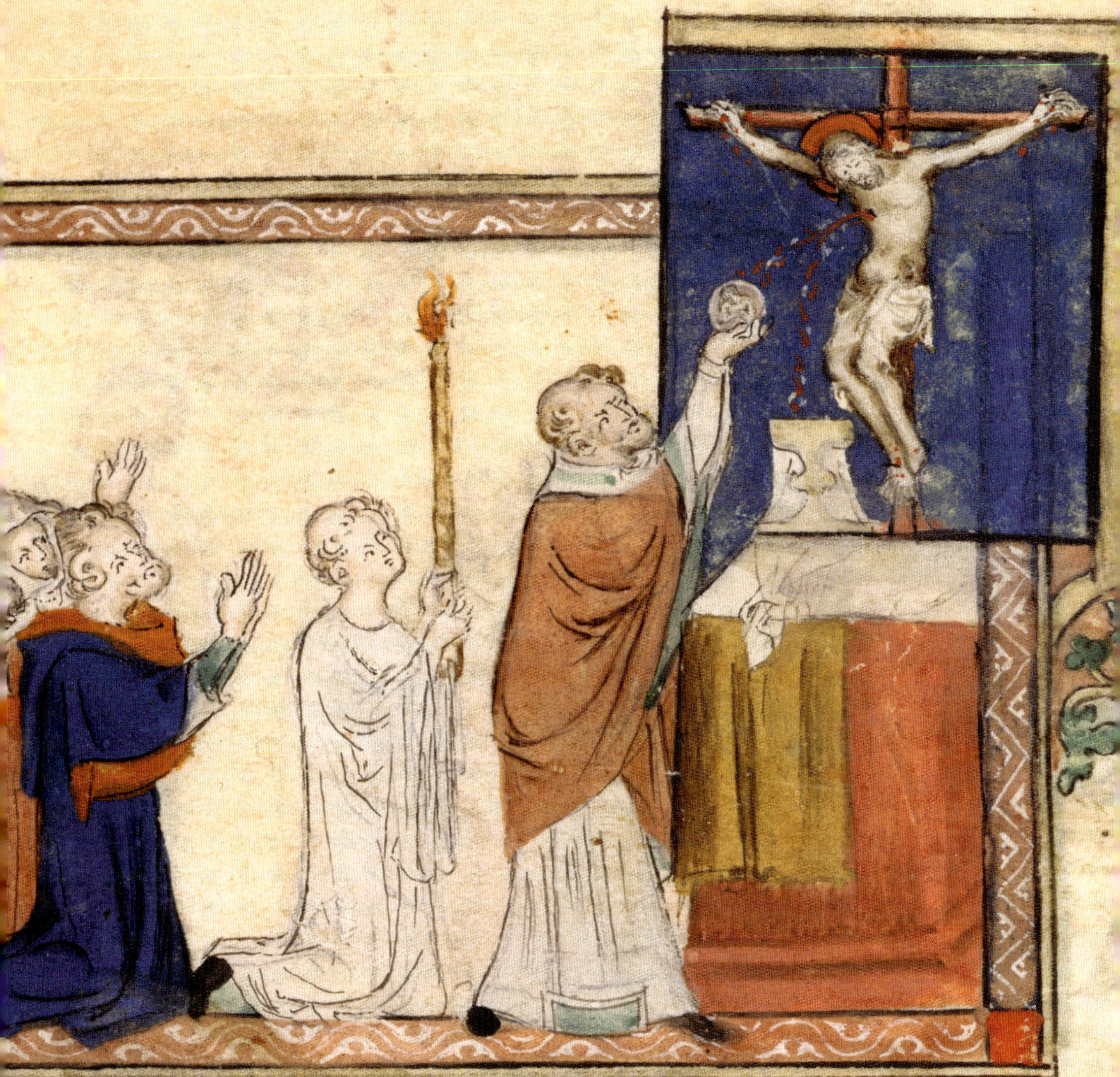

os especiales besoignes si com
l prendra·

CHAPTER THREE

Translating the Eucharist

Sacramentum pietatis huic mundo creditum aliena specie licet occultatum verumptamen veritate est amministratum.

(The sacrament of piety, entrusted to this world, although hidden under a foreign outward form, was nevertheless administered in truth.)

—Second vespers antiphon,
office for the feast of Corpus Christi

In the earliest office composed for the feast of Corpus Christi, liturgical song celebrated the Eucharist's paradoxical status.[1] A visible sign of the sacred reality of Christ's corporeal presence on the altar, the sacrament was not what it appeared to be. Bread and wine, consecrated in the Mass, became Christ's body and blood in truth (*veritate*), and yet that sacred truth remained paradoxically hidden (*occultatum*) by the very condition of sacramental visibility. The species of wafer and wine, visibly persisting after the consecration, were simultaneously a sign pointing to Christ's sacred presence and the *aliena specie* (foreign outward forms) that occluded sensory apperception of the true body on the altar. As countless liturgical commentaries, theological summae, and learned canons insisted, this phenomenal paradox was faith's opportunity to possess religious truth: "Veritas autem dum corpus Christi et sanguis et in veritate interius creditur" (It is truth, when the body and blood of Christ are inwardly believed in truth).[2]

An insistence on the imperceptible as soteriologically superior was something of a truism in the thirteenth century, designed to reassure the faithful that the disjunction between the seen and the salvific was not a problem. And yet, as liturgy and canon law acknowledged, questions—like the accidents of the bread and wine—continued to persist after the consecration: "Forte dicas, quomodo vera caro, quomodo verus sanguis, qui similitudinem non video carnis, non video sanguinis veritatem" (Perhaps you might say, how [can it be] true flesh, how [can it be] true blood? I do not

Detail from Fig. 42

see the appearance of flesh; I do not see the truth of blood).[3] The Eucharist was indeed a problem.

Radically collapsing the categories of sacred sign and sacred signified into one material and divine presence, the Eucharist brought unprecedented pressure to bear on traditional accounts of faith as a belief in unseen sacred truths. The sacrament was known to the eyes—even tangibly tested by the communicant's mouth and teeth—and yet it remained an article of faith, an object to be apprehended by the willed adhesion of creance, rather than the experimental knowledge of savoir. As the pastoral reform movement further involved the laity in the sacramental life of the church, particularly in the linked practices of penance and communion, the apparent paradox of the sacrament of the altar only became more visible—literally and conceptually—to the lay faithful. Indeed, the visibility and prestige of the Eucharist in thirteenth- and fourteenth-century Christian culture made the related questions of its ontology and semiosis pressing issues for clerical, monastic, and lay Christians alike.

In the high and later Middle Ages the problems posed by the paradox of the Eucharist were usually framed in terms of the relationship between the visible and the invisible, between finite matter—fractured by sacerdotal hands—and the uncreated *esse* of divinity, between mundane appearance and spiritual reality. Although a long tradition of Christian theological writing, beginning with Paul, had struggled with these issues, they became particularly thorny after the "recovery" and translation of the Aristotelian corpus challenged established conceptions of substance and accidents in the late twelfth and thirteenth centuries.[4]

At the same time, late medieval artists and viewers struggled to make sense of the Eucharist's power and apparent paradox with a different set of resources and, at times, with divergent aims. This chapter examines how two of these resources—visual representation and vernacular language—were employed to translate Eucharistic truth from the Latinate spaces of ritual performance and theological debate to the surface of the painted page. This visual translation of the sacrament was not simply an extension of a sacred and saving sight beyond the framework of the liturgy and the architectural space of the church. It was also an intervention in a sacramental situation with profound implications for the relationship between seeing and salvation, between vision and divine verities in the later Middle Ages.

The chapter begins by tracing ecclesiastic efforts to establish a normative vision of the Eucharist. The sacramental spectacle that emerged from this process in the early thirteenth century was a performance designed with a lay audience in mind, and elite lay devotees responded, appropriating aspects of Eucharistic performance to their own, spiritually ambitious ends. The continuation of the chapter is devoted to a close analysis of one ambitious response to the Eucharist's paradoxical and privileged sacramental situation: an illustrated Mass tract embedded within a compendium of spiritual instruction, painted in the mid-1320s by the Queen Mary Psalter Master for a lay patron. The Mass tract's images, and the texts that accompany them, make a sustained argument about the relationship between seeing and the apprehension of sacred truth; my analysis explores how these claims, framed by the manuscript's other texts and images, encouraged a sacramental mode of vision, not only of the Mass and the Eucharist but also of painted representation.

Defining a "Normative" Vision of the Mass

The medieval "design" of the Eucharist, as Miri Rubin has aptly termed it, was a long, heterogeneous, and, at times, highly contested historical process.[5] Unlike the detailed prescriptions provided for ritual performance in the Jewish Bible, the New Testament provided little in the way of specific instruction for the ritual conduct of the Eucharist. Significantly, both the Gospel accounts of the Last Supper and Paul's writings on the Eucharist affirm the sacramental identity of bread and wine with Christ's body without specifying the precise manner by which these material elements came to be a sacrament.[6] As a result, the protagonists of the first major chapter in the medieval design of the Eucharist took up the question of the nature of the sacrament and attempted to illuminate the special relationship it necessarily involved between the visible species and their invisible, transformed status as the body and blood of Christ.

By a kind of historiographical shorthand, this stage in the design of the Eucharist is often identified with the so-called controversy between the Eucharistic theologies of Paschasius Radbertus (c. 785–c. 860) and Ratramnus (d. 868), two monks of Corbie who have come to represent the "realist" or "physicalist" position and the "symbolic" or "spiritualist" position, respectively.[7] The precise terms of each monk's explication of the Eucharist's ontology and of Eucharistic change need not detain us here; the historical context of their contributions is, however, of some interest for an assessment of the subsequent, late medieval phase of the Eucharist's design.

As Rachel Fulton has emphasized, both men were writing out of, and for, a context of liturgical standardization and widespread conversion.[8] Two historical factors were largely responsible for the novel attention brought by Paschasius and Ratramnus to the question of Eucharistic change and its relationship to the historical body of Christ:

> On the one hand, the Carolingian project of standardization provoked a new consciousness not only of the liturgy as ritual but also of the discrepancies within the interpretive tradition, particularly among

> the descriptions provided by the Fathers such as Ambrose and Augustine—discrepancies that it now became incumbent upon the theologians to resolve. On the other hand, the project of education, including the education of the laity, enjoined upon the clergy an ideal not only of Christian unity but also of comprehension: it was not enough, the Frankish bishops insisted, for the people to simply participate in the rituals of the universal Church; they must also understand them.[9]

Despite their significant theological differences, both monks shared a common concern: the elucidation of Eucharistic being and significance for those who were still struggling to fully comprehend and accept the sacrament in all its apparent paradoxicality, be they the Saxon novices at Corbie or the lay emperor. A preoccupation with liturgical uniformity and reform characterized the broader context for Paschasius and Ratramnus's inquiries into Eucharistic ontology and change; an engagement with the profound conversion demanded of the Christian faithful prompted their theological interventions.

In the centuries between Paschasius and Ratramnus's inauguration of significant and systematic consideration of Eucharistic being and meaning and the Fourth Lateran Council in 1215, the sacramental worldview of the Western church underwent a series of profound revisions and transformations. In the eleventh century, the teaching of Berengar of Tours (c. 999–1088) and the impassioned—often vituperative—responses it provoked fundamentally altered the terrain of Eucharistic inquiry, effectively requiring subsequent interpreters to integrate Aristotelian conceptions of substance, quantity, and quality, the strictures of *Grammatica,* and eventually, a host of conciliar and synodal decrees into their elucidations of Eucharistic ontology.[10]

In the wake of this veritable revolution in Eucharistic discourse, theologians and churchmen increasingly paired considerations of the Eucharist's ontology with investigations of Eucharistic causality. The elaboration of a properly sacramental theology—in which the Eucharist was afforded an exceptional status—by the circle of Peter the Chanter once again emphasized the sacrament's material elements and attempted to parse their relationship to sacramental meaning and power.[11] In short, the design of the Eucharist was very much in flux during the high Middle Ages, or, perhaps more accurately, it should be said that these centuries witnessed a proliferation of Eucharistic designs, transmitting a "tradition of diversity," as Gary Macy aptly describes it, to Eucharistic theology and practice in the thirteenth and fourteenth centuries.[12]

In the period extending from the mid-twelfth century to the first quarter of the thirteenth century, two intertwined historical developments collaboratively exerted a profound effect on the design of the late medieval Eucharist.[13] The compilation and dissemination of a series of canon law collections and their commentaries offered a legal and conceptual framework for the regulation of the church and its liturgical practice; at the same time, as we examined in chapter 1, the pastoral reform movement took the enthusiasm for regulation into the provinces and dioceses and promoted a vision of the priesthood in which sacerdotal performance played a decisive part. Although both efforts were principally directed toward secular and monastic churchmen, their prescriptions and mandates concerned all strata of European society.

The historical context of this stage in the ongoing design of the Eucharist might well be characterized in the terms that have been applied to the ninth-century phase of the sacrament's design: liturgical reform and conversion. In the high and the later Middle Ages, however, legislative revision of liturgical practice focused on sacramental ritual—particularly the celebration of the Eucharist—and the conversion pursued by reformers in Europe was a perpetual interior conversio, increasingly expected of laymen and laywomen.[14]

Illuminated manuscripts of canon law provide an important glimpse of the regulated and refashioned spectacle of Eucharistic celebration promoted by legal and conciliar reform. Although the first major collection of canon law, Gratian's *Concordia discordantium canonum* (also called the *Decretum Gratiani*), had received its standard tripartite structure by the middle of the twelfth century, canon law continued to undergo revision and expansion throughout the twelfth and thirteenth centuries.[15] These additions were codified in the *Quinque compilationes antiquae* (produced c. 1188–1226), the *Decretales* of Pope Gregory IX (promulgated in 1234), the *Liber Sextus* commissioned by Pope Boniface VIII (promulgated in 1298), and finally the *Constitutiones Clementinae* (compiled for Pope Clement V in 1312 but promulgated in 1317 by Pope John XXII).[16]

The compilation, promulgation, and study of an ever-expanding body of canon law required the constant production of manuscripts and the creation of appropriate visual programs for new legal texts.[17] Among the images provided for canon law manuscripts, representations of the Mass signaled the beginning of *De consecratione,* the third part of the *Concordia discordantium canonum,* and also marked the start of *De vita et honestate clericorum,* the third book of the *Decretales.* In both texts, the ritual performance of the Mass was selected as an iconic précis of the privileges and responsibilities of clerical status.[18]

In a *Decretum* manuscript, likely produced in northern France during the first quarter of the fourteenth century, *De consecratione* (Concerning Consecration) is prefaced by an unusually detailed statement of sacerdotal power (fig. 27).[19] In the upper left compartment of the miniature, we see two bishops asperging a church during its ritual dedication. In the quadrant directly below, a small male figure enters another edifice.

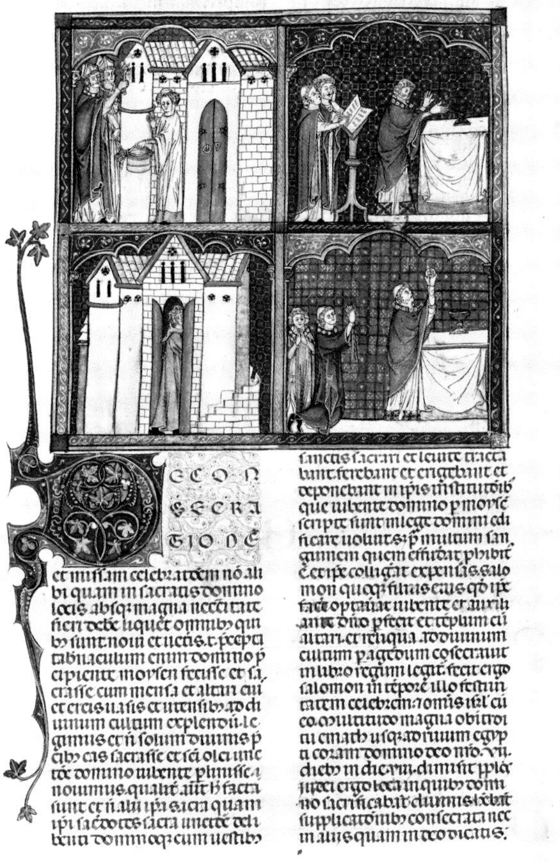

Fig. 27. De consecratione *in a* Decretum *manuscript, c. 1300–1330. Cambridge, Fitzwilliam Museum MS 262, f. 139r (detail): 435 x 285 mm.*

OPPOSITE: Fig. 28. De vita et honestate clericorum *in a leaf from a* Decretales *manuscript, c. 1330–1340. Cambridge, Fitzwilliam Museum, Marlay Cutting Fr. 2: 474 x 309 mm.*

This building seems to be a work in progress: the stepped profile of the masonry at its east end reveals that its apse has yet to be completed.[20] In the upper and lower compartments on the right side of the image we witness the celebration of the Mass. Above, two tonsured clerics sing from an open book on a lectern as the celebrant stands before them, hands outstretched to the chalice set on the altar. Below, we have arrived at the moment of the elevation. As the priest raises the consecrated wafer high above his head, the chalice remains on the altar. On the left side of the compartment the lectern has disappeared; in its place two clerics kneel with joined hands, adoring the elevated host.

The miniature's quadripartite structure is an innovation; typically, *Decretum* manuscripts feature a single Mass scene, usually depicting the moment of the elevation, as a visual frontispiece to *De consecratione.* In the Fitzwilliam *Decretum,* however, the illuminator has responded to cues provided in the first of *De consecratione*'s five distinctions. The first chapter of the first *distinctio,* which begins directly below the image, opens by declaring its topic: "De [ecclesiarum] consecratione, et missarum celebrationem non alibi quam in sacratis Domino locis absque magna necessitate fieri debere" (Concerning the consecration [of churches] and the celebration of Masses [which] ought not to be celebrated in places other than those hallowed to the Lord, save in cases of great necessity).[21] The following chapter asserts the prerogatives of the ordained, emphasizing their ministerial relationship to sacred space, ritual implements, and offerings.[22] In short, the legal architecture of *De consecratione* begins by defining a special relationship between the sacerdotal class, sacerdotal space, and sacerdotal ritual. In the miniature devised as a frontispiece for *De consecratione* in the Fitzwilliam *Decretum* manuscript, a quadripartite composition articulates a bipartite summary of this line of argument. In the left half of the illumination, ecclesiastical space is identified as the arena of sacerdotal—or more specifically, episcopal—authority. In the right half of the painting, the celebration of the Eucharist is displayed as the performance that defines the special status of the priest and the sacral space of the altar.

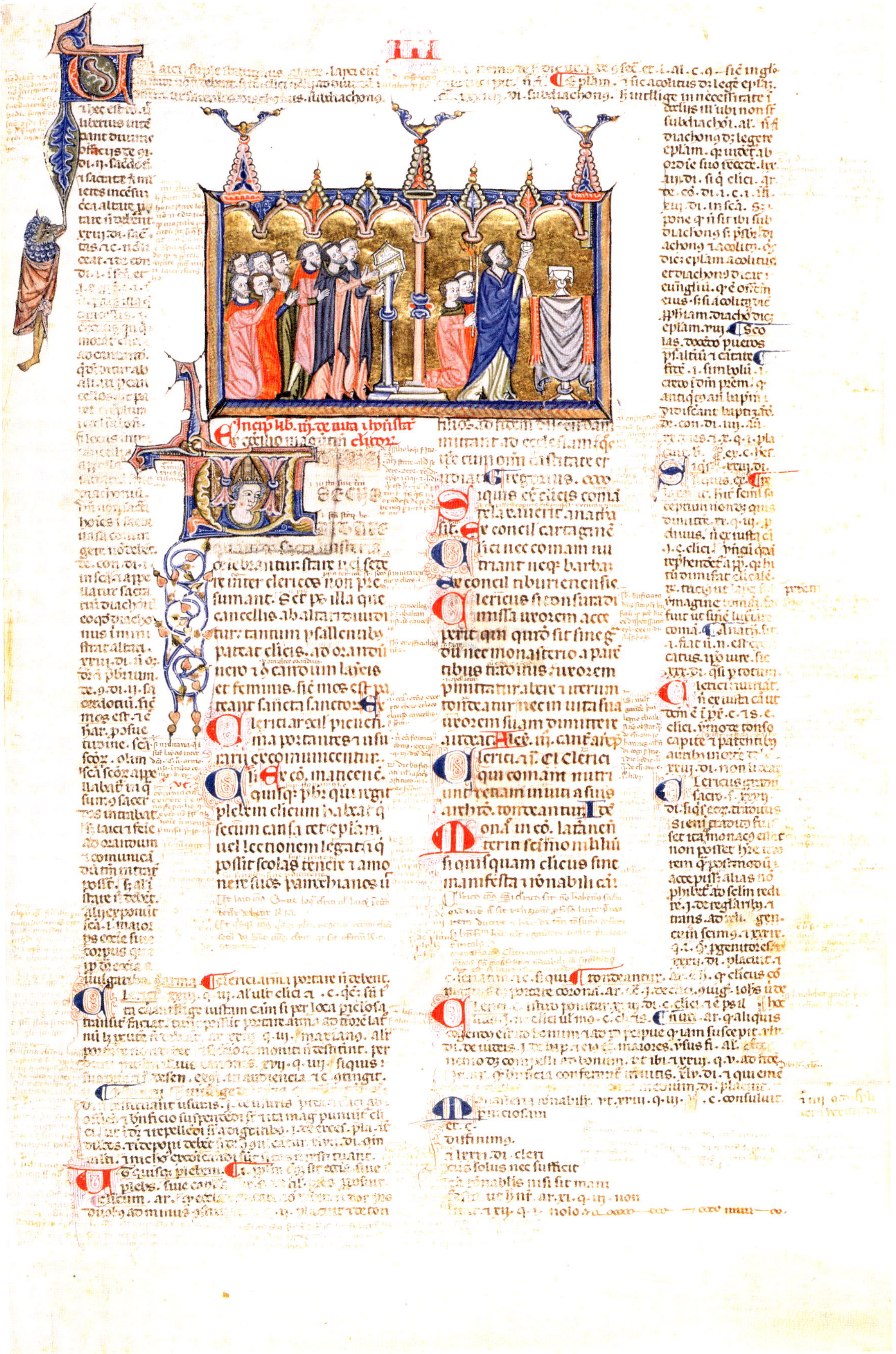

celebrantur. stare vel sede-
re inter clericos non pre-
sumant. Sed pars illa que
cancellis ab altari dividi-
tur: tantum psallentibus
pateat clericis. ad orandum
vero et communicandum laicis
et feminis. sicut mos est pa-
teant sancta sanctorum.
siquis ex clericis comam
relaxaverit anathema
sit.
Clerici nec comam nu-
triant neque barbam
Clericus si tonsuram di-
missa uxorem acce-
perit
nec monasterio a par-
entibus traditus
uxorem suam dimiserit
qui comam nutri-
unt
si quisquam clericus sine
manifesta et rationabili causa

A panoramic view of paradigmatic sacerdotal performance likewise marks the beginning of *De vita et honestate clericorum* (Concerning the Life and Honorableness of the Clergy), the third book of Gregory IX's *Decretales,* in a single leaf from a fourteenth-century manuscript produced in the south of France (fig. 28).[23] Although this two-column-wide miniature incorporates the basic compositional elements found in the *Decretum* miniature's right-hand compartments, the vision of the Mass it offers its viewer is significantly reinflected.

Despite the separative effect of the column interposed between the left and right halves of the painted scene, the ritual performance described in the image is—in quasi-Pauline terms—a unified and unifying scene. As the celebrant elevates the consecrated wafer, every figure arrayed against the miniature's burnished gold-leaf ground is physically oriented toward his gesture at the altar. The priest, singled out chromatically by the intense blue of his chasuble, is clearly the protagonist—if not the hero—of the moment represented in the image. Within the integrated composition, however, the celebrant is not simply a sacerdotal figure but also a pastoral one. Reading the image from right to left—that is, from the epicenter of sacrality to its outermost point of radiation—the viewer encounters kneeling candle bearers, a trio of singing clerics, and finally a dense cluster of five kneeling men. The leading figure in this group is distinguished by his tonsure. His four companions, however, bear no mark of clerical or monastic status; presumably they figure the lay congregation, on whose behalf the celebrant exercises his sacerdotal labor and privilege.

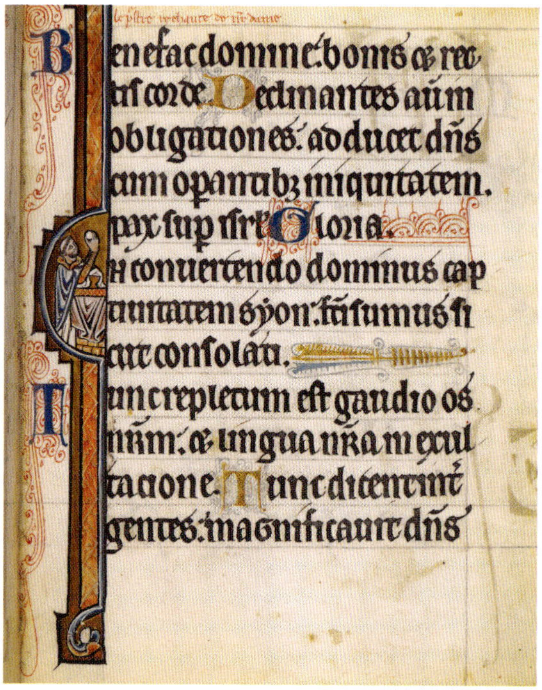

Fig. 29. The elevation of the host in the de Brailes Hours, c. 1240, f. 56r (detail). London, BL, Add. MS 49999: 150 x 123 mm.

Designed as a visual preface to a text of church law compiled for clerical readers, the representation of the Mass in the *Decretales* leaf (like the miniature prefacing the *De consecratione* text; see fig. 27) provides a metonymic statement of clerical identity. Within this miniature, however, the terms employed to predicate clerical excellence have been expanded into a kind of visual *sic et non.* The paradigmatic cleric is presented as a celebrant, the inhabitant of the most sacral of spaces, the handler of the most potent of sacraments. The miniature thus positively defines clerical identity in terms of its ritual performance, its proximity to the sacral center of sacred space. Within the fictive architecture of the image's frame, however, clerical identity is simultaneously

negatively defined by means of a kind of visual dialectic. The celebrant is *not* the congregant: he does not look like the congregants, he does not repeat their gestures, he does not share the crowded space afforded for their kneeling adoration.[24]

When illuminators constructed visual prefaces for *De vita et honestate clericorum* they clearly had the Mass scenes used as frontispieces for *De consecratione* in mind; through this iconographic repetition the two texts were intervisually related, much as they took up overlapping legal issues.[25] The prefatory images that introduce *De consecratione* and *De vita et honestate clericorum* do not represent the sacramental conferral of holy orders, nor do they typically provide a generic view of Eucharistic ritual. The moment chosen as an epitomizing statement of clerical authority and difference is the elevation of the host, when the consecrated wafer is displayed in its transformed state.[26]

Significantly, as illuminators first devised visual prefaces for these legal assertions of clerical prestige, they looked to the very liturgical books employed in sacerdotal performance. In the thirteenth and fourteenth centuries, a representation of the elevation could be found in the initial C of Psalm 97 ("Cantate domino canticum novum") illuminated in Liège Psalters and Psalter-Hours.[27] The English illuminator William de Brailes painted an elevation scene in the historiated initial I of Psalm 125:1 ("In convertendo dominus captivitatem Syon") at the hour of Vespers for the Office of the Holy Spirit in a book of hours he completed circa 1240 (fig. 29).[28] Missals, as might well be expected, employed representations of the elevation in the initial T of the "Te igitur," the opening words of the Canon of the Mass; a splendid example is provided by the Tiptoft Missal (c. 1311–1322; fig. 30).[29] Following the introduction of the feast of Corpus Christi in 1264, the elevation was also represented in miniatures introducing the Corpus Christi office in Breviaries.[30] In short, the visual models to which illuminators turned when they devised prefatory miniatures for these legal statements of clerical authority and difference were themselves part of the apparatus of sacerdotal office. Studying *De vita et honestate clericorum* in an illuminated copy of the *Decretales,* such as the book to which the Fitzwilliam leaf once belonged, the clerical viewer encountered an idealized and

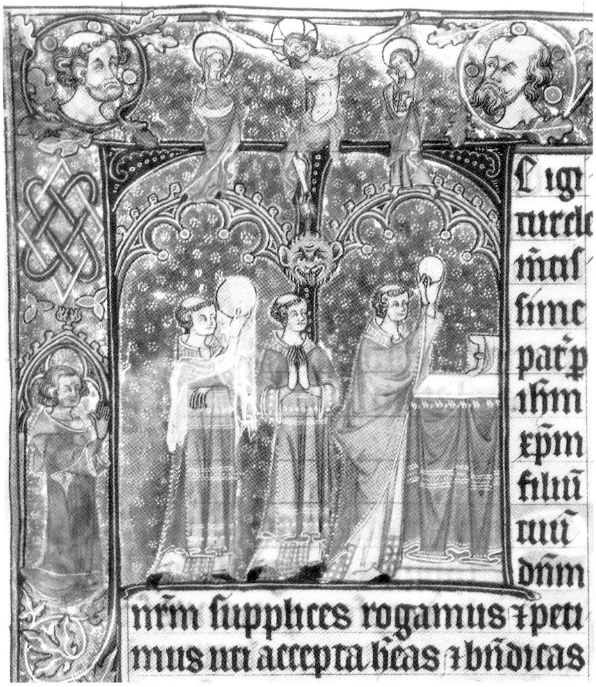

Fig. 30. The Tiptoft Missal's elevation of the host, c. 1311–1332. New York, Pierpont Morgan Library, MS M.107, f. 142r (detail): 415 x 300 mm. Gift of J. P. Morgan (1867–1943), 1924.

normative representation of the Mass that referenced the visual (and textual) supporting materials of that sacerdotal performance.

Despite this concatenation of intervisual allusions, the immediate referent or authority for the vision of Eucharistic celebration offered by the *Decretales* leaf's miniature should be sought not in the *realia* of contemporary liturgical performance (although its privileging of the moment of the elevation reveals the image to be very much a product of its time), but rather in the prescriptive language of the canon inscribed directly below it:

> Ut laici secus altare, quando sacra mysteria celebrantur . . . stare vel sedere inter clericos non praesumant; sed pars illa, quae cancellis ab altari dividitur, tantum psallentibus pateat clericis. Ad orandum vero et communicandum laicis et feminis, sicut mos est, pateant sancta sanctorum.[31]
>
> (That laypeople, when the holy mysteries are celebrated . . . should not presume to stand near the altar, nor to sit among the clergy; but rather that part [of the church] which is divided from the altar by the chancel [screen or rail] should be open to singing clerics only. But, as is customary, the nave [*sancta sanctorum*] should be open to laypeople and women for the purpose of praying or communicating.)[32]

The orthopractical discourse of this legal text and its visual preface describe the Mass as a ritual context for integration *and* distinction. The laity's presence within the miniature's representation of paradigmatic performance contributes to the securing of sacerdotal status and differentiation. The figures of lay Mass-goers have become integral components of the leaf's textual and visual promulgation of a normative vision of the Mass. Within the *Decretales* leaf's unified composition, these kneeling laymen collectively provide a necessary final term in a vision of the Mass that is principally about the visible display of regularized sacerdotal performance.

Manuscript collections of canon law, such as the *Decretum* and the *Decretales,* provided an important means of realizing the "universal" reforms mandated by general councils, and they were disseminated with didactic commentaries throughout Europe. The student audience for these manuscripts included clerics destined for the cura animarum, who brought the lessons they had learned in the faculties back to their provinces and dioceses, and even to centers of secular power.[33] In the late twelfth and thirteenth centuries, both the content of illuminated law books and their reader-viewers were concerned with the regularization of sacerdotal performance and its pastoral effects on Christian community. The "universal" discourse of the canon law collections and their commentaries found its local corollary in the legislation of provincial councils and diocesan synods.

Although no comparable tradition of illumination survives for the manuscript record of the statutes promulgated by medieval councils and synods, the substance of their legislation reveals that archbishops and bishops were not unaware of the power of visible display and the need for increasing standardization of ecclesiastical spectacle. If we approach the pastoral legislation produced by archbishops and bishops in thirteenth-century England much as we did the miniatures painted for manuscripts of the *Decretum* and the *Decretales,* that is, as orthopractical discourses that produce a reformed and regulated vision of sacerdotal practice, there is much we can learn about the vision of the Mass that English ecclesiastics were attempting to shape in the wake of the general Interdict (1208–1214) and the Fourth Lateran Council.

The general Interdict resulted from a conflict between King John and Innocent III over the promotion of Stephen Langton to the See of Canterbury.[34] After a disputed election following the death of Archbishop Hubert Walter in July 1205, several appeals, and a hearing in Rome, Innocent III consecrated Langton, cardinal of St. Chrysogonus, as archbishop of Canterbury in June 1207.[35] Claiming that the Pope's consecration of Langton had violated his privileges, causing "damage to his royal right and dignity," King John refused to confirm Langton's promotion and forbade him entry into England.[36] The standoff between king and pontiff resulted in Innocent III laying a general Interdict upon England and Wales in March 1208 and excommunicating John in November 1209.[37]

As C. R. Cheney has described it, the terms of the *forma interdicti* pronounced by Innocent III amounted to "a ban upon celebration of the mass, upon sacramental ceremonies and liturgical practices in church, and upon the administration of sacraments elsewhere, except for baptism, which was always allowed, marriage, which was a sacrament even when it could not be solemnized by a priest, and the absolution of the dying."[38] In practice, the Interdict was applied variously throughout the kingdom and was also modified, at various points, by papal direction.[39] Nonetheless, the Interdict's effects were visible, auditory, and otherwise palpable. From March 23, 1208, until July 2, 1214, altars were stripped, churches seemed bare and empty, there was no elevation of the host to be witnessed, the dead were buried outside of consecrated ground, and bells no longer rhythmically punctuated the day: the spiritual landscape of England was transformed.[40]

The terms of the Interdict mandated a withdrawal of ecclesiastical ritual and spiritual services from the kingdom and, by that removal, the creation of radical spiritual absences. In this way, the general Interdict was designed to punish by withholding the church's spiritual benefits, creating a situation that was spiritually (and politically) intolerable.[41] Nonetheless, as Paul Binski has observed, the period of the Interdict also "created an opportunity for reflection," a collective meditation that bore fruit in a subsequent period of renewed church construction.[42] It also provoked, and perhaps even made possible, a concerted effort to reconceive the spectacle of the Mass in terms of its audience.

Carolyn Marino Malone has suggested that the laity in England "may have been especially sensitive to devotional stimuli" when the Interdict was finally relaxed in 1214.[43] Certainly, the renewal of the full array of liturgical rituals—with their sights, sounds, and smells—must have collaborated with the pastoral mandates of a series of English synods and councils, arguably beginning as early as Archbishop Hubert Walter's legatine Council of York in 1195, to focus clerical and lay attention on the Mass in a newly invigorated fashion.[44] Indeed, thirteenth-century conciliar and synodal legislation suggests that the spectacle of the Mass, and the laity's vision of that spectacle, was very much on the minds of English archbishops and bishops.

Stephen Langton's first statutes for the diocese of Canterbury (July 1213 x 1214) contain a series of prescriptions regarding the Eucharist and the celebration of Mass. Langton's measures would become standard in subsequent English legislation: the Eucharist should be kept in a clean pyx; it should not be reserved for more than seven days; any reserved hosts should be consumed by the celebrant during Mass on the eighth day; the priest should be certain that he consumes a consecrated host (rather than one that has not yet been consecrated); the altar cloths, corporal, sindon, and other *panni* should be clean and adequate; likewise, the church should be outfitted with a *calicem argenteum* (silver chalice) and *vasis decentibus et honestis* (fitting and worthy vessels); and books and vestments should also be suitable and sufficient to the church's needs.[45]

Langton's statutes touching on the viaticum reveal a similar concern for the conduct and appearance of Eucharistic ritual. The archbishop decreed that when the Eucharist is to be taken to the sick, it should be carried in a clean and *honesta* (worthy) pyx, lined with a linen bursa and covered with a linen cloth; both a light and a cross should precede the Eucharist.[46] The procession Langton mandates is not simply a visual affair; he decrees that the Eucharist should also be preceded by bells "ad cuius sonitum excitetur devotio audientium" (so that at their sounding the devotion of listeners is roused).[47] In the normative vision outlined by Langton's statutes, the spectacle of the Eucharist is staged for the benefit of its audience in churches and streets alike.

Further statutes explicitly address the Eucharist's lay audience. The lay faithful of Canterbury are required to complete their own performance within the framework of the Mass: "Moneantur autem laici quod reverenter se habeant in consecratione eucharistie, et flectant genua maxime tempore quando post elevationem hostia sacra dimittitur" (Let the laity be admonished that they should comport themselves reverently at the consecration of the Eucharist, and let them kneel especially during that time when, after the elevation, the sacred host is dispensed).[48] In addition to acting as reverent witnesses to the consecration, Langton also requires the laity to participate in the Mass through their own well-regulated communion. In a series of measures concerning the sacrament of penance, the archbishop indicates that the laity should be admonished to prepare for communion through confession and abstinence and further notes, "ut ter in anno, scilicet in Pascha, Natali, Pentecoste, communicent, prius tamen preparati per aliquantulam abstinentiam de consilio sacerdotis faciendam et per confessionem" (they [the laity] should communicate three times a year, namely at Easter, Christmas, and Pentecost, first having prepared through some small abstinence prescribed by the counsel of the priest and through confession).[49]

As Binski has observed, no surviving set of English statutes issued in the century following the Fourth Lateran Council transmits the Council's decrees in toto.[50] By contrast, the substance of Langton's pre-Lateran IV provisions for the display and handling of the Eucharist in the Mass and as viaticum, his prescriptions concerning the proper appearance of the clergy, and his instructions concerning lay communion and lay response to the elevation were repeated (with few exceptions) in English statutes over the course of the thirteenth century. The influence of the Fourth Lateran Council's pastoral orientation may be discerned less in the incorporation of individual canons or fragments of canons into diocesan statutes than in an increased sensitivity to, or concern for, the proper appearance of Eucharistic ritual *and* the proper understanding of what it means to consecrate and communicate.[51] Collectively, the statutes reveal that the appearance or spectacle of Eucharistic celebration (in the Mass) and Eucharistic exhibition (through the procession of the viaticum) continued to preoccupy pastoral legislators.

The evidence of the statutes also suggests that questions of Eucharistic meaning and audience were never far from the minds of English bishops and archbishops during this period. Indeed, the legislation promulgated by thirteenth-century English councils and synods suggests that the laity's response to Eucharistic ritual was very much part of the reformist "Eucharistic design" pursued by bishops and archbishops. Although the canons of the Fourth Lateran Council did not address lay conduct at the elevation of the host, subsequent English statutes, following Stephen Langton's example, legislated on precisely this point. Bishop Quinel's 1287 statutes for the diocese of Exeter, which we have already encountered in chapter 2, provide a late, relatively comprehensive treatment of what was supposed to happen at the elevation:

> Quia vero per hec verba: Hoc est enim corpus meum, et non per alia, panis transsubstantiatur in corpus, prius hostiam non levet sacerdos donec ipsa plene protulerit, ne pro creatore creatura a populo veneretur. Hostia autem ita levetur in altum ut a fidelibus circumstantibus valeat intueri. Per hoc etenim fidelium devotio excitatur et fidei meritum suscipit incrementum. Parochiani solicite exhortentur ut in levatione corporis Christi nedum reverenter se inclinent sed genua flectant et creatorem suum adorent omni devotione et reverentia; ad quod per campanelle pulsationem primitus excitentur, et in levatione ter tangatur campana maior.[52]
>
> (But since through these words—*Hoc est enim corpus meum*—and not through others, the bread is changed in substance into the body [of Christ], the priest must not raise the host until he has pronounced them completely, lest a created thing should be adored by the people as the creator. Then the host should be raised so high that it may be seen by all the attending faithful. For indeed, through this [the elevation] the devotion of the faithful is roused and faith's reward is increased. Let parishioners be earnestly exhorted that they should not merely bow [*se inclinent*] at the elevation of Christ's body, but rather they should kneel and adore their creator with devotion and reverence; to which [response] they should first be roused through the ringing of a little bell and at the elevation a bigger bell should be rung three times.)

Quinel's text reads like a prescriptive ekphrasis of the idealizing visions of Eucharistic ritual represented in the prefatory miniatures executed for *Decretum* and *Decretales* manuscripts. The normative vision of the Mass encoded in the universal register of canon law, and in its images of sacerdotal excellence, is here realized in the idiom of local legislation.

In the idealized conception of the Mass promulgated by Quinel's statute, however, the elevation is not framed in terms of heroic sacerdotal performance; it has become a moment for the laity's exhibition of spiritual excellence. This Eucharistic performance involves a proper object—the consecrated host—and an audience for its spectacular display that is not simply a passive body of viewers, but rather a collectivity exhibiting its attention, its reverence, through a prescribed bodily decorum.[53] The laity's visible, gestural display is, in this statutory formulation, a signifying act. Although the elevated host clearly dominates this vision of the Mass, within the statute's imagined mise en scène the elevation is also a setting for the performance of lay reverence, devotion, and spiritual excellence.

Effected through the decorum of reverence and the provision of a riveting object for devout vision, the integration of lay parishioners in the spectacle of the Mass imagined in Quinel's statutes (and in many others in the period) was an ambitious pastoral ideal, an idealizing prescription, rather than a description of actual practice. The work of scholars such as Miri Rubin and Sarah Beckwith has, however, taught us that Eucharistic ritual could be a profoundly contentious arena, in which the "sacrament of unity" provoked social fraction, occasioned dispute, and could be effectively occluded by the hustle and bustle of lay conversation and commerce.[54] Nonetheless, the testimony of images like the representation of the Butler family, lords of Wren (Shropshire), at Mass in their book of hours suggests that for all the contention that may often have attended the Mass—or perhaps because of it—late medieval laypeople could and did see a place for themselves within the ritual framework of the elevation (fig. 31).[55] Indeed, in this full-page prefatory miniature the Butler family appropriated the authority of images such as those used to preface *De consecratione* and *De vita et honestate clericorum* to their own ends.

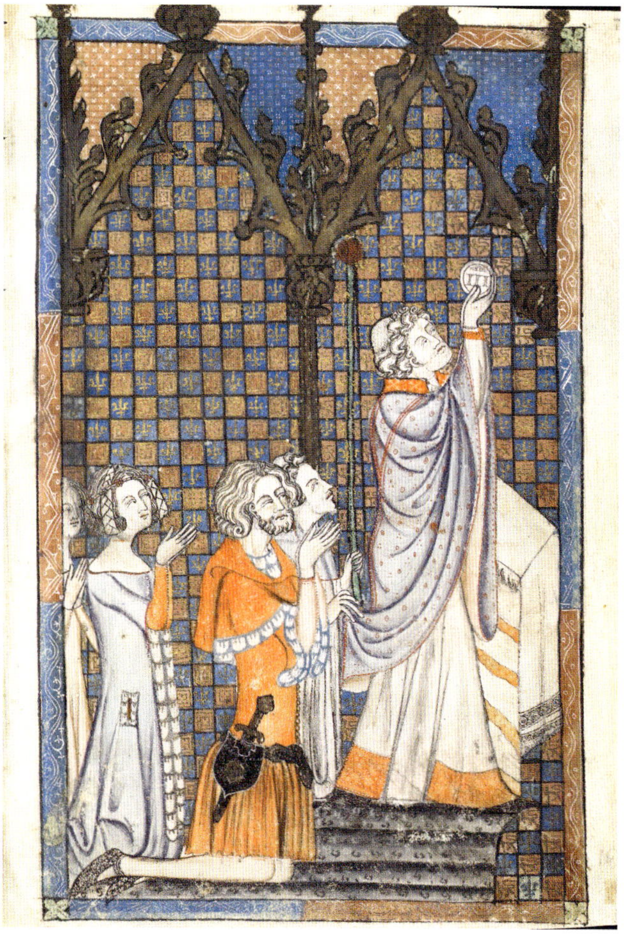

Fig. 31. The Butler family attends to the elevation of the host, c. 1340–1350. Baltimore, Walters Art Museum, MS W.105, f. 15r: 210 x 140 mm.

At the moment of the elevation, the eyes of all the figures painted within the miniature are turned to the host, elevated high above the priest's head. Within the cramped architectural setting of the painting, the kneeling figures of the Butler family inhabit the foreground; on their knees before the consecrated host, they are nonetheless in possession of the fictive space. And we cannot fail to recognize that the subject of the miniature is not the elevation of the host, per se; it is instead the Butlers and the excellence of their devotion, their proximity to the Eucharist, and their possession of sacred space. Gazing at the miniature, the original viewer (almost certainly a member

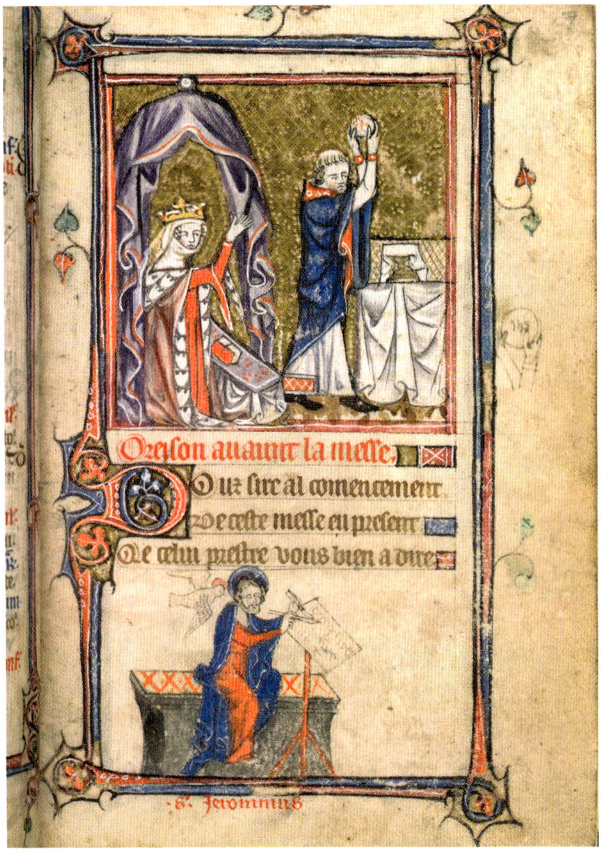

Fig. 32. *The elevation of the host in the Taymouth Hours, c. 1325–1335. London, BL, Yates Thompson MS 13, f. 7r: 168 x 110 mm.*

or members of the Butler family) encountered an alternative vision of the Mass, one that resembled the orthopractical representations of legal and liturgical manuscripts, but with a signifying shift of emphasis: the elevation scene in this manuscript might well be titled *De vita et honestate laicorum* (Concerning the Life and Honorableness of the Laity), or perhaps *Butlerorum*.

The Butlers were not alone in their appropriation of the elevation. In the Taymouth Hours, the elevation takes place as a kind of command performance (fig. 32).[56] Beneath a voluminous canopy, a crowned woman kneels with a book set before her. As she raises her hands in prayer, she echoes the gesture of the priest who elevates the host before her. A strangely potent, even audacious, visual punning is accomplished in this image: the strong diagonal that leads from the kneeling woman to the celebrant effects more than one parallelism between each half of the miniature. Just as the crowned laywoman echoes the celebrant in her exhibition of reverence, so the canopy surmounting her form slyly echoes the veil covering the chalice on the altar. At the same time, her sharply canted prie-dieu repeats the trapezoidal form of the steeply slanted desk on which the prophet Jeremiah writes his inspired text below the vernacular text block.[57] In this image, visual representation renders divinely inspired prophetic composition, sacerdotal performance, and queenly devotion as analogous terms in a calculus of spiritual performance. The crowned laywoman's book of vernacular devotion is made a pendant to Jeremiah's scriptural text, and yet, we see that she has turned from text to host, from reading to looking.

As if the starting point or efficient cause of this authorizing representation of lay spiritual excellence was not plain enough, in the outer margin of the folio we find a sketch of two schematic hands holding up a round disk inscribed with the letters "ihs,"—a sacred monogram of the name Jesus Christ—which served as a marginal instruction for the illuminator.[58] The persistent presence of this visual shorthand for the elevation on the page serves as a pointed reminder that the nominal focal point of the composition—and of the spiritual economy that it promotes—should be the Corpus Christi. And yet, as in the Butlers' book of hours, the lay devotee shares the pictorial stage, and the *corpus reginae*'s proximity to the Eucharist asserts her patronal appropriation of the Mass and the sacred body at its center.

The Taymouth and Butler Hours translate the elevation of the host from a sacerdotal register into the hands—quite literally—of elite lay reader-viewers. In both manuscripts, this appropriation of the elevation-as-representation takes place within the framework of paraliturgical devotion. The incorporation of elevation miniatures into prayer books designed for lay reader-viewers witnesses not only to the success of the normative vision of the Mass promoted by ecclesiastical reformers but also to appropriation and refashioning of that vision by lay elites. Such images reveal that the elevation of the host was a moment of real importance for lay spiritual and social self-fashioning; they also suggest that the lay patrons of these images conceived of the elevation much as Bishop Quinel had—as a moment of looking and showing.

The emergence of the elevation of the host as the high point of Eucharistic ritual in miniatures painted for clerical and elite lay audiences alike is an index of the effectiveness of efforts to "redesign" the sacrament and its ritual performance in the later Middle Ages. This normative vision of the sacrament, however, provoked further changes in how late medieval devotees saw the consecrated host, and in what that seeing signified. Framed by clerical performance, the Eucharist emerged in the thirteenth and fourteenth centuries as a focal point and catalyst for a range of epistemological and visual practices with profound implications for the translation of religious truth to ambitious lay audiences.

In the remainder of this chapter I turn to a manuscript that accomplishes a virtuosic translation of the Mass into vernacular text and visual representation, offering its elite lay beholder an education in how to look at the Mass and see religious truth. Within the Mass tract, and within the compendium to which it belonged, the pursuit of religious truth is framed as a process of epistemological formation, an emphasis echoed in contemporary theorizations of Eucharistic reception. What kind of truth was visible on the altar? How should one see a sacrament, and what might sacramental truth look like? These were persistent questions about a seemingly paradoxical situation: in the pages that follow I suggest that they were, perhaps, questions best answered by images.

The Mass in Text and Images

The Mass tract that concerns the rest of this chapter is but one component of a manuscript produced in England, likely in London or East Anglia, in the mid-1320s.[59] Two fragments of the original manuscript have been identified (Paris, BnF, MS fr. 13342 [henceforth BnF fr. 13342], and Oxford, Bodleian Library, MS Douce 79).[60] Considered

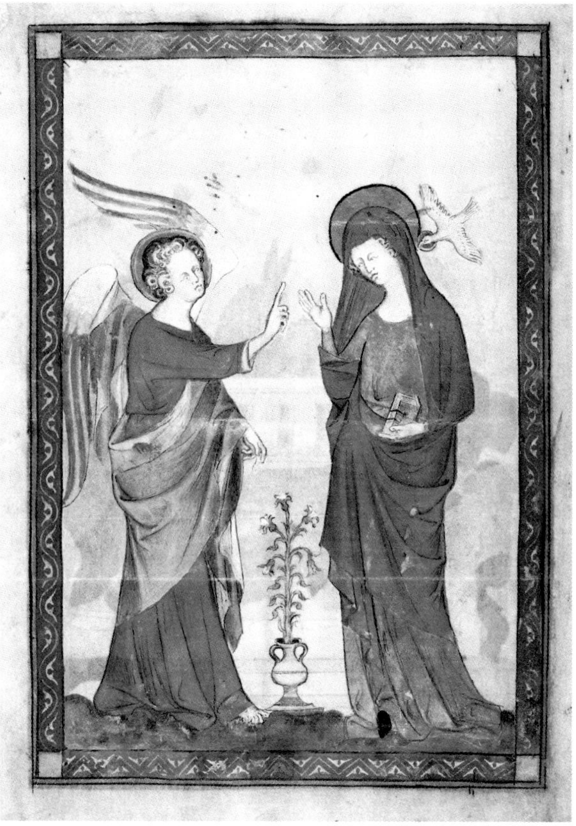

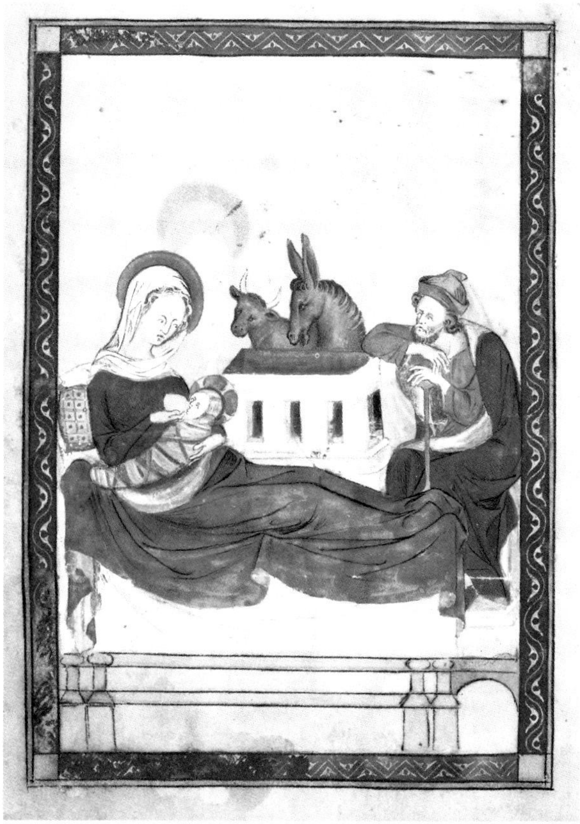

Fig. 33. The Annunciation, mid-1320s. Oxford, University of Oxford, Bodleian Library, MS Douce 79, f. 2r: 210 x 133 mm.

Fig. 34. The Nativity, mid-1320s. Oxford, University of Oxford, Bodleian Library, MS Douce 79, f. 2v.

together, these two sections indicate that the manuscript from which they derive was a deluxe compendium of at least seven texts suitable for the spiritual formation and practice of a layperson, embellished with four full-page images, a series of fourteen large miniatures, a full complement of inhabited and decorated initials, as well as marginal drolleries and foliate borders.[61]

In its fourteen folios, the Oxford fragment contains four full-page miniatures depicting the Annunciation, the Nativity, Mary's Assumption, and her Coronation (figs. 33-36).[62] Folios 4r–13v preserve an unidentified (and incomplete) Anglo-Norman text touching on episodes from the lives of Adam, Eve, and Solomon, coupled with an account of the Passion and the True Cross. The Paris fragment consists of fifty-three folios containing six texts: the Anglo-Norman *Dialogue del piere et del filz,* now incomplete (folios 1r–27v);[63] the Anglo-Norman *Mirour de seinte eglyse,* a translation of St. Edmund of Abingdon's *Speculum Ecclesiae* (folios 28r–44v);[64] the Mass tract to be considered here (folios 45r–48v);[65] the Latin Psalter of St. Jerome (folios 49r–51v; incomplete at end);[66] and two Christocentric prayers in Latin (folio 52r).[67]

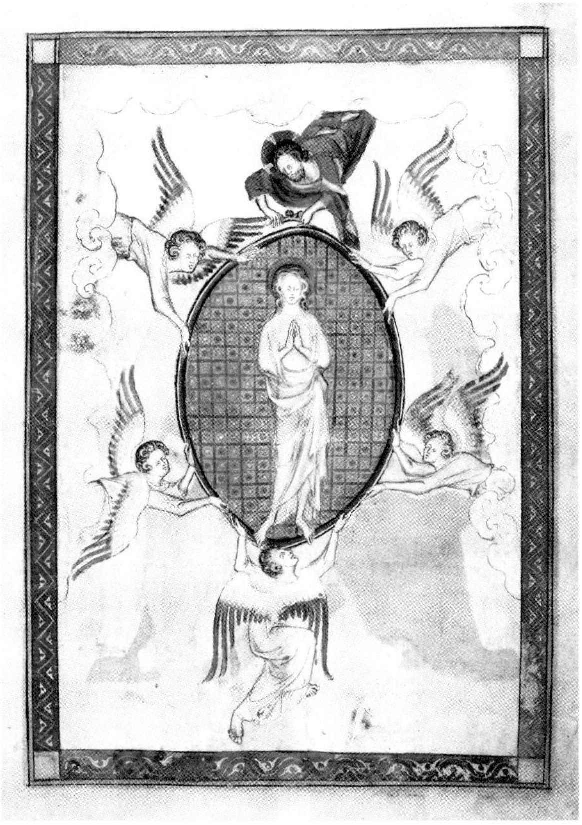

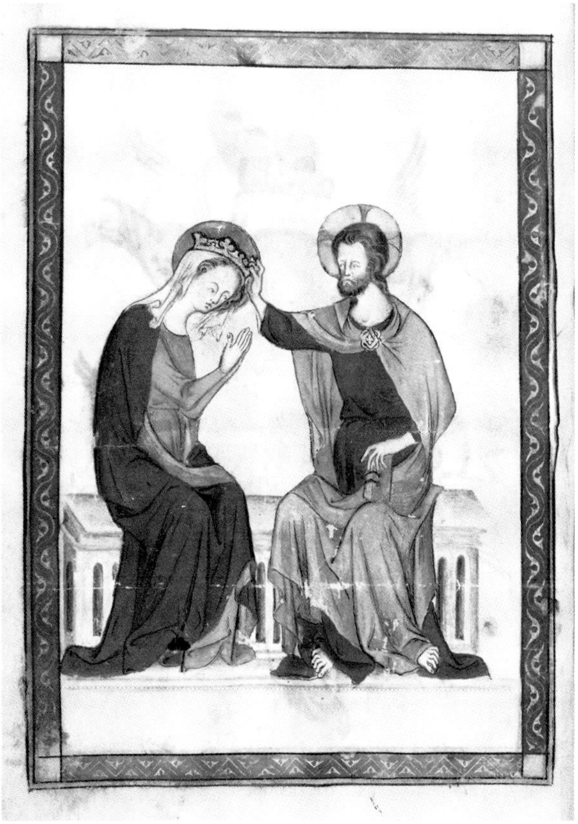

Fig. 35. The Virgin Mary's Assumption, mid-1320s. Oxford, University of Oxford, Bodleian Library, MS Douce 79, f. 3r.

Fig. 36. The Virgin Mary's Coronation, mid-1320s. Oxford, University of Oxford, Bodleian Library, MS Douce 79, f. 3v.

The illumination of both fragments of the manuscript is the work of members of the Queen Mary Psalter group, the preeminent English illuminators of their day.[68] In a series of studies of the Queen Mary Psalter workshop's oeuvre, Lynda Dennison has attributed the miniatures in the Oxford-Paris fragments to the hand of the Queen Mary Psalter Master himself.[69] The Paris Mass tract may very well have been the illuminator's final masterpiece.

The quality and patronage of other manuscripts illuminated by the Queen Mary Psalter Master and his collaborators indicate that these manuscript painters were highly prized artists, working for elite clients in the first and second decades of the fourteenth century. The attribution of the Mass tract's illumination to the Queen Mary Psalter Master thus implies London as a likely center for the manuscript's patronage and production, and suggests that the intended recipient of the manuscript was a person of considerable prestige.[70]

The original manuscript from which these two fragments derive was a deluxe object, encompassing a range of works that are as theological in their tenor as they are devotional. Although we may never be certain for whom the Oxford-Paris volume was produced, and its fragmentary state makes it difficult to ascertain precisely how and where the book was meant to be read and viewed, the illustrated Mass tract preserved in BnF fr. 13342 does allow us to make one significant claim about the manuscript's anticipated audience: the intended reader-viewer for this book was a layperson. The Mass tract's texts and images address only those components of the liturgy of the Mass that were audible, and perhaps visible, to a lay congregant.

Although the Mass tract follows the ritual progress of the Mass in the sequence of its images and texts, the treatise is not an exposition of sacerdotal performance. Instead, the Mass tract provides an ordo for the lay devotee's corporeal, intellectual, and spiritual participation in the Mass.[71] The Mass tract orients the lay Mass-goer within the progress of ritual and provides him or her with a series of meditative and gestural activities for the principal "acts" of this liturgical performance. As an examination of the tract's texts and images will reveal, a sustained (if concentrated) sacramental theology is also articulated within this "script" for devout lay engagement in the Mass.[72]

"CEO QE VOUS DEVEZ FERE E PENSER A CHASCON POINT DE LA MESSE"

A rubricated inscription written above the frame of the tract's first image tersely identifies the didactic aims of the texts and paintings that follow: "Ceo qe vous devez fere e penser a chascon point de la messe. Primerement al Confiteor" (That which you must do and think at each point of the Mass. Firstly, at the *Confiteor*) (fig. 37).[73] The words and paintings that follow trace the progression of the Eucharistic ritual from the lay devotee's perspective, engaging the beholder in a simulated vision of the Mass that is also a progressive account of the efficacy of spiritually intent ways of seeing. Like the liturgical ordo of the Mass itself, the tract's texts and images describe an unfolding action, a movement from a ritual "before state" to a spiritual "after state" that subtly delineates a causal account of how vision might be transformed within the sacramental frame. Like the fictive laypeople who populate the tract's paintings, if we want to better understand this powerful account of vision's transformation, we too must start at the ritual beginning and attend closely to what follows.

CONFITEOR

The Mass tract begins in the fore-Mass with the *Confiteor,* a general confession of sin that the celebrant offers at the altar in the first person (literally, "I confess"), as a representative of the Christian community assembled in the Mass.[74] One of several preparatory actions performed by the celebrant and his assistants before the Mass proper, in the Mass tract the Confiteor also marks the first moment of lay participation in the ritual celebration. Employing the imperative mode, an inscription inserted within the space

Fig. 37. Confiteor and introit in the Mass tract, mid-1320s. Paris, BnF, MS fr. 13342, f. 45r: 205 x 130 mm.

Ceo qe vous deuez fere et penser a chascon point de la messe. Primerement al Confiteor.

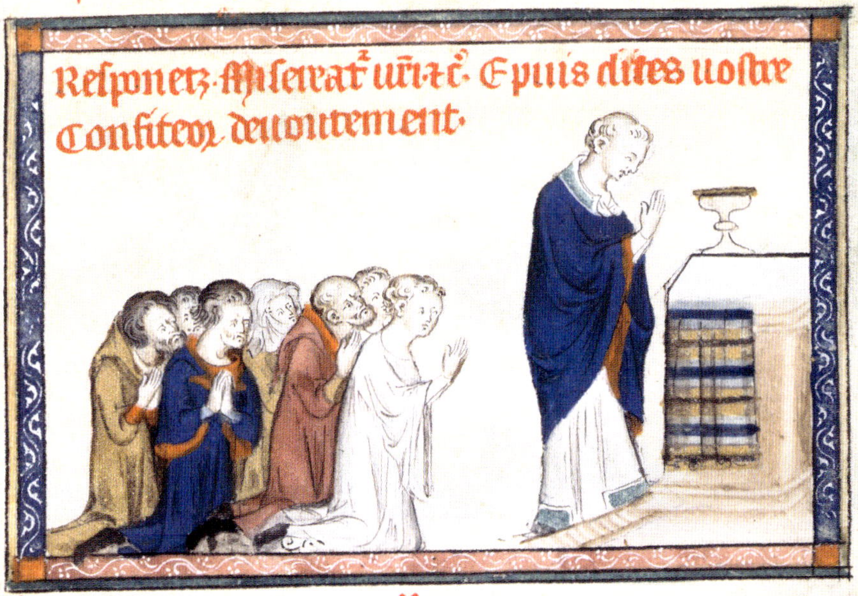

Al Entre de la messe.

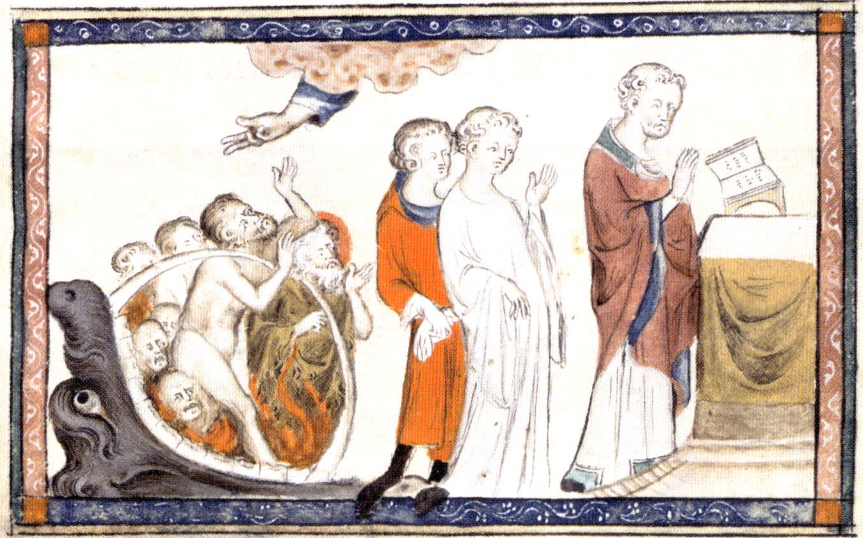

Pensez du desir qe les seintz patriarches et prophetes auoient qe nostre seignor venist pur eals reyndre.

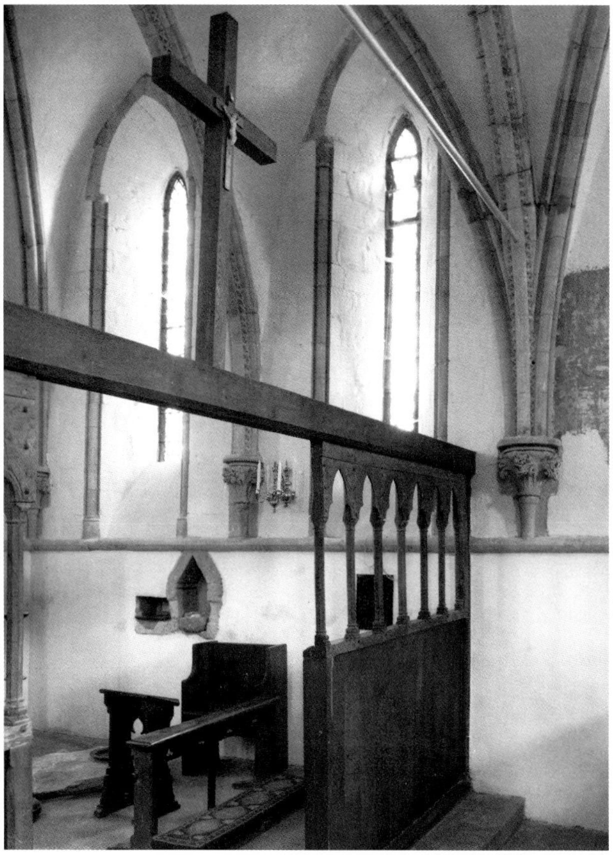

Fig. 38. Choir screen, St. Leonard's Church, Kirkstead (Lincolnshire), c. 1230–1240

of the first painted frame instructs the reader-viewer: "Responetz *Misereatur vestri etc.* E puis dites vostre *Confiteor* devoutement" (Respond *Misereatur vestri*, etc. And then say your *Confiteor* devoutly) (see fig. 37).[75]

The treatise's first miniature describes the space of the Mass quite minimally. The celebrant stands before a clothed altar bearing a chalice; the altar and a low step delineated economically before it are the only indications of setting provided for the viewer. The miniature instead emphasizes the communal nature of the ritual. A minutely individualized group of six laypeople—five men and a veiled woman—kneel behind the priest; the deacon, in white, kneels at the front of this group. Presenting a didactic view of the laity in an act of penitential preparation, the miniature renders the laity's devout recital of the Confiteor as a variant of, or pendant to, the priest's ritual preparation. Although the lay figures are depicted on their knees, their gestures and textually prescribed response—as well as the absence of any architectural barrier—make them inhabitants of the same space of ritual preparation as the celebrant who stands at the altar before them.

Already in this, the Mass tract's first miniature, representation departs from reality. The proximity of the lay congregants to the celebrant and the altar hardly reflects what we know of the hierarchically demarcated space of late medieval churches.[76] In the actual built environment of an early fourteenth-century English church, the laity would almost certainly have been segregated from the space of the high altar. Moreover, lay vision of the celebrant was often interrupted, mediated, and framed by a rood screen demarcating the clerical spaces of choir and altar from the lay space of the nave, such as the simple wooden screen preserved in the church of St. Leonard at Kirkstead (Lincolnshire), thought to date as early as circa 1230–1240 (fig. 38).[77] The miniature's close juxtaposition of lay Mass-goers and officiating clergy is a visual fiction that collapses the discrete spaces of lay and clerical performance into a unified zone of communal participation.[78]

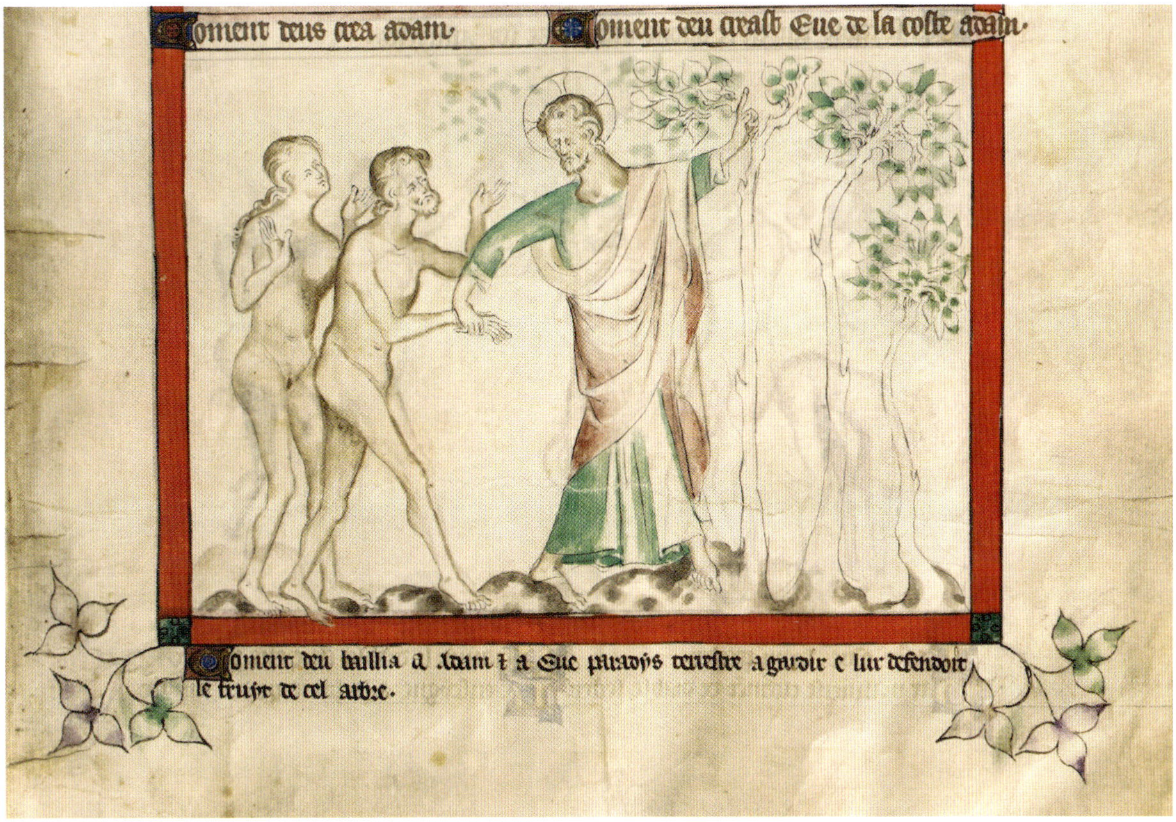

Fig. 39. God takes Adam by the hand in the Queen Mary Psalter, c. 1310–1320. London, BL, Royal MS 2.B.VII, f. 3r: 277 x 175 mm.

INTROIT

In the Mass tract's second image and text, liturgical ritual has progressed to the moment of the introit, a choral chant intoned at the beginning of the Mass, whose texts were proper, that is, specific to the day in the liturgical calendar (see fig. 37).[79] The tract instructs the reader-viewer to "Pensez du desir qe les seintz patriarches et prophetes avoient qe nostre seignor vensist pur eus reyndre" (Consider the desire that the Holy Patriarchs and Prophets had that our Lord should come to ransom them).[80] The image set immediately above this terse directive leaves no doubt that the Mass tract's visual program is a prescriptive, idealizing, even interpretive effort.

In the text written below the painting, a diminutive male head looks up, out of the initial he inhabits to the miniature above, linking textual exhortation and the arresting image that precedes it. In this second miniature, the minimally defined space of Eucharistic ritual is invaded by a monstrous Hell Mouth from which several figures emerge, among them John the Baptist, haloed and clothed in a hairy garment on the far right, and a man whose naked form is framed by the Hell Mouth's curving tusks.

If we turn to the manuscript that gave the Queen Mary Psalter Master his name, we find confirmation for an identification of this naked male figure as Adam (fig. 39). In his cameo in the Mass tract, Adam, like the figures behind him, does not look with John the Baptist toward the altar. The first man and his Old Testament descendants appeal to the hand of God as it descends from the upper bar of the frame to bless their liberation.

As the Hell Mouth yawns and releases its captives, the celebrant, deacon, and a single youth stand before the altar. The priest and his two companions remain conspicuously oblivious to the dramatic scene of rescue and release taking place behind them. The pictorial space of the miniature is implicitly divided into two orders of reality. On the right, the conduct of the Mass is represented in a more or less extrinsic, mundane manner. On the left, however, the meditation prescribed in the Mass tract's Anglo-Norman text is made visible for the manuscript's reader-viewer. The Hell Mouth is not represented as a visionary irruption within the painted frame; rather, it is a visual fiction, an image within an image provided as a visual aid to focus and fix the lay reader-viewer's pious attention. It also offers a lesson in liturgical exegesis.

Collaboratively, the terse vernacular instruction and the spectacular image above it communicate a well-established understanding of the introit's allegorical significance within the Mass. As the great thirteenth-century liturgist William Durandus explained, the introit expresses "uaticinia prophetarum et desiderium sanctorum patrum cum preconiis, Filii Dei aduentum et incarnationem expectantium" (the prophecies of the prophets and the ardent desire of the holy fathers longing for and awaiting the coming of the Son of God and his incarnation with prayers).[81] This well-established liturgiological interpretation of the introit likely motivated the content of vernacular instruction and visual representation in the lower half of the page.[82] In this way, the Mass tract provides the reader-viewer not simply with a meditative script but also with a way of seeing ritual action in relation to its allegorical or exegetical significance, an authorized mode of perception that frames devout participation as an hermeneutic exercise.

KYRIE ELEYSON

The Mass tract's next miniature introduces an emphatically visionary note into the treatise's visual narrative (fig. 40). The upper image on folio 45v marks the initial threefold singing of the *Kyrie eleyson,* a Greek phrase ("Lord have mercy") sung in every Mass as an appeal to the deity's clemency.[83] The short paragraph of text accompanying the painting exhorts the lay reader-viewer to "Pensetz la franchise dieu le piere a faire nous bien et sa pacience a soffrir nos maus et sa pité come il est prest a nous pardoner mes qe nous le voiloms prier" (Think about the liberality of God the Father in favoring us, and

Fig. 40. Kyrie eleyson *and* Christe eleyson *in the Mass tract, mid-1320s. Paris, BnF, MS fr. 13342, f. 45v.*

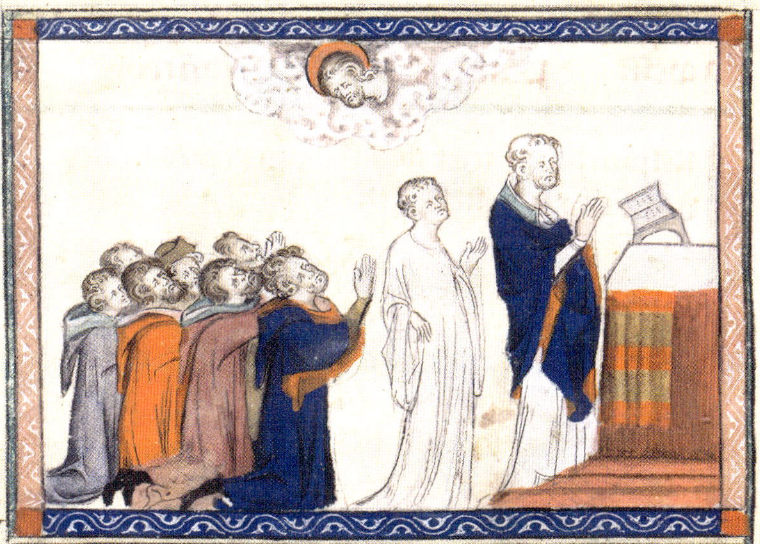

Al·iij·foiz·Kyriel·

Pensetz la franchise dieu le piere a faire no[us] bien & sa pacience a soffrir nos maus & sa pite come il est prest a no[us] p[ar]doner mes q[ue] no[us] le voloms prier.

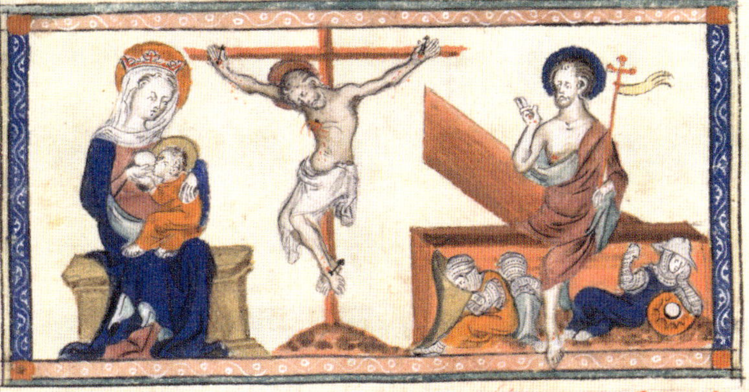

Pensetz la humilite de Al·iij·foiz·Xpeleyson· sa encarnacion & de sa nessance la deboneirete de sa vie & de sa mort la douzor de sa resurrection Et de sa assencion·

his patience in suffering our sins, and his mercy; for he is ready to pardon us, if only we should wish to implore him).[84]

In the image above the text, kneeling lay congregants direct their gaze upward for the first time. The head of God appears in a delicate cloud bank, marking the split between the laity and the clergy like a point of punctuation. In tandem with the textual instruction below it, the miniature describes a moment of devout dialogue. As the priest at the altar intones the first Kyrie, supplicating God on behalf of his flock, the laypeople behind him entreat God directly, fixing their eyes on the divine visage that condescends toward them from a cloud bank.

Within the image, two visual cues suggest that this appearance of the deity participates in a different ontological register than that of the Hell Mouth and its inhabitants in the prior miniature. First, the lay congregants in this miniature are distinctly represented looking up at the head of God, rather than at the priest at the altar. The Queen Mary Psalter Master has taken some pains to ensure that the congregants appear aware of this divine presence in their midst. Second, the cloud bank that surrounds the head of God marks it as a visionary apparition. In this fashion, the artist distinguishes the visible apparition of the deity from the visualization of an immaterial meditative subject, such as the Hell Mouth in the previous miniature. This iconographic differentiation of the visionary from the meditative is reinforced by the second miniature and text on this verso.

CHRISTE ELEYSON

An inscription set below the frame identifies this image with the singing of the Greek phrase *Christe eleyson* ("Christ have mercy"), which is intoned three times immediately after the Kyrie eleyson and usually followed by a repeated threefold intonation of the Kyrie.[85] At the singing of the Christe eleyson the tract exhorts its reader-viewer to "Pensetz la humilité de sa encarnacion et de sa nessance la deboneireté de sa vie et de sa mort la douzor de sa resurection et de sa assension" (Consider the humility of his incarnation and birth, the goodness of his life and death, and the sweetness of his Resurrection and Ascension).[86] As Binski has noted, the meditations prescribed by the Mass tract at this point closely echo the meditative subjects associated with the contemplation of Christ's humanity by St. Edmund of Abingdon's *Mirour de seinte eglyse,* the text that precedes the Mass tract in this volume.[87] Indeed, on folio 39r of the manuscript, the *Mirour* instructs the reader,

> De sa humanité dois tu penser treis choses. La humilité de sa incarnacion la dozour de sa conversacion et la charité de sa passion. Mes ceo ne poez tu fere a une foiz. Pour ceo ieo ai destincté par les

set hores du jor qe tu chantes a moustier qe nul' hore ne te eschape que tu ne soies ducement en deu occupé. Bien dois tu savoir qe chascon' houre ad double meditacion. Une de la passion. Une autre de autre soison.[88]

(Concerning his humanity, you ought to consider three things: the humility of his Incarnation, the sweetness of his way of life, and the charity of his Passion. But you cannot do all this at one time. Therefore I have separated [these meditations] among the seven hours of the day that you sing in the church [or monastery] so that no hour should escape you in which you have not sweetly occupied yourself with God. Indeed, you should know that each hour has a double meditation: one concerning the Passion, another concerning another period of time.)

The *Mirour*'s textual program for meditation assigns different moments from the Passion narrative and from other *soisons* (periods) from Christ's life. As the text notes, these meditative subjects have to be parceled out; they cannot be considered simultaneously.

Within the Queen Mary Psalter Master's miniatures, however, precisely this kind of simultaneous representation of devotional subjects is possible. Dispensing with the delineation of fictive liturgical space, the second miniature on folio 45v visually translates the meditative subjects prescribed by the *Mirour de seinte eglyse* and by the text of the Mass tract as three familiar iconographic types: the crowned Virgin nursing the Christ child; Christ on the cross; and the resurrected and victorious Christ, stepping out of the tomb beyond the sleeping soldiers to trespass the lower bar of the painted frame. Isolated against the reserved parchment ground these three sacred figures momentarily shift the attention of the visual program from a narration of the conduct of liturgical ritual to the iconic mode of the Christocentric devotional image.

In the interval between the upper Kyrie eleyson miniature and the lower Christe eleyson image, the ritual progress of the Mass advances and the mode of visualization deemed appropriate to it changes as well. Beginning in the Carolingian era, liturgical exegetes interpreted the Kyrie eleyson as addressing God the Father and the Christe eleyson as beseeching Christ.[89] This interpretation finds visual expression in the transition from the Kyrie eleyson image to the image accompanying the Christe eleyson. In the lower Christe eleyson miniature, altar, celebrant, and congregation vanish, and with them the notional space of the Mass's serial progress is transformed into the atemporal space of the devotional image. The narrative mode that structures the tract as a whole is, however, revised rather than refused by the Christe eleyson miniature. As the vernacular text written below the miniature makes clear, the juxtaposition of these three images-within-an-image encodes a Christological narrative: reading from left to right, the miniature arrays an iconographic précis of the tripartite structure of the culmination of Christ's *vita* (Incarnation, Passion, Resurrection-Ascension).

No cloud bank frames these three Christological subjects. As in the representation of the Hell Mouth on the recto of the folio, in this image the viewer is provided with an iconographic translation of the meditative subjects verbally set forth by the text written below the frame. Through this tripartite iconographic repertoire the Queen Mary Psalter Master provides a visual corollary to the text's prescribed devotions and delineates a terse, iconic précis of Christ's life as a visual accompaniment to a Christocentric liturgical chant.

Significantly, the miniature's iconographic shorthand rendering of Christ's biographical narrative echoes elements of the *vita Christi* sung in the Mass in the form of the Credo (Niceno-Constantinopolitan Creed):

> Credo . . . in unum dominum Jesum Christum . . . Qui propter nos homines, et propter nostram salutem descendit de cælis. Et incarnatus est de Spiritu Sancto ex Maria virgine, et homo factus est. Crucifixus etiam pro nobis sub Pontio Pilato: passus, et sepultus est. Et resurrexit tertia die. . . .
>
> (I believe . . . in one Lord Jesus Christ . . . who for us men and for our salvation came down from heaven, and was incarnate by the Holy Ghost of the Virgin Mary, and was made man, and was crucified also for us under Pontius Pilate. He suffered and was buried, and the third day he rose again. . . .)[90]

As we noted in chapter 1, the Credo was a major component of the pastoral syllabus, a formulary of knowledge and belief to which the laity were held to account. Although in the early Middle Ages, the recital of the Credo in the Mass had been a vernacular performance in which clergy and laity collaborated, by the later Middle Ages, the Credo had become a clerical choral piece, complicated by polyphony and no longer involving lay voices.[91]

The representation of the signing of the Credo would, were it included in the tract, have followed the Christe eleyson miniature; significantly, the Mass tract does not provide an image for this ritual profession of sacred truths. In keeping with the treatise's focus on a lay experience of the Mass, the Credo is excluded from the tract's episodic account. In the Christe eleyson miniature, however, the reader-viewer contemplates a condensation of the Christic tenets of the faith, both as they are performed in the Christe eleyson chant and as they are sung in the Credo. In this way, the painting solicits the viewer's religious knowledge, their mastery of the *vita Christi* and its significance, and gives delicately rendered outward form to those saving truths. As it recuperates the Credo's verbal performance of religious knowledge, the painting translates this clerical recital of sacred truth into a scene of visual recognition and meditation, designed for lay eyes.

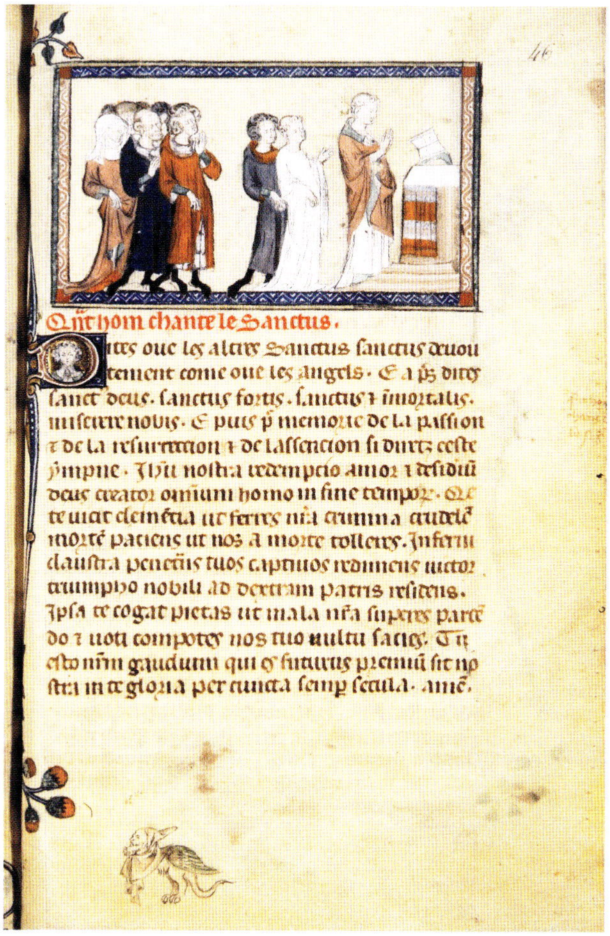

Fig. 41. The Sanctus *is sung in the Mass tract, mid-1320s. Paris, BnF, MS fr. 13342, f. 46r.*

SANCTUS

As the reader-viewer turns to the facing recto, they return to the fictive space of the liturgy delineated in the Mass tract's first three miniatures (fig. 41). The treatise has arrived at the singing of the *Sanctus,* a hymn invoking the deity's holiness, sung at the end of the Preface. The singing of the Sanctus also served as a signal for the beginning of the Canon of the Mass, a phase of the ritual in which the celebrant and ministers prepare and consecrate the Eucharistic bread and wine.[92]

The Mass tract's textual treatment of this moment begins with a transcription of the Sanctus hymn, prefaced by the exhortation, "Dites ové les altres *Sanctus sanctus* devoutement come ové les angels" (Devoutly say with the others, *Holy holy,* as if with the angels).[93] The command to sing "as if with the angels" is an explicit evocation of the liturgical chant's verbatim recapitulation of the song of praise sung by seraphim to the deity, as described in Isaiah 6:3 and Apocalypse 4:8. In this way, the Mass tract frames the Sanctus as a song performed by a company of adorers that embraces not only the clergy and laity but also the angelic host in heaven. Discussing the significance of the Sanctus, Pamela Sheingorn has suggested that for Christians, singing the seraphic hymn of praise "dissolved not only the boundaries separating heaven and earth, but also those separating time and eternity, for they participated in the 'Eternal Mass in the Heavenly Jerusalem.'"[94] The Mass tract's text takes this conception a step further.[95]

As the Anglo-Norman passage continues, the reader-viewer is asked to recite a further *ympne* (hymn) in which he or she addresses God, saying, "Ipsa te cogat pietas ut mala nostra superes parcendo et voti compotes nos tuo vultu sacies" (Piety itself compels you so that with mercy you overcome our sins and, our wishes fulfilled, you satisfy us with your countenance).[96] Having joined the angelic choirs in the singing of the Sanctus, the devotee is now exhorted to proclaim his or her confidence in a future union realized not through song but through vision. In the words of this ympne, it is the vision of God's *vultus*—his gaze or countenance—that satisfies the lay reader-viewer. This perceptual prerogative, promised to the devotee in the language of liturgy, is a privilege that the Mass tract's images grant to the fictive lay Mass-goers depicted within their painted frames. Indeed, already in the first miniature in this opening, the image for the singing of the Kyrie eleyson, the Queen Mary Psalter Master represented lay devotees and deity in a relationship of reciprocal contemplation.

Although the Mass tract's instructions for the singing of the Sanctus stress the cooperation of the Church Militant and the Church Mystical in the Sanctus's praise of God, the Sanctus miniature (unlike the Kyrie eleyson that faces it across the gutter) does not exploit the iconographic potential of this liturgical moment. By contrast, the Sanctus miniature describes this spiritually charged liturgical performance in a relatively mundane visual idiom. The elegantly swayed bodies of the lay congregants are grouped on the left side of the image. Standing alertly, they attend to the celebrant at the altar who performs the Sanctus from an open book placed upon the altar. At the center of the image the deacon faces the altar, his hipshot posture echoed closely by the laypeople who stand behind him. This resolutely extrinsic representation of the singing of the Sanctus in no way prepares the viewer for the opening that follows.

THE ELEVATION

For a lay congregant in fourteenth-century England, the Mass culminated in the elevation of the consecrated Eucharist. Beyond the three festal communions prescribed to the laity by statute and customary practice alike, for many laypeople it was the sight of the consecrated wafer—raised aloft by the celebrant before the altar—that gave access to the Eucharist. In the Mass tract, the importance of this moment warrants a miniature that spans both verso and recto in an integrated, oversized composition on folios 46v–47r (fig. 42). In the Queen Mary Psalter Master's ambitious image, the rectangular fields defined by painted borders on verso and recto are transformed into schematic, abstracted architectural cross-sections through the inclusion of two aedicules that extend into the gutter. On the verso two boys gather in the first of these arched apertures; just across the inner fold, their confrère stands on tiptoe, his form stretched tautly, as he rings a bell to announce the moment of the elevation. The sanctus bell itself also contributes to this moment of heightened attention and visual drama; the Queen Mary Psalter Master paints the bell at mid-ring, swinging out of an arched opening in the bell tower above.

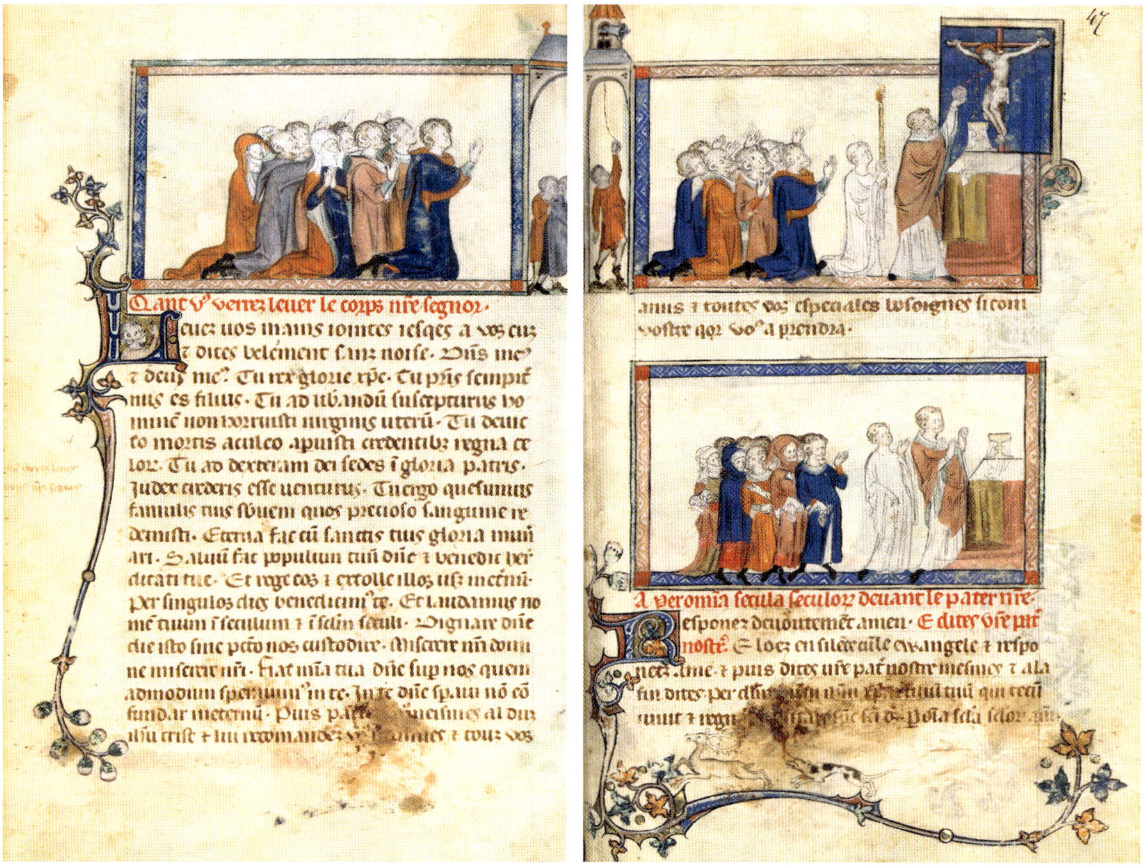

Fig. 42. The elevation of the host in the Mass tract, mid-1320s. Paris, BnF, MS fr. 13342, ff. 46v–47r.

As the sanctus bell is rung, all eyes turn to the host, held high by the celebrant at the altar. On the left side of this extended composition, a group of laywomen and men kneel with raised hands as they adore the host. In the portion of the miniature on the facing recto, a second group of lay congregants kneel in adoration behind the deacon, who holds a large lit taper to better illuminate their view of the elevated host. On the far right side of the image, the crucified body of Christ appears above the altar (fig. 43). This corpus is not a crucifix; the crucified body that the Queen Mary Psalter Master painted in this image is iconographically distinct from the crucifix shown to a dying man in the representation of last rites that he illuminated in the Psalter of Richard of Canterbury (fig. 44).[97] In the Mass tract's miniature, the corpus is not an inert sculpture; crucified upon the altar, Christ's body emits streams of blood and water that arc toward wafer and chalice.

Christ's spectacular bleeding body was not originally a component of this image.[98] The figure of Christ is an addition to the miniature that transgresses the

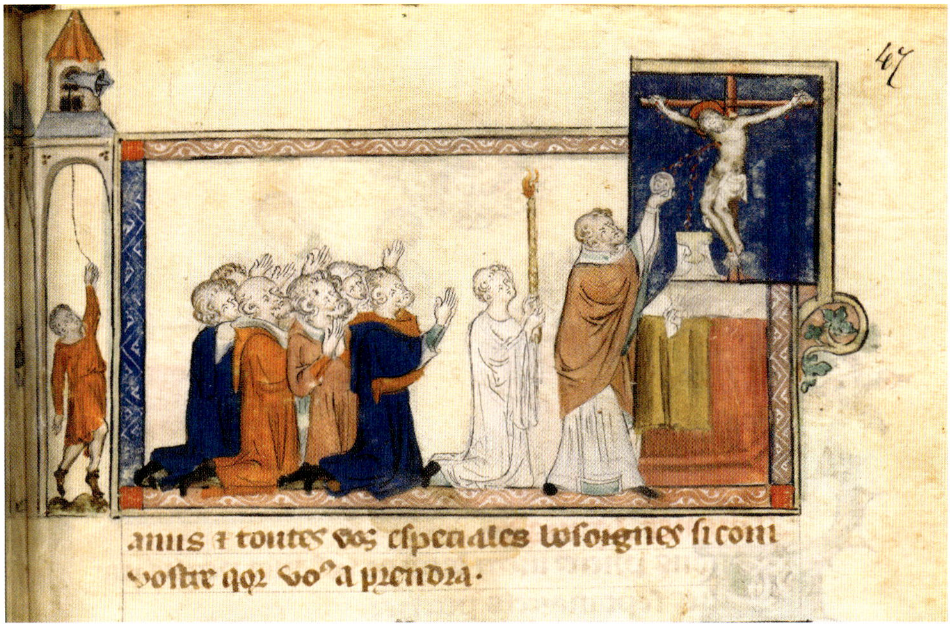

Fig. 43. Christ's spectacular sacramental body in the Mass tract, mid-1320s. Paris, BnF, MS fr. 13342, f. 47r (detail).

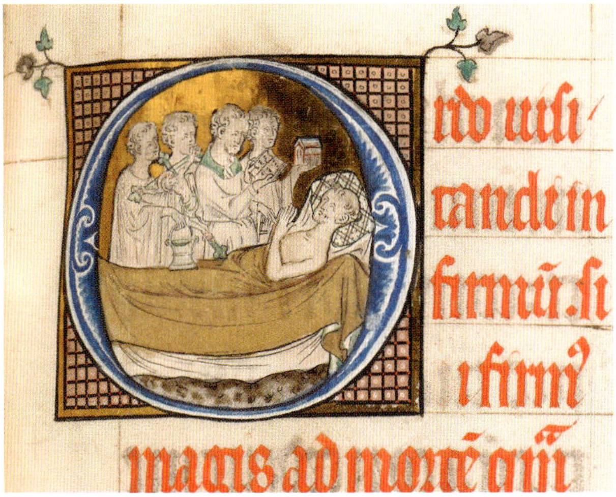

Fig. 44. Last rites: the crucifix is brought to a dying man in the Psalter of Richard of Canterbury, c. 1310–1320. New York, Pierpont Morgan Library, MS G.53, f. 150r (detail): 320 x 210 mm. Gift of the Trustees of the William S. Glazier Collection, 1984.

established bounds of its frame (see fig. 43). As if the original elevation image, teeming with a multitude of seeing subjects and subjects to be seen, was not sufficiently charged with the visual and the visionary, the Queen Mary Psalter Master returned to his composition and burdened its visual economy further. Placed against the only solid pigment ground to be found in the entirety of the Mass tract's visual program, Christ's crucified body demands the viewer's attention.

The text that accompanies the elevation miniature instructs the reader in their conduct at the moment of the elevation: "Quant vous verrez lever le corps notre segnor. Levez vos main jointes jesqes a vos euz et dites belement sanz noise. *Dominus meus et deus meus . . .*" (When you shall see the body of our Lord raised, raise your clasped hands up to your eyes and say graciously, without clamor, *My Lord and my God . . .*).[99] In the lengthy Latin prayer prescribed by the text, the devotee addresses Christ with a series of creedal statements, derived from the *Te Deum* hymn, that affirm his works of salvation. Following this confessional passage, the reader-viewer is instructed to petition Christ for his aid,

beseeching him, "Eterna fac cum sanctis tuis gloria munerari" (Make [your servants] to be numbered among your saints in eternal glory).[100] As if to justify these demands, the tract exhorts the lay devotee to proclaim, "Et laudamus nominem tuum in seculum et in seculum seculi" (And we praise your name for eternity, world without end).[101]

In these elevation prayers, as elsewhere in the text, the treatise employs a motivated macaronic approach in its prescription of devout practice and expression. Anglo-Norman is used to prescribe bodily gesture and pious meditation; Latin, however, remains the language of direct address to the deity. The Mass tract's provision of Latin texts, not only for the standard responses required by the Mass but also for additional, accessory "personal" prayers, is a linguistic extension of its Pauline emphasis on the Mass as a unifying, collective ritual. Within the linguistic program of the Mass tract, the lay devotee's direct petitioning of the deity employs the Latin language of scripture, ecclesiastical ritual, and religious authority. Considered within the broader context of the Mass tract's text-image program, these Latin petitions and proclamations assert the incorporation of the lay devotee in a relationship of ecclesial *unitas* by means of his or her visually intent form of Eucharistic devotion: an integration of the Divine and the faithful within a single ritual—and painted—frame.

At the moment of the elevation, text and image collapse the distance between the faithful and the Divine, between the laity and the object of their veneration. The prayers prescribed for the elevation cast the petitioner as one of Christ's intimates, seeking membership in the community of heaven. This textual insistence on the actual and anticipated proximity of devotee and divinity is given dramatic visual form in the elevation miniature (see fig. 42). The lay congregants within the image engage in a direct and doubled contemplation of Christ. They see Christ in the consecrated host raised high for their inspection, and, simultaneously, Christ is made visibly present in the crucified corpus that exudes water and blood upon the Eucharistic elements.

The addition of Christ's body to the painting was not a crude attempt at visual clarification, designed to prevent a possible misunderstanding of the miniature. For a layperson in the early fourteenth century, the Mass culminated in the elevation of the consecrated Eucharist, and fourteenth-century viewers would certainly have understood the sacrificial dimension of the liturgy. Indeed, the symbolic and doctrinal significance of the elevation of the host—and the sacramental transformation that it proclaims—are explained within the manuscript itself.

In the section of the Paris volume devoted to St. Edmund of Abingdon's *Mirour de seinte eglyse,* the reader is explicitly instructed in the significance of the Eucharistic celebration. In the meditations prescribed for Vespers, the *Mirour* tells the reader to consider

> coment a cel houre dona nostre segnor son corps et son sanc en semblance de payn et de vin. pur ceo qe nous avoms hydour de manger char et boivre sanc d'omme. Pur ceo dona il a nous son corps et son sanc. en semblance de tel manger et de tiel boivre com nous soumes a coustomés de user pur conforter nostre fraelté et pur edefier nostre creance pur ceo qe nous veom une chose et croiom une altre. E pur ceo qant vous aprochez le auter pur estre acomuingé auxi recevez illoec son corps vraiment com le receustes de sa cousté.[102]
>
> (how our Lord gave his body and his blood in the semblance of bread and wine, because we would be horrified to eat the flesh and to drink the blood of a man. For this reason he gave us his body and his blood in the semblance of such food and drink as we are accustomed to consume, in order to strengthen our frailty and to build up our faith, in that we see one thing and we believe another. And therefore, when you approach the altar to be communicated, receive his body there truly as if you received it from his side.)

The *Mirour de seinte eglyse* encourages its reader to receive the Eucharist as if it were emanating directly from Christ's side: that is, as if the consecrated host were the blood and water that flowed during the Crucifixion according to John 19:34.[103] The *Mirour*'s textual evocation of the blood and water shed by Christ's body is echoed, quite directly, by the representation of the crucified corpus in the Mass tract's elevation miniature.

The minute drops of water that spring from Christ's wound in this image are not ubiquitous features of fourteenth-century English representations of the Crucified. Their presence in the image becomes more intelligible, and more signifying, if we consider that they are stressed in the *Mirour*'s discussion of the Eucharist, a passage that occurs only three folios before the beginning of the Mass tract in the Paris volume.[104]

What, in the end, does this supplementary representation of Christ above the altar signify? What is the status of the figure of the Crucified? And why was it necessary to add Christ's bleeding body to this image when he was already visibly present in the form of the elevated host? I would suggest that the figure of Christ crucified *had to be* inserted in this image because the visual triangulation of raised host, veiled chalice, and crucified body was essential to the broader claims of the Mass tract's pictorial cycle.[105]

The image constructs a parallax view. Christ is represented in the visible species of consecrated wafer and wine, and, simultaneously, Christ is rendered as the bleeding body whose incarnate and divine reality guarantees the Eucharist's sacramentality. These are two continuous, but semantically differentiated, orders of presence that, in turn, imply the operation of two modes of vision within the miniature's frame. Gazing upon the Eucharist, the fictive lay congregants painted in the image are confronted not simply with the consecrated host but also with the very corpus whose redemptive sacrifice undergirds the sacramental reality and efficacy of the Eucharist.

If we consider the progress of the Mass tract's visual program up to this point we find three modes of representation, and thus of vision, at work. The iconographic repertoire of the Hell Mouth and the Christological subjects provides an external visualization of meditative subjects prescribed to the mind or heart at prayer. Other miniatures in the Mass tract's picture cycle delineate a mundane view of the Mass that stresses the outward progress of liturgical action. The treatise's elevation miniature builds from these two representational modes to assert the spiritual efficacy of devout vision within the sacramental framework of the Mass. Juxtaposing the visible species of the sacrament, that is, the host and chalice, with the actively bleeding body of Christ crucified, the miniature promotes devout vision's ability to penetrate beyond the visible to the invisible mysterium of the sacrament.

The rhetorical claim of the miniature is clear: properly prepared and intent vision binds the viewer to the sacred object of their sight in a relationship of perceptual proximity that is, simultaneously, an encounter with the second person of the Trinity. In the Mass tract's elevation miniature, to see the Eucharist is to see Christ, not as an apparition encircled by numinous clouds but as the fully human and fully divine savior present in the sacrament.

Apart from the three festal communions prescribed by English statutes, lay Mass-goers usually received Christ through the eyes rather than the mouth. Just as the moment of the elevation of the host was the culmination of the ritual drama of the Mass for the laity, so too the Mass tract makes the elevation the high point of its own representational drama. Through its texts and images it constructs the layperson's encounter with the Eucharist as a charged visual confrontation in which a vision of the sacrament involves seeing beyond—or through—the host to Christ's bleeding body.

Like the small figure with upraised hands in the initial L of the verso's text, the manuscript's reader-viewer is implicated in the labor and the rewards of the mode of vision promoted by the Mass tract's representation of the elevation (fig. 45). Considered in conjunction with the textual prayers it accompanies, the Queen Mary Psalter Master's expansive painting of the elevation leaves no doubt as to the means of communication and transformation at work within its frame. Indeed, the economy of salvation in which the reader-viewer is exhorted to proclaim their confidence is explicitly represented as a visual economy. Devout vision, the image seems to announce, is predicated on its divine object. In the elevation miniature this precept is realized through a virtuosic orchestration of vision:

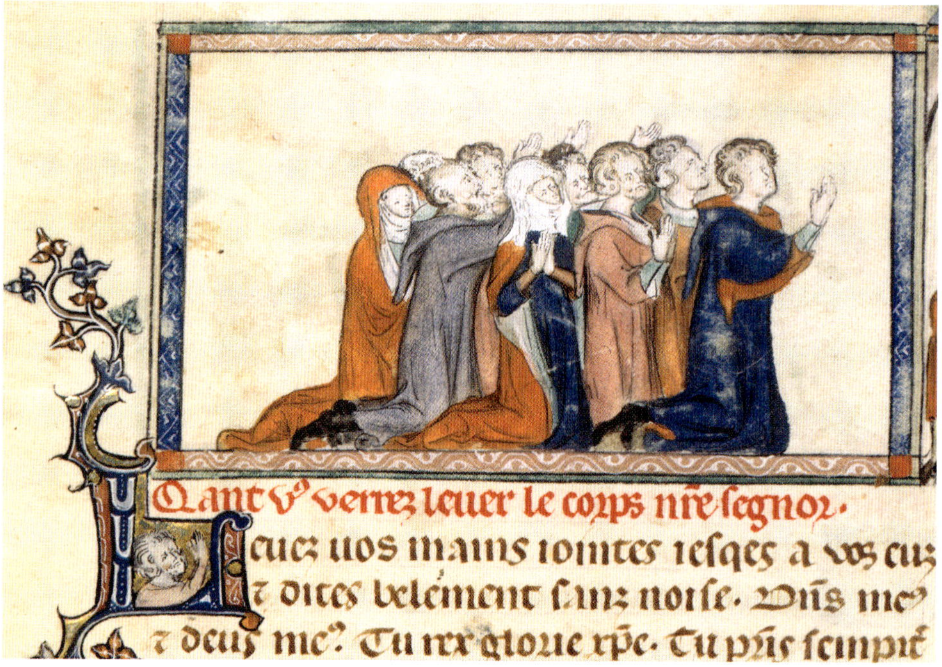

Fig. 45. Adoration of the host from within the letter in the Mass tract, mid-1320s. Paris, BnF, MS fr. 13342, f. 46v (detail).

as the reader-viewer contemplates text and image—with its fictive lay viewers, Eucharist, and crucified corpus—he or she is interpellated into a sacramentally unified community.

Encouraged by the Mass tract's texts and images to seek Christ in the Mass and the manuscript page, the reader-viewer accompanies the tract's painted lay congregants as they make their way through the manuscript's representation of liturgical ritual. Like these fictive Mass-goers, the reader-viewer must continue to the tract's end before their spiritually intent vision receives its full reward.

PER OMNIA SECULA SECULORUM AND PATER NOSTER

After the high drama of the elevation miniature, the second smaller painting on folio 47r provides a point of release within the picture cycle (see fig. 42). Here, as the rubric indicates, the final moment of the consecration of the Eucharist is represented. Addressing the altar, the celebrant performs the concluding doxology of the consecration, *per omnia secula seculorum* (world without end), to which the assembled congregants respond, *amen.*[106] As the Anglo-Norman text indicates, this final moment of the Canon is designated for the laity's assent and adhesion: after declaiming *amen,* the lay reader-viewer is instructed to recite the Pater Noster.

Christ's crucified corpus has disappeared within the accompanying image; the altar bears only a veiled chalice. Standing in a dense group behind the Eucharistic ministers, the lay Mass-goers seem distinctly relaxed, a marked contrast to their rigidly fixed attention in the miniature above. Although two men at the front of this group gaze steadily at the altar, their fellow congregants turn to each other and seem to converse. A woman at the far left of the group strikes a stylish, somewhat amusing pose as she holds a small dog in the crook of her arm. In a departure from the text's injunction that the Gospel should be heard *en silence,* the Queen Mary Psalter Master's rendering of this chatty group of laypeople injects a note of quotidian garrulousness into the Mass tract's liturgical narrative.[107]

THE COMMUNION CYCLE

Turning the page, the reader-viewer encounters three images devoted to the three-fold intonation of the *Agnus dei,* a chant acclaiming the Eucharistic lamb of God, which accompanies the fraction and mixture of the Eucharistic species and the priest's

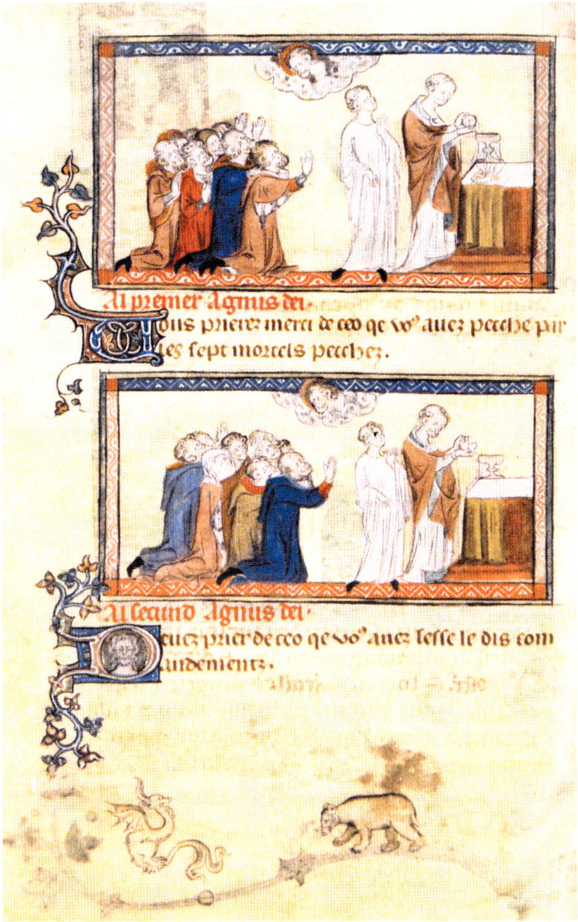

Fig. 46. First and second singings of the Agnus dei *in the Mass tract, mid-1320s. Paris, BnF, MS fr. 13342, f. 47v.*

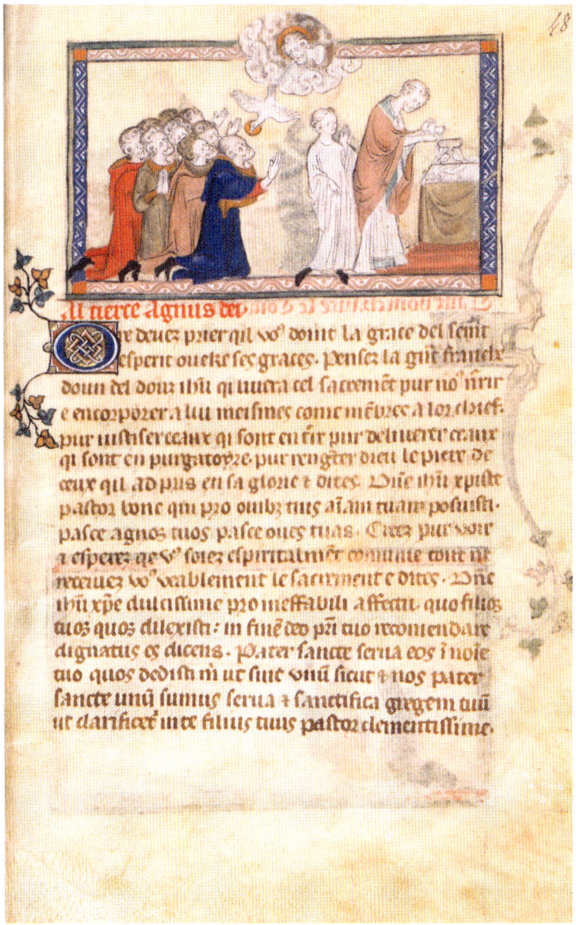

Fig. 47. The third singing of the Agnus dei *in the Mass tract, mid-1320s. Paris, BnF, MS fr. 13342, f. 48r.*

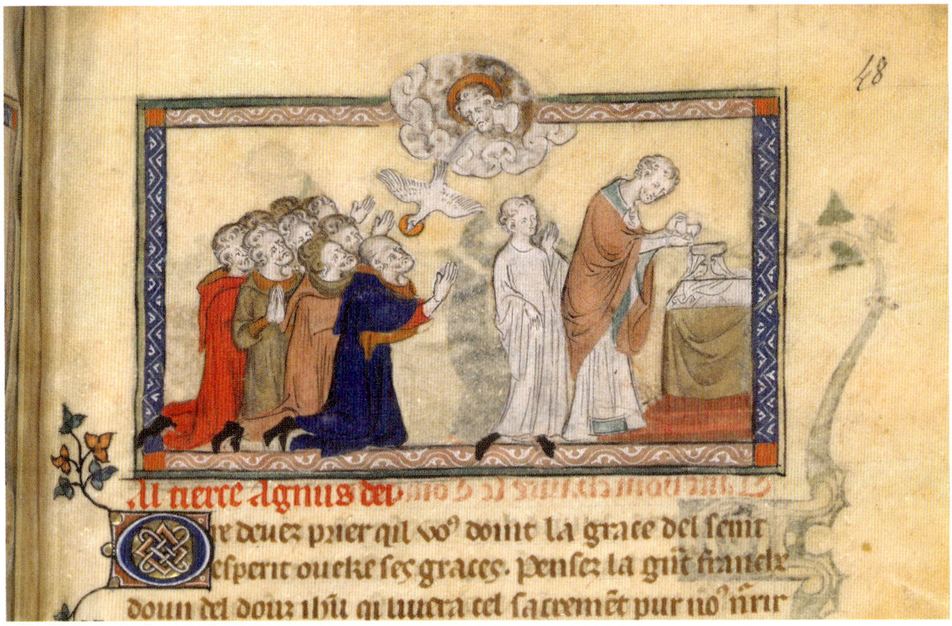

Fig. 48. The third singing of the Agnus dei *in the Mass tract, mid-1320s. Paris, BnF, MS fr. 13342, f. 48r (detail).*

communion (figs. 46 and 47).[108] Each of these three images is accompanied by a short text specifying how the devotee should address the deity. At the first singing of the Agnus dei the text instructs the reader-viewer to beg God's mercy for their mortal sins.[109] At the second intonation of the chant the reader-viewer is exhorted to pray because they have forsaken the Ten Commandments.[110] The penitential emphases of these textual injunctions mirror the tenor of the Agnus dei chant itself, which invokes the Eucharistic lamb's redemption of humanity's sins: "agnus dei qui tollit peccata mundi . . ." (lamb of God, who takes away the sins of the world . . .).

In the miniatures that accompany the first and second recitals of the *Agnus dei,* the minutely rendered progress of liturgical ritual is upstaged by a spiritual encounter that takes place behind the backs of the celebrant and his assistant (see fig. 46). In the first of these images, the priest holds the consecrated host before the chalice. His flock, however, do not attend to their pastor; they beseech God directly. Likewise, in the lower miniature, the fractured host displayed by the celebrant is altogether ignored by the lay devotees, who—once again—address their gaze and prayers to the apparition of God's countenance in the cloud above them. As the Agnus dei is intoned for a third and final time, the cloud bank surrounding the divine countenance bursts across the miniature's frame and the Dove of the Holy Ghost descends from Christ's head, like a breath, toward the lay congregants below (fig. 48).

Just as this third miniature in the Agnus dei sequence significantly increases the dramatic quotient of the supernatural visitation occurring behind the clergy's backs, the text it prefaces is significantly longer and more spiritually ambitious than its predecessors:

> Ore devez prier qu'il vous doint la grace del seint esperit oveke ses graces. Pensez la grant franche doun del douz Ihesu qui livera cel sacrement pur nous nourir e encorporer a lui meismes come membres a lor chief. pur justiser ceaux qi sont en terre pur deliverer ceaux qi sont en purgatoyre. pur rengrater dieu le piere de ceux qi ad pris en sa gloire e dites. *Domine ihesu criste pastor bone qui pro ovibus tuis animam tuam posuisti. pasce agnos tuos pasce oves tuas.* Creez pur voir e esperez qe vous soiez espiritalment comunié tout ne receivez vous veablement le sacrement e dites. *Domine ihesu christe dulcissime pro ineffabili affectu. quo filios tuos quos dilexisti: in finem deo patri tuo recomendare dignatus es dicens. Pater sancte serva eos in nomine tuo quos dedisti mihi ut sint unum sicut et nos pater sancte unum sumus serva et sanctifica gregem tuum ut clarificetur in te filius tuus pastor clementissime.*[111]
>
> (Now you must pray that he may give you the grace of the Holy Spirit with its graces. Think of the great generous gift of sweet Jesus who confers this sacrament in order to nourish us and incorporate us in him as limbs to their head, to justify those who are on earth, to deliver those who are in purgatory, to give thanks to God the Father for those he has taken to his glory; and say, "O Lord Jesus Christ, oh good pastor who laid down your soul for your sheep, feed your lambs, feed your sheep." Truly believe and hope that you shall be spiritually communicated even if you only receive the sacrament visually and say, "O sweetest Lord Jesus Christ, for the sake of the ineffable feeling of love with which you loved your sons, in the end you deigned to recommend [them] to your father God, saying, O Holy Father, save those ones, in your name, whom you gave to me so that they may be one just as we, O Holy Father, are one; preserve and sanctify your flock so that in you, most merciful pastor, your son might be made illustrious.")[112]

Exploiting the kind of instantaneous analogy only possible in visual representation, the miniature prefacing this text asserts a daring equivalence: just as the priest receives and consumes the consecrated host, so the laity receives the Holy Spirit with its host-like halo, aligned horizontally with the fractured wafer. In this fashion the image

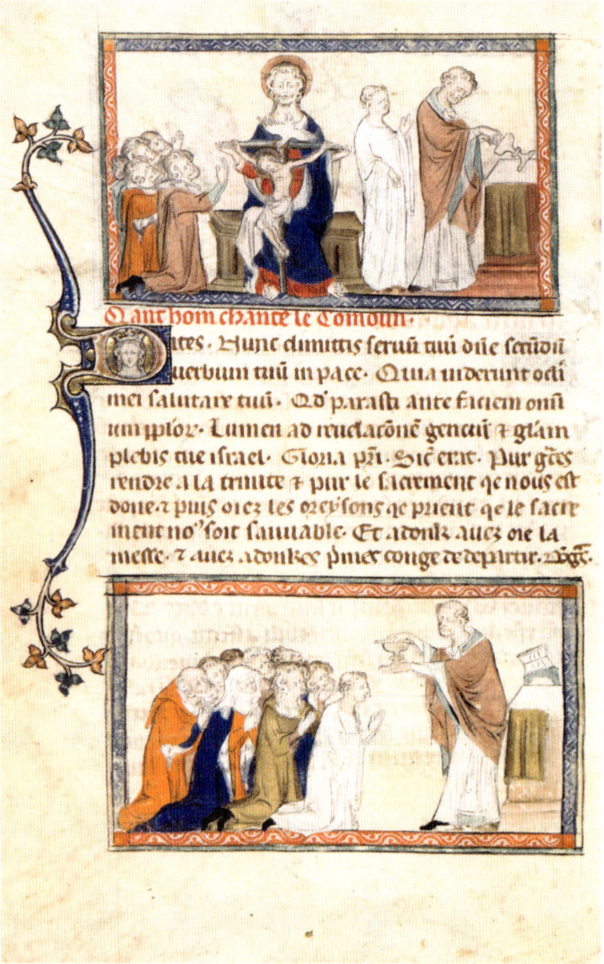

Fig. 49. *Communion with the Trinity in the Mass tract, mid-1320s. Paris, BnF, MS fr. 13342, f. 48v.*

renders the "grace del seint esperit" referenced in the text, a visual, even visible pendant to the consecrated host: as the sacramental host is to the priest, so the grace of the Holy Spirit is to the laity.

The procession of divine persons that emanates from the head of the deity, through the haloed Dove, to the lay congregants below defines a diagonal axis of transmitted grace and reciprocal vision, a post-elevation Trinity that incorporates lay Mass-goers into a unity of devout vision. This very unification is evoked by the text when it instructs the reader to consider how Christ gave us the Eucharist in order to "nous nourir e encorporer a lui meismes come membres a lor chief" (nourish and incorporate us in him, as limbs to their head).[113] Translated from text to image, this divine nourishment is cast as the mutual regard of deity and devotees.

In the lengthy prayer below this astonishing image, the efficacy of spiritually intent looking is explicitly promoted to the Mass tract's reader-viewer. The treatise urges its audience to "Creez pur voir e esperez qe vous soiez espiritalment comunié tout ne receivez vous veablement le sacrement" (Truly believe and hope that you shall be spiritually communicated even if you only receive the sacrament visually).[114] This is an audacious—but not unprecedented—claim that identifies seeing the consecrated host as a form of communion. Considered in tandem with the visible claims made in the image prefacing this passage—and in the Mass tract's visual program as a whole—this promotion of ocular communion implicitly asserts the visible sacrament's power to communicate itself by means of vision. This assertion depends, reciprocally, on the capacity of *vision* to effectively communicate sacramental presence.

The treatise's next image offers a visible proof for the efficacy of a devout vision of the Eucharist. In this, the Mass tract's penultimate miniature, the deity makes a final appearance (fig. 49). Assuming an emphatically Eucharistic and trinitarian form, the divinity appears as a Throne of Mercy in which the first person of the Trinity holds

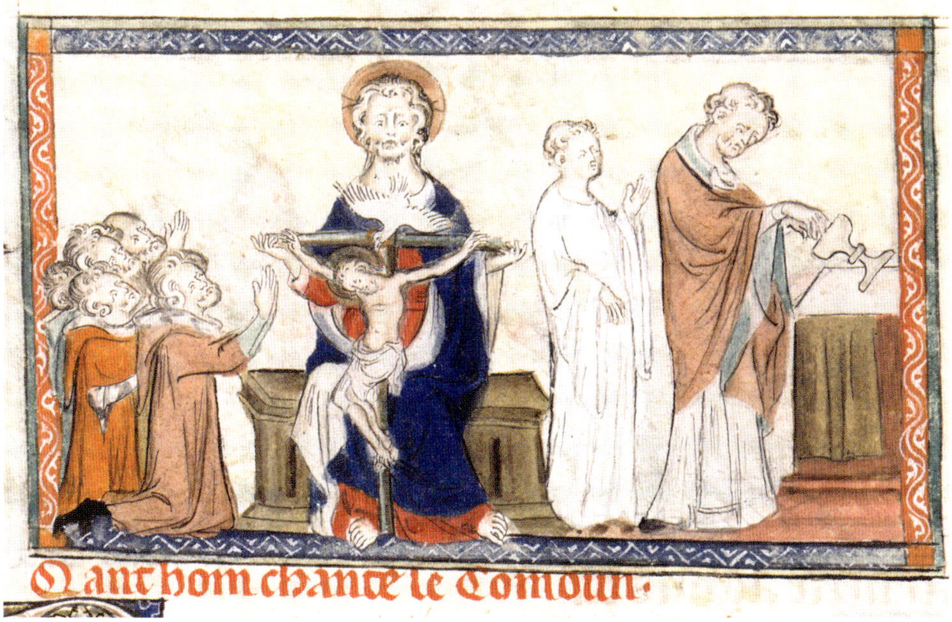

Fig. 50. The Throne of Mercy in the Mass tract, mid-1320s. Paris, BnF, MS fr. 13342, f. 48v (detail).

the crucified form of the second person, while the Dove of the Holy Ghost hovers between them.[115]

In the space between the third incantation of the Agnus dei and this first image on folio 48v, the Mass tract's visual cycle has progressed from the preparation for communion to a moment directly following the priest's communion. In the first of folio 48v's two images, the priest is represented rinsing (or wiping) the chalice at the altar. Having communicated on behalf of the congregation, he now completes a ritual cleansing of the liturgical vessels.

As the celebrant concludes the communion rite, the laity assists at a different, yet visually parallel, culmination of liturgical ritual. Priest and deacon are thoroughly upstaged by the massive Throne of Mercy painted at the center of the pictorial field (fig. 50). The clergy's inattention to this trinitarian apparition is rendered even more inexplicable by the attentiveness of the lay congregants kneeling in the far left corner of the image. The Trinity is given an unusually solid, even material appearance in this miniature. Like the kneeling lay figures beside it, the Throne of Mercy overlaps the frame, projecting out of pictorial space. Although the Trinity is not surrounded by a cloud bank, the fixed attention of the lay devotees who kneel in adoration before the Throne of Mercy leaves no doubt that it is very much the object of their devout vision. The access to the deity promised by the Mass—and by the Mass tract—is realized in the massive presence of the Trinity at the center of the painting's fictive ritual space.

Presented in hieratic frontality, the principal figure of the Throne of Mercy is both an object of vision and a visionary agent. As the first person of the Trinity looks out across the limits of the painted frame, his painted form offers the viewer an unimpeded vision of divinity. Turning to the Mass tract's final textual passage, inscribed immediately below the image, the manuscript's viewer may proclaim, in the words of the *Nunc dimittis* (Canticle of Simeon): "*Quia viderunt oculi mei salutare tuum. Quod parasti ante faciem omnium populorum. Lumen ad revelacionem gencium et gloriam plebis tue israel. Gloria Patri. Sicut erat.* Pur graces rendre a la trinité e pur le sacrement qe nous est doné" ("Because my eyes have seen your salvation. Which you prepared before the face of all the peoples. A light for the revelation of the peoples and the glory of your people Israel. Glory to the Father. As it was." To give thanks to the Trinity and for the sacrament which is given to us).[116] This final passage would have the reader-viewer confidently affirm the chief claim advanced in the image painted above and in the Mass tract's visual program as a whole: namely, that lay participation in the Mass finds its reward in a sacramental encounter that is nothing less than a direct contemplation of the saving divinity.

Over the course of the tract, the central mystery of the Mass—the realization of Christ's salvific presence among his people—is framed as a visual encounter. Moving from the elevation miniature to this communion miniature, the treatise asserts that spiritually intent contemplation of the *sacramentum* will lead the lay devotee to a dialogic encounter with the Trinity. In this penultimate image, the fictive lay inhabitants of the Mass tract's pictorial space have arrived at the apex of their devotional itinerary, and, simultaneously, the tract confronts its flesh-and-blood reader-viewer with the deity's countenance.

The viewer's vision of the miniature aligns him or her with the adoring lay throng painted on the parchment: both the painted laypeople and the lay reader-viewer look at the Trinity and contemplate sacramental grace given visible form. Although the priest and the deacon do not actively participate in this economy of mutual regard, their sacerdotal labor at the altar is its guarantor, simultaneously authenticating the nature of the theophany enjoyed by lay vision and enclosing it within the ritual structure of the Eucharistic liturgy.

"Et adonk avez oié la messe et avez adonkes primes congé de departir"

In the Mass tract's final image, theophanic revelation cedes the pictorial field to the priest as the lay congregation, with the deacon at its head, kneels to receive the final benediction from the celebrant (see fig. 49). The Mass having ended, the priest offers the people a customary blessing, accompanied by the sign of the cross, a gesture made with a hallowed object, in this case the chalice and paten employed in the Mass.[117]

The lines of the text inscribed above the image indicate that the laity's participation in the Mass should end on a note of hope and thanks: "puis oiez les oreysons qe prient qe le sacrement nous soit sauvable. Et adonk avez oié la messe et avez adonkes primes congé de departir. *Deo gratias*" (then listen to the prayers that ask that the sacrament should be salvific for us. And then you have heard the Mass and at that time you should take your leave. *Thanks be to God*).[118] In this, the Mass tract's final miniature, the Queen Mary Psalter Master returns to a more quotidian, extrinsic mode of representation as he depicts the lay congregation gazing intently at the Eucharistic vessels employed in the final benediction of the people. Nonetheless, this too is a moment of devout vision: the tract concludes with the visual assertion that even objects of human facture can be sanctified and, in turn, sanctifying.

"Quia viderunt oculi mei": The Trinity in the Mass and the Efficacy of Vision

The Mass tract preserved in BnF fr. 13342 constructs the Eucharistic rite as a space for shared, sacralized vision and—through text and image—it proclaims the reality and efficacy of such seeing to its lay reader-viewer. This devotional and didactic program is punctuated by a dramatic staging of the elevation, but the arc of its narrative and the economy of vision it encodes do not culminate in the raising of the host.

Instead, the tract continues to develop the privileges and rewards of devout vision in increasingly trinitarian terms throughout the texts and images of the communion cycle following the elevation. The visionary apex of the tract comes in the form of a Throne of Mercy placed in the midst of liturgical space. Within the ritual progress of the treatise's didactic representation of the Mass, the lay devotee's vision rests not in the elevation but rather in a post-communion encounter with an emphatically Eucharistic representation of the Trinity. Significantly, it is only in the Throne of Mercy miniature that the deity looks out from the pictorial field to confront the viewer directly. The culmination of the Mass tract's program is formally constructed as a moment of shared vision: both text and image implicate not only the fictive lay congregation but also the reader-viewer in this direct contemplation of the Divine.

What then is the significance of the Throne of Mercy's appearance within the tract's serial staging of visionary subjects? Why should the Trinity appear as the culminating sacral vision within this exposition of the Mass? The treatise itself answers these questions by asserting the sacrament's power to effect the unification, incorporation, and sanctification of spiritually prepared beholders. In this respect, the Mass tract's account of the Eucharist as a sacrament of unity is Pauline in its emphases and quite traditional in its confidence in the mystical and ecclesial union promised to faithful communicants. By contrast, the tract's promotion of the *vision* of the host as a saving and satisfying sight, and its claim that a properly devout contemplation of the consecrated Eucharist will lead the viewer to a vision of the Trinity—a prefiguration of the beatific vision—distinguish it as a very contemporary production.[119]

Although lay reception of the Eucharist in the Middle Ages was famously restricted, recent scholarship has reexamined the so-called *mysterium depopulatum*—a Mass in which laypeople were confined to the role of passive witnesses to ecclesiastical performance—and where scholarship influenced by Reformation polemic had seen the exclusion of the laity from the altar, we may now recognize a more complex environment, encompassing multiple modes of access to the sacrament with a multitude of attendant demands and rewards.[120]

THE SACRAMENT AND ITS RECEPTIONS

Thirteenth-century teaching about the Eucharist is often associated with a preoccupation with ontology, with the real presence and its transubstantive realization in the consecrated wafer and wine. Contemporary Eucharistic theology was, however, equally concerned with the semiological dimension of the sacrament, that is, with its exceptional status as an efficacious sign, a sign that effected what it signified. Scholastic accounts of Eucharistic substance and presence went hand in glove with sustained efforts to define the epistemological requirements of Eucharistic reception. Although late medieval distinctions of Eucharistic ontology do not map perfectly onto contemporary distinctions of modes of Eucharistic reception, these two lines of analyses, and the sacramental truths they treat, are best examined in tandem.

In broad strokes, scholastic theologians distinguished three principal elements in the sacrament of the altar: the *sacramentum,* the *res et sacramentum,* and the *res tantum.*[121] The term *sacramentum* typically referred to the species of bread and wine, in their capacity as visible signs. *Res et sacramentum* was understood to designate the true body and blood of Christ, substantially present after the consecration but also signified by the persistent visible appearance of the bread and wine. The res et sacramentum was thus both a substantial and spiritual entity, identified with the historical and ascended body of Christ in his Eucharistic mode of presence. The *res tantum* described the mystical union in which devotee and deity were conjoined by the sacrament, a union that encompassed not only the individual communicant but also the entire church of the faithful, transformed into the *corpus mysticum* (mystical body). The res tantum was thus both a referent of the sacrament and the spiritual state produced by worthy sacramental reception. Considered in itself, the Eucharist encompassed all three of these ontological states or elements.

In the thirteenth and fourteenth centuries theological consideration of how, precisely, the Eucharist was received resulted in an analytic decomposition of this complex ontological unity. Interest in the possible permutations of sacramental reception led to a tripartite distinction of the Eucharist's being in relation to the "quality" of the communicant. As Gary Macy has elucidated, thirteenth- and early fourteenth-century explorations of Eucharistic reception effectively shifted the terms of analysis from the metaphysical to the semiotic.[122] In this line of analysis, accounts of the mode of being of the Eucharist became analytically subordinated to a series of questions about the mode of understanding, the intention, and the epistemological capacity of the communicant.[123]

Thirteenth- and fourteenth-century theologians articulated a range of arguments about how the Eucharist was received; indeed, lively debate about sacramental reception animated theological investigation throughout the period. Without denying the very real and significant diversity of opinions in the period, we can, nonetheless, identify several recognized modes of Eucharistic reception. The principal modes of reception discussed by theologians corresponded roughly to the accepted tripartite account of the Eucharist's ontology (sacramentum, res et sacramentum, and res tantum).

The Eucharist could be received sacramentally (*sacramentaliter*), that is, as a sign of a sacred truth. This mode of reception involved the physical reception of the consecrated species and, it was generally agreed, required the recipient to be intellectually capable of understanding the bread and wine's status as signifiers as well as his or her willed intention to receive them not simply as bread and wine but as such sacred signs.

A second recognized mode of communication involved receiving the Eucharist spiritually (*spiritualiter*).[124] This account of Eucharistic reception argued that the res tantum—union with the deity, and incorporation in the corpus mysticum—was not necessarily tied to physical ingestion of the sacrament, but instead depended on the realization of faith in charity.[125] The epistemological and spiritual prerequisites for spiritual communion were considerable: sufficient understanding of the faith, acceptance of Christ's real presence in the sacrament, genuine penitence coupled with a desire to avoid further sin, and an inner devotion to Christ.[126]

In the 1220s Alexander of Hales described a third mode of reception, a form of communion that was, spiritually speaking, not a *communio* at all. Describing this taking of the Eucharist as "secundum quod est sacramentum solum" (according to how it is a sign only), Alexander described a physical ingestion of the consecrated wafer and wine without faith, that is, without an acceptance of the veridicality of the species' reference to an invisible, but present, divine truth.[127] According to Alexander this mode of reception realized a *unio speciei tantum*, a union with the outward forms of wafer and wine alone.[128] It granted no access to the true body of Christ, nor did it effect the res tantum of ecclesial and mystical incorporation. Associating this scenario explicitly with Jews and pagans, Alexander argued that although unbelievers were, by virtue of being human, capable of recognizing and understanding signs, they were still incapable of receiving the Eucharist "sacramentaliter" because they had no understanding (*cognitio*) of the sacred truth under the sacramental sign.[129]

Alexander of Hales's third form of reception foregrounds the important role that strictly epistemological considerations played in thirteenth- and fourteenth-century Eucharistic theology. Without the intellectual comprehension of the sacred referentiality of the Eucharist, without understanding and assenting to its status as the visible sign of an invisible sacred truth, the communicant was excluded from the economy of grace, union, and mystical incorporation.

And Alexander was not alone in insisting that valid and worthy Eucharistic reception required real epistemological effort. In the first half of the fourteenth century Nicholas of Lyra unequivocally restricted sacramental reception in relation to the recipient's understanding of the sacred truth of Christ's real presence in the Eucharist.[130] For Nicholas, epistemological competency was the sine qua non of true communication; on that basis he insisted that the mentally disturbed should be given the Eucharist only if they could demonstrate their recognition of the sacrament qua sacrament by an act or sign of devotion (*actus et signa devotionis*).[131] In this way, Nicholas required both the intellectual recognition of the sign and the devotee's ability to produce a countersign, an outward manifestation of the act of understanding.

The ideal mode of Eucharistic reception, late medieval theologians agreed, involved taking communion "sacramentaliter et spiritualiter." With a full knowledge of the faith and a belief in Christ's real presence in the sacrament, unimpeded by sin and possessed of an inner devotion to Christ, the communicant would receive the material sacrament *and* its spiritual benefits: incorporation in Christ, incorporation in *ecclesia*, and the sacrament's attendant benefits (often called its fruits).[132] When the Fourth Lateran Council made the reception of the Eucharist an annual obligation for the faithful, it bound communion to confession and so, by extension, to the communicant's capacity for epistemological participation in the sacrament. In this fashion, the Council's prescription may be read as requiring reception of the Eucharist sacramentaliter et spiritualiter, a mode of sacramental participation with serious epistemological stakes.

OCULAR COMMUNION, VISUAL RECEPTION

Despite pastoral requirements of annual (or thrice-annual) sacramental reception, and a general valorization of communion sacramentaliter et spiritualiter in the later Middle

Ages, spiritual communion—that is, a worthy reception of the Eucharist without physical ingestion of the consecrated species—continued to find favor among later medieval devotees. Initially established in the twelfth century by writings associated with the school of Laon, spiritual reception appears to have gained new currency (and new practitioners) over the course of the thirteenth century.[133] Although many late medieval discussions of spiritual communion do not identify a special role for vision in this nonmaterial mode of reception, contemporary evidence reveals that seeing became a preeminent and privileged vehicle for Eucharistic encounter, and one recognized by ecclesiastic authorities.

In the thirteenth century, statutes and liturgical treatises dictated that immediately after the celebrant consecrated the host he should raise it up, "ut a fidelibus circumstantibus valeat intueri" (so that it may be seen by all the attending faithful).[134] Although the earliest statute to mandate the elevation of the host is found in the synodal issued for Paris before 1208, like so much pastoral legislation in the period, the Parisian decree simply codified an already established practice.[135] In its contemporary effect, however, the Parisian decree intervened in an ongoing debate concerning the moment of consecration.[136] By institutionalizing the elevation of the host immediately following the priest's pronunciation of the phrase *hoc est corpus meum*, the synod implicitly affirmed the efficacy of the first consecration formula pronounced over the wafer. In this fashion—whether by design or simply in its effect—the Parisian decree on the elevation exerted some influence over a theological debate that would continue long after the promulgation of the synod's legislation.[137] Following the argument advanced by Edouard Dumoutet, historians have also discerned an effort to satisfy and control a deep-seated popular desire for the sight of the consecrated Eucharist in the Parisian synod's instructions.[138] In this view, the regularization of the elevation of the host guaranteed the faithful a vision of the consecrated wafer and simultaneously averted the danger of idolatry that might result from any adoration of the wafer in its preconsecrated state.[139]

In its intent, immediate effect, and considerable influence, the Paris synod's legislation is but one index of the thirteenth century's preoccupation with the host. In its insistence on making the host visible, not simply to the clergy at the altar but to all the faithful attending the ritual celebration, however, the Parisian synodal effectively encouraged a particular form of this Eucharistic fixation, a development with serious implications not simply for the sacrament but also for vision itself. Catalyzed by the privileged visibility of the host, late medieval doctrinal debate, devout desire, and devotional practice converged in a novel, theologically charged mode of vision: ocular communion.[140]

In the thirteenth and fourteenth centuries, ocular communion remained one among several acknowledged forms of spiritual communion. Requiring a vision of the consecrated host as a catalyst for spiritual communion, the practice of ocular communion actually restricted the conditions under which such sacramental encounter could take place.[141] Nonetheless, and in spite of the profound suspicion of vision that pervaded much theological, pastoral, and popular literature in the period, this visually determined mode of Eucharistic reception became widely accepted and practiced from the thirteenth century onward.[142]

Like all forms of spiritual communion, the efficacy of ocular communion depended upon the preparation and intention of its practitioner. Much recent scholarly attention to this form of Eucharistic reception has emphasized the visual and affective dimensions of ocular communion. Stressing the importance of forms of affective piety to the practice and experience of a visual reception of the consecrated host, interpreters have associated this form of sacramental reception with other late medieval forms of devotion to the wounded and suffering Christ and the affective responses they solicited from beholders. As Charles Caspers notes regarding the inclusion of Passion-centered images within church space, "These artistic expressions easily permit us to interpret the passion image as, in part, a visual support for the meditation on the passion which served as preparation for communion."[143]

In this analysis, the visual inventory of devotional images represented in the Mass tract's Christe eleyson miniature might be understood as an affective prompt, a tripartite visualization of Christ's incarnate biography designed to solicit an emotive mediation from the beholder (see fig. 40). As I have emphasized, however, the iconographic inventory that accompanies the Christe eleyson chant is also a visual précis of Christic elements of the pastoral syllabus, a visualization of required religious knowledge as much as a goad to pious feeling. As in other contemporary practices of spiritual communion, ocular communion required considerable epistemological preparation and labor; we have yet to fully explore how images contributed to that intellectual participation in the sacrament, to the thinking and knowing that were prerequisites for worthy reception through the eyes. In the Mass tract and the practice of Eucharistic reception it promotes, the devotee's epistemological capacity to look at the visible and to see sacred truth, to discern the ineffable in the material, is as much at stake as their affective preparation for Eucharistic reception. Within its unfolding account of the Mass, the tract consistently advocates a mode of knowing through seeing that is, simultaneously, a mode of seeing as knowing. To fully understand the epistemological burden and promise of the spiritual-visual practice valorized and prescribed by the Mass tract, we must briefly recontextualize its lessons in looking within their manuscript context.

An Epistemological Frame for Sacramental Seeing: The Mass in the Manuscript

Although the blow-by-blow account of Eucharistic ritual represented in the Mass tract's folios has captivated art-historical attention, it was, originally, but one component in a larger compendium designed to shape, guide, and promote the religious knowledge and practice of its owner. The manuscript's current fragmentary state precludes any definitive claims concerning the full array of texts and images it possessed when it was made in the 1320s, but what survives strongly suggests that intellectual formation and visual piety were thoroughly intertwined moral-spiritual practices for the volume's original owner.

The survival of four full-page paintings from the compendium, today kept in the Bodleian Library at Oxford, implies that the manuscript once possessed a prefatory cycle of Marian images, a form of visual preface more commonly associated with contemporary psalters and psalter-hours. Taking the form of an Annunciation, Nativity, Assumption of the Virgin, and Coronation of the Virgin, each vignette from Mary's life was painted on one surface of a single bifolium (see figs. 33–36). Presented in the same mode as the Christe eleyson miniature's terse summation of the *vita Christi,* these Marian illuminations offered the original book owner a more monumental series of iconic images. Unaccompanied by tituli or other inscriptions, and without any direct relation to the volume's extant texts, the full-page paintings of Mary invited a meditative gaze.

By contrast, the fragmentary text that once was bound with these Marian images begins with a lively Anglo-Norman narrative description of Adam and Eve's life after the Fall, of the account of their lives that their son Seth inscribed on tablets of stone and silver, and of Solomon's discovery and veneration of these tablets. Continuing, the text takes up the story of the true cross and the provenance of the thirty pieces of silver received by Judas, and terminates (incompletely) in an animated debate between Judas and his mother. Full of dialogue and narrative detail, even in its current fragmentary state the text offers an entertaining and edifying excursus into the biblical landscape, tracing the origins and afterlife of a series of legendary artifacts with recurrent roles in salvation history. An entertaining lesson in sacred history, the text also sketches a kind of soteriology elaborated via sacred objects, a material archeology of revelation and salvation extending from the first father and mother to the world of St. Helena's Constantinople and, by implication, to the relic-filled world of the later Middle Ages.

The compendium itself included one such artifact of divine intervention in the world: the Psalter of St. Jerome. An abridgement of the full psalter that was thought to have been dictated to Jerome by an angel and the Holy Spirit, the Psalter of St. Jerome provided devotees with a Latin florilegium of psalm verses, strung together for more convenient and efficient recitation. In the compendium, the inhabited initial V of the psalter's first phrase ("Verba mea auribus percipe domine"; Ps. 5:2) depicts the psalter's inspired origins: as the full-length figure of an angel dictates to Jerome, the Dove of the Holy Spirit whispers in the church father's ear. This authorizing account of the text's provenance is also rehearsed by a titulus at the top of the page: "Beatus ierominus hoc modo disposuit hoc psalterium ubi angelus domini docuit eum per spiritum sanctum" (Blessed Jerome arranged this psalter in this fashion when an angel of the Lord instructed him, through the Holy Spirit). Presented as a text with divine origins, the Psalter of St. Jerome subtly extends the artifactual soteriology of the fragmentary Anglo-Norman narrative into the religious regimen promoted by the compendium as whole.

Like the Mass tract, with which it is bound today, the Psalter of St. Jerome attests to the importance of Latin-language prayer and petition within the manuscript's program for lay spiritual excellence. Latin is also the language in which the devotee is invited to address God in the two prayers that currently terminate the Parisian part of the original book. What remains of the acephalous first prayer petitions God for protection from enemies and detractors, and requests the aid of the Paraclete and the extension of divine and angelic mercy. Complementing the Mass tract, the second prayer beseeches Christ as incarnate and judging deity to preserve the devotee's firm faith in the real presence at the hour of his or her death. As the prayer seeks to conserve correct Eucharistic belief it also, by implication, begs for the salvific epistemological and sacramental reception of the host that the Mass tract stages so persuasively.

The manuscript's insistence on the role of intellectual formation in the pursuit of salvation is most evident in the *Dialogue del piere e del fiz* and the *Mirour de seinte eglyse*—the two vernacular treatises that fill the bulk of the compendium's surviving folios—and in the pendant miniatures that preface each text (see figs. 51 and 52). The *Dialogue del piere e del fiz,* as its title suggests, takes the form of a familial question-and-answer session in which a generic son queries his father about a series of catechetical and theological topics, ranging from the nature, administration, and efficacy of the sacraments to the difference between creance and savoir, the existence of good and evil, the spiritual value of tribulation, humanity's possession of the imago dei, the value of worldly goods, and the extent of the devil's power over humanity. Surveying current moral-theological topics that exceed the confines of the catechetical syllabus, the *Dialogue* emphatically associates the mastery of religious knowledge with the possession and profession of correct belief.

The *Mirour de seinte eglyse,* by contrast, pursues religious knowledge within a program for meditative ascent. In this vernacular translation-adaptation of St. Edmund of Abingdon's *Speculum ecclesiae,* the reader is initiated into a more systematic program for spiritual excellence, focused primarily on fostering a meditative *cognois-*

sance (comprehension) of human limitation, of God as known through creation, of God as comprehended in scripture, and finally of God in himself. In a final section, the treatise offers a short guide to amicable and humble living that takes the reader from contemplative heights to the quotidian labor of Christian existence. Despite its anagogic emphases, the *Mirour* is concerned with the active practice of virtue, catechesis, and outward acts of piety. So, for example, the section of the treatise devoted to the contemplation of God in scripture reviews and expounds the pastoral syllabus; indeed, this *secund degré de contemplacion* is entirely concerned with the truths deemed necessary to salvation.[144]

Although the *Dialogue* and the *Mirour* offer distinct programs for spiritual formation—the one modeled after the pedagogy of the classroom, the other after the anagogical meditations of an aspiring contemplative—the paintings that preface each treatise are pendants. In the image set above the beginning of the *Dialogue* we witness a moment of lay religious instruction: a capped layman sits in an imposing chair and gestures didactically to the throng of youths who sit before him (fig. 51). One boy stands at the head of this group, taking up the role of the young interlocutor named in the treatise's title. The scene that introduces the *Mirour* describes an ecclesiastic reflection of this pedagogical vignette (fig. 52). At the top of a short flight of steps, an archbishop—certainly an evocation of the tract's sainted author, Edmund of Abingdon, archbishop of Canterbury—addresses an adult audience composed of tonsured clerics, hooded men, and women in wimples. Gesturing toward his auditors, the archbishop exemplifies reformist ideals of pastoral pedagogy. The men and women sitting before him are also exemplars of religious excellence, model listeners who attend to their pastor's every word and gesture their assent to his instruction.

From one miniature to the next, the viewer recognizes that religious instruction begins within the simple architectural setting inhabited by the lay teacher and his youthful students and continues beneath the cusped ecclesiastically coded arcade inhabited by St. Edmund and his flock. In both images, intellectual formation is promoted as a pastoral effort that defines Christian community and promotes spiritual excellence. In these images, as in the texts they preface, epistemological exertion is promoted as an essential preparation for the devotee desiring a fuller cognoissance of the deity and of religious truth. And in the small inhabited initials painted at the start of both the *Dialogue* and the *Mirour* the reader-viewer is offered a proleptic glimpse of the rewards earned by the diligent student of religious truth (figs. 53 and 54). Within the contours of each letterform, the lesson writ large in the miniature above is recapitulated, with a significant change: within each didactic initial, teacher and student are joined by the figure of the deity. Subtly, each juxtaposition of miniature and initial promotes a vision of

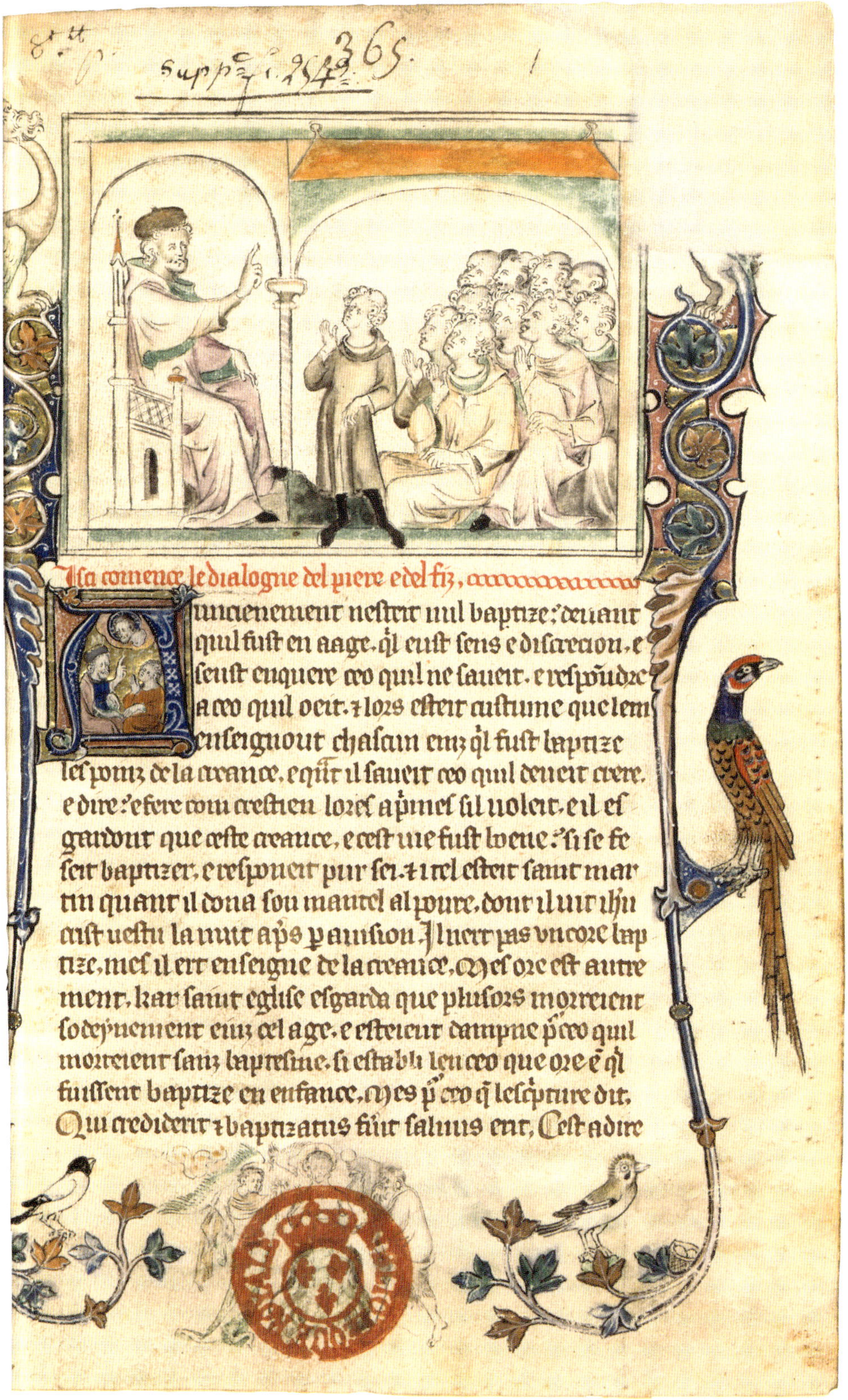

Fig. 51. Lay pedagogy in the Dialogue del piere e del fiz, *mid-1320s. Paris, BnF, MS fr. 13342, f. 1r.*

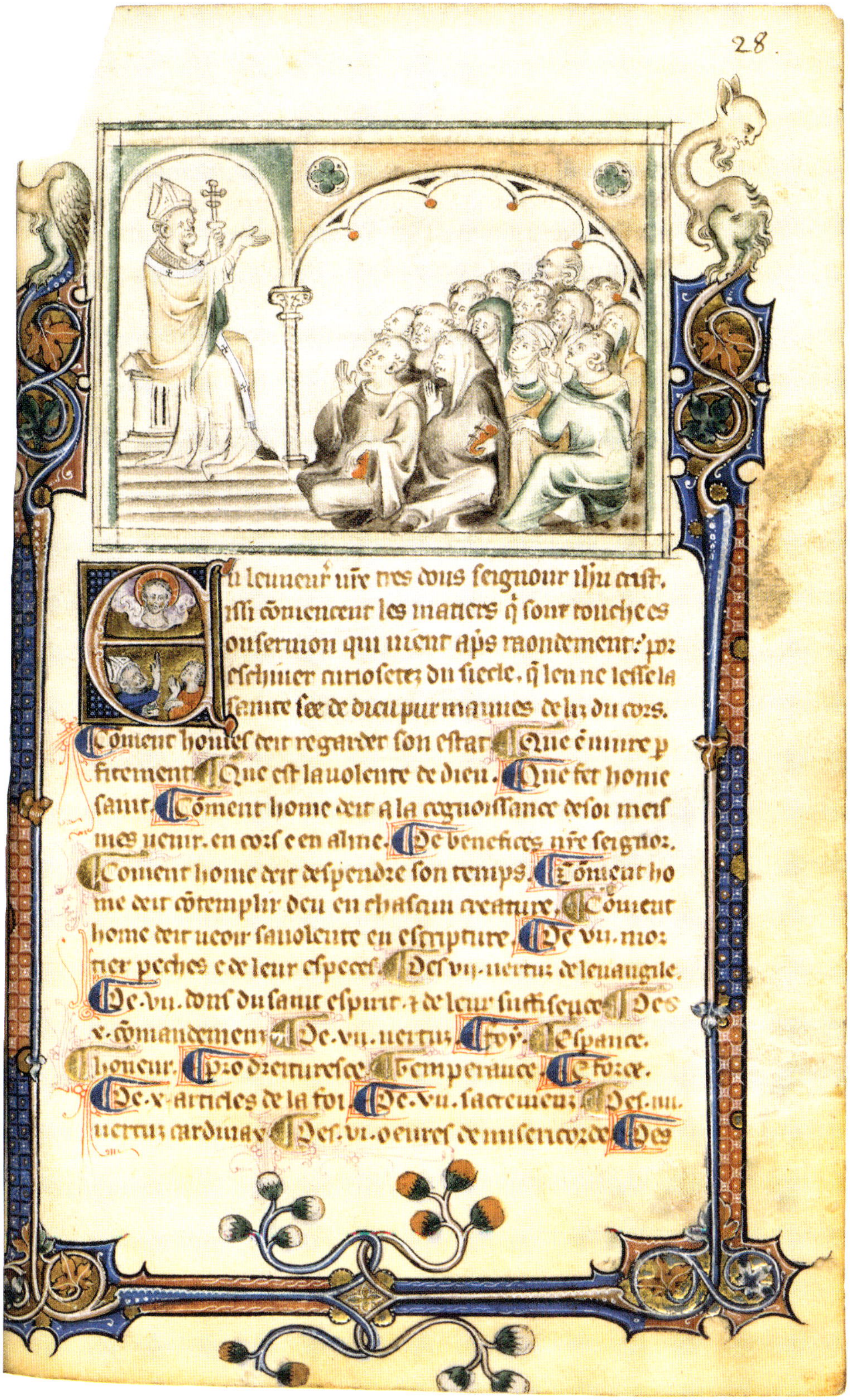

Fig. 52. The archbishop instructs his flock in the *Mirour de seinte eglyse*, mid-1320s. Paris, BnF, MS fr. 13342, f. 28r.

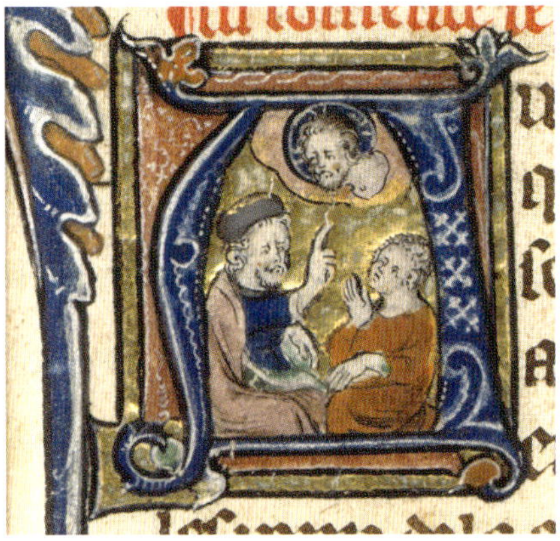

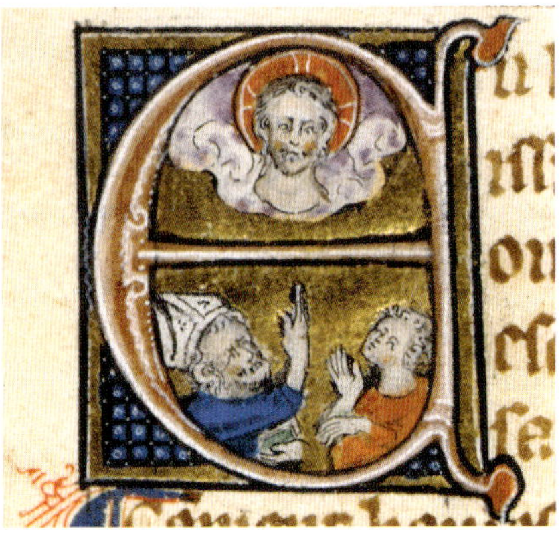

religious instruction not simply as a perfective process but even as a privileged colloquy with the Divine.

Considered together, as they would have been by the manuscript's original owner, the texts and images that today constitute—if fragmentarily—the Oxford-Paris compendium clearly once claimed that religious truth was well within the lay devotee's grasp. From the monumental representations of the Virgin that likely opened the volume to its narration of an artifactual account of salvation history and its valorization of a demanding curriculum of moral-theological formation, the compendium insisted that salvation could be pursued by reading, looking, thinking, and praying. Within the original volume's broader didactic and devotional project, vision emerges as a particularly privileged mode of epistemological and devotional ascent. Although the miniatures introducing the *Dialogue* and the *Mirour* represent religious instruction as an oral and auditory exchange, the compendium was itself an artifact designed to instruct the eye, first and foremost. It is the surface of the manuscript page that serves as the site of didactic formation and visual revelation, and as the textual and visual point of departure for the pious recitals prescribed by several of the compendium's texts.

Fig. 53. The deity attends a lesson in the Dialogue del piere e del fiz, *mid-1320s. Paris, BnF, MS fr. 13342, f. 1r (detail).*

Fig. 54. The deity—didactic topic and divine tutor in the Mirour de seinte eglyse, *mid-1320s. Paris, BnF, MS fr. 13342, f. 28r (detail).*

In the Mass tract, the compendium's emphasis on the epistemological and devotional efficacy of vision is refocused and reorganized around an exceptional sacramental object and its ritual framework. Authorized by the presence of the Divine in the Mass, the vision solicited, coached, and even required by the Mass tract is a mode of seeing religious truth, a mode of perception and reception in which epistemological and devotional labor are radically blurred and rewarded. A final, ideal term in the Mass tract's lyrical exposition of how human vision could become a truly sacramental vision, the perception of the Divine in the visible is visually translated as a quasi-beatific apperception of the Trinity in the midst of the Mass. This trinitarian revelation is both the sacrament's transcendent referent and sacramental vision's ideal object; it is also the epiphanic terminus toward which all of the compendium's texts and images urge the reader-viewer.

Conclusion: Looking at the Page, Seeing Eucharistic Truth

The Mass provides a framework—perhaps the only possible framework—for the compendium's staging of the idealized limits of vision. Although the Mass tract fulfills its ostensible purpose, providing the layperson with a series of meditations and actions to be performed within the context of the Eucharistic rite, its didactic project extends far beyond the outward decorum of dominical obligation.

The Queen Mary Psalter Master's paintings translate the spectacle of ritual—and a visual encounter with the sacrament within the liturgy—into a pictorial cycle that subtly, but assertively, blurs the boundaries between orders of representation, signification, and presence. Employing visual means to describe the visible and invisible being and power of the Eucharist, the illuminator collapses distinctions between the spiritual and the seeable within the pictorial field, and thus attempts to visually initiate the reader-viewer into a way of looking that discerns the *verum corpus* (true body) in the visible species upon the altar. In this way, the Mass tract's miniatures are best understood as describing and prescribing a sacramentalization of the reader-viewer's vision.

Within the structure, rhetoric, and argumentative logic of the Mass tract, the artist's representation of sacramental ritual claims the status of a paradoxically veridical simulacrum: a simulacrum that does not deceive, but rather, through its reflective agency, transmits the originary signified through a series of visual relays until it arrives in the eye of the manuscript's viewer.[145] Undergirding this economy of visual transmission is nothing less than a conviction in the real power of sacralized vision to find the visionary and the beatific in the visual and, reciprocally, a promotion of the human-made image as kind of *imitatio sacramenti,* a "third-order" sacramentum that may participate (if only by extension) in a semiosis authorized with reference to the Eucharist's exceptionality.

The miniatures in the Mass tract are, in the end, beautiful fictions. Executed in the refined idiom of the Queen Mary Psalter Master's celebrated style, these paintings put aesthetic excellence in the service of an ambitious theological argument. I would suggest that the artistic excellence of the manuscript's paintings is essential to the Mass tract's theological argument. As it attempts to represent a Eucharist that was, at once, visually and materially mundane (in its visible appearance as wafer and wine) and the sum of perfection (in theological and devotional terms), the Mass tract's pictorial cycle must proclaim its own excellence and disguise its artifice in one stroke. Blurring the boundary between the sacramental mode of vision it promotes and the reader-viewer's vision of the manuscript page, the Queen Mary Psalter Master's work translates the sacrament not simply as an object of vision but also as the catalyst and authority for an ambitious mode of seeing and showing religious truth.[146]

In a penetrating critique of established art-historical interpretations of the late medieval iconographic type generally identified as the "The Mass of Saint Gregory," Caroline Walker Bynum disputes any facile identification of the iconography as a "depiction" of transubstantiation:

> Because eucharistic presence was understood as involving substance, not accidents (regardless of how exactly the term "substance" was understood), transubstantiation as a technical notion was not depictable; however change was understood, what changed was what was *not* seen. Hence, if the presence evoked by the Gregorymass is theologically or devotionally correct, it must be a presence beyond; Gregory's vision, which the viewer sees, must itself be only a visual prod to encounter with an unseen.[147]

Bynum's rigorous and stimulating rereading of the Gregorymass is entirely persuasive, yet her assertion that a transubstantiated Eucharistic presence was fundamentally "not depictable" warrants closer scrutiny. The evidence of the Mass tract suggests that in the first half of the fourteenth century, the Queen Mary Psalter Master was not stymied by the disjunction between Eucharistic substance and accidents when he contributed paintings to this compendium. By contrast, the ambitious sequence of images he painted reveals that it was precisely the invisible and unseen substance of the Mass that captured his artistic attention and provoked a representational tour de force. The Mass tract does not refute Bynum's thesis so much as it asks us to reconsider what form the representation of Eucharistic presence—in all its transubstantive paradox—*could take* in the later Middle Ages.

To understand the full charge of the Mass tract's visual discourse, we must recognize that it does not localize Eucharistic presence in the consecrated wafer alone; rather, it proposes a paradigm of Eucharistic encounter that is fundamentally processual. The deity's presence in the Mass is an extended affair, centered on the elevation of the host but not limited to that moment. The host, in this account, is certainly a transformative object: it marks the culmination of the sacramental narrative and it effectively defines the Mass, from the layperson's perspective, as a ritual framework for visual encounter with the Divine. Within the argumentative arc of the Mass tract's texts and images, however, Eucharistic presence is never definitively reified in the host. The divine presence desired by the laity and encountered in the Eucharist persists beyond the elevation, finally assuming the form of a Eucharistically inflected Trinity that occupies the space between the faithful and the altar.

The appearance of the Trinity in the tract's penultimate miniature is the crowning statement of its representational response to the challenge of making a religious mysterium visible. In this image divine presence is realized in the space between devout viewers and the ritual focal point for their vision, the altar. The Queen Mary Psalter Master responds to the challenge of representing a Eucharistic presence defined by the disjunction between the visible and the ineffable through a series of images that relocate that presence in the very process of looking itself.

This guide to the Mass in texts and images does not promote the consecrated host as a transparent object through which Christ is visibly encountered. Instead, it invites its audience to learn to look at (and hear) the ordinary, extrinsic "accidents" of ritual—be it the singing of the Sanctus, the elevation of the host, or the priest's rinsing of the chalice—and to understand that process of looking as an experience of Eucharistic truth.

No less than scholastic *distinctiones* of Eucharistic substance and accidents, the Mass tract's miniatures confront the fundamental challenge of the sacrament: its conjunction of the imperceptible and the visible, its fusion of the Divine and the material, its dialectic of superabundant presence and apparent absence. But whereas late medieval theologians insisted on the opacity of the consecrated host—its occlusion of the divine presence under its visible species—the Mass tract's visual program invites its viewers to reform and reorient their way of seeing, to learn a new way of looking, so that the act of looking itself becomes a form of sacramental apprehension and participation. The Queen Mary Psalter Master's paintings propose that it is possible to look at the accidents of the Mass and see, in their midst, the truth of Eucharistic presence.

Bynum is certainly correct in asserting that "images never illustrate theology . . . first and foremost because images (even highly didactic images) never merely illustrate."[148] The Queen Mary Psalter Master's images are not illustrations of an extrinsic theology, nor are they simply illustrations of ritual practice. They are instead an ambitious visual discourse that involves the viewer in a dialogic consideration of how to look at the sacrament sacramentally. The artifice of these representations, their character as visual fictions—formally emphasized by the illuminator's characteristic wash technique, his refusal of any elaborate delineation of architectural setting, and his embrace of the reserved parchment ground—are essential to the tract's larger rhetorical and didactic goal. These miniatures proclaim, rather than elide, their status as representations; it is their very image-ness that allows them to model a mode of vision that can encompass seeing visible accidents and seeing God.

Rather than attempting to efface the visible disjunction between the consecrated wafer and the divine presence *sub speciebus,* the Queen Mary Psalter Master instead exploits visual representation's ability to concatenate referents within a single frame. His paintings confront—even exult—in the coexistence of the visible and the invisible within the ritual progress of the Mass. As visual fictions they are not bound by the constraints of phenomenal vision or apparent reality, and it is precisely their status as images that allows them to visibly translate Eucharistic truth in all its apparent paradoxicality.

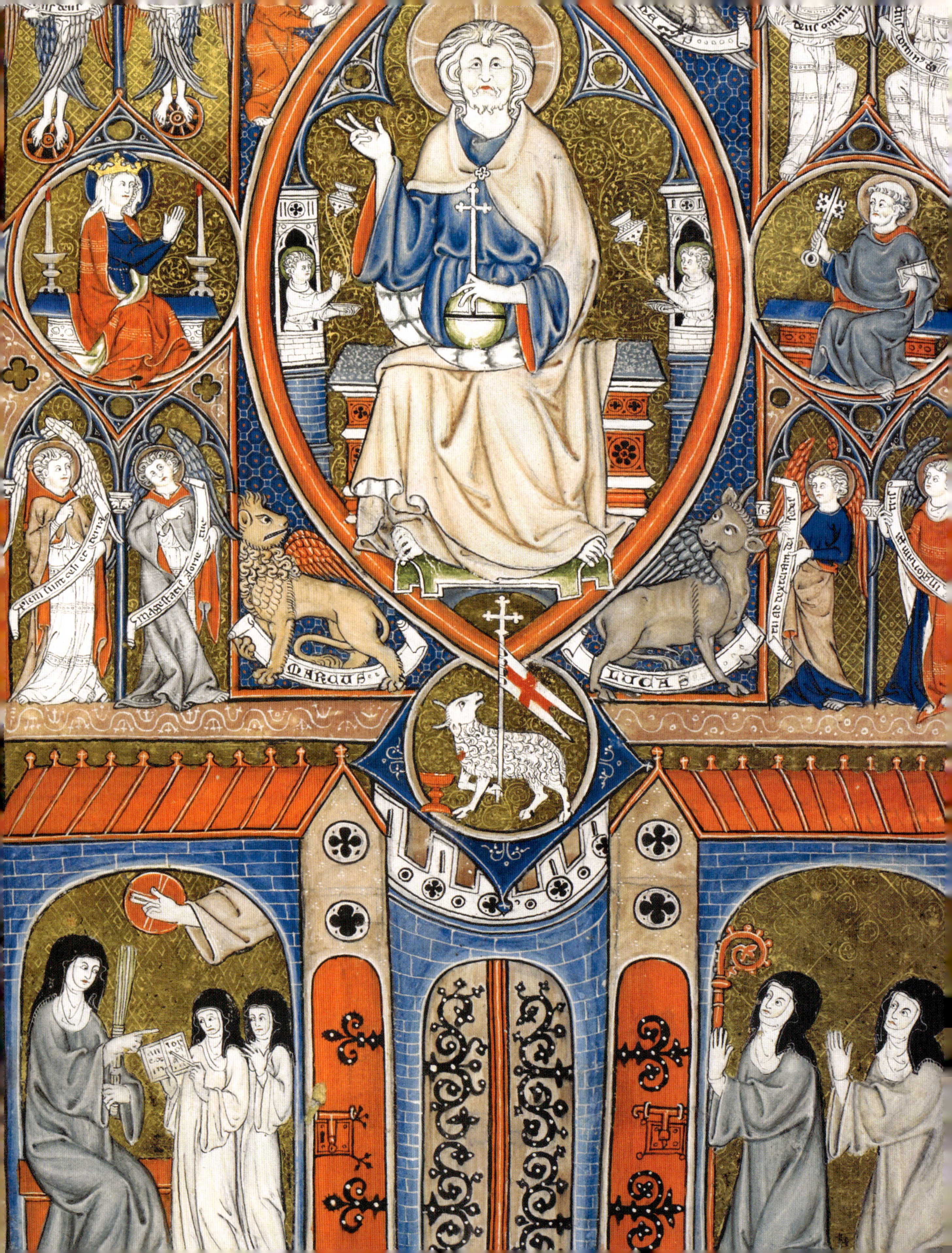
MARCUS
LUCAS

CHAPTER FOUR

Translating the Cloister

Les cloîtres anciens sur leurs grandes murailles
Étalaient en tableaux la sainte Vérité
Dont l'effet, réchauffant les pieuses entrailles,
Tempérait la froideur de leur austérité.

En ces temps où du Christ florissaient les semailles,
Plus d'un illustre moine, aujourd'hui peu cité,
Prenant pour atelier le champ des funérailles,
Glorifiait la Mort avec simplicité.

—Mon âme est un tombeau que, mauvais cénobite,
Depuis l'éternité je parcours et j'habite;
Rien n'embellit les murs de ce cloître odieux.

Ô moine fainéant! quand saurai-je donc faire
Du spectacle vivant de ma triste misère
Le travail de mes mains et l'amour de mes yeux?
—Charles Baudelaire, "Le mauvais moine"

Comparing his soul to a hateful cloister, Charles Baudelaire put a coda to a venerable theme. Within *Les fleurs du mal, le mauvais moine* is but one of a series of personae adopted by the poet as he constructs a poetic edifice capable of containing "deux postulations simultanées, l'une vers Dieu, l'autre vers Satan" (two simultaneous postulations, one toward God, the other toward Satan).[1] As Baudelaire rings the changes on the trope of the cloister-as-prison, his poem retains a certain fantasy of cloisters past as paradisiacal places in which truth acquired visible form.[2] This cloister fantasy is no baudelairian invention. Its contrapuntal presence in the poet's lament

Detail from Fig. 73

echoes, if distantly, a twelfth-, thirteenth-, and fourteenth-century claustral ideal, an ideal realized then, as in the nineteenth century, not only in stone and timber but also in the fabric of metaphor, fantasy, devotion, and—no less—images.

In a miniature painted in the last decade of the thirteenth century the claustral ideal takes vivid form (see fig. 73 and page 160). In the lower register, the figures of nuns and novices perform a tableau vivant of monastic discipline and devotion behind the closed doors of their convent. The female community's paradigmatic performance is rewarded with a theophany that fills the tracery space above them. Attended by the heavenly court, Christ, enthroned in majesty, presides over the enclosed community below him. In no uncertain terms, the illumination proclaims the excellence and authority of the claustral model. For whom was it painted? Where can this exemplary abbey be found?

The Old French treatise introduced by this image answers these questions in its first sentence: "La sainte abbaïe et la religion doit estre fondee esperituelment en la conscience" (The holy abbey and religion must be spiritually founded in the conscience).[3] The *Sainte abbaïe* treatise describes the fabrication of a claustral space in the conscience, made by the virtues and inhabited by them, subject to attack by vice and rescued by grace. The allegorical construction prescribed by the text is, in its own terms, a campaign of interior edification: the architecture of the devout soul is constructed by the exercise of virtue, the rigors of penitential purgation, and the elevating labor of devotion.

The *Sainte abbaïe* treatise and its prefatory painting are just two components from a larger work, a manuscript that contained five texts and a suite of full-page miniatures. Collectively, the book's texts and images delineate a program for spiritual improvement that takes the space of the cloister as a paradigm for the reformed interiority of the reader-viewer. In this chapter I explore how this exemplary manuscript translates the soul as a series of architectural allusions, refashioning the self as an architectonic space perfected by moral scrutiny and sanctified by sacramental participation. Significantly, this translation is undertaken on behalf of a lay reader-viewer for whom the cloister remained a spiritual ideal rather than a quotidian reality.

Christian notions of the moral-spiritual self as a sanctified structure have their foundations in biblical texts.[4] This scriptural legacy was mined, reworked, and elaborated throughout the Middle Ages in texts made for the dedication of material churches, in liturgical commentary on church architecture, and in a series of cloister allegories that appeared on the scene in the twelfth century.[5] When canonical and monastic authors wrote cloister allegories they undertook an exegesis of the architecture in which they lived, worked, studied, and prayed. As Nicole Rice has argued, texts and images that make the cloister allegorically or metaphorically available as a model for the interiority of uncloistered readers and viewers effect an even more audacious appropriation.[6]

The transformation of an invisible claustral ideal into a visible object for the physiological and spiritual vision of unenclosed viewers goes even further: it makes metaphor visible and asserts the theological and spiritual efficacy of visual representation.

As the claustral ideal moved from the restricted linguistic ambient of Latin to the wider—although hardly popular—audiences for vernacular texts, it was fundamentally unmoored from its quotidian referents; it became a metaphor, a simulation, an invisible, interiorized spiritual state. It became an imagined template for the soul, a standard of spiritual perfection to be achieved inwardly by unenclosed women and men. The transformation of the claustral model—from built architecture and architectural exegesis to a textual and visual exemplar for the perfected moral-spiritual self—attests to an important shift in spiritual self-fashioning that blurred the boundary between spiritual "professionals" and spiritual "amateurs" in the last centuries of the Middle Ages. In the case of the manuscript to be considered in this chapter, it also speaks to the appropriative spiritual ambitions of late medieval lay elites, to their aspiration to modes of spiritual excellence and authority associated with the monastic cloister.

The later Middle Ages were preoccupied with distinguishing *species* from *substantia,* outward appearance from the invisible substance of reality.[7] This concern is most fully articulated, and theorized, in theological debate and deliberation about the relationship between accidents and substance in the consecration of the Eucharist. It is, however, also implicated in contemporary attempts to affirm and control social distinction, frequently inseparable from spiritual distinction. Responding to the perception that appearances might be deceiving, the sumptuary legislation of the French monarchy attempted to police coded social display.[8] Likewise, the codes of dress prescribed for members of religious orders were an important means by which the spiritual and legal prerogatives that attached to religious profession were asserted visually.[9] When late medieval monarchs and ecclesiastics sought to codify these visible indices of identity, affiliation, and status, they were attempting to intervene not only in the visual coding of social station and authority but also in a moral-spiritual landscape where outward appearances were no longer reliable indices of the *homo interior.*

Deluxe literature of spiritual formation offered lay elites a compelling means of reconciling the inner and outer Christian, of asserting claims to worldly *and* spiritual excellence. The *Sainte abbaïe* cloister allegory, and the texts and paintings with which it was once bound, makes such a promise to its reader-viewer, promoting an ambitious program of interior edification. In its texts and images, the original reader-viewer encountered an extended mobilization of architectural metaphors for the spiritual self, chief among them the privileged paradigm of the cloister. What did it mean to make a cloister of one's soul in the last decade of the thirteenth century? What role could images play in this architectural translation of the self? These questions invite us to enter the *Sainte abbaïe* and the images that accompany it.

Court and Cloister

Today the *Sainte abbaïe* treatise is the first of four texts of spiritual instruction, each prefaced by a full-page illumination, bound together in a volume preserved at the British Library (London, BL, Yates Thompson MS 11; henceforth YT 11).[10] The allegorical abbey and the image that introduces it did not, however, enjoy pride of place in their original manuscript setting. The thirteenth-century volume for which they were executed instead opened with a regal compilation of text and image: the *Somme le roi*.[11] Fortuitously, the *Somme* that once formed the first part of the *Sainte abbaïe* manuscript is also preserved in the British Library (London, BL, Add. MS 28162; henceforth Add. 28162).[12]

A bespoke Old French summa of moral and theological instruction, the *Somme le roi* was compiled in 1279 for the Capetian king Philippe III by his Dominican confessor, Laurent d'Orléans (c. 1220/1228–c. 1300).[13] The compendium quickly became a high-prestige and highly influential "best seller" of medieval didactic literature.[14] No illustrated copies of the text survive from Philippe III's reign (1270–1285).[15] It was during the reign of his son, Philippe IV (1285–1314),[16] that a program of fifteen images was added to the text, initiating a long tradition of luxuriously illuminated exemplars.[17]

The four earliest illuminated *Somme le roi* manuscripts all date from the last decade of the thirteenth century.[18] In each book we find the same compilation of text and image, an indication that the visual program devised for the treatise in the 1290s was transmitted with a great degree of consistency.[19] Richard and Mary Rouse have argued convincingly that the provision of images for this regal compilation was itself a royal project, originating at the Capetian court in Paris and disseminated outward through gifts and patronal emulation.[20]

Dated stylistically to the mid-1290s, the *Somme le roi–Sainte abbaïe* manuscript was almost certainly produced within a year or two of the creation of the *Somme*'s program of images.[21] Two of the four earliest illustrated *Somme le roi* manuscripts have been associated with royal owners.[22] Belonging to this first phase in the production of illustrated *Somme le roi* manuscripts, the *Somme le roi–Sainte abbaïe* volume provided its reader with a luxuriously illuminated version of the text at a time when perhaps only Philippe IV and his queen, Jeanne de Navarre, possessed such a copy.

Unlike its contemporaries, however, the *Somme le roi–Sainte abbaïe* was provided with three additional full-page paintings.[23] The visual extravagance of the manuscript, and its inclusion of an illuminated *Somme le roi* at this very early date, indicate that the book owner's desire for salvation was entwined with this-worldly concerns; the manuscript documents an awareness of, and access to, the latest thing in regal patronage. The three additional full-page illuminations that prefaced other tracts in the manuscript made it the most copiously illuminated *Somme le roi* volume of its day. The *Somme le roi–Sainte abbaïe* manuscript was a book that even a king might envy.

In the manuscript's original state, the *Somme le roi*'s lessons in moral theology were followed by the theological allegory of the *Sainte abbaïe* treatise, a progress that took the reader-viewer from the regal architecture of the king's vernacular summa to the interior cloister of the spiritually adept soul.[24] The *Sainte abbaïe* treatise and its prefatory image of conventual theophany would have reoriented the manuscript's original reader-viewer, preparing him or her for the instruction in spiritual purification, sacramental theology, and mystical union offered by the manuscript's three remaining treatises.[25]

The tract placed after the *Sainte abbaïe* treatise takes the form of an exegetical letter.[26] Ostensibly concerned with defining four manners of love, the text quickly turns to an effusive discussion of *leal amour,* or "perfect charity." Relating the three-day journey described in Exodus 8:27 to Paul's rapture through the three heavens and the six wings of the seraphim, the treatise delineates a tripartite itinerary of spiritual perfection that includes an exposition of the sacraments of baptism, penance, and the Eucharist.

The treatise that follows discusses the three states of good souls: penitence, devotion, and contemplation.[27] The text identifies each state with one of "the three feasts that Holy Church celebrates on the day of the Epiphany": the Adoration of the Magi, Christ's Baptism in the River Jordan, and the Wedding at Cana.[28] Describing an itinerary of spiritual perfection, the tract stresses internal discernment and an active engagement in the exterior works of charity and devotion.

The manuscript's final treatise proclaims the utility of tribulation, properly endured.[29] Detailing the twelve benefits conferred by tribulation, the text outlines a theological justification of suffering. Throughout the text, the reader is exhorted to consider the operations of divine love, the necessity of purgation, and the eternal rewards that await the perfected soul.

The tracts that were once appended to the London *Somme le roi* radically extend the *Somme*'s program of spiritual formation. Exploring the rigors of ascesis and purgation, discussing the mysterium of the sacraments, and initiating the reader-viewer into the mystagogy of contemplative union, the four treatises that now form YT 11 provide an ambitious curriculum for spiritual perfection.

Until the second half of the nineteenth century, the *Somme le roi* and *Sainte abbaïe* volumes formed a single codex.[30] When this original manuscript was divided, it was almost certainly with the market in mind. The volume must have represented a terrible temptation to its owner. The manuscript's miniatures are painted on one side only of single leaves; each of these painted singletons was bound facing a discrete textual subunit in the originary volume. This codicological structure made it possible to divide the manuscript cleanly at the end of any of its tracts without a loss of text or image: the collation of the manuscript was ideally suited to fragmentation.[31]

Like many witnesses to the text, the London *Somme le roi* preserves a closing formula in the last folio of the treatise: "Cest livre compila et parfist uns freres de l'ordre des preescheors a la requeste dou Roi de france phelippe en L'an de L'incarnacion ihesu crist. Mil deus cenz et soissante et Neuf [*sic*] Deo Gracias" (A brother of the order of preachers compiled and completed this book at the request of King Philippe of France in the year of the Incarnation of Jesus Christ One thousand two hundred and sixty-nine [*sic*]).[32] The final lines of the *Somme le roi* proclaim the text's regal pedigree and mark the closure of the compilation as a self-contained textual unit. This closing formula defined an ideal point at which the manuscript might be divided by its nineteenth-century owner. Written to fill 145 folios, the *Somme le roi* section of the original book could be neatly severed from the rest of the volume in order to produce two manuscripts for the market from a single original.

The nineteenth-century fragmentation of the *Somme le roi–Sainte abbaïe* manuscript did not simply rupture the integrity of the thirteenth-century volume. It also effected a conceptual split within the object that continues to influence the manuscript's reception, even to the present day. The separation of the *Somme le roi* from the other textual and visual components of its original manuscript context effectively severed "court" from "cloister." Twentieth-century interpretations of Add. 28162 and YT 11 have, in turn, replicated this segregation of the regal from the monastic.

Discussions of the two volumes that once formed the *Somme le roi–Sainte abbaïe* manuscript have not attempted to interpret either manuscript in relation to its pendant part. Focusing instead on either the *Somme le roi* or the images bound in the *Sainte abbaïe* volume, art-historical interpretations have effectively disregarded the fact that they once formed a single manuscript. Add. 28162 has been addressed as an important early witness to the illustrated *Somme le roi* tradition, and its visual program has been employed as a stylistic point of reference in discussions of thirteenth- and fourteenth-century northern French illumination, with particular reference to the Renaud de Bar manuscripts and the artistic character of Lorraine manuscript painting.[33] Assimilated into the stemmatics of stylistic interpretation and adduced as an important witness to royal patronage of text and image, the London *Somme le roi* has been ranged under the rubric of the court, and the theological import of its texts and images has been rendered largely invisible.

The images in the *Sainte abbaïe* volume have been the object of greater scholarly attention. The general consensus, first articulated by M. R. James in 1898, sees its first three images as illustrations of text.[34] Thus, the manuscript's first miniature has been discussed as a visualization of the *Sainte abbaïe* cloister allegory (see fig. 73), and the figures of nuns who populate the second of the *Sainte abbaïe* volume's miniatures have been interpreted as a further representation of this female community (see fig. 79). The volume's third miniature, representing the quadripartite spiritual progress of a female penitent, has also been understood as an illustration of the text that it prefaces, the *Three States of Good Souls* treatise (see fig. 80).

Divorced from the *Somme le roi* component of the originary manuscript, the *Sainte abbaïe* volume's illuminations have frequently been evoked as paradigmatic expressions of conventual self-fashioning. Its first three miniatures have even become touchstones of a kind for art-historical discussions of female piety and the visual environment of late medieval convent life.[35] Richard and Mary Rouse's discovery of the *Somme le roi–Sainte abbaïe* manuscript in a 1463 inventory from the Cistercian convent of Maubuisson (Notre-Dame-la-Royale), founded by Blanche of Castile in 1241, seemed, once and for all, to confirm the interpretive consensus that the manuscript must have been made for a female religious.[36] Nevertheless, I would suggest that the appearance of the manuscript in a convent inventory almost two hundred years after it was produced is evidence only that the book *came* to be part of the visual environment of the Maubuisson community, not that it was destined for cloistered eyes from the beginning. Despite a scholarly desire to see a *speculum claustri* in the *Sainte abbaïe* volume, its images confound rather than confirm a desire to read audience from representation. In the miniature accompanying the *Sainte abbaïe* treatise, we find no attempt to identify any of the female figures by name or heraldic device. The anonymity of these nuns distinguishes them from their sisters in equally luxurious manuscripts produced for or by convent communities. Indeed, the convent community represented within the *Somme le roi–Sainte abbaïe* manuscript, like the manuscript as whole, is conspicuously unencumbered by any identificatory references, individual or corporate. The book in which these nuns are represented has no relationship to liturgical performance. The folios of the *Somme le roi–Sainte abbaïe* manuscript do not transmit a rule, calendar, or litany, nor is any other indication of local use, community, or conventual *memoria* preserved in the manuscript. Instead, the fictive nuns inhabit a compendium of prose treatises dominated by a vernacular summa devised for a male monarch. Indeed, the audience anticipated by the *Somme le roi* is explicitly identified as a lay audience.[37]

The impulse to read a cloistered audience from the *Somme le roi–Sainte abbaïe* manuscript's representations of claustral devotion is understandable, but it overlooks both the allegorical character of the *Sainte abbaïe* treatise and the appropriative character of its prefatory image. The *Somme le roi–Sainte abbaïe* manuscript is a major

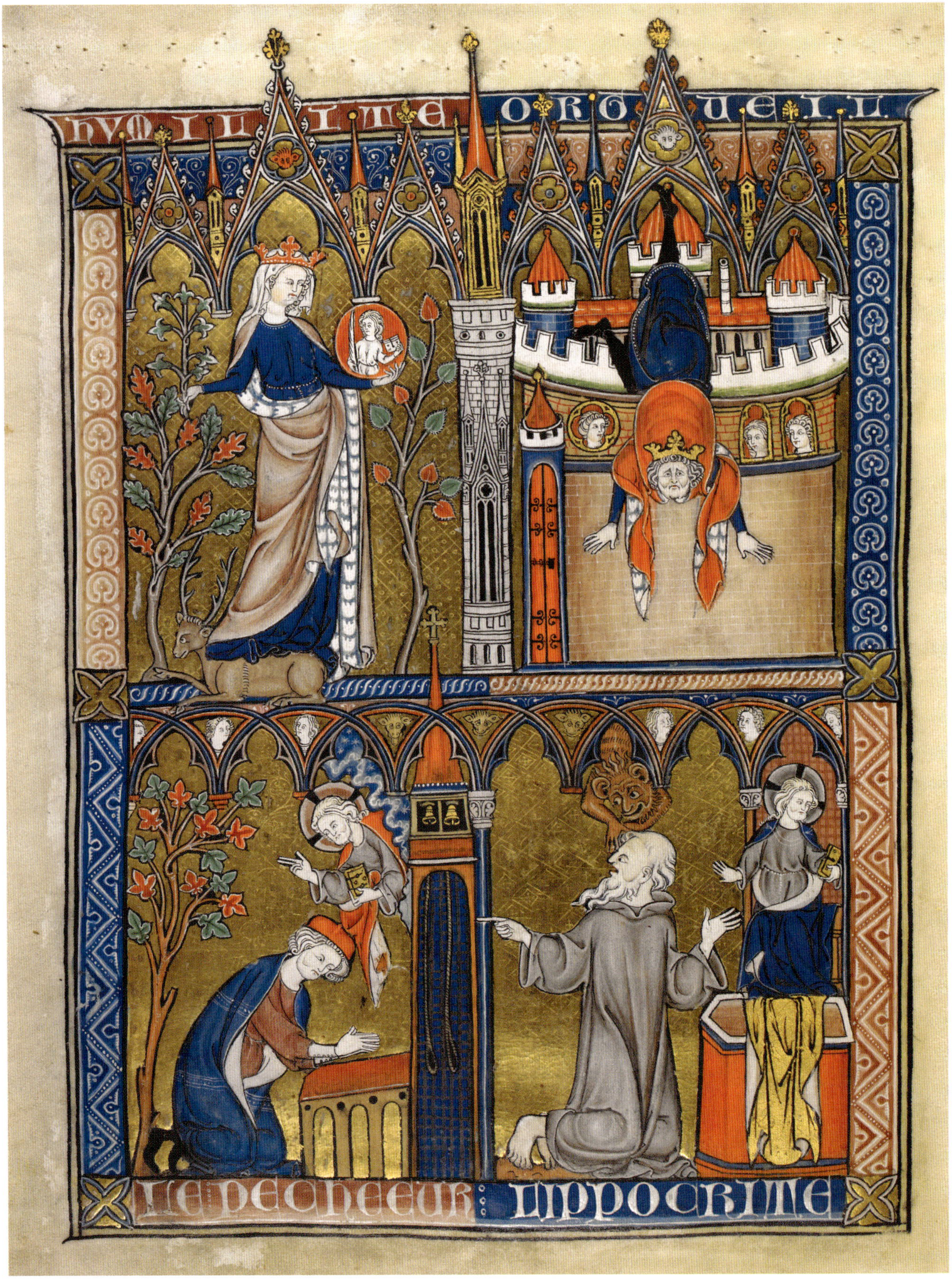

HUMILITE
ORGUEILL
LE PECHEEUR
LIPPOCRITE

monument of illuminated didactic literature, constructed in part with the material of antecedent traditions of spiritual formation, but fashioned in a new style for a new community in a changing moral-spiritual landscape. Without a contemporary ex libris, inventory record, or other external documentation of the manuscript, we cannot be certain for whom the *Somme le roi–Sainte abbaïe* manuscript was made. Close consideration of its texts and images, however, can tell us much about the religious knowledge and spiritual ambitions that were solicited and rewarded by the volume's texts and images.

OPPOSITE: *Fig. 55. Humility looks on as Pride takes a fall in the* Somme le roi, *c. 1294. London, BL, Add. MS 28162, f. 5v: 248 x 184 mm.*

The Gift Virtue Miniatures: Objects for the Moral Eye

In the miniatures devised for each of the *Somme le roi*'s seven chapters on the Gift Virtues, pictorial space is assimilated to the moral space of the conscience, a space inhabited by interrelated representations of virtue and vice. In this way painting outwardly pictures the penitential drama of sin and its remedies, making moral conflict visible on the page and soliciting a tropological gaze. In each of the miniatures, architectural framing devices organize the pictorial space into four compartments. The first of the four quadrants (in the upper left of each image) is inhabited by the personification of the virtue treated in the tract that follows. Each virtue is a crowned woman, holding an emblematic disc and standing upon a defeated beast. A titulus inscribed in the upper segment of the frame leaves no doubt as to the identity of these personifications.

Fig. 56. Varieties of amity and the ill effects of hatred in the Somme le roi, *c. 1294. London, BL, Add. MS 28162, f. 6v.*

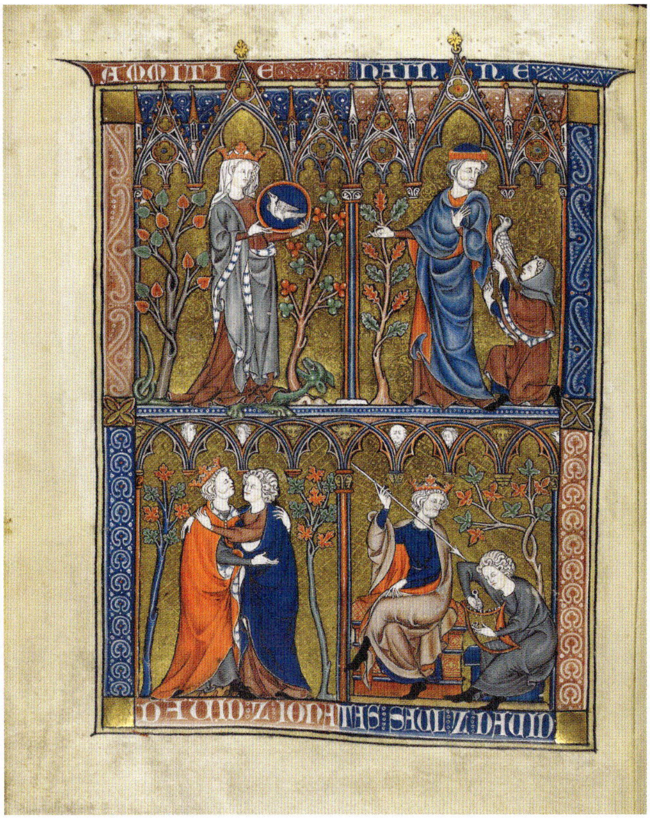

Vice is displayed in flagrante in the upper right compartment of each miniature. In the image prefacing the tract on Humility, Pride takes a fall in the form of the Old Testament King Ochozias (4 Kings 1; fig. 55). Avarice's exemplar, a miser, transfers coins from a strong box with demonic encouragement (see fig. 59). The vignette designed for *Hainne* (Hatred) is less readily understood (fig. 56).[38] Gesturing toward the personification of *Amistié* (Amity), an elegant man in contemporary dress looks over his shoulder at a kneeling servant who offers him a hawk. The figure of Hainne, like that of the avaricious miser, cannot be identified with any scriptural

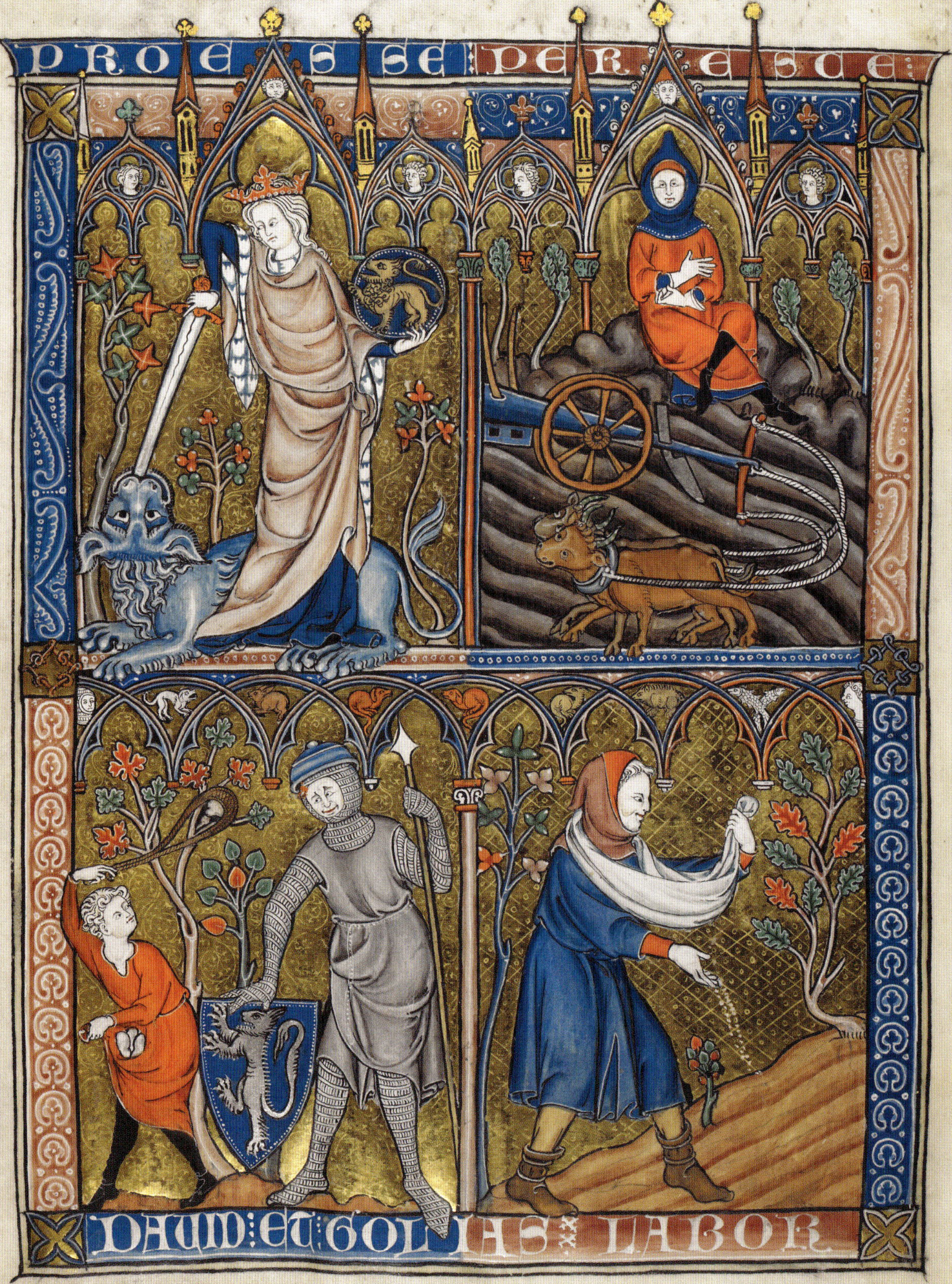
PROESSE
PERESCE
DAVID ET GOLIAS
LABOR

source. Instead both figures visibly show what they are, not through the lexicon of attributes or emblems, but rather through the vivid demonstration of figural representation.

The lower quadrants of each Gift Virtue miniature are given over to visual exempla of virtue and vice in action. Frequently, the lower left quadrant contains an exemplification of the virtue personified above it, and the lower right quadrant contains a further exemplification of the vice with which it is vertically aligned. So Jonathan and David's embrace exemplifies Amistié's outward manifestation, and Saul's contorted figure, with spear at the ready, provides a fitting demonstration of the consequences of Hatred (see fig. 56). There are, however, exceptions to this schematic rule within the cycle of Gift Virtue miniatures. The industrious sower in the *Proesce* (Prowess, Valor) miniature is a rebuke rather than a reiteration of the lazy peasant who figures *Peresce* (Sloth) in the quadrant above him (fig. 57).[39] Similarly, it is difficult to understand how the scene of Moses separating the quarreling Israelites (Exod. 2:13) in the lower right quadrant of the *Equité* (Righteousness) miniature relates to the vice of *Felonnie* (Perfidy) above (fig. 58).[40]

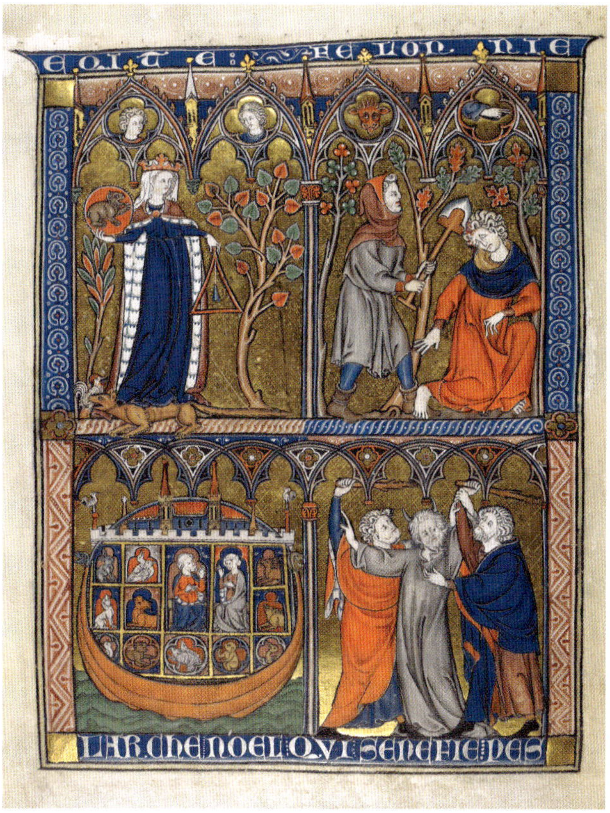

Fig. 58. Placid Equité and the agitations of Felonnie in the Somme le roi, *c. 1294. London, BL, Add. MS 28162, f. 7v.*

In certain of the Gift Virtue miniatures, the lower left and right quadrants are paired to form an integrated register of moral antitheses. In the *Humilité* miniature, the parable of the Pharisee and the Publican (Luke 18:10–14) provides a distant source text for the figures of the sinner and the hypocrite that inhabit the image's third and fourth compartments (see fig. 55). Even as the apparition of Christ blesses the repentant sinner's prayer, a demonic crony eggs on the hermit-hypocrite's mockery. The statue of Christ on the hypocrite's altar turns away from this display in disgust, providing an art-into-life exemplar for the viewer's own response.

Although the *Somme le roi*'s Gift Virtue tracts make frequent use of scriptural scenes in their didactic visualization of moral rectitude and depravity, the biblical episodes given visible form do *not* illustrate the scriptural references marshaled by the tracts they preface. At times, the choice of biblical subjects for the lower quadrants of the Gift Virtue miniatures seem to defy exegetical interpretation.

OPPOSITE: *Fig. 57. Industry and idleness in the* Somme le roi, *c. 1294. London, BL, Add. MS 28162, f. 8v.*

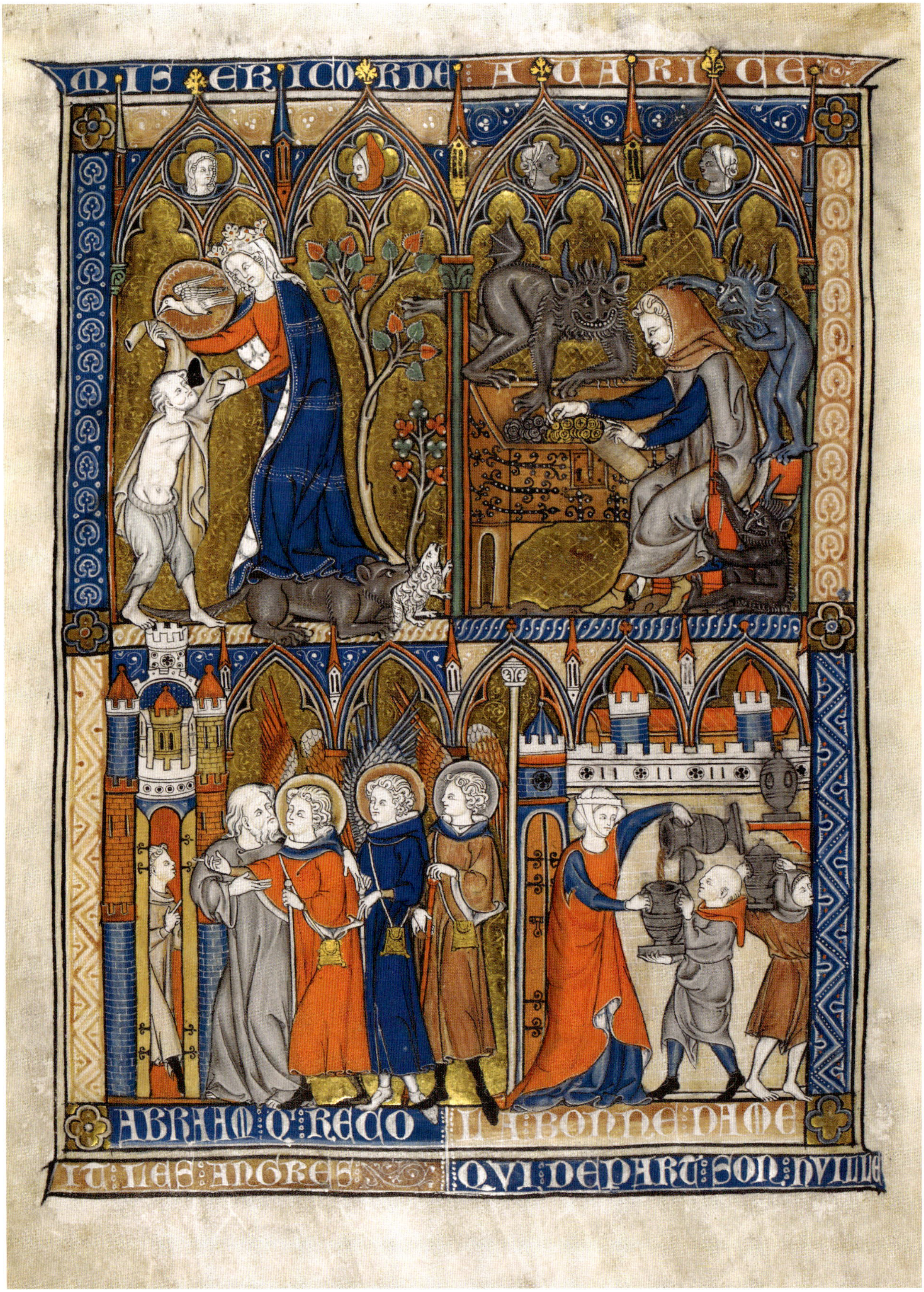
MISERICORDE
AVARICE
ABRAHAM Q' RECO
IT LES ANGRES
LA BONNE DAME
QVI DEPART SON HVILLE

In the *Misericorde* (Mercy, Compassion) miniature, to take but one example, the lower left quadrant represents Abraham's welcome of the three angels, described in Genesis 18 (fig. 59).[41] The Patriarch's hospitality clearly echoes Mercy's generous distribution in the quadrant directly above. A more obscure scriptural episode is visualized in the lower right compartment of the image. The titulus inscribed in the frame below this vignette reads, "La bonne dame qui depart son huille" (The good woman who distributes her oil); the scene depicted is that of the widow and the oil from 4 Kings 4:1–7. In its scriptural context the episode is a miracle story: the prophet Elisha miraculously provides the widow of a God-fearing man with an endless supply of oil; this material bounty allows the widow to pay her debts and to save her two sons from enslavement to her creditors. The good widow, rescued by the prophet, is hardly a figure of the vice of Avarice depicted directly above her; from an iconographic perspective, her role in the Misericorde image is far from self-evident. The scriptural source for the image is, moreover, never referenced in the *Somme le roi.*

As the Misericorde miniature demonstrates, the repertoire of scriptural vignettes visualized in the *Somme*'s Gift Virtue miniatures is an autonomous discourse that cannot be elucidated by recourse to the *Somme* text itself. It would seem that the designers of the *Somme*'s visual program did not scour the major textual monuments of tropological exegesis as they devised a sequence of images for the compendium.[42] Instead, they turned their eyes toward the surfaces of ecclesiastical space and found their *auctoritates* in the struggle for moral rectitude displayed on a monumental scale.

Appropriating the Authority of Monumental Virtues

In the twelfth and thirteenth centuries, virtue and vice invaded the public face of ecclesiastical edifices, and the *Somme le roi*'s personified virtues emulate the monumental personifications carved for a number of church facades in the period. The conceptual framework and formal rhetoric of the manuscript's Gift Virtue miniatures, however, mark the London *Somme le roi*'s visual program as an appropriative reworking of the sculpture executed for a specific edifice: Notre-Dame de Paris.

Devised in the shadow of Paris's great cathedral, the *Somme le roi*'s cycle of Gift Virtue miniatures profited from the cathedral chapter's investment in moral theology and moralizing visual display. The *Somme*'s Gift Virtue miniatures do not, however, simply rehearse the authoritative pronouncements of ecclesiastical sculpture. Selectively appropriating well-established and more recent monumental visualizations of virtue and vice, the manuscript's images reconfigure these borrowings in order to construct innovative visual objects for the moral gaze.

Fig. 59. Merciful distributions and avaricious hoarding in the Somme le roi, *c. 1294. London, BL, Add. MS 28162, f. 9v.*

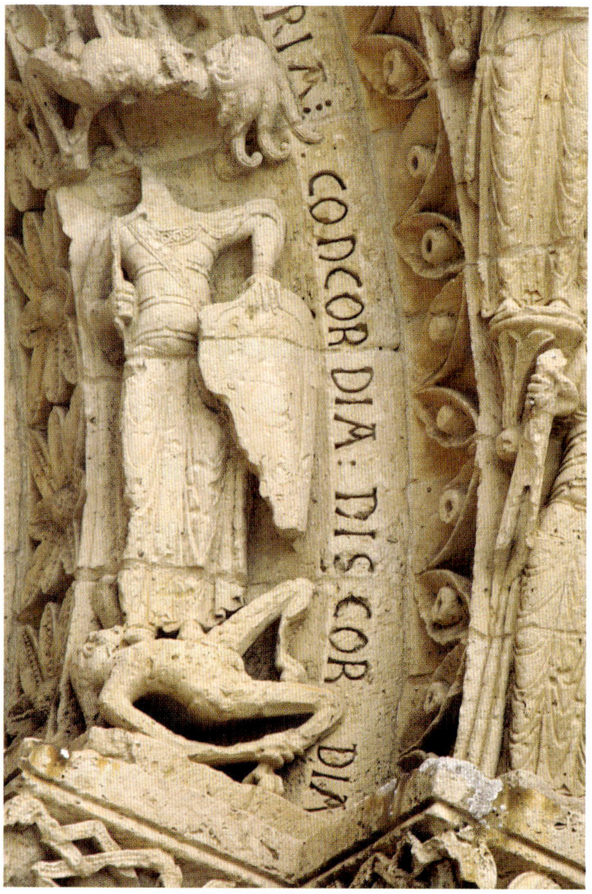

The full-length figures of the *Somme* virtues, placidly trampling bestial forms underfoot, are skillful appropriations of the figures of the Virtues Triumphant carved for a series of French church portals in the twelfth and thirteenth centuries.[43] In the archivolts of the west portal of Saint-Pierre-de-la-Tour at Aulnay (c. 1130–1160), the virtues are triumphant warrior-maidens who keep vigil at the church's entrance (fig. 60).[44] In a further development of this iconographic scheme, the vices also acquire human forms, as witnessed by the left portal of Laon Cathedral's west front (c. 1195–1205; fig. 61).[45] Almost a century later, this anthropomorphic and quotidian visualization of moral combat acquired a startling contemporaneity in the sculpture of the northern portal of Strasbourg Cathedral's west facade (c. 1280–1300; fig. 62).[46] The Strasbourg virtues, completed only a year or two after Laurent d'Orléans compiled the text of the *Somme le roi,* are crowned, courtly personifications who wage a kind of virtuous class warfare with vices given the contorted forms of bourgeois women.[47]

Fig. 60. Concordia tramples Discordia underfoot at Aulnay. Archivolt figures, west portal, Saint-Pierre-de-la-Tour, Aulnay, c. 1130–1160.

These sculptural programs recast the psychomachian tradition, with its emphasis on armed virtue, bellicose vice, and the heat of the moral battlefield, into a display of virtuous conquest rather than ongoing moral struggle.[48] In the sculptures of Aulnay and Laon, virtue has already triumphed and the vices are both defeated and dwarfed by rectitude. At Strasbourg, the dramatic quotient of moral conflict no longer attaches to a narrative of pitched battle, but instead inheres in the blurring of temporal boundaries: vice defeated resembles nothing more than the viewer.

OPPOSITE: Fig. 61. The armed virtues subjugate the vices at Laon. Angels, virtues and vices, and Marian scenes; right archivolts, left portal, west facade, Cathedral of Notre-Dame, Laon, c. 1195–1205.

The *Somme le roi*'s painted personifications are diminutive younger sisters of the triumphant virtues devised for these monumental programs. The conceptual framework of the *Somme*'s Gift Virtue miniatures, however, is indebted to an alternative monumental scheme for the representation of moral rectitude and depravity. In the decades between the completion of the archivolt virtues at Laon and the execution of the Strasbourg virtues, a new approach to the theorization and representation of virtue and vice made itself felt in Paris through the teaching of Notre-Dame's chapter

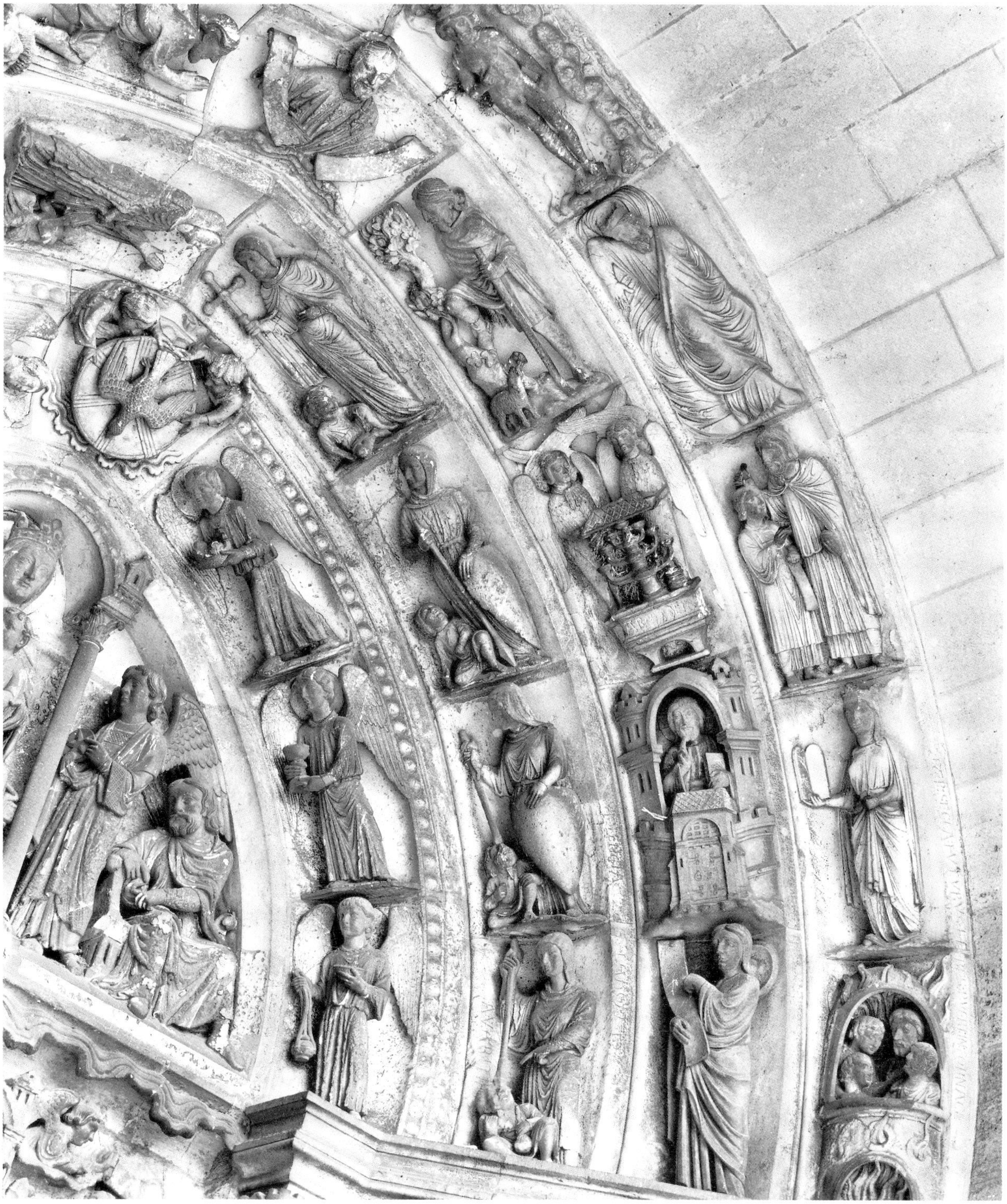

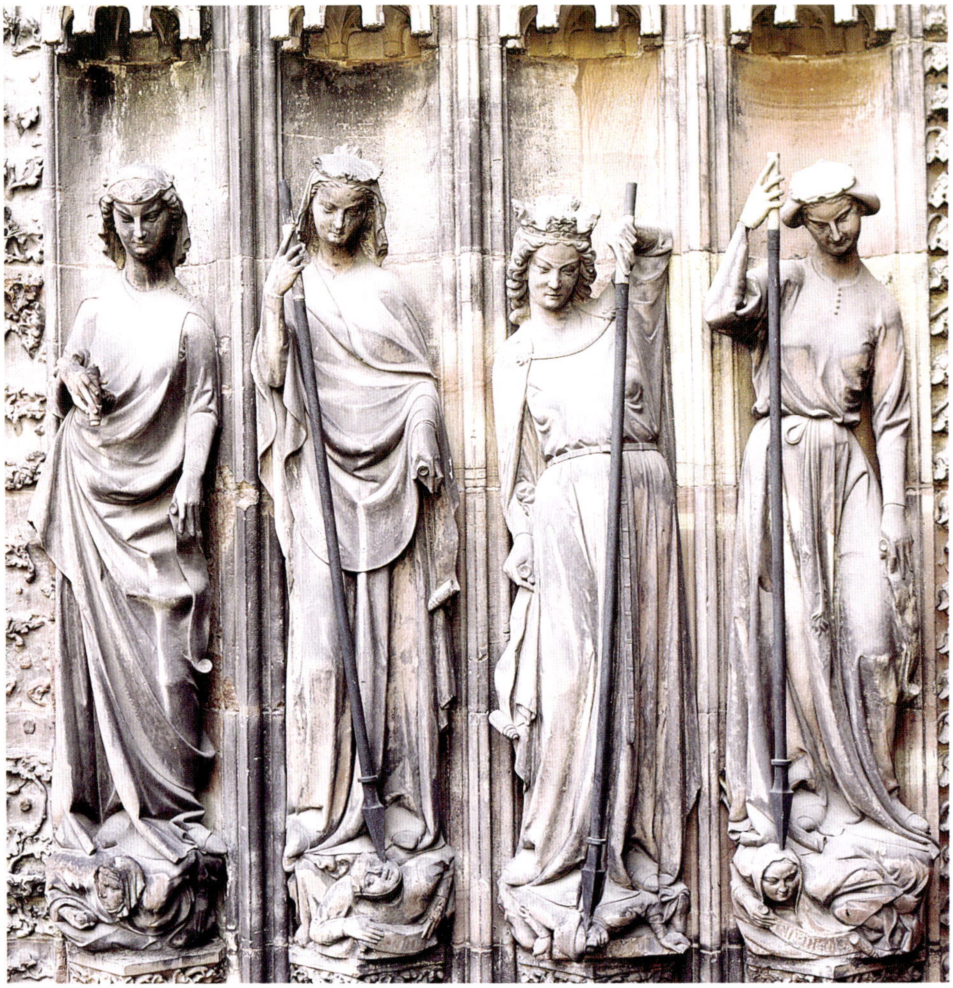

Fig. 62. The virtues put the vices in their places at Strasbourg. Left jamb, north portal, west facade, Cathedral of Notre-Dame, Strasbourg, c. 1280–1300.

and through the visual instruction of the plinth reliefs carved for the central portal of the cathedral's west facade (c. 1220; figs. 63 and 64).[49] These reliefs, situated at eye level, abandon the psychomachian paradigm and install the virtues and vices in a new moral setting.[50]

The Notre-Dame reliefs sever virtue from vice. The virtues no longer wage a battle for moral superiority; in both conceptual and spatial terms, superiority has become their attribute. Notre-Dame's twelve enthroned virtues are personifications holding emblematic disks and seated within trilobe arches above each of their opposed vices. Dignified by their elevated placement and enclosed in architectural niches bounded by pairs or compound triplets of classicizing columns projecting outward in relief, the Notre-Dame virtues are endowed with didactic *auctoritas*.

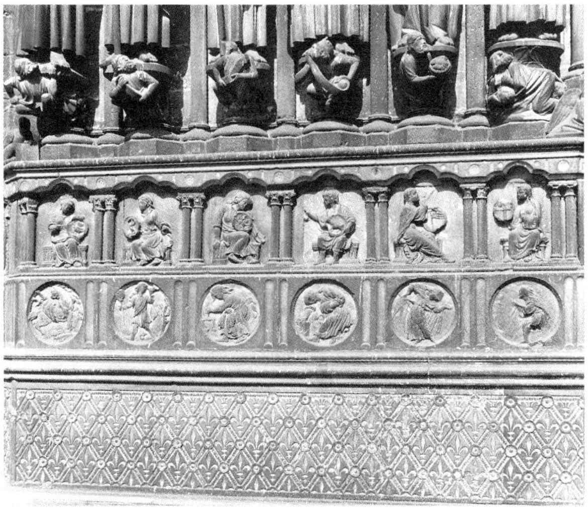

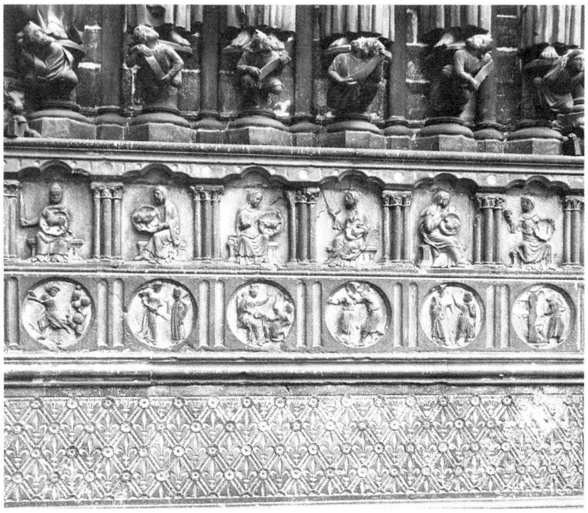

Fig. 63. Virtue arrayed above vice in Paris. North plinth, central portal, west facade, Cathedral of Notre-Dame, Paris, c. 1220.

Fig. 64. Virtue arrayed above vice in Paris. South plinth, central portal, west facade, Cathedral of Notre-Dame, Paris, c. 1220.

By contrast, vice runs wild through the Notre-Dame reliefs. In the plinth program, vice is a disruptive force animating the lower array of twelve reliefs. In this register, a series of vicious dramas unfolds within the circumference of recessed medallions. *Superbia* (Pride) is exemplified by a figure tumbling from the thrashing form of a horse barely contained by its relief setting (fig. 65). In the medallion for *Ignavia* (Cowardice), a diminutive hare strikes such fear in a youth that he flees the circular confines of the relief (fig. 66). Town and gown conflict also finds a place in this knaves' gallery: a bishop threatened by a layman provides an exemplum for *Contumacia* (Insolence) that upbraids the viewer in decidedly clerical tones (fig. 67).[51]

The negative disarray that characterizes the vice reliefs at Notre-Dame is further emphasized by the treatment of the surface that bonds each set of six medallions into a continuous band. The interstices between the circular spaces of vicious action are carved with two vertical lozenges that mimic the form of the columns dividing the virtues directly above them. Just as the circular space inhabited by each vicious episode is recessed from the plinth surface, so the sculptured frame that binds them into a malign community is defined by these punctuating anti-columns of negative space.[52] At Notre-Dame, the virtues inhabit a clearly defined architectural arcade; vice, however, takes place in a series of spaces defined by the absence of architectural form.

The reliefs of Notre-Dame's west facade were a privileged means of public communication for the cathedral chapter. The cathedral's west front was the most accessible of the building's entrances. The Porte Rouge, on the north side of the edifice, and the symmetrically placed southern passage facing the episcopal precinct were restricted

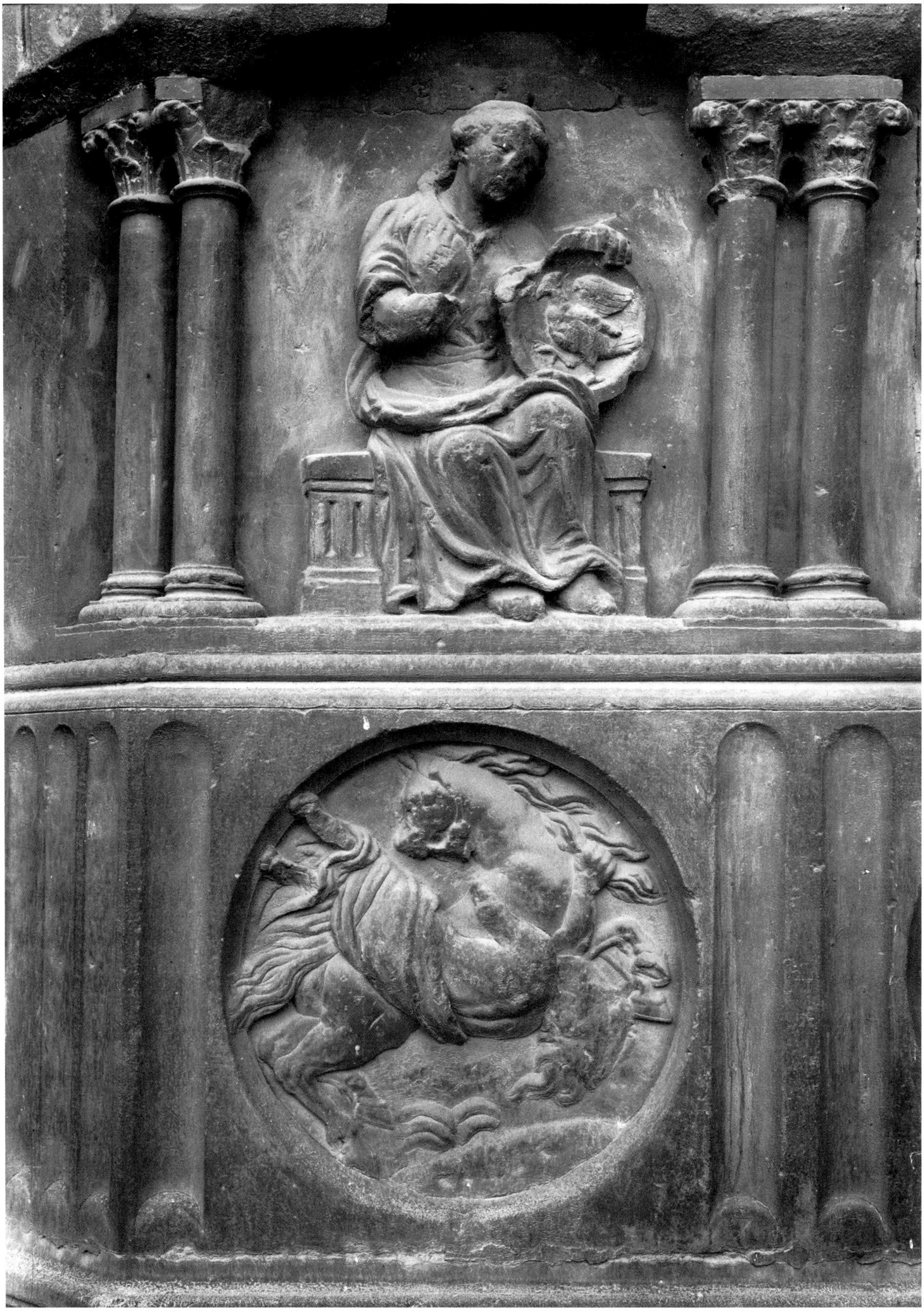

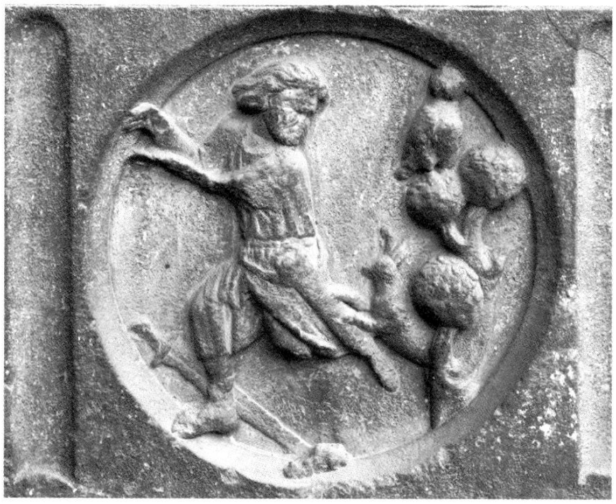

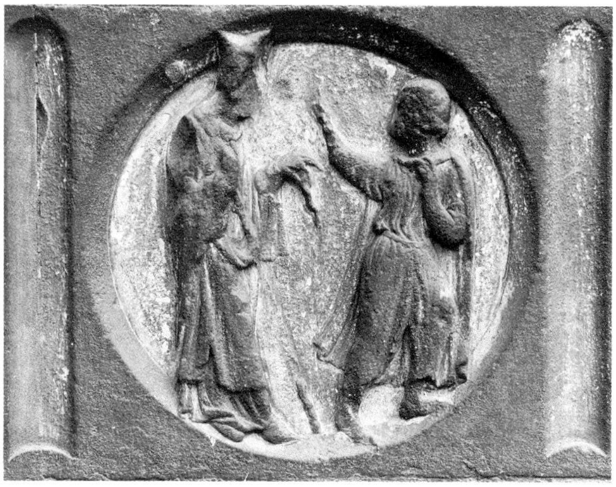

Fig. 66. The absurdity of Ignavia *in Paris. Plinth medallion, central portal, west facade, Cathedral of Notre-Dame, Paris, c. 1220.*

Fig. 67. Contumacia: *lay impudence speaks out of turn in Paris. Plinth medallion, central portal, west facade, Cathedral of Notre-Dame, Paris, c. 1220.*

OPPOSITE: Fig. 65. Parisian Superbia *untamed. Plinth medallion, central portal, west facade, Cathedral of Notre-Dame, Paris, c. 1220.*

points of entry with sculptural programs that addressed the particular concerns and interests of the cathedral chapter and the bishop, respectively.[53] By contrast, the three portals of the cathedral's west facade faced the busy cathedral parvis and the rue Neuve Notre-Dame, the center of a thriving community of book producers by the 1220s.[54]

Through the sculptural programs of the west facade, including the virtue and vice reliefs, the cathedral chapter attempted to exhort the Parisians who passed or entered their church.[55] Michael Camille aptly described the vicious lower array as confronting viewers with a "personal decision between one or the other, between the higher and the lower."[56] The pedagogy of the Notre-Dame reliefs, however, does not rest in the Socratic querying of the viewer, *which do you choose?* In sensitive explorations of the theological underpinnings and argument of the reliefs, Bruno Boerner has made compelling connections between the sculptural program of Notre-Dame's central portal and the moral theology developed by members of the cathedral chapter in the first decades of the thirteenth century.[57]

As Boerner suggests, it was during this period that capitular theologians, such as Peter the Chanter, Prevostin of Cremona, Peter of Poitiers, and Stephen Langton, developed a distinctive conception of virtue, one that intimately connected it with the operation of grace.[58] When the circle of Peter the Chanter took up the related question of sin, they stressed its contingent nature. Arguing that the gravity of sin varies according to its circumstances and objects, members of the cathedral chapter emphasized the variable quality of vice and its realization in finite, varied human action.[59] According to capitular theologians, the virtuous act derives from a virtuous *habitus* that is itself a work of grace, a divine gift.[60] Accordingly, virtuous acts are not subject to the casuistic quantifications and qualifications applied to vice: virtue, as an *opus gratie* (work of grace),

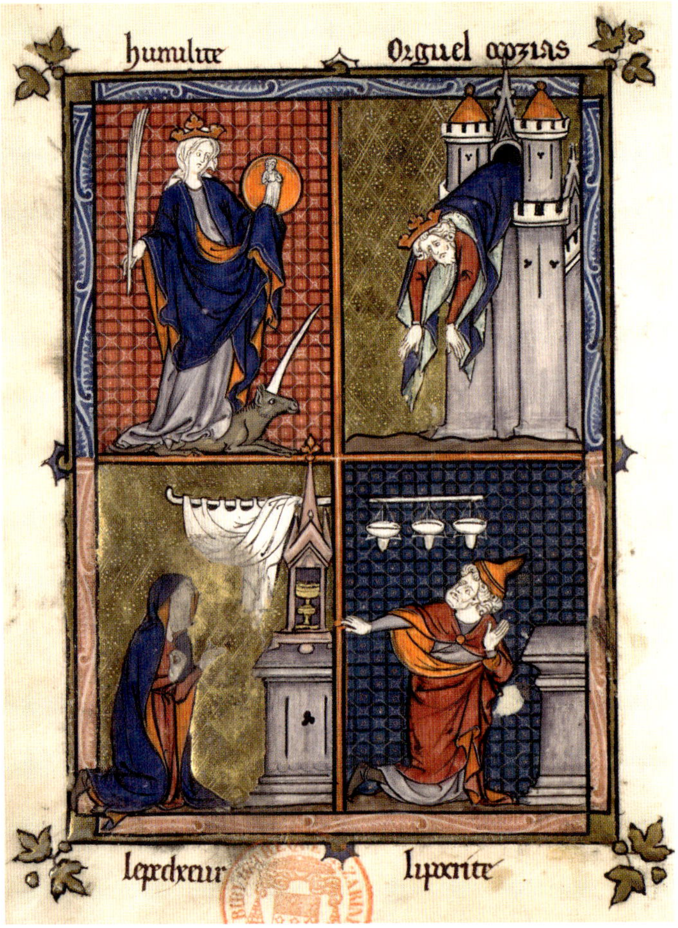

Fig. 68. Virtue personified and vice exemplified: Humility and Pride in a Somme le roi*, 1295. Paris, Bibliothèque Mazarine, MS 870, f. 89v: 194 x 133 mm.*

possesses power and merit in itself.[61] The vices, however, have no soteriological being or value in themselves; vice comes into existence and is culpable as it is realized in human action.

The plinth program of Notre-Dame's central portal makes visible central tenets of the cathedral chapter's novel moral theology. The self-contained, personified forms of the virtues demonstrate the self-sufficiency and self-definition of virtue as an opus gratie.[62] By contrast, the vices, refused the self-identification of personification, appear to the viewer as they appear within the moral-theological framework developed by members of the cathedral chapter—that is, as finite moments of action in the world, caused by human agents.[63] The differentiated framing of the plinth reliefs appends a determinative gloss to the sculptural program's *distinctio* of virtue and vice. The virtuous register is defined by the positive relief of architectural form; vice, however, is bound only by the geometrical constraints of the recessed medallion form in a register punctuated not by columns but by columnar voids.[64]

The miniatures devised for the *Somme le roi*'s Gift Virtue tracts have been identified as the "most conspicuous examples" of the influence exerted by the Notre-Dame plinth reliefs in the later decades of the thirteenth century.[65] Interpreters have emphasized how the *Somme le roi*'s miniatures represent viciousness in the act, rather than *in esse,* thus perpetuating the paradigm established at Paris. This basic representational principle—that the virtues are personified and the vices exemplified—governs the Gift Virtue miniatures in all of the four earliest illustrated *Somme le roi* manuscripts (figs. 68–70). Beyond this point of consonance, however, the pictorial program devised for the *Somme le roi* diverges in significant ways from its Parisian inspiration. The quadripartite organization of the picture field, the exemplification of virtue in action, and the use of scriptural vignettes collectively distinguish the visual template devised for the

OPPOSITE: *Fig. 69. Virtue personified and vice exemplified: Humility and Pride in a* Somme le roi*, dated 1294. Paris, BnF, MS fr. 938, f. 74r: 270 x 190 mm.*

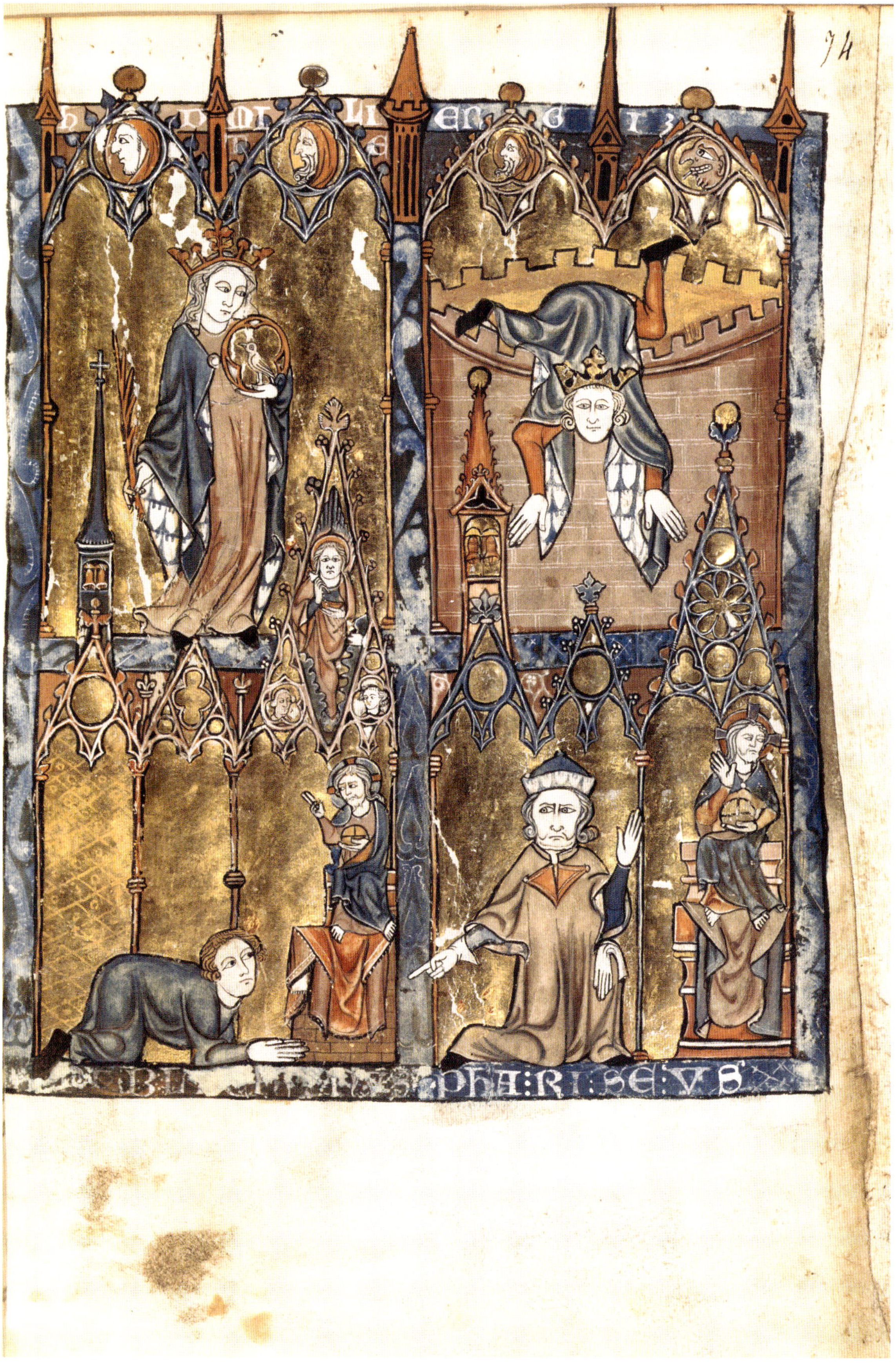
PHARISEVS

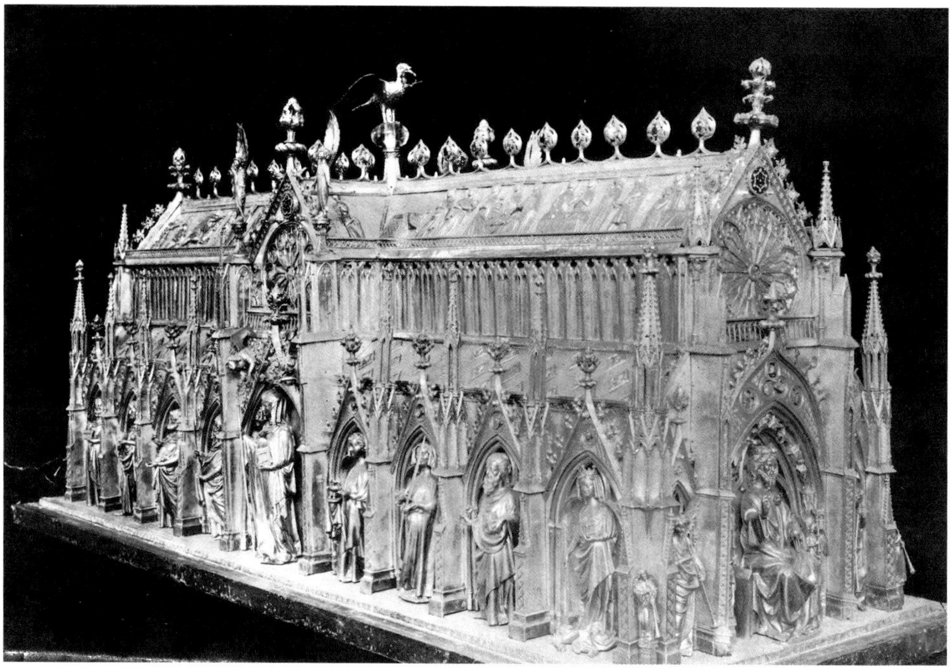

Fig. 71. Gothic monumentality on a small scale. The reliquary châsse of St. Gertrude of Nivelles, begun 1272, completed by May 30, 1298, destroyed by bombardment May 14, 1940.

Constructing the Moral Interior

> . . . li premiers degrez de ceste vertu [Equité] est que li hons soit bons juges de son cuer meismes car il doit entrer dedenz soi et regarder sa conscience et bien examiner ses pensees et ses volentez queles eles sunt bones ou mauvaises.[75]
>
> (. . . the first degree of this virtue [Righteousness] is that a man should be a good judge of his own heart, for he should enter within himself and inspect his conscience, and he should closely examine his thoughts and desires, [to see] whether they are good or bad.)

Fig. 72. A "super-shrine turned outside-in." Interior view of the Upper chapel, Sainte-Chapelle, Paris, c. 1239–1248.

This exhortation to enter one's conscience and to inspect its moral contents is but one of a series of references in the *Somme le roi* to an architectonic conception of the moral-spiritual interior. The moral-theological curriculum in which the *Somme le roi* engages its reader is a process of edification in a doubled sense: as the reader-viewer masters the syllabus of the virtues, he or she simultaneously constructs a more perfect moral interior. In a discussion of the gift of *Science,* which nourishes the virtue of Equity, the *Somme* explains,

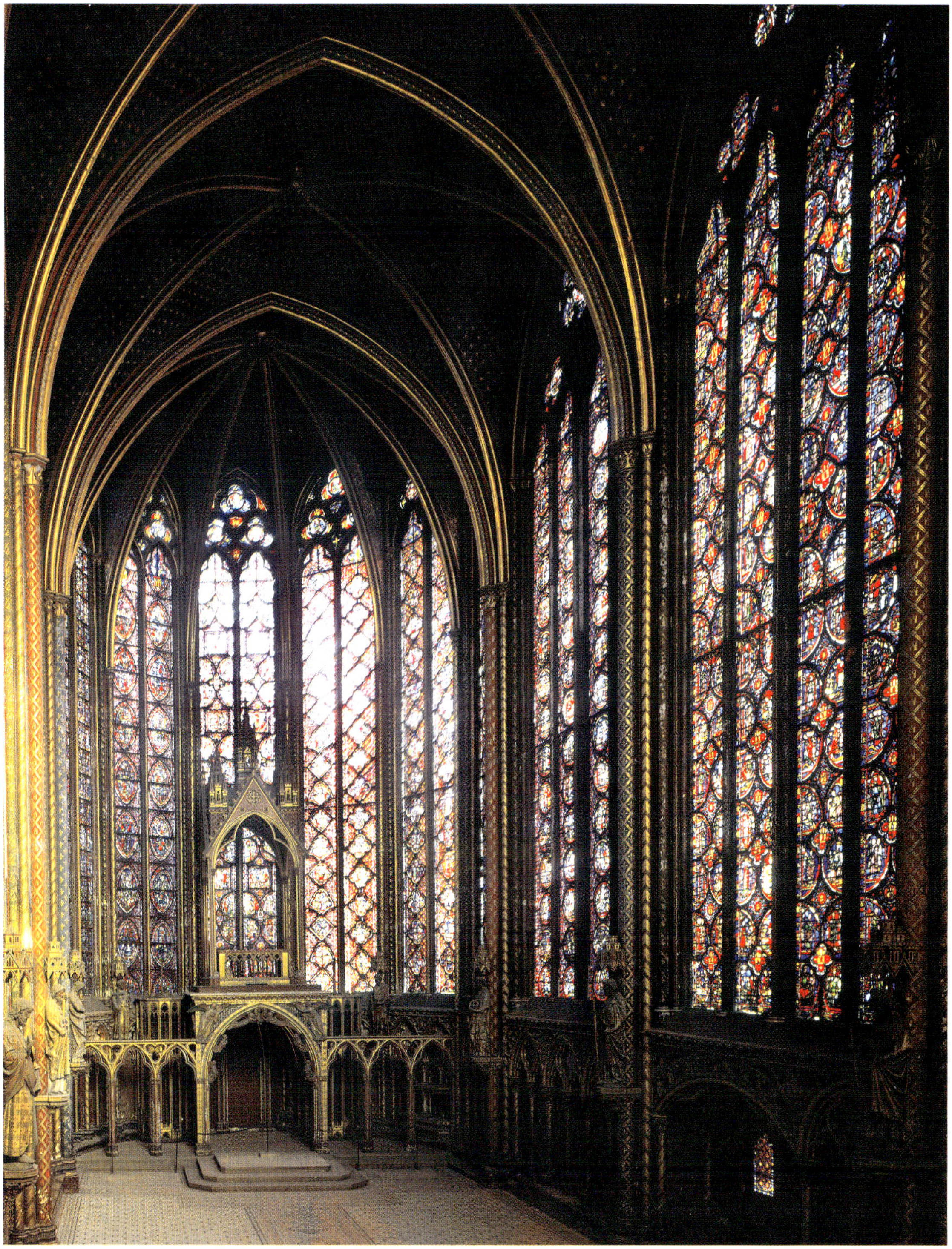

> Cist dons est li maistres des oeuvres c'est a dire des vertuz d'ome car il fait tout a point et a regle et a plonc et a livel. Il prent premierement son point et sa bonne et ce est ce que li saiges dist de quanque tu commenceras garde a la fin a quel chief tu en vendras. Aprés il tient sa lingne par quoi il va droite voie et par droite entencion non mie comme li serpenz ou comme li goupilz. Aprés il fait tout a livel car il fait le mur igal et onni car la vie des bons il aimme sanz trouver nouveletez. Aprés il aprueve souvent son oevre au plonc car il prent garde que sa tour ne pende ne ne cline ne a destre par prosperité ne a senestre par adversité.[76]
>
> (This gift is the master of works, that is, of the virtues of man. For in all things he works with a [fixed] point, a rule, with a plumb line and with a level. First he takes his point and his square and this is what the wise man says: "whatever you shall begin, at its conclusion attend to what end [or point] you shall come." Afterward, he takes his line, by which he travels the straight path with upright intention, not at all like the serpent or the fox. Afterward, he works perpendicularly, for he makes the wall equal and even; for he loves the life of good men, without finding strangeness. Afterward, he often tests his work with the plumb line, for he takes care that his tower does not list or incline; neither to the right, through prosperity, nor to the left, through adversity.)[77]

Permeated by a dense doublespeak, the passage models the effect of knowledge within the moral interior after the mason's careful work.[78] *Science* (knowledge) is both a master of works and the very body of knowledge that constructs the perfected interior of the righteous man. Within the edificatory paradigm that informs the *Somme le roi,* man, as a moral creature, cannot avoid building interior structures. The *Somme le roi* exhorts its reader, and viewer, to the proper kind of construction.

Unlike the *Sainte abbaïe* treatise, the *Somme le roi* is not a building allegory, nor does it provide the reader with a sustained discussion or development of any allegorical edifice. Architectural metaphor and analogy are, instead, recurrent motifs in the *Somme,* employed to figure and fashion the moral-spiritual interior. Just as the compendium's program of paintings makes sustained use of architectural framing to structure the relationship between virtue and vice within the bounded space of moral display, so too the *Somme le roi*'s constituent tracts describe a series of interior structures to which they direct the reader in pursuit of moral perfection: the castle or fortress, the house or chamber, and the cloister. Collectively, these metaphoric structures approximate a didactic itinerary wherein the *Somme* introduces the reader-viewer into progressively more interior spaces—an inward movement that is, implicitly, an itinerary of spiritual ascent.

CASTLE

Fortified against the besieging forces of fortune, misfortune, sensory temptation, and innate vice, the castle of the heart and body is, inevitably, the most contested of the *Somme le roi*'s interior structures.[79] The heart's fortification is dangerously perforated by the five senses, and the *Somme* exhorts the reader to police the sensory boundaries of the self through the exercise of the faculty of Reason and the cultivation of the virtue of Equité.[80] The dangers that beset the *Somme*'s castle of the heart are not, however, exclusively identified with the sensory world beyond the space of the self: the vices are also treacherous inhabitants of the inner castle; left unchecked, they will certainly betray the heart or soul. Above all, the *Somme* argues that it is the oversight of the virtues and the establishment of their regime of rectitude that can best protect the castle of the heart from viciousness, both extrinsic and interior.

In the *Somme*'s discussion of the virtue of *Chasteé* (Chastity) the castle trope is initially reconceived as a Marian structure:

> la virge marie estoit touz jorz reposte et ot poour quant li angeles s'apparut a li. Mes la poour de deu est en cele la tresorerie qui garde le tresor de virginité que deables d'enfer ne le puisse embler car ele garde les portes dou chastel ou est cist tresors enclos. Les portes dou chastel dou cuer ou est li tresors de virginité sunt li sens dou cors ces portes garde la poour nostre seigneur que eles ne soient ouvertes a l'enemi par vaine curiosité de vooir ou d'oïr ou de paller ou d'aler en compaignies soupeconneuses car curiositez especiaument de vooir et d'oïr les vanitez dou monde est souvent voie a pechié de luxure.[81]
>
> (the Virgin Mary was always hidden away and she was afraid when the angel appeared to her. But in her, Fear of God is the treasurer who preserves the treasure of virginity so that the Devil of Hell may not carry it off, for she [Fear of God] guards the doors of the castle in which this treasure is enclosed. The doors of the castle of the heart, in which the treasure of virginity is [contained], are the senses of the body. Fear of our Lord guards these doors so that they should not be opened to the enemy by vain curiosity in seeing, hearing, or speaking, or by traveling in questionable company. For curiosity, especially in seeing and hearing the vanities of the world, is often a path to the sin of luxury.)

In the last decade of the thirteenth century, to compare the Virgin to a castle containing a treasure guarded by *Timor Dei* (Fear of God) was simply to marshal a complex of motifs invested with the patina of established orthodox use.[82] In the continuation of the passage, however, the *Somme le roi* reorients this inherited material.

Beginning with the paradigmatic closed body—the Virgin Mary—the tract again identifies the entrances to the castle of the heart with the five senses. The text thus assimilates the virginal castle to the fortress described in connection with the virtue of Equité, with one significant difference: the castle of the heart is now understood to contain the treasure of virginity, and its guardian is not Righteousness, but rather the Gift of the Fear of the Lord. In one stroke, the *Somme le roi* assimilates the special status of virginity, per se, to a state of spiritual vigilance and enclosure. The castle of the virginal body becomes the castle of the heart, and a proper relationship to the divinity ensures its closure. Corporeal enclosure, in this context, is not defined as an inviolate and impenetrable body, but rather as a sensorium turned away from the vanities of the world.[83] This inward turn takes the reader from the fortified architecture of the interior castle to the domestic spaces of the house of the heart.[84]

HOUSE

The first of the *Somme le roi*'s references to the interior house occurs in its treatise on the Pater Noster. In an exposition of Christ's precept—"the kingdom of God is within you" (Luke 17:21)—the text explains,

> Or enten bien comment ce puet estre quant dex done une grace que on apele l'esperit d'entendement ou cuer aussi comme li solauz oste les tenebres de la nuit et gaste les nues et le bruilllet dou matin ausi gaste cis esperiz toutes les tenebres dou cuer et li monstre ses pechiéz et ses defauz si que cil qui doit estre touz nez trueve lors tant de defautes et de pouties et de poudre sanz nombre ausi comme li rais dou soleil monstre les pouties et les poudretes qui sunt aval la maison.[85]
>
> (Now understand well how this can be: when God gives a grace in the heart that is called the Spirit of Understanding, just as when the sun removes the shadows of night and destroys the clouds and the fog of morning, so too this spirit destroys the shadows of the heart and demonstrates to it its sins and its failings so that it, which should always be clean, then finds so many flaws and filth and dust immeasurable, just as the ray of the sun shows the filth and the dust that are in the house.)

Although the house of the heart remains an implicit structure in this exegesis, it effectively usurps the text's initial exegetical locus—the kingdom of God—and reframes the evangelical promise in terms that evoke domestic space.

Grace-filled inspection of the sullied moral-spiritual interior prompts the penitent to action. The *Somme le roi* describes how the filth found within the heart causes the devotee to turn against himself until "il commence cel cuer a netoier a force et a giter hors toutes ces ordures qui li toloient la veue deu en lui et ce fait il o la pele de veraie confession" (he begins to cleanse this heart by force and to cast out all these foul things that take from him the vision of God in him, and he does this with the shovel of true confession).[86] The sacrament of confession is the means of purifying the heart; through self-examination and an active engagement in the work of penance the heart is cleansed.

In the section of the *Somme* dedicated to the virtue of Proesce the movement from mortal sin to repentance is rhetorically dilated as a permutating process of descent and purification. Initially, the Christian is a chevalier who wins the *bataille ou cuer* (battle in the heart) through an exercise of Prowess's component qualities: magnanimity, faith, confidence, patience, constancy, magnificence, and the desire for justice.[87] When the text turns to repentance (the first branch of Proesce), the glorified spiritual warrior is subjected to a radical transformation: he becomes a robber, a betrayer, a murderer—in short, the antithesis of the chivalric ideal:

> Cil qui deu a correcié par pechié mortel il doit gemir dou parfont dou cuer si que li cuers fonde touz en larmes et a granz doleurs et a granz souspirs doit crier a deu merci comme son larron comme son murtrier comme son traiteur qui a deservi le gibet d'enfer. . . . Aprés il est traitres a deu car le chatel de son cuer et de son cors que il li avoit baillié en garde il la rendu a son anemi mortel c'est au deable. Bien doit donques grant duel mener qui est en tel point et souvent de ses larmes son lit laver c'est sa conscience ou li serpenz venimeus se gist. Tex larmes chacent le deable fors dou cuer aussi comme l'iaue chaude chace le chien de la cuisine. Aprés la repentance doit venir la confession. C'est la bone chamberiere qui netoie l'ostel et giete toute l'ordure hors au balai de la langue si comme parole david ou sautier [Ps. 50:9].[88]
>
> (He who has angered God through mortal sin ought to groan from the depths of his heart so that the heart entirely melts in tears and great suffering; and with great sighs the heart must cry for mercy from God, as his thief, his murderer, his betrayer who has deserved the gallows of hell. . . . Afterward he is God's betrayer, for he has handed over the castle of his heart and his body, which God entrusted to his care, to his mortal enemy, the devil. Truly he who is in this state should mourn greatly and with his tears [he should] wash his bed, that is, his conscience, in which the poisonous serpent lies. Such tears

> chase the devil out of the heart just as hot water chases the dog from the kitchen. After repentance should come confession. It is the good chambermaid who cleans the house and ejects all filth with the broom of the tongue, just as David says in the psalter [Ps. 50:9].)

Not only does the framework of repentance abase the Christian, it also compels him to move inward. The fortified military architecture of the castle of the heart and body is displaced by the bedchamber of the conscience. This space of rest and repose (of a tear-soaked variety) is, in turn, subjected to a further rhetorical demotion, becoming the more humble and menial space of the kitchen. By the end of this process, the text has effaced the landscape of the battlefield with quotidian images of hot water, running dogs, and zealous chambermaids: the spiritual knight has become a female servant and the castle is now a kitchen. This inward progress through a descending scale of social status is, simultaneously, a movement of spiritual ascent. It is only by penetrating the inner spaces of the heart and conscience that the repentant soul comes to the purifying work of confession, and through confession to absolution.

Confession is provided with its own locus within the *Somme le roi*'s architectural topography of the moral-spiritual interior:

> Li pechierres doit entrer en son ostel c'est en son cuer non mie en trespassant comme li jouglerres qui ne demeure mie volentiers en son ostel car il n'a pire ostel dou sien. Mes ileques doit demourer et regarder touz ses defauz de quoi il doit rendre conte a deu et raison et a son prevost c'est a son confessor. Et doit penser de soi aussi comme s'il fust ajournez a conter de ses recoites et de ses mises par devant son seignor.[89]
>
> (The sinner must enter into his house, that is, into his heart, not at all by passing through as does the *jongleur,* who never willingly stays in his [own] house, for there is no house worse than his own. But there he [the sinner] must remain and he must consider all his flaws, concerning which he must account to God, and to Reason, and to his *prévôt,* that is, his confessor. And he must consider himself just as if he was summoned to account for his receipts and expenditures before his lord.)

The passage casts confession in terms that evoke the management of the aristocratic household. Like a good steward, the penitent must diligently survey the interior household. Taking stock of its contents, he prepares to account to the deity for his management of his moral-spiritual self. Although confession does not return the Christian to the chivalric status that he enjoyed in the first folios of the Proesce tract, it does restore to him a certain mastery of the moral-spiritual interior. This control or expertise is focused in diligent introspection; it is not the mastery of ownership, but rather a managerial care of the self, undertaken as a service owed to the deity.

The final space within the *Somme le roi*'s house of the heart is assimilated to the middle term in the text's threefold preparation of the moral-spiritual interior: purification, prayer, perfection.

> La tierce chose qui doit estre en oraison est devocion de cuer c'est alever le cuer a deu sanz penser ailleurs. Dont nostre sires dist *quant tu prieras deu entre dedenz ta couche* c'est dedenz ton cuer *et clo l'uis dessus toi* [Matt. 6:6, slightly modified]. C'est a dire met hors toutes pensees charneles et ordes et mondaines et einsi prie ton pere dou ciel en repost.[90]
>
> (The third thing that must be in prayer is devotion of heart, that is, to raise the heart to God without straying thoughts [*penser ailleurs*]. Thus our Lord says: *when you shall pray to God, enter within your bedchamber,* that is, within your heart, *and close the door upon yourself* [Matt. 6:6, slightly modified]. That is, evict all carnal, filthy, and worldly thoughts and thus, in repose, pray to your Father in heaven.)

The *Somme le roi*'s exhortation to pray within the closed space of the bedchamber of the heart occurs within a larger, architecturally modeled prescription. As the tract explains, "Oroisons est mout puissanz vers deu quant ele est apoiee de iiij choses comme de iiij pilers" (Prayer is very powerful before God when it is supported on four things, as on four pillars).[91] The *Somme* identifies the fourfold basis of prayer with "droite foi" (correct faith), "esperance d'avoir ce que l'en requiert" (the hope of having what one requests), "devocion de cuer" (devotion of the heart), and the "ij eles qui la portent devant deu. Ces ij eles sunt jeune et aumosne" (two wings that bear it [prayer] before God. These two wings are fasts and alms).[92]

The text's discussion of the four supports of prayer evokes the account of the cherubim concealing the tabernacle and the four pillars of setim wood supporting the tabernacle veil in Exodus 25:18–20 and 26:32. Embedding a description of the bedchamber of the heart—the Christian's innermost space of prayer—within a larger architectonic structure, exegetically derived from the fittings of the tabernacle, the innermost space of the Exodus temple, the *Somme le roi* does not simply elevate the domestic space of the Christian moral-spiritual interior; it sanctifies it.[93]

CLOISTER

The first of the *Somme le roi*'s two allusions to the interior cloister occurs in the treatise's exposition of the Pater Noster. Examining the phrase "Give us today our daily bread," the text explains,

> Or samble que ce soit mout petite chose que nos demandons. Mes certes mout est grant chose. Quant on requiert a un abbé le pain de s'abbaïe on requiert la fraternité et part et compaignie et droit en touz les biens qui sunt leanz. C'est li pains de celui beneoit convent *li pains dou ciel li pains des angeles* [Ps. 77:24–25, slightly modified] li pains delitables li pains de vie pardurable car il done bone vie et garde l'arme sanz morir. . . . Nous l'apelons nostre pain cotidien. C'est a dire de chascun jour car ce est la cotidiene distribucions que dex done a ses chanoines chascun jour qui font son servise et chantent ses heures. C'est a touz bons cuers qui chascun jour doucement par veraie amor font memoire et remembrance de sa passion. Le gros de la provende nos prendrons en nostre aoust ou ciel quant nos le verrons a descouvert en sa biauté si com il est.[94]
>
> (Now it seems that this is a very small thing that we ask. But certainly it is a very great thing. When one asks an abbot for the bread of his abbey, one asks for fellowship, participation, community, and a just claim in all the goods that are there. This is the bread of that blessed convent, *the bread of heaven, the bread of angels* [Ps. 77:24–25, slightly modified], the delicious bread, the bread of eternal life. For it confers a good life and it keeps the soul from dying. . . . We call it our quotidian bread, that is to say, [our bread] of each day. For this is the distribution that God gives each day to his canons who perform his service and sing his hours; that is, [he gives it] to all good hearts who sweetly, with true love, remember and commemorate his passion daily. We shall take up the greater part of the prebend in our harvest in heaven, when we shall see him uncovered in his beauty, just as he is.)

In the words of the Pater Noster the Christian petitions not simply for daily sustenance but for membership in a divine convent, which the *Somme* explicitly models after a chapter of canons. The Eucharist is the catalyst that transforms the devotee from pious petitioner to a member of the heavenly community, and in return for the Eucharistic distribution, the devotee must perform an interiorized, affective divine service. Just as canons fill the choir with liturgical song at the canonical hours, so too all Christians should pray the Pater Noster and fill their hearts with an intent memory

of Christ's Passion. Evoking the institutional and economic framework of ecclesiastical benefices through the language of *distribucions* and *provende*, the *Somme le roi* tropologically interprets these features of church hierarchy in a way that both spiritualizes the economic basis of clerical status and makes that status spiritually available to all Christians who fulfill the basic requirements of the faith.

The community joined by the lay devotee is a superior foundation. It is a blessed convent whose members include the angels, its prebends provide for eternal life, and its welcoming abbot is Christ himself. The treatise also identifies the prior of the interior abbey:

> Cist dons [*Science*] est prieux ou cloistre de l'arme qui garde l'ordre et fait garder par tout. Primes ou cuer a ij costez l'entendement et la volenté la raison et l'affection. Quant cil dui costé s'acordent il font mout de melodie et mout biau servise c'est quant volentez veut quanque entendemenz enseigne de bien et affections sent ce que raisons entent.[95]
>
> (This gift [Knowledge] is the prior in the cloister of the soul, who preserves order and makes it to be preserved everywhere. Firstly, in the heart there are two sides: understanding and will; reason and affection. When these two sides harmonize they make much melody and a very beautiful service, that is, when the will wants whatever the understanding teaches concerning the Good, and affection feels that which reason intends.)

Serving as the spiritual abbey's prior, Knowledge oversees the antiphonal cooperation of the soul's faculties. When Will and Affection obey the dictates of Understanding and Reason, the interior cloister is filled with an internal harmony analogous to the well-ordered chant of the monastic or capitular choir.

In the *Somme le roi*'s inner cloister the proper governance of the moral-spiritual self is supervised by religious knowledge, an intellectual management of interiority that makes devout prayer and affective meditation possible. It is precisely this moral-spiritual expertise that the *Somme le roi* as a whole aims to inculcate in its royal and aristocratic readers. Installed within a purged and perfected architecture of interiority, the *Somme*'s reader-viewer inhabits the cloister of the soul as a monastic, not in habit but in virtuous habitus.

In the remainder of this chapter I turn from the *Somme le roi* to the texts and images that once followed it. As we shall see, these texts extend the royal summa's religious instruction in new, more spiritually ambitious directions. But it is the three full-page paintings punctuating the remainder of the volume that most decisively intervene

in its program of spiritual edification. Delineating a tripartite argument, these images take the architectural repertoire of the *Somme le roi* and visually refashion it into an architecture for theophany.

Inhabiting La Sainte Abbaïe

The *Sainte abbaïe* treatise is a cloister allegory in three acts: construction, installation, and reformation. The first section of the treatise describes how the Holy Spirit sends various virtues to establish a conventual compound in the conscience. This interior abbey is erected in a penitential landscape, next to the "iaue courant de larmes et de pleurs" (flowing water of tears and crying).[96] After Truth and Love have purged the building site by means of confession and the protection of the heart's purity, other virtues arrive and begin construction:

> Quant la place est bien purgiee si couvient faire les fondemenz larges et parfonz et ce feront ij damoiseles humilitez qui les fera parfonz et povretez qui les fera granz et larges et getera la terre d'une part et d'autre en largement doner quanque ele ara. . . . Damoisele obedience d'une part et misericorde d'autre feront les murs granz et hauz. Tant de bones oevres comme nos faisons et tant d'aumosnes comme nos donons autant de pierres metons nos en noz edefices. . . . Damoisele pacience et damoisele force feront les pilers por soustenir et pour apoier que nus venz de tribulacion ne de temptacion ou de parole cuisant ou de grant domaige ne les puisse abatre.[97]
>
> (When the place is truly purged then it is necessary to make the foundations broad and deep, and two demoiselles shall do this: Humility, who shall make them deep, and Poverty, who shall make them large and broad and shall remove the earth from one side and the other by generously giving whatever she shall have. . . . Demoiselle Obedience on one side, and Mercy on the other, shall make the walls large and high. As many good works as we do and as many alms as we give, so many stones do we place in our buildings. . . . Demoiselle Patience and demoiselle Force shall make the pillars to support and prop up [the building], so that no wind of tribulation or temptation, or of stinging speech, or of great injury should be able to knock them down.)

As the text assigns a constructive labor to each of these personified virtues, it clarifies their role within the interior cloister. The allegory transforms Poverty into a distributive virtue, a form of Christian largesse. Pairing Obedience and Mercy, the text has them construct the abbey's walls through the twinned labors of good works and alms.

Having completed the conventual church, the virtues' work continues apace: Confession builds the chapterhouse, Preaching erects the refectory, and Prayer makes the chapel "qui doit estre haute par douce contemplacion et dessevree de touz soussiz du monde" (that must be lofty in sweet contemplation and detached from all worldly cares).[98] The abbey complex is completed by Compassion, Devotion, and Meditation, who construct the infirmary, cellar, and granary, respectively.[99]

The text's second section begins with an account of the Trinity's involvement in the life of the interior cloister, couched in language that evokes the endowment of an abbey, the liturgical dedication of its church, and the institutional supervision of its community by an appointed visitor:

> Or i couvient metre des vertuz des graces et des dons du saint esperit qui de ceste religion est garde et visiterres. Dieus li peres ceste abbaïe fonda par sa poissance. *Psalmus. Fundavit eam altissimus* [Ps. 86:5]. Li filz deu l'ordena par sa sapience. *Apostolus. Que a deo sunt ordinata* [*sic*] *sunt* [Rom. 13:1, modified]. *Et psalmus. Omnia in sapientia fecisti* [Ps. 103:24]. Li sainz esperiz la garde et la visite par sa bonté et s'amour et sa vaillance dont nous chantons. *Veni creator spiritus et cetera* [hymn].[100]
>
> (Now it is necessary to install the virtues, the graces, and the gifts of the Holy Spirit, who is the warden and visitor of this religious house. God the Father founded this abbey through his power. *Psalm. The Highest founded her* [Ps. 86:5]. The Son of God consecrated it through his wisdom. *Apostle. And those things that exist through God are ordained of God* [Rom. 13:1, modified]. And *Psalm. You made all things in wisdom* [Ps. 103:24]. The Holy Spirit protects and visits her through his goodness, love, and virtue, of whom we sing. *Come creator spirit, etc.* [hymn].)

The text's concise review of the interior abbey's "institutional history" is profoundly authorizing. Not only does the *Sainte abbaïe* cast the claustral refashioning of the spiritual interior as a recapitulation of the original creation, it also claims divine patronage for this inner structure. Founded by God the Father and consecrated by Christ, the soul-as-abbey is the beneficiary of the Holy Spirit's continuing oversight. The prestige of the interiorized convent surpasses that of any royal foundation or reformed order.

The treatise turns next to the inhabitants of the abbey. The highest officers are identified first: Charity is the abbess, Holy Wisdom is the prioress, and Humility serves as the abbey's subprioress. In the folios that follow, an additional nineteen personified virtues are discussed: among them, Discretion is the treasurer, Prayer is the cantor and Jubilation accompanies her, Penitence is the convent's cook, Sobriety reads the lives

of the Father during meals, Fear is the portress, Honesty is the novice mistress, and Courtesy and Simplicity receive the abbey's guests.

The *Sainte abbaïe* pays particular attention to three inhabitants of the interior convent: Devotion, Meditation, and Zeal (*Jalousie*). Devotion, the builder of the cellar in the construction phase of the allegory, is identified as the convent's cellarer in the text's second section. In her cellar she keeps three kinds of good wine, interpreted as three memorial subjects: the remembrance of God and of the joy of paradise, the remembrance of the passion and death of Christ and of the martyrs, and the remembrance of hell's unending torments.[101] Meditation, the builder of the convent granary, becomes its *guernetiere* (granary keeper):

> Ceste damoisele garde le bon grain de froment qui est rouges par dehors et si est blans dedenz et fenduz en costé dont li bons pains est faiz. C'est ihesu criz nostre sauveor qui fu rouges dehors du sanc qu'il espandi pour nous et blans par dedenz par purté de innocence et fenduz au costé du fer de la lance. C'est li pains que nous recevons ou sacrement de l'autel. Li guerniers doit estre seur le celier. Aussi meditation seur devocion.[102]
>
> (This demoiselle keeps the good wheaten grain that is red on the outside, white within, and split open in the side, from which the good bread is made; that is, Jesus Christ our savior who was red without with the blood that he poured out for us, and white within with the purity of innocence, and split open in the side with the blade of the lance. This is the bread that we receive in the sacrament of the altar. The granary ought to be above the cellar; so too, meditation [is] above devotion.)

The stores overseen by these personifications recapitulate the criteria for membership in the *Somme le roi*'s cloister of the soul. The *Sainte abbaïe,* however, inscribes Devotion and Meditation in an explicitly hierarchical relationship. Devotion is necessary to the abbey's proper functioning, but her cellar and its memorial contents play a supporting role; the Eucharistic substance guarded by Meditation occupies a more elevated position within the pious architecture of the inner abbey.

The text's discussion of the *Sainte abbaïe*'s sacristan, Jalousie, is also an occasion for significant allegorical elaboration. The text explains that Jalousie is always awake and ready to do good. She is principally responsible for the convent bell (*auloge*), by which she summons the virtuous community to the worship of God in the divine service. Jalousie's vigilant bell ringing leads the treatise to consider other kinds of bells:

Et devons savoit [*sic*] qu'il i a auloge de vile pour esveillier les paisanz c'est le cor si a auloge de cité pour esveillier les marcheanz c'est la gueste qui corne le jour et auloge de religion qui chiet aus matines et auloge de contemplacion et de saint beguinaige cest jalousie et amor de perfection. Si est mainte foiz avenu en religion que avant que l'auloge de matines sonast que maintes persones avoient plouré maintes larmes devant deu de doleur et de contriction quant a soi de pitié et de compassion quant a leur prochien d'amour et de devocion quant a deu car li auloges d'amour les avoit esveilliez. Hé beneoite soit l'ame que amour esveille car ele n'est pas pereceuse ne endormie et tele ame chante en cantiques quant je dor et mon cuer veille. *Ego dormio et cor meum vigilat* [Sg. 5:2]. C'est a dire quant je dor por mon cors reposer mes cuers veille en jalousie en soussi et en desir de deu amer. Tele ame a touz jorz l'auloge de son cuer tendu et estendu a deu. Et pour ce si puet bien dire et chanter. J'ai un cuer a clochetes esveillié pour bien amer.[103]

(And we should know that there is a bell of the town to wake the peasants, this is the horn; and there is a bell of the city to wake the merchants, this is the watchman who trumpets the day; and there is a bell of religion that rings at matins and a bell of contemplation and of the holy beguinage and this is jealousy and the love of perfection. Thus it often happens in religion that before the matins bell sounds, many people have cried many tears before God: [tears] of sadness and contrition with respect to themselves; [tears] of pity and compassion for their neighbors; and [tears] of love and devotion toward God, for the bell of love had woken them. Oh, blessed is the soul that love has woken, for she is not lazy, nor asleep. Such a soul sings in the Song of Songs: when I sleep and my heart keeps watch. *I sleep and my heart watcheth* [Sg. 5:2]. That is to say, when I sleep to repose my body, my heart keeps watch in zeal, cares, and the desire to love God. Such a soul always has the bell of her heart held out and stretched toward God. And thus she can truly say and sing: I have a heart woken by bells to love well.)

The passage sketches a landscape, full of sounds and summons. It is, at once, a social and a spiritual landscape, dotted with towns, cities, churches, and monasteries. Above all, it is a landscape permeated by an intense piety, in which the *sainte beguinaige* occupies pride of place and the semireligious penitent becomes the *Sponsa* (Bride) of the Song of Songs, summoned by the bell of love to a desirous encounter with God.[104]

In the treatise's third and final section, four vicious newcomers arrive at the abbey and allegorical exegesis is displaced by a burst of allegorical narrative. The story is one of negligence, invasion, and rescue. An evil usurer (*mauvais userier*), the Devil of

Hell, connives to introduce his four daughters into the abbey.[105] His scheme succeeds because the portress, *Peeur* (Fear), is negligent and fails to guard the abbey's many gates, doors, windows, and other entrances.[106] The Devil's daughters are a hideous quartet of vicious personifications: Envy, Presumption, Murmur-and-Detraction, and False Judgment. Described as half-blind, hunchbacked, stammering, and lame, respectively, their presence throws the abbey into confusion: "si que par ces quatre filles a ce mauvais userier laides et mauvaises est toute l'abbaïe et la religion de cuer troublee et destourbee" (thus by these four ugly and evil daughters of this evil usurer the entire abbey and the religion of the heart is troubled and disturbed).[107]

In response to the inner turmoil provoked by the Devil's disfigured daughters, Charity, the abbess, takes action:

> Mes ma dame charitez l'abbaesse quant ele voit et apercoit ceste chose si doit tantost soner chapitre et assambler tout le couvent et damoisele discrecion leur donra conseil que eles aillent toutes en oroison et prient le saint esperit que il par sa grace les viegne visiter car granz mestiers leur est et adonc doivent chanter en grant devocion. *Veni creator spiritus et cetera* [hymn] qui doucement et volentiers vendra et descendra. Et quant ce vendra a cest ver. *Hostem repellas longius* il les getera hors de l'ordre comme mauvaises garces i ces iiij filles a ce mauvais userier les filles au deable. Et einsi sera l'abbaïe ordenee et renformee comme devant.[108]
>
> (But my lady Charity, the abbess, when she sees and perceives this, must immediately ring the bell for chapter and assemble the entire convent. And demoiselle Discretion shall counsel them that they should all go to prayer and beseech the Holy Spirit that he, by his grace, should come visit them, for their need is great, and then in great devotion they ought to sing, *Come creator spirit, etc.* [hymn], who, sweetly and willingly, shall come and descend. And when [their singing] shall come to this verse, *You repel the enemy afar,* he shall throw them out of the order like evil sluts, these four daughters of that evil usurer, the daughters of the Devil. And thus the abbey shall be put in order and reformed, as [it was] before.)

A signifying change of tense takes place in this passage. The description of the infiltration of the abbey is couched in a vivid present tense; when the abbess rallies the nuns in chapter, however, the future tense is introduced and governs the action of prayer and divine rescue that follows. This shift of tense locates the reader at the midpoint of the narrative: the interior abbey *is* invaded by vice; prayer and rescue, however, are

prescribed and promised *in futuro*. The curious temporal disjunction contained in the *Sainte abbaïe*'s narrative culmination is an extension of a doubled temporal reference found in the first sentence of the treatise's narrative section:

> Mais aucune foiz est avenu et avient souvent que quant ceste abbaïe est si bien fondee gardee et ordenee et dex i est si bien serviz comme vous oez que la portiere par negligence et par sa defaute i laisse entrer et demourer quatre filles a un mauvais userier.[109]
>
> (But it happened once, and it happens often, that when this abbey is so well founded, protected, and put in order, and God is so well served there—as you have heard—that the portress, through her negligence and failure, permits four daughters of an evil usurer to enter and stay.)

The *Sainte abbaïe*'s narrative conclusion describes an infiltration and rescue of the interior abbey that happens not once, but often. Although the allegory's description of life within the interior convent may not evoke the siege conditions that frequently inform the *Somme le roi*'s conceptions of moral interiority, the *Sainte abbaïe* nonetheless defines the inner cloister as dangerously permeable. Fear, the portress, cannot be trusted to keep out the vices; the only remedy for their incursion, the treatise implies, is fervent prayer and the operation of grace.

Whose Cloister? Tradition and Innovation

The *Sainte abbaïe* appropriates and refashions a claustral ideal that had previously been restricted to the Latinate discourse of clerical and monastic authors and their clerical and monastic audiences. Transposing the terms and literary forms employed by antecedent texts to the vernacular language it employs and the vernacular audience it addresses, the *Sainte abbaïe* treatise synthetically masters and refashions this tradition.

The *Sainte abbaïe* owes its greatest debt to the extended architectural exegesis of texts like Hugh of Folieto's *De claustro animae* (c. 1153) and Jean of Saint-Jean-des-Vignes's identically titled treatise (c. 1179). It is in comparison with these treatises that the innovative character of the *Sainte abbaïe*'s translation of the claustral ideal emerges most clearly.[110] In Hugh's and Jean's treatises, the cloister and the architectural compound surrounding it are taken as a kind of "built text" to be prescriptively interpreted as a guide to the virtues, practices, and inner states appropriate to professed life. Hugh states,

> Hujus claustri ambitus, virtutum columnis decoratur, sustentatur patientiae basibus, ac regula justitiae quadratur, virtutum coadjacentibus

officinis munitur, muro boni operis, claustri septa forinsecus ambiuntur, quae clauso silentii ostio vagae mentis gressum prohibent.[111]

(The enclosure of this cloister is adorned with the columns of the virtues, sustained on the bases of patience, squared by the rule of justice, fortified with the adjacent workshops [*coadjacentibus officinis*] of the virtues, surrounded by the wall of good work [and], outwardly, with the enclosure of the cloister, which [two fortifications], when the door of silence is closed, restrain the movement of the errant mind.)

For Hugh and Jean, the cloister is a place of stability, a fixed template to be internalized by those men who live inside its walls.[112] The *De claustro animae* treatises are not concerned with *how* one builds the spiritual cloister, nor do they discuss the installation of the virtues as officers in the spiritual cloister. For the authors and anticipated audiences of the *De claustro animae* treatises, the cloister is already built and the virtues are intrinsic components of the claustral regime. The tension that pervades these Latin texts is instead generated by their desire to fix the wandering mind or affect within the confines of the *stabilitas* demanded by regular discipline.

The *De claustro animae* treatises exhort their readers to read the architecture that surrounds them exegetically so that they may conform their inner life to the authority of the material cloister in which they live, work, read, and pray.

Sicut ex quatuor lateribus claustri materialis structura fieri solet, sic in quatuor virtutibus animi quadratura claustri spiritualis per similitudinem assignari potest, quae sunt contemptus sui, contemptus mundi, amor Dei et amor proximi. . . . Dum enim defectus carnis assiduos cernimus, dum quotidianos occasus animi videmus, tunc quasi in latere claustri, quod ad occasum respicit, sedemus. . . . Recedente sole crescunt tenebrae, minuitur claritas, sic recedente sole justitiae, miserae mentis caecitas advenit. Ille vero, qui profundae noctis tenebras, id est, saecularium difficiles culpas, et eorum corda frigida, gelu desperationis concreta considerat, quasi in latere claustri sedet, quod ad Septentrionem spectat. . . . In latere vero claustri, quod ad meridiem respicit, sumus, quando ardente charitatis sole, divinae majestatis lumen prae nimia claritate tenuiter videmus. . . . Non est igitur quo divertat animus, qui inter haec quatuor virtutum munimina manet constitutus. Non enim ad carnis voluptatem, non ad mundi vanitatem, non ad odium proximi, non ad contemptum Dei.[113]

(Just as the structure of the material cloister is wont to be made from four sides, so, by analogy [*per similitudinem*], the quadrangle of the spiritual cloister can be assigned [*assignari*] to four virtues of the soul, which are contempt of self, contempt of the world, love of God, and love of one's fellow man. . . . For while we perceive the constant failings of the flesh, for so long as we see the daily decline of the soul, then we sit as if in the side of the cloister that faces the setting sun. . . . As the sun recedes, shadows grow, brightness is diminished; thus as the sun of justice recedes, the blindness of the wretched mind arrives. But he who considers the shadows of deep night, that is, the difficult sins of worldly men and their cold hearts, hardened with the frost of despair, it is as if he sits in the side of the cloister that looks toward the North. . . . And we are in the side of the cloister that faces toward the South when, with the sun of charity burning, we acutely see the light of the divine majesty because of its brightness beyond measure. . . . Therefore, there is nothing in which the spirit who remains settled among these defenses of the four virtues might diverge. For [he may not turn] to the desire of the flesh, nor to the vanity of the world, nor to a hatred of his fellow man, nor to a contempt of God.)

When Hugh of Folieto evokes the movement of sunlight across the cloister's walls as a *similitudo* to be assigned to the proper disposition of the soul, he draws upon an experience of the cloister that he assumes his audience shares. For Hugh and Jean the cloister is not only an architectural model for the properly ordered soul; it is also the place within the monastery designated for individual *lectio,* the place where their treatises will be read.[114] The *De claustro animae* treatises are hermeneutic exercises in regular living that ask their monastic readers to reconcile the spiritual self to the authoritative precepts of the architectural environment that surrounds them.

With few exceptions, twelfth- and thirteenth-century Latin cloister allegories and exegeses were works written for the interrelated purposes of conformation and reformation. They prescribe a normative vision of the cloister to novices and established monks alike. In this respect, these works should be understood as remedial texts, designed to initiate brothers-in-training into the requirements of life under a rule and to recall erring brothers to an authentically regular conversio.[115] The *Sainte abbaïe* is also a reformist text, but the audience it exhorts and the claustral ideal it pursues distinguish its vernacular instruction from the Latin texts whose authority it appropriates.

Refashioning and reorienting an established allegorical tradition, the *Sainte abbaïe* translates the founding principles of regular life into active and contemplative practices

accessible to readers living in the world beyond the monastery's walls. The vernacular treatise's transformation of the architecture and discipline of monasticism is nowhere more evident than in its exposition of enclosure itself:

> Or couvient faire le cloistre a quatre corons pour ce a il nom cloistre que il doit estre clos et bien gardez. Fille veuz tu estre bien religieuse. Tien te close garde ton cloistre clo ton cuer de mauvaisement penser tes eulz de folement regarder tes oreilles de males paroles escouter ta bouche de rire legierement et de folement paller. Cele qui se tient close en ces quatre choses est bien religieuse.[116]
>
> (Now it is necessary to make the cloister with four corners; thus is it called a cloister because it must be closed and well guarded. Daughter, do you wish to be truly religious? Keep yourself closed, guard your cloister; close your heart from evil thinking, your eyes from foolishly looking, your ears from hearing evil speech, your mouth from laughing lightly and speaking foolishly. She who keeps herself closed in these four things is truly religious.)

The import of the *Sainte abbaïe*'s exegesis of the cloister's four walls comes into sharper focus in comparison with the exegesis of the *claustrum* provided by a twelfth-century monk of Petershausen:

> De Claustro. *Fores* quippe *erant clausae propter metum Iudaeorum* [John 20:19]. Exceptis enim exterioribus ianuis, quae in monasteriis its sunt clausae, ut nullus eas audeat etiam apertas transgredi, interiores fores tanta clausura sunt munitae, ut raro quisquam eas, etiamsi velit, valeat aperire. Nonne tibi videntur fores tunc bene clausae, quando os a loquendo, aures a vano auditu, manus a malis operibus, pedes vero a vago incessu cohibentur? Velit nolit, monachus tali claustro religatus erit. *Fores,* inquit, *clausae erant.* Hinc primo videtur claustri nomen exortum, quod utique, sicut diximus, manere semper debet intus et exterius undique clausum.[117]
>
> (Concerning the cloister: *The doors,* indeed, *were shut for fear of the Jews* [John 20:19]. Excepting the outer doors, which in monasteries are closed in such a fashion that even were they opened no one would dare to cross them, the inner doors in such an enclosure are so secured that seldom, even if he wished to, is anyone strong enough to open them. Do not the doors seem well closed to you then, when they restrain the mouth from speaking, the ears from vain listening,

> the hands from evil works, and indeed the feet from aimless walking? Whether he wishes or not, the monk shall be bound in such a cloister. *The doors,* he says, *were shut.* From this, the name of "cloister" seems to have first arisen, because certainly, as we said, it must always remain, within and without, closed in every respect.)

Although both expositions of enclosure prescribe a regime of outward decorum in strikingly similar language, the *Sainte abbaïe*'s interpretation of the cloister effectively evaporates its protective and confining walls and, in the process, promotes an alternative definition of authentic conversio and authentic enclosure. The *Sainte abbaïe*'s cloister is no longer the experiential space of monastic restraint; it is instead the regulated space of the self in the world. Most significantly, perhaps, in the *Sainte abbaïe*'s terms to be truly religious is to be *religieuse.*

The explicitly female audience anticipated by the vernacular treatise marks the *Sainte abbaïe* as an appropriative translation of the claustral ideal to an audience composed not of monastic *fratres* but devout *filles.* The feminine form of address employed by the text is but one component in the treatise's decidedly gendered reorientation of the claustral ideal.[118] The *Sainte abbaïe* insistently valorizes the sainte beguinaige, associating it with *amour de perfection:* was the "fille" addressed by the vernacular treatise expected to build her interior cloister within the semi-enclosed space of the beguinage? The text's emphasis on a pious integration of both the active and contemplative lives, and, above all, its vernacular translation and adaptation of key elements of the monastic conversio make the *Sainte abbaïe* a cloister allegory with particular sympathy to the spiritual ambitions and ideals of thirteenth-century *mulieres religiosae.*[119]

Addressed to a reader who is *not* assumed to live within claustral walls, the interior abbey described by the *Sainte abbaïe* is a destination rather than a point of departure. Beginning in the sacrament of confession and culminating in the infusion of grace, the *Sainte abbaïe* tract differs from its monastic exemplars most significantly in its anxiety about the profound permeability of the inward convent. For the vernacular allegory's reader the perfected internal cloister is no impenetrable refuge, but rather a place requiring constant maintenance and reorientation toward the Divine.

In their hour of need, the allegorical convent community assembles in the chapter house and petitions the Holy Spirit by singing the *Veni creator spiritus;* at the start of the hymn's fifth verse, "Hostem repellas longius" (You repel the enemy afar), the divinity comes to their aid.[120] Although the Veni creator spiritus hymn was sung on a variety of liturgical occasions, it was most closely associated with the feast of Pentecost.[121] Playing on the hymn's liturgical referent, the *Sainte abbaïe* subtly conflates the Holy Ghost's descent into the abbey with the descent of the Holy Ghost upon the apostles (Acts 2:1), an event celebrated in the feast of Pentecost. Assembled in the interior chapter house, a space explicitly identified with the sacrament of confession in the treatise's first section, the abbey's virtuous inhabitants receive an apostolic charism from their divine visitor. As the apostles' miraculous speech is assimilated to the confessional speech of the penitent soul, the confessor's purifying absolution is glossed as nothing less than the advent of the Divine in pastoral practice. The construction and inhabitation of the interior abbey is, in the end, not a withdrawal from the outward ministrations of the cura animarum; it is, instead, an extension of that extrinsic regime into the hidden places of the spiritual-moral self. In its conclusion, the *Sainte abbaïe* treatise claims nothing less than the authority of divine patronage and pentecostal supervision for the immaterial, interior enclosure it promotes. The full-page miniature that prefaces the *Sainte abbaïe* treatise takes that authorizing assertion as its point of departure.

Divine Presence in the Cloister of the Soul: Theophany

When a full-page miniature is placed before the beginning of a text it is usually understood to be a summarizing preface to, or recapitulation of, the textual content that follows. Without exception, the painting that faces the *Sainte abbaïe* treatise has been interpreted according to these perceived conventions of medieval text-image arrangement—that is, either as an illustration of the allegory that follows it or as a prefatory statement of that allegory's instruction (fig. 73). The image in question, however, is hardly a conventional image.

Although the figures of nuns in the miniature's lower register invite comparison with the *Sainte abbaïe*'s inventory of personifications, they cannot be neatly reconciled with the text. Unlike the *Somme le roi*'s virtues, identified by tituli and attributes, these female figures are refused the insignia of personification.[122] Placed before the *Sainte abbaïe* treatise, the painting is, in fact, a pictorial sequel to the text it faces. Subverting conventional expectations, the miniature makes an anticipatory visual argument that begins where the vernacular text leaves off.

The space of the image is architecturally demarcated into two zones. In the lower register a crenellated central portal is flanked by two buildings, each inhabited by the figures of nuns. The arched apertures in these buildings are concessions to the voyeuristic gaze, allowing the viewer access to the spiritual labor undertaken behind closed claustral doors. Two activities occupy the lower register of the miniature—disciplined instruction and engaged devotion—the very activities in which each text in the *Somme le roi–Sainte abbaïe* manuscript engages the reader.

Fig. 73. Theophany within the architecture of the soul, c. 1294. London, BL, Yates Thompson MS 11, f. 1v: 245 x 180 mm.

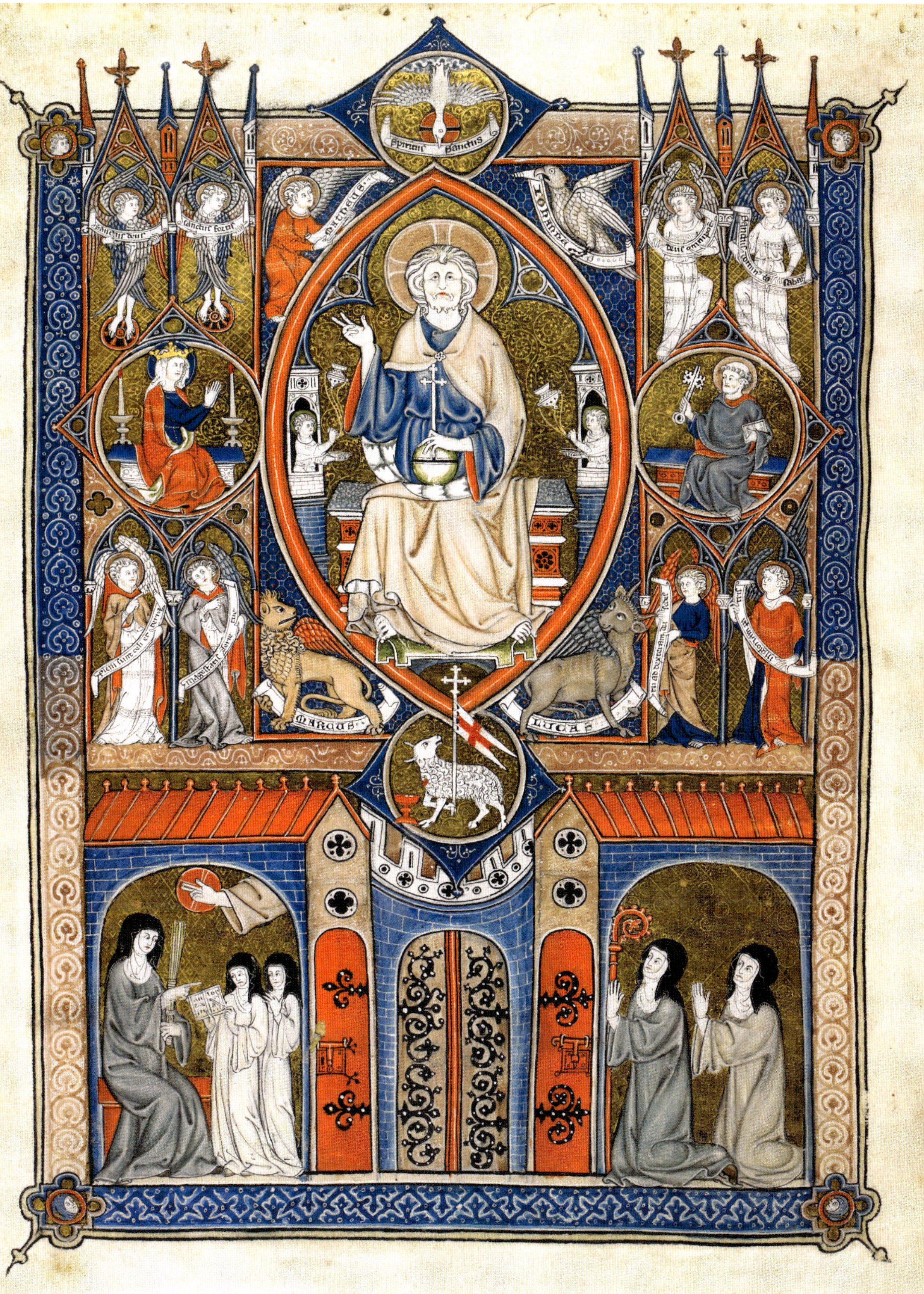
MARCUS
LUCAS

In the convent's schoolroom, or perhaps its *locutorium,* the novice mistress supervises her pupils much as the manuscript would instruct its audience. This claustral instruction is approved by the deity, whose hand blesses the teacher and her students. Although the abbess, identified by her crosier, and her sister-companion in the second conventual building do not receive this metonymic benediction, as they look up toward the center of the upper register their devotion receives its own reward. Within the cloister of the soul, disciplined study earns God's approbation and engaged prayer merits a *visio dei.*

The theophany to which the abbess and her companion direct their devotion is framed by gothic tracery, a filigree-like setting for the heavenly court. At the center of the upper register, Christ sits enthroned in majesty. Staring out of the image, the deity reiterates the benediction given the scene of claustral study in the register below, implicating the manuscript's reader-viewer in this community of blessed learning. The openwork embrasure of the upper register is inhabited by four pairs of angels. Seraphim, distinguished by their six wings and the wheels upon which they float, occupy the upper left pair of trilobe arches surmounted by gables and pinnacles. The upper right tabernacles house a second pair of angels, dressed in white albs; two further sets of angels stand in the lower range of arches, which support the pierced planes of the spandrels above them.

Interposed within the left and right vertical segments of this two-storied angelic array, the Virgin Mary and St. Peter sit on altar-like benches, framed by circular apertures set within pierced diamond-shaped planes. Together with the Holy Ghost and the paschal lamb, they form a cruciform arrangement of plaques that breaks the outer bounds of the upper register's tracery embrasure. At the center of this crux, Christ presides over the heavenly court arrayed about him, flanked by diminutive angelic thurifers who lean out of towers to offer incense before the deity's throne. The image is completed by the four evangelist symbols, who display their names inscribed on banderoles as they contemplate the deity from the spandrels of the rectangular field surrounding the mandorla. Fusing the architectural delineation of a monumental elevation with the planar forms of enameled metal work, the upper register pulls out all the microarchitectural stops to proclaim the sacrality of its painted contents.

Divine presence dominates the miniature's architecture of interiority. The tripled instantiation of Holy Ghost, Christ in Majesty, and Lamb of God defines a strong vertical axis that breaks the upper frame of the miniature and terminates below in the closed portal at the center of the lower register's conventual complex. Surmounted with white crenellation and ornamented with sinuous metalwork vine scrolls, the cloister's closed door stamps its architecture as a fortified *hortus conclusus,* a paradisiacal zone penetrable by the deity alone.

How does God enter this claustral space? The *Sainte abbaïe* treatise asserts that the inner cloister is rescued and reformed by the pentecostal ingress of the Holy Spirit; in this painting of the soul-as-convent, however, it is the *Agnus Dei* (Lamb of God) that bridges the divide between the space of the soul's spiritual labor and the theophanic display above. Equipped with the victorious standard of the resurrected Christ and a Eucharistic chalice, the Lamb of God forges a sacramental bond between the court of heaven and the enclosed architecture of the soul's faculties. In no uncertain terms, the theophanic miniature promotes the Eucharist as the means by which God takes his magisterial place within the cloister of the soul.

The Eucharistic tenor of the image is made explicit in the proclamations held by angels in each corner of the upper register.[123] Three interrelated liturgical texts serve as sources for the praise that fills the heavenly court: the *Trisagion* sung during the Veneration of the Cross on Good Friday; the Te Deum hymn, sung within the divine office at the end of matins on Sundays and on feasts of nine or twelve lessons; and the Sanctus, in which the Preface of the Mass culminates.[124] All three texts are acclamations that address the divinity with the predicate "Holy!"

Sung antiphonally during the Veneration of the Cross on Good Friday, the *Trisagion* is a Greek and Latin refrain.[125] The banderoles held by the seraphim in the upper left corner of the image recapitulate the Trisagion's first two phrases: "sanctus deus," "sanctus fortis" (Holy God, Holy [God] of strength). The third part of the Latin text of the Trisagion does not appear within the image.[126] In its place, the words "deus omnipotens" (omnipotent God) are inscribed on the banderole held by the first of the two angels in the upper right corner of the painting.

The phrase "deus omnipotens" occurs only ten times in the Vulgate.[127] Within the context of the image, the phrase must, I think, be identified with its first occurrence in the Apocalypse. In Apocalypse 4:8 John describes seeing "quattuor animalia singula eorum habebant alas senas et in circuitu et intus plena sunt oculis et requiem non habent die et nocte dicentia sanctus sanctus sanctus Dominus Deus omnipotens qui erat et qui est et qui venturus est" (four living creatures, each of which had six wings, and round about and within they are full of eyes and they rested not day and night, saying, Holy, holy, holy, Lord God Almighty, who was, and who is, and who is to come).[128] The acclamation proclaimed by the four living creatures is itself a recapitulation of the seraphim's praise of the deity witnessed by Isaiah (Isa. 6:1–3). The inscription "deus omnipotens" on the third angelic banderole moves the miniature's collective praise of the deity from the textual framework of the Trisagion to the unending heavenly worship of the deity witnessed by John and Isaiah.

The text held by the fourth angel confirms this reading. Paired with the angel holding the "deus omnipotens" scroll, this angel proclaims, "sanctus dominus deus sabatus" (Holy Lord God *Sabatus*), a latinization of the phrase "sanctus dominus deus sabaoth," declaimed by the seraphim in Isaiah 6:3. Although the Vulgate's translation of Isaiah dispensed with the transliterated Hebrew *sabaoth*, preferring its Latin equivalent (*exercitium*), the Latin liturgy retained *sabaoth* in two texts: the Te Deum hymn and the Sanctus. The banderole held by the fourth angel in the image thus acts as a textual hinge between the seraphic praise witnessed by Isaiah and the liturgical praise of the Te Deum and the Sanctus. The banderoles held by the four angels who occupy the lower range of arches extend this evocation of the liturgy: each angelic scroll is inscribed with a text taken from the Te Deum or the Sanctus.[129]

As songs of ritual praise, the Te Deum and the Sanctus were deliberate emulations of the heavenly liturgy described in John's Revelation and Isaiah's prophetic text. Emphasizing the continuity between these liturgical songs and the words proclaimed by the four living creatures and the seraphim, the angelic banderoles in the theophanic miniature assert the principal theological claim of the liturgy itself: the praise sung to the deity by Christian worshippers is not merely authorized by its recapitulation of scriptural text; rather, it is substantially identical with the worship described by John and Isaiah. Christian liturgy is a temporal performance declaimed in unison with the eternal praise of the heavenly choirs.

Although the Te Deum and the Sanctus were assigned to different liturgical moments (the divine office and the Mass, respectively), for medieval worshippers they were intimately related texts; as Pamela Sheingorn observes, "the text of the Te Deum describes the singing of the 'Sanctus.'"[130] Performed at the end of matins, the Te Deum references both the eternal praise sung in heaven by the four living creatures and the seraphim *and* the temporal praise of the deity sung by the community of the faithful in the Mass. As the Sanctus is sung in the Mass, heaven and earth, the eternal and the temporal, merge in an integrated praise of God, and it is in the Mass that Christ, spiritually and substantially present in the Eucharist, receives this acclamation from all of *ecclesia*.[131]

Within the miniature, this Eucharistic unification of heaven and earth is made visible most emphatically in the figure of the victorious lamb and its chalice. Bridging the divide between the heavenly register above and the conventual register below, the Agnus Dei represents Christ in the guise of the paschal lamb sacrificed in the Eucharist. The figure of the lamb also acts as a kind of word illustration referencing the Agnus dei chant sung immediately before communion within the Canon of the Mass.[132] Asserting that Christ comes to the soul in the form of the Eucharistic lamb, the image identifies the Mass as the occasion for his arrival in the cloister of the soul.[133]

The *Sainte abbaïe* treatise describes the influx of divine presence in the soul as a recapitulation of the Pentecost event, and so emphasizes the role of the Holy Spirit in the grace-filled supervision and reform of the interior cloister. The full-page miniature that faces the vernacular treatise does not neglect the Holy Spirit's participation in the deity's descent into the interior cloister, but it reframes that participation in terms of the Eucharist and the Eucharistic liturgy.

Medieval liturgists interpreted the verse of the Sanctus held by the miniature's fifth angel, "pleni sunt coeli et terra gloria tua" (heaven and earth are full of your glory), as an echo of a scriptural text, "spiritus Domini replevit orbem terrarum" (the Spirit of the Lord hath filled the whole world; Wisdom 1:7), designated for the feast of Pentecost.[134] The perceived interrelationship of these two liturgical texts conflates the reception of pentecostal grace with the reception of the Eucharist, and so glosses both events as figuring the revelation of the deity's full glory in the visio dei already enjoyed by the heavenly court and promised to the faithful.[135] The miniature's theophanic display, centered on the vertical axis formed of the Dove of the Holy Spirit, the Maiestas Domini, and the Agnus Dei, makes this intersection of the temporal and the eternal, of theophanic revelation and Eucharistic reception, visible to a viewer who contemplates neither heaven nor the host, but instead gazes at the painted page.

The liturgical conflation of pentecostal descent and Eucharistic reception accomplished by the miniature's central axis and its florilegium of inscriptions also informs the painting's unusual arrangement of the Virgin Mary and St. Peter on either side of Christ enthroned. Medieval Maiestas representations accompanied by figures other than those of the evangelist symbols or angels were more frequently flanked by the Virgin and John the Baptist, or the Virgin and John the Evangelist. The miniature's grouping of the Virgin seated between two lit candles, the Maiestas, and St. Peter holding his keys is a highly unusual arrangement and one that carries a very specific charge.

Although scripture does not name the Virgin in the group of Christ's followers who received the Holy Spirit (Acts 2:1–4), medieval artists did not hesitate to place her at the center of their Pentecost scenes, making her Peter's female opposite number within the college of the apostles. The pentecostal resonance of this pairing of the Virgin and Peter surely informed their inclusion in the London manuscript's miniature. An even more suggestive iconographic parallel to the *Somme le roi–Sainte abbaïe* manuscript's theophanic composition is, however, provided by an enameled coffer, produced in the first decade of the thirteenth century.[136]

On the front face of this Limousin casket, the Virgin and St. Peter flank the figure of Christ, enthroned in majesty (fig. 74). Both Mary and Peter are provided with insignia that specify their offices within ecclesia: the Virgin holds a scepter terminating in a fleur-de-lis, identifying her with the flowering branch from the tree of Jesse, prophesied in Isaiah 11:1–3, and Peter holds the keys of apostolic authority. Seven apostles are

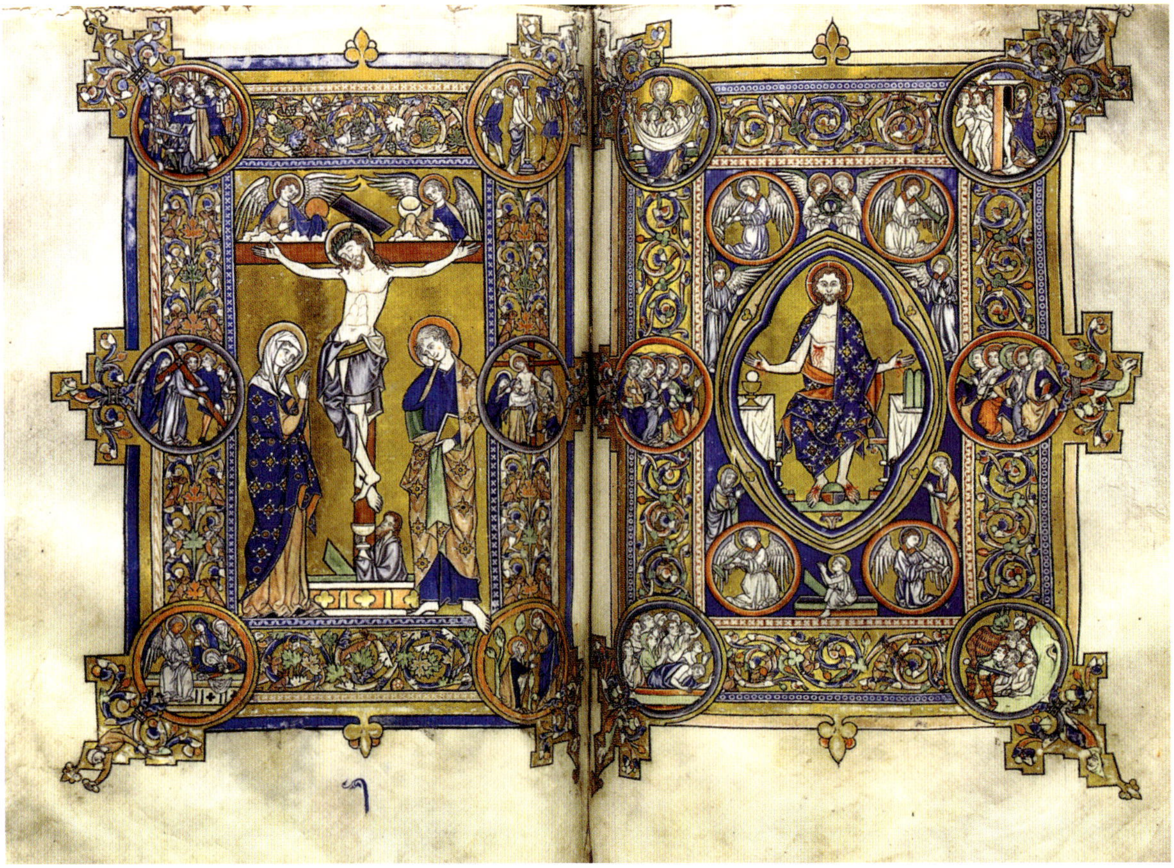

Fig. 77. Crucifixion and Maiestas for the Canon of the Mass; missal, c. 1250. Arras, Bibliothèque municipale, MS 38 (58), ff. 105v–106r: 350 x 245 mm.

the inclusion of a Maiestas at the center of the theophanic miniature; through the appropriation of an iconographic formula closely associated with the Canon of the Mass, the miniature invests its theological argument with liturgical authority. Or perhaps the authority appropriated iconographically should be described as paraliturgical. An image painted for a book of hours provides an illuminating parallel to the *Somme le roi–Sainte abbaïe* manuscript's theophanic miniature.

One of two full-page miniatures from an extensive, and unusual, visual program in an early fourteenth-century book of hours, the image describes an elaborate architectural elevation inhabited by the celestial polity (fig. 78).[138] Pride of place is given to the Virgin Mary, who sits with her son in a central niche. Although the image evokes scenes of the Coronation of the Virgin, its emphasis is less on the Virgin's exceptional merits than on her place at the head of the community of the blessed.[139]

A series of compartments within the heavenly edifice house the apostles, crowned female virgins, male and female saints, martyrs, musician angels, and angelic

thurifers. The corners of the composition explode in cusped medallions inhabited by larger angels, including the seraphim described by Isaiah. In halved medallions on either side of the outer frame, the figures of *Ecclesia* triumphant and dejected *Synagoga* bookend this celestial display, reminding the viewer that his or her salvation is framed by the supersession of the Old Law and the inauguration of the sacramental age of grace.

Although the miniature in this book of hours was painted more than a decade after the *Somme le roi–Sainte abbaïe* manuscript's theophanic miniature, both images draw from a common repertoire of visual tropes, established in the Carolingian period, to affirm the *rapprochement* of the heavenly and the earthly communities within the framework of liturgical celebration. In the fourteenth-century book of hours, the representation of a liturgically unified ecclesia, iconographically appropriated from liturgical use-books, authorizes paraliturgical devotions—forms of meditation and prayer that the personal prayer book encourages its reader-viewer to pursue in the vicinity of, or in tandem with, church ritual.

The *Somme le roi–Sainte abbaïe* manuscript is a very different kind of book. Its vernacular texts and didactic images were compiled for the edification of the reader-viewer, a moral-spiritual labor that complemented—but did not coincide with—the ritual time and space of liturgical celebration and paraliturgical participation. Nonetheless, the theophanic miniature's iconographic appropriations reveal the painting's ambitious pretensions. Here visual signifiers of liturgical celebration and paraliturgical participation are mobilized in a manuscript that is not a prayerbook, but instead contains texts designed to cultivate spiritual excellence by didactic means. In this miniature any tidy distinction between liturgy, paraliturgy, and the intellectual labor of instruction is profoundly blurred.

When the artists who executed the *Somme le roi–Sainte abbaïe* manuscript's visual program began work on the theophanic miniature and the images that follow it, they were confronted with a new problem. Unlike the *Somme le roi,* the manuscript's final suite of texts had never before received visual prefaces or pendants; the manuscript's illuminators no longer had an established visual program from which to work. Extending the signifying microarchitectural repertoire of the *Somme le roi*'s visual cycle, the illuminators completed an additional series of full-page miniatures that reoriented the manuscript's textual and visual program in a new, emphatically sacramental direction.

The theophanic miniature argumentatively appropriates elements from the visual repertoire of the liturgy and paraliturgy in order to confer an explicitly Eucharistic gloss on the mysterium of God's presence in the soul. In this image, the architecture of interiority is visually redefined as a claustral space designed for the theophany of Eucharistic reception. The manuscript's two subsequent images extend this theological argument yet further.

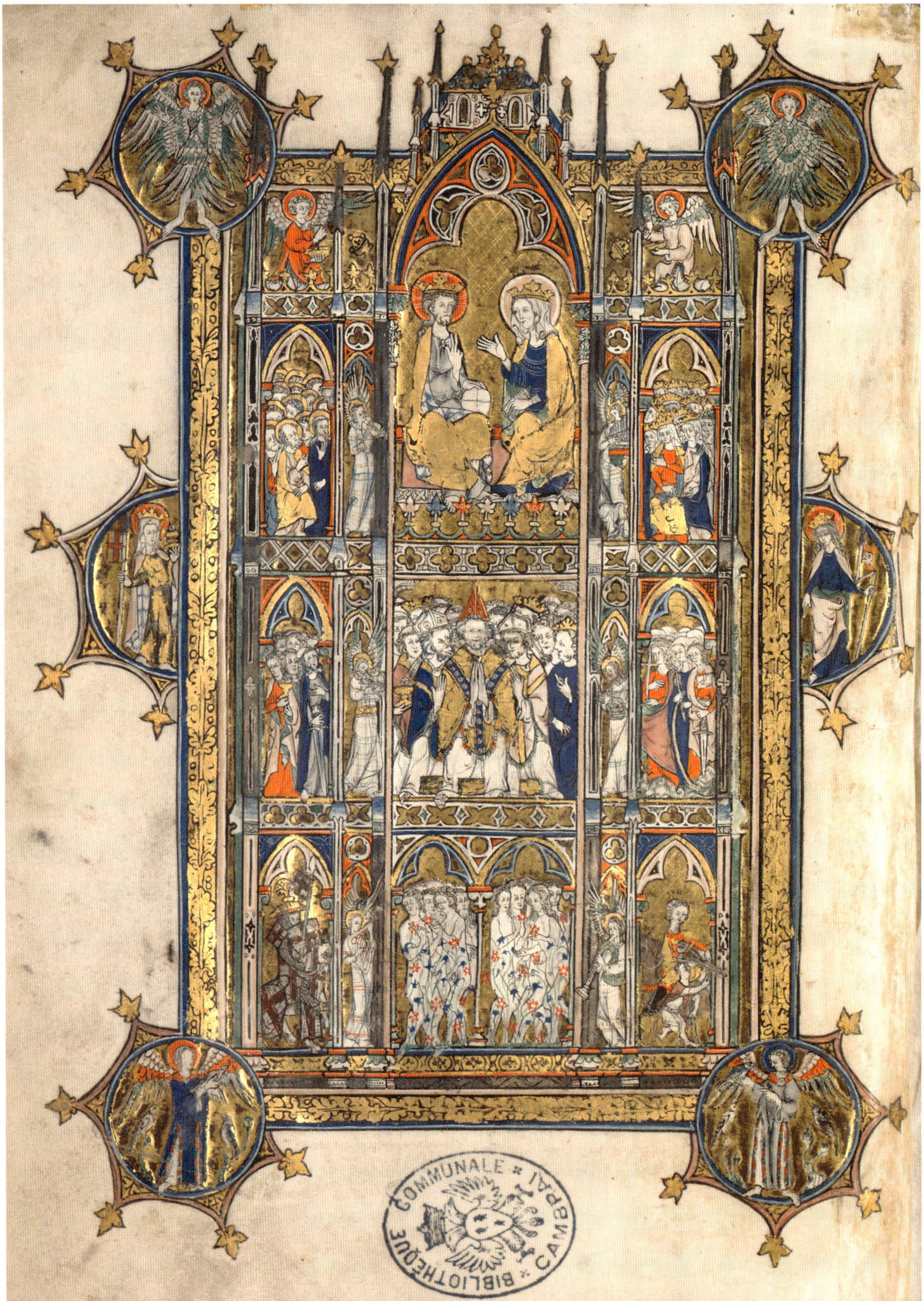
BIBLIOTHEQUE COMMUNALE CAMBRAI

Divine Presence in the Cloister of the Soul: The Liturgy of Participation

The figures of nuns who inhabit the painting prefacing the *Four Loves and the Three Heavens* treatise invite the viewer to see the image as a sequel to the theophanic miniature that precedes it (fig. 79). The residential and pedagogical space of the convent, introduced in the theophanic miniature, is represented in this subsequent image by an arcade filling the lower register and by the blue masonry buildings at the left side of the upper register. The distanced vista of the upper register is dominated, however, by a detailed cutaway view of the abbey's church, a high gothic cathedral in miniature.

In the lower register of the image, a Mass procession wends its way through a series of intersecting round arches that evoke the arcaded space of the cloister walk. Customary processional order is ignored by the miniature: in its fictive procession, the abbess occupies the place of honor usually reserved for the celebrant.[140] Framed by two slender red columns, the priest and the deacon, carrying the Gospel book, nonetheless remain the focal point of the figural grouping. The celebrant's brilliant blue cope, with its intense red lining, forms a chromatic center point within the muted palette of gray and pale brown habits that surround him. Moreover, the convent's celebrant is no ordinary priest; his halo distinguishes him as both saint and presbyter. It is, therefore, all the more puzzling that nothing in the image allows us to identify this priest-saint. In the absence of a titulus or distinctive habit under his cope, the tonsured celebrant remains an anonymous figure of male spiritual authority. The image is not an example of visual hagiography; its emphases lie elsewhere.

An acolyte carrying a processional cross at the head of the procession is followed by the smaller figures of two nuns holding lit candles. Together with the legible text of the choir books held by the nuns who follow, these ceremonial details conclusively identify the liturgical occasion for the convent's solemn procession. Each choir book displays the phrase "Suscepimus deus" (Ps. 47:10), the incipit of the introit for the Feast of the Purification of the Virgin (also called the Feast of the Presentation), in which the church commemorates the fulfillment of the Virgin's ritual obligation and the presentation of her son in the temple.[141]

On the Feast of the Purification, candles were exorcised, blessed, and distributed to churchgoers. Once lit, the candles were carried in procession to the Mass as a symbolic evocation of the entrance of Christ as the divine light into the church. The ritual significance of the Purification procession was proclaimed by the singing of the antiphon "Lumen ad revelationem gentium" (A light to the revelation of the people; Luke 2:32).[142] The *Somme le roi–Sainte abbaïe* manuscript's miniature describes just this liturgical moment in its lower register. As they sing the introit for the Feast of the Purification, "Suscepimus deus misericordiam tuam in medio templi tui" (We have received your

Fig. 78. The heavenly polity housed in a book of hours, c. 1310–1315. Cambrai, Médiathèque municipale, MS 87, f. 17v: 250 x 177 mm.

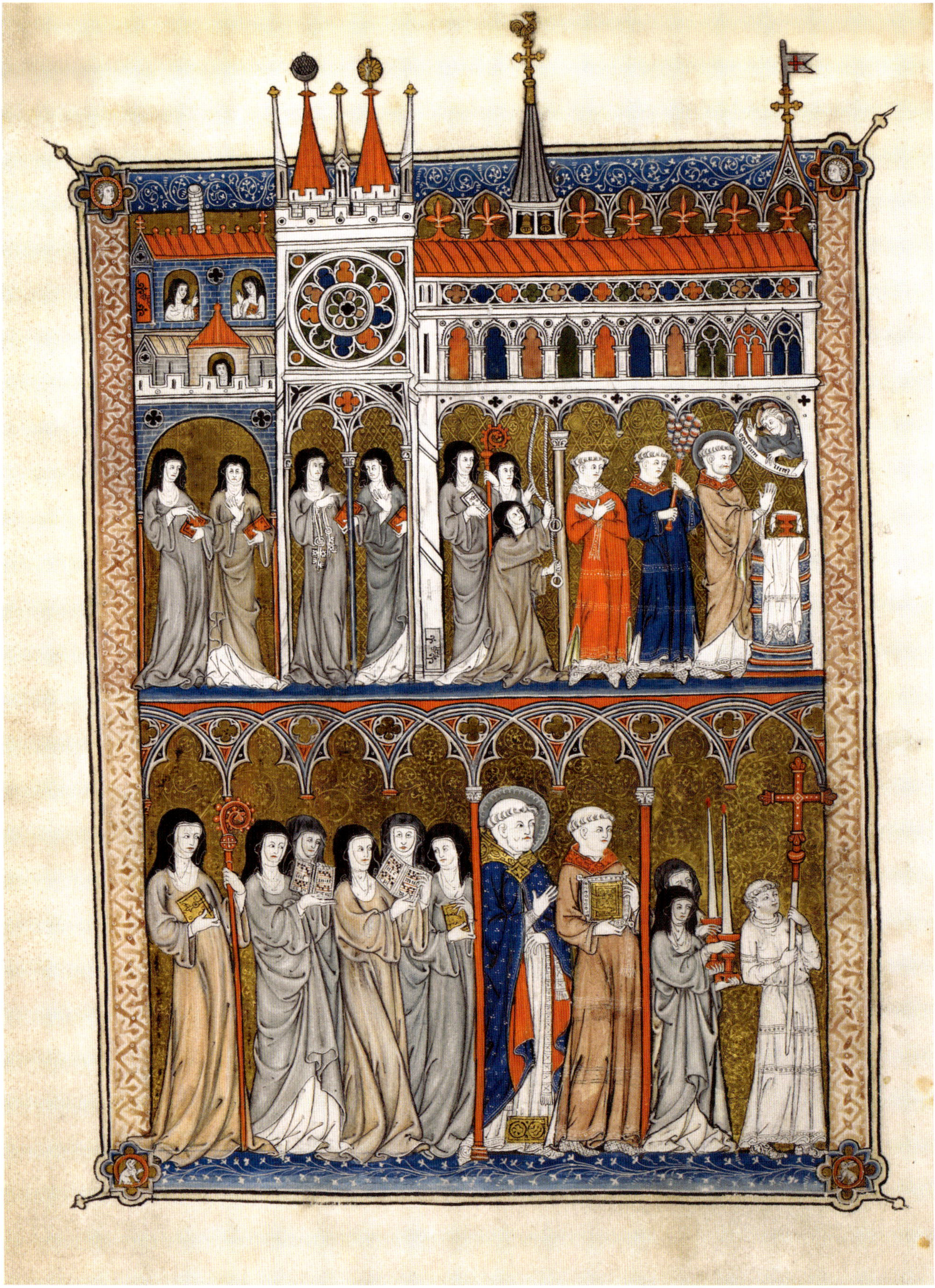

mercy, O God, in the midst of your temple; Ps. 47:10), the convent community prepares to receive Christ in the Eucharist.

The confident tenor of the introit receives a wondrous reply in the upper register of the painting as Christ appears in the conventual church upon and above the altar. Blessing the Eucharistic species and the abbey community, Christ holds a banderole inscribed "Ego sum vita" (I am life), a distillation of his promise to the disciples after the last supper: "Ego sum via et veritas et vita nemo venit ad Patrem nisi per me" (I am the way and the truth and the life. No man cometh to the Father, but by me; John 14:6).[143]

In its scriptural context, Christ's affirmation of his salvific power assures the disciples that they will be able to follow him into the *domo Patris,* the heavenly home of his father. The miniature translates both the content and the context of Christ's authoritative pronouncement into the space and liturgical framework of the contemporary church. The last supper, in which Christ instituted the Eucharist, becomes the Mass, the ritual reiteration of that paschal meal; the messianic promise to the disciples is made an affirmation of the salvific power of the Eucharist as the means by which all Christians travel the path of salvation.

Several visual cues indicate that Christ's figural appearance occurs at a very precise liturgical moment. The nun-sacristan's ringing of the bells, the flabellum held by the deacon standing immediately behind the priest, and the chalice covered with a folded white corporal collectively announce that the Mass has arrived at the moment of the consecration of the Eucharist.[144] Within the image, Christ's mystical presence above the altar is a visual guarantee of his real presence upon the altar.

Although the celebrant and the abbey community seem unaware of Christ's mystical appearance in their midst, the architectural space of the altar responds to the deity's presence. Above the altar the triforium lights are elaborated with tracery, distinguishing them from the simple trilobe apertures that surmount the nave; their three-light structure articulates a trinitarian gloss on the mystery of Eucharistic presence, couched in the visible language of architectural form.[145]

The painting's insistence on Christ's real presence in the Eucharist is not, however, the sum of its visual exhortation, nor is the lower register's evocation of the Feast of the Purification incidental to the miniature's theological argument. What is at stake in the image is a particular lesson in sacramental reception, and the miniature exploits the liturgical symbolism of the Feast of the Purification miniature to communicate its theological instruction.

As the fictive convent community processes to the church, they reiterate two biblical itineraries: the Holy Family's journey to the temple for Mary's ritual purification and Christ's ritual presentation, and Simeon's divinely inspired visit to the temple in

Fig. 79. Eucharistic celebration in the inward convent, c. 1294. London, BL, Yates Thompson MS 11, f. 6v.

search of the savior. As the Cistercian abbot Guerric of Igny (1138–1156) explains in his first sermon for the Feast of the Purification,

> Quis enim hodie, cereum ardentem gestans in manibus, non statim illius beati senis recordetur, qui hodie accipiens Iesum in ulnas suas, Verbum in carne tamquam lumen in cera, ipsum esse lumen ad illuminationem gentium perhibebat? Erat profecto et ipse *lucerna ardens et lucens* [John 5:35] testimonium perhibens de lumine, qui ad hoc ipsum in Spiritu, quo plenus erat, venit in templum: ut, suscipiens *misericordiam tuam, Deus, in medio templi tui* [Ps. 47:10; introit for Feast of the Purification], praedicaret ipsam esse misericordiam et lumen populi tui.[146]
>
> (For who today, bearing a lighted candle in [his] hands, does not immediately remember that blessed old man [i.e., Simeon] who, receiving Jesus in his arms today, the word in flesh just as a light in wax, affirmed him to be a light for the illumination of the people? For truly he himself [i.e., Simeon] was a *burning and shining lamp* [John 5:35], bringing forth testimony about the light, who, in the Spirit with which he was full, for this very reason came into the temple so that, receiving *your mercy, O God, in the midst of your temple* [Ps. 47:10; introit for Feast of the Purification], he might declare it to be your mercy and a light to your people.)[147]

Referencing the "Lumen ad revelationem gentium" antiphon, Guerric interprets the lit candles carried in the festal procession as visible tokens of Simeon's shining witness to Christ's divinity and of Christ's illuminating divinity itself. With Mary, the faithful bear Christ, the light, into the church; with Simeon, they are illuminated witnesses to Christ's divine illumination of his church.

Liturgical participation in the Feast of the Purification is also a figure of communal participation in salvation for Guerric's fellow Cistercian, Bernard of Clairvaux (1090–1153). In his first sermon for the Feast of the Purification, Bernard writes:

> David, rex et propheta, *exsultavit ut videret diem istum; vidit, et gavisus est* [John 8:56, modified]. Alioquin si non viderat, unde psallebat: *Suscepimus,* inquit, *Deus, misericordiam tuam in medio templi tui* [Ps. 47:10; introit for Feast of the Purification]? Suscepit hanc misericordiam Domini David, suscepit Simeon, suscepimus et nos, et *quicumque sunt praeordinati ad vitam* [Acts 13:48, modified]: siquidem

Christus heri, et hodie, et in aeternum [Hebr. 13:8, modified]. In medio enim templi misericordia est, non in angulo aut diversorio, quia *non est personarum acceptio apud Deum* [cf. 2 Par. 1:7; Acts 10:34; Rom. 2:11; Eph. 6:9; Co1. 3:25; 1 Pet. 1:17]. In communi posita est, offertur omnibus, et nemo illius expers, nisi qui renuit.[148]

(David, king and prophet, *rejoiced that he might see that day: he saw and he rejoiced* [John 8:56, modified]. Otherwise, if he had not seen, why then did he sing: *We have received,* he says, *O God, your mercy in the midst of your temple* [Ps. 47:10; introit for Feast of the Purification]? David received this mercy of the Lord, Simeon received [it], and we ourselves, and *all those who are predestined for life* [Act. 13:48, modified], have received it; since indeed *Christ* [exists]—*yesterday, today, and forever* [Hebr. 13:8, modified]. For mercy is in the midst of the temple, not in a corner or a lodging place, because there is no respect of persons with God [cf. 2 Par. 19:7; Acts 10:34; Rom. 2:11; Eph. 6:9; Co1. 3:25; 1 Pet. 1:17]. God's mercy is placed in common, it is offered to all, and no one is deprived of it, save he who refuses [it].)

Bernard, like Guerric, invites his audience to identificatory participation. Finding in Simeon a type for all faithful Christians, Bernard makes the Feast of the Purification a terrestrial paradigm for the merciful encounter with divinity that awaits the saved. Simultaneously, Bernard asserts that in the liturgical framework of the feast's celebration the faithful—as a community—already encounter God's mercy in the midst of the Christian temple when they, like Simeon before them, receive Christ on the altar. As a symbolic and ceremonial setting for Eucharistic encounter, the Feast of the Purification proclaims the corporate unification worked by Christ's presence in ecclesia.

The mystical, sacramental, liturgical, and ecclesiastical integration of the Christian community achieved through Christ's real presence in the Eucharist is the *thema* visibly elaborated by the *Somme le roi–Sainte abbaïe* manuscript's Mass miniature. The image is a representation of the Purification unlike any other in medieval art. Rather than representing the historical event of the Purification as a prefiguration for the Eucharistic celebration of the church, the image works in a liturgical mode, inviting its viewer to discern the *figura* of scriptural event in the ritual present tense.

The miniature's visual evocation of the liturgy is not an end in itself: liturgical referents are employed as an internal, interpretive apparatus by which the image visibly elucidates the mysterium of sacramental participation and Eucharistic encounter. The painting provides a simulated ideal monastic community for its viewer: contemplating the image, the viewer joins the fictive convent in their festal celebration.

And yet, how could the viewer, scrutinizing this lavish representation of a conventual solemnity, fail to recognize that his or her vision of the Mass surpasses that enjoyed by the nuns and the celebrant? Together with the painted nuns and Eucharistic ministers, the viewer contemplates Christ's body and blood in the Eucharistic species upon the altar. The mystical appearance of the figure of Christ above the altar, however, goes unnoticed by the abbey community: it is the image's viewer alone who sees beyond the appearance of the consecrated chalice, and so perceives the painting's full sacramental theophany. Within its representation of monastic liturgical performance, the image translates an encounter with the visible sacrament as a visual apperception of that sacrament's invisible substance. Incorporated into a fictive community of liturgical performance, the viewer of this miniature receives an exceptional vision of God's mercy in the midst of the abbey church, a structure that figures both ecclesia and interiority.

It is the image's fiction, its capacity to reimagine liturgy and sacrament, that insistently privileges the book owner's viewpoint. Representation rewards the viewer in this image, offering him or her a vision that penetrates beyond liturgical signifiers to the very sacramental signified at the heart of the Mass. In this way the visible fiction of the image trumps liturgical *realia,* and the viewer sees beyond the nuns and celebrant, encountering not only Eucharistic appearances but even sacramental substance within the painted frame.

From Sacrament to Divine Enclosure: Two Textual Itineraries for Contemplative Ascent

The text that follows the Mass miniature has only the most tenuous relationship to the illumination that introduces it. Like its prefatory miniature, the *Four Loves and the Three Heavens* treatise emphasizes proper participation in Christian community as the foundation of spiritual progress. In the text, however, community is defined with reference to four manners of love, an ascendant scale of charity that begins in a self-interested love of one's fellow man and culminates in leal amour, a perfect charity that loves human creatures in God alone.[149] Subjecting leal amour to further exposition, the treatise explains that it encompasses three spiritual loves, exegetically identified with Paul's rapture through the three heavens.[150] In the tract's discussion of the first heaven the divergent didactic trajectories of text and image briefly intersect.

The *Four Loves and the Three Heavens* treatise identifies the first heaven with "l'amour dont dex nous aimme" (the love with which God loves us), a love expressed on earth through the sacraments.[151] The treatise then discusses several of the sacraments in the order in which they are received by the faithful: baptism, confirmation, the

Eucharist (preceded by a brief digression on penance), and extreme unction.[152] Among the sacraments, the Eucharist receives the most extensive, even effusive, exposition.[153]

Discussing Christ's real presence in the consecrated bread and wine, the text rehearses an oft-repeated admonition:

> Encor le fait pour ce que nostre foiz a plus grant merite car se nous veissiens ce que nous creons tele creance ne deserviroit mie merite. Mes por ce est granz nostre merite que nos creons ce que nous ne povons vooir. Il est ore tans de croire et apres ceste vie sera tans de vooir.[154]
>
> (And also he does this [i.e., God maintains the appearance of the bread and wine in the consecrated species] so that our faith should have greater reward; for if we were to see that which we believe, such belief would deserve no reward at all. But for this reason is our reward great, that we believe what we cannot see. It is now the time to believe and after this life it will be the time to see.)

The treatise promises its audience that creance's victory over the contrary testimony of vision will win them salvation. The faith praised by the text is the faith of the miniature's fictive nuns, who greet Christ's presence upon the altar although they do not see him above the altar. As the treatise continues, however, the text makes a brief and unexpected detour from this well-trod catechetical path:

> Nequedent il i a de teles ames qui en ceste vie le voient et sentent mes ce est en esperit et especial don que dex done a ses amis. Et sanz ce puet on bien avoir salut qu'en n'a pas selonc le sentement mes selonc la foi.[155]
>
> (Nevertheless there are such souls who see and sense him in this life, but this is in spirit, and [it is] a special gift that God gives to his beloved ones. And without this, one can truly have salvation, which one has not according to sensory perception but according to faith.)

Hemmed in by caveats and admonishments, the treatise allows for a visual apperception of Christ's presence in the Eucharist. Although the tract insists that seeing the deity *en esperit* is not necessary to salvation, it privileges this Eucharistic theophany as an exceptional gift, a mark of special distinction conferred by God on his *amis*.

In this respect, we can see how the tract's prefatory image exceeds the terms of the tract's verbal instruction. In the painting, an intent gaze discovers Christ in and

Implicitly evoking the Pauline *speculum in enigmate* (1 Cor. 13:12), the treatise explains that even a soul who has become a fervent Sponsa may encounter her divine bridegroom only "couvertement." The tract promotes the sacraments, particularly the Eucharist, as necessary mediators between the soul and her creator. Sacramental encounter with divinity is veiled, indirect, and partial; it is, however, no less necessary or sweet to the soul.

Here again we can see an obvious tension between visual and textual instruction. In the image that prefaces this passage no enigma intervenes between viewer and divinity, and the sacrament is hardly a veil for divine presence within the pictorial field. Instead the Eucharist is figured as a two-part event, a display of species and deity together at the altar. Painted representation offers the viewer an unobstructed, naked vision of the host and the Divine, a theophany that surpasses the conventional limits of theophany, as rehearsed by the text.

In the *Four Loves and the Three Heavens* tract, the soul's perfection culminates in the third heaven, a spiritual state in which the soul leaves behind all of creation, including her self, in order to come to rest within the divinity:

> Mes encore veut dex que vous passez outre si comme il dist a abraham que il issist de la maison son pere car il veut que vous oubliez vos meismes et anges et archanges et toutes creatures qui sunt en ciel et en terre si entrez dedenz deu meismes c'est ce que il dist ou sautier. *Audi filia et vide et cetera* [Ps. 44:11]. Fille dist il oi et voi et encline t'oreille et oublie ton pueple et la maison de ton pere et dont couvoitera li rois ta beauté. Il li rueve veoir escouter et regarder pour connoistre les biens que dex a faiz en li et aus autres ames et en aprés veut que ele oublie son pueple c'est soi meismes et les autres ames qui avec li sunt en terre et encor veut que ele oublie la maison son pere ce est toute la compaignie des anges si que ele soit entierement enclose en deu et dont sera ele si bele ce dist que li rois couvoitera sa biauté. Or povez vooir qu'il ne veut mie que ele demeure au premier ciel ne au secont mes que ele trespasse jusques au tierz ciel.[159]
>
> (And yet, God wants you to pass beyond [the second heaven], just as he said to Abraham that he should leave the house of his father, for he wants you to forget yourself, and the angels and archangels, and all creatures that exist in heaven and earth, and so to enter within God himself; this is what he says in the psalter. *Listen daughter and see, et cetera* [Ps. 44:11]. Daughter, he says, listen and see, and lend your ear, and forget your people and the house of your father, and thus the king shall greatly desire your beauty. He asks her to see, to listen, and to look, in order to know the good things that God has done in

> her and in the other souls who are with her on earth; and, moreover, he wants her to forget the house of her father, this is all the company of the angels, so that she should be entirely enclosed in God; and thus she shall be so beautiful, it says, that the king shall greatly desire her beauty. Now you can see that he does not desire that she should remain in the first heaven, nor in the second, but that she should pass beyond, even to the third heaven.)

God's desire for the soul is a radically transformative love that desires—even demands—that she should ascend beyond herself, and beyond all of creation, until she attains a complete absorption within the deity, the most radical of enclosures. At the end of the *Four Loves and the Three Heavens* treatise, the author revisits this *unité d'esperit,* only to emphasize that it surpasses human understanding and speech. Speaking directly to the reader, he acknowledges the limits of his own didactic authority:

> les granz estoupes et li destourbiex qui me sunt venu seur le col me deffendent que je n'en die neant et pour ce n'ose je plus avant paller devant ce que dex me donra plus de pais et me metra en autre estat. Mes vous qui estes enclos en nostre seigneur a cui il a revelé ses secrez fichiez i voz esperiz si vous saoulez des delices vostre espous et si en departez a nous qui sommes mendianz des mietes qui chient de vostre table.[160]
>
> (the great deceits and troubles that have fallen upon me forbid that I should say anything, and for this reason I do not dare to speak further until God shall give me greater peace and shall put me in another state. But you who are enclosed in our Lord, to whom he has revealed his secrets, fix there your spirit, and sate yourself on the delights of your spouse and thus share with us, who are beggars, the crumbs that fall from your table.)

In this concluding address, the tract's author not only affirms his confidence in the possibility of complete union with the deity, but even expresses his conviction that his reader has already attained this divine enclosure. Fixed and enclosed in the deity, the reader now surpasses the author in spiritual authority.

The image of the spiritual banquet, from which the author of the *Four Loves and the Three Heavens* treatise begs a few crumbs, recurs in the final, contemplative stage of spiritual perfection discussed by the *Three States of Good Souls* tract. The tract takes the wedding feast in Cana (John 2:1–11) as a scriptural figure for the banquet of contemplation, the nuptial feast in honor of the soul and her divine bridegroom. The soul comes to the banquet through an ascesis that begins and ends in love:

> Einsi sunt cil mort par amors qui pour l'amour de deu ont veincuz les travauz et les langors des temptacions et sunt aussi comme mort au monde. . . . Beneuree est l'ame qui a pasees les langors d'amors et parmi le repos de cele douce mort est venue a la vie d'amors que mais ne la couvient mendiier ne mengier son pain en travail ne en doleur ainz a tout trespassé si siet comme espouse avec son ami ihesu crist aus noces de galilee ou ele est aemplie de delices esperituels et voit son ami face a face.[161]
>
> (Thus are those ones dead through love, who, for the love of God, have conquered the labors and languors of temptations and [they] are as if dead to the world. . . . Blessed is the soul who has passed beyond the languors of love and amid the repose of this sweet death has come to the life of love, so that never more need she beg or eat her bread in labor or pain, for thus she has passed beyond entirely and so she sits as a bride with her beloved, Jesus Christ, at the wedding in Galilee where she is filled with spiritual delights and she sees her beloved face to face.)

The *Three States of Good Souls* treatise does not, however, describe the journey to God as a linear progress, comedically completed in the soul-bride's nuptial visio dei. The tract instead emphasizes the soul's oscillation between the heights of contemplation and the oppression of sin and temporal cares. The treatise prescribes reading, meditation, prayer, graciousness (*deboneretez*), charity, and discretion as the soul's only means of preparing for the arrival of the bridegroom.[162]

The *Four Loves and the Three Heavens* treatise and the *Three States of Good Souls* tract prescribe spiritual itineraries that begin in purgation and culminate in a nuptial enclosure in God. Despite their common emphases, however, the ordering of the texts in the manuscript implicitly encodes an ascending spiritual progression. In keeping with the tenor, if not the specific argument, of the Mass miniature that prefaces it, the *Four Loves and the Three Heavens* treatise promotes the transformative power of sacramental participation. The *Three States of Good Souls* treatise makes the sacrament of penance a necessary, but preliminary, point of departure for an initiation into the more elevated spiritual states of devotion and contemplation. In the codicological and conceptual space between these two treatises, and between the degrees of spiritual progress they encode, the *Somme le roi–Sainte abbaïe* manuscript's final image offers the reader-viewer an independent vision of spiritual ascent (fig. 80).

Fig. 80. From confession to contemplative enclosure: a laywoman apprehends divinity, c. 1294. London, BL, Yates Thompson MS 11, f. 29r.

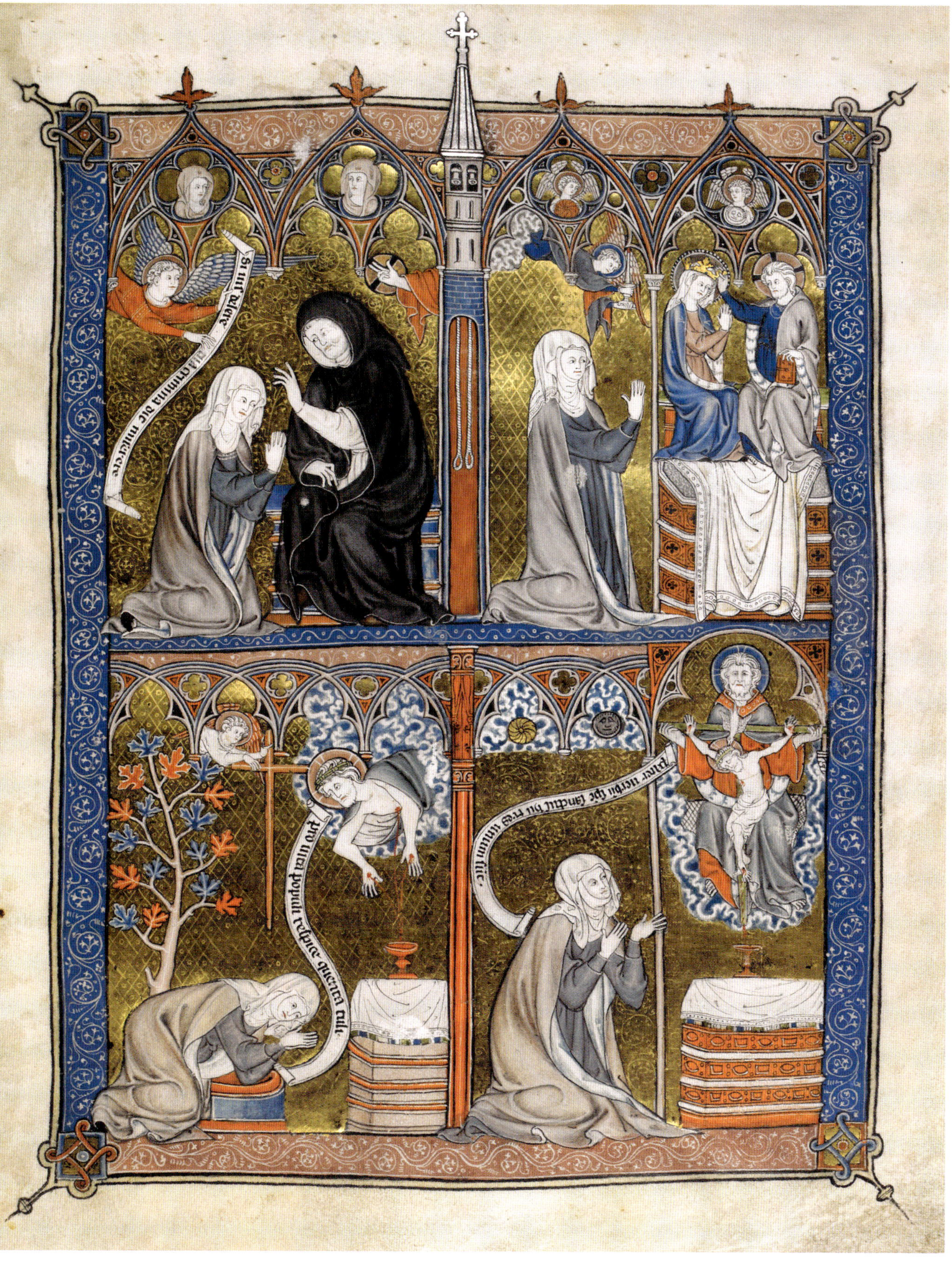

The Devotee in the Presence of the Deity: Sacramental Encounter as Contemplative Enclosure

The manuscript's final image stages a drama of spiritual ascent in four acts. The heroine of this mystical narrative wears a blue robe, a pale brown mantle, and the simple white veil and wimple of the modest, unprofessed matron. In this image—the culmination of the manuscript's visual program and, arguably, the most spiritually ambitious of its paintings—the apex of mystical progress is attained not by a nun or a saint, but rather by an anonymous laywoman, distinguished only by her devotion.[163]

The image's account of mystical ascent has an emphatically sacramental point of departure: in the upper left quadrant of the painting, the laywoman and a Dominican friar enact a scene of confession. In the upper right corner of this quadrant, the friar's gesture of absolution is echoed discretely by the hand of God. The deity's metonymic presence goes unobserved by the woman and her confessor. The quadrant does not describe a moment of theophany, but rather it visually asserts the sacramental nature of confession: it is the deity, present in the sacrament, who works the remission of the laywoman's sins. The celestial authority of sacramental absolution is also marked by the appearance of an angel who acts as a kind of ventriloquist glossator, enclosing the moment of confession with a banderole inscribed, "Si vis delere tua crimina dic Miserere" (If you wish to efface your sins say the *Miserere*). The speech scroll addresses the female penitent in the doubled voices of confessor and divine creator, assigning her a particular penance: she must recite Psalm 50, one of the seven penitential psalms.

Although the psalms formed the bedrock of the divine office from the earliest days of Christian monasticism, by the thirteenth century they had also become an important component of the daily devotions of lay, particularly female, elites.[164] Compiled, in whole or in part, with other accessory texts in books of devotion tailored to the needs of extra-monastic audiences, psalm texts punctuated the devotional day of both court and cloister in the later Middle Ages. Although the miniature invokes the devotional utility of the psalms most explicitly in the angel's banderole, the influence of psalm-based devotion may be discerned throughout the image; it was in the visual programs devised for psalm-based prayer books that the manuscript's illuminators found authoritative models for their innovative composition.[165]

The *Somme le roi–Sainte abbaïe* manuscript's scene of confession is echoed in an English psalter, illuminated circa 1325–1335 (fig. 81).[166] Inhabiting the initial for the Canticle of Isaiah (Isa. 12:1–6), the figure of a female penitent, whispering in the ear of her Franciscan confessor, embodies the prophet's song: "Confitebor tibi domine quoniam iratus es mihi" (I will confess to you, O Lord, because you were angered with me).[167]

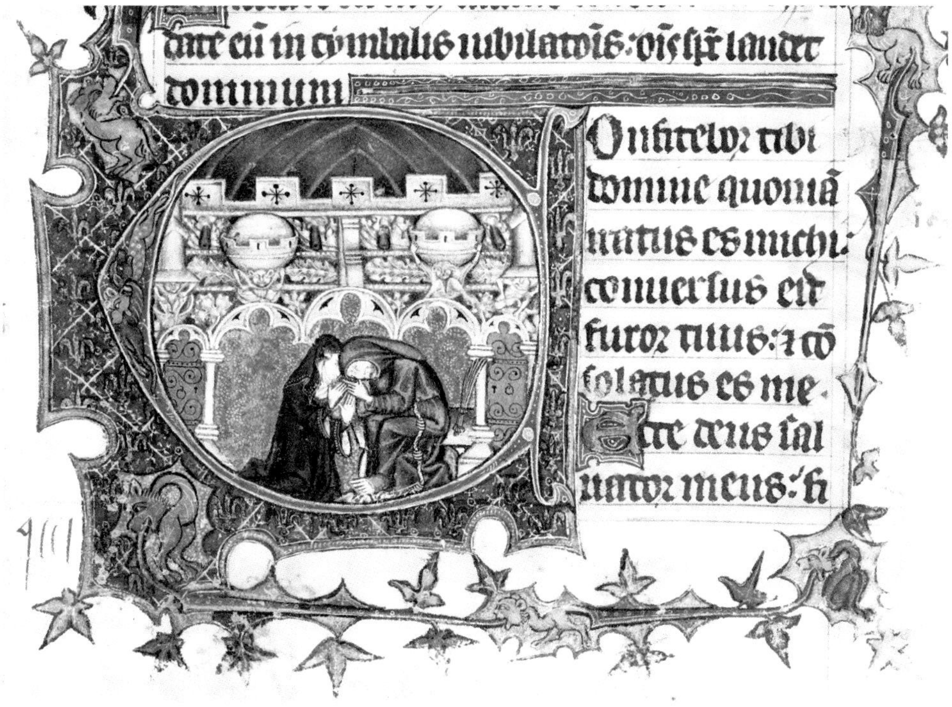

Fig. 81. Whispered confession in an English psalter, c. 1325–1335. Oxford, University of Oxford, Bodleian Library, MS Douce 131, f. 126r (detail): 233 x 155 mm.

The initial for the first penitential psalm (Ps. 6) in a Thérouanne psalter-hours, executed in the 1280s, represents a female devotee kneeling before an altar (fig. 82).[168] Above the veiled chalice on the altar, the hand of God reaches out from the rippling edge of a cloud to bless her devotion. The psalm initial encloses the precise combination of elements that the *Somme le roi–Sainte abbaïe* manuscript's final miniature distributes among its four quadrants: penitential psalm, female supplicant, altar, Eucharistic offering, and divine apparition (see fig. 80). In the psalter-hours, the inhabited initial represents an ideal form of prayer for a praying viewer; the *Somme le roi–Sainte abbaïe* manuscript's miniature reconfigures the component parts of this ideal in order to visualize a spiritual itinerary surpassing the terms, and perhaps even the normative ideals, of the devotional routines codified in prayer books.

The manuscript's final miniature frames its narrative of mystical ascent within a quadripartite setting that deliberately emulates the architectural embrasures of the *Somme le roi*'s Gift Virtue miniatures. As in the *Somme*'s miniatures, microarchitectural framing transforms the image's four quadrants into an intercommunicating series of spaces in which exterior affect becomes an index of interior transformation and the visual rhetoric of architectural form and ornament encloses the laywoman's ascent to God within a larger, signifying structure.

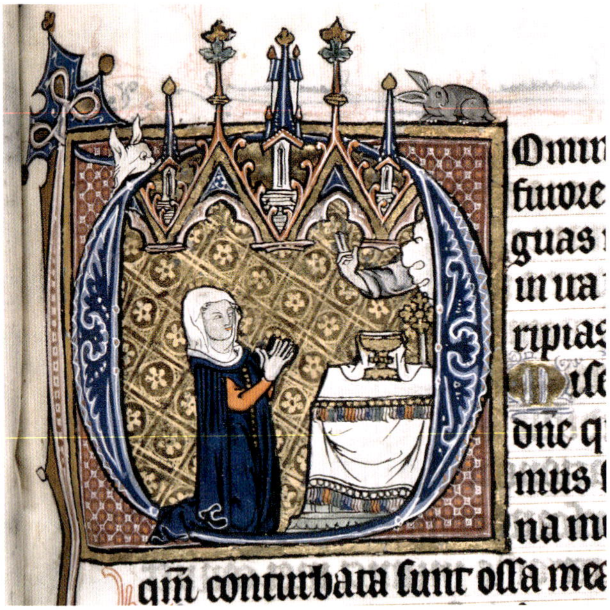

Fig. 82. *The ideal of psalm-based devotion in a Thérouanne psalter-hours, c. 1280s. Marseille, Bibliothèque municipale, MS 111, f. 40r (detail): 195 x 135 mm.*

One element of the miniature's micro-architecture specifically references two other images in the manuscript's visual program. The bell tower marking the divide between the miniature's upper left and right quadrants recalls the bell tower that looms over the repentant sinner in the *Somme le roi*'s Humilité miniature and the belled steeple of the manuscript's Mass miniature (see figs. 55 and 79).[169] The still ropes and soundless bells painted in the two penitential vignettes are marked visual counterpoints to the church bells rung vigorously by the nun-sacristan at the moment of the consecration. The repentant sinner and the penitent laywoman perform their devotions outside of the framework of corporate liturgical celebration. Like the blessed soul discussed in the *Sainte abbaïe* treatise, these repentant figures are summoned to prayer by the internal bells of the heart; with her they can say, "J'ai un cuer a clochetes esveillié pour bien amer" (I have a heart woken by bells to love well).[170]

Stirred to penance and absolved, the laywoman benefits from the sacramental *imitatio Christi* of her confessor, a confluence of pastoral and divine authority that is made visible by the Dominican's mimetic repetition of the deity's gesture. In the second quadrant of the miniature, the laywoman herself participates in the authorizing economy of spiritual imitatio as she kneels before an altar bearing a statue of the Coronation of the Virgin. The devotee's mimetic emulation of Mary's sculpted figure signals the efficacy of her visually intent devotion: contemplation conforms her to the object of her pious vision.

In this second quadrant, an angel holding a lit candle, the apparatus of sacrality, further dignifies the laywoman's prayer. A dense complex of allusions is concentrated in this angelic gesture. The angelic candle bearer figures a celestial facilitation and approbation of the woman's visual piety. The candle offered before the statue on behalf of the lay penitent also evokes the lights provided for statues, altars, and liturgical use in parish and cathedral churches by lay parishioners, both in life and by testamentary bequest in the later Middle Ages.[171] Above all, the light brought to the female figure's prayer before the Virgin and her son is a metaphoric figure for spiritual *illuminatio*, the divine penetration and elevation of the soul.

The sun and moon held by diminutive angels in the quatrefoil *oculi* of the quadrant's arcade establish a temporal frame for the laywoman's image-based devotion. Although her prayer before the statuary group is assisted by an angel, it is visually situated within the ordinary progress of day and night. As signs of the dramatic eclipse that preceded Christ's death on the cross (Matt. 27:45; Mark 15:33; Luke 23:44–45), the sun and moon were also conventional attributes of the Crucifixion (see fig. 77). Within the manuscript's final miniature these celestial lights reprise their role as a portent; in this image they do not announce the historical moment of Christ's death, but instead signal the mystical recapitulation of Christ's sacrifice that erupts in the painting's third quadrant.

In the miniature's lower left compartment, the laywoman cowers in proskynesis, averting her eyes from Christ's startling appearance. Wearing the crown of thorns and bleeding copiously into the chalice on the altar, Christ assumes the form of an inverted, visionary man of sorrows whose Eucharistic presence overwhelms the devotee. The rippling cloud bank surrounding Christ marks his appearance within the arcaded space of the quadrant as a visible and visionary event. Behind the unseeing woman, a tree sprouts green and red leaves, a further sign that the space of quotidian devotion has been utterly transformed by Christ's mystical *adventus*. A third supernatural element completes this scene of theophany: in the space between Christ's wounded figure and the miraculous tree, an angel displays a simple red cross. The conjunction of living tree and ruddy cross glosses this Eucharistic theophany in terms of the salvation won by Christ's passion. This visual commentary is voiced imperatively in the sinuous speech scroll that stretches from Christ to the woman below him. With divine authority Christ commands her: "pro vita populi respice quanta tuli" (look how much I bore for the sake of the life of the people).[172]

In the image's final scene the laywoman obeys Christ's command and looks. In a final burst of the cloud bank that spans the lower register, Christ reappears above the altar within a trinitarian Throne of Mercy. The Trinity's presence transforms the architecture about it. The regular rhythm of the register's arcade is broken as the final bay expands to accommodate the divine apparition laterally and vertically, transgressing the internal border above it. In this attenuated space, the altar is also transformed; it is a *mensa gemmata*, a sacrificial table encrusted with gems.[173]

Transfixed by the imposing apparition of the Trinity that floats above chalice and altar, the laywoman raises her hands in wonder. Devotee and triune deity are linked by a curving banderole that proclaims, "pater verbum spiritus sanctus hii tres unum sunt" (Father, Word, Holy Spirit, these three are one). Significantly, we cannot be sure who affirms the mysterium of the Trinity. The words inscribed on the banderole are written in the same direction as those uttered by Christ in the previous quadrant, as if they emanated from the Trinity. And yet, the inscription, derived from the *comma Johanneum*

(1 John 5:7–8), is a distanced, dogmatic statement that makes the Trinity's unity the object, rather than the origin, of its affirmation.[174]

The ambiguity that attaches to this utterance is deliberate; it is inseparable from—even constitutive of—the miniature's theology of perfection. As the speech scroll curves about the woman's form, it trespasses the slender column that separates her from the space of the altar and the visionary apparition above it. Within the quadrant, the lay devotee's apprehension—both visual and epistemological—of the truth of divinity is inscribed in the authorized and authorizing language of Latinate catechesis.

The trinitarian apparition that interpellates the female devotee takes an emphatically Eucharistic form. As God the Father hieratically presents his crucified son to the laywoman, and to the viewer, blood drips from Christ's feet into the chalice placed on the altar below. This vision of the Trinity is a vision of the trinitarian presence in the Eucharist; the image renders the laywoman's apprehension of the reality of God's threefold unity as a communion with Communion.

The painting's staging of spiritual ascent is pervaded by a dialectic of seeing and not seeing, of corporeal and spiritual vision and their material and ineffable objects. In the first two quadrants, the laywoman pursues salvation with the means available to the active life: confession, prayer, and visual piety. In this upper register, contemplation of the Virgin's sculpted form conforms the female devotee to her feminine exemplar, yet she does not discern God's presence in the sacrament, nor does she greet the angel who attends her at prayer. In the lower register of the image, devotion's labor is surpassed by the revelation of divine presence. The distinction between the visible and the invisible that pervades the upper register is now obliterated by Christ's redoubled presence as visionary apparition and visible, yet wholly divine, Eucharist. The vision that the laywoman cannot bear to contemplate is simultaneously supersensible and sacramentally signified. In the miniature's final quadrant, the sacrament's exceptional conjunction of the material and the transcendent transforms not only the architectural space around it but even the laywoman herself. In the presence of the Trinity, the female figure confronts the fundamental mystery of the sacrament: the union of the human and the Divine, the material and the sacred, signifier and signified.

The *Somme le roi–Sainte abbaïe* manuscript's final miniature describes spiritual ascent as a process that begins and ends in forms of sacramental participation. It is the practice of confession, the sine qua non of Eucharistic reception after the Fourth Lateran Council, that inaugurates the female penitent's spiritual ascent. The manuscript sounds its most triumphant note in an image of penitential theophany, an encounter with divinity provoked by sin's remediation rather than the stability of conventual life, and in

the final quadrant of this last image, enclosure is, at last, fully translated. No longer a function of metaphoric architecture, the manuscript's final painting figures enclosure as a theophanic encounter initiated by sacramental participation, a spectacular apprehension of divine truth articulated in the language of catechesis.

Conclusion: Translation and Enclosure

> Igitur claustrum est omnibus omnia; scilicet principibus, bellorum procellas fugientibus, est portus salutis; negotiatoribus, aestum curarum declinantibus, est refrigerii obumbraculum; servis vel arctatis, a nimio labore cessantibus, est lectus quietis; militibus hostes suos fugientibus, est certum asylum, ut firmum castrum; indoctis, schola virtutum inexercitatis, exercitium diversarum artium, vagis vel criminosis carcer, imo hospitium; inexpertis caminus probationis, poenitentibus infernus purgans, rebellibus infernus crucians, sapientibus et charitate ferventibus paradisus affluens deliciis, aeternis eos replens divitiis.[175]
>
> (Therefore the cloister is all things to all people; namely, to princes fleeing the tempests of wars, it is a haven of safety; to merchants shunning the scorching heat of cares, it is the shade of consolation; to slaves or the oppressed, retiring from excessive labor, it is a bed of rest; to soldiers fleeing their enemies, it is a secure refuge; to the unlearned, unpracticed in the school of the virtues, it is the exercise of diverse arts; to the wandering or guilty, a prison, nay rather, a hospice; to the inexperienced, a testing forge; to the penitent, a purifying hell; to the rebellious, a crucifying hell; to the wise and to those [who are] fervent in charity, a paradise overflowing with delights, filling them with eternal riches.)

In his *De vita claustrali* (On the claustral life), Honorius Augustodunensis (c. 1080–c. 1156) promotes the cloister as a universal panacea, an antidote to the burdens and infirmities that pervade every walk of life. Within its walls princes, merchants, slaves, and the unlearned are freed from the diversity of their troubles and weaknesses by the purifying, reformist, and salvific regime of life under a rule. The *stabilitas* of the cloister is a constant in this equation. For Honorius, the issue at stake is not whether the cloister can be built, or how it must be built, but rather, will troubled men enter its doors?

The *Somme le roi–Sainte abbaïe* manuscript perpetuates many of Honorius's claims for claustral living; it proceeds, however, from a very different set of assumptions. Underlying the manuscript's textual and visual promotion of the claustral ideal is the implicit assumption that the doors of the material cloister are shut. The material enclosure of regular community does not define a refuge or regime within which the manuscript's reader-viewer reads and views. The *Somme le roi–Sainte abbaïe* manuscript is, in the end, no more (or less) idealizing of claustral life than Honorius and other promulgators of the claustral ideal, but the vernacular manuscript promotes the claustral ideal as a metaphoric exemplar for interiority, rather than an architectural destination. For the *Somme le roi–Sainte abbaïe* manuscript, the cloister is not found; it must be made.

In its translations of the cloister, the manuscript privileges the process of edification because, unlike the intended readers of so many Latin cloister treatises and allegories, its anticipated reader-viewers do not enjoy a quotidian vision of the architecture to which their spiritual selves are to be conformed. The *Somme le roi–Sainte abbaïe* manuscript's audience must learn to construct a more perfect moral-spiritual interior from the materials available to the mixed or active life: good works, penance, pious devotion, theological engagement, and sacramental participation.

Although the manuscript's program of spiritual edification owes much to the pastoral syllabus, the *Somme le roi–Sainte abbaïe* manuscript ambitiously surpasses this catechetical baseline. Offering its reader-viewer a thoroughly theological initiation into the arcana of moral discernment, contemplative ascent, and even mystical union, the manuscript makes its most radical arguments in images. The theological sophistication of the *Somme le roi–Sainte abbaïe* manuscript's illuminations and the theological audacity of its three final images, newly devised for the manuscript and never repeated, stamp the manuscript's visual program as a profoundly ambitious translation of the cloister or, more precisely, the convent.

The spiritual culture of female monasticism in the later Middle Ages fostered intensely visual forms of piety—a piety, moreover, that encompassed affective response *and* theological sophistication.[176] Convents also played a major part in the efflorescence of vernacular works of devotion and theology.[177] It has long been argued that many characteristic practices of late medieval lay piety had their origins in the spiritual traditions—and innovations—of female monasticism. The example of the *Somme le roi–Sainte abbaïe* manuscript suggests that the migration of vernacular texts of spiritual instruction and the cultivation of a theology-in-images were hardly the result of a "trickle-down" spirituality. The manuscript's texts and images reveal a deliberate appropriation of theological and spiritual ideals associated with conventual milieus for a lay audience beyond the walls of monastic enclosure.

The *Somme le roi–Sainte abbaïe* manuscript subjects enclosure to the most radical of transformations. Disassociated from the ideals of material confinement and hermetically sealed virginity, the manuscript translates enclosure as a state of constant interior reform, of perpetual spiritual refashioning—in short, as a product of moral-spiritual artifice. The manuscript does not, however, prescribe the construction and constant renovation of the interior cloister as an end in itself. The preparation of a claustral interiority is, instead, promoted as a necessary prerequisite for divine indwelling. In its texts and images, the manuscript urges the reader-viewer to refashion his or her soul into an architecture designed for theophany.

The manner and means of the deity's entrance into the soul are described most cogently and compellingly by the manuscript's three final images. A diffuse textual discourse on contemplation and the soul's union with God is concentrated, refined, and extended in these miniatures. They visually re-translate the claustral ideal, transforming its instrumental status as an exemplar for reformed interiority into a metaphoric account of the soul's apprehension—both visual and epistemological—of divinity.

As the *Somme le roi–Sainte abbaïe* manuscript's final painting describes mystical progress as an ascent from sacrament to sacramental vision—culminating in an epiphanic encounter with sacramental truth—it asserts an axiom that implicitly authorizes all of the manuscript's images: namely, that the ineffable may be realized visually. This is an implicit, but no less triumphant, avowal of the spiritual efficacy and excellence of all works of visual pastoralia, a profession of faith in things seen.

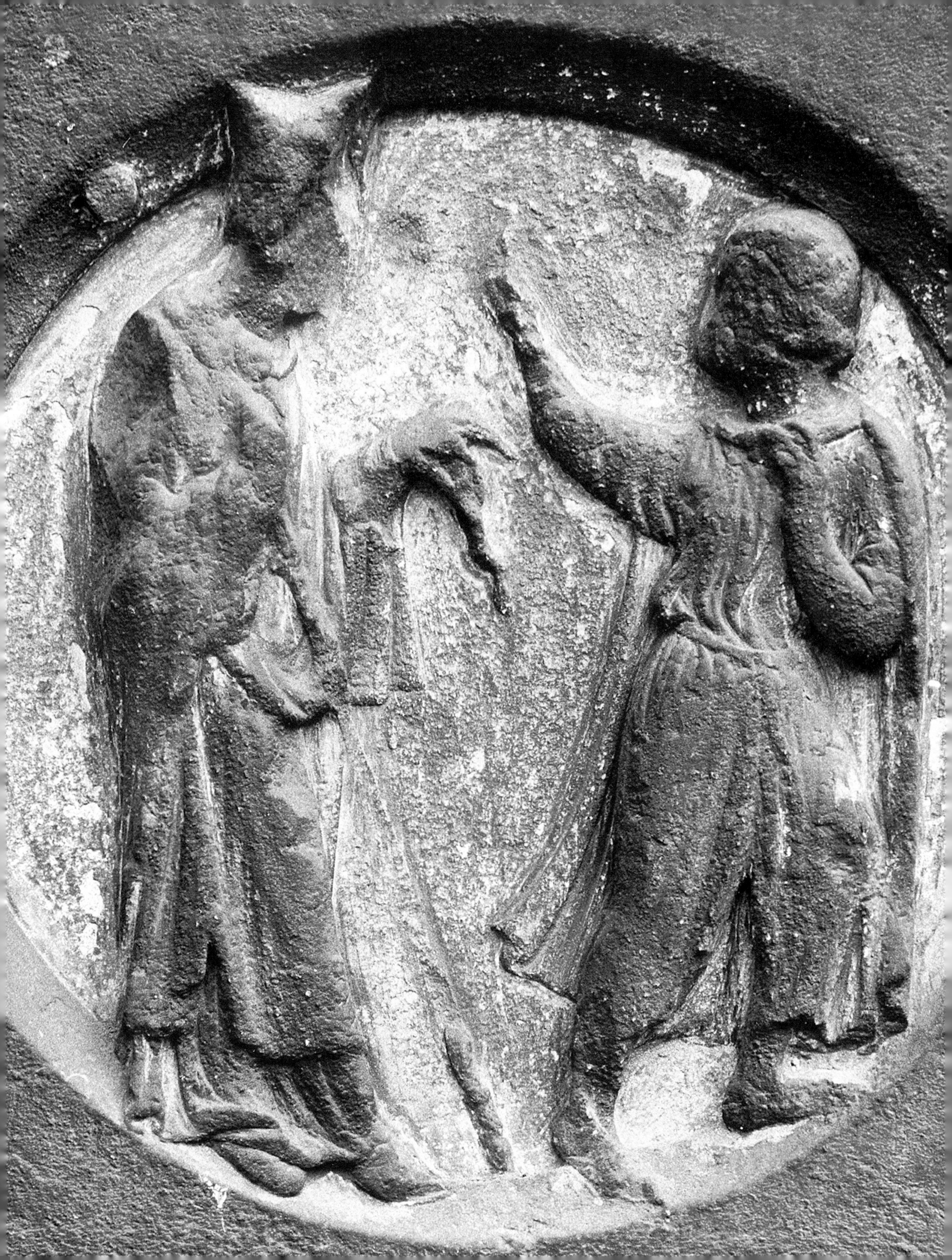

Conclusion

Le moyen âge a conçu l'art comme un enseignement.
Tout ce qu'il était utile à l'homme de connaître . . .
lui était enseigné par les vitraux de l'église ou par les statues du porche.

(The Middle Ages conceived of art as a lesson.
All that was useful for man to know . . . was taught to him
by church windows and the statutes of the [church] porch.)
—Émile Mâle

At close of the nineteenth century, Émile Mâle discerned in the monumental surfaces of France's great cathedrals a kind of plein-air schoolroom for an undifferentiated medieval laity. Hardening a fantasy of immutable doctrine into stony forms or else discerning the reflection of a unitary clerical *pensée* in the lustrous polychromy of stained glass, Mâle advanced a vision of medieval art as fundamentally didactic.[1] In Mâle's thirteenth century, *doctrine* emanated from ecclesiastic authorities and was translated (*traduite*) by artists—if confusedly—to a *sainte plèbe* whose vernacular language was still incapable of abstract thought.[2] He wrote, "Au moyen âge, toute forme est le vêtement d'une pensée. . . . La forme ne peut se séparer de l'idée qui la crée et qui l'anime" (In the Middle Ages, every form is the garment of a thought. . . . The form cannot separate itself from the idea that created it and animates it).[3]

For Mâle, medieval religious art was the materialization of a transcendent, fundamentally stable religious truth in historical and visible form, a process of translation he described in terms of fidelity and docility. A sworn witness to truth, Mâle's religious image was fashioned by thought as if from within, a visible expression of those *grandes idées directrices* that seemed, to the French iconographer, to change not at all in the later Middle Ages.[4] In this analysis, religious truth—a distinguished species of the genus meaning—always precedes form; visually translated, religious truth (or

Detail from Fig. 67

meaning) acquires a more or less accurate outward aspect, a more or less faithful material expression.

This is, of course, an understanding of religious truth and sacred signification that Mâle appropriated from Latinate medieval theology. It was this conception of religious truth as always a priori—existing before and beyond human language and the limits of the visible—that paradoxically authorized the very possibility of translating divine verities into visible form and simultaneously insisted upon the limitations of the sensible and of human artifice in the face of divine mysteries. This medieval conception of religious truth has surfaced again and again in the preceding chapters as a historical artifact and source of authorization for the medieval project of visual translation. It is not, however, an account that can in any way prepare us for our first, second, or one hundredth encounter with the illuminations discussed in this book. It cannot explain the elegant specificity of the Lambeth Apocalypse's allegory of penitence, it does not address the edificatory power of the *Somme le roi–Sainte abbaïe* manuscript's simulated architecture, it does not exhaust the transformation of vision worked in the Paris Mass tract's miniatures or the complicated, even contradictory account of religious knowledge asserted by the figure of Sainte Eglise and her book of devinitei in Blanche of Castile's Bible moralisée.

As the analyses of individual chapters and the broader argument of this book have, I hope, demonstrated, the visual translation of religious truth performed by the manuscripts I have examined—and by many other works of medieval art—was transformative. By this I mean that it was a process accomplished in the making of visible forms—in all their visual and material specificity—and in the beholder's encounter with them. Accordingly, these paintings and the visual programs to which they belong are irreducibly formal interventions in the discursive production of truth and religious authority. The specific visible appearance of each painting, its manual delineation, the precise details of its material realization on the manuscript page, even its apparent revision or emulation of anterior visual models—these are not merely persistent accidents to be seen beyond, a captivating surface behind which the powerful substance of meaning is concealed. To say that these images translated religious truth is, in my account, to insist that they—quite literally—transformed it.

When these manuscripts were painted, did their illuminators have in mind a radical transformation of modes of religious knowing, the dismantling of a textual monopoly on sacred verities, the inauguration of a new chapter in the history of the image or the visibility of religious truth? Without sharing Mâle's nostalgia for an imagined era of docile artists, I think the response to this largely rhetorical question must be negative.[5] As members of an increasingly organized and robust community of commercial bookmen, the illuminators of these books worked within a larger system of visual production: they used existing models when they could, devised new compositions from the fragments of antecedent images, and worked within established stylistic modes. In this respect, the miniatures they painted are best understood both as rarefied constituents of a "mainstream" tradition of artistic practice and religious discourse, and, simultaneously, as reinventions of those orthodoxies, providing them with new resources capable of new feats of discursive production, truth formation, and revelation.

Collaborating with vernacular texts, the paintings I have interpreted in the preceding chapters effectively revised powerful and long-standing Christian conceptions of the role of epistemology and the sensible in the practice of faith and the pursuit of salvation. Collectively, they amount to a sustained assertion of the semantic efficacy and authority of visual representation and a compelling argument for the spiritual efficacy of vision, not least the beholder's vision of the painted page.

And so, the object of this study is not the truths congealed or concealed in late medieval painting, but rather the religious truths formed by painting in the later Middle Ages. The visual translation of religious truth that I have traced within and across the heterogeneous group of manuscripts examined in the preceding pages was a process, one that began in the making of visible forms and continued in the perceptual and hermeneutic space between the visible object and its beholder. No static codification of religious truth, each manuscript is better understood as a material practice, a dialogic intervention that spoke to its privileged beholder about his or her salvation, transforming religious knowledge into a way of seeing, translating religious truth into visible forms, and soliciting the book owner's ambition, thought—even his or her dread and delight—in response. These manuscripts were demanding objects, books that made claims upon artists and beholders, involving laymen and women in the epistemological refashioning of the self, in spiritually powerful ways of looking, in the pursuit of salvation and the production of religious truth. That images made by human hands were entrusted with this labor testifies to the power of the work of art in the later Middle Ages.

ABBREVIATIONS

A-N L: Dean, Ruth J., and Maureen Barry McCann Boulton. *Anglo-Norman Literature: A Guide to Texts and Manuscripts.* Anglo-Norman Text Society Occasional Publications Series, 3. London: Anglo-Norman Text Society from Birkbeck College London, 1999.

BL: London, British Library

BnF: Paris, Bibliothèque nationale de France

C&S I (II): Whitelock, D. M., M. Brett, and C. N. L. Brooke, eds. *Councils & Synods: Vol. I, A. D. 871–1204; Part II, 1066–1204.* Oxford: Clarendon Press, 1981.

C&S II (I): Powicke, F. M., and C. R. Cheney, eds. *Councils & Synods: Vol. II, A.D. 1205–1313; Part I, 1205–1265.* Oxford: Clarendon Press, 1964.

C&S II (II): Powicke, F. M., and C. R. Cheney, eds. *Councils & Synods: Vol. II, A.D. 1205–1313; Part II, 1265–1313.* Oxford: Clarendon Press, 1964.

DEC (1): Tanner, Norman P., ed. *Decrees of the Ecumenical Councils,* vol. 1. London: Sheed & Ward; Washington, D.C.: Georgetown University Press, 1990.

EGM (1): Morgan, Nigel. *Early Gothic Manuscripts: Part 1, 1190–1250.* A Survey of Manuscripts Illuminated in the British Isles, 4. London: Harvey Miller; New York: Oxford University Press, 1982.

GM (1): Sandler, Lucy Freeman. *Gothic Manuscripts, 1285–1385, Part 1.* A Survey of Manuscripts Illuminated in the British Isles, 5. London: Harvey Miller; Oxford: Oxford University Press, 1986.

GM (2): Sandler, Lucy Freeman. *Gothic Manuscripts, 1285–1385, Part 2.* A Survey of Manuscripts Illuminated in the British Isles, 5. London: Harvey Miller; Oxford: Oxford University Press, 1986.

SLR: Frère Laurent. *La somme le roi.* Edited by Edith Brayer and Anne-Françoise Leurquin Labie. Paris: Société des anciens textes français; Abbeville: F. Paillart, 2008.

SSF 1: Pontal, Odette, ed. *Les statuts synodaux français du XIIIe siècle: Tome 1, Les statuts de Paris et le synodal de l'Ouest (XIIIe siècle).* Collection de documents inédits sur l'histoire de France; Série in-8o, 9. Paris: Bibliothèque nationale, 1971.

SSF 3: Avril, Joseph, ed. *Les statuts synodaux français du XIIIe siècle: Tome 3, Les statuts synodaux angevins de la seconde moitié du XIIIe siècle: Précédés d'une étude sur la législation synodale angevine.* Collection de documents inédits sur l'histoire de France; Série in-8o, 19. Paris: Éditions du Comité des Travaux historiques et scientifiques, 1988.

SSF 4: Avril, Joseph, ed. *Les statuts synodaux français du XIIIe siècle: Tome 4, Les statuts synodaux de l'ancienne province de Reims.* Collection de documents inédits sur l'histoire de France; Série in-8o, 23. Paris: Éditions du Comité des Travaux historiques et scientifiques, 1995.

NOTES

INTRODUCTION

1. For discussion of antecedent antiscopic and iconoclastic traditions, see Tryggve N. D. Mettinger, *No Graven Image;* Alain Besançon, *The Forbidden Image,* 13–146.
2. On medieval conceptions of idolatry, see Irven M. Resnick, "Idols and Images"; Michael Camille, *The Gothic Idol;* Jean Wirth, "Faut-il adorer les images?"
3. On medieval representation's relationships to "optical truth" and other realities, see Max Dvořák, *Idealism and Naturalism in Gothic Art;* Jean Wirth, *L'image médiévale,* 267–299; Madeleine Caviness, "'The Simple Perception of Matter'"; Madeleine Caviness, "Images of Divine Order."
4. On the Gregorian dictum, with extensive further bibliography, see Herbert L. Kessler, "Gregory the Great and Image Theory"; Cynthia Hahn, "Visio Dei."
5. For a foundational exploration of medieval visual representation as theological argument, see the studies collected in Herbert L. Kessler, *Spiritual Seeing.*
6. David Freedberg, *The Power of Images;* Hans Belting, *Likeness and Presence;* Hans Belting, *Das Bild und sein Publikum im Mittelalter.*
7. The literature on medieval theories and practices of vision is extensive and still growing; see, for example, Jean-Claude Schmitt, "L'imagination efficace"; Herbert L. Kessler, *Seeing Medieval Art,* 165–179 (esp.); Cynthia Hahn, "Vision"; Thomas Lentes, "'As far as the eye can see . . .'"; Jeffrey Hamburger, "Seeing and Believing"; Jeffrey Hamburger, "Speculations on Speculation"; Madeleine Caviness, "Images of Divine Order"; Caroline Walker Bynum, "Seeing and Seeing Beyond"; Cynthia Hahn, "Visio Dei."
8. The representation of sacred history, including hagiographic narratives, has also been a topic of considerable interest: Suzanne Lewis, "Narrative"; Suzanne Lewis, *Reading Images;* Cynthia Hahn, *Portrayed on the Heart.*
9. There have, of course, been important exceptions to this generalizing rule in the last thirty years, and my own analysis is deeply indebted to these alternate accounts of medieval religious representations; see, for example, Cynthia Hahn, "Visio Dei"; Michael Camille, "Before the Gaze"; Jean-Claude Schmitt, "Imago: De l'image à l'imaginaire"; Jean-Claude Schmitt, "Les images classificatrices"; Madeleine Caviness, "Images of Divine Order." For a recent collection of essays exploring the intersection and, at times, fusion of medieval art and theology that offers a range of accounts for religious images in the period, see Jeffrey Hamburger and Anne-Marie Bouché, *The Mind's Eye.*
10. Jean Wirth, *L'image à l'époque gothique,* 205.
11. Michel Foucault, *Histoire de la sexualité,* vol. 1, 78–84 (esp.).
12. "Depuis le Moyen Age au moins, les sociétés occidentales ont placé l'aveu parmi les rituels majeurs dont on attend la production de vérité: réglementation du sacrement de pénitence par le Concile de Latran, en 1215, développement des techniques de confession qui s'en est suivi . . . l'aveu est devenu, en Occident, une des techniques les plus hautement valorisées pour produire le vrai": Michel Foucault, *Histoire de la sexualité,* vol. 1, 78–79.
13. Nicole R. Rice, "Spiritual Ambition and the Translation of the Cloister." Rice focuses on late fourteenth-century Middle English texts and their receptions, but as her own analysis of the French origins of *The Abbey of the Holy Ghost* indicates, a consideration of Anglo-Norman and Old French literature of spiritual instruction clearly indicates that the phenomenon of lay spiritual ambition predates its manifestation in Middle English literature. In her recent book, Rice employs the term "spiritual aspiration": Nicole R. Rice, *Lay Piety and Religious Discipline,* 17–46 and passim. For reasons that will, I think, become clear over the course of this introduction and the chapters that follow, I prefer the more assertive and allusively status-conscious term "ambition" in relation to the claims and promises made by the manuscripts I discuss and the receptions they solicited from their reader-viewers.
14. ". . . ad exstirpanda vitia et plantandas virtutes, corrigendos excessus, et reformandos mores, eliminandas haereses, et roborandam fidem": Innocent III, *Regesta sive epistolae,* 824B.
15. Norman P. Tanner, *DEC (1),* 239 [9].
16. See, for example, the insistence that new synodal legislation be promulgated to the laity in the vernacular in statutes issued for Cambrai (1278): Joseph Avril, *SSF 4,* 106 [17]. In statutes issued for Chichester (1245 x 1252), Bishop Richard de Wich mandated that priests should transmit the syllabus of catechetical knowledge to the laity *in lingua materna:* F. M. Powicke and C. R. Cheney, *C&S II (1),* 465 [70]. Throughout the period, priests were required to teach the laity the verbal forma for baptism in the vernacular, so that they would be prepared to administer the sacrament in the case of an emergency; for two early and influential examples of such legislation, see Eudes de Sully's statutes for Paris (before 1208) and Richard Poore's statutes for Salisbury (1217 x 1219): F. M. Powicke and C. R. Cheney, *C&S II (1),* 69 [23]; Odette Pontal, *SSF 1,* 54 [7].
17. Paul Binski, *Becket's Crown.*
18. Leonard E. Boyle, "Fourth Lateran Council." See also Joseph Goering, *William de Montibus,* 58–99. Dieter Harmening has proposed an alternative taxonomy for pastoralia: Harmening, "Katechismusliteratur."
19. Leonard E. Boyle, "Summae confessorum," 230.
20. For a helpful survey of the flowering of Anglo-Norman pastoralia in the period, see Mary Dominica Legge, *Anglo-Norman Literature,* 206–242.
21. Leonard E. Boyle, "Fourth Lateran Council," 35–36.
22. Claire Sherman has considered how illustrations "constituted another level of the translation" in manuscripts of Nicole Oresme's Aristotle translations, made for Charles V: Sherman, *Imaging Aristotle,* xxii, and passim. Anne Hedeman has also employed the paradigm of visual translation in her study of the role of illuminations in Laurent de Premierfait's translations of Boccaccio in the first decade of the fifteenth century: Hedeman, *Translating the Past,* xii, 33–34, 35, 53, 77, 84–85, 208–209, and passim. Sherman and Hedeman's analyses demonstrate how fourteenth- and fifteenth-century translators made use of visual representation to clarify, amplify, and at times complicate their textual translations and to elucidate ancient authorities, history, and unfamiliar ideas for a contemporary audience. As the arguments of individual chapters will make clear, I see the strategy of visual translation pursued in the manuscripts I examine as a more autonomous practice, whose "source" is primarily identified with religious truths understood as transcending any textual instantiations. From a sprawling literature on linguistic forms of translation in the Middle Ages I found the following studies particularly instructive: Rita

Copeland, *Rhetoric, Hermeneutics, and Translation in the Middle Ages;* Ruth Morse, *Truth and Convention in the Middle Ages,* 179–248 (esp.). Ruth Evans, Andrew Taylor, Nicholas Watson, and Jocelyn Wogan-Browne have offered useful criticism of the distinctions that should be made between theories of translation and "vernacular theory," particularly in relation to the significance of anticipated audience for much vernacular textual production in the later Middle Ages: Evans, Taylor, and Watson, "The Notion of Vernacular Theory."

23. Particularly prompted by Franz Bäuml's claims and Michael Camille's suggestions, several medievalists have explored the notion that the visual might itself be understood as a kind of "vernacular" in the later Middle Ages or that there might be such a thing as a "vernacular style" of illumination that shared characteristics now attributed to vernacular texts or audiences. I remain unconvinced that either of these constructs is adequate to the polysemy, sophistication, and heterogeneity of the evidence, both visual and verbal. In my experience, close analysis of images in individual vernacular-language manuscripts and close reading of the texts they accompany quickly dismantle any totalizing category of "vernacularity," be it stylistic, rhetorical, semiotic, or social-historical. For Bäuml's and Camille's discussions of the possible vernacularity of late medieval images, see Bäuml, "Varieties and Consequences of Medieval Literacy and Illiteracy," 259–265 (esp.); Camille, "The Language of Images." See also Camille, "Visualising in the Vernacular," in which a rather more nuanced account of the possible relationship between vernacular language and visual representation is advanced.
24. Thomas Aquinas, *Summa theologiae*, vol. 4, Ia, Q. 16, a. 5 (p. 88).
25. In the later Middle Ages four Creeds were in use; in addition to the Nicene-Constantinopolitan and Apostles' Creeds, the *Quicumque vult,* or Pseudo-Athanasian Creed, was included in Breviaries for recital at Prime, and Lateran IV also issued a creedal statement, known by its incipit *Firmiter Credimus,* to which I will return in chapter 1. J. N. D. Kelly, *Early Christian Creeds.*
26. London, BL, Royal MS 15.D.II, f. 56r–v; Pierre de Peckham, *La lumere as lais,* vol. 2, L. 4, D. xi, c. lviii, ll. 7405–7416 (p. 11). For clarity of sense, and in keeping with the reading attested by Hesketh's base manuscript (without variants), I have emended the manuscript's "trere" to "[c]rere"; it seems likely that the scribe of f. 56v simply confused the similar letterforms of initial lowercase *t* and *c.*
27. This axiom is beautifully condensed by Augustine: "credere non potest nisi volens." Augustine, *In Iohannis evangelium tractatus CXXIV,* Tractatus XXVI, 2 (p. 260).
28. Paris, BnF, MS fr. 4509, f. 1r; Lionel J. Friedman, *Text and Iconography for Joinville's Credo,* 29.
29. London, BL, Royal MS 15.D.II, ff. 74v–75r; Pierre de Peckham, *La lumere as lais,* vol. 2, L. 5, D. iii, c. xix, ll. 9749–9764 (p. 78). For clarity of sense, I have emended the manuscript's "crez" to "[t]rez"; for a similar example of scribal confusion of *c* and *t* see note 26 above.
30. I'm grateful to Maureen Boulton for her improving comments on this translation.
31. Augustine, *In Iohannis evangelium tractatus CXXIV,* Tractatus XL, 9 (p. 355).
32. Hebrews 11:6 was a touchstone for medieval discussions of faith; see, for example, Peter Lombard, *In Epistolam ad Hebraeos,* c. xi (cols. 490C–492D).
33. Malcolm Vale, *The Princely Court,* 3.
34. This was a change not simply of linguistic practice but also of contemporary perceptions and theorizations of langue d'oïl, as Serge Lusignan has explored in several studies: Lusignan, *Parler vulgairement;* Lusignan, "Le Français et le Latin aux XIIIe–XIVe siècles"; Lusignan, "Langue française et société du XIIIe au XVe siècle"; Lusignan, *La langue des rois au moyen age.* The increasing intellectual and semantic authority of langue d'oïl is palpable in the efflorescence of vernacular didactic texts in the period, an important category of textual production neglected by Lusignan but well documented in Jürgen Beyer, *La littérature didactique.*
35. On the linguistic landscape of late medieval England, with reference to further bibliography, see William Rothwell, "The Role of French in Thirteenth-Century England"; Tony Hunt, "Anglo-Norman: Past and Future"; Susan Crane, "Anglo-Norman Cultures in England"; John Frankis, "The Social Context of Vernacular Writing"; M. B. Parkes, "The Literacy of the Laity"; M. T. Clanchy, *From Memory to Written Record,* 151–201 (esp.). See also the varied contributions in Jocelyn Wogan-Browne et al., *Language and Culture in Medieval Britain.*
36. M. T. Clanchy, *From Memory to Written Record,* 170–174 (esp. 170). The use of Anglo-Norman in the royal administration is also examined by Serge Lusignan, *La langue des rois au moyen age,* 163–177.
37. This is amply demonstrated by the many didactic texts treating matters mundane, moral, and theological, cataloged in Ruth J. Dean and Maureen Barry McCann Boulton, *A-N L.* See also Nicholas Watson and Jocelyn Wogan-Browne, "The French of England"; Jocelyn Wogan-Browne, "'Our Steward, St Jerome.'" As Linda Georgianna has trenchantly observed, the "vexed politics of the vernacular" that would critically shape the production and reception of vernacular theology and pastoralia after 1400 are conspicuously not evident in the late twelfth- through fourteenth-century linguistic landscape of England: Georgianna, "Vernacular Theologies." For the landmark assessment of the post-1400 situation of vernacular theology, to which Georgianna responds, see Nicholas Watson, "Censorship and Cultural Change."
38. For a critical assessment of the situation of Middle English within the landscape of linguistic authority in late medieval England and in modern historiography of "vernacular theory," see Ruth Evans, Andrew Taylor, and Nicholas Watson, "The Notion of Vernacular Theory." The late medieval conjunction of Middle English text and visual representation has begun to attract serious attention, but much work remains to be done. See, for example, the focused examinations pursued by Kathryn Kerby-Fulton and Denise Louise Despres, *Iconography and the Professional Reader;* Jessica Brantley, *Reading in the Wilderness;* Richard K. Emmerson, "Visualizing the Vernacular"; Jessica Brantley, "Images of the Vernacular in the Taymouth Hours."
39. For a broad reassessment of "court culture" in the later Middle Ages that attends to the quotidian multilingualism of many late medieval courts, see Malcolm Vale, *The Princely Court,* 282–294.
40. Several recent studies have foregrounded the importance of the book of hours in the later Middle Ages: Claire Donovan, *The de Brailes Hours;* John Higgitt, *The Murthly Hours;* Paul Saenger, "Books of Hours and the Reading Habits"; Eamon Duffy, *Marking the Hours;* Kathryn A. Smith, "The Neville of Hornby Hours"; Kathryn A. Smith, *Art, Identity, and Devotion in Fourteenth-Century England.*
41. See, for example, the prefatory statements of purpose examined by Geneviève Hasenohr, "Les prologues des textes de dévotion."
42. Mary Dominica Legge's work remains the most helpful orientation to the antecedents and general contours of Anglo-Norman pastoralia in the period: Legge, *Anglo-Norman*

Literature, 176–275 (esp.); Legge, *Anglo-Norman in the Cloisters*. For the continental material, the third and fourth volumes of Charles Victor Langlois's *La vie en France au moyen âge* are still instructive. See also the extensive corpus of texts, designed for moral-spiritual instruction, documented in Jürgen Beyer, *La littérature didactique*.

43. Delisle's 1893 essay remains essential reading: Léopold Delisle, "Livres d'images."
44. Olivier Collet, "Du 'manuscrit de jongleur' au 'recueil aristocratique'"; Jacques Monfrin, "Des premiers apparitions du français dans les manuscrits"; Ian Short, "L'avènement du texte vernaculaire."
45. The medieval "miscellany" has provoked considerable discussion and debate. In 1989 Julia Boffey and John Thompson proposed a taxonomic distinction between the miscellany and the anthology: Boffey and Thompson, "Anthologies and Miscellanies." Nonetheless, within a single volume devoted to medieval miscellanies, Ralph Hanna identified "miscellaneity" as a key characteristic of late medieval vernacular manuscript production, whereas Barbara Shailor argued against the imprecision of the term "miscellany" when confronted with the codicological character of many compendia: Hanna, "Miscellaneity and Vernacularity"; Shailor, "A Cataloger's View." Other scholars have preferred the term "anthology": Seth Lerer, "Medieval English Literature and the Idea of the Anthology." Francophone scholarship, emphasizing the codicological determination of the structure and contents of manuscripts composed of multiple texts and images, has employed the less-contested term "recueil": Geneviève Hasenohr, "Les recueils littéraires français du XIIIe siècle"; Ian Short, "L'avènement du texte vernaculaire." In this study I use the term "compendium" to refer to a manuscript containing multiple texts and images written or painted for it and bound together in a single campaign. In some of the manuscripts to be discussed, constituent textual or visual components form discrete codicological units within a codex; in other exemplars, constituent texts and images trespass the limits of individual quires.
46. Bespoke vernacular compendia, particularly volumes intended for spiritual instruction, have attracted growing attention and invite a considered reevaluation of claims for the "miscellaneity" of vernacular manuscript production, tout court. See, for example, Vincent Gillespie, "Vernacular Books of Religion"; Vincent Gillespie, "*Lukynge in haly bukes*"; Sylvia Huot, "Polytextual Reading"; Adelaide Bennett, "A Book Designed for a Noblewoman"; Andrew Taylor, "Manual to Miscellany"; Sylvia Huot, "A Book Made for a Queen."
47. Lucy Freeman Sandler, *GM (1)*, 37–40.

CHAPTER 1. FROM NECESSARY TRUTHS TO SPIRITUAL AMBITIONS

1. On the "sign of the book" in the Bibles moralisées, with a brief consideration of this medallion, see Michael Camille, "Visual Signs of the Sacred Page," 115–116 (esp.). Camille's suggestion that the manuscript was designed as a "visual manual" (p. 126) of exegesis for clerical use has been rejected by subsequent interpreters.
2. John Lowden, *The Making of the Bibles Moralisées*, vol. 1, 1. In the characteristic layout of a Bible moralisée, each page is divided into eight small medallions, displayed in two columns. The roundels are grouped in pairs: one represents a scriptural passage, while its pendant depicts an exegetical interpretation, always in tropological or moral terms, of that biblical text. This pairing of scriptural source and moralizing commentary is continued in the textual components of the page. A short text accompanies each image, either a paraphrase of scripture or a brief tropological interpretation of a given scriptural passage. In the Bible moralisée discussed in this chapter, Vienna, Österreichische Nationalbibliothek, Cod. Vind. 2554 (henceforth Vienna 2554), the "reading" order of the medallion pairs (scriptural and exegetical) is from left to right and then, below, from left to right again. Each commentary roundel is placed directly below its scriptural roundel. The conventional notation for this arrangement is
A B
a b
C D
c d
in which capital letters denote scriptural medallions and lowercase letters denote commentary medallions. Vienna 2554 has been reproduced in facsimile, with commentary, three times: Reiner Haussherr, *Bible moralisée: Codex Vindobonensis 2554;* Gerald B. Guest, *Bible moralisée: Codex Vindobonensis 2554;* Reiner Haussherr, *Bible moralisée: Faksimile-Ausgabe*. Vienna 2554's 131 folios (344 x 260 mm) have been trimmed considerably, it has suffered a loss of an unknown number of leaves, and it has been rebound erroneously and foliated variously. Folio references given here correspond to the twentieth-century refoliation of the manuscript, the system currently in use by the Österreichische Nationalbibliothek and most scholars.
3. I follow John Lowden's proposed dating of the manuscript: Lowden, *The Making of the Bibles Moralisées*, vol. 1, 50–54. For further discussion of the current codicological state of the manuscript and a proposed reconstruction of the original order of its quires and folios, see Lowden, *The Making of the Bibles Moralisées*, vol. 1, 12–22, 285–286 (App. 1). Robert Branner heroically attributed the illumination of each page of Vienna 2554 (as well as the three other thirteenth-century Bibles moralisées) to individual "hands" and "shops" of illuminators: Branner, *Manuscript Painting in Paris*, 39–41, 42–47, 160–161. As Lowden notes, Branner's attributions require some critical reassessment, a process that Branner himself began but was prevented from seeing through: Lowden, *The Making of the Bibles Moralisées*, vol. 1, 33–42. For the identification of Blanche of Castile as the patron or intended recipient of Vienna 2554, see Lowden, *The Making of the Bibles Moralisées*, vol. 1, 52. Blanche's role as patron or recipient of the manuscript is examined further by Tracy Chapman Hamilton, "Queenship and Kinship in the French *Bible moralisée*"; Gerald B. Guest, "Picturing Women in the First *Bible moralisée*."
4. Following Vienna 2554, three other Bibles moralisées were produced for royal recipients in the first half of the thirteenth century: Vienna, Österreichische Nationalbibliothek, Codex 1179 (one volume, Latin); Toledo Cathedral Treasury and New York, Pierpont Morgan Library, MS M.240 (originally three volumes, Latin with added French); Oxford, Bodleian Library, MS Bodley 270b, BnF, MS lat. 11560, and BL, Harley MSS 1526–1527 (originally three volumes, Latin). For further discussion, see John Lowden, *The Making of the Bibles Moralisées*, vol. 1. As will be clear, my understanding of the production and patronage of Vienna 2554 is indebted to Lowden's magisterial investigation of the manuscript and its place in the broader tradition of Bibles moralisées: Lowden, *The Making of the Bibles Moralisées*, vol. 1, 11–54.
5. Vienna 2554, f. 1r.
6. Gerald B. Guest translates *tote devinitei* as "the whole divinity": Guest, *Bible moralisée: Codex Vindobonensis 2554*, 54. *Devinitei* is translated as "Holy Writ" in John Lowden,

The Making of the Bibles Moralisées, vol. 1, 50. It should be noted, however, that Frédéric Godefroy and the Tobler-Lommatzsch *Altfranzösisches Wörterbuch* give "theology" as the primary meaning of *devinitei:* Godefroy, *Dictionnaire de l'ancienne langue française,* vol. 2, 700; Adolf Tobler and Erhard Lommatzsch, *Altfranzösisches Wörterbuch,* vol. 2, col. 1969. Katherine Tachau likewise translates *devinitei* as "theologia": Tachau, "God's Compass and 'Vana Curiositas,'" 24.

7. The elevation of the host in the Mass is first textually attested in statutes issued for the diocese of Paris before 1208: Odette Pontal, *SSF 1,* 82 [80]. I will return to the elevation of the host and its significance for the laity in chapter 3.
8. John Lowden's analysis of the texts inscribed in Vienna 2554's Ruth cycle reveals several serious gaffes in relation to the scriptural source text and notable omissions: Lowden, *The Making of the Bibles Moralisées,* vol. 1, 200–201.
9. The progress of Vienna 2554's production, from the selection of bifolia to illumination to the inscription of the short texts, is carefully reconstructed in John Lowden, *The Making of the Bibles Moralisées,* vol. 1, 22–27, 30–33, 42–47.
10. As Richard and Mary Rouse have noted, "The history of illuminated manuscripts in Paris in the first half of the thirteenth century is dominated by the production of the Moralized Bibles." They estimate that the production of the first four Bibles moralisées "provided recurrent employment over some thirty years for a small army of book-producers" and involved the painting of more than 13,000 images: Rouse and Rouse, *Manuscripts and Their Makers,* vol. 1, 33. On Vienna 2554's plausible contribution—as inspiration, rather than source text—to Parisian scriptural translation see C. R. Sneddon, "On the Creation of the Old French Bible."
11. Although Yves Christe and others have argued for close relationships between the early Bibles moralisées and the windows of the Sainte-Chapelle, John Lowden suggests that the relationship must be understood more flexibly, as part of a larger Capetian ideological project, often articulated in terms of Biblical history: Lowden, "Les rois et reines de France en tant que 'public' des Bibles moralisées."
12. James Heinlen, *The Ideology of Reform,* 9, 196–197; Gerald B. Guest, *Bible moralisée: Codex Vindobonensis 2554,* 21.
13. Although James Heinlen first recognized the post–Lateran IV reform movement as an important context for the production of Vienna 2554, he understood the manuscript as "an instrument of Church propaganda directed toward the French kings." I do not share his conception of the manuscript as a monovocal ecclesiastical discourse: Heinlen, *The Ideology of Reform,* 1. Describing a mode of reception for the Bible moralisée that involved "discussion" as well as questions and answers "between a king or queen and his or her favorite chaplain or confessor," John Lowden remarks, "I am not sure that we have a term for this kind of use of a book": Lowden, "'Reading' Images and Texts in the *Bibles moralisées,*" 515–516. I suggest in this chapter, and explore further in chapter 2, that such a dialogic mode of reception can best be described as "pastoral."
14. Boyle described the "second wave" of pastoralia production as beginning circa 1260; the example of Vienna 2554 (as well as three Latin-language Bibles moralisées that were subsequently produced in the first half of the century) suggests that this periodization may need to be reexamined, at least in relation to royal patronage and audiences: Leonard E. Boyle, "Fourth Lateran Council," 34–35. Guest's analysis of the sustained discourse on vice and its effects in Vienna 2554 reveals the clear pastoral orientation of the volume: Gerald B. Guest, "'The Darkness and the Obscurity of Sins,'" 103 (esp.).
15. "Unde ad teneram rudium erudiendam infantiam qui tanquam adhuc edentuli ad hostium pulsant theologie et ad cibum solidiorem prouectiorum frugalis percipiendum, questiones morales et tam de fide quam de ceteris uirtutibus institutas pro posse nostro deo annuente prosequemur": V. L. Kennedy, "Robert Courson on Penance," 294. This passage serves as a preamble to the section of de Courson's *Summa* that is devoted to the sacrament of penance. My partial translation follows that proposed in Leonard E. Boyle, "Inter-Conciliar Period," 47. De Courson's treatment of penance is discussed further by Bella Millett, "*Ancrene Wisse* and the Conditions of Confession," 197–198.
16. Joseph Avril, "Remarques sur un aspect de la vie religieuse paroissiale," 346–347; Henri Maisonneuve, *La morale chrétienne d'après les conciles;* John Blair and Richard Sharpe, *Pastoral Care before the Parish.*
17. The larger historical narrative and major historiographical assessments are surveyed in Uta-Renate Blumenthal, *The Investiture Controversy.* For a recent introduction to this period of reform with greater attention to its pastoral dimensions, see Kathleen G. Cushing, *Reform and Papacy in the Eleventh Century.*
18. Stephan Kuttner, *Harmony from Dissonance;* Knut Wolfgang Nörr, "Institutional Foundations of the New Jurisprudence"; Stanley Chodorow, *Christian Political Theory and Church Politics.*
19. Giles Constable, *The Reformation of the Twelfth Century,* 257–295. See also Giles Constable, "Renewal and Reform"; Marie-Dominique Chenu, *L'éveil de la conscience;* Caroline Walker Bynum, *Jesus as Mother,* 36–43, 82–109; Caroline Walker Bynum, *Docere Verbo et Exemplo,* 77–93, 181–197, and passim.
20. Odon Lottin's six-volume study is unsurpassed in its synthetic treatment of the theological developments: Lottin, *Psychologie et morale aux XIIe et XIIIe siècles.* See also Joseph de Ghellinck, *Le mouvement théologique du XIIe siècle;* Philippe Delhaye, "L'enseignement de la philosophie morale au XIIe siècle"; Wendelin Knoch, *Die Einsetzung der Sakramente durch Christus.*
21. Paul Binski, *Becket's Crown,* 29–31, 62–65, 179–181; W. A. Pantin, *The English Church in the Fourteenth Century,* 9–11, 14–21; Barbara Hutchinson, "Robert Grosseteste: The Role of Education," 27–30.
22. Leonard E. Boyle, "Notes on the Education of the *Fratres Communes,*" 249.
23. M. Michèle Mulchahey, *"First the Bow Is Bent";* Leonard E. Boyle, "Notes on the Education of the *Fratres Communes.*"
24. Bert Roest, *Franciscan Literature of Religious Instruction;* Bert Roest, *A History of Franciscan Education,* 1–117 (esp. 67–81), 272–324; Jean-Marc Goglin, *L'enseignement de la théologie,* 5–63.
25. John C. Moore, *Pope Innocent III and His World,* 228–251; Raymonde Foreville, *Latran I, II, III et Latran IV,* 227–317; Brenda Bolton, "A Show with a Meaning"; Marion E. Gibbs and Jane Lang, *Bishops and Reform,* esp. 94–173.
26. Innocent III, *Regesta sive epistolae,* epistola XXX (col. 824A).
27. On the historical antecedents of the pastoral reform codified in Lateran IV, see Leonard E. Boyle, "Inter-Conciliar Period"; Joseph Goering, *William de Montibus,* 58–99; John W. Baldwin, *Masters, Princes, and Merchants.*
28. Leonard E. Boyle, "Fourth Lateran Council," 31.
29. Innocent III invited ecclesiastic and civil authorities from all of Europe to the Council, and actual attendance was quite significant:

412 bishops attended the Council, and 71 ecclesiastic superiors, including archbishops, primates, and patriarchs, were also in attendance: Brenda Bolton, "A Show with a Meaning," 59. Raymonde Foreville provides a list of ecclesiastic personnel and represented jurisdictions: Foreville, *Latran I, II, III et Latran IV*, 391–395.

30. Innocent III, *Sermones de diversis*, Sermo VI (cols. 678C–678D).
31. English translation from Innocent III, *Between God and Man*, 62.
32. Norman P. Tanner, *DEC (1)*, 242–243 [14–16].
33. Norman P. Tanner, *DEC (1)*, 243 [17], 248–249 [29], 264 [63], 265 [66].
34. On Innocent's academic formation and early works, see Helene Tillmann, *Pope Innocent III*, 1–19; John C. Moore, *Pope Innocent III and His World*, 3–11.
35. Leonard E. Boyle, "The Constitution 'Cum ex eo.'"
36. Norman P. Tanner, *DEC (1)*, 240 [11]. For the Third Lateran Council's legislation on this point, see Tanner, *DEC (1)*, 220 [18].
37. English translation from Norman P. Tanner, *DEC (1)*, 240 [11].
38. On clerical education in the period, see Friedrich Wilhelm Oediger, *Über die Bildung der Geistlichen*, 46–57; John Raymond Shinners, "University Study Licenses"; R. N. Swanson, "Universities, Graduates and Benefices"; W. A. Pantin, *The English Church in the Fourteenth Century*, 105–122; Barbara Hutchinson, "Robert Grosseteste: The Role of Education"; A. G. Little, "The Education of the Clergy"; Leonard E. Boyle, "The Constitution 'Cum ex eo.'"; Boyle, "Aspects of Clerical Education."
39. Norman P. Tanner, *DEC (1)*, 236–237 [6].
40. Norman P. Tanner, *DEC (1)*, 236 [6]. The English translation is Tanner's.
41. Norman P. Tanner, *DEC (1)*, 237–238 [7–8].
42. Norman P. Tanner, *DEC (1)*, 250 [33].
43. Paul Binski, *Becket's Crown*, 152.
44. Raymonde Foreville, "La réception des conciles généraux," 252.
45. On the copying, dissemination, and possession of *synodalia*, see Odette Pontal, *SSF 1*, LXVI–LXVII; C. R. Cheney, "Legislation of the Medieval English Church."
46. Richard Poore (1217 x 1219): F. M. Powicke and C. R. Cheney, *C&S II (I)*, 96 [114]; Alexander of Stavensby (1224 x 1237): F. M. Powicke and C. R. Cheney, *C&S II (I)*, 214 [27]; William de Blois (1229): F. M. Powicke and C. R. Cheney, *C&S II (I)*, 179 [51]; Walter de Cantilupe (1240): F. M. Powicke and C. R. Cheney, *C&S II (I)*, 319 [94]; Richard de Wich (1253): F. M. Powicke and C. R. Cheney, *C&S II (I)*, 466–467 [79]; Peter Quinel (1287): F. M. Powicke and C. R. Cheney, *C&S II (II)*, 1058–1059 [56]; Eudes de Sully (before 1208): Odette Pontal, *SSF 1*, 84 [87]; Nicolas Gellent (1262 and 1269): Joseph Avril, *SSF 3*, 82 [1], 84 [4], 98 [1]; Guillaume le Maire (1293 and 1312): Joseph Avril, *SSF 3*, 164 [1], 232 [2], 252 [8].
47. For Walter de Cantilupe's provision, see F. M. Powicke and C. R. Cheney, *C&S II (I)*, 319 [94]. For Guillaume le Maire's decree, see Joseph Avril, *SSF 3*, 164–167 [1].
48. Joseph Avril, *SSF 3*, 110 [3], 130 [1] (renewal in 1276).
49. Joseph Avril, *SSF 3*, 130 [1].
50. It should be stressed that the celebration of the Eucharist represented a special epistemological burden for pastors: Friedrich Wilhelm Oediger, *Über die Bildung der Geistlichen*, 55–56. As chapter 3 will explore, late medieval Eucharistic theology came to extend aspects of that onus to the lay faithful as well.
51. Odette Pontal, *SSF 1*, 54–70 [7–48]. The dating of the complete sequence of statutes has been the subject of some controversy. The statutes as they survive are the product of multiple phases of legislative promulgation, likely covering the period 1204 (or 1205)–1214, that is, extending into the episcopate of Pierre de Nemours; for further discussion, see Odette Pontal, *SSF 1*, 40–50 (esp. 48–50).
52. Odette Pontal, *SSF 1*, 190–226 [75–122]. "Synodal de l'Ouest" is Pontal's appellation for a group of statutes initially promulgated in Angers and subsequently adopted in the provinces of Tours and Rouen. These statutes are traditionally attributed to Bishop Guillaume de Beaumont, yet, as Pontal notes, we do not have a manuscript witness from his lifetime: Odette Pontal, *SSF 1*, 106–111.
53. F. M. Powicke and C. R. Cheney, *C&S II (I)*, 67–81 [20–64], 85–91 [78–95].
54. F. M. Powicke and C. R. Cheney, *C&S II (I)*, 71–75 [33–46].
55. Odette Pontal, *SSF 1*, 226–237 [123–134].
56. F. M. Powicke and C. R. Cheney, *C&S II (II)*, 900–905 [9].
57. Pecham's condensed pastoral manual proved to be extremely influential, not least because it formed the basis of Archbishop John Thoresby's 1357 Latin *Injunctions*, translated into English by John of Catterick (or Gaytryge) as the *Lay Folk's Catechism*: R. N. Swanson, "The Origins of the *Lay Folks' Catechism*"; W. A. Pantin, *The English Church in the Fourteenth Century*, 193–194, 211–212. Thoresby's *Injunctions* and the *Lay Folk's Catechism* have been edited: Thomas Frederick Simmons and Henry Edward Nolloth, *The Lay Folks' Catechism*. The immediate circulation of *Ignorantia sacerdotum* is also discussed, with further bibliography, in F. M. Powicke and C. R. Cheney, *C&S II (II)*, 887–888.
58. F. M. Powicke and C. R. Cheney, *C&S II (II)*, 900–901 [9].
59. Elisabeth Gössmann, *Glaube und Gotteserkenntnis im Mittelalter*, 38–42.
60. Peter Lombard, *Sententiae*, L. III, D. 25, c. 2 (pp. 154–155).
61. English translation from Peter Lombard, *The Sentences*, bk. 3, 108.
62. For further discussion of the concept of implicit faith and its implications for the laity, see Jean Wirth, "La naissance du concept de croyance," 17–20; John Van Engen, "Faith as a Concept of Order"; Jean-Claude Schmitt, "Du bon usage du 'Credo,'" 340–343 and passim; John Van Engen, "The Christian Middle Ages," 545–548.
63. John Van Engen notes a shift in clerical expectations beginning in the twelfth century and becoming particularly evident from the mid-thirteenth century, but argues that "cognitive profession remained largely the preserve of churchmen and, more particularly still, the small number of university educated men": Van Engen, "Faith as a Concept of Order," 43. I would suggest that the vernacular evidence paints a different picture, at least for literate, book-owning laypeople in France and England.
64. "Lors vient moyses si prent un voil et le met devant sa chiere et parole a son pueple et li dist les commandemenz Deu et li pueples l'escoute et si l'entent": Vienna 2554, f. 26v.
65. Vienna 2554, f. 26v.
66. English translation slightly modified from Gerald B. Guest, *Bible moralisée: Codex Vindobonensis 2554*, 84.
67. Michael Camille proposes a different reading of the veil, seeing in it a visual sign of the laity's inability to apprehend the spiritual meaning of scripture. Accordingly he glosses the commentary roundel below as staging the laity's handling of the "lowly vernacular" letter, rather than the *logos*: Camille, "Visual Signs of the Sacred Page," 126–127.
68. Like Camille, James Heinlen interpreted the medallion in relation to Stephen Langton's emphasis on the importance of "simple discourse" in preaching addressed to lay audiences: Heinlen, *The Ideology of Reform*, 152–158. As subsequent chapters reveal, I am

not convinced that elite lay audiences should be assimilated to the undifferentiated *simplici* imagined by clerics, nor do the manuscripts examined in this study support the notion that the laity were denied access to theological "subtlety."

69. Although I derive the term "textual community" from Brian Stock, I construe the catalytic role of the interpreter, around whom a textual community forms, to include interpretive functions or positions (e.g., pastoral catechesis, the "voice" of the didactic text, the argument of images), as well as individual historical interpreters: Stock, *The Implications of Literacy,* esp. 88–240. As Yves Christe notes, the lay figures represented in this medallion are all "personnes de qualité"; like Camille, however, he sees the medallion as focused not on the distinguished laity's reception of the text, but rather on the clerical adaptation of that lesson to the assumed limitations of a lay audience: Christe, "Grossement," 342–345.
70. The Old French "paraphrase" reads, "Lors lor commande moyses qe il crient merci a Deu et qe il facent offrande de lor or et de lor bestes et il si font et dex lor pardone": Vienna 2554, f. 26v. By contrast, as James Heinlen observed, the Vulgate makes no mention of the injunction to beg God's mercy and specifies that the Israelites' offerings consisted of various materials, including but not limited to gold, destined to be used in the fabrication of the tabernacle, its furnishings, and priestly garments: Heinlen, *The Ideology of Reform,* 147 (n. 100).
71. Vienna 2554, f. 26v. The singular form of the first verb in the sentence ("il se face") is, perhaps, best explained as a direct textual response to the single figure of the lay penitent in the medallion. English translation slightly modified from Gerald B. Guest, *Bible moralisée: Codex Vindobonensis 2554,* 84.
72. Victor Leroquais identified this iconography as first appearing in missals and pontificals in the first half of the thirteenth century: Leroquais, *Les sacramentaires et les missels,* vol. 1, xxxviii–xxxix. For further discussion of the iconography, see Edouard Dumoutet, *Le Christ selon la chair,* 105–110; F. O. Büttner, *"Ad Te, Domine, Levavi Animam Meam."*
73. Princeton, Princeton University Library, Garrett MS 41, f. 5r; a concise description of the manuscript is available from the Princeton Index of Christian Art Database. See also Joan Naughton, "Friars and Their Books at Saint Louis de Poissy," 92.
74. Norman P. Tanner, *DEC (1),* 245 [21].
75. Norman P. Tanner, *DEC (1),* 245 [21].
76. Norman P. Tanner, *DEC (1),* 245 [21]. The English translation is Tanner's.
77. For further discussion of the frequency and timing of lay communion before Lateran IV, see Louis Braeckmans, *Confession et communion,* 1–4, 9–63; Alexander Murray, "Confession before 1215"; Joseph Avril, "Remarques sur un aspect de la vie religieuse paroissiale"; Peter Browe, "Die öftere Kommunion der Laien"; Peter Browe, "Die Pflichtkommunion der Laien."
78. Stephen Langton mandated confession and communion thrice yearly in his first statutes for Canterbury (1213 x 1214): F. M. Powicke and C. R. Cheney, *C&S II (I),* 32 [43]. For additional examples of this prescription in English statutes, see Bishop Richard Poore's statutes for Salisbury (1219 x 1218) and Bishop Fulk Basset's statutes for London (1245 x 1259): F. M. Powicke and C. R. Cheney, *C&S II (I),* 72 [38], 639 [28]. In France, early fourteenth-century statutes for Cambrai anticipate lay communicants at Easter, Pentecost, and All Saints: Joseph Avril, *SSF 4,* 159 [71]. Synodal statutes for Soissons, dated by Avril to 1280–1300, also prescribe thrice yearly confession and communion to the laity: Joseph Avril, *SSF 4,* 295 [37]. For a longer view of this phenomenon, see Peter Browe, "Die öftere Kommunion der Laien."
79. Peter Browe, "Zum Kommunionempfang des Mittelalters."
80. Antecedent traditions of penitential preparation for communion are discussed by Peter Browe, "Die Kommunionvorbereitung."
81. Norman P. Tanner, *DEC (1),* 245 [21].
82. Norman P. Tanner, *DEC (1),* 245 [21].
83. On liturgical professions of faith and the liturgy as a framework for creedal formation, see Éric Palazzo, "Foi et croyance au moyen âge."
84. Joseph Avril, *SSF 4,* 84 [54].
85. F. M. Powicke and C. R. Cheney, *C&S II (I),* 465 [70].
86. Jean-Claude Schmitt, "Du bon usage du 'Credo,'" 248–352 (esp.). Beginning in the thirteenth century, statutes are not content to simply prescribe the faithful's recital of the Apostles' Creed but also provide curates with the means of expounding the Creed to parishioners: Jean Longère, "Comment expliquer le symbole des apôtres?" 168.
87. Joseph Avril, *SSF 4,* 123 [111].
88. F. M. Powicke and C. R. Cheney, *C&S II (I),* 213 [20]. The scriptural reference in brackets is my addition to the passage, but I derive it from a note to the text in Powicke and Cheney's edition.
89. Gellent: Joseph Avril, *SSF 3,* 146–148; le Maire: Joseph Avril, *SSF 3,* 216–219 [2].
90. Joseph Avril, *SSF 3,* 216–218 [2].
91. Odette Pontal, *SSF 1,* 84 [84]. Eudes de Sully's legislation on preaching postdates by several decades an established Parisian practice of addressing students and the laity in sermons: Jean Longère, "La prédication et l'instruction des fidèles," 411.
92. F. M. Powicke and C. R. Cheney, *C&S II (I),* 465 [70].
93. Joseph Avril, *SSF 4,* 330 [43].
94. Joseph Avril, *SSF 4,* 330 [43].
95. F. M. Powicke and C. R. Cheney, *C&S II (I),* 269 [8].
96. F. M. Powicke and C. R. Cheney, *C&S II (I),* 269 [8].
97. To take but one example, Bishop William Raleigh's statutes for the diocese of Winchester (issued c. 1247) repeat verbatim Grosseteste's precepts regarding both the education of pueri and the examination and instruction to be conducted in confession: F. M. Powicke and C. R. Cheney, *C&S II (I),* 405 [10].
98. Vienna 2554, f. 22v.
99. I have modified the English translation from Gerald B. Guest, *Bible moralisée: Codex Vindobonensis 2554,* 78.
100. Vienna 2554, f. 22v.
101. English translation from Gerald B. Guest, *Bible moralisée: Codex Vindobonensis 2554,* 78.
102. F. M. Powicke and C. R. Cheney, *C&S II (II),* 900 [9]. The scriptural references in brackets are my addition to the passage, but I derive them from the notes to the text in Powicke and Cheney's edition.
103. English translation from John Raymond Shinners and William J. Dohar, *Pastors and the Care of Souls in Medieval England,* 127. I have supplied italics for scriptural quotations.
104. Discussed and edited in Mary Dominica Legge, "John Pecham's *Jerarchie.*" See also Mary Dominica Legge, *Anglo-Norman Literature,* 225–226; Mary Dominica Legge, *Anglo-Norman in the Cloisters,* 81–82; Paul Binski, *Becket's Crown,* 268–269; Jocelyn Wogan-Browne, "'Our Steward, St Jerome,'" 149–157.
105. Mary Dominica Legge, "John Pecham's *Jerarchie,*" 80.
106. The Pseudo-Dionysian text had recently been re-translated, with a new commentary, by Robert Grosseteste (c. 1235–1245) and

continued to attract scholastic attention: John Carmi Parsons, "Of Queens, Courts, and Books," 180.

CHAPTER 2. TRANSLATING THE MODUS CONFITENDI

1. Princeton, Princeton University Library, Taylor Medieval MS 1 (243 ff., 245 x 125mm). Adelaide Bennett kindly confirmed this reading of the banderole within the initial. For a more comprehensive examination of the manuscript's textual and visual program, see Bennett, "A Book Designed for a Noblewoman." The manuscript and its visual program are also discussed in Jocelyn Wogan-Browne, "'Our Steward, St Jerome,'" 148–149; Paul Binski, *Becket's Crown,* 187–188.
2. As Adelaide Bennett has noted, Joan's husband, Baron Robert Tateshal the Fifth (1247–1298), was one of a group of Lincolnshire correspondents who supported the failed attempt to have Grosseteste canonized in 1286–1287. Despite the failure of this campaign Joan's compendium refers to the late Bishop of Lincoln as "Seint Robert": Bennett, "A Book Designed for a Noblewoman," 167.
3. Evelyn Anne Mackie, "Scribal Intervention and the Question of Audience," 63. Mackie's 2002 dissertation provides the most recent edition of the *Château d'amour;* future publication of the edition is planned: Mackie, *Robert Grosseteste's Chasteu d'amur.* For further discussion of the text, see also Mackie, "Robert Grosseteste's Anglo-Norman"; Paul Binski, *Becket's Crown,* 182–188; Christiania Whitehead, "A Fortress and a Shield."
4. I have found Bakhtin's discussions of dialogue and the dialogical a helpful analytic corrective to deterministic accounts—both medieval and modern—of the practices of confession and catechesis: M. M. Bakhtin, "The Problem of Speech Genres"; M. M. Bakhtin, "From the Prehistory of Novelistic Discourse"; M. M. Bakhtin, "Discourse in the Novel."
5. For an exploration of "dialogic form" as a means of reforming lay spiritual authority in three Middle English spiritual guides, see Nicole R. Rice, *Lay Piety and Religious Discipline,* 47–80.
6. On the "cura sui" or "culture de soi," with particular attention to the classical tradition, see Michel Foucault, *Histoire de la sexualité,* vol. 3, 53–85 (esp.). My thanks to Rebecca Zorach for reminding me of Foucault's use of this terminology.
7. Alexander Murray, "Confession before 1215"; Henry Charles Lea, *A History of Auricular Confession;* Peter Biller and A. J. Minnis, *Handling Sin;* Pierre Michaud-Quantin, *Sommes de casuistique et manuels de confession.*
8. Sarah Hamilton, *The Practice of Penance.*
9. Cyrille Vogel, *Les "Libri paenitentiales";* John Thomas McNeill and Helena Margaret Gamer, *Medieval Handbooks of Penance.*
10. This practice of penance, often (but not unproblematically) referred to as "private" penance, coexisted in the period with a different mode of penitential satisfaction, usually identified as "public" penance: Mary C. Mansfield, *The Humiliation of Sinners.* The hearing of confessions by laypeople is also of considerable historical interest but cannot be discussed here: Amédée Teetaert, *La Confession aux laïques.*
11. Peter Abelard, *Ethics,* 88, ll. 6–10; 89 (English translation). Cited and discussed by Susan R. Kramer, "'We Speak to God with Our Thoughts,'" 33.
12. Peter Abelard, *Ethics,* 98, ll. 13–15; 99 (English translation). Cited and discussed by Susan R. Kramer, "'We Speak to God with Our Thoughts,'" 35.
13. D. E. Luscombe, *The School of Peter Abelard,* 198–213 and passim. See also R. Baron, "Note sur l'énigmatique 'Summa Sententiarum.'"
14. The key passage is, "Quid ergo super his sentiendum? Quid tenendum? Sane quod sine confessione oris et solutione poenae exterioris peccata delentur, per contritionem et humilitatem cordis. Ex quo enim proponit, mente compuncta, se confessurum, Deus dimittit; quia ibi est confessio cordis, etsi non oris, per quam anima interius mundatur a macula et contagio peccati commissi, et debitum aeternae mortis relaxatur . . . Sicut enim praecepta est nobis interior poenitentia, ita et oris confessio et exterior satisfactio, si adsit facultas; unde nec vere poenitens est, qui confessionis votum non habet": Peter Lombard, *Sententiae,* vol. 2 [Lib. III and IV], L. IV, D. 17, c. 1 (pp. 345, 346). The Lombard's conception of penance is explored further by Marcia L. Colish, *Peter Lombard,* vol. 2, 583–609.
15. On scholastic discussions of sacramental signification, see Irène Rosier-Catach, *La parole efficace.*
16. Bernhard Poschmann, *Penance and the Anointing of the Sick,* 168–183; Ludwig Ott, "Das Opusculum des hl. Thomas von Aquin *De forma absolutionis.*"
17. Thomas Aquinas, *Summa theologiae,* vol. 60, Q. 84, a. 3 (pp. 10–19).
18. Thomas Aquinas, *Summa theologiae,* vol. 60, Q. 84, a. 1 (pp. 2–7). This analogical extension of the relationship between form and matter is further discussed by Nicole Bériou, "La confession dans les écrits," 266.
19. This trope is so ubiquitous in discussions of penance, confession, and absolution from the eleventh century forward that Boyle regards it as "hackneyed" and Bériou as a "metaphore classique" and "un motif banal": Nicole Bériou, "La confession dans les écrits," 270; Leonard E. Boyle, "Summae confessorum," 232.
20. Norman P. Tanner, *DEC (1),* 245 [21]. The English translation is Tanner's.
21. Norman P. Tanner, *DEC (1),* 245. I have modified Tanner's English translation to read more literally, and so to foreground the metaphoric language describing the exchange between penitent and confessor.
22. Nicole Bériou, "La confession dans les écrits," 274–278.
23. Nicole Bériou, "La confession dans les écrits," 275.
24. See, for example, the statutes issued in the Synodal de l'Ouest (1216 x 1219) and those promulgated by Bishop Alexander of Stavensby for the diocese of Coventry and Lichfield (1224–1237): F. M. Powicke and C. R. Cheney, *C&S II (I),* 209–210 [1]; Odette Pontal, *SSF 1,* 190–192 [76].
25. F. M. Powicke and C. R. Cheney, *C&S II (II),* 982–1077. Quinel's summula is an expanded revision of the penitential treatise referenced by Bishop Walter de Cantilupe in his statutes for the diocese of Worcester (1240): Joseph Goering and Daniel S. Taylor, "The Summulae of Bishops Walter de Cantilupe (1240) and Peter Quinel (1287)."
26. F. M. Powicke and C. R. Cheney, *C&S II (II),* 1062 [1].
27. F. M. Powicke and C. R. Cheney, *C&S II (II),* 1062 [2].
28. F. M. Powicke and C. R. Cheney, *C&S II (II),* 1063 [3–4].
29. F. M. Powicke and C. R. Cheney, *C&S II (II),* 1063 [5].
30. F. M. Powicke and C. R. Cheney, *C&S II (II),* 1063 [4].
31. The distinction between external and internal sins was often elaborated in relation to discussions of the difference between extrasacramental and sacramental penance: Dallas G. Denery, *Seeing and Being Seen,* 40–44.
32. F. M. Powicke and C. R. Cheney, *C&S II (II),* 1062 [1].
33. F. M. Powicke and C. R. Cheney, *C&S II (II),* 1074–1075 [33–34].
34. F. M. Powicke and C. R. Cheney, *C&S II (II),* 1069 [20].

35. D. W. Robertson Jr., "A Note on the Classical Origin of 'Circumstances.'"; D. W. Robertson Jr., "The Cultural Tradition of Handlyng Synne," 170–172; Dallas G. Denery, *Seeing and Being Seen,* 36 (esp. n. 81), 58–63; Thomas N. Tentler, *Sin and Confession,* 116–120.
36. F. M. Powicke and C. R. Cheney, *C&S II (II),* 1071 [27].
37. F. M. Powicke and C. R. Cheney, *C&S II (II),* 1069 [21].
38. Dallas G. Denery, *Seeing and Being Seen,* 50.
39. F. M. Powicke and C. R. Cheney, *C&S II (II),* 992 [5].
40. Jacqueline Murray, "The Absent Penitent"; Alexander Murray, "Counselling in Medieval Confession"; Dallas G. Denery, *Seeing and Being Seen,* 51–57; Thomas N. Tentler, *Sin and Confession,* 82–95. Visual exemplars of confessional comportment are discussed in Ann Elijenholm Nichols, "The Etiquette of Pre-Reformation Confession in East Anglia."
41. See, for example, Eudes of Sully's recommendation of the use of circumlocution when inquiring about "unusual sins": Odette Pontal, *SSF 1,* 62 [26].
42. "De aliis inusitatis non requirat nisi per circumstantias et a longe, ut per hoc expertis, dum eorum recensetur memoria, detur materia confitendi, inexpertis, dum celantur incognita, occasio delinquendi non pandatur": F. M. Powicke and C. R. Cheney, *C&S II (II),* 994 [5]. For further discussion of the prevalence of this advice, see D. W. Robertson Jr., "The Cultural Tradition of Handlyng Synne," 172–175.
43. Norman P. Tanner, *DEC (1),* 245 [21]. The English translation is Tanner's.
44. In this connection, Dallas Denery's analysis of the literature and techniques employed by the Dominican order in the formation of novices, preachers, and confessors reveals the extent to which the inculcation of an awareness of the self-as-representation was inseparable from practices of self-examination and a consciousness of the self as always visible to others: Denery, *Seeing and Being Seen,* 19–38.
45. Dallas G. Denery, *Seeing and Being Seen,* 74.
46. Thomas N. Tentler, "The Summa for Confessors"; Leonard E. Boyle, "The Summa for Confessors"; Leonard E. Boyle, "Summae confessorum."
47. See, for example, Lea's 1896 polemic that "the Europe of the middle ages and the faithful of Latin Christianity to-day are what the teaching of the confessional has made them": Henry Charles Lea, *A History of Auricular Confession,* vol. 2, 414.
48. Arguably, the most influential account of the confessional production of sinners remains Michel Foucault, *Histoire de la sexualité,* vol. 1, 78–84 (esp.).
49. Alexander Murray, "Counselling in Medieval Confession." The pedagogic character of this dialogue and its relationship to the didacticism of the classroom is further explored by Marjorie Curry Wood and Rita Copeland, "Classroom and Confession."
50. Jutta Seyfarth, *Speculum virginum.* On the *Speculum virginum* manuscripts, with further bibliography, see also Eleanor Simmons Greenhill, *Die geistigen Voraussetzungen der Bilderreihe des Speculum virginum;* Morgan Powell, *The Mirror and the Woman,* 99–280; Constant J. Mews, *Listen, Daughter: The Speculum Virginum.*
51. Seyfarth's *L* manuscript, BL, Arundel MS 44 (129 ff., 280 x 185 mm) once belonged to a certain Magister Hugo, resident of the Cistercian Abbey of Eberbach: *Krone und Schleier: Kunst aus mittelalterlichen Frauenklöstern* 316–317 (No. 205a); Jutta Seyfarth, *Speculum virginum,* 56*–60*. For further discussion of the manuscript see Nigel F. Palmer, *Zisterzienser und ihre Bücher,* 76–80, 206–207, 281, and passim.
52. Morgan Powell, "The *Speculum virginum,*" 114.
53. Morgan Powell, "The *Speculum virginum,*" 114.
54. Jutta Seyfarth, *Speculum virginum,* Epist., ll. 47–50 (pp. 2–3).
55. English translation from Janice M. Pinder, "The Cloister and the Garden," 160.
56. Jutta Seyfarth, *Speculum virginum,* Lib. IV, ll. 18–23 (p. 85).
57. English translation from Morgan Powell, "The *Speculum virginum,*" 123.
58. Paris, BnF, MS fr. 9220 (henceforth BnF fr. 9220): Ransom dates the manuscript to 1290–1300: Carol Lynn Ransom, *Cultivating the Orchard,* 23.
59. The folios of BnF fr. 9220 measure 440 x 310 mm; for further codicological discussion of the manuscript see Carol Lynn Ransom, *Cultivating the Orchard,* 17–23. The first systematic description of the manuscript's contents was published by Arthur Långfors, "Notice du manuscrit français 9220." More recently, the manuscript has been described in Patrick M. de Winter, *La bibliothèque de Philippe le Hardi,* cat. no. 7. See also Lynn Ransom, "The *Speculum theologie* and Its Readership"; Jean-Claude Schmitt, "Les images classificatrices"; Hélène Bouget, "Le *Miroir de vie et de mort.*"
60. BnF fr. 9220, f. 1r. Other than this inscription, the recto is blank.
61. The image and its principal arboreal elements are glossed by two two-line vernacular verse inscriptions, placed in the upper left and right corners of the framed pictorial space. The first, on the left, reads, "Li miroirs de vie et de mort / Ki met a terre foible et fort." The second inscription, on the right, asserts, "Et s'est li arbres de pechiés / dont tous li mons est entechiés."
62. Hélène Bouget also discerns a mise en abîme in the manuscript, but she associates it with the "quasi-totalité des planches" in which the viewer finds "une démultiplication des diverses connaissances du monde, et en même temps une mise en perspective de ces diverses connaissances": Bouget, "Le *Miroir de vie et de mort,*" 111.
63. BnF fr. 9220, f. 10r.
64. Mâle's commentary is written in response to the only other known exemplar of the image, found in Paris, Bibliothèque Sainte-Geneviève, MS 2200, f. 164r (dated by a colophon to 1277): Emile Mâle, *L'art religieux du XIIIe siècle,* 145. The precise relationship between the two manuscripts has yet to be thoroughly explored.
65. Hélène Bouget identifies this figure as "un humain" who attempts to climb "l'échelle de la *mors humana*": Bouget, "Le *Miroir de vie et de mort,*" 115. I think the figure carrying the coffin must be Mors humana herself, whose grammatical gender is feminine. Moreover, although the Latin transcript of the Devil's exhortation poses several problems, I think it must be construed as an address to the figure of Mors as she hastens toward Vita mundi: "Dum sit in hac sorde, rogo, mors, vitam cito morde, [?]Ut evat [*sic*?] hancque feri, te rogo firmiter i": BnF fr. 9220, f. 10r. Lynn Ransom also identifies the figure on the ladder as "Death": Ransom, *Cultivating the Orchard,* 177.
66. The first line of the inscription, like several others in the image, presents considerable difficulties; it would seem that the Latin has become somewhat garbled. I am grateful to Anthony Adams for his help with this proposed translation.
67. On the *Speculum theologiae* compilation and its diagrams see Lynn Ransom, "The *Speculum theologie* and Its Readership"; Fritz Saxl, "A Spiritual Encyclopaedia"; Lucy Freeman Sandler, *The Psalter of Robert de Lisle,* 23–27, 107–115, and passim. The principal evidence adduced by Ransom for Franciscan involvement in the conception and design of the *Vrigiet* includes the addition of the *arbor amoris* and the *lignum vitae* diagrams (the

latter derived from Bonaventure's text); the presence of a Franciscan friar in the illustrated hymn found on f. 3v and of St. Francis in the *lignum vitae* image of f. 9v; and the emphasis throughout the manuscript on an affective approach to Christological devotion, centered on Christ's Passion: Lynn Ransom, "Innovation and Identity"; Carol Lynn Ransom, *Cultivating the Orchard*, 203–242.

68. Lionel J. Friedman, *Text and Iconography for Joinville's Credo,* 2. This titular description of the work appears in its final paragraph: Paris, BnF, MS n. a. fr. 4509 (henceforth BnF naf 4509), f. 14r. For further discussion of the text see Alfred Foulet, "When Did Joinville Write His Vie de Saint Louis?" 242–243; Lionel J. Friedman, *Text and Iconography for Joinville's Credo;* Lionel J. Friedman, "Observations on the Style of Joinville's 'Credo'"; Lionel J. Friedman, "On the Structure of Joinville's 'Credo.'"
69. Citations of the tract are made from the manuscript, followed by references to Friedman's publication of the text: BnF naf 4509, f. 14r; Lionel J. Friedman, *Text and Iconography for Joinville's Credo,* 51. We will revisit Joinville's statement of purpose in further detail.
70. The manuscript is today preserved in two continuously foliated volumes (Paris, BnF, MSS n. a. fr. 4509–4510); 124 ff., 192 x 130 mm: Henri Auguste Omont, *Catalogue général des manuscrits français,* 201–202. See also Lionel J. Friedman, *Text and Iconography for Joinville's Credo,* 2–3. Two further manuscripts preserve fragments of the visual program devised for the Credo: the outline drawings preserved in BnF, MS lat. 11907 and the fully painted pages interpolated into a missal for the use of Reims, Saint Petersburg, National Library of Russia, MS Lat.Q.v.1.78: Yolanta Zaluska and François Boespflug, "L'église et les sacrements dans le Credo de Joinville"; H.-F. Delaborde and P. Lauer, "Un projet de décoration murale inspiré du Crédo de Joinville"; Jaroslav Folda, *Crusader Art in the Holy Land*, 500–503; Jaroslav Folda, *Crusader Manuscript Illumination at Saint-Jean d'Acre,* 103–111; Tamara Pavlovna Voronova and Alexander Sterligov, *Western European Illuminated Manuscripts,* 53–66.
71. BnF naf 4509, f. 1v; Lionel J. Friedman, *Text and Iconography for Joinville's Credo,* 30.
72. Lionel J. Friedman, *Text and Iconography for Joinville's Credo,* 6–7.
73. BnF naf 4509, f. 1v; Lionel J. Friedman, *Text and Iconography for Joinville's Credo,* 31.
74. BnF naf 4509, f. 2r; Lionel J. Friedman, *Text and Iconography for Joinville's Credo,* 31.
75. BnF naf 4509, f. 2r; Lionel J. Friedman, *Text and Iconography for Joinville's Credo,* 32.
76. BnF naf 4509, f. 2r; Lionel J. Friedman, *Text and Iconography for Joinville's Credo,* 32.
77. BnF naf 4509, ff. 3v, 8r.
78. Lionel J. Friedman, *Text and Iconography for Joinville's Credo,* 3.
79. The one exception to this rule is the miniature devised for Joinville's account of the "Old Saracen" and the captive crusaders: BnF naf 4509, f. 7v. For further discussion of this episode and its image in the manuscript, see Lionel J. Friedman, *Text and Iconography for Joinville's Credo,* 40–41, 70–72.
80. BnF naf 4509, f. 10r; Lionel J. Friedman, *Text and Iconography for Joinville's Credo,* 45.
81. BnF naf 4509, f. 10v; Lionel J. Friedman, *Text and Iconography for Joinville's Credo,* 45.
82. BnF naf 4509, f. 11r; Lionel J. Friedman, *Text and Iconography for Joinville's Credo,* 47. I am grateful to Daisy Delogu for her kind review of my proposed translation.
83. The anointing of the French kings took place within the coronation liturgy; for further discussion see Jacques Le Goff et al., *Le sacre royal.*
84. BnF naf 4509, f. 1r; Lionel J. Friedman, *Text and Iconography for Joinville's Credo,* 29.
85. BnF naf 4509, f. 1r; Lionel J. Friedman, *Text and Iconography for Joinville's Credo,* 29.
86. BnF naf 4509, f. 1r; Lionel J. Friedman, *Text and Iconography for Joinville's Credo,* 29.
87. I have followed Friedman's expansion of the manuscript reading "au briois" to "aubrigois": Lionel J. Friedman, *Text and Iconography for Joinville's Credo,* 29.
88. BnF naf 4509, f. 1r: Lionel J. Friedman, *Text and Iconography for Joinville's Credo,* 29.
89. BnF naf 4509, f. 1r; Lionel J. Friedman, *Text and Iconography for Joinville's Credo,* 29–30.
90. BnF naf 4509, f. 1r; Lionel J. Friedman, *Text and Iconography for Joinville's Credo,* 30.
91. BnF naf 4509, f. 1v; Lionel J. Friedman, *Text and Iconography for Joinville's Credo,* 30.
92. For further discussion of patristic and medieval understandings of faith, see John Van Engen, "Faith as a Concept of Order"; Jean Wirth, "La naissance du concept de croyance"; Jean-Claude Schmitt, "Du bon usage du 'Credo'"; Elisabeth Gössmann, *Glaube und Gotteserkenntnis im Mittelalter.*
93. BnF naf 4509, f, 14r; Lionel J. Friedman, *Text and Iconography for Joinville's Credo,* 51.
94. K. M. Openshaw, "Weapons in the Daily Battle."
95. London, Lambeth Palace Library, MS 209 (henceforth Lambeth 209) comprises fifty-six folios (272 x 196 mm); for a detailed codicological and paleographic examination of the codex, see Nigel Morgan, *The Lambeth Apocalypse,* 101–119. Occupying f. ii verso and ff. 40r–53v, the additional full-page images to be discussed here are described in Nigel Morgan, *The Lambeth Apocalypse,* 49–71. Although Eleanor de Quincy has emerged as the preferred patron-recipient for the manuscript in its expanded second state, Morgan has argued that Margaret de Quincy (d. 1281), countess of Derby and wife of William III Ferrers cannot be entirely excluded from consideration: Morgan, *The Lambeth Apocalypse,* 76–79.
96. Suzanne Lewis, *Reading Images,* 292; Kathryn A. Smith, *Art, Identity, and Devotion in Fourteenth-Century England,* 175. My translation of the inscription agrees with that proposed by Nigel Morgan, *The Lambeth Apocalypse,* 259.
97. As Nigel Morgan has noted, the rapprochement of trinitarian teaching and Eph. 6 effected in the diagram is also elaborated in an antecedent *postilla* on Ephesians composed by Hugh of St. Cher (c. 1200–1264): Morgan, *The Lambeth Apocalypse,* 63 (n. 62). For further discussion of Paul's spiritualized armor, and its transmission in the Middle Ages, see Michael Evans, "An Illustrated Fragment of Peraldus's Summa of Vice," 17–19.
98. The scutum fidei appears in the dicta preserved in Durham, Durham Cathedral Library, MS A.III.12, f. 14v: Suzanne Lewis, *The Art of Matthew Paris in the Chronica Majora;* Paul Binski, *Becket's Crown,* 183.
99. Michael Evans, "An Illustrated Fragment of Peraldus's Summa of Vice," 22, 24.
100. BL, Cotton MS Julius D. VII, f. 3v; discussed further in Paul Binski, *Becket's Crown,* 184; Suzanne Lewis, *The Art of Matthew Paris in the Chronica Majora,* 195–196; Suzanne Lewis, *Reading Images,* 293; Michael Evans, "An Illustrated Fragment of Peraldus's Summa of Vice," 22–24.
101. The scutum fidei diagram also appears in a more stripped-down form in the margins of Matthew Paris's earlier *Chronica majora,* Cambridge, Corpus Christi College, MS 16, f. 45v: Suzanne Lewis, *The Art of Matthew Paris in the Chronica Majora,* 194–197; Michael Evans, "An Illustrated Fragment of Peraldus's Summa of Vice," 22–24; Suzanne Lewis, *Reading Images,* 293.

102. Nigel Morgan, *The Lambeth Apocalypse,* 63 (n 62).

103. Norman P. Tanner, *DEC (1),* 230–233 [1–2].

104. The codex (hereafter Harley 3244) comprises 192 ff. measuring 278 x 170 mm, and also includes an illuminated bestiary (ff. 36r–71v); the textual contents of the volume are listed in the entry for the manuscript in the British Library's online catalog of illuminated manuscripts: http://prodigi.bl.uk/illcat/welcome.htm. See also the description of the manuscript in Michael Evans, "An Illustrated Fragment of Peraldus's Summa of Vice," 43–45; Nigel Morgan, *EGM (1),* 127–128 (no. 80). The compendium's three full-page images, as well as other of its texts, have been misbound since the fifteenth century; Evans proposes a reconstruction of the original order of the manuscript's quires: Evans, "An Illustrated Fragment of Peraldus's Summa of Vice," 38–40.

105. Michael Evans, "An Illustrated Fragment of Peraldus's Summa of Vice," 14. The manuscript is the only identified exemplar of Peraldus's much-circulated text to include images.

106. The text is preserved in Toulouse, Bibliothèque municipale, MS 418; the text has not yet been edited but it is discussed at length by M. Michèle Mulchahey, *"First the Bow Is Bent,"* 113–126; Raymond Creytens, "L'Instruction des novices Dominicains"; C. Douais, *Essai sur l'organisation des études dans l'ordre des Frères Prêcheurs,* 17–23. I plan to explore the volume's twenty images, designed in direct response to its text, in a future study.

107. M. Michèle Mulchahey, *"First the Bow Is Bent,"* 117–118.

108. Michael Evans, "An Illustrated Fragment of Peraldus's Summa of Vice," 19–20. See also Paul Binski's comments on Grosseteste's adept use of chivalric motifs in his *Château d'amour:* Binski, *Becket's Crown,* 182–184.

109. Paul Binski, *Becket's Crown,* 184. See also Joachim Bumke's more expansive consideration of the tradition of moral-religious understandings of knighthood: Bumke, *Courtly Culture,* 290–311.

110. On the identification of Eleanor de Quincy as the manuscript's patron, see Nigel Morgan, *The Lambeth Apocalypse,* 73–82. This representation of the female patron kneeling before the Virgin parallels the image of the friar kneeling before Christ in Harley 3244 quite suggestively. Michael Evans noted that motifs shared by the two manuscripts were sufficient "to suggest a relationship": Evans, "An Illustrated Fragment of Peraldus's Summa of Vice," 28.

111. Suzanne Lewis, *Reading Images,* 292.

112. Suzanne Lewis, *Reading Images,* 292–293.

113. I borrow this phrase from K. M. Openshaw, "Weapons in the Daily Battle."

114. This visual insistence on the textile character of the relic-referent distinguishes the Lambeth Veronica from other early English exemplars of the iconography. The other early English representation of the Veronica to emphasize its textile character is found in a commentary miniature on f. 13r of the Gulbenkian Apocalypse (Lisbon, Museu Calouste Gulbenkian, MS L.A. 139), a manuscript that has been related on other grounds to the Lambeth Apocalypse.

115. The classic accounts of the Veronica remain Karl Pearson, *Die Fronica;* Ernst von Dobschütz, *Christusbilder,* 197–262; Hans Belting, *Likeness and Presence,* 208–224 and passim.

116. For a succinct analysis of the origin of the Veronica as an individual image and its relationship to the Mandylion, see Gerhard Wolf, "From Mandylion to Veronica." See also Gerhard Wolf, *Schleier und Spiegel,* 12–51.

117. The first reference to a representation of Christ's face on the sudarium relic dates from a late twelfth-century French chronicle: Gerhard Wolf, "From Mandylion to Veronica," 167. Christoph Egger reviews the earliest textual accounts of the relic in Rome: Egger, "Papst Innocenz III. und die Veronica," 192–195. The exceptional ontological-semiological status of the Veronica and its significance as a paradigm for medieval and Renaissance conceptions of the image are brilliantly explored by Gerhard Wolf, *Schleier und Spiegel.* My discussion of the Veronica represented in the Lambeth Apocalypse is indebted to Wolf's analyses. See also Jean Wirth's recent discussion of the tension between relic and image in the case of the Veronica: Wirth, *L'image à l'époque gothique,* 54–60.

118. The attribution to Innocent III is first made by Matthew Paris in the *Chronica maiora;* Christoph Egger has cast serious doubts on this ascription: Egger, "Papst Innocenz III. und die Veronica," 198–202 (esp.). See also Solange Corbin, "Les offices de la Sainte Face," 27–30. Innocent's promotion of the Veronica in Rome is examined by Brenda Bolton, "Advertise the Message."

119. In addition to the Lambeth Apocalypse, the other early English witnesses to the prayer accompanied by a representation of the Holy Face are Cambridge, Corpus Christi College, MS 16, f. 53v (Matthew Paris's *Chronica maiora,* c. 1240–53; the Veronica is a pasted addition); BL, Arundel MS 157 (psalter-hours c. 1200–1210, to which the representation of the Veronica was added c. 1240); BL, Add. MS 44874, f. 6v (Evesham Psalter, c. 1250–1260?); BL, Royal MS 2.A.XXII, f. 221v (the Veronica is one of five drawings added to the Westminster Psalter c. 1250); Paris, Bibliothèque de l'Arsenal, MS 135, f. 152v (missal dated c. 1260–1270); and London, Lambeth Palace Library, MS 368, f. 95v (psalter made for Norwich Cathedral Priory): Nigel Morgan, *The Lambeth Apocalypse,* 68. As Morgan notes these witnesses suggest a Benedictine milieu as the point of origin for the English transmission of the prayer and image, perhaps the Abbey of St. Albans. See also Suzanne Lewis, *The Art of Matthew Paris in the Chronica Majora,* 126–131.

120. Flora Lewis, "The Veronica," 100 (n. 4).

121. Lambeth 209, f. 53v.

122. Lambeth 209, f. 53v.

123. Jeffrey Hamburger argues for the Veronica as an exemplar of both religious and artistic imitation and links such *imitatio* to a recovery of divine *vestigia* in the soul: Jeffrey Hamburger, "'Frequentant Memoriam Visionis Faciei Meae,'" 239–240 (esp.).

124. Gerhard Wolf, "From Mandylion to Veronica," 179.

125. Composed of sixty-four folios (337 x 248 mm), Paris, BnF, MS fr. 400 (henceforth BnF fr. 400) contains an impressive program of 274 images executed in a line and wash technique: Paulin Paris, *Les manuscrits françois de la Bibliothèque du roi,* vol. 3, 352–360 (no. 70113.3); François Avril and Patricia Danz Stirnemann, *Manuscrits enluminés d'origine Insulaire,* 166–169 (no. 208). The contents of the volume are (ff. 1r–22v) *Le Miroir de la Salvation humaine,* a highly abridged Anglo-Norman prose adaptation of the *Speculum humanae salvationis* here presented as a series of 170 images, arranged four to a page (save ff. 1v and 2v, which each feature one large image only) accompanied by a single column of vernacular exposition below; (ff. 23r–40v) a text-image "litany" of saints composed of two trinitarian images and seventy-one full-length representations of saints, each accompanied by an Anglo-Norman explanation of the relevant feast day and a short related Latin prayer until f. 28v when the textual program is abandoned; (ff. 41r–48v) the

Seven Sorrows and Nine Joys of the Virgin, each of which is provided with a half-page image and a vernacular exposition below; (ff. 49r–52v) recapitulations and expositions of items from the pastoral syllabus (to be examined in detail); (ff. 53r–56r) representations of each of the Vices as a social type mounted on a symbolic animal and holding a symbolic bird, each figure enclosed within a complexly arranged inscribed banderole and accompanied by a paragraph of vernacular exposition; (ff. 56v) a short unidentified Anglo-Norman text identified by a titulus as treating "lez pechez du qoer, de la bouche, du fait, et de omission" (incipit: "lez pecchez del quoer et du pensé sont folye penser . . ."; explicit: ". . . ne lez bonez mandementz garder et cetera"); and (ff. 57r–64v) an Anglo-Norman treatise on estate management that combines Walter of Henley's *Housbondrie,* the anonymously authored tract of the same title, and some additional chapters on accounting, with two initial chapters treating issues of moral-spiritual rectitude. For further orientation to the textual contents of BnF fr. 400, with bibliography, see Ruth J. Dean and Maureen Barry McCann Boulton, *A-N L,* nos. 394, 395, 675, 677, 740 (d.1), 763. The little attention that has been paid to the manuscript has focused on its representations of the mounted Vices as social types (rather than personifications), a precocious exemplar of this iconography: Johann Reidemeister, *Superbia und Narziss,* 64, 68 (erroneously identifying the manuscript as a French production); Emile Mâle, *L'art religieux de la fin du moyen age en France,* 329–332 (dating the manuscript to 1390); Mireille Vincent-Cassy, "Quelques réflexions sur l'envie et la jalousie"; Mireille Vincent-Cassy, "Un modèle français." For the most recent notice of the manuscript's *Miroir de la Salvation humaine,* see Heather M. Flaherty, *The Place of the Speculum Humanae Salvationis,* 11, 79–80, 81 (n. 37 and n. 39), 89–90, 505.

126. The additional items include charity, patience, mercy, generosity, avoidance of occasions for sin, upright intention, and flight from temporal goods.

127. "Responsio: Dicendum quod haec est differentia inter consilium et praeceptum, quod praeceptum importat necessitatem, consilium autem in optione ponitur ejus cui datur; et ideo convenienter in lege nova, quae est lex libertatis, supra praecepta sunt addita consilia; non autem in veteri lege, quae erat lex servitutis. Oportet igitur quod praecepta novae legis intelligantur esse data de his quae sunt necessaria ad consequendum finem aeternae beatitudinis, in quem lex nova immediate introducit; consilia vero oportet esse de illis per quae melius et expeditius potest homo consequi finem praedictum": Thomas Aquinas, *Summa theologiae,* vol. 30, Q. 108, a. 4 (pp. 60–63: Latin and English translation).

128. BnF fr. 400, f. 49r.

129. The medieval iconographic tradition is surveyed in Ruth Mellinkoff, *The Horned Moses in Medieval Art and Thought.*

130. On the recto of the page, Moses is described in parallel terms: "Lez dys comandementz del auncien testament nous moustre dieuz par son prophete moyses en disant . . ." (God shows us the Ten Commandments of the Old Testament through his prophet Moses, in saying . . .): BnF fr. 400, f. 49r.

131. In BnF fr. 400 several unfinished folios demonstrate that, after ruling, the volume's images were first completed and then its texts written. This sequence is most clear in the unfinished "litany and suffrages" section of the volume (ff. 23r–40v), but it may also be discerned in the pages discussed here, in which the disposition of texts (other than the ruled vernacular text block) is dictated by the artist's work on the page.

132. "Respondeo dicendum, quod articuli fidei distinguuntur dupliciter. uno modo quantum ad ipsa credibilia; et sic sunt quatuordecim: alio modo quantum ad ipsos qui articulos distinxerunt; et sic sunt duodecim secundum numerum duodecim apostolorum": Thomas Aquinas, *Opera omnia,* vol. 1, lib. 3, d. 25, q. 1, a. 2 co (p. 350). In the *Summa theologiae* Aquinas employs both the fourteen-part distinction of the articles and the two-part organizational scheme (explicitly related to Christ's two natures) that we find in BnF fr. 400: "quaedam pertinent ad majestatem divinitatis; quaedam vero pertinent ad mysterium humanitatis Christi . . . Et ita sunt septem articuli ad divinitatem pertinentes. Similiter etiam circa humanitatem Christi ponuntur septem articuli": Aquinas, *Summa theologiae,* vol. 31, Q. 1, a. 8, co (p. 42).

133. BnF fr. 400's apostolic attributions do not correspond to those listed by Aquinas in his Sentence commentary, nor have I been able to identify the manuscript's scheme elsewhere. At least fifteen different ways of dividing and attributing the articles in the Middle Ages have been identified: Bertrand-Georges Guyot, "L'attribution des articles de la foi aux apôtres"; James D. Gordon, "The Articles of the Creed and the Apostles"; Curt F. Bühler, "The Apostles and the Creed."

134. Although the inclusion of individual apostles in conjunction with the Credo was a well-established iconographic tradition in the later Middle Ages, BnF fr. 400's representation of the content of the Apostles' Creed in purely Christological terms is quite unusual. Representations of the content of the Credo in the period more frequently visualize individual articles, the approach employed in Joinville's *Romans,* to take but one example: François Boespflug, "Symboles de foi et apôtres au Credo"; François Boespflug, "Autour de la traduction picturale du Credo."

135. Similarly stressing how the figures of apostles in representations of the Credo "integrate" the beholder in the community of faith, François Boespflug argues that the apostles figure the authority of the church and thus solicit the viewer's "docilité": Boespflug, "Symboles de foi et apôtres au Credo," 260. I understand this opening rather differently: with the apostles clearly subordinated to each representation of the deity, the beholder is interpellated by Christ and so joins the *collegium apostolorum* in an act of witnessing and professing the faith.

136. Known as the Welles Apocalypse or the Greenfield Apocalypse, the manuscript (London, BL, Royal MS 15.D.II; henceforth Royal 15.D.II) is described in Lucy Freeman Sandler, *GM (1),* 39–40 (no. 34). For further discussion of Royal 15.D.II, see Mary Dominica Legge, *Anglo-Norman Literature,* 216, 237; Donald Drew Egbert, "The So-Called 'Greenfield' *La Lumiere As Lais.*" The *Lumere as lais* has been edited by Glynn Hesketh: Pierre de Peckham, *La lumere as lais.*

137. With the exception of the eight-line initial, featuring a curly-haired youth, that introduces the main section of the *Lumere* (f. 5v), all of the eight-line initials appear in the Apocalypse section of the volume. In these folios, the mise en page shifts from thirty-nine lines to nineteen lines per page, so the increased height of the initial corresponds to an increased size of text letter; nonetheless, the ostentatious effect of these inhabited initials is remarkable.

138. The *Lumere*'s author has also been referred to as Peter of Peckham, Peter of Pecham, and Peter of Fetcham; for further discussion of the text's authorship and dating see Pierre de Peckham, *La lumere as lais,* vol 3, 1–5. Matthias Hessenauer (whose work

Hesketh appears not to know) advances a less-cautious interpretation of the evidence: Hessenauer, *La Lumière as lais,* 16–29.

139. For further discussion of Honorius's life and works, including a determinative rejection of the older appellation "Honorius of Autun," see Valerie I. J. Flint, *Honorius Augustodunensis.*

140. Matthias Hessenauer, *La Lumière as lais,* 44–111; Pierre de Peckham, *La lumere as lais,* vol. 3, 12–18. Pierre's use of other sources, largely pastoral in orientation, is further discussed by Matthias Hessenauer, *La Lumière as lais,* 145–155.

CHAPTER 3. TRANSLATING THE EUCHARIST

Epigraph: The Hague, Koninklijke Bibliotheek, MS 70.E.4, f. 90v, as transcribed in Barbara R. Walters, Vincent J. Corrigan, and Peter T. Ricketts, *The Feast of Corpus Christi,* 175.

1. The so-called *Animarum cibus* office has been variously attributed to Juliana of Mont Cornillon in collaboration with a certain young monk named John, and to her confessor John of Lausanne, a canon of Saint-Martin, Liège: Barbara R. Walters, Vincent J. Corrigan, and Peter T. Ricketts, *The Feast of Corpus Christi,* xviii, 7–8, 61–62; Miri Rubin, *Corpus Christi,* 189.

2. Lection for matins in the Animarum cibus office for the feast of Corpus Christi, preserved in The Hague, Koninklijke Bibliotheek, MS 70.E.4, as transcribed (without folio reference) in Barbara R. Walters, Vincent J. Corrigan, and Peter T. Ricketts, *The Feast of Corpus Christi,* 139. The lection is itself a slightly modified quotation from the *Decretum:* Emil Friedberg, *Corpus iuris canonici: Vol. 1, Decretum, De consecratione,* D. 2, c. 82 (col. 1348). On the polysemy of Eucharistic *veritas,* see also Henri de Lubac, *Corpus mysticum,* 210–247.

3. Emil Friedberg, *Corpus iuris canonici: Vol. 1, Decretum, De consecratione,* D. 2, c. 43 (col. 1329), quoted, in modified form, in a lection for matins in the Animarum cibus office for the feast of Corpus Christi preserved in The Hague, Koninklijke Bibliotheek, MS 70.E.4, as transcribed (without folio reference) in Barbara R. Walters, Vincent J. Corrigan, and Peter T. Ricketts, *The Feast of Corpus Christi,* 145.

4. Irène Rosier-Catach, *La parole efficace,* 59–62, 211–214, and passim; Gary Macy, "The 'Dogma of Transubstantiation' in the Middle Ages," 98–99, 181.

5. Miri Rubin, *Corpus Christi,* 12–82, and passim.

6. The key scriptural texts are Matthew 26:26–29, Mark 14:22–26, Luke 22:14–23, and 1 Corinthians: Ellen Bradshaw Aitken, "τα δρωμενα και τα λεγονενα"; Andrew Brian McGowan, "'Is There a Liturgical Text in This Gospel?'"

7. Macy suggests that the so-called ninth-century controversy may be more the product of historical retrospection than Carolingian theological conflict: Gary Macy, *The Theologies of the Eucharist,* 21–22. For further discussion of the early influence of Paschasius's and Ratramnus's writings on the Eucharist, see Jean Paul Bouhot, *Ratramne de Corbie;* Gary Macy, *The Theologies of the Eucharist,* 21–35.

8. Rachel Fulton, *From Judgment to Passion,* 9–59, esp. 11.

9. Rachel Fulton, *From Judgment to Passion,* 11.

10. Brian Stock, *The Implications of Literacy,* 273–315; Gary Macy, "Berengar's Legacy as Heresiarch"; Gary Macy, "The Theological Fate of Berengar's Oath of 1059"; Miri Rubin, *Corpus Christi,* 17–35.

11. See, for example, Peter the Chanter's systematizing discussion of the sacraments: Petrus Cantor, *Summa de sacramentis,* 13–182. For an overview of the theological contributions of Peter the Chanter and his circle, see John W. Baldwin, *Masters, Princes, and Merchants,* vol. 1, 47–59.

12. Gary Macy, *The Theologies of the Eucharist,* 18–43.

13. Although my discussion focuses on developments in the second half of the twelfth century and following, the foundation for much of this institutional reform—both legal and liturgical—must be identified with the so-called Gregorian reform movement initiated in the eleventh century: Brian Stock, *The Implications of Literacy,* 30–59.

14. The importance of crusade in this context cannot be overstated; it cannot, however, be treated here.

15. The *Decretum* circulated in two recensions, the first dating from circa 1139 and the second from no later than 1150: Anders Winroth, *The Making of Gratian's Decretum.* For a concise review of the *Decretum*'s contents and structure in the mid-twelfth century, see also Susan L'Engle, "The Texts," 15–16.

16. Peter Clarke, "The Growth of Canon and Civil Law Studies," 27–28; Susan L'Engle, "The Texts," 15–18.

17. The visual material is surveyed in Anthony Melnikas, *The Corpus of the Miniatures in the Manuscripts of Decretum Gratiani.* See also Susan L'Engle and Robert Gibbs, *Illuminating the Law.*

18. Susan L'Engle, "Legal Iconography," 82, 89, 95–96. The illumination of *De consecratione* is surveyed briefly, with numerous illustrations, in Anthony Melnikas, *The Corpus of the Miniatures in the Manuscripts of Decretum Gratiani,* vol. 3, 1175–1202.

19. Cambridge, Fitzwilliam Museum, MS 262 (174 ff., 435 x 285 mm). The manuscript's text has been dated to circa 1300 and its illumination to circa 1310–1330; there is, as yet, no consensus about the localization of the manuscript. Robert Gibbs has described the manuscript as possessing northern French traits (particularly its text), but firmly associates its miniatures with the Tickhill Psalter group: Susan L'Engle and Robert Gibbs, *Illuminating the Law,* 146–152 (cat. no. 8).

20. Susan L'Engle and Robert Gibbs, *Illuminating the Law,* 150. The masonry-in-progress painted in this quadrant may be a visual response to a textual passage that occurs slightly later in this first of *De consecratione*'s distinctions: "Omnes basilicae cum missa debent semper consecrari. Et ecclesiae destructae, ubi autem plures sunt, quam necesse sit, aut maioris magnitudinis, quam ut ex rebus ad eas pertinentibus restaurari possint, episcopi prouidentia modus inueniatur, qualiter consistere possint": Emil Friedberg, *Corpus iuris canonici: Vol. 1, Decretum, De consecratione,* D. 1, c. 69 (cols. 1294–1295).

21. Emil Friedberg, *Corpus iuris canonici: Vol. 1, Decretum, De consecratione,* D. 1, c. 1 (col. 1293).

22. Emil Friedberg, *Corpus iuris canonici: Vol. 1, Decretum, De consecratione,* D. 1, c. 2 (cols. 1293–1294).

23. Cambridge, Fitzwilliam Museum, Marlay Cutting Fr. 2. Likely produced in southern France, the leaf (474 x 309 mm) has been dated to circa 1330–1340: Susan L'Engle and Robert Gibbs, *Illuminating the Law,* 204–206 (cat. no. 15).

24. The visual assertion of clerical prerogative articulated in these miniatures (and in a host of similar miniatures executed for other canon law codices) in terms of a sacerdotal monopolization of Eucharistic space may be a more radical claim than has hitherto been noted. As Gary Macy has pointed out, ample evidence suggests that "there was no necessary connection between consecration and sacramental ordination" in the middle of the twelfth century: Gary Macy, "The Eucharist and Popular Religiosity," 173. Certainly, many of the elements in the late medieval design of

the Eucharist were, at least in part, intended to reinforce distinctions between the laity and the clergy that were relatively recent social-spiritual constructions; for further discussion, see also Gary Macy, "The 'Invention' of Clergy and Laity in the Twelfth Century."

25. There is, of course, a certain literalism to the choice of scenes for each frontispiece: both the ritual dedication of a church and the ritual offering of the Eucharist are "consecrations."
26. Miri Rubin provides a succinct summary of the range of manuscripts in which elevation scenes were painted, with further examples: Rubin, *Corpus Christi,* 131–134.
27. See, for example, New York, Pierpont Morgan Library, MS M.94, f. 90r (c. 1250–1274; illuminated in Cologne). For the visual programs devised for Liège Psalters-Hours, often identified as Psalters of Lambert le Bègue, see Judith Oliver, *Gothic Manuscript Illumination in the Diocese of Liege.* The examples of elevation scenes executed for liturgical manuscripts discussed in this note and in the notes following were identified by means of the online database of the Index of Christian Art; full records with further bibliography and images may be accessed through the Index of Christian Art at Princeton University.
28. BL, Add. 49999, f. 56r; discussed further in Nigel Morgan, *EGM (1),* 119–121 (no. 73); Claire Donovan, *The de Brailes Hours,* esp. 91.
29. New York, Pierpont Morgan Library, MS M.107, f. 142r. The manuscript is described further in Lucy Freeman Sandler, *GM (2),* 84–86 (no. 78). For further discussion of elevation scenes in missals, see Miri Rubin, *Corpus Christi,* 138–139.
30. As in a Breviary illuminated, in part, by a follower of Jean Pucelle in the third quarter of the fourteenth century: New York, Pierpont Morgan Library, MS M.75, f. 302r. The development of new visual programs to accompany the Corpus Christi office in liturgical manuscripts is explored in Miri Rubin, *Corpus Christi,* 204–208.
31. Emil Friedberg, *Corpus iuris canonici: Vol. 2, Decretalium collectiones,* Lib. 3, Tit. I, *De vita et honestate clericorum,* c. 1 (col. 449).
32. The gloss on this passage helps clarify some syntactical and terminological ambiguity: "Dicitur in hoc capitulo, quod laici non debent sedere in choro inter clericos, quando cantantur diuina officia, sed in sancta sanctorum. Nota, quod laici inter clericos sedere non debent. Item ecclesia debet habere duas partes, scilicet chorum, qui per cancellos diuiditur ab altari, et sancta sanctorum, id est, partem inferiorem ecclesiae, quae vulgariter dicitur, nauis ecclesiae" (It is said in this chapter that laypeople should not sit in the choir among the clergy when the divine offices are sung, but [they should sit] in the *sancta sanctorum.* Note that laypeople must not sit among the clergy. *Item,* the church ought to have two parts: namely, a choir, which is separated from the altar by the chancel [screen], and a *sancta sanctorum,* that is the lower part of the church, which is popularly called the nave [literally, "ship," "vessel"] of the church): *Corpus juris canonici emendatum et notis illustratum. Gregorii XIII. pont. max. iussu editum,* vol. 2, lib. 3, tit. 1, c. 1 (col. 991).
33. Joseph Goering, *William de Montibus,* 64–67; Peter Clarke, "The Growth of Canon and Civil Law Studies," esp. 29–34. After 1298 this phenomenon was encouraged by Boniface VIII's *Cum ex eo* constitution which established a system of episcopal licenses for university study, allowing clergy who were not yet priests access to further education: Leonard E. Boyle, "Aspects of Clerical Education"; Leonard E. Boyle, "The Constitution 'Cum ex eo.'"
34. For a helpful examination of the theorization and application of interdicts in the thirteenth century, with extensive consideration of the general Interdict of 1208, see Peter Clarke, *The Interdict in the Thirteenth Century.*
35. C. R. Cheney, *Pope Innocent III and England,* 147–154; M. D. Knowles, "The Canterbury Election of 1205–6."
36. C. R. Cheney, *From Becket to Langton,* 94. See also C. R. Cheney, *Pope Innocent III and England,* 298–302.
37. On the excommunication, see C. R. Cheney, *Pope Innocent III and England,* 319–322.
38. C. R. Cheney, "A recent view," 162. From the initial imposition of the Interdict on Sunday, March 23, 1208, until late in 1212 even the viaticum was withheld: F. M. Powicke and C. R. Cheney, *C&S II (I),* 11. See also Peter Clarke, *The Interdict in the Thirteenth Century,* 130–168.
39. C. R. Cheney, "A Recent View," 161–168 (esp.); C. R. Cheney, *Pope Innocent III and England,* 303–307.
40. Carolyn Marino Malone provides a compelling account of the spiritual and sensory impact of the Interdict, with further bibliography: Malone, *Façade as Spectacle,* 186. Although Innocent III relaxed the prohibition on the celebration of Mass for monastic houses in 1209, no such concession was made for secular churches and their lay parishioners in the years from 1208 to 1213: C. R. Cheney, "A Recent View," 163. It must be noted that according to Roger of Wendover, Archbishop Stephen Langton mitigated aspects of the Interdict after his return to England and King John's absolution (in July 1213): F. M. Powicke and C. R. Cheney, *C&S II (I),* 19. Following John's absolution, Langton celebrated a Mass in the king's presence on July 20, 1213; as C. R. Cheney notes, Innocent III reproached the archbishop for this act: Cheney, "A Recent View," 167.
41. For contemporary theorization and justification of the use and efficacy of interdicts, see Peter Clarke, *The Interdict in the Thirteenth Century,* 14–58.
42. Paul Binski, *Becket's Crown,* 62–64 (esp. 64).
43. Carolyn Marino Malone, *Façade as Spectacle,* 186.
44. D. M. Whitelock, M. Brett, and C. N. L. Brooke, *C&S I (II),* 1048–1052.
45. Reservation in a clean pyx: F. M. Powicke and C. R. Cheney, *C&S II (I),* 27 [14]; seven-day reservation of host: F. M. Powicke and C. R. Cheney, *C&S II (I),* 27 [14]; consumption of reserved hosts by priest: F. M. Powicke and C. R. Cheney, *C&S II (I),* 27 [14]; priest must know whether host is consecrated: F. M. Powicke and C. R. Cheney, *C&S II (I),* 27 [14]; clean and adequate cloths for the Mass: F. M. Powicke and C. R. Cheney, *C&S II (I),* 28 [15], 29 [18]; adequate and fitting vessels, books, and vestments for the Mass: F. M. Powicke and C. R. Cheney, *C&S II (I),* 29 [18].
46. F. M. Powicke and C. R. Cheney, *C&S II (I),* 28 [17].
47. F. M. Powicke and C. R. Cheney, *C&S II (I),* 28 [17]. The measures Langton prescribes are hedged with the stipulation *post solutum scilicet interdictum* or *post solutionem interdicti,* clearly indicating that the archbishop was consciously shaping these Eucharistic practices in advance of their reintroduction: F. M. Powicke and C. R. Cheney, *C&S II (I),* 27 [14], 28 [17].
48. F. M. Powicke and C. R. Cheney, *C&S II (I),* 33 [45].
49. F. M. Powicke and C. R. Cheney, *C&S II (I),* 32 [43].
50. Paul Binski, *Becket's Crown,* 152.
51. Paul Binski, *Becket's Crown,* 155–157; R. N. Swanson, "Medieval Liturgy as Theatre."
52. F. M. Powicke and C. R. Cheney, *C&S II (II),* 990 [4].

53. Quinel's prescriptions for clerical and lay comportment are part of a broader phenomenon emphasizing corporeal *habitus* as an integral component of spiritual practice: Jean-Claude Schmitt, *La raison des gestes,* 289–320, 330–355 (esp.); Paul Binski, *Becket's Crown,* 199–200; Jean-Claude Schmitt, "Entre le text et l'image"; Richard C. Trexler, "Legitimating Prayer Gestures"; Kathryn A. Smith, "Book, Body, and the Construction of the Self in the Taymouth Hours," 177–184 (esp.).
54. Sarah Beckwith, *Christ's Body,* esp. 34–35; Miri Rubin, *Corpus Christi,* 1–11; Miri Rubin, "What Did the Eucharist Mean." Rubin and Beckwith propose fundamental revisions of John Bossy's landmark analysis of the Mass as an occasion for the formation of late medieval community through a process of "social fusion": Bossy, "The Mass as a Social Institution, 1200–1700." By contrast, Eamon Duffy has offered an account of the Mass in late medieval England that attempts to rehabilitate conceptions of ritual as a site for social integration: Duffy, *The Stripping of the Altars,* esp. 2–3, 91–130.
55. Dated circa 1340–1350, the manuscript is today preserved (with losses) in Baltimore, Walters Art Museum, MS W.105 (56 ff., 210 x 140 mm) and Stockholm, Nationalmuseum, MSS B.1726 and B.1727 (two detached leaves): Lucy Freeman Sandler, *GM (2),* 130–131 (no. 117). For further discussion of the manuscript, see Michael Camille, *The Gothic Idol,* 215; Kathryn A. Smith, *Art, Identity, and Devotion in Fourteenth-Century England,* 117; J. J. G. Alexander and Paul Binski, *Age of Chivalry,* 255 (cat. no. 152); Roger S. Wieck, *Time Sanctified,* 106, 116, 222 (cat. no. 112).
56. Composed of 195 folios (168 x 110 mm), the Taymouth Hours (London, BL, Yates Thompson MS 13) continues to provoke debate. Lucy Freeman Sandler suggests that the manuscript may have been produced in London, circa 1325–1335: Sandler, *GM (2),* 107–109 (no. 98). Kathryn Smith, who is preparing a book-length study of the Taymouth Hours, dates the manuscript to the "early 1330s": Smith, "Book, Body, and the Construction of the Self in the Taymouth Hours," 174. Suzanne Lewis's proposal that the manuscript was made for Isabelle of France and that the crowned female figure who appears in the visual program should be identified as Isabelle has not been universally accepted: Lewis, "The Apocalypse of Isabella of France," 233–234. For further discussion of the manuscript see also Anne Rudloff Stanton, *The Queen Mary Psalter,* 196–204; Anne Rudloff Stanton, "Isabelle of France and her Manuscripts," 242–245; Jessica Brantley, "Images of the Vernacular in the Taymouth Hours"; Kathryn A. Smith, "Chivalric Narratives and Devotional Experience in the Taymouth Hours"; Linda Brownrigg, "The Taymouth Hours"; Richard K. Emmerson, "Visualizing the Vernacular"; Sylvia Huot, "Polytextual Reading," 218–222.
57. As Linda Brownrigg first remarked, the figure of Jeremiah in the bas-de-page is modeled after the figure of Jerome painted in the opening initial of the Psalter of St. Jerome in the manuscript that forms the focus of the remainder of this chapter (Paris, BnF, MS fr. 13342 [henceforth BnF fr. 13342], f. 49r): Brownrigg, "The Taymouth Hours," 236–237. The relationship between the two manuscripts is explored further in Kathryn A. Smith, "Book, Body, and the Construction of the Self in the Taymouth Hours," 178–180.
58. Kathryn A. Smith, "Book, Body, and the Construction of the Self in the Taymouth Hours," 178.
59. A convincing case has been made for dating the manuscript to circa 1325 by Lynda Dennison, "An Illuminator of the Queen Mary Psalter Group," 298, 305. Earlier notices of the manuscript proposed circa 1310–1325 as the likely period for its production: Lucy Freeman Sandler, *GM (2),* 67–68 (no. 58); J. J. G. Alexander and Paul Binski, *Age of Chivalry,* 236–237 (no. 110), 453–454 (no. 572).
60. Although the relationship between the two extant fragments of the manuscript is well known, art-historical attention has, with few exceptions, focused on the Mass tract found in BnF fr. 13342: Melanie Holcomb, *Pen and Parchment,* 159–161 (no. 48); Kathryn A. Smith, "Book, Body, and the Construction of the Self in the Taymouth Hours," 178–180; Ann Elijenholm Nichols, "The Bread of Heaven," 47; Lynda Dennison, "An Illuminator of the Queen Mary Psalter Group," 290–291; Judith Oliver, "Image et dévotion: Le rôle de l'art dans l'institution de la Fête-Dieu," 159, 164; Moshe Barasch, "Elevatio," 52–53; Anne Rudloff Stanton, *The Queen Mary Psalter,* 20, 57, 80, 196, 198 (n. 14); Francis Wormald, "Some Pictures of the Mass"; Jean-Claude Schmitt, *La raison des gestes,* 350–353; Paul Binski, *Becket's Crown,* 197–201; François Avril and Patricia Danz Stirnemann, *Manuscrits enluminés d'origine Insulaire,* 143–145 (cat. no. 179). An interpretive guide to the Mass tract has been published online by the VW-Forschungsgruppe "Kulturgeschichte und Theologie des Bildes im Christentum" of the Westfälische Wilhelms-Universität (SFB 496, Teilprojekt A4): http://www.uni-muenster.de/Kultbild/missa/themen/laienmesse_1.html.
61. The four full-page miniatures (foliated 2 and 3) from the Oxford section of the manuscript (Oxford, Bodleian Library, MS Douce 79; henceforth Douce 79) are currently matted and framed under glass. The ten surviving text folios of Douce 79 have been bound separately: iv + 1^{2} (modern paper replacement for full-page miniatures) + 2^{6} (a regular quaternion lacking its first and second folios) + 3^{4} + ii. These folios are both foliated (4–13; final modern flyleaves foliated 14–15) and paginated (odd numbers only, 1–19); they measure 210 x 133 mm. The Paris fragment (BnF fr. 13342) currently consists of fifty-three folios (205 x 130 mm). The volume's tight binding precludes a reliable collation of the manuscript, but it would seem that the first three quires (ff. 1–24) and the fifth quire (ff. 31–38) are composed of regular gatherings of eight folios (four conjoined bifolios) with catchwords in the lower margin of each final folio. The fourth quire (ff. 25–30), currently consisting of six folios, would seem to have lost its innermost bifolium (catchword preserved on f. 30v). I have not been able to determine the quire structure of the volume's final fifteen folios. It should be noted that the catchword preserved at the end of the fifth quire (f. 38v) does not match the first words of f. 39r (currently the first folio of quire six); clearly some loss has been suffered at this point. In short, the structure of BnF fr. 13342 can only be approximated as: ii + 1–3^{8}, 4^{6}, 5^{8}, 6–$?^{?}$. The fragmentary current state of the compendium makes it impossible to know how many texts and images it originally contained. It seems likely that the four surviving full-page miniatures now in Oxford are but a fraction of a larger prefatory cycle.
62. Otto Pächt and J. J. G. Alexander, *Illuminated Manuscripts in the Bodleian,* vol. 3, 49–50 (no. 539, S.C. 21653); Lucy Freeman Sandler, *GM (2),* 68 (no. 59).
63. First noted by Paul Meyer, this text, which circulated in England and France in multiple redactions, awaits an edition: Ruth J. Dean and Maureen Barry McCann Boulton, *A-N L,* 347–348 (no. 632); Paul Meyer, "Trois nouveaux manuscrits des sermons français de Maurice de Sully," 254, 257–261. The treatise

is discussed (with extensive excerpts) by Charles Victor Langlois, *La vie en France: Vol. 4, La vie spirituelle: Enseignements, méditations et controverses,* 47–65.

64. The *Mirour* has been edited, with a very helpful introduction to the text, by A. D. Wilshere, *Mirour de Seinte Eglyse.* The text in BnF fr. 13342 belongs to Wilshere's "A," or "religious" recension, a textual tradition designed for female religious readers; as Wilshere notes, BnF fr. 13342 presents some divergences from the "A" family, but Wilshere feels that these are defects rather than revisions: Wilshere, *Mirour de Seinte Eglyse,* xi–xii. In three manuscripts the *Mirour* is followed by a set of instructions for devout thought and prayer at Mass, possibly also authored by St. Edmund of Abingdon: Ruth J. Dean and Maureen Barry McCann Boulton, *A-N L,* 392 (no. 720). The Mass tract included in BnF fr. 13342 is, however, a distinct text.
65. According to Dean and Boulton, the tract is attested only in BnF fr. 13342: Ruth J. Dean and Maureen Barry McCann Boulton, *A-N L,* 392–393 (no. 722). The text of the Mass tract was first published by Francis Wormald, "Some Pictures of the Mass." I will cite my own transcriptions from the manuscript.
66. Victor Leroquais describes the Psalter of St. Jerome as composed of a series of verses taken from different Psalms, seemingly strung together without any overarching scheme: Leroquais, *Les psautiers,* vol. 1, xiii. Pierre Salmon, by contrast, suggests that the text is a "réunion systématique de textes des psaumes, avec omission de certains versets, mais en s'en tenant strictement au texte biblique": Salmon, "Psautiers abrégés," 76.
67. The beginning of the first of these two prayers is lost, with only its final seventeen lines remaining (on f. 52r); the second prayer begins, "Domine Ihesu Christe qui ex voluntate patris cooperante spiritu sancto de beata maria virgine corporis nostri fragilitatem sumpsisti . . ." and ends ". . . cum vera cordis contricione et cum percepcione corporis et sanguinis sui. Qui vivis et regnas cum deo patre et spiritu sancto per omnia secula seculorum amen."
68. There is a growing literature on the Queen Mary Psalter (BL, Royal MS 2.B.VII) and the corpus of manuscripts related to it stylistically: Bruce Watson, "The East Anglican Problem"; Anne Rudloff Stanton, "Notes on the Codicology of the Queen Mary Psalter"; Kathryn A. Smith, "History, Typology and Homily"; Lynda Dennison, "An Illuminator of the Queen Mary Psalter Group"; O. S. Pickering, "Some Similarities between Queen Mary's Psalter and the Northern Passion"; Michael A. Michael, "Oxford, Cambridge and London," esp. 112–114; Anne Rudloff Stanton, *The Queen Mary Psalter;* George F. Warner, *Queen Mary's Psalter;* Lynda Dennison, "'Liber Horn,' 'Liber Custumarum'"; Anne Rudloff Stanton, "*La Genealogye Comence*"; Anne Rudloff Stanton, "From Eve to Bathsheba and Beyond"; Michael A. Michael, "The Harnhulle Psalter-Hours."
69. Lynda Dennison attributes the inhabited initial and the foliate border painted on the first text folio of the Psalter of St. Jerome (f. 49r) to the "Ancient 6" Master, an illuminator named for his work in London, Library of Dr. Williams, MS Ancient 6. For further discussion of this artist's work and his collaboration with the Queen Mary Psalter Master, see Lynda Dennison, "An Illuminator of the Queen Mary Psalter Group." Dennison affirms that the illumination of the other miniatures, initials, and borders in Douce 79 and BnF fr. 13342 may be securely attributed to the Queen Mary Psalter Master.
70. Lucy Freeman Sandler preferred London-Westminster as a likely localization for manuscripts made by the Queen Mary Psalter Master and his collaborators; more recently Michael Michael has also identified East Anglia or Kent as possible points of origin for the manuscript: Sandler, *GM (1),* 30–32; Michael, "Urban Production of Manuscript Books," 185–186. For a documentary perspective on the late medieval book trade in London, see C. Paul Christianson, *A Directory of London Stationers and Book Artisans,* 13–44 (esp.).
71. Moshe Barasch's assertion that the treatise "consists of a collection of instructions given to the priest as to how to celebrate Mass correctly" is mistaken; as Francis Wormald recognized, the tract is certainly designed for the use of a layperson: Wormald, "Some Pictures of the Mass," 45; Barasch, "Elevatio," 52.
72. As my discussion of the Mass tract's images should make clear, I do not concur with Paul Binski's assessment that the work eschews a theoretical, "doctrinal," or "rhetorical" engagement with the gestural performance expected of lay Mass-goers: Paul Binski, *Becket's Crown,* 200. My understanding of the hermeneutic orientation of the tract is also shared by the SFB 496, Teilprojekt A4's analysis: http://www.uni-muenster.de/Kultbild/missa/themen/laienmesse_2.html.
73. BnF fr. 13342, f. 45r.
74. Josef A. Jungmann, *Missarum sollemnia,* vol. 2, 47–62.
75. BnF fr. 13342, f. 45r.
76. Recent arguments have shown that the demarcation of church interiors did not constitute an impermeable division of space, but rather functioned to frame and mediate multiple viewpoints and experiences of ecclesiastical space in the Middle Ages: Jacqueline E. Jung, "Beyond the Barrier"; Richard Marks, *Image and Devotion in Late Medieval England,* 157–185; Eamon Duffy, *The Stripping of the Altars,* 109–116.
77. Discussed with further bibliography in Francis Bond, *Screens and Galleries,* 87; Lucy Archer, *Architecture in Britain and Ireland,* 196, pl. 223.
78. Paul Binski also remarks on the absence of many of the markers of social distinction that one would expect to encounter in English church space of the period: Binski, *Becket's Crown,* 200–201.
79. In the later Middle Ages the introit typically consisted of an antiphon, a psalm verse, and the *Gloria patri* with repeated antiphon: John Harper, *The Forms and Orders of Western Liturgy,* 115. For further discussion, see Josef A. Jungmann, *Missarum sollemnia,* vol. 2, 72–87.
80. BnF fr. 13342, f. 45r.
81. Guillaume Durand, *Rationale Divinorum Officiorum, I–IV,* Lib. IV, c. V, 1 (p. 267).
82. Liturgiological interpretations of the introit are explored further by Margot Fassler, "The Meaning of Entrance"; Margot Fassler, "Liturgy and Sacred History," 501–502. Schmitt proposes that the Hell Mouth is included in the image as a reminder that the celebrant's entry symbolizes Christ's descent into limbo and that the Mass liberates sinners just as Christ liberated the justified: Jean-Claude Schmitt, *La raison des gestes,* 352.
83. Josef A. Jungmann, *Missarum sollemnia,* vol. 2, 87–103.
84. BnF fr. 13342, f. 45v.
85. Josef A. Jungmann, *Missarum sollemnia,* vol. 2, 94–97, 102.
86. BnF fr. 13342, f. 45v.
87. Paul Binski, *Becket's Crown,* 198. For further discussion of the meditations prescribed by the *Mirour* for each of the canonical hours, see Helen P. Forshaw, "St Edmund's *Speculum*"; Michel Zink, "L'Expression de la contemplation dans le *Mirour de seinte eglyse*"; Mother Mary Philomena, "St. Edmund of Abingdon's Meditations"; Jocelyn Wogan-Browne, *Saints' Lives and Women's Literary Culture,* 187.

88. BnF fr. 13342, f. 39r; A. D. Wilshere, *Mirour de Seinte Eglyse,* 20.10–17 (pp. 58–59).
89. Josef A. Jungmann, *Missarum sollemnia,* vol. 2, 97.
90. Latin text and English translation in John Harper, *The Forms and Orders of Western Liturgy,* 266–267.
91. Josef A. Jungmann, *Missarum sollemnia,* vol. 2, 233–247.
92. Josef A. Jungmann, *Missarum sollemnia,* vol. 3, 37–47. The ritual actions and texts performed in the Canon of the Mass, as a whole, are elucidated in Josef A. Jungmann, *Missarum sollemnia,* vol. 3, 5–197.
93. BnF fr. 13342, f. 46r.
94. Pamela Sheingorn, "The Te Deum Altarpiece," 179.
95. As Pierre Alain Mariaux has noted, this insistence on the collapse of heavenly and temporal liturgies in the singing of the *Sanctus* has a long history: Mariaux, "'Faire Dieu,'" 99.
96. BnF fr. 13342, f. 46r.
97. New York, Pierpont Morgan Library, MS G.53, f. 150r; 320 x 210 mm, dated circa 1310–1320 and made for Richard, a monk of St. Augustine's Abbey, Canterbury: Lucy Freeman Sandler, *GM (2),* 66–67 (no. 57).
98. The style and finesse of the painting of the crucified corpus in this miniature is consistent with work securely attributed to the Queen Mary Psalter Master. As François Avril and Patricia Stirnemann indicate, it seems clear that the illuminator returned to the miniature after a first campaign of work and added the figure of Christ crucified on the cross: Avril and Stirnemann, *Manuscrits enluminés d'origine Insulaire,* 144.
99. BnF fr. 13342, f. 46v.
100. BnF fr. 13342, f. 46v.
101. BnF fr. 13342, f. 46v.
102. BnF fr. 13342, ff. 41v–42r. The manuscript reading exhibits significant variance from both the A- and B-texts edited by A. D. Wilshere: Wilshere, *Mirour de Seinte Eglyse,* 26.12–13, 17–30 (pp. 70–73).
103. Here the *Mirour* closely echoes Richard Poore's statutory admonition (1217 x 1219) that the faithful should be taught that in the Eucharist they receive Christ's body as it hung on the cross and his blood as it flowed from his side: "Nam hoc accipiunt proculdubio sub panis specie quod pro nobis pependit in cruce, hoc accipiunt in calice quod effusum est de Christi latere": F. M. Powicke and C. R. Cheney, *C&S II (I),* 77–78 [55].
104. If, as I think is likely, the unified elevation scene executed across the opening of ff. 46v–47r must have been planned and painted across a single unbound bifolium, this would suggest that ff. 46v–47r must define the center of a quire. Given that the majority of the Paris volume's quires are organized in the traditional structure of four bifolia, it would seem likely that the elevation miniature spans the innermost bifolium of a quire composed of ff. 43–50. Accordingly, the last folio of the *Mirour* (f. 44v) would belong to the same quire as the beginning of the Mass tract (f. 45r) and the elevation opening (ff. 46v–47r). Thus, the codicological and conceptual proximity of the *Mirour*'s discussion of the sacrament of the altar and the Mass tract's extended instruction in Eucharistic participation would have been the result of a highly planned design for the compendium as a whole. Given the difficulties posed by the Paris volume's current binding, this proposal regarding the structure of the volume's final fifteen folios must remain tentative.
105. I do not share Moshe Barasch's conviction that the elevation miniature is principally about sacerdotal proximity or fusion with Christ: Barasch, "Elevatio," 53. Barasch does not seem to be aware that Christ's bleeding body is an addition to the original composition.
106. Josef A. Jungmann, *Missarum sollemnia,* vol. 3, 196–197.
107. BnF fr. 13342, f. 47r. The injunction to listen to the Gospel in silence that appears in this passage is curious. According to the established conduct of the Mass, the Gospel reading occurs before the Credo; I have not been able to resolve what the *ewangele* mentioned in the text refers to.
108. Josef A. Jungmann, *Missarum sollemnia,* vol. 3, 261–269. The fraction, commixtion, and celebrant's communication are discussed in: Josef A. Jungmann, *Missarum sollemnia,* vol. 3, 228–248 281–290.
109. "Al premer *Agnus dei.* Vous prierez merci de ceo qe vous avez pecché par les sept mortels pecchez" (At the first *Agnus dei:* You shall ask for forgiveness because you have sinned through [committing] the seven deadly sins): BnF fr. 13342, f. 47v.
110. "Al second *Agnus dei.* Devez prier de ceo qe vous avez lessé le dis comandementz" (At the second *Agnus dei:* You should pray because you have abandoned [or neglected] the ten commandments): BnF fr. 13342, f. 47v.
111. BnF fr. 13342, f. 48r.
112. I am grateful to Maureen Boulton for her kind review of my translation.
113. BnF fr. 13342, f. 48r.
114. BnF fr. 13342, f. 48r.
115. The iconographic and theological associations of the Trinity and the Eucharist in the later Middle Ages are signaled, with a brief consideration of this image, in François Boespflug, "Eucharistie et Trinité dans l'art médiéval," 1143–1144 (esp.).
116. BnF fr. 13342, f. 48v.
117. On this practice, see Peter Browe, "Der Segen mit Reliquien der Patene und Eucharistie," 233–234 (esp.). As Josef Jungmann notes, the sacerdotal use of the chalice and paten in the final blessing is a practice particularly well attested in northern Europe in the fourteenth century: Jungmann, *Missarum sollemnia,* vol. 3, 382–383. I cannot concur with Jean-Claude Schmitt's reading of this miniature as a depiction of the communion of the people: Schmitt, *La raison des gestes,* 353. The fact that the lay figures are never represented physically receiving the Eucharist is, in fact, crucial to the Mass tract's project and entirely in keeping with contemporary practices, as I will examine.
118. BnF fr. 13342, f. 48v.
119. The beatific vision was a topic of considerable controversy at the end of the thirteenth and beginning of the fourteenth centuries: Christian Trottmann, *La vision béatifique.* Ann Nichols explores how gazing at the Eucharist was understood to prefigure the beatific vision, primarily with reference to English sources (including the Mass tract examined here): Nichols, "The Bread of Heaven." On the representation of the beatific vision in medieval art, see Cynthia Hahn, "Visio Dei"; Jérôme Baschet, "Vision béatifique et représentations du paradis (XIe–XVe siècle)"; Lucy Freeman Sandler, "Face to Face with God."
120. Gary Macy, "The Eucharist and Popular Religiosity"; Gary Macy, "Reception of the Eucharist According to the Theologians"; Charles Caspers, "*Meum summum desiderium est te habere,*" 131–132. For a reassessment of how we might understand the role of congregants in the medieval Mass that revises older conceptions of the so-called mysterium depopulatum, see Gerard Lukken, "Les transformations du rôle liturgique du peuple."
121. My admittedly generalizing characterization of these aspects of scholastic theology of the Eucharist is indebted to Gary Macy, "Reception of the Eucharist According to the Theologians"; David Burr, *Eucharistic Presence and Conversion.*

122. Gary Macy, "Reception of the Eucharist According to the Theologians."

123. Two notable exceptions to this rather gross rule must be acknowledged: both Albertus Magnus and Thomas Aquinas maintained the analytic priority of a metaphysical account of the Eucharist. This commitment leads both thinkers, albeit in importantly different ways, to advance views of reception that were rejected by their peers (for example, that Christ would remain truly present in the sacrament, even in the stomach of an animal or unbeliever): Gary Macy, "Reception of the Eucharist According to the Theologians," 43, 45.

124. The chief biblical and patristic authorities marshaled in support of spiritual communion are reviewed by Jef Lamberts, "Liturgie et spiritualité de l'eucharistie au XIIIe siècle," 90–93.

125. Gary Macy, "Reception of the Eucharist According to the Theologians," 37; Gary Macy, "The Eucharist and Popular Religiosity," 175–177.

126. Charles Caspers, "The Western Church during the Late Middle Ages," 88.

127. Alexander of Hales, *Quaestiones disputatae "antequam esset frater,"* vol. 2, 966–967 (no. 199). Discussed in Gary Macy, "Reception of the Eucharist According to the Theologians," 37–38.

128. "Item, alia est unio speciei tantum, ut in iis qui manudcant secundum quod est sacramentum solum, sicut panem aliquem, ut Iudaei vel pagani": Alexander of Hales, *Quaestiones disputatae "antequam esset frater,"* vol. 2, 967 (no. 199).

129. Responding to an objection concerning the mode of reception by Jews and pagans, Alexander asserts, "dico quod plus est in hac manducatione [by Jews and pagans] quam in manducatione irrationalis creaturae, quia unio est ibi in natura. Tamen quia non est ibi cognitio rei sub specie, et cum manducatio sacramentalis importet accipere species et attingere rem quae est sub sacramento fide, non manducant sacramentaliter": Alexander of Hales, *Quaestiones disputatae "antequam esset frater,"* vol. 2, 970 (no. 210).

130. "Si queras Numquid idem est sumere sacramentum et sacramentaliter sumere. Dico quod non quia sumere sacramentaliter addit supra sumere sacramentum modum sumendi videlicet quod referat signum in signatum suum credendo et si opus est confidendo ore quod sub illis speciebus veraciter contineatur corpus Christi quod non facit infidelis nec etiam brutum": Nicholas of Lyra, *Dicta de sacramentis* (Cologne, 1495), unpaginated; discussed and cited in Gary Macy, "Reception of the Eucharist According to the Theologians," 50, 58 (n. 57). See also Gary Macy, "The Eucharist and Popular Religiosity," 177–179.

131. "Si autem sit amentes sic quod non fit furiosus sed tantummodo loquens inania et a vero sensu alienatus. Adhuc distinguendum est, quia vel pretendit actus et signa deuotionis tunc potest ei ministrari, si vero nullum actum aut signum deuotionis pretendit, recurredum [*sic:* recurrendum] est ad tempus precedens passionem quia si tunc petierit et deuotionem pretenderit et obstet aliquid aliud periculum, licite potest sibi dari": Nicholas of Lyra, *Dicta de sacramentis* (Cologne, 1495), unpaginated; discussed and cited in Gary Macy, "Reception of the Eucharist According to the Theologians," 50, 58 (n. 58).

132. Eamon Duffy, *The Stripping of the Altars,* 95–102; Charles Caspers, "*Meum summum desiderium est te habere,*" 140–141.

133. On the twelfth century: Gary Macy, *The Theologies of the Eucharist,* 73–82. On the thirteenth century: Charles Caspers, "*Meum summum desiderium est te habere,*" 137; Charles Caspers, "The Western Church during the Late Middle Ages," 87–88.

134. Peter Quinel's Statutes for Exeter (1287): F. M. Powicke and C. R. Cheney, *C&S II (II),* 990 [4].

135. "Precipitur presbyteris ut, cum in canone misse inceperint 'Qui pridie,' tenentes hostiam, ne elevent eam statim nimis alte, ita quod viderit possit a populo, sed quasi ante pectus detineant donec dixerint 'Hoc est corpus meum' et tunc elevent eam ita quod possit ab omnibus videri" (It is prescribed to priests that, when in the canon of the Mass they begin [with the words] "Qui pridie," holding the host, they should not raise it up immediately to such a great height that it may be seen by the people, but they should hold it about chest-height until they shall have said "Hoc est corpus meum" and then they should raise it up so that it may be seen by all): Odette Pontal, *SSF 1,* 82 [80]. V. L. Kennedy questioned the attribution of the decree to Eudes de Sully, suggesting that his successor Pierre de Nemours may have been responsible for mandating the elevation: Kennedy, "The Moment of Consecration"; Kennedy, "The Date of the Parisian Decree on the Elevation." Odette Pontal, the editor of the Parisian synodal, however, rejects Kennedy's argument and gives Eudes de Sully authorship of the legislation: Pontal, *SSF 1,* 47–50. See also Peter Browe, "Die Elevation in der Messe." On the practice of Eucharistic elevation in the twelfth century, see V. L. Kennedy, "The Moment of Consecration," 121. For a broad consideration of the antecedents and significance of the elevation, as well as other gestures of display within the Canon of the Mass, see Josef A. Jungmann, *Missarum sollemnia,* vol. 3, 123–135, 190–195.

136. Herbert Thurston argued that the Parisian decree was a deliberated response to Peter the Chanter's teaching that the consecration of the bread was not completed until the pronunciation of the forma concerning the wine: Thurston, "The Origin of the Elevation." V. L. Kennedy rejects this explanation, but Odette Pontal reaffirms it: Pontal, *SSF 1,* 49; Kennedy, "The Moment of Consecration."

137. Despite the influence of the Parisian decree in France and abroad, significant diversity of practice and theological opinion on the moment of the consecration and on the simultaneity (or succession) of the transformation of the bread and wine persisted: Josef A. Jungmann, *Missarum sollemnia,* vol. 3, 125.

138. Edouard Dumoutet, *Le désir de voir l'hostie,* 46 and passim.

139. Josef A. Jungmann, *Missarum sollemnia,* vol. 3, 123–135 (esp. 124).

140. Suzannah Biernoff, *Sight and Embodiment in the Middle Ages,* 133–164 (esp. 140–144); Charles Caspers, "The Western Church during the Late Middle Ages."

141. By contrast, William of St-Thierry insisted that spiritual communion was available to the properly prepared and desirous devotee anywhere, at any time: Charles Caspers, "*Meum summum desiderium est te habere,*" 136–138.

142. For medieval discussions of vision as both spiritually efficacious and suspect, see Jeffrey Hamburger, "Seeing and Believing."

143. Charles Caspers, "The Western Church during the Late Middle Ages," 95.

144. A. D. Wilshere, *Mirour de Seinte Eglyse,* c. 7–19 (pp. 22–57).

145. Although one can hardly use the word "simulacrum" without summoning the specters of Deleuze and Baudrillard, it is the theorization of simulacra and similitudines that took place between Plato and Deleuze that is most relevant to an understanding of the medieval Eucharist's complex semiosis. As Michael Camille has observed, the Middle Ages possessed simulacra—both "good" and "bad"—in abundance: Michael Camille, *The Gothic Idol,* 42–44.

146. Developed autonomously, my analysis of the significance of Eucharistic modes of being and seeming (as they were theorized in the later Middle Ages) for the argument and status of these paintings (and certain modes of visual representation, more broadly construed) converges with the argument advanced by Jean Wirth in his recent reassessment of the status of the image in the "long thirteenth century": Wirth, *L'image à l'époque gothique,* 27–33 (esp.).

147. Caroline Walker Bynum, "Seeing and Seeing Beyond," 210.

148. Caroline Walker Bynum, "Seeing and Seeing Beyond," 231–232.

CHAPTER 4. TRANSLATING THE CLOISTER

Epigraph: Charles Baudelaire, "Le mauvais moine," *Les fleurs du mal,* in *Oeuvres complètes,* vol. 1, 15–16. Virginie Greene kindly reminded me of Baudelaire's participation in the claustral tradition that I examine in this chapter.

1. Charles Baudelaire, *Mon Couer mis à nu,* XI, 19, in *Oeuvres complètes,* vol. 1, 682.

2. For the topos of the cloister as prison, see Jean Leclercq, "Le cloître est-il un prison?"; Joan M. Ferrante, "Images of the Cloister—Haven or Prison."

3. London, BL, Yates Thompson MS 11 (olim Add. MS 39843), f. 2r A (henceforth YT 11). Janice Pinder and Kathryn Hall are preparing an edition and translation of various recensions of the *Sainte abbaïe* text, with further commentary. It is a pleasure to thank Jan Pinder for her kind responses to several queries. A transcription of the text, as preserved in YT 11 (misdated to 1300), is available in Cornelia Logemann, *Heilige Ordnungen,* 415–418 (App. 3). My analysis of the treatise is based exclusively on the state of the text preserved in YT 11.

4. The principal scriptural sources for Christian conceptions of spiritual edification are discussed in Anno Schoenen, "Aedificatio."

5. Jill Mann, "Allegorical Buildings in Mediaeval Literature"; Christiania Whitehead, *Castles of the Mind,* 61–86; Gerhard Bauer, *Claustrum animae;* Roberta Douglas Cornelius, *The Figurative Castle.*

6. My discussion of the translation of the cloister is indebted to Nicole Rice's analysis of several later Middle English texts, including *The Abbey of the Holy Ghost,* a translation-adaptation of the *Sainte abbaïe* treatise: Rice, *Lay Piety and Religious Discipline,* 17–46; Rice, "Spiritual Ambition and the Translation of the Cloister." Rice understands the Middle English *Abbey of the Holy Ghost* as "using literary form to enforce a self-imposed 'sense of limits' on lay religious identity and practice"; by contrast, my interpretation of YT 11 argues for an inflation of lay spiritual expectations, culminating in the appropriation of forms of contemplative spiritual authority associated with claustration: Rice, *Lay Piety and Religious Discipline,* 21. This difference between the two cloister allegories is also noted by Rice; she observes that the Middle English tract "offers English readers a guide . . . leaving less room for the 'regulated improvisations' that the French text had encouraged": Rice, *Lay Piety and Religious Discipline,* 21.

7. Late medieval conceptions of the difference between appearance and substance (or existence), with particular attention to the problem of visual error or ambiguity, are examined in Dallas G. Denery, *Seeing and Being Seen,* 96–168 (esp.).

8. Sarah-Grace Heller, "Anxiety, Hierarchy and Appearance"; Alan Hunt, *Governance of the Consuming Passions,* 25–28 and passim.

9. The religious habit is also taken as an intelligible and truthful mark of identity by the author of the twelfth-century *Libellus de diversis ordinibus et professionbius qui sunt in aecclesia:* Giles Constable and Bernard Smith, *Libellus de diversis ordinibus,* 50, 51. The importance of clothing and appearance are further discussed in relation to twelfth-century reform in Giles Constable, *The Reformation of the Twelfth Century,* 188–194.

10. YT 11: circa 1294, 82 ff., 245 x 180 mm; text in two columns, twenty-eight lines. Collation: vii + 1^{8+2} + $2\text{–}3^{8}$, 4^{8+1}, $5\text{–}6^{8}$, 7^{12+1}, 8^{12}, 9^{2}, 10^{4} + v. Secundo folio: "siterres. Dieus li peres." The manuscript is provided with four full-page miniatures, painted on one side only of singletons: ff. 1v, 6v, 29r, 52v (a misbound image of Christ teaching the Pater Noster, from London, BL, Add. MS 28162 [henceforth Add. 28162]).

11. The *Somme le roi* has been edited, with a substantial introduction and bibliography: Frère Laurent, *SLR.* The title of the text is a fourteenth-century creation: Richard H. Rouse and Mary A. Rouse, *Manuscripts and Their Makers,* vol. 1, 145. Because I am interested in the text-image program as it was encountered by its late medieval reader-viewer in the manuscript once formed by YT 11 and Add. 28162, my textual analysis and transcriptions reflect manuscript readings rather than Brayer and Leurqin-Labie's edition. I have, however, provided cross-references to Brayer and Leurqin-Labie's edition whenever possible.

12. Add. 28162: circa 1294, 147 ff., 248 x 184 mm; text in two columns, twenty-eight lines. Collation: vi + 1^{6} + 2^{5} + 3^{6+1} + $4\text{–}6^{8}$ + $7\text{–}8^{6+1}$ + $9\text{–}11^{8}$ + 12^{4+3} + 13^{8} + 14^{4+3} + $15\text{–}18^{8}$ + 19^{6+2} + 20^{4+1} + i. Secundo folio: "les autres feste sollempnes" (f. 12r). Quires one and two consist entirely of singletons, illuminated with full-page miniatures on one side only. These folios have been removed from their original positions (facing each tract within the *Somme* compilation) and displaced en masse to the front of the volume. One leaf from this visual cycle (the image of Christ teaching the Pater Noster) is currently misbound as f. 52v in YT 11. In addition to the works cited in the select bibliography provided by the British Library's online catalog (http://www.bl.uk/catalogues/illuminatedmanuscripts/record.asp?MSID=18452&CollID=58&NStart=11), the principal notices of Add. 28162 and YT 11 are *Krone und Schleier: Kunst aus mittelalterlichen Frauenklöstern,* 384 (no. 273); Kathleen L. Scott, *Tradition and Innovation in Later Medieval English Manuscripts,* 78–81; Léopold Delisle, *Recherches sur la librairie de Charles V,* vol. 1, 239–240; Jean-François Auguste comte de Bastard d'Estang, *Études de symbolique chrétienne,* 29–33, 68, 163–164 (nn. 45–49), 183–187 (nn. 102–103); Eric George Millar, *An Illuminated Manuscript of La Somme Le Roy,* 15–17, pls. 27–31; Eric George Millar, *Souvenir de l'exposition de manuscrits français à peintures,* 23, pls. xx–xxi; Henry Yates Thompson, *Illustrations from One Hundred Manuscripts,* vol. 1, pls. 6–9; Georg Vitzthum, *Die Pariser Miniaturmalerei,* 224–226, pls. xlvii–xlviii.

13. A biographical and bibliographical introduction to Laurent (or Lorens) d'Orléans is provided in Frère Laurent, *SLR,* 14–23.

14. More than ninety witnesses to the text survive. The *Somme* was also translated into most of the European vernaculars and abridged and adapted in a series of derivative texts: Frère Laurent, *SLR,* 23–27; W. Nelson Francis, *The Book of Vices and Virtues,* xix–xl; Richard H. Rouse and Mary A. Rouse, *Manuscripts and Their Makers,* vol. 1, 145–146. Although interpreters have long recognized that the *Somme* is itself a compilation, there is little consensus concerning how the compendium is structured: Frère Laurent, *SLR,* 10–11; Ellen Kosmer, *A Study of the Style and Iconography of a Thirteenth-Century Somme le Roi,* 14–15, 287–299; Leo Carruthers, *La*

somme le roi et ses traductions anglaises, 7–12. I am concerned with how the *Somme le roi–Sainte abbaïe* manuscript was visually and codicologically structured as a singular object. In the manuscript, the *Somme le roi* is clearly demarcated as a compilation-within-a-compilation: internal textual divisions are distinguished by means of large painted initials at the start of sub-tracts and by the full-page miniatures set opposite each sub-tract. The manuscript's mise en page thus asserts that the *Somme* is composed of fifteen tracts; the internal structure discerned by interpreters of the *Somme* (as a text) is ignored by the textual-visual construction of the *Somme le roi–Sainte abbaïe* manuscript.

15. Richard H. Rouse and Mary A. Rouse, *Manuscripts and Their Makers,* vol. 1, 146–148, 165.
16. During Philippe III's lifetime, Laurent d'Orléans served as the king's confessor and as tutor to his children, among them the future king, Philippe IV. After Philippe III's death (1285), Laurent would seem to have enjoyed significant favor with his former charge: Frère Laurent, *SLR,* 16–21.
17. Richard H. Rouse and Mary A. Rouse, *Manuscripts and Their Makers,* vol. 1, 146. Ellen Kosmer's 1974 dissertation remains the most comprehensive art historical investigation of the tradition of illuminated exemplars of the *Somme le roi:* Kosmer, *A Study of the Style and Iconography of a Thirteenth-Century Somme le Roi.* See also J. J. G. Alexander, *Medieval Illuminators,* 115–118; Kosmer, "Gardens of Virtue"; Kosmer, "The 'noyous humoure of lecherie.'" There is no evidence that Laurent d'Orléans was involved in designing the program of images that came to be added to his *Somme le roi* during the reign of Philippe IV.
18. Paris, BnF, MS fr. 938 (dated 1294; henceforth BnF fr. 938); Add. 28126 and YT 11 (the *Somme le roi–Sainte abbaïe* manuscript, dated to the mid-1290s); London, BL, Add. MS 54180 (c. 1295); Paris, Bibliothèque Mazarine, MS 870 (dated 1295): Richard H. Rouse and Mary A. Rouse, *Manuscripts and Their Makers,* vol. 1, 146.
19. Seven illuminated *Somme le roi* manuscripts preserve instructions to the illuminator specifying the iconographic content of images and their placement. No extant witness contains the full set of instructions, and when individual instructions are preserved they are not always strictly followed by illuminators: Ellen Kosmer, *A Study of the Style and Iconography of a Thirteenth-Century Somme le Roi,* 20–22, 300–327; Richard H. Rouse and Mary A. Rouse, *Manuscripts and Their Makers,* vol. 1, 146–147, 164–165.
20. Richard H. Rouse and Mary A. Rouse, *Manuscripts and Their Makers,* vol. 1, 161, 170.
21. The dating of Add. 28162 depends on two points of reference: the visual program's stylistic affinities with other illuminated works from the 1290s and its close iconographic relationship to BnF fr. 938, an illuminated *Somme le roi* dated internally to 1294. It must be noted that although BnF fr. 938 and Add. 28162 are—in stylistic terms—very different productions, the visual cycles executed for these two *Somme* manuscripts share iconographic peculiarities that appear in no other illuminated *Sommes.* On the basis of their shared idiosyncratic iconography, Ellen Kosmer proposed that BnF fr. 938 and Add. 28162 belong to a "North French family": Kosmer, *A Study of the Style and Iconography of a Thirteenth-Century Somme le Roi,* 264–268, 286a ("Chart B"). The precise localization of the style of illumination in BnF fr. 938 remains an open question.
22. BL, Add. MS 54180, and Paris, Bibliothèque Mazarine, MS 870: Richard H. Rouse and Mary A. Rouse, *Manuscripts and Their Makers,* vol. 1, 148–154.
23. Of the four earliest illuminated manuscripts containing the *Somme le roi,* only one—Paris, Bibliothèque Mazarine, MS 870—is provided with a painting beyond the *Somme*'s complement of fifteen miniatures (an inhabited initial at the start of the *Miroir de l'âme*): Richard H. Rouse and Mary A. Rouse, *Manuscripts and Their Makers,* vol. 1, 152–153. Sean Field has suggested that the *Miroir de l'âme* (in its original Latin-language state) was composed for Blanche of Castile: Field, "From *Speculum anime* to *Miroir de l'âme*"; Field, "Reflecting the Royal Soul."
24. The French *Sainte abbaïe* treatise (surviving in multiple states) is discussed in Nicole R. Rice, *Lay Piety and Religious Discipline,* 17–28; Kathleen Chesney, "Notes on Some Treatises of Devotion," 13–17; Roberta Douglas Cornelius, *The Figurative Castle,* 51–55; Geneviève Hasenohr, "Aperçu sur la diffusion et la réception de la littérature de spiritualité," 60–61. The *Abbey of the Holy Ghost,* a Middle English adaptation-translation of the *Sainte abbaïe* treatise, and a related tract, *The Charter of the Abbey of the Holy Ghost,* have recently received considerable scholarly attention: Nicole R. Rice, *Lay Piety and Religious Discipline,* 17–28, 136–140; Christiania Whitehead, *Castles of the Mind,* 76–84; Christiania Whitehead, "Making a Cloister of the Soul"; Julia Boffey, "*The Charter of the Abbey of the Holy Ghost*"; Nicole R. Rice, "Spiritual Ambition and the Translation of the Cloister."
25. The codicological structure of YT 11 is such that we cannot be absolutely certain that the current order of texts in the volume preserves the original order of the undivided manuscript. As the *Sainte abbaïe* treatise and the tract following it in YT 11 share f. 7r (in the first quire), we can be certain that they were in the same sequence in the original volume. Likewise, the second and third tracts in YT 11 share f. 28v, indicating that the order of these texts has not been altered. The fourth tract in YT 11, however, is contained discretely in an autonomous codicological unit of three quires (currently quires 7–10) and so, in the absence of catchwords, we cannot be certain of its placement in the original volume. The secundo folio reference for the original manuscript discovered by Richard and Mary Rouse in a 1463 inventory (to be discussed further) does, however, prove beyond a doubt that the *Somme le roi* was the first text in the order of the original volume's contents: Rouse and Rouse, *Manuscripts and Their Makers,* 155.
26. The treatise is untitled in YT 11. It begins, "Vous vouliez que je vous envoiaisse chose qui confortast vostre ame mes je fais le contraire . . ." (f. 7r A), and ends, ". . . Et cil qui fu conjoinz a nostre char en terre nous parmaint par sa bonté a cele parfaite conjoncion d'esperit ou ciel ihesu criz li filz deu. Qui vivit et regnat deus per omnia secula seculorum. Amen" (f. 28v A).
27. A prefatory rubric identifies the tract as *li livres de l'estat de l'ame.* The text begins, "Trois estaz de bones ames sunt que nous trouvons en la sainte escriture. Li premiers est des commencanz qui sunt en servaige de cremeur . . ." (f. 28r A). The text ends, ". . . Or prions donc ihesu crist que il nous doint si lui querre et desirrer que nous le puissons trouver lassus en son regne et avoir parfaite joie en la vision de sa face parmanablement sanz fin. Amen" (f. 51v A). The text is misidentified as "Les heures de l'estat de l'ame" in Jeffrey Hamburger, *The Rothschild Canticles,* 140. Gia Toussaint's brief discussion of this treatise is the only published commentary on the text: Toussaint, *Das Passional,* 153–155, 175.
28. "Cist troi estat sunt senefiez par les trois festes que sainte eglise fait le jour de la tiephaine. Li premiers est entenduz par les offrandes qui furent faites en bethleem. Li

seconz par le bautesme de flun jordain. Li tierz par les noces de galilee": YT 11, f. 28v B–30r A.

29. This treatise, commonly identified as the *Livre de tribulacion,* has been identified as a translation-adaptation of the longer version of the *Tractatus de tribulatione.* The shorter version has been printed among Peter of Blois's works as Petrus Blesensis, *De duodecim utilitatibus tribulationis.* The attribution to Peter of Blois is no longer accepted: Alexandra Barratt, *The Book of Tribulation,* 26–27. The French manuscript tradition is discussed in Alexandra Barratt, *The Book of Tribulation,* 7–31. The text in YT 11 begins, "Da nobis domine auxilium de tribulatione. A toi ame livree aus temptacions et aus tribulacions de ceste vie est adrecié la doctrine de ceste parole et a ce que tu apreignes a connoistre de quex mestiers tribulacions servent aus saiges . . ." (f. 53r A). The text ends, ". . . car par ce il t'assenera a cele gloire a la quele il est ores assenez. Or di donques a ton dieu. Da nobis domine auxilium de tribulatione. Amen" (f. 81v A). The remainder of f. 81v is filled with a summary listing of each of the twelve services rendered by tribulation; this list ends, "Li douziemes si est que eles te tesmoignent a avoir l'amour de ton creatour" (f. 81v B).

30. At present, the provenance of the manuscript cannot be completely reconstructed. As will be discussed further, Richard and Mary Rouse identified the *Somme le roi–Sainte abbaïe* manuscript in a 1463 inventory from the convent of Maubuisson (Notre-Dame-la-Royale, near Pontoise): Rouse and Rouse, *Manuscripts and Their Makers,* vol. 1, 155–157. Further information regarding the provenance of YT 11 is available from the British Library's online main manuscripts catalog (http://www.bl.uk/catalogues/manuscripts) and its catalog of illuminated manuscripts (http://www.bl.uk/catalogues/illuminatedmanuscripts/record.asp?MSID=18452&CollID=58&NStart=11). The fate of the *Somme le roi* portion of the original manuscript after it left the collection of Jean-François Auguste comte de Bastard et d'Estang is more obscure. In 1869, or shortly before, the Librairie Bachelin-Deflorenne possessed Add. 28162: *Le bibliophile français: Gazette illustrée des amateurs de livres, d'estampes et de haute curiosité,* 31 and unnumbered plate. An anonymous ink notation on f. 1r also notes, "Purchased of Mr. G. Attenborough, 12 June 1869." I have not been able to identify G. Attenborough. In a corrigendum sheet inserted in his catalog of the Yates Thompson manuscripts, M. R. James reports, "The portion of the MS now in the British Museum [i.e., Add. 28162], Mr Warner [keeper of manuscripts at the British Museum at the time] tells us, was formerly in the possession of a Mrs Sowerby, and belonged before that to Bachelin-Deflorenne (so written)": James, *A Descriptive Catalogue of Fifty Manuscripts from the Collection of Henry Yates Thompson,* unpaginated corrigendum sheet. I have not been able to identify Mrs. Sowerby. If the annotation on f. 1r is in her hand, it would seem that circa 1869, Add. 28162 passed rather rapidly through the hands of the Librairie Bachelin-Deflorenne and G. Attenborough and was acquired by Mrs. Sowerby before 1898 (when James published his catalog of the Yates Thompson manuscripts). There is no reason to think, as Kathleen Chesney and several other scholars have, that YT 11 once belonged to Jean duc de Berry and passed to his niece Marie de Bourbon: Chesney, "Notes on Some Treatises of Devotion," 14.

31. In addition to the four miniatures that have been lost from the *Somme le roi*'s visual cycle, the manuscript may also have lost a final image, placed before the treatise on tribulation. The original existence of this miniature remains an open question; see Richard H. Rouse and Mary A. Rouse, *Manuscripts and Their Makers,* vol. 1, 366, n. 79.

32. Add. 28162, f. 145r B.

33. The illumination of several manuscripts associated with the patronage (or ownership) of Renaud de Bar, Bishop of Metz, has been singled out as particularly close to the style of the painting in the *Somme le roi–Sainte abbaïe* manuscript: Patrick M. de Winter, *La bibliothèque de Philippe le Hardi,* 82, 204, fig. 30; Pamela Hemzik, *Illuminated Moral and Devotional Compilations,* 135, 143–145, 219–222; Patrick M. de Winter, "Une réalisation exceptionnelle"; Georg Vitzthum, *Die Pariser Miniaturmalerei,* 224–226. Although the *Somme le roi–Sainte abbaïe* manuscript's illumination has been stylistically localized to northeastern France, possibly Lorraine (Metz?), the artists responsible for the manuscript's paintings could, quite plausibly, have been active in Paris. François Avril suggests that the *Somme le roi–Sainte abbaïe* illuminators may have been among the painters employed by Marie de Brabant, the stepmother of Philippe le Bel: *L'art au temps des rois maudits: Philippe le Bel et ses fils, 1285–1328: Paris, Galeries nationales du Grand Palais, 17 mars–29 juin 1998,* 282. A consensus on the number of illuminators involved in the execution of the full-page paintings has yet to be reached. Several scholars have argued that the first three paintings in YT 11 are by a different "hand" than those found in Add. 28162. From an inspection of both Add. 28162 and YT 11, I suspect that this distinction of "hands" is more a matter of models than "masters": the paintings in Add. 28162 were almost certainly executed after an exemplar (either a lost witness to the *Somme*'s visual program or a model book); by contrast, the images painted for the subsequent tracts were bespoke creations (to be discussed further). I would argue that the "hand A"/"hand B" distinction should instead be understood as a visual trace of the different working methods required of a collaborative group of artists responsible for the original set of fifteen paintings. Although I discern at least two artists at work in the full-page paintings, I concur with Richard and Mary Rouse in seeing their contributions as deliberately harmonized: Rouse and Rouse, *Manuscripts and Their Makers,* vol. 1, 155. It would seem that a unified approach to the handling of physiognomy, proportion, drapery, vegetal and architectural motifs, and a relatively consistent palette was sought in the execution of the manuscript's full-page miniatures. The beginning of each tract is also marked with a large (five- to seven-line) initial, filled with vegetal and zoomorphic elements. These large initials appear to be the work of a single artist. The small heads that inhabit numerous of the manuscript's two-line initials also reveal an effort to maintain a formal consistency between the original volume's full-page illuminations and its smaller painted elements.

34. M. R. James, *A Descriptive Catalogue of Fifty Manuscripts from the Collection of Henry Yates Thompson,* 228, 231. Richard and Mary Rouse's analysis is the exception to this rule; they characterize each of the *Somme le roi–Sainte abbaïe* manuscript's three final images as "relevant to its accompanying texts only in the most general sense": Rouse and Rouse, *Manuscripts and Their Makers,* vol. 1, 156. Although I concur with their assertion that the presence of nuns in the manuscript's miniatures "does not reflect the texts but, instead, represents the wishes of the manuscript's patron," I do not share their conviction that the book owner was herself a

nun: Rouse and Rouse, *Manuscripts and Their Makers,* vol. 1, 156.

35. Jeffrey Hamburger, *The Visual and the Visionary,* 131–132; Jeffrey Hamburger, *The Rothschild Canticles,* 6; Hans Belting, *Likeness and Presence,* 44, 412–414.
36. Richard H. Rouse and Mary A. Rouse, *Manuscripts and Their Makers,* vol. 1, 155–157, esp. 155–156.
37. The *Somme le roi* not only addresses concerns of particular interest to laypeople (virtuous marriage, sinful and sinless sex, the regulation of secular fashion, the moral dangers that beset princes, etc.), the text also explicitly asserts that it is intended for the edification of the laity. In its discussion of the vice of avarice, the *Somme* explains, "Ce sunt les branches d'avarice. Assez i a des autres mais eles apartienent plus aus clerz que aus lais. Et cist livres est plus faiz pour les lais que pour les clerz qui sevent les escritures" (These are the branches of avarice. There are many more, but they pertain more to clerics than to the laity. And this book is made more for the laity than for clerics, who know scripture): Add. 28162, f. 30v A; Frère Laurent, *SLR,* c.36 §219–221 (p. 146). A further example of the compilation's consciousness of its lay audience is provided by its discussion of simony. The *Somme* explains, "Mout i a des autres pechiez de divers kas de symonie mais il apartienent plus aus clers que aus lais. Et cist livres est plus faiz pour les lais que pour les clers qui ont les livres. Mes toutes voies est il mestiers aus laies persones que il se gardent de cestui pechié en trois kas" (There are many more sins [deriving] from different types of simony, but they pertain more to clerics than to the laity. And this book is made more for the laity than for clerics, who have books. Nevertheless, it is necessary that laypeople should keep themselves from this sin in three cases): Add. 28162, f. 28v B; Frère Laurent, *SLR,* c.36 §153–155 (p. 142–143).
38. Among illuminated *Somme le roi* manuscripts, the figure of Hatred is an iconographic variant particular to Add. 28162 and BnF fr. 938. In the two other "first-phase" illustrated manuscripts of the text (Ellen Kosmer's "Parisian family"), the second quadrant is inhabited by a figure labeled *Hely,* presumably the prophet Ely. The identificatory titulus "Hainne" is present only in the *Somme le roi–Sainte abbaïe* manuscript: Kosmer, *A Study of the Style and Iconography of a Thirteenth-Century Somme le Roi,* 103–105 (pt. I), 265 (pt. I).
39. On the moral and ideological representation of labor and idleness in medieval art, see Michael Camille, *Mirror in Parchment,* esp. 178–231; Michael Camille, "Labouring for the Lord"; J. J. G. Alexander, "Labeur and Paresse."
40. Although the vignette painted for this quadrant of the image casts Moses as a peacemaker, it is worth noting that the larger scriptural context for the scene is concerned with Moses's violence. Exodus 2:11–12 recounts how Moses furtively slew an Egyptian and hid him in the sand. Immediately following Moses's intervention in the quarrel between the two Israelites, one of the men turns on Moses, saying, "Who hath appointed thee prince and judge over us: wilt thou kill me, as thou didst yesterday kill the Egyptian?" (Exod. 2:14). Although nothing in the quadrant would seem to indict Moses, the alignment of the vignette with the vice of *Felonnie* above it, suggests that the scriptural backstory of the scene depicted in the miniature's lower right quadrant was not irrelevant to the design of the image as a whole.
41. The *Somme le roi* does reference Abraham's reception of the angel-visitors in its tract on Mercy, the section of the text prefaced by the miniature depicting the Patriarch: Add. 28162, f. 108v B. Several of the scriptural vignettes included in the Gift Virtue miniatures are also referenced by the *Somme;* none of these textual references occur in proximity to a relevant prefatory image, nor does the *Somme* contextualize these scriptural episodes in a fashion that is consonant with the visual arguments of its full-page miniatures.
42. I have not been able to identify any external textual sources for the combinations of scriptural vignettes depicted in the Gift Virtue miniatures.
43. The relationship between the forms of the personified virtues in the visual cycle devised for the *Somme le roi* and antecedent monumental sculpture has been noted by several commentators: Adolf Katzenellenbogen, *Allegories of the Virtues and Vices,* 84; Jennifer O'Reilly, *Studies in the Iconography of the Virtues and Vices,* 56–57, 181–182.
44. On the sculpture of the west portal at Saint-Pierre-de-la-Tour, see Linda Seidel, *Songs of Glory,* 48–55; Ferdinand Werner, *Aulnay de Saintonge,* 6–15.
45. Willibald Sauerländer, *Gothic Sculpture in France,* 425–428, pls. 70–71. See also Boerner's concise review of the Prudentian visual tradition and the treatments of the virtues and vices at Aulnay and Laon: Bruno Boerner, *Par caritas par meritum,* 122–124.
46. Adolf Katzenellenbogen, *Allegories of the Virtues and Vices,* 19–20; Paul Williamson, *Gothic Sculpture,* 193–195.
47. Adolf Katzenellenbogen observed that these subdued women have been given the form of "burgher's [*sic*] wives": Katzenellenbogen, *Allegories of the Virtues and Vices,* 20.
48. For Prudentius's *Psychomachia* and the *longue durée* of its visual tradition, see Joanne S. Norman, *Metamorphoses of an Allegory;* Jennifer O'Reilly, *Studies in the Iconography of the Virtues and Vices,* 1–82; Adolf Katzenellenbogen, *Allegories of the Virtues and Vices,* 1–13.
49. Citing Willibald Sauerländer's 1959 article, Bruno Boerner assigns a date as early as 1200–1210 for the reliefs: Boerner, "Réflexions sur les rapports," 58. Sauerländer, however, subsequently redated the plinth reliefs to circa 1220: Sauerländer, *Gothic Sculpture in France,* 457.
50. The plinth reliefs were subject to significant, if "surprisingly sympathetic," restoration in the eighteenth century: Willibald Sauerländer, *Gothic Sculpture in France,* 453. My discussion of the Notre-Dame reliefs focuses on components of the carving that were not affected by the eighteenth-century intervention in the portal: Willibald Sauerländer, "Die Kunstgeschichtliche Stellung"; Daniel D. Reiff, "Viollet le Duc and Historic Restoration."
51. I have adopted Adolf Katzenellenbogen's identification of each of the scenes: Katzenellenbogen, *Allegories of the Virtues and Vices,* 76. It should be noted that Willibald Sauerländer identifies Katzenellenbogen's *Contumacia* as an exemplification of *Inoboedientia,* and he identifies the second figure in the medallion as a monk, rather than a layman: Sauerländer, "Die Kunstgeschichtliche Stellung," 14. I concur with Katzenellenbogen that this figure represents a layman; a comparison with the vignette identified by Katzenellenbogen as visualizing *Ira* (right plinth, second medallion from the doorway) reveals that the figure of a monk in that scene is clearly distinguished from the smaller figure in the *Contumacia* roundel.
52. Willibald Sauerländer notes the exclusively negative definition of the vicious space of the lower reliefs as a deliberate contrast to the positive, projecting embrasures that enclose the virtues: Sauerländer, "Die Kunstgeschichtliche Stellung," 7.
53. Michael T. Davis, "Splendor and Peril," 35 and passim. Cecilia Gaposchkin argues that the

Porte Rouge program and the canons' cloister would have been far more accessible than Davis suggests: Gaposchkin, "The King of France and the Queen of Heaven," 60–61.

54. Richard H. Rouse and Mary A. Rouse, *Manuscripts and Their Makers,* vol. 1, 14, 19–23, map 5.
55. Michael T. Davis, "Canonical Views," 108–109.
56. Michael Camille, *The Gothic Idol,* 9.
57. Bruno Boerner, *Par caritas par meritum;* Bruno Boerner, "Réflexions sur les rapports."
58. Bruno Boerner, *Par caritas par meritum,* 91–100, 107–114, 137–178. In the discussion of the cathedral chapter's teaching on virtue that follows, I refer exclusively to their definition and exposition of the so-called Catholic Virtues, rather than the so-called Political or Aristotelian Virtues. The distinction of, and potential interrelationship between, these two classes of virtues were, however, topics treated in tandem by the circle of Peter the Chanter and other contemporary theologians. For a magisterial examination of competing definitions and classifications of the virtues in the period, see Odon Lottin, *Psychologie et morale aux XIIe et XIIIe siècles,* vol. 3, pt. 2. The definitive study of Peter the Chanter and his circle is John W. Baldwin, *Masters, Princes, and Merchants.*
59. Bruno Boerner, "Réflexions sur les rapports," 60, 91–100.
60. The arguments pursued by Peter the Chanter and his circle make a critical distinction between virtue *in habitu* and *in usu:* Odon Lottin, *Psychologie et morale aux XIIe et XIIIe siècles,* vol. 3, pt. 2, 129–131.
61. In this connection it should be noted that the Notre-Dame theologians emphasize the unity of the virtues: Odon Lottin, *Psychologie et morale aux XIIe et XIIIe siècles,* vol. 3, pt. 2, 135.
62. Bruno Boerner, "Réflexions sur les rapports," 62.
63. Bruno Boerner refers to the representations of vice in the plinth program as displaying "la culpabilité des actions concrètes, représentées comme telles dans le cycle": Boerner, "Réflexions sur les rapports," 62.
64. On this point, see also the analysis in Willibald Sauerländer, "Die Kunstgeschichtliche Stellung," 7.
65. Jennifer O'Reilly makes this claim for illustrated *Somme le roi* manuscripts, generally: O'Reilly, *Studies in the Iconography of the Virtues and Vices,* 181.
66. BnF fr. 938, the other member of Ellen Kosmer's "North French" *Somme le roi* family, also takes up and revises the Notre-Dame plinth program. Although Kosmer briefly notes the "iconographic" use of microarchitectural framing and representation in the "North French" visual programs, she does not interpret this microarchitecture as a signifying pictorial element: Kosmer, *A Study of the Style and Iconography of a Thirteenth-Century Somme le Roi,* 267 (pt. I).
67. Ellen Kosmer interprets the female figure as a "reassuring example for those in doubt about charitable giving": Kosmer, *A Study of the Style and Iconography of a Thirteenth-Century Somme le Roi,* 134 (pt. I). Although I agree with Kosmer that an antithetical relationship is established between the image's upper and lower right quadrants, I find little in the image or the *Somme le roi* text to support her reading of the quadrant as a commentary on charitable giving. Surely the emphasis in this scriptural vignette is on the good woman as a *recipient* of God's mercy and, by extension, a *participant* in the economy of grace, rather than as a behavioral exemplar for hesitant almsgivers.
68. The space inhabited by the female figure is identified as an interior by a small shelf supporting a third vessel, painted at the far right side of the compartment; this detail indicates that the good woman pours out her oil within the enclosure of her home.
69. BL, Add. MS 54180, is composed of 208 folios (183 x 124 mm). The illumination of the manuscript is traditionally given to the illuminator known as Master Honoré, and Mary and Richard Rouse have argued convincingly that the volume belonged to Philippe IV. For further discussion and bibliography, see Rouse and Rouse, *Manuscripts and Their Makers,* vol. 1, 127–154.
70. François Bucher, Peter Kurmann, and James Bugslag have explored the relationship between macroarchitecture (particularly that of cathedrals) and the microarchitecture of metalwork: Bucher, "Micro-Architecture"; Kurmann, "Cathédrale miniature ou reliquaire monumental?"; James Bugslag, "The Shrine of St. Gertrude de Nivelles." In a brief discussion, Harvey Stahl also points to the intervisual referentiality of fictive framing in late medieval manuscript painting: Stahl, "Heaven in View," esp. 220–227. More recently, Achim Timmermann has investigated the dynamic microarchitecture of Eucharistic sacrament houses: Timmermann. *Real Presence.* I was not able to consult the essays collected in Christine Kratzke and Uwe Albrecht, *Mikroarchitektur im Mittelalter.*
71. For considerations of "cross-media" allusion and influence in manuscript painting, see Karen Gould, "Illumination and Sculpture in Thirteenth-Century Amiens"; Carl F. Barnes Jr., "Cross-Media Design Motifs in XIIIth-Century France"; Karen Gould, "Jean Pucelle and Northern Gothic Art."
72. The Nivelles châsse was irreparably damaged by bombardment on May 14, 1940. Today the shrine survives in over 300 fragments. An exhibition at the Schnütgen Museum and the Musée Cluny examined the shrine from a variety of perspectives (with comprehensive bibliography) and provided detailed documentation of the chasse, before and after it was devastated by bombing: *Un trésor gothique: La châsse de Nivelles: Cologne, Schnütgen-Museum, 24 novembre 1995–11 février 1996: Paris, Musée national du moyen age, Thermes de Cluny, 12 mars–10 juin 1996,* 15–16.
73. Robert Branner, "The Painted Medallions," 8.
74. In other words, the metaphoric comparison cultivated by the microarchitectural repertoire functions as a comparison-substitution, emphasizing the formal and semantic similarity between the fictive enclosure of the painted page and the liturgically consecrated material enclosure of the church, shrine, or reliquary. For the substitutional and comparative operation of metaphor, see Roman Jakobson, "Two Aspects of Language."
75. Add. 28162, f. 84v B; Frère Laurent, *SLR,* c.55 §67–69 (p. 264).
76. Add. 28162, f. 83r B; Frère Laurent, *SLR,* c.55 §13–17 (p. 261).
77. My translation of this passage has benefited from the generous advice of Virginie Greene and Daisy Delogu. The errors that remain are entirely my own.
78. This passage bears comparison with the analogy between scriptural *lectio* and the mason's work in Hugh of Saint-Victor's *Didascalicon:* "respice opus caementarii. collocato fundamento, lineam extendit in directum, perpendiculum demittit, ac deinde lapides diligenter politos in ordinem ponit. alios deinde atque alios quaerit . . . ecce ad lectionem venisti, spirituale fabricaturus aedificium. iam historiae fundamenta in te locata sunt: restat nunc tibi ipsius fabricae bases fundare. linum tendis, ponis examussim, quadros in ordinem collocas, et circumgyrans quaedam futurorum murorum vestigia figis" (Take a look at what the mason does. When the foundation has been laid, he stretches out his string in a straight line, he drops his perpendicular,

and then, one by one, he lays the diligently polished stones in a row. Then he asks for other stones, and still others. . . . See now, you have come to your [reading], you are about to construct the spiritual building. Already the foundations of the story have been laid in you: it remains now that you found the bases of the superstructure. You stretch out your cord, you line it up precisely, you place the square stones into the course, and, moving around the course, you lay the track, so to say, of the future walls). Latin edition: Hugh of Saint-Victor, *Didascalicon,* Lib. VI, c. 4 (pp. 118, 119, 120). English translation from Mary Carruthers, *The Craft of Thought,* 20.

79. As an analogic edifice, the castle belongs to the *Somme*'s repertoire of interiorized structures; as a motif derived from the lexicon of combat and warfare it participates in the *Somme*'s sustained cultivation of chivalric and military images for the moral and spiritual combat of Christian life.
80. Add. 28162, f. 85r A; Frère Laurent, *SLR,* c.55 §81–86 (p. 362).
81. Add. 28162, f. 130r A; Frère Laurent, *SLR,* c.58 §539–544 (p. 362).
82. Christiania Whitehead, *Castles of the Mind,* 92–100.
83. The *Somme le roi*'s conception of virginity finds many parallels in late medieval texts of spiritual guidance. Virginity, in the Middle Ages, was never exclusively defined as a state of imperforate or sexually inexperienced anatomy: Anke Bernau, Sarah Salih, and Ruth Evans, *Medieval Virginities;* Jocelyn Wogan-Browne, *Saints' Lives and Women's Literary Culture;* Cindy L. Carlson and Angela Jane Weisl, *Constructions of Widowhood and Virginity.*
84. Medieval conceptions of the heart as a house, with particular attention to the German tradition, are reviewed by Gerhard Bauer, "Herzklosterallegorien"; Gerhard Bauer, *Claustrum animae.* See also Kurt Ruh, "Das geistliche Haus."
85. Add. 28162, f. 60v A; Frère Laurent, *SLR,* c.51 §164–168 (p. 216).
86. Add. 28162, f. 60v B; Frère Laurent, *SLR,* c.51 §176–177 (p. 217).
87. Add. 28162, ff. 90r A–92v B; Frère Laurent, *SLR,* c.56 §1–159 (pp. 273–281).
88. Add. 28162, ff. 93v B–94r A; Frère Laurent, *SLR,* c.56 §201–214 (pp. 283–284).
89. Add. 28162, f. 94v A; Frère Laurent, *SLR,* c.56 §228–231 (p. 285).
90. Add. 28162, f. 120r B; Frère Laurent, *SLR,* c.58 §197–199 (p. 341).
91. Add. 28612, f. 119r A; Frère Laurent, *SLR,* c.58 §144 (p. 338).
92. Add. 28162, ff. 119r A, 120r B, 123r B–123v A; Frère Laurent, *SLR,* c.58 §145, 149, 197, 306–307 (pp. 338, 341, 347).
93. The penetration of the space of the tabernacle evoked in this passage is something of a commonplace in Latin appropriations of the Temple compound as a template for spiritual progress: Christiania Whitehead, *Castles of the Mind,* 10–27. Although the *Somme le roi* emulates its Latinate predecessors in modeling the inner space of devout prayer after the innermost space of the tabernacle, the *Somme*'s architectural itinerary does not culminate in this locus, but rather progresses further into the enclosed space of the interior cloister.
94. Add. 28162, ff. 61v A–62v A; Frère Laurent, *SLR,* c.51 §207–208, 210–211, 241–243 (pp. 219, 220–221).
95. Add. 28162, ff. 83r B–83v A; Frère Laurent, *SLR,* c.55 §18–21 (p. 262).
96. YT 11, f. 2r B.
97. YT 11, ff. 2r A–2v A.
98. YT 11, f. 2v B.
99. YT 11, f. 2v B.
100. YT 11, ff. 2v B–3r A.
101. "Li vin blanc sunt la remembrance de dieu et de la joie de paradis. Li vermaus et li rosez de la passion et de la mort ihesu crist et des martyrs. Li ferrez des tormenz d'enfer qui durent sanz fin" (The white wines are the remembrance of God and of the joy of paradise. The red and rosé wines [are the remembrance] of the passion and death of Christ and the martyrs. The fortified[?] wines [are the remembrance] of the torments of hell that last without end): YT 11, f. 3v A.
102. YT 11, ff. 4r B–4v A.
103. YT 11, ff. 4v B–5r A.
104. For the category of the "semireligious" in the later Middle Ages—that is, persons not living under a rule or formally affiliated with a religious order, yet adhering to a model of religious life—see Kaspar Elm, "Die Stellung der Frau," 14–17; Bella Millett, "*Ancrene Wisse* and the Book of Hours."
105. YT 11, ff. 5r B, 5v B, 7r A.
106. YT 11, ff. 5r B, 5v A.
107. YT 11, f. 5v B.
108. YT 11, ff. 5v B, 7r A.
109. YT 11, f. 5r B.
110. Hugo de Folieto, *De claustro animae.* Hugh of Folieto's cloister exegesis is discussed by Janice M. Pinder, "The Cloister and the Garden," 166–169; Christiania Whitehead, *Castles of the Mind,* 62–66. On Jean of Saint-Jean-des-Vignes, with an edition of his *De claustro animae* treatise, see Guy Oury, "Le *De claustro animae* de Jean, prieur de Saint-Jean-des-Vignes."
111. Hugo de Folieto, *De claustro animae,* col. 1087D. In his *De claustro animae,* Jean of Saint-Jean-des-Vignes makes extensive use of Hugh of Folieto's *De claustro* treatise; accordingly, my analysis will concentrate on Hugh's work and I will cite, whenever possible, parallel passages in Jean's text from Guy Oury's edition. The elements of the material cloister are interpreted (by means of a citation of Hugh of Folieto) in the first lines of Jean's treatise: Oury, "Le *De claustro animae* de Jean, prieur de Saint-Jean-des-Vignes," 437.
112. The spiritual and spatial significances of monastic *stabilitas* are discussed further by Adalbert de Vogüé, "Persévérer au monastère jusqu'à la mort."
113. Hugo de Folieto, *De claustro animae,* col. 1088D–1089B. The corresponding passage in Jean's *De claustro animae* is far more concise: Guy Oury, "Le *De claustro animae* de Jean, prieur de Saint-Jean-des-Vignes," 437.
114. Monastic customaries specify the cloister as a place for reading: Mary Carruthers, *The Craft of Thought,* 87, 108, 272; Paul Meyvaert, "The Medieval Monastic Claustrum," 54–55.
115. Mary Carruthers and Christiania Whitehead have both noted the coincidence of reformist architectural exegesis and building campaigns focused on the renovation and reform of material structures; a sustained examination of the relationship between these two reform-oriented modes of edification has yet to be undertaken: Carruthers, *The Craft of Thought,* 224–230, 257–261; Whitehead, *Castles of the Mind,* 62. See also the insightful discussion of reform of self, reform of *communitas,* and architectural reform as interrelated elements in a broader "rhetoric of reform" in Giles Constable, *The Reformation of the Twelfth Century,* 125–167.
116. YT 11, f. 2v A–B.
117. Jean Leclercq, "Le cloître est-il un prison?" 415, n. 36.
118. Leo Carruthers has stressed that the virtues that construct and populate the interior abbey are *demoiselles* by virtue of their grammatical gender: Carruthers, "In Pursuit of Holiness outside the Cloister," 221–222. I would, nevertheless, suggest that the *Sainte abbaïe* (as found in YT 11) is a female convent by design rather than linguistic accident.

119. On the beguines and other mulieres religiosae in the period see Herbert Grundmann, *Religious Movements in the Middle Ages,* 139–152; Walter Simons, *Cities of Ladies;* Barbara Newman, *From Virile Woman to Woman Christ,* 137–167. For the northern French context see Bernard Delmaire, "Les béguines dans le Nord de la France."

120. The complete text of the *Veni creator spiritus* is edited in Guido Maria Dreves and Clemens Blume, *Analecta hymnica,* vol. 50, 103–104 (no. 144). The *Veni creator* and medieval commentary on the hymn are examined in detail by Heinrich Lausberg, *Der Hymnus "Veni Creator Spiritus."*

121. The hymn could also have paraliturgical associations; see, for example, its unusual visualization within the initial for Sext of the Holy Spirit in Hawisia de Bois's book of hours (New York, Pierpont Morgan Library, MS M.700), elucidated by Kathryn A. Smith, *Art, Identity, and Devotion in Fourteenth-Century England,* 110–113.

122. The presence of identifying banderoles for the Dove of the Holy Ghost and each of the evangelist symbols in the upper register of the image indicates that the omission of tituli for the figures of the nuns in the lower register is deliberate.

123. From left to right, top to bottom, these angelic banderoles read, "sanctus deus," "sanctus fortis," "deus omnipotens," "sanctus dominus deus sabatus," "pleni sunt celi et terra," "magestatis glorie tue," "tu ad dexteram dei sedes," and "in gloriam patris."

124. On the *Te Deum,* see John Harper, *The Forms and Orders of Western Liturgy,* 83–84. A certain confusion of terminology has arisen around the term *Sanctus.* Sung three times in the Mass, the *Sanctus* is sometimes referred to as the *Tersanctus;* some historians of the liturgy also use the term *Tersanctus* to refer to the *Trisagion* recited within the rites for the Veneration of the Cross on Good Friday. I will refer to the Good Friday text as the *Trisagion,* and to the tripled singing of the *Sanctus* in the Mass simply as the *Sanctus.* For a historical examination of the *Sanctus,* beginning with its origins in Jewish thought and texts and extending to the present day, see Bryan D. Spinks, *The Sanctus in the Eucharistic Prayer.*

125. J. W. Tyrer, *Historical Survey of Holy Week,* 128–133.

126. The Latin text of the third intonation is, "Sanctus et immortalis, miserere nobis" (Holy and immortal [God], have mercy on us).

127. Gen. 17:1, 35:11, 48:3; Oratio Manesse 1; Tob. 13:4; Apoc. 4:8, 11:17, 15:3, 16:7, 21:22.

128. I have modified slightly the English translation of the Douay-Rheims Bible.

129. The phrase on the first banderole ("pleni sunt celi et terra") is found in both the *Sanctus* and the *Te Deum;* the remaining three banderoles derive from the *Te Deum;* the fourth banderole ("in gloriam patris") gives a variant reading of the *Te Deum*'s tenth line ("in gloria patris").

130. Pamela Sheingorn, "The Te Deum Altarpiece," 182.

131. Pamela Sheingorn, "The Te Deum Altarpiece," 179.

132. Word illustration, usually associated with the illumination of psalters, has been the subject of considerable recent attention: Felix Heinzer, *Wörtliche Bilder;* Lucy Freeman Sandler, "The Images of Words"; Mary Carruthers, *The Book of Memory,* 226–229.

133. The eschatological overtones of this image cannot be explored here. For a discussion of a similar visual conjunction of sacramental revelation within an evocation of the apocalyptic nuptials of the lamb see Harvey Stahl, "Heaven in View," 215 (esp.).

134. Josef A. Jungmann, *Missarum sollemnia,* vol. 3, 45, n. 39.

135. Josef A. Jungmann, *Missarum sollemnia,* vol. 3, 45, n. 39.

136. Limoges, Musée municipale de l'Évêché, Inv. 52-267; 131 x 203 mm. The casket once belonged to the treasury of the Abbey of Grandmont: Jean Maury, Marie-Madeleine Gauthier, et al., *Limousin roman,* 287–288. The coffret was one of a group of twenty-six works stolen from the Musée municipale on December 31, 1980; it has not been recovered.

137. Arras, Bibliothèque municipale, MS 38 (58): a missal made circa 1250 for the Augustinian Canons of Mont-Saint-Éloi. For further discussion, see Aden Kumler, "Faire translater," 96-97; Jeffrey Hamburger, "Body vs. Book," 130-131.

138. Cambrai, Bibliothèque municipale, MS 87: composed of 240 folios (250 x 170 mm), dated to circa 1310–1315 and tentatively localized to Cambrai: *L'art au temps des rois maudits: Philippe le Bel et ses fils, 1285–1328: Paris, Galeries nationales du Grand Palais, 17 mars–29 juin 1998,* 310–311 (no. 210); Peter H. Brieger and Philippe Verdier, *Art and the Courts,* vol. 1, 89–90 (no. 180), vol. 2, 43 (pl. 26); *Un trésor gothique: La châsse de Nivelles: Cologne, Schnütgen-Museum, 24 novembre 1995–11 février 1996: Paris, Musée national du moyen age, Thermes de Cluny, 12 mars–10 juin 1996,* 378 (no. 51, fig. 64). The manuscript's unusual visual program is examined further by Harvey Stahl, "Heaven in View."

139. Strikingly, Mary occupies the place normally reserved for Christ in scenes of the Coronation of the Virgin: Harvey Stahl, "Heaven in View," 207–209 and passim.

140. William Durandus's comments about processional order are discussed by Ruth Ellis Messenger, "Processional Hymnody," 186. Honorius of Regensburg also discusses the symbolic import of correct processional order in his *Gemma animae*: Margot Fassler, "Liturgy and Sacred History," 499.

141. Richard H. Rouse and Mary A. Rouse, *Manuscripts and Their Makers,* vol. 1, 156. The text of the introit is taken from Psalm 47:10. In light of her perpetual virginity, not all medieval exegetes agreed that Mary was obligated to participate in the ritual purification prescribed in Leviticus 12 for women who had given birth. Mary's fulfillment of the ritual obligation was, however, commonly advanced as proof of the Virgin's humility and obedience; see, for example, the discussion in Jacobus de Voragine, *The Golden Legend,* vol. 1, 144.

142. Ruth Ellis Messenger, "Processional Hymnody," 186, 191; Andrew Hughes, *Medieval Manuscripts for Mass and Office,* 289–290. The candles blessed and processed to Mass on the Feast of the Purification were subsequently brought home by churchgoers; they would be used by women who gave birth in the coming year for their own churching: Penny Howell Jolly, "Learned Reading, Vernacular Seeing," 444. Eamon Duffy and Richard Marks discuss the laity's participation in liturgical and extraliturgical celebrations of the Feast: Duffy, *The Stripping of the Altars,* 15–22; Marks, *Image and Devotion in Late Medieval England,* 164.

143. The scriptural passage is a touchstone for medieval conceptions of the *ordines* of the elect—the varied paths to salvation available to Christians; see, for example, the exegesis of the phrase in the twelfth-century *Libellus de diversis ordinibus et professionibus qui sunt in ecclesia:* Giles Constable and Bernard Smith, *Libellus de diversis ordinibus,* 16, 17.

144. On the ringing of bells to mark the moment of consecration, see Miri Rubin, *Corpus Christi,* 58–60.

145. The signifying hierarchy of architectural vocabulary employed in the miniature is discussed by Jeffrey Hamburger, *The Visual and the Visionary,* 44.
146. Guerric d'Igny, *Sermons,* vol. 1, 310, ll. 52–61.
147. I have consulted John Morson's and Hilary Costello's translations of this passage, but the translation here is my own: Guerric d'Igny, *Sermons,* vol. 1, 311; Guerric d'Igny, *Liturgical Sermons,* vol. 1, 101.
148. Bernard de Clairvaux, *Sermons pour l'année,* 258, 260. The scriptural references in brackets are my addition to the passage, but I derive them from the notes to the text of this edition.
149. YT 11, ff. 7r–12r.
150. The three loves explored by the text are the love with which God loves us, the love of the angels (for God), and, finally, the love with which the deity loves itself: YT 11, f. 12v A. The related questions of how human beings love and whether a person may naturally love another more than him- or herself were live issues in thirteenth-century academic circles, particularly at the University of Paris, where the debate involved the fraught issue of interpreting the Aristotelian corpus: Thomas M. Osborne, *Love of Self and Love of God in Thirteenth-Century Ethics.*
151. YT 11, f. 12v A.
152. In its discussion of these sacraments the text touches upon several *menu sacrament* (little sacraments): holy water, ashes, Easter palms and flowers, and blessed candles: YT 11, ff. 21r B–21v B.
153. Of the thirty text columns dedicated to the sacraments, the Eucharist receives a full nineteen: YT 11, ff. 16v B–21r B.
154. YT 11, ff. 19v B.
155. YT 11, ff. 20r A.
156. YT 11, ff. 25v B–26r A.
157. In its citation of Sg. 2:3 the text alters the Vulgate's "quam desideraveram" to read "quem desideraveram," thus changing the gender of the desired beloved from female to male; this alteration of the text may perhaps be an indication that the treatise anticipates a female reader. Certainly, the text's substitution of the masculine form emphasizes that the beloved desired by the Sponsa is Christ.
158. YT 11, f. 20r B–20v A.
159. YT 11, f. 13r A–B.
160. YT 11, ff. 28r B–28v A.
161. YT 11, ff. 41v B–42r A.
162. YT 11, ff. 48v B–51r B.
163. This female figure has frequently been identified as a nun: Richard Marks, *Image and Devotion in Late Medieval England,* 17–18 (manuscript misidentified as "Yates Thompson 2"); Hans Belting, *Likeness and Presence,* 412; Richard H. Rouse and Mary A. Rouse, *Manuscripts and Their Makers,* vol. 1, 156; Jeffrey Hamburger, *The Rothschild Canticles,* 6, 140; Jeffrey Hamburger, *The Visual and the Visionary,* 131–134. A careful comparison of her attire with that worn by the figures of nuns in the two preceding images reveals, however, that she is quite deliberately distinguished from the convent community by her garments and white veil. Cornelia Logemann, Gia Toussaint, and Michael Camille prefer to see her as a figure of "the soul": Logemann, *Heilige Ordnungen,* 168 (n. 366); Toussaint, *Das Passional,* 153–154; Camille, "'Him whom you have ardently desired you may see,'" 148–149. (It should be noted that elsewhere Camille refers to the figure simply as a "Dominican nun": Camille, *Gothic Art,* 120–123.) Although Logemann's, Toussaint's, and Camille's interpretations of the figure as a surrogate for the soul are closer to the mark than readings that see her as a particularized surrogate for a monastic reader-viewer, I would suggest that the miniature's argumentative insistence on a progress from corporeal vision (second quadrant) to a more supernatural mode of encounter (in the second and third quadrants) must be taken seriously. Her corporeal *and* spiritual engagement in the progress of contemplative ascent is essential to the miniature's sacramental theology.
In my view, the female protagonist of this image is neither an anonymous nun nor a personification of *anima;* rather, she is an *embodied* fictive exemplar for the lay viewer. I concur with F. O. Büttner's description of the figure as simply "die Gläubige": Büttner, *"Ad Te, Domine, Levavi Animam Meam,"* 336.
164. Adelaide Bennett, "The Transformation of the Gothic Psalter."
165. On the importance of illuminated psalters to visual innovation in the twelfth and thirteenth centuries, see Jeffrey Hamburger, *The Rothschild Canticles,* 15–16.
166. Oxford, Bodleian Library, MS Douce 131: 138 ff., 233 x 155 mm. This psalter survives in a significantly mutilated state: Lucy Freeman Sandler, *GM (2),* 117–118 (no. 106). J. J. G. Alexander suggests that the manuscript may have been intended for Edward III: Alexander, "Painting and Manuscript Illumination," 142–143.
167. Typically placed after the psalms in psalters, the Canticles were assigned to the hour of matins in the divine office, with different Canticles to be recited on different days of the week. The Canticle of Isaiah was assigned to the hour of Lauds on Mondays: John Harper, *The Forms and Orders of Western Liturgy,* 257; James Mearns, *The Canticles of the Christian Church,* 51.
168. Marseille, Bibliothèque municipale, MS 111: 160 ff., 195 x 135 mm. The manuscript once formed a single codex with a Franciscan psalter (BnF, MS lat. 1076): *L'art au temps des rois maudits: Philippe le Bel et ses fils, 1285–1328: Paris, Galeries nationales du Grand Palais, 17 mars–29 juin 1998,* 308–309 (no. 209 A and B). This initial is also discussed by Richard Marks, *Image and Devotion in Late Medieval England,* 220.
169. A helpful question from Beatrice Kitzinger concerning the repetition of the motif of the bell tower prompted me to consider more fully its significance in this miniature.
170. YT 11, ff. 4v B–4r A. This passage is discussed previously.
171. David Postles, "Lamps, Lights and Layfolk"; Richard Marks, *Image and Devotion in Late Medieval England,* esp. 60–61, 161–164; Eamon Duffy, *The Stripping of the Altars,* 134, 146–148.
172. I have silently corrected the text ("quenta") inscribed on the banderole. As noted by Gia Toussaint, Christ's command in this miniature closely echoes a similar exhortation, found on f. 9r of the *Passionale* of Abbess Kunigunde, "Vide quanta pro te Dei Filius sustinuit" (See how much the Son of God bore for your sake!): Toussaint, *Das Passional,* 154, 178. The *Passionale*'s exhortation occurs in the body of a text column and, it should be noted, addresses the reader not in the persona of the savior, but rather in the didactic voice of a spiritual guide; by contrast, the *Somme le roi–Sainte abbaïe* manuscript's miniature text effects a bolder claim for direct communication between Christ and the lay devotee.
173. Jeffrey Hamburger, *The Visual and the Visionary,* 132, 134. Hamburger sees the transformation of the altar and its architectural enclosure as indications that the Trinity "belongs to a different decorative as well as ontological order; it quite literally transcends its physical boundaries": Hamburger, *The Visual and the Visionary,* 134.
174. On the *comma Johanneum* see Raymond Edward Brown, *The Epistles of John,* 775–787.
175. Honorius Augustodunensis, *De vita claustrali,* 1248C.

176. As Jeffrey Hamburger's study of the Rothschild Canticles reveals, high theology and intensely affective mysticism could—and did—go hand in glove in the Middle Ages: Hamburger, *The Rothschild Canticles.*

177. The significance of female convents and religious women for the development of theological and devotional literature in the vernacular has been most fully examined in the German context; see, for example, Herbert Grundmann, *Religious Movements in the Middle Ages,* 187–201; Gertrud Jaron Lewis, *By Women, for Women, about Women;* Marie-Luise Ehrenschwendtner, *"Puellae litteratae."*

CONCLUSION

Epigraph: Emile Mâle, L'art religieux du XIIIe siècle en France, i.

1. "Nous essaierons de montrer comment les artistes ont traduit la pensée des docteurs": Emile Mâle, L'art religieux du XIIIe siècle en France, iii–iv.
2. This sentence is a pastiche of terms and phrases employed in the preface to the first edition of the text: Emile Mâle, L'art religieux du XIIIe siècle en France, i, iii, vi, xiii–xiv.
3. Emile Mâle, L'art religieux du XIIIe siècle en France, iii.
4. Emile Mâle, L'art religieux du XIIIe siècle en France, v–vi.
5. "Il suffit de les [medieval artists] montrer comme ils furent vraiment: simples, modestes, sincères. Ils nous plaisent mieux ainsi. Ils furent les interprètes dociles d'une grande pensée, qu'ils mirent tout leur génie à bien comprendre" (It suffices to show them [medieval artists] as they truly were: simple, modest, sincere. They please us better that way. They were docile interpreters of a great thought, which they focused all their talent on understanding): Emile Mâle, L'art religieux du XIIIe siècle en France, 499.

BIBLIOGRAPHY

Abelard, Peter. *Ethics.* Translated and edited by D. E. Luscombe. Oxford Medieval Texts. Oxford: Clarendon Press, 1971; reprint, 1979.

Aitken, Ellen Bradshaw. "τα δρωμενα και τα λεγονενα: The Eucharistic Memory of Jesus' Words in First Corinthians." *Harvard Theological Review* 90, no. 4 (1997): 359–370.

Alexander, J. J. G. "*Labeur* and *Paresse*: Ideological Images of Medieval Peasant Labour." *Art Bulletin* 72, no. 3 (1990): 436–452.

———. *Medieval Illuminators and Their Methods of Work.* New Haven: Yale University Press, 1992.

———. "Painting and Manuscript Illumination for Royal Patrons in the Later Middle Ages." In *English Court Culture in the Later Middle Ages,* edited by V. J. Scattergood and J. W. Sherborne, 141–162. New York: St. Martin's Press, 1983.

Alexander, J. J. G., and Paul Binski, eds. *Age of Chivalry: Art in Plantagenet England, 1200–1400.* London: Royal Academy of Arts; Weidenfeld and Nicolson, 1987.

Alexander of Hales. *Quaestiones disputatae "antequam esset frater."* Edited by the Collegium S. Bonaventurae. 3 vols. Bibliotheca Franciscana scholastica Medii Aevi, 19–21. Quaracchi, Florence: Ex Typographia Collegii S. Bonaventurae, 1960.

Aquinas, Thomas. *Opera omnia: Ut sunt in Indice Thomistico, additis 61 scriptis ex aliis medii aevi auctoribus.* Edited by Roberto Busa. *Vol. 1, In Quattuor Libros Sententiarum.* Stuttgart-Bad Cannstatt: Frommann-Holzboog, 1980.

———. *Summa theologiae: Vol. 4, Knowledge in God (1a. 14–18).* Translated by Thomas Gornall. [Cambridge?]: Blackfriars; London: Eyre & Spottiswoode; New York: McGraw-Hill, 1964.

———. *Summa theologiae: Vol. 30, The Gospel of Grace (1a2ae. 106–114).* Translated by Cornelius Ernst. [Cambridge?]: Blackfriars; New York: McGraw-Hill; London: Eyre & Spottiswoode, 1972.

———. *Summa theologiae: Vol. 31, Faith (2a2ae. 1–7).* Translated by T. C. O'Brien. [Cambridge?]: Blackfriars; New York: McGraw-Hill; London: Eyre & Spottiswoode, 1974.

———. *Summa theologiae: Vol. 60, Penance (3a. 84–90).* Translated by Reginald Masterson and T. C. O'Brien. [Cambridge?]: Blackfriars; New York: McGraw-Hill; London: Eyre & Spottiswoode, 1966.

Archer, Lucy. *Architecture in Britain and Ireland, 600–1500.* London: Harvill Press, 1999.

Augustine. *In Iohannis evangelium tractatus CXXIV.* Edited by Radbodus Willems. Corpus Christianorum. Series Latina, vol. 36, part 8. Turnhout: Typographi Brepols, 1954.

Avril, François, and Patricia Danz Stirnemann. *Manuscrits enluminés d'origine insulaire VIIe–XXe siècle.* Paris: Bibliothèque nationale, 1987.

Avril, Joseph, ed. *Les statuts synodaux français du XIIIe siècle: Tome 3, Les statuts synodaux angevins de la seconde moitié du XIIIe siècle: Précédés d'une étude sur la législation synodale angevine.* Collection de documents inédits sur l'histoire de France; Série in-8o, 19. Paris: Éditions du Comité des Travaux historiques et scientifiques, 1988.

———, ed. *Les statuts synodaux français du XIIIe siècle: Tome 4, Les statuts synodaux de l'ancienne province de Reims.* Collection de documents inédits sur l'histoire de France; Série in-8o, 23. Paris: Éditions du Comité des Travaux historiques et scientifiques, 1995.

———. "Remarques sur un aspect de la vie religieuse paroissiale: La pratique de la confession et de la communion du Xe au XIVe siècle." In *L'encadrement religieux des fidèles au moyen-age et jusqu'au Concile de Trente: La paroisse, le clergé, la pastorale, la dévotion,* 345–363. Paris: Ministère de l'éducation nationale; Éditions du Comité des Travaux historiques et scientifiques, 1985.

Bakhtin, M. M. "Discourse in the Novel." In *The Dialogic Imagination: Four Essays,* edited by Michael Holquist, 259–422. Austin: University of Texas Press, 1981.

———. "From the Prehistory of Novelistic Discourse." In *The Dialogic Imagination: Four Essays,* edited by Michael Holquist, 41–83. Austin: University of Texas Press, 1981.

———. "The Problem of Speech Genres." In *Speech Genres and Other Late Essays,* edited by Caryl Emerson and Michael Holquist, 60–102. Austin: University of Texas Press, 1986.

Baldwin, John W. *Masters, Princes, and Merchants: The Social Views of Peter the Chanter and His Circle.* 2 vols. Princeton: Princeton University Press, 1970.

Barasch, Moshe. "'Elevatio': The Depiction of a Ritual Gesture." *Artibus et historiae* 24, no. 48 (2003): 43–56.

Barnes, Carl F., Jr. "Cross-Media Design Motifs in XIIIth-Century France: Architectural Motifs in the Psalter and Hours of Yolande de Soissons and in the Cathedral of Notre-Dame at Amiens." *Gesta* 17, no. 2 (1978): 37–40.

Baron, R. "Note sur l'énigmatique 'Summa Sententiarum.'" *Recherches de théologie ancienne et médiévale* 25 (1958): 26–42.

Barratt, Alexandra, ed. *The Book of Tribulation.* Middle English Texts, 15. Heidelberg: Carl Winter Universitätsverlag, 1983.

Baschet, Jérôme. "Vision béatifique et représentations du paradis (XIe–XVe siècle)." *Micrologus* 6 (1998): 73–93.

Bastard d'Estang, Jean-François Auguste, comte de. *Études de symbolique chrétienne: Rapports sur les crosses de Tiron et de Saint-Amand de Rouen, faits, en 1856 et 1857, au Comité de la langue, de l'histoire et des arts de la France, section d'archéologie.* Paris: Imprimerie impériale, 1861.

Baudelaire, Charles. *Oeuvres complètes.* Edited by Claude Pichois. [Nouvelle éd.] 2 vols. Bibliothèque de la Pléiade, 1. Paris: Gallimard, 1975.

Bauer, Gerhard. *Claustrum animae: Untersuchungen zur Geschichte der Metapher vom Herzen als Kloster: Bd. 1, Entstehungsgeschichte.* Munich: W. Fink, 1973.

———. "Herzklosterallegorien." In *Die deutsche Literatur des Mittelalters: Verfasserlexikon,* edited by Kurt Ruh, 1154–1167. Berlin: De Gruyter, 1981.

Bäuml, Franz H. "Varieties and Consequences of Medieval Literacy and Illiteracy." *Speculum* 55, no. 2 (1980): 237–265.

Beckwith, Sarah. *Christ's Body: Identity, Culture, and Society in Late Medieval Writings.* London: Routledge, 1993.

Belting, Hans. *Das Bild und sein Publikum im Mittelalter: Form und Funktion früher Bildtafeln der Passion.* Berlin: Mann, 1981.

———. *Likeness and Presence: A History of the Image before the Era of Art.* Translated by Edmund Jephcott. Chicago: University of Chicago Press, 1994.

Bennett, Adelaide. "A Book Designed for a Noblewoman: An Illustrated *Manuel des Péchés* of the Thirteenth Century." In *Medieval Book Production: Assessing the Evidence: Proceedings of the Second Conference of the Seminar in the History of the Book to 1500, Oxford, July 1988,* edited by Linda L. Brownrigg, 163–181. Los Altos Hills, Calif.: Anderson-Lovelace, 1990.

———. "The Transformation of the Gothic Psalter in Thirteenth-Century France." In *The Illuminated Psalter: Studies in the Content, Purpose and Placement of Its Images,* edited by F. O. Büttner, 211–221. Turnhout: Brepols, 2004.

Bériou, Nicole. "La confession dans les écrits théologiques et pastoraux du XIIIe siècle: Médication de l'âme ou démarche judiciaire?" In *L'Aveu, antiquité et moyen-âge: Actes de la table ronde organisée par l'École française

de Rome avec le concours du CNRS et de l'Université de Trieste, Rome, 28–30 mars 1984, 261–282. Rome: École française de Rome, 1986.
Bernard de Clairvaux. *Sermons pour l'année: Tome 1.2, De Noël à la Purification de la Vierge.* Translated by Marie-Imelda Huille. Edited by Jean Leclercq, Henri Rochais, and C. H. Talbot. Oeuvres complètes, XV.2; Sources chrétiennes, 481. Paris: Cerf, 2004.
Bernau, Anke, Sarah Salih, and Ruth Evans, eds. *Medieval Virginities.* Religion and Culture in the Middle Ages. Cardiff: University of Wales Press, 2003.
Besançon, Alain. *The Forbidden Image: An Intellectual History of Iconoclasm.* Translated by Jane Marie Todd. Chicago: University of Chicago Press, 2000.
Beyer, Jürgen, ed. *La littérature didactique, allegorique et satirique. Grundriss der romanischen Literaturen des Mittelalters,* 6.2. Heidelberg: Carl Winter Universitätsverlag, 1970.
Biernoff, Suzannah. *Sight and Embodiment in the Middle Ages.* [New Middle Ages.] Basingstoke: Palgrave Macmillan, 2002.
Biller, Peter, and A. J. Minnis, eds. *Handling Sin: Confession in the Middle Ages.* York Studies in Medieval Theology, 2. Woodbridge, Eng.: York Medieval Press, 1998.
Binski, Paul. *Becket's Crown: Art and Imagination in Gothic England, 1170–1350.* New Haven: Published for the Paul Mellon Centre for Studies in British Art by Yale University Press, 2004.
Blair, John, and Richard Sharpe, eds. *Pastoral Care before the Parish.* Studies in the Early History of Britain. Leicester: Leicester University Press, 1992.
Blumenthal, Uta-Renate. *The Investiture Controversy: Church and Monarchy from the Ninth to the Twelfth Century.* Middle Ages Series. Philadelphia: University of Pennsylvania Press, 1988.
Boerner, Bruno. *Par caritas par meritum: Studien zur Theologie des gotischen Weltgerichtsportals in Frankreich—am Beispiel des mittleren Westeingangs von Notre-Dame in Paris.* Freiburg: Universitätsverlag, 1998.
———. "Réflexions sur les rapports entre la scolastique naissante et les programmes sculptés du XIIIe siècle." In *De l'art comme mystagogie: Iconographie du Jugement dernier et des fins dernières à l'époque gothique: Actes du Colloque de la Fondation Hardt tenu à Genève du 13 au 16 février 1994,* edited by Yves Christe, 55–69. Poitiers: Université de Poitiers, Centre national de la recherche scientifique, Centre d'études supérieures de civilisation médiévale, 1996.
Boespflug, François. "Autour de la traduction picturale du Credo au moyen âge (XIIe–XVe siècle)." In *Rituels: Mélanges offerts à Pierre-Marie Gy, O.P.,* edited by Eric Palazzo, 55–84. Paris: Editions du Cerf, 1990.
———. "Eucharistie et Trinité dans l'art médiéval d'Occident (XIIe–XVe siècle)." In *Pratiques de l'eucharistie dans les Églises d'Orient et d'Occident (antiquité et moyen âge): Actes du séminaire tenu à Paris, Institut catholique (1997–2004),* edited by Nicole Bériou, Béatrice Caseau, and Dominique Rigaux, 1111–1167. Paris: Institut d'études augustiniennes, 2009.
———. "Symboles de foi et apôtres au Credo: Quelques réflexions sur leurs functions respectives." In *Pensée, image et communication en Europe médiévale: À propos des stalles de Saint-Claude,* edited by Pierre Lacroix, Andrée Renon, Marie-Claude Mary, et al., 257–262. Besançon: ASPRODIC, 1993.
Boffey, Julia. "*The Charter of the Abbey of the Holy Ghost* and Its Role in Manuscript Anthologies." *Yearbook of English Studies* 33 (2003): 120–130.
Boffey, Julia, and John J. Thompson. "Anthologies and Miscellanies: Production and Choice of Texts." In *Book Production and Publishing in Britain, 1375–1475,* edited by Jeremy Griffiths and Derek Albert Pearsall, 279–315. Cambridge: Cambridge University Press, 1989.
Bolton, Brenda. "Advertise the Message: Images in Rome at the Turn of the Century." In *The Church and the Arts: Papers Read at the 1990 Summer Meeting and the 1991 Winter Meeting of the Ecclesiastical History Society,* edited by Diana Wood, 117–130. Oxford: Published for the Ecclesiastical History Society by Blackwell Publishers, 1992.
———. "A Show with a Meaning: Innocent III's Approach to the Fourth Lateran Council, 1215." In *Innocent III: Studies on Papal Authority and Pastoral Care,* 53–67. Aldershot, Eng.: Variorum, 1995.
Bond, Francis. *Screens and Galleries in English Churches.* [Church Art in England, 1] London: H. Frowde, 1908.
Bossy, John. "The Mass as a Social Institution, 1200–1700." *Past and Present* 100 (1983): 29–61.
Bouget, Hélène. "Le *Miroir de vie et de mort:* Une enluminure du *Vrigiet de Solas.*" In *Miroirs et jeux de miroirs dans la littérature médiévale,* edited by Fabienne Pomel, 109–124. Rennes: Presses universitaires de Rennes, 2003.
Bouhot, Jean Paul. *Ratramne de Corbie: Histoire littéraire et controverses doctrinales.* Paris: Études augustiniennes, 1976.
Boyle, Leonard E. "Aspects of Clerical Education in Fourteenth-Century England." In *Pastoral Care, Clerical Education and Canon Law, 1200–1400,* 19–32. London: Variorum Reprints, 1981.
———. "The Constitution 'Cum ex eo' of Boniface VIII." In *Pastoral Care, Clerical Education and Canon Law, 1200–1400,* 263–302. London: Variorum Reprints, 1981.
———. "The Fourth Lateran Council and Manuals of Popular Theology." In *The Popular Literature of Medieval England,* edited by Thomas J. Heffernan, 30–43. Knoxville: University of Tennessee Press, 1985.
———. "The Inter-Conciliar Period 1179–1215 and the Beginnings of Pastoral Manuals." In *Miscellanea Rolando Bandinelli Papa Alessandro III,* edited by Filippo Liotta, 45–56. Siena: Accademia senese degli intronati, 1986.
———. "Notes on the Education of the *Fratres Communes* in the Dominican Order in the Thirteenth Century." In *Pastoral Care, Clerical Education and Canon Law, 1200–1400,* 249–267. London: Variorum Reprints, 1981.
———. "The Summa for Confessors as a Genre and Its Religious Intent." In *The Pursuit of Holiness in Late Medieval and Renaissance Religion: Papers from the University of Michigan Conference,* edited by Charles Edward Trinkaus and Heiko Augustinus Oberman, 126–130. Leiden: Brill, 1974.
———. "Summae confessorum." In *Les genres littéraires dans les sources théologiques et philosophiques médiévales: Définition, critique et exploitation: Actes du Colloque international de Louvain-la-Neuve, 25–27 mai 1981,* 227–237. Louvain-la-Neuve: Institut d'Études médiévales de l'Université Catholique de Louvain, 1982.
Braeckmans, Louis. *Confession et communion au moyen âge et au Concile de Trente.* Recherches et synthèses. Section de morale, 6. Gembloux: J. Duculot, 1971.
Branner, Robert. *Manuscript Painting in Paris during the Reign of Saint Louis: A Study of Styles.* California Studies in the History of Art, 18. Berkeley: University of California Press, 1977.
———. "The Painted Medallions in the Sainte-Chapelle in Paris." *Transactions of the American Philosophical Society,* n.s. 28, part 2 (1968): 1–42.
Brantley, Jessica. "Images of the Vernacular in the Taymouth Hours." *English Manuscript Studies, 1100–1700* 10 (1989): 83–113.
———. *Reading in the Wilderness: Private Devotion and Public Performance in Late Medieval England.* Chicago: University of Chicago Press, 2007.

Brieger, Peter H., and Philippe Verdier, eds. *Art and the Courts: France and England from 1259 to 1328*. 2 vols. Ottawa: National Gallery of Canada, 1972.

Browe, Peter. "Die Elevation in der Messe." *Jahrbuch für Liturgiewissenschaft* 9 (1929): 20–66.

———. *Die Eucharistie im Mittelalter: Liturgiehistorische Forschungen in kulturwissenschaftlicher Absicht*. Münster: Lit, 2003.

———. "Die Kommunionvorbereitung im Mittelalter." In *Die Eucharistie im Mittelalter*, 173–218.

———. "Die öftere Kommunion der Laien im Mittelalter." In *Die Eucharistie im Mittelalter*, 67–88.

———. "Die Pflichtkommunion der Laien im Mittelalter." In *Die Eucharistie im Mittelalter*, 39–50.

———. "Der Segen mit Reliquien der Patene und Eucharistie." In *Die Eucharistie im Mittelalter*, 233–238.

———. "Zum Kommunionempfang des Mittelalters." In *Die Eucharistie im Mittelalter*, 19–31.

Brown, Raymond Edward. *The Epistles of John*. Anchor Bible. Garden City, N.Y.: Doubleday, 1982.

Brownrigg, Linda. "The Taymouth Hours and the Romance of *Beves of Hampton*." *English Manuscript Studies, 1100–1700* 1 (1989): 222–241.

Bucher, François. "Micro-Architecture as the 'Idea' of Gothic Theory and Style." *Gesta* 15, no. 1–2 (1976): 71–89.

Bugslag, James. "The Shrine of St. Gertrude de Nivelles and the Process of Gothic Design." *RACAR (Revue d'art canadienne / Canadian Art Review)* 20, no. 1–2 (1993): 16–28.

Bühler, Curt F. "The Apostles and the Creed." *Speculum* 28, no. 2 (1953): 335–339.

Bumke, Joachim. *Courtly Culture: Literature and Society in the High Middle Ages*. Translated by Thomas Dunlap. Berkeley: University of California Press, 1991.

Burr, David. *Eucharistic Presence and Conversion in Late Thirteenth-Century Franciscan Thought*. Transactions of the American Philosophical Society. Philadelphia: American Philosophical Society, 1984.

Büttner, F. O. "*Ad Te, Domine, Levavi Animam Meam:* Bildnisse in der Wortillustration zu Psalm 24:1." In *Miscellanea codicologica F. Masai: Dicata MCMLXXIX*, edited by P. Cockshaw, Monique-Cécile Garand, and Pierre Jodogne, 331–343. Ghent: E. Story-Scientia S.P.R.L., 1979.

Bynum, Caroline Walker. *Docere Verbo et Exemplo: An Aspect of Twelfth-Century Spirituality*. Harvard Theological Studies, 31. Missoula, Mont.: Scholars Press, 1979.

———. *Jesus as Mother: Studies in the Spirituality of the High Middle Ages*. Publications of the UCLA Center for Medieval and Renaissance Studies, 16. Berkeley: University of California Press, 1982.

———. "Seeing and Seeing Beyond: The Mass of St. Gregory in the Fifteenth Century." In *The Mind's Eye: Art and Theological Argument in the Middle Ages*, edited by Anne-Marie Bouché and Jeffrey Hamburger, 208–240. Princeton: Princeton University Press, 2006.

Camille, Michael. "Before the Gaze: The Internal Senses and Late Medieval Practices of Seeing." In *Visuality Before and Beyond the Renaissance: Seeing as Others Saw*, edited by Robert S. Nelson, 197–223. Cambridge: Cambridge University Press, 2000.

———. *Gothic Art: Glorious Visions*. New York: Harry N. Abrams, 1996.

———. *The Gothic Idol: Ideology and Image-Making in Medieval Art*. Cambridge: Cambridge University Press, 1989.

———. "'Him whom you have ardently desired you may see': Cistercian Exegesis and the Prefatory Pictures in a French Apocalypse." In *Studies in Cistercian Art and Architecture*, edited by Meredith P. Lillich, 137–160. Kalamazoo, Mich.: Cistercian Publications, 1987.

———. "Labouring for the Lord: The Ploughman and the Social Order in the Luttrell Psalter." *Art History* 10, no. 4 (1987): 423–454.

———. "The Language of Images in Medieval England, 1200–1400." In *Age of Chivalry: Art in Plantagenet England, 1200–1400*, edited by J. J. G. Alexander and Paul Binski, 33–40. London: Royal Academy of Arts; Weidenfeld and Nicolson, 1987.

———. *Mirror in Parchment: The Luttrell Psalter and the Making of Medieval England*. Chicago: University of Chicago Press, 1998.

———. "Visual Signs of the Sacred Page: Books in the *Bible moralisée*." *Word and Image* 5, no. 1 (1989): 111–130.

———. "Visualising in the Vernacular: A New Cycle of Early Fourteenth-Century Bible Illustrations." *Burlington Magazine* 130, no. 1019 (1988): 97–106.

Carlson, Cindy L., and Angela Jane Weisl, eds. *Constructions of Widowhood and Virginity in the Middle Ages*. New Middle Ages. New York: St. Martin's Press, 1999.

Carruthers, Leo. "In Pursuit of Holiness outside the Cloister: Religion of the Heart in *The Abbey of the Holy Ghost*." In *Models of Holiness in Medieval Sermons: Proceedings of the International Symposium (Kalamazoo, 4–7 May 1995)*, edited by Beverly Mayne Kienzle, 211–227. Louvain-la-Neuve: Fédération internationale des Instituts d'études médiévales, 1996.

———. *La somme le roi et ses traductions anglaises: Étude comparée*. Publications de l'Association des médiévistes anglicistes de l'enseignement supérieur, 12. Paris: Association des médiévistes anglicistes de l'enseignement supérieur, 1986.

Carruthers, Mary. *The Book of Memory: A Study of Memory in Medieval Culture*. Pbk. ed. Cambridge Studies in Medieval Literature, 10. Cambridge: Cambridge University Press, 1992.

———. *The Craft of Thought: Meditation, Rhetoric, and the Making of Images, 400–1200*, Cambridge Studies in Medieval Literature, 34. Cambridge: Cambridge University Press, 1998.

Caspers, Charles. "*Meum summum desiderium est te habere:* L'eucharistie comme sacrement de la rencontre avec Dieu pour tous les croyants (ca. 1200–ca. 1500)." In *Fête-Dieu (1246–1996)*, edited by André Haquin, 127–151. Louvain-la-Neuve: Institut d'études médiévales de l'Université Catholique de Louvain, 1999.

———. "The Western Church during the Late Middle Ages: *Augenkommunion* or Popular Mysticism?" In *Bread of Heaven: Customs and Practices Surrounding Holy Communion: Essays in the History of Liturgy and Culture*, edited by Charles Caspers, Gerard Lukken, and Gerard Rouwhorst, 83–97. Kampen: Kok Pharos, 1995.

Caviness, Madeleine. "Images of Divine Order and the Third Mode of Seeing." *Gesta* 22, no. 2 (1983): 99–120.

———. "'The Simple Perception of Matter' in Representations, ca. 1180–1280: Narrative Mode or Gothic Style?" *Gesta* 30, no. 1 (1991): 48–64.

Cheney, C. R. *From Becket to Langton: English Church Government, 1170–1213*. Ford Lectures, 1955. Manchester: Manchester University Press, 1956.

———. "Legislation of the Medieval English Church." *English Historical Review* 50, no. 198 (1935): 193–224.

———. *Pope Innocent III and England*. Päpste und Papsttum, 9. Stuttgart: Hiersemann, 1976.

———. "A Recent View of the General Interdict on England, 1208–1214." In *Studies in Church History: Papers Read at the Third Winter and Summer Meetings of the Ecclesiastical History Society*, edited by G. J. Cuming, 159–168. Leiden: Brill, 1966.

Chenu, Marie-Dominique. *L'éveil de la conscience dans la civilisation médiévale.* Conférences Albert-le-Grand. Montreal: Institut d'études médiévales Albert-le-Grand, 1969.
Chesney, Kathleen. "Notes on Some Treatises of Devotion Intended for Margaret of York (MS. Douce 365)." *Medium Aevum* 20 (1951): 11–39.
Chodorow, Stanley. *Christian Political Theory and Church Politics in the Mid-twelfth Century: The Ecclesiology of Gratian's Decretum.* Publications of the Center for Medieval and Renaissance Studies, UCLA, 5. Berkeley: University of California Press, 1972.
Christe, Yves. "Grossement." In *Autour de Guillaume d'Auvergne (+1249),* edited by Franco Morenzoni and Jean-Yves Tilliette, 341–367. Turnhout: Brepols, 2005.
Christianson, C. Paul. *A Directory of London Stationers and Book Artisans, 1300–1500.* New York: Bibliographical Society of America, 1990.
Clanchy, M. T. *From Memory to Written Record, England, 1066–1307.* 2nd ed. Oxford: Blackwell, 1993.
Clarke, Peter. "The Growth of Canon and Civil Law Studies, 1070–1535." In *Illuminating the Law: Legal Manuscripts in Cambridge Collections,* edited by Susan L'Engle and Robert Gibbs, 22–38. London: Harvey Miller, 2001.
———. *The Interdict in the Thirteenth Century: A Question of Collective Guilt.* Oxford: Oxford University Press, 2007.
Colish, Marcia L. *Peter Lombard.* 2 vols. Brill's Studies in Intellectual History, 41. Leiden: Brill, 1994.
Collet, Olivier. "Du 'manuscrit de jongleur' au 'recueil aristocratique': Réflexions sur les premières anthologies françaises." *Le moyen age* 113, no. 3–4 (2007): 481–499.
Constable, Giles. *The Reformation of the Twelfth Century.* Cambridge: Cambridge University Press, 1996.
———. "Renewal and Reform in Religious Life: Concepts and Realities." In *Renaissance and Renewal in the Twelfth Century,* edited by Robert Louis Benson, Giles Constable, and Carol Dana Lanham, 37–67. Cambridge, Mass.: Harvard University Press, 1982.
Constable, Giles, and Bernard Smith, eds. *Libellus de diversis ordinibus et professionibus qui sunt in aecclesia.* Oxford Medieval Texts. Oxford: Clarendon Press, 1972.
Copeland, Rita. *Rhetoric, Hermeneutics, and Translation in the Middle Ages: Academic Traditions and Vernacular Texts.* Cambridge Studies in Medieval Literature, 11. Cambridge: Cambridge University Press, 1991.
Corbin, Solange. "Les offices de la Sainte Face." *Bulletin des études portugaises* 11 (1947): 1–65.
Cornelius, Roberta Douglas. *The Figurative Castle: A Study in the Mediaeval Allegory of the Edifice with Especial Reference to Religious Writings.* PhD diss., Bryn Mawr College, 1930.
Corpus juris canonici emendatum et notis illustratum. Gregorii XIII. pont. max. iussu editum. 3 parts in 4 volumes. Rome: In aedibus Populi Romani, 1582. Electronic edition: UCLA Digital Library Program, *Corpus Juris Canonici (1582),* http://digital.library.ucla.edu/canonlaw.
Crane, Susan. "Anglo-Norman Cultures in England, 1066–1460." In *The Cambridge History of Medieval English Literature,* edited by David Wallace, 35–60. Cambridge: Cambridge University Press, 1999.
Creytens, Raymond. "L'instruction des novices Dominicains au XIIIe siècle d'après le MS. Toulouse 418." *Archivum Fratrum Praedicatorum* 20 (1950): 114–193.
Cushing, Kathleen G. *Reform and Papacy in the Eleventh Century: Spirituality and Social Change.* Manchester Medieval Studies. Manchester: Manchester University Press, 2005.
Davis, Michael T. "Canonical Views: The Theophilus Story and the Choir Reliefs at Notre Dame, Paris." In *Reading Medieval Images: The Art Historian and the Object,* edited by Elizabeth Sears and Thelma K. Thomas, 103–116. Ann Arbor: University of Michigan Press, 2002.
———. "Splendor and Peril: The Cathedral of Paris, 1290–1350." *Art Bulletin* 80, no. 1 (1998): 34–66.
de Ghellinck, Joseph. *Le mouvement théologique du XIIe siècle.* 2nd ed. Museum Lessianum, Section historique, 10. Bruges: Éditions "De Tempel," 1948.
de Lubac, Henri. *Corpus mysticum: L'eucharistie et l'église au moyen âge.* 2nd ed. Paris: Aubier, 1949.
de Vogüé, Adalbert. "Persévérer au monastère jusqu'à la mort: La stabilité chez saint Benoît et autour de lui." *Collectanea cisterciensia: Revue de spiritualité monastique* 43, no. 4 (1981): 337–365.
de Winter, Patrick M. *La bibliothèque de Philippe le Hardi, duc de Bourgogne (1364–1404): Étude sur les manuscrits à peintures d'une collection princière à l'époque du "style gothique international."* Paris: Éditions du Centre National de la Recherche Scientifique, 1985.
———. "Une réalisation exceptionnelle d'enlumineurs français et anglais: Le bréviaire de Renaud de Bar, évêque de Metz." In *Actes du 103e congrès des Sociétés savantes (1978),* 27–62. Paris, 1980.
Dean, Ruth J., and Maureen Barry McCann Boulton. *Anglo-Norman Literature: A Guide to Texts and Manuscripts.* Anglo-Norman Text Society Occasional Publications Series, 3. London: Anglo-Norman Text Society from Birkbeck College London, 1999.
Delaborde, H.-F., and P. Lauer. "Un projet de décoration murale inspiré du Crédo de Joinville." *Monuments Piot* 16 (1909): 61–84.
Delhaye, Philippe. "L'enseignement de la philosophie morale au XIIe siècle." *Mediaeval Studies* 11 (1949): 77–99.
Delisle, Léopold. "Livres d'images destinés à l'instruction religieuse et aux exercises de piété des laïques." *Histoire littéraire de la France* 31 (1893): 213–285.
———. *Recherches sur la librairie de Charles V, roi de France, 1337–1380.* 2 vols. Paris, 1907; reprint, Amsterdam: Gérard Th. van Heusden, 1967.
Delmaire, Bernard. "Les béguines dans le Nord de la France au premier siècle de leur histoire (vers 1230–vers 1350)." In *Les religieuses en France au XIIIe siècle,* edited by Michel Parisse, 121–162. [Nancy]: Presses Universitaires de Nancy, 1985.
Denery, Dallas G. *Seeing and Being Seen in the Later Medieval World: Optics, Theology And Religious Life.* Cambridge Studies in Medieval Life and Thought, 4th ser., vol. 63. Cambridge: Cambridge University Press, 2005.
Dennison, Lynda. "An Illuminator of the Queen Mary Psalter Group: The Ancient 6 Master." *Antiquaries Journal* 66, no. 2 (1986): 287–314.
———. "'Liber Horn,' 'Liber Custumarum' and Other Manuscripts of the Queen Mary Psalter Workshops." In *Medieval Art, Architecture and Archaeology in London,* edited by Lindy Grant, 118–134. [London]: British Archaeological Association, 1990.
Dobschütz, Ernst von. *Christusbilder: Untersuchungen zur christlichen Legende.* Texte und Untersuchungen zur Geschichte der altchristlichen Literatur, Bd. 18. Leipzig: J. C. Hinrichs, 1899.
Donovan, Claire. *The de Brailes Hours: Shaping the Book of Hours in Thirteenth-Century Oxford.* Toronto Medieval Texts and Translations, 7. Toronto: University of Toronto Press, 1991.
Douais, C. *Essai sur l'organisation des études dans l'ordre des frères Prêcheurs au treizième et au quatorzième siècle (1216–1342): Première province de Provence-Province de Toulouse, avec de nombreux textes inédits et un état du personnel enseignant dans cinquante-cinq couvents du midi de la France.* Paris: A. Picard; Toulouse: E. Privat, 1884.
Dreves, Guido Maria, and Clemens Blume, eds. *Analecta hymnica Medii Aevi,* vol. 50. New York: Johnson Reprint, 1961.

Duffy, Eamon. *Marking the Hours: English People and Their Prayers, 1240–1570.* New Haven: Yale University Press, 2006.
———. *The Stripping of the Altars: Traditional Religion in England, c. 1400–c. 1580.* New Haven: Yale University Press, 1992.
Dumoutet, Edouard. *Le Christ selon la chair et la vie liturgique au moyen-âge.* Paris: G. Beauchesne, 1932.
———. *Le désir de voir l'hostie et les origines de la dévotion au Saint-Sacrement.* Paris: G. Beauchesne, 1926.
Durand, Guillaume. *Rationale Divinorum Officiorum, I–IV.* Edited by Anselmus Davril and T. M. Thibodeau. Corpus Christianorum. Continuatio Mediaevalis, 140. Turnhout: Brepols, 1995.
Dvořák, Max. *Idealism and Naturalism in Gothic Art.* [Notre Dame, Ind.]: University of Notre Dame Press, 1967.
Egbert, Donald Drew. "The So-Called 'Greenfield' *La Lumiere As Lais* and *Apocalypse,* Brit. Mus., Royal MS. 15 D II." *Speculum* 11, no. 4 (1936): 446–452.
Egger, Christoph. "Papst Innocenz III. und die Veronica: Geschichte, Theologie, Liturgie und Seelsorge." In *The Holy Face and the Paradox of Representation: Papers from a Colloquium Held at the Bibliotheca Hertziana, Rome, and the Villa Spelman, Florence, 1996,* edited by Herbert L. Kessler and Gerhard Wolf, 182–203. Bologna: Nuova Alfa, 1998.
Ehrenschwendtner, Marie-Luise. "*Puellae litteratae:* The Use of the Vernacular in the Dominican Convents of Southern Germany." In *Medieval Women in Their Communities,* edited by Diane Watt, 49–71. Toronto: University of Toronto Press, 1997.
Elm, Kaspar. "Die Stellung der Frau in Ordenswesen, Semireligiosentum und Häresie zur Zeit der heiligen Elisabeth." In *Sankt Elisabeth: Fürstin, Dienerin, Heilige: Aufsätze, Dokumentation, Katalog; Herausgegeben von der Philipps-Universität Marburg in Verbindung mit dem Hessischen Landesamt für Geschichtliche Landeskunde,* 7–28. Sigmaringen: Thorbecke, 1981.
Emmerson, Richard K. "Visualizing the Vernacular: Middle English in Early Fourteenth-Century Bilingual and Trilingual Manuscript Illustrations." In *Tributes to Lucy Freeman Sandler: Studies in Illuminated Manuscripts,* 187–204. London: Harvey Miller, 2007.
Evans, Michael. "An Illustrated Fragment of Peraldus's Summa of Vice: Harleian MS 3244." *Journal of the Warburg and Courtauld Institutes* 45 (1982): 14–68.
Evans, Ruth, Andrew Taylor, and Nicholas Watson. "The Notion of Vernacular Theory." In *The Idea of the Vernacular: An Anthology of Middle English Literary Theory, 1280–1520,* edited by Jocelyn Wogan-Browne, Nicholas Watson, Andrew Taylor, and Ruth Evans, 314–330. University Park: Pennsylvania State University Press, 1999.
Fassler, Margot. "Liturgy and Sacred History in the Twelfth-Century Tympana at Chartres." *Art Bulletin* 75, no. 3 (1993): 499–520.
———. "The Meaning of Entrance: Liturgical Commentaries and the Introit Tropes." In *Reflections on the Sacred: A Musicological Perspective,* edited by Paul Brainard, 8–18. [New Haven]: Yale Institute of Sacred Music Worship and the Arts, 1994.
Ferrante, Joan M. "Images of the Cloister—Haven or Prison." *Mediaevalia* 12 (1989 [for 1986]): 57–66.
Field, Sean L. "From *Speculum anime* to *Miroir de l'âme:* The Origins of Vernacular Advice Literature at the Capetian Court." *Mediaeval Studies* 69 (2007): 59–110.
———. "Reflecting the Royal Soul: The *Speculum anime* Composed for Blanche of Castile." *Mediaeval Studies* 68 (2006): 1–41.
Flaherty, Heather M. *The Place of the Speculum Humanae Salvationis in the Rise of Affective Piety in the Later Middle Ages.* PhD diss., University of Michigan, 2006.
Flint, Valerie I. J. *Honorius Augustodunensis.* Authors of the Middle Ages, 2.5–6. Aldershot, Eng.: Variorum, 1995.
Folda, Jaroslav. *Crusader Art in the Holy Land: From the Third Crusade to the Fall of Acre, 1187–1291.* New York: Cambridge University Press, 2005.
———. *Crusader Manuscript Illumination at Saint-Jean d'Acre, 1275–1291.* Princeton: Princeton University Press, 1976.
Foreville, Raymonde. "La réception des conciles généraux dans l'église et la province de Rouen au XIIIe siècle." In *Droit privé et institutions régionales: Études historiques offertes à Jean Yver,* 243–253. Paris: Presses universitaires de France, 1976.
———. *Latran I, II, III et Latran IV.* Histoire de conciles oecuméniques, 6. Paris: Éditions de l'Orante, 1965.
Forshaw, Helen P. "St. Edmund's *Speculum:* A Classic of Victorine Spirituality." *Archives d'histoire doctrinale et littéraire du moyen âge* 47 (1972): 7–40.
Foucault, Michel. *Histoire de la sexualité.* 3 vols. Bibliothèque des histoires. Paris: Gallimard, 1976–1984.
Foulet, Alfred. "When Did Joinville Write His Vie de Saint Louis?" *Romanic Review* 32, no. 3 (1941): 233–243.
Francis, W. Nelson, ed. *The Book of Vices and Virtues: A Fourteenth Century English Translation of the Somme Le Roi of Lorens d'Orléans.* London: Published for the Early English Text Society by H. Milford, Oxford University Press, 1942.
Frankis, John. "The Social Context of Vernacular Writing in Thirteenth Century England: The Evidence of the Manuscripts." *Thirteenth Century England* 1 (1986): 175–184.
Freedberg, David. *The Power of Images: Studies in the History and Theory of Response.* Chicago: University of Chicago Press, 1989.
Frère Laurent. *La somme le roi.* Edited by Edith Brayer and Anne-Françoise Leurquin Labie. Paris: Société des anciens textes français; Abbeville: F. Paillart, 2008.
Friedberg, Emil, ed. *Corpus iuris canonici.* Editio lipsiensis secunda ed. 2 vols. Graz: Akademische Druck-u. Verlagsanstalt, 1959.
Friedman, Lionel J. "Observations on the Style of Joinville's 'Credo.'" *Romance Philology* 8 (1954–1955): 272–278.
———. "On the Structure of Joinville's 'Credo.'" *Modern Philology* 51, no. 1 (1953): 1–8.
———. *Text and Iconography for Joinville's Credo.* Mediaeval Academy of America Publication, 68. Cambridge: Mediaeval Academy of America, 1958.
Fulton, Rachel. *From Judgment to Passion: Devotion to Christ and the Virgin Mary, 800–1200.* New York: Columbia University Press, 2002.
Gaposchkin, M. Cecilia. "The King of France and the Queen of Heaven: The Iconography of the Porte Rouge of Notre-Dame of Paris." *Gesta* 39, no. 1 (2000): 58–72.
Georgianna, Linda. "Vernacular Theologies." *English Language Notes* 44, no. 1 (2006): 87–94.
Gibbs, Marion E., and Jane Lang. *Bishops and Reform, 1215–1272, with Special Reference to the Lateran Council of 1215.* Oxford Historical Series. London: Oxford University Press, 1934.
Gillespie, Vincent. "*Lukynge in haly bukes: Lectio* in Some Late Medieval Spiritual Miscellanies." In *Spätmittelalterliche geistliche Literatur in der Nationalsprache,* edited by James Hogg, 1–27. Salzburg: Institut für Anglistik und Amerikanistik, Universität, Salzburg, 1984.
———. "Vernacular Books of Religion." In *Book Production and Publishing in Britain, 1375–1475,* edited by Jeremy Griffiths and Derek Albert Pearsall, 317–344. Cambridge: Cambridge University Press, 1989.
Godefroy, Frédéric. *Dictionnaire de l'ancienne langue française.* 10 vols. Vaduz: Scientific Periodicals Establishment; New York: Kraus Reprint, 1961.

Goering, Joseph. *William de Montibus (c. 1140–1213): The Schools and the Literature of Pastoral Care.* Toronto: Pontifical Institute of Mediaeval Studies, 1992.
Goering, Joseph, and Daniel S. Taylor. "The *Summulae* of Bishops Walter de Cantilupe (1240) and Peter Quinel (1287)." *Speculum* 67, no. 3 (1992): 576–594.
Goglin, Jean-Marc. *L'enseignement de la théologie dans les ordres mendiants à Paris au XIIIe siècle.* Paris: Éditions franciscaines, 2002.
Gordon, James D. "The Articles of the Creed and the Apostles." *Speculum* 40, no. 4 (1965): 634–640.
Gössmann, Elisabeth. *Glaube und Gotteserkenntnis im Mittelalter.* Handbuch der Dogmengeschichte, 1. 2b. Freiburg: Herder, 1971.
Gould, Karen. "Illumination and Sculpture in Thirteenth-Century Amiens: The Invention of the Body of Saint Firmin in the Psalter and Hours of Yolande of Soissons." *Art Bulletin* 59, no. 2 (1977): 161–166.
———. "Jean Pucelle and Northern Gothic Art: New Evidence from Strasbourg Cathedral." *Art Bulletin* 74, no. 1 (1992): 51–74.
Greenhill, Eleanor Simmons. *Die geistigen Voraussetzungen der Bilderreihe des Speculum virginum: Versuch einer Deutung.* Beiträge zur Geschichte der Philosophie und Theologie des Mittelalters: Texte und Untersuchungen, 39.2. Münster: Aschendorff, 1962.
Grundmann, Herbert. *Religious Movements in the Middle Ages: The Historical Links between Heresy, the Mendicant Orders, and the Women's Religious Movement in the Twelfth and Thirteenth Century, with the Historical Foundations of German Mysticism.* Notre Dame: University of Notre Dame Press, 1995.
Guerric d'Igny. *Liturgical Sermons,* vol. 1. Cistercian Fathers Series, 8. Spencer, Mass.: Cistercian Publications, 1970.
———. *Sermons,* vol. 1. Edited by John Morson and Hilary Costello. Sources chrétiennes, 166. Paris: Éditions du Cerf, 1970.
Guest, Gerald B. *Bible moralisée: Codex Vindobonensis 2554, Vienna, Österreichische Nationalbibliothek.* Manuscripts in Miniature, 2. London: Harvey Miller, 1995.
———. "'The Darkness and the Obscurity of Sins': Representing Vice in the Thirteenth-Century *Bibles moralisées.*" In *In the Garden of Evil: The Vices and Culture in the Middle Ages,* edited by Richard Newhauser, 74–103. Toronto: Pontifical Institute of Mediaeval Studies, 2005.
———. "Picturing Women in the First *Bible moralisée.*" In *Insights and Interpretations: Studies in Celebration of the Eighty-Fifth Anniversary of the Index of Christian Art,* edited by Colum Hourihane, 106–130. Princeton: Index of Christian Art, Department of Art and Archaeology, Princeton University, in association with Princeton University Press, 2002.
Guyot, Bertrand-Georges. "L'attribution des articles de la foi aux apôtres dans la littérature pastorale latine des XIIIe–XIVe siècles." In *Pensée, image et communication en Europe médiévale: À propos des stalles de Saint-Claude,* edited by Pierre Lacroix, Andrée Renon, Marie-Claude Mary, et al., 179–184. Besançon: ASPRODIC, 1993.
Hahn, Cynthia. *Portrayed on the Heart: Narrative Effect in Pictorial Lives of Saints from the Tenth through the Thirteenth Century.* Berkeley: University of California Press, 2001.
———. "Visio Dei: Changes in Medieval Visuality." In *Visuality Before and Beyond the Renaissance: Seeing as Others Saw,* edited by Robert S. Nelson, 169–196. Cambridge: Cambridge University Press, 2000.
———. "Vision." In *A Companion to Medieval Art: Romanesque and Gothic in Northern Europe,* edited by Conrad Rudolph, 44–64. Malden, Mass.: Blackwell, 2006.
Hamburger, Jeffrey. "Body vs. Book: The Trope of Visibility in Images of Christian-Jewish Polemic." In *Ästhetik des Unsichtbaren: Bildtheorie und Bildgebrauch in der Vormoderne,* edited by David Ganz, Thomas Lentes and Georg Henkel, 113–145. Kultbild, 1. Berlin: Reimer, 2004.
———. "'Frequentant Memoriam Visionis Faciei Meae': Image and Imitation in the Devotions to the Veronica Attributed to Gertrude of Helfta." In *The Holy Face and the Paradox of Representation: Papers from a Colloquium Held at the Bibliotheca Hertziana, Rome, and the Villa Spelman, Florence, 1996,* edited by Herbert L. Kessler and Gerhard Wolf, 229–246. Bologna: Nuova Alfa, 1998.
———. *The Rothschild Canticles: Art and Mysticism in Flanders and the Rhineland circa 1300.* Yale Publications in the History of Art. New Haven: Yale University Press, 1990.
———. "Seeing and Believing: The Suspicion of Sight and the Authentication of Vision in Late Medieval Art and Devotion." In *Imagination und Wirklichkeit: Zum Verhältnis von mentalen und realen Bildern in der Kunst der frühen Neuzeit,* edited by Klaus Krüger and Alessandro Nova, 47–69. Mainz am Rhein: Philipp von Zabern, 2000.
———. "Speculations on Speculation: Vision and Perception in the Theory and Practice of Mystical Devotion." In *Deutsche Mystik im abendländischen Zusammenhang: Neu erschlossene Texte, neue methodische Ansätze, neue theoretische Konzepte; Kolloquium, Kloster Fischingen 1998,* edited by Walter Haug and Wolfram Schneider-Lastin, 351–408. Tübingen: Niemeyer, 2000.
———. *The Visual and the Visionary: Art and Female Spirituality in Late Medieval Germany.* New York: Zone Books; Cambridge, Mass.: MIT Press, 1998.
Hamburger, Jeffrey, and Anne-Marie Bouché, eds. *The Mind's Eye: Art and Theological Argument in the Middle Ages.* Princeton: Princeton University Press, 2006.
Hamilton, Sarah. *The Practice of Penance, 900–1050.* Royal Historical Society Studies in History. Woodbridge, Eng.: Royal Historical Society; Rochester, N.Y.: Boydell Press, 2001.
Hamilton, Tracy Chapman. "Queenship and Kinship in the French *Bible moralisée:* The Example of Blanche of Castile and Vienna ÖNB 2554." In *Capetian Women,* edited by Kathleen Nolan, 177–208. New York: Palgrave Macmillan, 2003.
Hanna, Ralph, III. "Miscellaneity and Vernacularity: Conditions of Literary Production in Late Medieval England." In *The Whole Book: Cultural Perspectives on the Medieval Miscellany,* edited by Stephen G. Nichols and Siegfried Wenzel, 37–51. Ann Arbor: University of Michigan Press, 1996.
Harmening, Dieter. "Katechismusliteratur: Grundlagen religiöser Laienbildung im Spätmittelalter." In *Wissensorganisierende und wissensvermittelnde Literatur im Mittelalter: Perspektiven ihrer Erforschung: Kolloquium, 5.–7. Dezember 1985,* edited by Norbert Richard Wolf, 91–102. Wiesbaden: L. Reichert, 1987.
Harper, John. *The Forms and Orders of Western Liturgy from the Tenth to the Eighteenth century: A Historical Introduction and Guide for Students and Musicians.* Oxford: Clarendon Press, 1991.
Hasenohr, Geneviève. "Aperçu sur la diffusion et la réception de la littérature de spiritualité en langue française au dernier siècle du moyen age." In *Wissensorganisierende und wissensvermittelnde Literatur im Mittelalter: Perspektiven ihrer Erforschung: Kolloquium, 5.–7. Dezember 1985,* edited by Norbert Richard Wolf, 57–90. Wiesbaden: L. Reichert, 1987.
———. "Les prologues des textes de dévotion en langue française (XIIIe–XVe siècles)." In *Les prologues médiévaux,* edited by Jacqueline Hamesse, 593–638. Turnhout: Brepols, 2000.
———. "Les recueils littéraires français du XIIIe siècle: Public et finalité." In *Codices miscellanearum: Brussels Van Hulthem colloquium 1999, Colloque Van Hulthem, Bruxelles, 1999,* edited by Ria Jansen-Sieben and Hans van

Dijk, 37–50. Brussels: Bibliothèque royale de Belgique, 1999.
Haussherr, Reiner. *Bible moralisée: Codex Vindobonensis 2554 der Österreichischen Nationalbibliothek.* Translated by Hans-Walter Stork (Old French Texts). Glanzlichter der Buchkunst, 2. Graz: Akademische Druck-u. Verlaganstalt, 1992.
———. *Bible moralisée: Faksimile-Ausgabe im Originalformat des Codex Vindobonensis 2554 des Österreichischen Nationalbibliothek.* Codices selecti XL–XL*. Graz: Akademische Druck-u. Verlagsanstalt, 1973.
Hedeman, Anne D. *Translating the Past: Laurent de Premierfait and Boccaccio's De casibus.* Los Angeles: J. Paul Getty Museum, 2008.
Heinlen, James. *The Ideology of Reform in the French Moralized Bible.* PhD diss., Northwestern University, 1991.
Heinzer, Felix. *Wörtliche Bilder: Zur Funktion der Literal-Illustration im Stuttgarter Psalter (um 830).* Wolfgang Stammler Gastprofessur, 13. Berlin: De Gruyter, 2005.
Heller, Sarah-Grace. "Anxiety, Hierarchy and Appearance in Thirteenth-Century Sumptuary Laws and the Roman de la Rose." *French Historical Studies* 27, no. 2 (2004): 311–348.
Hemzik, Pamela. *Illuminated Moral and Devotional Compilations and Lay Piety in Fourteenth-Century Metz.* PhD diss., Pennsylvania State University, 1995.
Hessenauer, Matthias. *La Lumière as lais: Pierre de Peckhams Vermittlung scholastischer Theologie.* Wissensliteratur im Mittelalter, 2. Wiesbaden: L. Reichert, 1989.
Higgitt, John. *The Murthly Hours: Devotion, Literacy and Luxury in Paris, England, and the Gaelic West.* British Library Studies in Medieval Culture. London: British Library and University of Toronto Press, in association with the National Library of Scotland, 2000.
Holcomb, Melanie, ed. *Pen and Parchment: Drawing in the Middle Ages.* New York: Metropolitan Museum of Art; New Haven: Yale University Press, 2009.
The Holy Bible: Douay-Rheims Version. Rev. ed. Translated by Bishop Richard Challoner. Rockford, Ill.: Tan Books, 2000.
Honorius Augustodunensis. *De vita claustrali.* In Migne, *Patrologia cursus completus: Series latina,* vol. 172, cols. 1247A–1248C.
Hugh of Saint-Victor. *Didascalicon de studio legendi.* Edited by Charles Henry Buttimer. Washington, D.C.: Catholic University Press, 1939.
Hughes, Andrew. *Medieval Manuscripts for Mass and Office: A Guide to Their Organization and Terminology.* Pbk. ed. Toronto: University of Toronto Press, 1995.
Hugo de Folieto. *De claustro animae.* In Migne, *Patrologiae cursus completus: Series latina,* vol. 176, cols. 1017B–1182D.
Hunt, Alan. *Governance of the Consuming Passions: A History of Sumptuary Law.* Houndmills: Macmillan; New York: St. Martin's Press, 1996.
Hunt, Tony. "Anglo-Norman: Past and Future." In *The Dawn of the Written Vernacular in Western Europe,* edited by Michèle Goyens and Werner Verbeke, 379–389. Louvain: Leuven University Press, 2003.
Huot, Sylvia. "A Book Made for a Queen: The Shaping of a Late Medieval Anthology Manuscript (B.N. fr. 24429)." In *The Whole Book: Cultural Perspectives on the Medieval Miscellany,* edited by Siegfried Wenzel, 123–173. Ann Arbor: University of Michigan Press, 1996.
———. "Polytextual Reading: The Meditative Reading of Real and Metaphorical Books." In *Orality and Literacy in the Middle Ages: Essays on a Conjunction and Its Consequences in Honour of D. H. Green,* edited by Mark Chinca and Christopher Young, 203–222. Turnhout: Brepols, 2005.
Hutchinson, Barbara. "Robert Grosseteste: The Role of Education in the Reform of Thirteenth Century English Society." *History of Education Quarterly* 5, no. 1 (1965): 26–39.
Innocent III. *Between God and Man: Six Sermons on the Priestly Office.* Translated by Corinne J. Vause and Frank C. Gardiner. Medieval Texts in Translation. Washington, D.C.: Catholic University of America Press, 2004.
———. *Regesta sive epistolae.* In Migne, *Patrologiae cursus completus: Series latina,* vol. 216, cols. 9A–992B.
———. *Sermones de diversis.* In Migne, *Patrologiae cursus completus: Series latina,* vol. 217, cols. 649B–690D.
Jacobus de Voragine. *The Golden Legend: Readings on the Saints,* vol. 1. Translated by William Granger Ryan. Princeton: Princeton University Press, 1993.
Jakobson, Roman. "Two Aspects of Language and Two Types of Aphasic Disturbances." In *On Language,* edited by Monique Monville-Burston, 115–133. Cambridge, Mass.: Harvard University Press, 1990.
James, M. R. *A Descriptive Catalogue of Fifty Manuscripts from the Collection of Henry Yates Thompson.* Cambridge, [Eng.]: University Press, 1898.
Jauss, Hans Robert, Erich Köhler, and Hans Ulrich Gumbrecht, eds. *Grundriss der romanischen Literaturen des Mittelalters.* 11 vols. Heidelberg: C. Winter Universitätsverlag, 1968–1993.
Jolly, Penny Howell. "Learned Reading, Vernacular Seeing: Jacques Daret's Presentation in the Temple." *Art Bulletin* 82, no. 3 (2000): 428–452.
Jung, Jacqueline E. "Beyond the Barrier: The Unifying Role of the Choir Screen in Gothic Churches." *Art Bulletin* 82, no. 4 (2000): 622–657.
Jungmann, Josef A. *Missarum sollemnia: Explication génétique de la messe romaine.* 3 vols. Théologie: Études publiées sous la direction de la Faculté de théologie S.J. de Lyon-Fourvière, 19–21. Paris: Aubier, 1952.
Katzenellenbogen, Adolf. *Allegories of the Virtues and Vices in Mediaeval Art from Early Christian Times to the Thirteenth Century.* Translated by Alan J. P. Crick. New York: W. W. Norton, 1964.
Kelly, J. N. D. *Early Christian Creeds.* London: Longmans Green, 1950.
Kennedy, V. L. "The Date of the Parisian Decree on the Elevation of the Host." *Mediaeval Studies* 8 (1946): 87–96.
———. "The Moment of Consecration and the Elevation of the Host." *Mediaeval Studies* 6 (1944): 121–150.
———. "Robert Courson on Penance." *Mediaeval Studies* 7 (1945): 291–336.
Kerby-Fulton, Kathryn, and Denise Louise Despres. *Iconography and the Professional Reader: The Politics of Book Production in the Douce Piers Plowman.* Medieval Cultures, 15. Minneapolis: University of Minnesota, 1999.
Kessler, Herbert L. "Gregory the Great and Image Theory in Northern Europe during the Twelfth and Thirteenth Centuries." In *A Companion to Medieval Art: Romanesque and Gothic in Northern Europe,* edited by Conrad Rudolph, 151–172. Malden, Mass.: Blackwell, 2006.
———. *Seeing Medieval Art.* Rethinking the Middle Ages, 1. Peterborough, Ont.: Broadview Press, 2004.
———. *Spiritual Seeing: Picturing God's Invisibility in Medieval Art.* Middle Ages Series. Philadelphia: University of Pennsylvania Press, 2000.
Knoch, Wendelin. *Die Einsetzung der Sakramente durch Christus: Eine Untersuchung zur Sakramententheologie der Frühscholastik von Anselm von Laon bis zu Wilhelm von Auxerre.* Beiträge zur Geschichte der Philosophie und Theologie des Mittelalters, n.F., 24. Münster: Aschendorff, 1983.
Knowles, M. D. "The Canterbury Election of 1205–6." *English Historical Review* 53, no. 210 (1938): 211–220.
Kosmer, Ellen. "Gardens of Virtue in the Middle Ages." *Journal of the Warburg and Courtauld Institutes* 41 (1978): 302–307.
———. "The 'noyous humoure of lecherie.'" *Art Bulletin* 57, no. 1 (1975): 1–8.

———. *A Study of the Style and Iconography of a Thirteenth-Century Somme le Roi (British Museum MS. Add. 54180) with a Consideration of Other Illustrated Somme Manuscripts of the Thirteenth-Century, Fourteenth-Century and Fifteenth-Century (Parts I–III).* PhD diss., Yale University, 1974.

Kramer, Susan R. "'We Speak to God with Our Thoughts': Abelard and the Implications of Private Communication with God." *Church History* 69, no. 1 (2000): 18–40.

Kratzke, Christine, and Uwe Albrecht, eds. *Mikroarchitektur im Mittelalter: Ein gattungsübergreifendes Phänomen zwischen Realität und Imagination: Beiträge der gleichnamigen Tagung im Germanischen Nationalmuseum Nürnberg vom 26. bis 29. Oktober 2005.* Leipzig: Kratzke, 2008.

Krone und Schleier: Kunst aus mittelalterlichen Frauenklöstern; Ruhrlandmuseum: Die frühen Klöster und Stifte 500–1200; Kunst-und Ausstellungshalle der Bundesrepublik Deutschland: Die Zeit der Orden 1200–1500. Munich: Hirmer, 2005.

Kumler, Aden. "*Faire translater, faire historier*: Charles V's *Bible historiale* and the Visual Rhetoric of Vernacular *Sapience*." *Studies in Iconography* 29 (2008): 90–135.

Kurmann, Peter. "Cathédrale miniature ou reliquaire monumental? L'architecture de la châsse de sainte Gertrude." In *Un trésor gothique: La châsse de Nivelles: Cologne, Schnütgen-Museum, 24 novembre 1995–11 février 1996: Paris, Musée national du moyen age, Thermes de Cluny, 12 mars–10 juin 1996,* 135–153. Paris: Réunion des musées nationaux, 1996.

Kuttner, Stephan. *Harmony from Dissonance: An Interpretation of Medieval Canon Law,* Wimmer Lecture 10. Latrobe, Pa.: Archabbey Press, 1960.

L'art au temps des rois maudits: Philippe le Bel et ses fils, 1285–1328: Paris, Galeries nationales du Grand Palais, 17 mars–29 juin 1998. Paris: Réunion des musées nationaux, 1998.

L'Engle, Susan. "Legal Iconography." In *Illuminating the Law: Legal Manuscripts in Cambridge Collections,* edited by Susan L'Engle and Robert Gibbs, 75–104. London: Harvey Miller, 2001.

———. "The Texts." In *Illuminating the Law: Legal Manuscripts in Cambridge Collections,* edited by Susan L'Engle and Robert Gibbs, 12–21. London: Harvey Miller, 2001.

L'Engle, Susan, and Robert Gibbs, eds. *Illuminating the Law: Legal Manuscripts in Cambridge Collections.* London: Harvey Miller, 2001.

Lamberts, Jef. "Liturgie et spiritualité de l'eucharistie au XIIIe siècle." In *Fête-Dieu (1246–1996),* edited by André Haquin, 81–95. Louvain-la-Neuve: Institut d'études médiévales de l'Université Catholique de Louvain, 1999.

Långfors, Arthur. "Notice du manuscrit français 9220 de la Bibliothèque nationale: Quatrains français sur le trône de Salomon, La vision de Saint Paul, vers latin de vie et de mort, etc." *Romania* 54 (1928): 413–426.

Langlois, Charles Victor. *La vie en France au moyen âge, du XIIe au milieu du XIVe siècle.* 4 vols. Paris: Hachette, 1924–1928.

Lausberg, Heinrich. *Der Hymnus "Veni Creator Spiritus."* Abhandlungen der Rheinisch-Westfälischen Akademie der Wissenschaften, 64. Opladen: Westdeutscher Verlag, 1979.

Le bibliophile français: Gazette illustrée des amateurs de livres, d'estampes et de haute curiosité, vol. 3. Paris: Librairie Bachelin-Deflorenne, 1869.

Le Goff, Jacques, Éric Palazzo, Jean-Claude Bonne, and Marie-Noël Colette. *Le sacre royal à l'époque de Saint Louis d'après le manuscrit latin 1246 de la BNF.* Le temps des images. Paris: Gallimard, 2001.

Lea, Henry Charles. *A History of Auricular Confession and Indulgences in the Latin Church.* 3 vols. London: Swan Sonnenschein, 1896.

Leclercq, Jean. "Le cloître est-il un prison?" *Revue d'ascétique et de mystique* 47, no. 4 (1971): 407–420.

Legge, Mary Dominica. *Anglo-Norman in the Cloisters: The Influence of the Orders upon Anglo-Norman Literature.* Edinburgh University Publications, Language and Literature, 2. Edinburgh: University Press, 1950.

———. *Anglo-Norman Literature and Its Background.* Oxford: Clarendon Press, 1963.

———. "John Pecham's *Jerarchie*." *Medium Aevum* 11 (1942): 77–84.

Lentes, Thomas. "'As far as the eye can see . . .': Rituals of Gazing in the Late Middle Ages." In *The Mind's Eye: Art and Theological Argument in the Middle Ages,* edited by Jeffrey F. Hamburger and Anne-Marie Bouché, 360–373. Princeton: Princeton University Press, 2006.

Lerer, Seth. "Medieval English Literature and the Idea of the Anthology." *PMLA* 118, no. 5 (2003): 1251–1267.

Leroquais, Victor. *Les psautiers, manuscrits latins des bibliothèques publiques de France,* vol. 1. Maçon: Protat frères, 1940–41.

———. *Les sacramentaires et les missels manuscrits des bibliothèques publiques de France.* 3 vols. Paris: n.p., 1924.

Lewis, Flora. "The Veronica: Image, Legend and Viewer." In *England in the Thirteenth Century: Proceedings of the 1984 Harlaxton Symposium,* edited by W. M. Ormrod, 100–106. Woodbridge, Eng.: Boydell Press, 1986.

Lewis, Gertrud Jaron. *By Women, for Women, about Women: The Sister-Books of Fourteenth-Century Germany.* Toronto: Pontifical Institute of Mediaeval Studies, 1996.

Lewis, Suzanne. "The Apocalypse of Isabella of France: Paris, Bibl. Nat. MS Fr. 13096." *Art Bulletin* 72 (1990): 224–260.

———. *The Art of Matthew Paris in the Chronica Majora.* California Studies in the History of Art, 21. Berkeley: University of California Press in collaboration with Corpus Christi College, Cambridge, 1987.

———. "Narrative." In *A Companion to Medieval Art: Romanesque and Gothic in Northern Europe,* edited by Conrad Rudolph, 86–105. Malden, Mass.: Blackwell, 2006.

———. *Reading Images: Narrative Discourse and Reception in the Thirteenth-Century Illuminated Apocalypse.* Cambridge: Cambridge University Press, 1995.

Little, A. G. "The Education of the Clergy: The Works of Friar John of Wales." In *Studies in English Franciscan history,* 158–192. Manchester: University Press; London: University Press; Longman's, Green, 1917.

Logemann, Cornelia. *Heilige Ordnungen: Die Bild-Räume der "Vie de Saint Denis" (1317) und die französische Buchmalerei des 14. Jahrhunderts.* Pictura et Poesis, 24. Cologne: Böhlau, 2009.

Longère, Jean. "Comment expliquer le symbole des apôtres? L'apport de quelques conciles et synodes médiévaux." In *Pensée, image et communication en Europe médiévale: À propos des stalles de Saint-Claude,* edited by Pierre Lacroix, Andrée Renon, Marie-Claude Mary, et al., 165–170. Besançon: ASPRODIC, 1993.

———. "La prédication et l'instruction des fidèles selon les conciles et les statuts synodaux depuis l'antiquité tardive jusqu'au XIIIe siècle." In *L'encadrement religieux des fidèles au moyen-age et jusqu'au Concile de Trente: La paroisse, le clergé, la pastorale, la dévotion,* 391–418. Paris: Ministère de l'éducation nationale; Éditions du Comité des Travaux historiques et scientifiques, 1985.

Lottin, Odon. *Psychologie et morale aux XIIe et XIIIe siècles.* 6 vols. Louvain: Abbaye du Mont César, 1942–1960.

Lowden, John. "Les rois et reines de France en tant que 'public' des Bibles moralisées: Une approche tangentielle à la question des liens entre les Bibles moralisées et les vitraux de la Sainte-Chapelle." In *La Sainte-Chapelle de Paris: Royaume de France ou Jerusalem céleste?:*

Actes du colloque (Paris, Collège de France, 2001), edited by Christine Hediger, 345–362. Turnhout: Brepols, 2007.

———. *The Making of the Bibles Moralisées.* 2 vols. University Park, Pa.: Pennsylvania State University Press, 2000.

———. "'Reading' Images and Texts in the *Bibles moralisées:* Images as Exegesis and the Exegesis of Images." In *Reading Images and Texts: Medieval Images and Texts as Forms of Communication: Papers from the Third Utrecht Symposium on Medieval Literacy, Utrecht, 7–9 December 2000,* edited by Mariëlle Hageman and Marco Mostert, 495–525. Turnhout: Brepols, 2005.

Lukken, Gerard. "Les transformations du rôle liturgique du peuple: La contribution de la sémiotique à l'histoire de la liturgie." In *Omnes Circumadstantes: Contributions towards a History of the Role of the People in the Liturgy: Presented to Herman Wegman on the Occasion of His Retirement from the Chair of the History of Liturgy and Theology in the Katholieke Theologische Universiteit Utrecht*, edited by Charles Caspers and Marc Schneiders, 15–30. Kampen: J. H. Kok, 1990.

Luscombe, D. E. *The School of Peter Abelard: The Influence of Abelard's Thought in the Early Scholastic Period.* Cambridge Studies in Medieval Life and Thought, n.s. 14. London: Cambridge University Press, 1969.

Lusignan, Serge. *La langue des rois au moyen age: Le français en France et en Angleterre.* Le noeud gordien. Paris: Presses universitaires de France, 2004.

———. "Langue française et société du XIIIe au XVe siècle." In *Nouvelle histoire de la langue francaise*, edited by Jacques Chaurand, 93–143. Paris: Editions du Seuil, 1999.

———. "Le Français et le Latin aux XIIIe–XIVe siècles: Pratique des langes et pensée linguistique." *Annales Économies Sociétés Civilisations* 42, no. 4 (1987): 955–967.

———. *Parler vulgairement: Les intellectuels et la langue française au XIIIe et XIVe siècles.* 2nd ed. Edited by Pierre Boglioni. Études médiévales. Montreal: Les Presses de l'Université de Montréal, 1987.

Mackie, Evelyn Anne. "Robert Grosseteste's Anglo-Norman Treatise on the Loss and Restoration of Creation, Commonly Known as *Le château d'amour:* An English Prose Translation." In *Robert Grosseteste and the Beginnings of a British Theological Tradition: Papers Delivered at the Grosseteste Colloquium Held at the Greyfriars, Oxford on 3rd July 2002,* edited by Maura O'Carroll, 151–179. Roma: Istituto storico dei Cappuccini, 2003.

———. *Robert Grosseteste's Chasteu d'amur: A Text in Context.* PhD diss., University of Toronto, 2002.

———. "Scribal Intervention and the Question of Audience: Editing *Le château d'amour.*" In *Editing Robert Grosseteste: Papers Given at the Thirty-Sixth Annual Conference on Editorial Problems, University of Toronto, 3–4 November 2000,* edited by Joseph Goering and Evelyn A. Mackie, 61–77. Toronto: University of Toronto Press, 2003.

Macy, Gary. "Berengar's Legacy as Heresiarch." In *Treasures from the Storeroom,* 59–80.

———. "The 'Dogma of Transubstantiation' in the Middle Ages." In *Treasures from the Storeroom,* 81–120.

———. "The Eucharist and Popular Religiosity." In *Treasures from the Storeroom,* 172–195.

———. "The "Invention" of Clergy and Laity in the Twelfth Century." In *A Sacramental Life: A Festschrift Honoring Bernard Cooke,* edited by Michael Horace Barnes and William P. Roberts, 117–135. Milwaukee, Wis.: Marquette University Press, 2003.

———. "Reception of the Eucharist According to the Theologians: A Case of Diversity in the 13th and 14th Centuries." In *Treasures from the Storeroom,* 36–58.

———. "The Theological Fate of Berengar's Oath of 1059: Interpreting a Blunder Become Tradition." In *Treasures from the Storeroom,* 20–35.

———. *The Theologies of the Eucharist in the Early Scholastic Period: A Study of the Salvific Function of the Sacrament According to the Theologians, c. 1080–c. 1220.* Oxford: Clarendon Press; New York: Oxford University Press, 1984.

———. *Treasures from the Storeroom: Medieval Religion and the Eucharist.* Collegeville, Minn.: Liturgical Press, 1999.

Maisonneuve, Henri. *La morale chrétienne d'après les conciles des Xe et XIe siècles.* Analecta mediaevalia namurcensia, 15. Louvain: Editions Nauwelaerts; Lille: Librairie Giard, 1963.

Mâle, Emile. *L'art religieux de la fin du moyen age en France: Étude sur l'iconographie du moyen âge et sur ses sources d'inspiration.* 2nd ed. Paris: Librairie Armand Colin, 1922.

———. *L'art religieux du XIIIe siècle en France: Étude sur l'iconographie du moyen âge et sur ses sources d'inspiration.* Paris: Ernest Leroux, 1898.

Malone, Carolyn Marino. *Façade as Spectacle: Ritual and Ideology at Wells Cathedral.* Studies in Medieval and Reformation Traditions, 102. Leiden: Brill, 2004.

Mann, Jill. "Allegorical Buildings in Mediaeval Literature." *Medium Aevum* 63, no. 2 (1994): 191–210.

Mansfield, Mary C. *The Humiliation of Sinners: Public Penance in Thirteenth-Century France.* Ithaca: Cornell University Press, 1995.

Mariaux, Pierre Alain. "'Faire Dieu': Quelques remarques sur les relations entre confection eucharistique et création d'image (IXe–XIIe siècles)." In *Asthetik des Unsichtbaren: Bildtheorie und Bildgebrauch in der Vormoderne,* edited by David Ganz, Thomas Lentes, and Georg Henkel, 95–111. [Berlin]: Reimer, 2004.

Marks, Richard. *Image and Devotion in Late Medieval England.* Stroud: Sutton, 2004.

Maury, Jean, Marie-Madeleine Gauthier, et al. *Limousin roman.* 3rd ed. La nuit des temps, 11. La Pierre-qui-Vire (Yonne): Zodiaque, 1990.

McGowan, Andrew Brian. "'Is There a Liturgical Text in This Gospel?': Institution Narratives and Their Early Interpretive Communities." *Journal of Biblical Literature* 118, no. 1 (1999): 73–87.

McNeill, John Thomas, and Helena Margaret Gamer. *Medieval Handbooks of Penance: A Translation of the Principal "Libri Poenitentiales" and Selections from Related Documents.* Records of Western Civilization. 1938; reprint, New York: Columbia University Press, 1990.

Mearns, James. *The Canticles of the Christian Church, Eastern and Western, in Early and Medieval Times.* Cambridge, [Eng.]: University Press, 1914.

Mellinkoff, Ruth. *The Horned Moses in Medieval Art and Thought.* California Studies in the History of Art, 14. Berkeley: University of California Press, 1970.

Melnikas, Anthony. *The Corpus of the Miniatures in the Manuscripts of Decretum Gratiani.* 3 vols. Corpus picturarum minutarum quae in codicibus manuscriptis iuris continentur, t. 1. Rome: [Institutum Gratianum]; Columbus, Ohio: Index of Juridical and Civic Iconography (distributor), 1975.

Messenger, Ruth Ellis. "Processional Hymnody in the Later Middle Ages." *Transactions and Proceedings of the American Philological Association* 81 (1950): 185–199.

Mettinger, Tryggve N. D. *No Graven Image? Israelite Aniconism in Its Ancient Near Eastern Context.* Coniectanea biblica. Old Testament Series, 42. Stockholm: Almqvist & Wiksell International, 1995.

Mews, Constant J., ed. *Listen, Daughter: The Speculum Virginum and the Formation of Religious Women in the Middle Ages.* New Middle Ages. Basingstoke: Palgrave, 2001.

Meyer, Paul. "Trois nouveaux manuscrits des sermons français de Maurice de Sully." *Romania* 28 (1899): 245–268.

Meyvaert, Paul. "The Medieval Monastic Claustrum." *Gesta* 12, no. 1-2 (1973): 53-59.

Michael, Michael A. "The Harnhulle Psalter-Hours: An Early Fourteenth-Century English Illuminated Manuscript at Downside Abbey." *Journal of the British Archaeological Association* 134 (1981): 81-99.

———. "Oxford, Cambridge and London: Towards a Theory for 'Grouping' Gothic Manuscripts." *Burlington Magazine* 130 (1988): 107-115.

———. "Urban Production of Manuscript Books and the Role of the University Towns." In *The Cambridge History of the Book in Britain*, edited by Nigel Morgan and Rodney M. Thomson, 168-194. Cambridge: Cambridge University Press, 2008.

Michaud-Quantin, Pierre. *Sommes de casuistique et manuels de confession au moyen âge (XII-XVI siècles).* Analecta mediaevalia Namurcensia, 13. Louvain: Nauwelaerts, 1962.

Migne, Jacques-Paul, ed. *Patrologiae cursus completus: Series latina.* 221 vols. Paris: Migne, 1844-1865.

Millar, Eric George. *An Illuminated Manuscript of La Somme Le Roy Attributed to the Miniaturist Honoré.* Oxford: Printed for the Roxburghe Club, 1953.

———. *Souvenir de l'exposition de manuscrits français à peintures organisée à la Grenville library (British Museum) en janvier-mars 1932: Étude concernant les 65 manuscrits exposés.* Paris: Société française de reproductions de manuscrits à peintures, 1933.

Millett, Bella. "*Ancrene Wisse* and the Book of Hours." In *Writing Religious Women: Female Spiritual and Textual Practices in Late Medieval England*, edited by Denis Renevey and Christiania Whitehead, 21-40. Cardiff: University of Wales Press, 2000.

———. "*Ancrene Wisse* and the Conditions of Confession." *English Studies* 80, no. 3 (1999): 193-215.

Monfrin, Jacques. "Des premiers apparitions du français dans les manuscrits à la constitution des grands receuils des XIIIe-XIVe siècles." In *La Présentation du livre: Actes du colloque de Paris X—Nanterre (4, 5, 6 décembre 1985)*, edited by Emmanuèle Baumgartner and Nicole Boulestreau, 295-311. Nanterre: Centre de recherches du Dép. de français de Paris X—Nanterre, 1987.

Moore, John C., ed. *Pope Innocent III and His World.* Aldershot, Eng.: Ashgate (prepared under the auspices of Hofstra University), 1999.

Morgan, Nigel J. *Early Gothic Manuscripts: Part 1, 1190-1250.* Survey of Manuscripts Illuminated in the British Isles, 4. London: Harvey Miller; New York: Oxford University Press, 1982.

———. *The Lambeth Apocalypse, Manuscript 209 in Lambeth Palace Library: A Critical Study.* London: Harvey Miller, 1990.

Morse, Ruth. *Truth and Convention in the Middle Ages: Rhetoric, Representation, and Reality.* Cambridge: Cambridge University Press, 1991.

Mother Mary Philomena. "St. Edmund of Abingdon's Meditations before the Canonical Hours." *Ephemerides Liturgicae* 3 (1964): 33-57.

Mulchahey, M. Michèle. *"First the Bow Is Bent in Study—": Dominican Education before 1350.* Studies and Texts, 132. Toronto: Pontifical Institute of Mediaeval Studies, 1998.

Murray, Alexander. "Confession before 1215." *Transactions of the Royal Historical Society*, 6th ser., vol. 3 (1993): 51-81.

———. "Counselling in Medieval Confession." In *Handling Sin: Confession in the Middle Ages*, edited by Peter Biller and A. J. Minnis, 63-77. Woodbridge, Eng.: York Medieval Press, 1998.

Murray, Jacqueline. "The Absent Penitent: The Cure of Women's Souls and Confessors' Manuals in Thirteenth-Centry England." In *Women, the Book, and the Godly: Selected Proceedings of the St. Hilda's Conference, 1993*, edited by Lesley Smith and Jane H. M. Taylor, 13-25. Woodbridge, Eng.: D. S. Brewer, 1995.

Naughton, Joan. "Friars and Their Books at Saint Louis de Poissy, a Dominican Foundation for Nuns." *Scriptorium* 52 (1998): 83-102.

Newman, Barbara. *From Virile Woman to WomanChrist: Studies in Medieval Religion and Literature.* Middle Ages Series. Philadelphia: University of Pennsylvania Press, 1995.

Nichols, Ann Elijenholm. "The Bread of Heaven: Foretaste or Foresight?" In *The Iconography of Heaven*, edited by Clifford Davidson, 40-68. Kalamazoo, Mich.: Medieval Institute Publications, 1994.

———. "The Etiquette of Pre-Reformation Confession in East Anglia." *Sixteenth Century Journal* 17, no. 2 (1986): 145-163.

Norman, Joanne S. *Metamorphoses of an Allegory: The Iconography of the Psychomachia in Medieval Art.* American University Studies. Series 9, History, 29. New York: P. Lang, 1988.

Nörr, Knut Wolfgang. "Institutional Foundations of the New Jurisprudence." In *Renaissance and Renewal in the Twelfth Century*, edited by Robert Louis Benson, Giles Constable, and Carol Dana Lanham, 324-338. Cambridge, Mass.: Harvard University Press, 1982.

O'Reilly, Jennifer. *Studies in the Iconography of the Virtues and Vices in the Middle Ages.* Outstanding Theses in the Fine Arts from British Universities. New York: Garland, 1988.

Oediger, Friedrich Wilhelm. *Über die Bildung der Geistlichen im späten Mittelalter.* Studien und Texte zur Geistesgeschichte des Mittelalters, 2. Leiden: Brill, 1953.

Oliver, Judith. *Gothic Manuscript Illumination in the Diocese of Liège (c. 1250-c. 1330).* 2 vols. Louvain: Uitgeverij Peeters, 1988.

———. "Image et dévotion: Le rôle de l'art dans l'institution de la Fête-Dieu." In *Fête-Dieu (1246-1996)*, edited by André Haquin, 153-172. Louvain-la-Neuve: Institut d'études médiévales de l'Université Catholique de Louvain, 1999.

Omont, Henri Auguste, ed. *Catalogue général des manuscrits français: Vol. 1, Nouvelles acquisitions françaises, Tome II, Nos. 3061-6500.* Paris: Ernest Leroux, 1900.

Openshaw, K. M. "Weapons in the Daily Battle: Images of the Conquest of Evil in the Early Medieval Psalter." *Art Bulletin* 75, no. 1 (1993): 17-38.

Osborne, Thomas M. *Love of Self and Love of God in Thirteenth-Century Ethics.* Notre Dame, Ind.: University of Notre Dame Press, 2005.

Ott, Ludwig. "Das Opusculum des hl. Thomas von Aquin *De forma absolutionis* in dogmengeschichtlicher Betrachtung." In *Festschrift Eduard Eichmann zum 70. Geburtstag: Dargebracht von seinen Freunden und Schülern in Verbindung mit Wilhelm Laforet*, edited by Martin Grabmann and Karl Hofmann, 99-135. Paderborn: Schöningh, 1940.

Oury, Guy. "Le *De claustro animae* de Jean, prieur de Saint-Jean-des-Vignes." *Revue d'ascétique et de mystique* 40, no. 4 (1964): 427-442.

Pächt, Otto, and J. J. G. Alexander. *Illuminated Manuscripts in the Bodleian Library, Oxford*, vol. 3. Oxford: Clarendon Press, 1973.

Palazzo, Éric. "Foi et croyance au moyen age: Les médiations liturgiques." *Annales, Histoire, Sciences Sociales* 53, no. 6 (1998): 1131-1154.

Palmer, Nigel F. *Zisterzienser und ihre Bücher: Die mittelalterliche Bibliotheksgeschichte von Kloster Eberbach im Rheingau unter besonderer Berücksichtigung der in Oxford und London aufbewahrten Handschriften.* Regensburg: Schnell & Steiner, 1998.

Pantin, W. A. *The English Church in the Fourteenth Century.* Pbk. ed. Notre Dame, Ind.: University of Notre Dame Press, 1963.

Paris, Paulin, ed. *Les manuscrits françois de la Bibliothèque du roi: Leur histoire et celle des textes allemands, anglois, hollandois, italiens, espagnols de la même collection*, vol. 3. Paris: Techener, 1840.

Parkes, M. B. "The Literacy of the Laity." In *The Mediaeval World*, edited by David Daiches and Anthony Thorlby, 555-577. London: Aldus Books, 1973.

Parsons, John Carmi. "Of Queens, Courts, and Books: Reflections on the Literary Patronage of Thirteenth-Century Plantagenet Queens." In *The Cultural Patronage of Medieval Women,* edited by June Hall McCash, 175–201. Athens: University of Georgia Press, 1996.

Pearson, Karl. *Die Fronica: Ein Beitrag zur Geschichte des Christusbildes im Mittelalter.* Strassburg: K. J. Trübner, 1887.

Peter Lombard. *Collectanea in Paulum Continuatio: In Epistolam ad Hebraeos.* In Migne, *Patrologiae cursus completus: Series latina,* vol. 192, cols. 399A–520A.

———. *The Sentences: Book 3, On the Incarnation of the Word.* Translated by Giulio Silano. Mediaeval Sources in Translation, 45. Toronto: Pontifical Institute of Mediaeval Studies, 2007.

———. *Sententiae in IV libris distinctae.* 3rd ed. 3 vols. Spicilegium Bonaventurianum, 4, 5. Grottaferrata: Editiones Collegii S. Bonaventurae ad Claras Aquas, 1971–1981.

Petrus Blesensis. *De duodecim utilitatibus tribulationis.* In Migne, *Patrologiae cursus completus: Series latina,* vol. 207, cols. 989A–1006B.

Petrus Cantor. *Summa de sacramentis et animae consiliis: Premère partie.* Edited by Jean Albert Dugauquier. Analecta mediaevalia namurcensia, 4. Louvain: Nauwelaerts, 1954.

Pickering, O. S. "Some Similarities between Queen Mary's Psalter and the Northern Passion." *Journal of the Warburg and Courtauld Institutes* 35 (1972): 135–144.

Pierre de Peckham. *La lumere as lais by Pierre d'Abernon of Fetcham.* Edited by Glynn Hesketh. 3 vols. Anglo-Norman Texts, 56–58. London: Anglo-Norman Text Society from Birbeck College, 1996–2000.

Pinder, Janice M. "The Cloister and the Garden: Gendered Images of Religious Life from the Twelfth and Thirteenth Centuries." In *Listen, Daughter: The Speculum Virginum and the Formation of Religious Women in the Middle Ages,* edited by Constant J. Mews, 159–179. Basingstoke: Palgrave, 2001.

Pontal, Odette, ed. *Les statuts synodaux français du XIIIe siècle: Tome 1, Les statuts de Paris et le synodal de l'Ouest (XIIIe siècle).* Collection de documents inédits sur l'histoire de France; Série in-8o, 9. Paris: Bibliothèque nationale, 1971.

———, ed. *Les statuts synodaux français du XIIIe siècle: Tome 2, Les statuts de 1230 à 1260.* Collection de documents inédits sur l'histoire de France; Série in-8o, 15. Paris: Bibliothèque nationale, 1983.

Poschmann, Bernhard. *Penance and the Anointing of the Sick.* Translated by Francis Courtney. New York: Herder and Herder, 1964.

Postles, David. "Lamps, Lights and Layfolk: 'Popular' Devotion before the Black Death." *Journal of Medieval History* 25, no. 2 (1999): 97–114.

Powell, Morgan. *The Mirror and the Woman: Instruction for Religious Women and the Emergence of Vernacular Poetics, 1120–1250.* PhD diss., Princeton University, 1997.

———. "The *Speculum virginum* and the Audio-Visual Poetics of Women's Religious Instruction." In *Listen, Daughter: The Speculum Virginum and the Formation of Religious Women in the Middle Ages,* edited by Constant J. Mews, 111–135. Basingstoke: Palgrave, 2001.

Powicke, F. M., and C. R. Cheney, eds. *Councils & Synods: Vol. II, A.D. 1205–1313; Part I, 1205–1265.* Oxford: Clarendon Press, 1964.

———, eds. *Councils & Synods: Vol. II, A.D. 1205–1313; Part II, 1265–1313.* Oxford: Clarendon Press, 1964.

Ransom, Carol Lynn. *Cultivating the Orchard: A Franciscan Program of Devotion and Penance in the Verger de Soulas (Paris, Bibliothèque nationale de France, fr. 9220).* PhD diss., University of Texas at Austin, 2001.

Ransom, Lynn. "Innovation and Identity: A Franciscan Program of Illumination in the *Verger de soulas* (Paris, Bibliothèque Nationale de France, Ms. fr. 9220)." In *Insights and Interpretations: Studies in Celebration of the Eighty-Fifth Anniversary of the Index of Christian Art,* edited by Colum Hourihane, 85–105. Princeton: Index of Christian Art, Department of Art and Archaeology, Princeton University, in association with Princeton University Press, 2002.

———. "The *Speculum theologie* and Its Readership: Considering the Manuscript Evidence." *Papers of the Bibliographical Society of America* 93 (1999): 461–483.

Reidemeister, Johann. *Superbia und Narziss: Personifikation und Allegorie in Miniaturen mittelalterlicher Handschriften.* Ars nova. Turnhout: Brepols, 2006.

Reiff, Daniel D. "Viollet le Duc and Historic Restoration: The West Portals of Notre-Dame." *Journal of the Society of Architectural Historians* 30, no. 1 (1971): 17–30.

Resnick, Irven M. "Idols and Images: Early Definitions and Controversies." *Sobornost* 7, no. 2 (1985): 35–51.

Rice, Nicole R. *Lay Piety and Religious Discipline in Middle English Literature.* Cambridge: Cambridge University Press, 2008.

———. "Spiritual Ambition and the Translation of the Cloister: *The Abbey* and *The Charter of the Holy Ghost.*" *Viator* 33 (2002): 222–260.

Robertson, D. W., Jr. "The Cultural Tradition of Handlyng Synne." *Speculum* 22, no. 2 (1947): 162–185.

———. "A Note on the Classical Origin of 'Circumstances' in the Medieval Confessional." *Studies in Philology* 43 (1946): 6–14.

Roest, Bert. *Franciscan Literature of Religious Instruction before the Council of Trent.* Studies in the History of Christian Traditions. Leiden: Brill, 2004.

———. *A History of Franciscan Education (c. 1210–1517).* Education and Society in the Middle Ages and Renaissance, 11. Leiden: Brill, 2000.

Rosier-Catach, Irène. *La parole efficace: Signe, rituel, sacré.* Paris: Éditions du seuil (avec le concours du Centre national du livre), 2004.

Rothwell, William. "The Role of French in Thirteenth-Century England." *Bulletin of the John Rylands Library* 58 (1975): 445–466.

Rouse, Richard H., and Mary A. Rouse. *Manuscripts and Their Makers: Commercial Book Producers in Medieval Paris, 1200–1500.* 2 vols. Turnhout: Harvey Miller, 2000.

Rubin, Miri. *Corpus Christi: The Eucharist in Late Medieval Culture.* Cambridge: Cambridge University Press, 1991.

———. "What Did the Eucharist Mean to Thirteenth-Century Villagers?" In *Thirteenth Century England IV: Proceedings of the Newcastle upon Tyne Conference 1991,* edited by P. R. Coss and S. D. Lloyd, 47–55. Woodbridge, Eng.: Boydell Press, 1991.

Ruh, Kurt. "Das geistliche Haus." In *Die deutsche Literatur des Mittelalters: Verfasserlexikon,* edited by Wolfgang Stammler, Karl Langosch, and Kurt Ruh, 1154–1167. Berlin: De Gruyter, 1980.

Saenger, Paul. "Books of Hours and the Reading Habits of the Later Middle Ages." In *The Culture of Print: Power and the Uses of Print in Early Modern Europe,* edited by Roger Chartier, 141–173. Princeton: Princeton University Press, 1989.

Salmon, Pierre. "Psautiers abrégés du moyen âge." In *Analecta liturgica: Extraits des manuscrits liturgiques de la Bibliothéque vaticane: Contribution à l'histoire de la priére chrétienne,* 67–119. Città del Vaticano: Biblioteca apostolica vaticana, 1974.

Sandler, Lucy Freeman. "Face to Face with God: A Pictorial Image of the Beatific Vision." In *England in the Fourteenth Century: Proceedings of the 1985 Harlaxton Symposium,* edited by W. M. Ormrod, 224–235. Woodbridge, Eng.: Boydell Press, 1986.

———. *Gothic Manuscripts, 1285–1385.* 2 parts. Survey of Manuscripts Illuminated in the British Isles, 5. London: Harvey Miller; Oxford: Oxford University Press, 1986.

———. "The Images of Words in English Gothic Psalters." In *Studies in the Illustration of the*

Psalter, edited by Brendan Cassidy and Rosemary Muir Wright, 67–86. Stamford: Shaun Tyas, 2000.

———. *The Psalter of Robert de Lisle in the British Library.* London: Harvey Miller; New York: Oxford University Press, 1999.

Sauerländer, Willibald. "Die Kunstgeschichtliche Stellung der Westportale von Notre-Dame in Paris: Ein Beitrag zur Genesis des hochgotischen Stils in der französischen Skulptur." *Marburger Jahrbuch für Kunstwissenschaft* 17 (1959): 1–56.

———. *Gothic Sculpture in France, 1140–1270.* Translated by Janet Sondheimer. New York: H. N. Abrams, 1973.

Saxl, Fritz. "A Spiritual Encyclopaedia of the Later Middle Ages." *Journal of the Warburg and Courtauld Institutes* 5 (1942): 82–142.

Schmitt, Jean-Claude. "Du bon usage du 'Credo.'" In *Faire croire: Modalités de la diffusion et de la réception des messages religieux du XIIe au XVe siecle: Table ronde, Rome, 22–23 juin 1979,* 337–361. Collection de l'École française de Rome, 51. Rome: École française de Rome, 1981.

———. "Entre le text et l'image: Les gestes de la prière de saint Dominique." In *Persons in Groups: Social Behavior as Identity Formation in Medieval and Renaissance Europe,* edited by Richard C. Trexler, 195–220. Binghamton, N.Y.: Medieval & Renaissance Texts & Studies, 1985.

———. "Imago: De l'image à l'imaginaire." In *L'image: Fonctions et usages des images dans l'Occident médiéval: Actes du 6e "International Workshop on Medieval Societies," Centro Ettore Majorana (Erice, Sicile, 17–23 octobre 1992),* edited by Jérôme Baschet and Jean Claude Schmitt, 29–37. Paris: Le Léopard d'Or, 1996.

———. "L'imagination efficace." In *Imagination und Wirklichkeit: Zum Verhältnis von mentalen und realen Bildern in der Kunst der frühen Neuzeit,* edited by Klaus Krüger and Alessandro Nova, 13–20. Mainz am Rhein: Philipp von Zabern, 2000.

———. *La raison des gestes dans l'Occident médiéval.* Bibliothèque des histoires. Paris: Gallimard, 1990.

———. "Les images classificatrices." *Bibliothèque de l'École des Chartes* 147 (1989): 311–341.

Schoenen, Anno. "Aedificatio: Zum Verständnis eines Glaubenswortes in Kult und Schrift." In *Enkainia: Gesammelte Arbeiten zum 800 jährigen Weihegedächtnis der Abteikirche Maria Laach am 24. August 1956,* edited by Hilarius Emonds, 14–29. Düsseldorf: Patmos-Verlag, 1956.

Scott, Kathleen L. *Tradition and Innovation in Later Medieval English Manuscripts.* London: British Library, 2007.

Seidel, Linda. *Songs of Glory: The Romanesque Facades of Aquitaine.* Chicago: University of Chicago Press, 1981.

Seyfarth, Jutta, ed. *Speculum virginum.* Corpus Christianorum. Continuatio Mediaevalis, 5. Turnhout: Brepols, 1990.

Shailor, Barbara A. "A Cataloger's View." In *The Whole Book: Cultural Perspectives on the Medieval Miscellany,* edited by Stephen G. Nichols and Siegfried Wenzel, 153–167. Ann Arbor: University of Michigan Press, 1996.

Sheingorn, Pamela. "The Te Deum Altarpiece and the Iconography of Praise." In *Early Tudor England: Proceedings of the 1987 Harlaxton Symposium,* edited by Daniel Williams, 171–182. Woodbridge, Eng.: Boydell Press, 1989.

Sherman, Claire Richter. *Imaging Aristotle: Verbal and Visual Representation in Fourteenth-Century France.* Berkeley: University of California Press, 1995.

Shinners, John Raymond. "University Study Licenses and Clerical Education in the Diocese of Norwich, 1325–35." *History of Education Quarterly* 28, no. 3 (1988): 387–410.

Shinners, John Raymond, and William J. Dohar, eds. *Pastors and the Care of Souls in Medieval England.* Notre Dame Texts in Medieval Culture, 4. Notre Dame: University of Notre Dame Press, 1998.

Short, Ian. "L'avènement du texte vernaculaire: La mise en receuil." In *Théories et pratiques de l'écriture au moyen âge: Actes du Colloque Palais du Luxembourg—Senat, 5 et 6 mars 1987,* edited by Emmanuèle Baumgartner and Christiane Marchello-Nizia, 11–24. Nanterre: Centre de Recherches du Département de français de Paris X; Saint-Cloud: Centre Espace-Temps-Histoire de l'E.N.S. Fontenay, 1988.

Simmons, Thomas Frederick, and Henry Edward Nolloth, eds. *The Lay Folks' Catechism, or The English and Latin Versions of Archbishop Thoresby's Instruction for the People.* Early English Text Society, Original Series, 118. Millwood: Kraus Reprint, 1972.

Simons, Walter. *Cities of Ladies: Beguine Communities in the Medieval Low Countries, 1200–1565.* Middle Ages Series. Philadelphia: University of Pennsylvania Press, 2001.

Smith, Kathryn A. *Art, Identity, and Devotion in Fourteenth-Century England: Three Women and Their Books of Hours.* London: British Library and University of Toronto Press, 2003.

———. "Book, Body, and the Construction of the Self in the Taymouth Hours." In *Negotiating Community and Difference in Medieval Europe: Gender, Power, Patronage, and the Authority of Religion in Latin Christendom,* edited by Katherine Allen Smith and Scott Wells, 173–197. Leiden: Brill, 2009.

———. "Chivalric Narratives and Devotional Experience in the Taymouth Hours." In *Negotiating Secular and Sacred in Medieval Art: Christian, Islamic, and Buddhist,* edited by Alicia Walker and Amanda Luyster, 17–54. Farnham, Eng.: Ashgate, 2009.

———. "History, Typology and Homily: The Joseph Cycle in the Queen Mary Psalter." *Gesta* 32, no. 2 (1993): 147–159.

———. "The Neville of Hornby Hours and the Design of Literate Devotion." *Art Bulletin* 81, no. 1 (1999): 72–92.

Sneddon, C. R. "On the Creation of the Old French Bible." *Nottingham Medieval Studies* 46 (2002): 25–44.

Spinks, Bryan D. *The Sanctus in the Eucharistic Prayer.* Cambridge: Cambridge University Press, 1991.

Stahl, Harvey. "Heaven in View: The Place of the Elect in an Illuminated Book of Hours." In *Last Things: Death and the Apocalypse in the Middle Ages,* edited by Caroline Walker Bynum and Paul H. Freedman, 205–232. Philadelphia: University of Pennsylvania Press, 2000.

Stanton, Anne Rudloff. "From Eve to Bathsheba and Beyond: Motherhood in the Queen Mary Psalter." In *Women and the Book: Assessing the Visual Evidence,* edited by Lesley Smith and Jane H. M. Taylor, 172–189. London: British Library; Toronto: University of Toronto Press, 1997.

———. "Isabelle of France and Her Manuscripts, 1308–58." In *Capetian Women,* edited by Kathleen Nolan, 225–252. New York: Palgrave Macmillan, 2003.

———. "*La Genealogye Comence:* Kinship and Difference in the *Queen Mary Psalter.*" *Studies in Iconography* 17 (1996): 177–214.

———. "Notes on the Codicology of the Queen Mary Psalter." *Scriptorium* 49, no. 2 (1995): 250–262.

———. *The Queen Mary Psalter: A Study of Affect and Audience.* Transactions of the American Philosophical Society, 91.6. Philadelphia: American Philosophical Society, 2001.

Stock, Brian. *The Implications of Literacy: Written Language and Models of Interpretation in the Eleventh and Twelfth Centuries.* Princeton: Princeton University Press, 1983.

Swanson, R. N. "Medieval Liturgy as Theatre: The Props." In *The Church and the Arts: Papers Read at the 1990 Summer Meeting and the 1991 Winter Meeting of the Ecclesiastical History Society,* edited by Diana Wood, 239–253. Oxford: Published for the Ecclesiastical History Society by Blackwell Publishers, 1992.

———. "The Origins of the *Lay Folks' Catechism.*" *Medium Aevum* 60, no. 1 (1991): 92–100.
———. "Universities, Graduates and Benefices in Later Medieval England." *Past and Present* 106 (1985): 28–61.
Tachau, Katherine H. "God's Compass and 'Vana Curiositas': Scientific Study in the Old French 'Bible Moralisée.'" *Art Bulletin* 80 (1998): 7–33.
Tanner, Norman P., ed. *Decrees of the Ecumenical Councils.* 2 vols. London: Sheed & Ward; Washington, D. C.: Georgetown University Press, 1990.
Taylor, Andrew. "Manual to Miscellany: Stages in the Commercial Copying of Vernacular Literature in England." *The Yearbook of English Studies* 33 (2003): 1–17.
Teetaert, Amédée. *La confession aux laïques dans l'Eglise latine depuis le VIIIe jusqu'au XIVe siècle: Étude de théologie positive.* Universitas catholica lovaniensis. Dissertationes ad gradum magistri in Facultate theologica consequendum conscriptae, ser. 2, t. 17. Wetteren: J. de Meester et fils; Paris: J. Gabalda, 1926.
Tentler, Thomas N. *Sin and Confession on the Eve of the Reformation.* Princeton: Princeton University Press, 1977.
———. "The Summa for Confessors as an Instrument of Social Control." In *The Pursuit of Holiness in Late Medieval and Renaissance Religion: Papers from the University of Michigan Conference,* edited by Charles Edward Trinkaus and Heiko Augustinus Oberman, 103–126. Leiden: Brill, 1974.
Thompson, Henry Yates. *Illustrations from One Hundred Manuscripts in the Library of Henry Yates Thompson.* 7 vols. London: Printed at the Chiswick Press, 1907–1918.
Thurston, Herbert. "The Origin of the Elevation." *Month* 148 (1926): 254–258.
Tillmann, Helene. *Pope Innocent III.* Translated by Walter Sax. Europe in the Middle Ages, 12. Amsterdam: Distributed by Elsevier North-Holland, 1980.
Timmermann, Achim. *Real Presence: Sacrament Houses and the Body of Christ, c. 1270–1600.* Architectura medii aevi. Turnhout: Brepols, 2009.
Tobler, Adolf, and Erhard Lommatzsch. *Altfranzösisches Wörterbuch,* vol. 2. Wiesbaden: Franz Steiner Verlag, 1915; reprint, 1989.
Toussaint, Gia. *Das Passional der Kunigunde von Böhmen: Bildrhetorik und Spiritualität.* Paderborn: Schöningh, 2003.
Trexler, Richard C. "Legitimating Prayer Gestures in the Twelfth Century: The *De Penitentia* of Peter the Chanter." *History and Anthropology* 1, no. 1 (1984): 97–126.
Trottmann, Christian. *La vision béatifique: Des disputes scolastiques à sa definition par Benoît XII.* Bibliothèque des écoles françaises d'Athènes et de Rome, fasc. 289. Rome: École française de Rome, 1995.
Tyrer, J. W. *Historical Survey of Holy Week, Its Services and Ceremonial.* Alcuin Club Collections, 29. London: Oxford University Press, 1932.
Un trésor gothique: La châsse de Nivelles: Cologne, Schnütgen-Museum, 24 novembre 1995–11 février 1996: Paris, Musée national du moyen age, Thermes de Cluny, 12 mars–10 juin 1996. Paris: Réunion des musées nationaux, 1996.
Vale, Malcolm. *The Princely Court: Medieval Courts and Culture in North-West Europe, 1270–1380.* Oxford: Oxford University Press, 2001.
Van Engen, John. "The Christian Middle Ages as an Historiographical Problem." *American Historical Review* 91, no. 3 (1986): 519–552.
———. "Faith as a Concept of Order in Medieval Christendom." In *Belief in History: Innovative Approaches to European and American Religion,* edited by Thomas A. Kselman, 19–67. Notre Dame: University of Notre Dame Press, 1991.
Vincent-Cassy, Mireille. "Quelques réflexions sur l'envie et la jalousie en France au XIVe siècle." In *Études sur l'histoire de la pauvreté: moyen age—XVIe siècle,* edited by Michel Mollat, 487–503. Paris: Publications de la Sorbonne, 1974.
———. "Un modèle français: Les cavalcades des sept péchés capitaux dans les églises rurales de la fin du XVe siècle." In *Artistes, artisans et production artistique au moyen age: Colloque international, Centre national de la recherche scientifique, Université de Rennes II, Haute-Bretagne, 2–6 mai 1983,* edited by Xavier Barral i Altet, 461–487. Paris: Picard, 1990.
Vitzthum, Georg. *Die Pariser Miniaturmalerei von der Zeit des hl. Ludwig bis zu Philipp von Valois und ihr Verhältnis zur Malerei in Nordwesteuropa.* Leipzig: Quelle & Meyer, 1907.
Vogel, Cyrille. *Les "Libri paenitentiales."* Typologie des sources du moyen age occidental, fasc. 27. Turnhout: Brepols, 1978.
Voronova, Tamara Pavlovna, and Alexander Sterligov. *Western European Illuminated Manuscripts of the 8th to the 16th Centuries in the National Library of Russia, St. Petersburg: France, Spain, England, Germany, Italy, the Netherlands.* Bournemouth: Parkstone Press; St. Petersburg: Aurora, 1996.
Walters, Barbara R., Vincent J. Corrigan, and Peter T. Ricketts. *The Feast of Corpus Christi.* University Park, Pa.: Pennsylvania State University Press, 2006.
Warner, George F. *Queen Mary's Psalter: Miniatures and Drawings by an English Artist of the 14th Century, Reproduced from Royal MS. 2 B. VII in the British Museum.* London: Printed for the Trustees, 1912.
Watson, Bruce. "The East Anglican Problem: Fresh Perspectives from an Unpublished Psalter." *Gesta* 13, no. 2 (1974): 3–16.
Watson, Nicholas. "Censorship and Cultural Change in Late-Medieval England: Vernacular Theology, the Oxford Translation Debate and Arundel's Constitutions of 1409." *Speculum* 70, no. 4 (1995): 822–864.
Watson, Nicholas, and Jocelyn Wogan-Browne. "The French of England: The *Compileison, Ancrene Wisse,* and the Idea of Anglo-Norman." *Journal of Romance Studies* 4, no. 3 (2004): 35–59.
Weber, Robert and Bonifatius Fischer, eds. *Biblia Sacra iuxta vulgatam versionem.* 4th ed. Stuttgart: Deutsche Bibelgesellschaft, 1994.
Werner, Ferdinand. *Aulnay de Saintonge und die romanische Skulptur in Westfrankreich.* Worms am Rhein: Wernersche Verlagsgesellschaft, 1979.
Whitehead, Christiania. *Castles of the Mind: A Study of Medieval Architectural Allegory.* Religion and Culture in the Middle Ages. Cardiff: University of Wales Press, 2003.
———. "A Fortress and a Shield: The Representation of the Virgin in the *Château d'amour* of Robert Grosseteste." In *Writing Religious Women: Female Spiritual and Textual Practices in Late Medieval England,* edited by Denis Renevey and Christiania Whitehead, 109–132. Cardiff: University of Wales Press, 2000.
———. "Making a Cloister of the Soul in Medieval Religious Treatises." *Medium Aevum* 67, no. 1 (1998): 1–29.
Whitelock, D. M., M. Brett, and C. N. L. Brooke, eds. *Councils & Synods: Vol. I, A. D. 871–1204; Part II, 1066–1204.* Oxford: Clarendon Press, 1981.
Wieck, Roger S. *Time Sanctified: The Book of Hours in Medieval Art and Life.* 2nd ed. New York: G. Braziller in association with the Walters Art Gallery, Baltimore, 2001.
Williamson, Paul. *Gothic Sculpture, 1140–1300.* Yale University Press Pelican History of Art and Index. New Haven: Yale University Press, 1995.
Wilshere, A. D., ed. *Mirour de Seinte Eglyse: St Edmund of Abingdon's Speculum Ecclesiae.* Anglo-Norman Texts, 40. London: Anglo-Norman Text Society, 1982.
Winroth, Anders. *The Making of Gratian's Decretum.* Cambridge Studies in Medieval Life and Thought, 4th ser., vol. 49. Cambridge: Cambridge University Press, 2000.

INDEX

Page numbers in **bold** refer to illustrations

Wirth, Jean. "Faut-il adorer les images? La théorie du culte des images jusqu'au concile de Trente." In *Iconoclasme: Vie et mort de l'image médiévale: Catalogue de l'exposition: Musée d'histoire de Berne, Musée de l'Oeuvre Notre-Dame, Musées de Strasbourg,* edited by Cécile Dupeux, Peter Jezler, and Jean Wirth, 28–37. [Paris]: Somogy, 2001.

———. *L'image à l'époque gothique (1140–1280).* Histoire. Paris: Les Éditions du Cerf, 2008.

———. *L'image médiévale: Naissance et développements, VIe–XVe siècle.* Paris: Méridiens Klincksieck, 1989.

———. "La naissance du concept de croyance (XIIe–XVIIe siècles)." *Bibliothèque d'Humanisme et Renaissance* 44, no. 1 (1983): 7–58.

Wogan-Browne, Jocelyn. "'Our Steward, St Jerome': Theology and the Anglo-Norman Household." In *Household, Women, and Christianities in Late Antiquity and the Middle Ages,* edited by Anneke B. Mulder-Bakker and Jocelyn Wogan-Browne, 133–165. Turnhout: Brepols, 2005.

———. *Saints' Lives and Women's Literary Culture, c. 1150–1300: Virginity and Its Authorizations.* Oxford: Oxford University Press, 2001.

Wogan-Browne, Jocelyn, Carolyn Collette, Maryanne Kowaleski, Linne Mooney, Ad Putter, and David Trotter, eds. *Language and Culture in Medieval Britain: The French of England, c. 1100–c. 1500.* Woodbridge, Eng.: York Medieval Press, 2009.

Wolf, Gerhard. "From Mandylion to Veronica: Picturing the 'Disembodied' Face and Disseminating the True Image of Christ in the Latin West." In *The Holy Face and the Paradox of Representation: Papers from a Colloquium Held at the Bibliotheca Hertziana, Rome, and the Villa Spelman, Florence, 1996,* edited by Herbert L. Kessler and Gerhard Wolf, 153–179. Bologna: Nuova Alfa, 1998.

———. *Schleier und Spiegel: Traditionen des Christusbildes und die Bildkonzepte der Renaissance.* Munich: W. Fink, 2002.

Wood, Marjorie Curry, and Rita Copeland. "Classroom and Confession." In *The Cambridge History of Medieval English Literature,* edited by David Wallace, 376–406. Cambridge: Cambridge University Press, 1999.

Wormald, Francis. "Some Pictures of the Mass in an English XIVth Century Manuscript." *Walpole Society* 41 (1966–1968): 39–45.

Zaluska, Yolanta, and François Boespflug. "L'église et les sacrements dans le *Credo* de Joinville." *Revue des sciences religieuses* 79, no. 2 (2005): 173–191.

Zink, Michel. "L'expression de la contemplation dans le *Mirour de seinte eglyse* de saint Edmond d'Abingdon." In *Plaist vos oïr bone cançon vallant? Mélanges offerts à François Suard,* edited by Dominique Boutet, Aimé Petit, Marie-Madeleine Castellani, and Françoise Ferrand, 1031–1040. Villeneuve d'Ascq: Université Charles de Gaulle-Lille 3, 1999.

ILLUSTRATION CREDITS

The photographers and the sources of visual material other than the owners indicated in the captions are as follows. Every effort has been made to supply complete and correct credits; if there are errors or omissions, please contact Yale University Press so that corrections can be made in any subsequent edition.

Figs. 1, 2, 4: © Österreichische Nationalbibliothek, Bildarchiv; figs. 3, 5: Princeton University Library; figs. 6–8: © The British Library Board (London, British Library, Arundel MS 44); figs. 9–13, 20–23, 37, 40–43, 45–54, 69: Bibliothèque nationale de France; figs. 14, 17–19: © Lambeth Palace Library, London, UK / The Bridgeman Art Library; figs. 15, 16: © The British Library Board (London, British Library, Harley MS 3244); figs. 24–26: © The British Library Board (London, British Library, Royal MS 15.D.II); figs. 27, 28: © Fitzwilliam Museum, Cambridge; fig. 29: © The British Library Board (London, British Library, Add. MS 49999); figs. 30, 44: The Pierpont Morgan Library, New York; fig. 31: © The Walters Art Museum, Baltimore; fig. 32: © The British Library Board (London, British Library, Yates Thompson MS 13); figs. 33–36, 81: Bodleian Library, University of Oxford; fig. 38: Photograph: Edwin Smith / RIBA Library Photographs Collection; fig. 39: © The British Library Board (London, British Library, Royal MS 2.B.VII); figs. 55–59: © The British Library Board (London, British Library, Add. MS 28162); fig. 60: Photograph: Marianne Lamor; fig. 61: © Hirmer Verlag, Munich; fig. 62: Photograph: Jean-Claude Billing, courtesy of La Fondation de l'Oeuvre Notre-Dame, Strasbourg; figs. 63, 64, 67: © The Courtauld Institute of Art, London; figs. 65, 66: Foto Marburg / Art Resource, NY; fig. 68: Bibliothèque Mazarine, Paris; fig. 70: © The British Library Board (London, British Library, Add. MS 54180); fig. 71: © KIK-IRPA, Brussels; fig. 72: Scala / Art Resource, NY; figs. 73, 79, 80: © The British Library Board (London, British Library, Yates Thompson MS 11); figs. 74–76: © Belzeaux-Zodiaque, Photothèque-Zodiaque, La Pierre-qui-Vire, 89630 Saint Leger Vauban, France; fig. 77: Médiathèque d'Arras; fig. 78: © Cambrai, Médiathèque municipale / IRHT-CNRS; fig. 82: BMVR Marseille

———. "The Origins of the *Lay Folks' Catechism.*" *Medium Aevum* 60, no. 1 (1991): 92–100.
———. "Universities, Graduates and Benefices in Later Medieval England." *Past and Present* 106 (1985): 28–61.
Tachau, Katherine H. "God's Compass and 'Vana Curiositas': Scientific Study in the Old French 'Bible Moralisée.'" *Art Bulletin* 80 (1998): 7–33.
Tanner, Norman P., ed. *Decrees of the Ecumenical Councils.* 2 vols. London: Sheed & Ward; Washington, D. C.: Georgetown University Press, 1990.
Taylor, Andrew. "Manual to Miscellany: Stages in the Commercial Copying of Vernacular Literature in England." *The Yearbook of English Studies* 33 (2003): 1–17.
Teetaert, Amédée. *La confession aux laïques dans l'Eglise latine depuis le VIIIe jusqu'au XIVe siècle: Étude de théologie positive.* Universitas catholica lovaniensis. Dissertationes ad gradum magistri in Facultate theologica consequendum conscriptae, ser. 2, t. 17. Wetteren: J. de Meester et fils; Paris: J. Gabalda, 1926.
Tentler, Thomas N. *Sin and Confession on the Eve of the Reformation.* Princeton: Princeton University Press, 1977.
———. "The Summa for Confessors as an Instrument of Social Control." In *The Pursuit of Holiness in Late Medieval and Renaissance Religion: Papers from the University of Michigan Conference,* edited by Charles Edward Trinkaus and Heiko Augustinus Oberman, 103–126. Leiden: Brill, 1974.
Thompson, Henry Yates. *Illustrations from One Hundred Manuscripts in the Library of Henry Yates Thompson.* 7 vols. London: Printed at the Chiswick Press, 1907–1918.
Thurston, Herbert. "The Origin of the Elevation." *Month* 148 (1926): 254–258.
Tillmann, Helene. *Pope Innocent III.* Translated by Walter Sax. Europe in the Middle Ages, 12. Amsterdam: Distributed by Elsevier North-Holland, 1980.
Timmermann, Achim. *Real Presence: Sacrament Houses and the Body of Christ, c. 1270–1600.* Architectura medii aevi. Turnhout: Brepols, 2009.
Tobler, Adolf, and Erhard Lommatzsch. *Altfranzösisches Wörterbuch,* vol. 2. Wiesbaden: Franz Steiner Verlag, 1915; reprint, 1989.
Toussaint, Gia. *Das Passional der Kunigunde von Böhmen: Bildrhetorik und Spiritualität.* Paderborn: Schöningh, 2003.
Trexler, Richard C. "Legitimating Prayer Gestures in the Twelfth Century: The *De Penitentia* of Peter the Chanter." *History and Anthropology* 1, no. 1 (1984): 97–126.
Trottmann, Christian. *La vision béatifique: Des disputes scolastiques à sa definition par Benoît XII.* Bibliothèque des écoles françaises d'Athènes et de Rome, fasc. 289. Rome: École française de Rome, 1995.
Tyrer, J. W. *Historical Survey of Holy Week, Its Services and Ceremonial.* Alcuin Club Collections, 29. London: Oxford University Press, 1932.
Un trésor gothique: La châsse de Nivelles: Cologne, Schnütgen-Museum, 24 novembre 1995–11 février 1996: Paris, Musée national du moyen age, Thermes de Cluny, 12 mars–10 juin 1996. Paris: Réunion des musées nationaux, 1996.
Vale, Malcolm. *The Princely Court: Medieval Courts and Culture in North-West Europe, 1270–1380.* Oxford: Oxford University Press, 2001.
Van Engen, John. "The Christian Middle Ages as an Historiographical Problem." *American Historical Review* 91, no. 3 (1986): 519–552.
———. "Faith as a Concept of Order in Medieval Christendom." In *Belief in History: Innovative Approaches to European and American Religion,* edited by Thomas A. Kselman, 19–67. Notre Dame: University of Notre Dame Press, 1991.
Vincent-Cassy, Mireille. "Quelques réflexions sur l'envie et la jalousie en France au XIVe siècle." In *Études sur l'histoire de la pauvreté: moyen age—XVIe siècle,* edited by Michel Mollat, 487–503. Paris: Publications de la Sorbonne, 1974.
———. "Un modèle français: Les cavalcades des sept péchés capitaux dans les églises rurales de la fin du XVe siècle." In *Artistes, artisans et production artistique au moyen age: Colloque international, Centre national de la recherche scientifique, Université de Rennes II, Haute-Bretagne, 2–6 mai 1983,* edited by Xavier Barral i Altet, 461–487. Paris: Picard, 1990.
Vitzthum, Georg. *Die Pariser Miniaturmalerei von der Zeit des hl. Ludwig bis zu Philipp von Valois und ihr Verhältnis zur Malerei in Nordwesteuropa.* Leipzig: Quelle & Meyer, 1907.
Vogel, Cyrille. *Les "Libri paenitentiales."* Typologie des sources du moyen age occidental, fasc. 27. Turnhout: Brepols, 1978.
Voronova, Tamara Pavlovna, and Alexander Sterligov. *Western European Illuminated Manuscripts of the 8th to the 16th Centuries in the National Library of Russia, St. Petersburg: France, Spain, England, Germany, Italy, the Netherlands.* Bournemouth: Parkstone Press; St. Petersburg: Aurora, 1996.
Walters, Barbara R., Vincent J. Corrigan, and Peter T. Ricketts. *The Feast of Corpus Christi.* University Park, Pa.: Pennsylvania State University Press, 2006.
Warner, George F. *Queen Mary's Psalter: Miniatures and Drawings by an English Artist of the 14th Century, Reproduced from Royal MS. 2 B. VII in the British Museum.* London: Printed for the Trustees, 1912.
Watson, Bruce. "The East Anglican Problem: Fresh Perspectives from an Unpublished Psalter." *Gesta* 13, no. 2 (1974): 3–16.
Watson, Nicholas. "Censorship and Cultural Change in Late-Medieval England: Vernacular Theology, the Oxford Translation Debate and Arundel's Constitutions of 1409." *Speculum* 70, no. 4 (1995): 822–864.
Watson, Nicholas, and Jocelyn Wogan-Browne. "The French of England: The *Compileison, Ancrene Wisse,* and the Idea of Anglo-Norman." *Journal of Romance Studies* 4, no. 3 (2004): 35–59.
Weber, Robert and Bonifatius Fischer, eds. *Biblia Sacra iuxta vulgatam versionem.* 4th ed. Stuttgart: Deutsche Bibelgesellschaft, 1994.
Werner, Ferdinand. *Aulnay de Saintonge und die romanische Skulptur in Westfrankreich.* Worms am Rhein: Wernersche Verlagsgesellschaft, 1979.
Whitehead, Christiania. *Castles of the Mind: A Study of Medieval Architectural Allegory.* Religion and Culture in the Middle Ages. Cardiff: University of Wales Press, 2003.
———. "A Fortress and a Shield: The Representation of the Virgin in the *Château d'amour* of Robert Grosseteste." In *Writing Religious Women: Female Spiritual and Textual Practices in Late Medieval England,* edited by Denis Renevey and Christiania Whitehead, 109–132. Cardiff: University of Wales Press, 2000.
———. "Making a Cloister of the Soul in Medieval Religious Treatises." *Medium Aevum* 67, no. 1 (1998): 1–29.
Whitelock, D. M., M. Brett, and C. N. L. Brooke, eds. *Councils & Synods: Vol. I, A. D. 871–1204; Part II, 1066–1204.* Oxford: Clarendon Press, 1981.
Wieck, Roger S. *Time Sanctified: The Book of Hours in Medieval Art and Life.* 2nd ed. New York: G. Braziller in association with the Walters Art Gallery, Baltimore, 2001.
Williamson, Paul. *Gothic Sculpture, 1140–1300.* Yale University Press Pelican History of Art and Index. New Haven: Yale University Press, 1995.
Wilshere, A. D., ed. *Mirour de Seinte Eglyse: St Edmund of Abingdon's Speculum Ecclesiae.* Anglo-Norman Texts, 40. London: Anglo-Norman Text Society, 1982.
Winroth, Anders. *The Making of Gratian's Decretum.* Cambridge Studies in Medieval Life and Thought, 4th ser., vol. 49. Cambridge: Cambridge University Press, 2000.